CATALOG OF LITTLE MAGAZINES

Catalog of Little Magazines

A COLLECTION IN THE RARE BOOK ROOM, MEMORIAL LIBRARY
UNIVERSITY OF WISCONSIN-MADISON

Compiled and edited by Robert F. Roeming

University of Wisconsin-Milwaukee

in cooperation with
MINITEX
University of Minnesota, Wilson Library
Minneapolis, Minnesota

THE UNIVERSITY OF WISCONSIN PRESS

Published 1979

The University of Wisconsin Press
114 North Murray Street
Madison, Wisconsin 53715

The University of Wisconsin Press, Ltd.
1 Gower Street
London WC1E 6HA, England

Copyright © 1979
The Board of Regents of the University of Wisconsin System
All rights reserved

Published through the Imprint Series
Monograph Publishing
University Microfilms International
Ann Arbor, Michigan 48106

Printed in the United States of America

Library of Congress Cataloging in Publication Data

Wisconsin. University—Madison. Library.
   Catalog of little magazines.

   1. Little magazines—Bibliography—Catalogs.
2. Wisconsin. University—Madison Library—Catalogs.
I. Roeming, Robert F. II. Title.
Z6944.L5W57 1979 [PN4836] 016.0705'72 79-5414
ISBN 0-299-08180-X

This Catalog was made possible by grants from the Research Collections Program
of the National Endowment for the Humanities

CONTENTS

Foreword   vii

Introduction   ix

Little Magazine Collection   1

Addendum   123

FOREWORD

The Catalog of Little Magazines provides scholars with a unique tool for utilizing one of the largest and most complete collections of little magazines in the United States. Established in 1958 when the University of Wisconsin-Madison acquired the little magazine library of Dr. Marvin Sukov, the Collection through substantial subsequent acquisitions now includes more than 3,650 titles. The growth and development of the Collection are a direct result of Dr. Sukov's continuing interest and the very special devotion of Felix Pollak, Curator of Rare Books from 1959 until 1974.

The significance of the Collection as a research source lies in the nature of the magazines themselves, which often form the first published record of new authors, new styles, and new ideas in literature, politics, and social appraisal.

Dr. Sukov's goal of a "complete and clean" library has been maintained in the efforts of the Library to obtain a comprehensive collection of complete runs that are preserved with the original covers and advertising material intact. The Collection is housed in the vault of the Rare Book Room of the Memorial Library. Although noncirculating, it is available for use in the reading room.

Librarians and other scholars should find this detailed catalog an indispensable tool in pursuing research in this or any other collection of little magazines.

Joseph H. Treyz
Director of Libraries
University of Wisconsin-Madison

INTRODUCTION

This catalog presents the holdings of the Sukov Collection of Little Magazines housed in the Rare Book Room of the Memorial Library of the University of Wisconsin-Madison. The first section is a record of issues held in the Collection as of October 31, 1977. A title current at that date can be assumed to have been augmented by subsequently published issues. The Addendum includes holdings of new titles added between November 1, 1977, and June 30, 1979.

The Collection of which this catalog is the record has not been gathered according to pre-established guidelines. Marvin Sukov, the young medical student of the early 1930's who created the base of this Collection, was simply curious about little magazines. As his zeal for collecting became more intense, he went farther and farther afield to gain as much variety in as many complete sets as he could find. The additional augmenting of this Collection makes it even more representative of the whole spectrum of little magazines.

DESCRIPTION OF THE CATALOG

The highly individualized nature of each little magazine made cataloging this Collection a significant challenge. The very term "little magazine" cannot be defined precisely. It must be explained by describing a variety of general characteristics which are not necessarily common to all little magazines. Some magazines began as "little" and maintained long and well established runs, ultimately losing any evidence of original littleness. Some began impressively endowed with both intellectual and financial substance, but were shortlived, often for lack of an audience. The idea of "audience" is again no criterion, since some of the titles in the Collection often give evidence of having been noncirculating monologs, inspired by a frenzy for self-expression in some less ephemeral form than speech. At times the combined faith and meagre fortunes of the devoted were sufficient to infuse a breath of life into a little magazine but inadequate to sustain it. The designation "magazine" should not suggest any particular form or physical appearance a little magazine may take. One issue in this Collection was partially destroyed because, although titled and numbered, it was a mere hexagonal pencil bearing a line of a poem printed on each of its faces. By the time it was retrieved from the library employee found using it, half of each line had been ground into the pencil sharpener.

Little magazines in this Collection include broadsides, folios of individual loose sheets, full- and tabloid-size newspapers, boxes of materials, posters, single-sheet issues, and imaginative creations, at times three-dimensional, in which physical form reinforces content. The various styles of production reflect the extent of financial resources available. Much of the Collection is mimeographed and often poorly reproduced on wretched paper. Some little magazines did not use the same format or the same means of production with any consistency.

Many of the little magazines in this Collection were voices of protest and of the underground. Their editors, perhaps to avoid persecution and arrest, may purposely have created an informational vacuum by not naming themselves, their supporting organizations, nor designating, at times, the places and the dates of publication. Moreover, in some cases, in order to increase the difficulty of identification or to underscore the message, the publication title was changed.

The average life of a little magazine in this Collection seems to have been about seven issues. Usually the fifth issue carried an apology for its late appearance, and an urgent plea for funds in the form of subscriptions or donations. The sixth issue warned that the disheartening financial response to the previous appeal gave small cause for optimism. The seventh issue carried the dire announcement that it was the last.

This catalog is evidence that the tangible accomplishments of little magazines have been impressive. In this Collection are recorded the beginning efforts of a considerable number of writers who today have acquired distinction, whether here in the United States or in English-speaking countries abroad. It also includes magazines that were principally concerned with social and political comment. Those that were vehicles of protest and revolt, often espousing no serious solution more positive than destruction and anarchy, also influenced language and its style. In magazines that vehemently opposed the Vietnam War, vituperation and blasphemy created a new language-orientation in which no conceivable expression was subjected to any censorship or definable taste.

The roots of the literary, cultural, and social phenomena of the twentieth century are laid bare in these magazines. And with that there is poetry, endless torrents of poetry, numberless untitled poems, in which some, especially the exuberantly youthful, describe without restraint every emotion and sensation experienced, while others of all ages, through constraints of form and language, in new as well as old modes and measures, rediscover the manifestations of beauty and harmony.

As a "tool for research" this catalog should serve well those who would study the first writings and the forming of contemporary English-language authors. It should also arouse the interest of those who would study protest movements, reaction to the Vietnam War and to the

Johnson administration, black culture and writing, feminism, the student revolt, and other social phenomena of the last quarter-century. In reading these little magazines one senses the moods, the attitudes, the pain, the rage, the euphoria, that brought these publications into being. No intimation of these emotional sources can be found in historical documents of the same periods. The testimony of the little magazines gives life to history and offers greater understanding of the human quality, the individual participation, which history summarizes.

Certainly these comments about the form and substance of little magazines describe chaos. And indeed these magazines often reflect the chaos of certain years when much had to be said and attention had to be gained by whatever means promised success. It is well to keep this in mind because the orderly appearance of this catalog is deceptive. What is incomprehensible even to me is that a well-organized and logically arranged catalog was produced from this large collection of totally incongruous material. The organization is evidence of the effectiveness of a computerized cataloging system that can accommodate so many widely disparate items. It is this revelation of a definable logical arrangement which makes this catalog of uniquely erratic materials readable and constantly surprising.

PROCEDURE

The primary concern of the National Endowment for the Humanities in lending support to this cataloging project was to ensure the addition of these titles to the national data bank maintained by CONSER (Conversion of Serials Project) and the reduction of all cataloging information to the MARC II (Machine Readable Cataloging) Format, both projects established and maintained under the aegis of the Library of Congress.

The terms of two grants provided by the National Endowment for the Humanities specified that the data concerning each title included in this catalog be processed by MINITEX (Minnesota Interlibrary Telecommunications Exchange), housed in the University of Minnesota Wilson Library in Minneapolis. MINITEX is a cooperative effort of libraries to create a machine-readable data base containing information about serials held in libraries throughout the states of Minnesota and North Dakota. The acceptance of MINITEX of the responsibility of processing the data of this catalog added several unique dimensions as well as complexities to the original concept. By adding these titles to its own data base, MINITEX has incorporated them into the Minnesota Union List of Serials (MULS). The second edition of MULS published in September 1977 includes those titles which were processed after the first phase of this cataloging was completed in the summer of 1976. Approximately 1,450 titles from the beginning of the alphabet through part of the letter K (including <u>Karyn</u>) have thus been included in that edition. Any subsequent editions of MULS will include all the titles of the first section of this catalog.

The process of verification of titles established by MINITEX provided for the addition of certain records to the Columbus, Ohio, data base maintained by OCLC (formerly Ohio College Library Center) and by using CONSER. This makes it possible, by use of a local terminal now commonly found in libraries throughout the United States, to call forth a display of the filed information concerning many of these titles.

The MINITEX procedures and capabilities offered the potential of including with each little magazine record an expanse of information in a universal format which allows for integration with other records as well as for updating and revision. Thus a search of the computer records, in order to find additional issues, for example, can be pursued by using the variety of data made available through this catalog.

The responsibility for the actual production of this catalog in its final form as camera-ready copy was assumed under contract by MINITEX, mandated by the National Endowment for the Humanities. Variations in format and in basic procedures of compiling records were completely controlled by the MINITEX System. All records were submitted with duplicate copies of those pages from each magazine which verified the required data. For each record MINITEX conducted a search in the computer data banks and various indexes, thus adding information not available in the original publications of the Collection. Without the search services thus rendered by MINITEX, the references and the cross references would have been extremely limited. It must, therefore, be recognized that the minimal errors and inconsistencies of format that occur are offset by the speed and thoroughness with which the catalog was produced.

FORMAT

The format of the records is that of the Minnesota Union List of Serials (MULS).

The title of the magazine, as the main entry, appears in bold roman type face, and may also include a subtitle or descriptive definition of function, if that information appears on the title page. Following in italics on the same line is the original place of publication with the imprint statement, which may be the name of the press, the association, the educational institution or other sponsoring agency.

The next line gives the ISSN (International Standard Serial Number) and the LCCN (Library of Congress Card Number) if available; following on the same line appear the beginning date, if it is known, and the end date, if cessation of the publication is verified.

Then follow general notes. This may include variations in the title and a record of the issues in which these occur, titles of related publications, and explanation of cessation of publication, suspension, and possible reinstatement.

The next line begins with "WU," which distinguishes the University of Wisconsin System from the contributing institutions of other states. The following notation "UWM (RBR)" identifies the University of Wisconsin-Madison, Rare Book Room. This coding makes it possible at all times to retrieve a listing of all the records of this specific Collection, to add to these records, and to modify them. Continuing on the same line, there follows the identification by volume and number of the individual issues held in the Collection. A final summary notation gives in parenthese the date of the first and the last issue of the holding.

In general all issues are identified by volume and number, to the extent that information is available. The dates of issues are given subsequently within a given range. If a searcher can identify an issue only by date, it is possbile by means of interpolation to deduce the colume and number, and thus determine whether it is in the Collection.

Each record is accompanied on the upper right by a unique seven-digit identification number which is an internal control number and is not significant in using this catalog.

Records given as <u>secondary entries</u> in roman type face, but not bold, are variant titles or names of sponsoring presses, organizations, associations or agencies. These are followed by a "See" notation (in bold roman), which includes the title of the magazine and the imprint to which reference is made.

The extent to which access to these magazines is increased by such secondary entries can be judged by referring to a record such as <u>Rocking Horse</u>. One can also gain access to this title through "Wisconsin. University-Madison" or through "Arden Club, Madison." In this case no ISSN nor LCCN is available, since this publication ceased in 1935. Or consider <u>The Far point</u>, which has both the ISSN and the LCCN, with cross reference to "Manitoba. University. Dept. of English" and to <u>Northern Light</u>. Through the latter it is linked to <u>Preview</u>, which is not listed by title because it is not represented in this Collection. This highly complex computerized system has at times thus identified multiple means of access to a specific title.

<u>The Far point</u> also is a model for a complete record, in which the specific cessation of publication is verified by the formula "Ceased publication with no. 7/8, Fall 1972/Spring 1973"; then, in the holdings, notation indicates that the set is complete in the Collection: "No. 1-8 (FAL/WIN1968-SPR1973)." Since entry into the MINITEX System is by coding information on format sheets, which is then transposed onto cassette magnetic tape by electric typewriter, a human factor must be taken into consideration. Variations, therefore, occur in the manner in which cessation of publication is noted. The notation "Ceased" (<u>Advance Guard</u>), "Ceased publication" (<u>Colonial Freedom News</u>), "No more published" (<u>American Parade</u>) indicate that no data is available to identify the last issue. At times such notations are based on correspondence which questions failure to receive issues.

In the MINITEX System, numerals file before letters. Therefore, the first entries under "A" are numeral titles filed on the first digit as the primary sort beginning with "0" (zero). But in addition cross references are supplied under the word form of the digits. This phenomenon demontrates the extent to which fine distinctions are made in the MINITEX System: "121" is cross referenced to "One hundred and twenty one" (sic) as well as to "One hundred twenty one." Similarly "365."

To the end that research may be better served, this catalog of the Collection is offered. Those magazines which are represented in the Collection but which have attained substance and now form part of the circulating collections of major libraries have not been included. The value of this catalog will be enhanced if it is used by librarians to evaluate and record their own holdings of little magazines. Through such inventories and analyses it will be possible to establish whether the location of issues missing from this Collection can be determined.

Fortunately, the utilization of an established computerized system makes it possible to add titles and issues, to identify them by place, and to adjust entries in the data bank. Ultimately it will be possible to produce cooperatively a combined catalog of little magazines in the United States, and possibly Canada, in which the holdings of all participating libraries will be recorded. Perhaps this vision can be extended to include the aspiration that this catalog may serve as a model to encourage similar compilations of information about little magazines published in languages other than English.

ACKNOWLEDGMENTS

The simple idea of compiling a catalog of one collection of little magazines soon became exceptionally complex. Without the support and advice of many this catalog would never have been produced. In the initial attempts to gain the attention of the National Endowment for the Humanities I was supported by Senator William Proxmire of Wisconsin, who has maintained a continuing interest in this project. When it became apparent that an involvement with MINITEX might be advantageous, further support was given by the then Senators from Minnesota, Hubert H. Humphrey and Walter Mondale. In the negotiations to gain funding for the continuation of the project into the second phase and bring it to completion, Senator Samuel I. Hayakawa of California added his support as one knowledgeable about little magazines and as the former editor of the Rocking Horse, published at the University of Wisconsin in the early thirties. Without their letters of support and recommendations the catalog would no doubt have remained an idea.

I am indebted equally to Dr. Margaret Child, Assistant Director, Research Collections Porgram, Division of Research Grants, of the National Endowment for the Humanities, who took the project under administrative control and carried it through the various processes by which an affirmative decision to fund the proposal was twice achieved. At all times she offered carefully reasoned advice to improve the methods by which the final catalog was completed and thus increase its value to scholarship as a research tool. It is also due to her good offices that the liaison with MINITEX was established so that my highly individualized proposal for computerization was converted into participation in a national system.

In like measure I acknowledge my complete dependence on Mrs. Alice Wilcox, Director of MINITEX, and Mrs. Lois Upham, then Program Director of MINITEX, who brought the catalog to completion in the form presented here, as well as to Ms Susan Zuriff, who maintained editorial supervision of the records. Also to COMPUTYPE of Minneapolis for special assistance in typesetting problem records and in effecting the overall composition.

In addition to the grants received from the National Endowment for the Humanities, substantial financial support was given by Dean William

F. Halloran and Associate Dean G. Micheal Riley, College of Letters and Science, Dean George W. Keulks and Associate Dean Norman P. Lasca, Graduate School, University of Wisconsin-Milwaukee; Dean E. David Cronin, College of Letters and Science, Dean Robert M. Bock, Graduate School, and Joseph P. Treyz, Director of Libraries, University of Wisconsin-Madison.

Gretchen Lagana, Curator of Rare Books, Memorial Library, University of Wisconsin-Madison, as well as former and present members of the department were most helpful in advising me during the drafting of the proposals and during the execution of the project.

Dr. Marvin Sukov, with whom I consulted during the period of planning, was equally gracious in offering historical information about his collecting experiences and in adding his recommendations to the funding proposals.

Finally my thanks are offered to Joseph P. Treyz for his constant support and interest, which he has continued to demonstrate in his foreword to this catalog.

Robert F. Roeming
University of Wisconsin-Milwaukee
Milwaukee, Wisconsin
June 30, 1979

A

0 to 9. *New York.* 1515049
ISSN: 0514-7360 Beg. date: 1967 End date: 1969
Ceased publication with no. 6, July 1969.
WU   UWM (RBR) No.1-6 (APR1967-JUL1969); suppl. no. 6.

10.5. *See* 10 point 5. Eugene, Ore., Oz Publications, Inc. 1511997

10 point 5. *Eugene, Ore., Oz Publications, Inc.* 1511984
WU   UWM (RBR) Spring, Winter, New Year 1975; Summer 1976; no.5 (SPR1977).

100. *Chicago.* 1505240
ISSN: 0471-6078 Beg. date: 1951 End date: 1952
"A magazine without illusions or delusions."
Ceased publication with vol. 2 no. 5, Nov. 1952.
WU   UWM (RBR) V.2 no.5 (NOV1952).

100 flowers. *Stanford, Calif.* 1505266
Beg. date: 1971
WU   UWM (RBR) No.1 (SPR1971).

121. *Little Neck, N.Y.* 1505281
"A little magazine of poetry."
WU   UWM (RBR) 1967: two issues.

12th street. *New York, Students of the New School for Social Research.* 1514724
"A quarterly."
WU   UWM (RBR) V.2 no.2-4 (SPR1948-SPR1949).

13th moon. *New York.* 1512017
ISSN: 0094-3320 LCCN: 76-647817 Beg. date: 1975
"Publication of the Writing Organization for Women at the City College of New York."
WU   UWM (RBR) V.1-v.3 no.2 (SPR/SUM1973-1977).

1933: a year magazine. *Philadelphia, J. Louis Stoll.* 1515064
Beg. date: 1933 End date: 1934
WU   UWM (RBR) Section 1-2 (JUN/DEC1933-Dec1933/APR1934).

21st century. *Sydney.* 1512619
ISSN: 0494-335X Beg. date: 1955
"The magazine of a creative civilization."
WU   UWM (RBR) No.1-2 (SEP1955-AUG1957).

3 arts quarterly. *London, Woodstock Gallery.* 1528286
ISSN: 0495-517X Beg. date: 1960 End date: 1960
Ceased publication with no. 4, Winter 1960.
WU   UWM (RBR) No.1-4 (SPR-WIN1960); unnumbered supplement.

3 (cent) pulp. *Vancouver, B.C., Pulp Press.* 1511969
Beg. date: 1972
WU   UWM (RBR) V.1 no.1-12,14-25; v.2-v.4 no.10 (NOV151972-1977).

365 days of the year. *Warndon, Worcester, Eng.* 1512045
WU   UWM (RBR) No.1-2 (APR-JUN1969).

The 3rd thing. *Edgewater, N.J.* 1512073
Beg. date: 1974
WU   UWM (RBR) No.1 (SUM1974).

4 elements. *St. Simons Island, Ga.* 1427796
Beg. date: 1975
"A poetry review."
WU   UWM (RBR) V.1 no.1-3 (OCT1975-SPR1976).

79 [cent] spread. *Carmel, Calif.* 1510858
Beg. date: 1968
WU   UWM (RBR) V.1 no.1-3 (JUL05-AUG231968).

A. *See* A b. London. 1441341

A; a journal of contemporary literature. *Laguna, N.M.* 1528308
ISSN: 0147-7196 LCCN: sc78-392 Beg. date: 1976
WU   UWM (RBR) V.1 no.1; v.2 no.1-2 (FAL1976-FAL1977).

A; an envelope magazine of visual poetry. *See* A b. London. 1441339

The A and T poetry review. *Greensboro, N.C., A and T Register, N.C. Agric. and Tech. State Univ. newspaper.* 1441129
Beg. date: 1968
WU   UWM (RBR) V.1 no.1 (FAL1968).

The A and T register. Poetry supplement. *Greensboro, N.C., North Carolina Agricultural and Technical State University.* 1468604
WU   UWM (RBR) May 4, 1973.

A b. *London.* 1441326
Beg. date: 1971
Title varies: no. 1, 1971/1972, A; an envelope magazine of visual poetry.
WU   UWM (RBR) No.1-2 (1971-1973).

A D [1950]. *New York A.D. Literary Association.* 1427818
ISSN: 0567-3593 LCCN: 58-28415 Beg. date: 1950 End date: 1952
Title includes date of issue.
Vol. 1 no. 1 has caption title: Anno Domini.
Founded by the A D Literary Foundation.
WU   UWM (RBR) V.1 no.1; v.2 no.1-3; v.3 1st, 3rd qtr. (FAL1950-AUT1951).

A D Literary Foundation. A D [1950]. *See* A D [1950]. New York A.D. Literary Association. 1427833

Aardvark. *Chicago, Aardvark Publications Inc.* 1429440
Beg. date: 1961
WU   UWM (RBR) V.2 no.4 (WIN1964).

Aavesh; a rejoinder of writings of Indian youth biased to liberated thinking. *New Delhi.* 1429453
ISSN: 0001-3064
Published twice a year alternately in Hindi and English.
WU   UWM (RBR) V.1 no.3 (1968).

Ab intra. *Belmont, Mass., Hellric Publications.* 1429466
Beg. date: 1971
WU   UWM (RBR) No.1-4 (1972-1976).

Abacus. *Madison, Wis.* 1429479
WU   UWM (RBR) Spring 1966.

Abbey. *See* Abbey; the journal of literary brouhaha. Columbia, Md., White Urp Press. 1441157

Abbey; the journal of literary brouhaha. *Columbia, Md., White Urp Press.* 1441144
Beg. date: 1970
WU   UWM (RBR) V.1 no.1-4; v.2 no.1 (no.1-5) (SPR1970-SPR1971); no.6,8-22 (NOV1971-1977).

Aberdeen. University. Student Representative Council. 1468632
Alma mater. *See* Alma mater. Aberdeen, Scot., The Langstane Press.

The Above ground review. *Greensboro, N.C., Triple Press.* 1429481
Beg. date: 1968
WU   UWM (RBR) V.1 no.1-3; v.2 no.1-3; v.3 no.1-2 (NOV1968-SUM1973).

Abraxas. *Madison, Wis., etc., Abraxas Press, etc.* 1429494
ISSN: 0361-1663 LCCN: sc76-05 Beg. date: 1968
Title varies: The Abraxas anthology.
Indexes: nos. 1-10, 1968-1974, in no. 10.
WU   UWM (RBR) V.1 no.1-2; v.2 no.1-2 (no.1-4) (1968-1970); no.5-13 (1971-1976).

Abraxas anthology. *See* Abraxas. Madison, Wis., etc., Abraxas Press, etc. 1429503

Abyss. *Somerville, Mass. etc., Abyss Publications, etc.* 1441746
ISSN: 0001-3722 Beg. date: 1967
WU   UWM (RBR) V.1 no.1-4; v.2 no.1-2 (1967-1969); ser. 2 v.3 no.1; v.4 no.1-3 (SPR1971-n.d.).

Academy. *Minneapolis, University of Minnesota, College of Liberal Arts, Honors Student Council.* 0006023
Beg. date: 1966
"Journal of the College of Liberal Arts."
WU   UWM (RBR) V.2 no.1-2; v.3 no.1,3; v.4 no.2; v.5 no.1; v.6 no.1-3; v.6 issue A (1967-1972).

Academy of American Poets. Poetry pilot. *See* Poetry pilot. 152924A
New York, Academy of American Poets.

Acadia University, Wolfville, Nova Scotia. Amethyst. *See* 1468658
Amethyst; student literary magazine. Wolfville, N.S., Students of Acadia University.

Acadia University, Wolfville, Nova Scotia. Students' Union. 1435632
Either/or. *See* Either/or. Wolfville, N.S., Acadia Students' Union.

Accent; a quarterly of new literature. *Urbana, Illinois.* 0007015
Beg. date: 1940 End date: 1960
Ceased with v. 20.
WU   UWM (RBR) V.1-20 (1940-1960).

Acorn. *New York.* 1429516
Beg. date: 1938
WU   UWM (RBR) V.1 no.1-2 (APR-SUM1938).

Acorn. Three Oaks, Mich.   0007500
   WU   UWM (RBR) No.1-2 (OCT1905-FEB1906).

Action Movement for the Crafts. Crafts review. *See* Crafts review. Tring, Eng., Action Movement for the Crafts.   1429321

Activist. Oberlin, Ohio, Students for a Democratic Society.   0010805
   Absorbed the Albatross, Spring 1963; caption title, vol. 3 no. 2- (Spring 1963-   ) Activist and the Albatross.
   WU   UWM (RBR) V.5 no.2; v.6-v.15 no.2 (no.12,14-36) (MAR1965-SPR1975).

Actual size. Detroit, Actual Size Press.   1429529
   ISSN: 0044-6122 Beg. date: 1969
   WU   UWM (RBR) Nov. 1969.

Adam. Los Angeles, Knight Pub. Corp.   1429531
   ISSN: 0001-8007
   WU   UWM (RBR) V.14 no.2 (FEB1970).

Adam, international review. London.   0011145
   ISSN: 0001-8015 LCCN: 67-94838
   Began publication 1929.
   WU   UWM (RBR) V.5 no.6 (JUL1933); v.10 no.123-v.11 no.132,146-149 (JUN1938-DEC1939); no.153-207,212-218, 224-238,244-249,251,258-393 (13th-39th year) (NOV1941-1975); v.40 no.394-396 (1976).

Adelphi... London, British periodicals limited.   0011418
   LCCN: 41-4743.
   Monthly, June 1923-June 1927; quarterly. Sept. 1927-Aug. 1930; monthly, Oct. 1930-1941 (irregular).
   Title varies: June 1923-June 1927, The Adelphi; Sept. 1927-Aug. 1930, The New Adelphi; Oct. 1930- The adelphi.
   Ceased with v. 31 no. 4.
   WU   UWM (RBR) V.1 no.1-2,5-8,10,12; v.2 no.1,3-4,6-9; v.4 no.2,7-9 (JUN1923-MAR1927); n. ser. v.2 no.1; v.3 no.4 (SEP1928-AUG1930); n. ser. (ser. 3) v.1 no.3; v.3 no.2-6; v.4 no.3; v.5 no.4; v.8 no.3; v.25 no.2-3; v.27 no.1-4; v.28 no.1,4; v.30 no.1,3 (DEC1930-MAY1954).

Adelphi Students' Library. Vision. *See* Vision. Sydney, Adelphi Students' Library.   1517351

Adept; a quarterly publication. *See* Adept quarterly. Houston.   1429557

The Adept quarterly. Houston.   1429544
   ISSN: 0001-818X Beg. date: 1965
   Title varies: vol. 1 no. 1, Spring 1965, Adept; a quarterly publication.
   WU   UWM V.1 no.1-2 (SPR1965-SPR/SUM1966).

Advance Guard. Denver.   0012005
   Ceased.
   WU   UWM (RBR) No.2-4 (1948).

Adventures in poetry. New York.   144116A
   ISSN: 0568-0155 Beg. date: 1968
   WU   UWM (RBR) No.1-9 (MAR1968-SPR1972). Kraus Reprint copies.

Aegis. Moorhead, Minn., Moorhead State College.   0945617
   Beg. date: 1973
   WU   UWM (RBR) No.1-3 (SPR1973-SPR1974).

Aerend; a Kansas quarterly. Hays, Kansas, Fort Hays Kansas State College.   0014108
   LCCN: 44-35323
   Indexes: vols. 1-10, 1930-1939, in v. 10.
   WU   UWM (RBR) V.1-21 (WIN1930-1950).

Aesop's feast. Denver, etc.   142956A
   ISSN: 0001-9577 Beg. date: 1968
   WU   UWM (RBR) V.1 no.1-4 (MAY1968-APR1972).

Aesthete 1925. New York.   1257053
   Beg. date: 1925 End date: 1925
   Issued as an answer to Aesthete: model 1924, by Ernest Boyd, which appeared in The American mercury for Jan. 1924.
   Ceased publication with vol. 1 no. 1, Feb. 1925.
   WU   UWM (RBR) 1925.

Aesthetics. Bombay, Youths' Art and Culture Circle.   1429572
   Beg. date: 1947
   WU   UWM (RBR) V.5 no.4; v.6 no.3 (OCT/DEC1951-SEP1952).

Africa, Latin America, Asia revolution. *See* Revolution. Paris, etc.   0014963

Africa south. *See* Africa south in exile. Cape Town, London.   0924678

Africa south in exile. Cape Town, London.   0924665
   ISSN: 0568-1170 Beg. date: 1956 End date: 1961
   Title varies: vol. 1-vol. 4 no. 4, Oct./Dec. 1956-July/Sept. 1960, Africa south.
   Ceased publication with vol. 6 no. 1, Oct./Dec. 1961.
   WU   UWM (RBR) V.1 no.1; v.2 no.1-4; v.3 no.1-3 (OCT/DEC1956-APR/JUN1959).

African revolution. *See* Revolution. Paris, etc.   0015431

Afro-Asian writings. *See* Lotus. Cairo, Permanent Bureau of Afro-Asian Writers.   1323490

Agenda. London.   001593A
   ISSN: 0002-0796 Beg. date: 1959
   "Agenda is a revival of the publication known originally as Four pages."
   WU   UWM (RBR) V.1-6; v.7 no.1,3; v.8-13; v.14 no.2-4; v.15 no.1 (1959-1977).

Aggie Weston's. Belper, Derbyshire, Eng.   1429598
   Beg. date: 1973
   WU   UWM (RBR) No.1-12 (WIN1973-1976).

The Agni review. Cranford, N.J.   1438818
   Beg. date: 1972
   WU   UWM (RBR) No.3-7 (1974-1977).

Agora. Belmont, N.C., Belmont Abbey College.   1432507
   WU   UWM (RBR) V.8 (MAY1967).

Agora. [Worcester, Mass., Worcester State College].   1429607
   LCCN: 72-622328 Beg. date: 1972
   WU   UWM (RBR) V.1 no.1; v.2 (APR1972-SPR1973).

Agricultural and Technical College at Morrisville. Gold rush. *See* Gold rush. Morrisville, N.Y., State University of New York, A and T College.   1436258

Aim. Charlotte, N.C., Aim Publications.   1429622
   ISSN: 0002-2128 Beg. date: 1969
   WU   UWM (RBR) V.1 no.1-2 (1969-1970).

Air. Vancouver, B.C.   1429635
   ISSN: 0044-6947 Beg. date: 1971
   Ceased publication.
   WU   UWM (RBR) No.1-2,4-24,27-29 (1971-1976).

Aisling; a quarterly of Irish and American poetry. San Francisco.   1429648
   Beg. date: 1973
   WU   UWM (RBR) No.2-7/8 (WIN1973/1974-SUM1974).

The Ajax. St. Louis, Mo. [etc.].   1429650
   Beg. date: 1916
   WU   UWM (RBR) V.47-52 (1963-1968).

Akros. Preston, Eng., etc., Akros Publications.   1429663
   ISSN: 0002-3728 Beg. date: 1966
   Title varies: -   Akros poets.
   Subtitle varies.
   WU   UWM (RBR) V.1-12 (no.2-35) (FEB1966-1977).

Akros poets. *See* Akros. Preston, Eng., etc., Akros Publications.   1429676

Alabama. University. Black warrior review. *See* Black warrior review. University, Ala., University of Alabama.   1433282

Alabama. University, Birmingham. Aura. *See* Aura. Birmingham, Ala.   143831A

Alabama College, Montevallo, Alabama. Montevallo review. *See* Montevallo review. Montevallo, Ala., Montevallo Press, Alabama College.   1496956

Alaska review. Anchorage, Alaska Methodist University.   0024564
   ISSN: 0002-4554 Beg. date: 1963
   WU   UWM (RBR) V.1-v.3 no.3; v.3 no.4-v.4 no.1 (no.12-13); no.15-17 (WIN1963-1973); special issue: v.4 no.2 (FAL1970).

Albatross. Madison, Wis., Albatross Press.   1429691
   WU   UWM (RBR) No.1 (1970); followed by another issue with no number or date.

Albatross. San Francisco.   1429689
   ISSN: 0568-8965 Beg. date: 1963
   WU   UWM (RBR) V.1 no.1 (DEC1963).

Albion. Manchester, Eng., Radical Press.   1429700
   WU   UWM (RBR) No.1-6 (n.d.-n.d.).

Albion. Oswestry, T. Owen and son, printers.   0025227
   Title changes: no. 1-3: New Saxon pamphlets; no. 4-5: New Saxon Review.
   WU   UWM (RBR) No.1-4 (n.d.-n.d.).

Alcaeus review. Carmichael, Calif. 1429713
Beg. date: 1974
WU UWM (RBR) V.1 no.1 ([1974]).

The Alchemist. Lasalle, Que. 1429726
Beg. date: 1974
WU UWM (RBR) No.1-3 (1974-1976).

Alcheringa; ethnopoetics. Boston, Boston University. 1117068
ISSN: 0044-7218 LCCN: 72-626511 Beg. date: 1970
Publication suspended between Spring/Summer 1973 and 1975; began new series with 1975.
Nos. 1-5, Fall 1970-Spring/Summer 1973, published in New York.
WU UWM (RBR) No.1-5 (AUT1970-SPR/SUM1973); n. ser. v.1 no.1; v.2 no.1-2; v.3 no.1 (1975-1977).

Aldebaran. Bristol, R.I., Roger Williams College. 1441761
Beg. date: 1971
WU UWM (RBR) V.1-3; v.6 no.2 (1971-1977).

Aldebaran review. Berkeley, Calif., Noh Directions Press. 1429739
ISSN: 0002-5089 Beg. date: 1967
WU UWM (RBR) No.1-23 ([1967]-1976).

Alembic. London, Share Publications. 1429741
WU UWM (RBR) No.2-5 (SPR/SUM1974-1976).

Alentour; a national magazine of poetry. [Lowell, Mass., The Beaver Press, etc.]. 1429754
LCCN: 42-48185 Beg. date: 1935 End date: 1942
Supersedes Caravel; a national magazine of new poetry.
Subtitle varies slightly.
Ceased publication with 1942.
WU UWM (RBR) Summer 1937-Fall 1940.

Aleph; a quarterly of the arts. Takoma Park, Md. 1429767
Beg. date: 1975
WU UWM (RBR) No.1-4 (1975-1976).

Alive. Guelph, Ont., etc., Alive Press Ltd., etc. 142977A
ISSN: 0044-7285 Beg. date: 1969 End date: 1974
Ceased publication.
United with Literature and ideology to form Alive magazine: literature and ideology.
WU UWM (RBR) Feb.-Nov. 1970; v.2 (no.1-9); v.3 (no.16-33) (1971-1973); n. ser. no.34-41,51-95 (n.d.-1977).

Alive magazine: literature and ideology. Guelph, Ont., Alive Production Collective. 1429782
ISSN: 0318-6512
Formed by the union of Alive and Literature and ideology, continuing the volume numbering of the former.
WU UWM (RBR) No.42-50 (1974-JUN1976).

The Alkahest. Atlanta, Franklin Printing and Pub. Co. 1429795
LCCN: 10-26529 Beg. date: 1896 End date: 1903
Volume numbering irregular.
Caption title: May 1869- , The Alkahest magazine.
Absorbed Things and Thoughts, Art and photography, and The Florida magazine with Nov. 1903.
Ceased publication with 1903.
WU UWM (RBR) V.1 no.1 (MAY1896); July 1896; v.1 no.4-6 (OCT-DEC1896); v.2 no.3 (APR1897).

Alkahest; American college poetry. Middletown, Conn., Wesleyan University Press. 0924819
ISSN: 0002-5488
Ceased publication.
WU UWM (RBR) No.1-5 (SPR1968-SPR1971).

Allegany poetry. Olean, N.Y., Allegany Mountain Press. 1429804
Beg. date: 1975
WU UWM (RBR) No.[1]-4 (n.d.-1976).

Allotrope. Kenton, Harrow, Middlesex, Eng. 1429817
ISSN: 0044-7366 Beg. date: 1971
WU UWM (RBR) One unnumbered, undated issue.

Alma mater. Aberdeen, Scot., The Langstane Press. 146862A
Beg. date: 1883
"Published by the Students' Representative Council of the University of Aberdeen".
WU UWM (RBR) V.61 no.2; v.64 no.1 (SUM1950-JAN1953).

Alpha. Borgerhout, Belgium. 1441185
WU UWM (RBR) No.14-15 (JUN1956-FEB1957).

Alpha. [n.p.]. 1438820
Beg. date: 1976
WU UWM (RBR) V.1 no.1-3 (OCT-DEC1976); Jan.-Apr. 1977.

Alphabet. London, Ontario. 0027570
ISSN: 0002-6425 LCCN: 64-44271
Ceased publication with no. 18/19.
Absorbed Waterloo review in July 1961.
"A semiannual devoted to the iconography of the imagination".
WU UWM (RBR) No.2-19 (JUL1961-JUN1971).

Also. Chicago. 142982A
ISSN: 0569-1273 Beg. date: 1950 End date: 1951
Ceased publication with Spring 1951?
WU UWM (RBR) Issue 1-2 (MAY1950-SPR1951).

Alta. Birmingham, Eng., University of Birmingham. 1429832
Beg. date: 1966
"The University of Birmingham review."
WU UWM (RBR) No.1-6 (AUT1966-SUM1968); v.2 no.7-9 (WIN1968/1969-AUT1969).

Amalgam. Hounslow, Middlesex, Eng. 1429860
WU UWM (RBR) No.4-5 (n.d.-n.d.).

The Amalgamated holding company. Milwaukee, The Amalgamated Holding Company. 1429873
WU UWM (RBR) V.1 no.1-3 (n.d.-n.d.).

Amaranthus. Grand Rapids, Mich., Pilot Press Books. 1429886
WU UWM (RBR) V.2 no.3,7 (SPR-WIN1972).

Amarillo College, Amarillo, Texas.   Penny poems from Amarillo College. *See* Penny poems from Amarillo College. Amarillo, Tex. 1499737

Amateur notes & quotes. *See* Writer's notes & quotes. Fullerton, Calif. [etc.]. 1515023

Amazing grace. London, Institute for Research in Art and Technology. 1429899
WU UWM (RBR) No.1-6 (n.d.-1972).

Amazon quarterly. Oakland, Calif., Amazon Press. 1429910
Beg. date: 1972
"A lesbian-feminist arts journal."
WU UWM (RBR) V.1 issue 2; v.1 no.5-v.2 no.2,4 (FEB1973-1974).

Ambience; the arts in North London. [London], Haringey Arts Council. 1429923
ISSN: 0002-6956 Beg. date: 1968
WU UWM (RBR) No.1-3; v.2 no.1-2 (OCT1968-SPR1971).

Ambit. London. 1429949
ISSN: 0002-6972 Beg. date: 1959
"A quarterly of poems, short stories, drawings and criticism."
WU UWM (RBR) No.1-71 (SUM1959-1977).

The Ambrosian review. Davenport, Iowa. 1429951
Beg. date: 1965
WU UWM (RBR) V.1 no.1 (FAL/WIN1965).

American. Washington, D.C., American University Student Association. 1429964
ISSN: 0516-8783 Beg. date: 1965
WU UWM (RBR) No.1; v.3 no.2; v.4 no.1; v.5 no.2; v.6 no.2 (n.d.-WIN1971).

American aphrodite; a quarterly for the fancy-free. [New York]. 143000A
LCCN: 52-30982 Beg. date: 1951
WU UWM (RBR) V.1 no.1-4; v.2 no.5-7; v.3 no.9 (1951-1953).

American art association of Paris. *See* Quartier Latin. London, Paris, New York, Iliffe and son. 0029422

The American autopsy. Springfield, Mass., Headquarters Pub. Co. 1441774
Beg. date: 1932 End date: 1932
Ceased publication with vol. 1 no. 1, Jan. 1932?
WU UWM (RBR) V.1 no.1 (JAN1932).

American bard. Madison, N.J., Los Angeles, R. Sharp. 0033957
LCCN: 35-9610 rev
Title varies: 1918-Mar. 1945, The Country bard.
WU UWM (RBR) V.1-17; v.18 no.1-3; v.19 no.2,4; v.20 no.1 (SPR1944-JAN/MAR1971).

American bookman; a quarterly of literary theory and criticism. New York, The Philosophical Library. 0034362
Ceased publication with vol. 1 no. 2, Fall 1944.
Absorbed by Philosophic abstracts.
WU UWM (RBR) V.1 no.1-2 (WIN-FAL1944).

American caravan, a yearbook of American literature. *New York, The Macaulay Company.*   0034726
LCCN: 27-19157
Title varies: 1927, The American caravan. 1928, The second American caravan. 1929, The New American caravan. 1931, American caravan. IV. 1936, The New Caravan.
WU   UWM (RBR) No.1-4 (1927-1931).

American Center for Students and Artists. Montparnasse review. *See* Montparnasse review. Paris, American Center for Students and Artists.   1496997

American courier; dedicated to the mental and material improvement of man. *Kansas City, Mo.*   1441787
End date: 1956
Title varies: -vol. 2 no. 5, -May 15, 1941, DeHart's courier; vol. 2 no. 6-10, June 1-Oct. 1, 1941, Kansas City courier.
Subtitle varies.
Ceased publication with vol. 17 no. 1, Jan. 1956.
WU   UWM (RBR) V.1 no.27,29,31; v.2 no.2,4-7,9-12; v.5 no.3-4,7-12; v.6; v.7 no.1-9,11-12; v.8 no.1-2,4-11; v.9 no.1-7,9-12; v.10 no.1-3, 6-12; v.11; v.12 no.1,4-5; v.15 no.6-7 (JAN011941-JUL011954).

American dialog. *New York.*   0037472
ISSN: 0002-8215 LCCN: 65-9901 Beg. date: 1964
Called also American Dialogue.
None published in 1970.
WU   UWM (RBR) V.7 no.1,3 (WIN-SUM1972).

American dialogue. *See* American dialog. *New York.*   1164306

American Friends of the Chinese People. *See* China today. *New York, Greenwood Reprint, 1968.*   0039456

American haiku. *[Platteville, Wisconsin, etc.].*   0040448
ISSN: 0569-4981 LCCN: 66-97799 Beg. date: 1963 End date: 1968
Semiannual.
Ceased publication with vol. 6, 1968.
WU   UWM (RBR) V.1-6 (1963-1968).

The American imago; a psychoanalytical journal for the arts and sciences. *Boston, H. Sachs.*   0041323
ISSN: 0065-860X LCCN: A41-2485 Beg. date: 1939
Indexed by Reader's guide to periodical literature.
Indexes: vols. 1-10, in v. 10.
WU   UWM (RBR) V.22 no.1-4 (SPR-WIN1965).

American International College. Literary Club. Criterion. *See* Criterion. Springfield, Mass., Literary Club, American International College.   1431606

American letters; a monthly review. *Charleston, S.C.*   1430012
Beg. date: 1948 End date: 1949
Ceased publication with June 1949.
WU   UWM (RBR) Dec. 1948-Apr. 1949; June 1949.

American liberal. *San Francisco.*   1430025
ISSN: 0517-3159 Beg. date: 1960 End date: 1962
Title varies: vol. 1 nos. 1-2, Jan.-Feb. 1960, California liberal; vol. 1 no. 3-vol. 3 no. 6, March 1960-June 1962, Californian.
Ceased publication with vol. 3 no. 10, Nov. 1962.
WU   UWM (RBR) V.1 no.3-10; v.2-v.3 no.10 (APR1960-NOV1962).

American Literary Association. *See* American poetry magazine. *[Milwaukee].*   0046852

American Literary Association. Creative youth. *See* Creative youth. Wauwatosa, Wis., American Literary Association.   1431515

American Literary League. Lantern. *See* Lantern. Brooklyn, N.Y.   1507657

American magazine. *See* American. Washington, D.C., American University Student Association.   1429977

The American Mercury, a monthly review. *New York, American Mercury Magazine.*   0048429
LCCN: 25-11667 Beg. date: 1924
Title varies: Dec. 1950-Feb. 1951, New American mercury.
Subtitle varies.
Indexed by Reader's guide to periodical literature.
WU   UWM (RBR) V.1-3 (no.1-12); v.7 (no.28) (1924-APR1926).

American mosaic; gems of creativity by today's mosaic authors. *Lansing, Mich., American Mosaic Literary Publications.*   1430053
WU   UWM (RBR) V.1 no.1 (FAL1975).

American parade. *Girard, Kansas, Haldeman-Julius Company.*   005013A
LCCN: 30-31838
No more published.
Title varies: vol. 1-2, Haldeman-Julius quarterly.
WU   UWM (RBR) V.1; v.2 no.1,3-4 (OCT1926-JUL/SEP1928).

American parade. *New York, The parade publishing company.*   0050142
LCCN: 26-3074.
Subtitle varies.
WU   UWM (RBR) V.1 no.1-4; v.3 no.1-2 (1926-MAR1929).

American poet. *Brooklyn, N.Y.*   0051106
Beg. date: 1941 End date: 1944
Publication suspended with v. 3 (March 1944).
WU   UWM (RBR) V.1 no.2-4,6-8,10-12; v.2 no.1,3-12; v.3 no.1-2 (MAY1941-MAY1943).

American poet. *Charleston, Ill., American Poets Fellowship Society.*   1508820
ISSN: 0003-0546 Beg. date: 1963
Title varies: - , American poets.
WU   UWM (RBR) V.1 no.1-5; v.2 no.1 (OCT1963-WIN1964/1965); Mar. 1965-Jan./Mar. 1971.

American Poetry Journal. *[Flushing, L. I., L. Twinem].*   0051119
LCCN: 41-3907
Cover-title.
Monthly, July 1933-June 1935; bimonthly, July/August 1935.
No more published.
WU   UWM (RBR) July 1933-Jan. 1935.

American Poetry-League. Bulletin. *Kingsville, Tex.*   1430066
WU   UWM (RBR) July, Oct. 1957; Oct. 1958; 1959; Jan./Mar.-Apr./June, Oct./Dec. 1960; July/Sept. 1961.

American poetry magazine. *[Milwaukee].*   0051121
LCCN: 33-20878 Beg. date: 1919 End date: 1956
Frequency varies.
Official organ of the American Literary Association.
Ceased publication with vol. 37 no. 4, 1956.
Supplements accompany some issues.
WU   UWM (RBR) V.1 no.11 (MAR1920); v.35 no.2-3; v.37 no.1,4 (1954-1956).

American poetry publisher. *St. Louis, Mo. [etc.].*   1430079
ISSN: 0402-0480 Beg. date: 1959
Title varies.
WU   UWM (RBR) V.1 no.4-5 (OCT-NOV/DEC1959).

The American poetry review. *Philadelphia.*   0932003
ISSN: 0360-3709 LCCN: sc 75-12 Beg. date: 1972
WU   UWM (RBR) V.1-v.3 no.5; v.4; v.5 no.2-6; v.6 no.1-5 (NOV/DEC1972-1977); Masterbooks no.1 (1972).

American poets. *See* American poet. Charleston, Ill., American Poets Fellowship Society.   1508846

American Poets Fellowship Society. American poet. *See* American poet. Charleston, Ill., American Poets Fellowship Society.   1508833

American Poets Fellowship Society. American poets. *See* American poet. Charleston, Ill., American Poets Fellowship Society.   1508859

American prefaces; a journal of critical and imaginative writing. *[Iowa City, University of Iowa Press].*   0051489
LCCN: 36-6640
Published under the auspices of the School of letters and with the cooperation of the School of journalism and the School of fine arts of the University of Iowa.
Index v. 1-5.
WU   UWM (RBR) V.1-v.5 no.9; v.6 no.2-4; v.7-8 (OCT1935-SUM1943).

American quarterly. *Minneapolis, etc. University of Minnesota Philadelphia Univ. of Penn.*   0052323
ISSN: 0003-0678 LCCN: 50-4992 Beg. date: 1949
1949-50 issues published by U. of M. Press for the program of American studies at the Univ. of Minn.
1951-date, published for the Committee on American Civilization of the University of Pennsylvania.
1952-date: official journal of the American Studies Association.
Indexed by Humanities index, International index, and Social sciences and humanities index.
WU   UWM (RBR) V.1 no.2 (SUM1949); v.16 no.2 pt.1, no.3-4 (SUM-WIN1964).

American Review. *New York, Bookman Publishing Company.* 0052806
Beg. date: 1933 End date: 1937
Supersedes Bookman with Apr. 1933.
WU   UWM (RBR) Kraus reprints: v.1-9 (1933-1937); originals: v.5 no.4-5; v.6 no.1-3 (SEP1935-JAN1936).

The American satiricon; a quarterly journal of sardonic commentary. *New York.* 1430081
ISSN: 0402-0804 Beg. date: 1956
WU   UWM (RBR) V.6-8 (SPR1959-WIN1961/1962).

American-Scandinavian foundation, New York. *See* 005324A
American-Scandinavian review. *New York, American-Scandinavian foundation.*

The American-Scandinavian review. *New York, American-Scandinavian foundation.* 0053280
ISSN: 0003-0910 LCCN: 16-23752 Beg. date: 1913 End date: 1974
Continued by Scandinavian review with vol. 63 no. 1, March 1975.
Indexed by International index, Public affairs information service, and Social sciences index.
WU   UWM (RBR) V.47 no.1 (MAR1959).

The American scholar. *New York, Phi Beta Kappa, Concord, New Hampshire, Rumford Press, etc.* 0053315
ISSN: 0003-0937 LCCN: 33-20171 Beg. date: 1932
Supersedes the Phi Beta Kappa Key.
Indexed by Humanities index, Public affairs information service, and Reader's guide to periodical literature.
WU   UWM (RBR) V.27 no.3-4; v.28-29; v.30 no.4; v.33 no.3 (SUM1958-SUM1964).

American School of Classical Studies at Athens. Gennadius Library. Griffon. *See* Griffon. *Athens, Greece, American School of Classical Studies at Athens. Gennadius Library.* 1442318

American Semantic Society. Journal. *See* Semantika. *St. Louis, Mo.* 1507161

American spectator. *New York.* 0057038
Monthly.
WU   UWM (RBR) V.1-4 (no.1-38,46) (NOV1932-JAN1937).

American Students' and Artists' Center. Parnassus. *See* Parnassus. *Paris, Parnassus Publications.* 1498431

American Studies Association. *See* American quarterly. *Minneapolis, etc. University of Minnesota Philadelphia Univ. of Penn.* 0057486

American stuff. *See* Direction. *Darien, Connecticut.* 0057536

American University, Washington, D.C. Student Association. American. *See* American. *Washington, D.C., American University Student Association.* 142998A

American University Student Association. American. *See* American. *Washington, D.C., American University Student Association.* 1429992

American Weave. *Cleveland.* 0059024
ISSN: 0003-1526 End date: 1971
With supplements.
Ceased publication with v. 33 (1971).
WU   UWM (RBR) V.14 no.2; v.18 no.2-4; v.19 no.2-4; v.20 no.1,4; v.21-31; v.32 no.1; v.33 (SPR1949-1971).

American writing [year]; the anthology and yearbook of the American non-commercial magazine. *Boston [etc.], Bruce Humphries, Inc. [etc.].* 1430094
LCCN: 43-11058 Beg. date: 1942
Title includes date of issue.
WU   UWM (RBR) 1943.

Americana, a magazine of pictorial satire. *New York, American Group, Inc.; etc.* 1441811
Beg. date: 1932 End date: 1933
Subtitle varies.
Ceased publication with n. ser. vol. 2 no.1, Nov. 1933.
WU   UWM (RBR) V.1 no.1-4 (FEB-JUL1932); n. ser. v. 1 no.1-9,11 (NOV1932-SEP1933).

Amethyst; student literary magazine. *Wolfville, N.S., Students of Acadia University.* 1468645
ISSN: 0569-9290 Beg. date: 1962 End date: 1964
Ceased publication with vol. 4 no. 1, Autumn 1964.
Superseded by Either/or with Fall 1965.
WU   UWM (RBR) V.1 no.1; v.2 no.1,3-4; v.3 no.1-3; v.4 no.1 (SPR1962-AUT1964).

Amherst College. Paideia. *See* Paideia. *Amherst, Mass., Amherst College.* 1498143

The Amphora. *San Francisco, The Headstone Press.* 1432589
Beg. date: 1970
WU   UWM (RBR) No.1-8 (SUM1970-1972).

Anaesthesia review. *Ann Arbor, Mich.* 1432591
WU   UWM (RBR) 1975, 1977.

Analecta. *Demarest, N.J.* 1432600
ISSN: 0569-9770 Beg. date: 1967 End date: 1968
Ceased publication with vol. 2 no. 2, Spring 1968.
WU   UWM (RBR) No.1; v.2 no.1-2 (FAL1967-SPR1968).

Analects. *[Greensboro, N. C.].* 006027A
Ceased.
WU   UWM (RBR) V.1 no.1-2 (OCT-SPR1960).

Anathema. *See* Nationalist quarterly. *Boston, Mass.* 1492293

Anchor review. *Garden City, N.Y., Doubleday.* 0060830
LCCN: 55-10207
Ceased with no. 3.
WU   UWM (RBR) No.1-2 (1955-1957).

Ancillary; being a casual literary appendix to each printed issue of The Sparrow magazine. *Corona, N.Y.* 1492096
Beg. date: 1954
WU   UWM (RBR) No.1 (JUN1954).

And. *London, Writers Forum.* 1438019
ISSN: 0570-0248 Beg. date: 1954
No. 1 issued in Hendon by Hendon Arts Together; nos. 2-3 by Arts Together.
WU   UWM (RBR) No.1-6 (1954-1973).

Andúril. *Cincinnati.* 1432613
Beg. date: 1967
WU   UWM (RBR) No.1 (JAN311967).

Anduril, magazine of fantasy. *Bushey, Eng.* 1432626
Beg. date: 1972
Nos. 1-2 subtitled: Bulletin of the Tolkien Society and magazine of fantasy.
WU   UWM (RBR) No.3 (NOV1972).

Angel hair. *Williamstown, Mass., The Chapel Press.* 1432641
ISSN: 0003-3057 Beg. date: 1966
WU   UWM (RBR) No.1-6 (SPR1966-SPR1969).

Angel hour. *San Jose, Calif., Spearman Publications.* 1432654
ISSN: 0003-3065 Beg. date: 1964
WU   UWM (RBR) Sept./Oct. 1965; no.12,14-17,19,24-25 (FAL1967-1975); suppl. (n.d.).

The Angels. *Central Islip, N.Y., J R D Publishing Co. Inc.* 143267A
ISSN: 0003-3103 Beg. date: 1964
WU   UWM (RBR) V.3-5 (SPR1966-AUT/WIN1968).

The Angels. *Los Angeles, Spearman Associates.* 1432667
ISSN: 0517-7634 Beg. date: 1964
WU   UWM (RBR) V.1 no.1 (1964).

The Anglo-Saxon review; a quarterly miscellany. Edited by Lady Randolph Spencer Churchill. *London and New York, John Lane; [etc.].* 0061785
LCCN: 25-13816
"Printed by Ballantyne, Hanson and Co. at the Ballantyne Press, London and Edinburgh."
The covers are reproductions of rare bookbindings. Each volume has "Note on the binding...By Cyril Davenport".
No more published.
WU   UWM (RBR) V.1-10 (JUN1899-SEP1901).

Anglo-Welsh review. *Pembroke Dock, Eng., Temby, Wales, [etc.].* 118596A
ISSN: 0003-3405 Beg. date: 1949
Title varies: v.1-v.5 no.22, 1949-1957, Dock leaves.
WU   UWM (RBR) V.1 no.3; v.2 no.4; v.3 no.7,10; v.5 no.13,15; v.13 no.32; v.14 no.34; v.15-25 (no.35-56) (DEC1950-SPR1976).

Angry penguins. *See* Angry penguins broadsheet. *Melbourne.* 1438062

Angry penguins. *Melbourne.* 006181A
WU   UWM (RBR) Sept. 1943; Fall, Dec. 1944; Dec. 1945; July 1946.

Angry penguins broadsheet. *Melbourne.* 143805A
Beg. date: 1946 End date: 1946
An annual issue, dated 1945, precedes this series.
Cover title: Angry penguins.
Ceased publication with no. 10, Dec. 1946.
WU   UWM (RBR) 1 issue (1946).

Animal world. *See* Snowy egret. *Battle Creek, Mich.* 1510557

Ann Arbor review. Ann Arbor, Mich.   0062240
    WU   UWM (RBR) No.1-13,17-20,23-26 (FAL1967-1977).

Anno Domini. See A D [1950]. New York A.D. Literary Association.   1427820

Annual annual. Los Angeles, Pacifica Foundation.   1432682
    Beg. date: 1965
    WU   UWM (RBR) [No.1] (1965).

Anon. [Ann Arbor].   1432704
    WU   UWM (RBR) 1968-1975.

Anon. Austin, Tex.?, Kolokol Press.   1441263
    Beg. date: 1970
    WU   UWM (RBR) No.1 (DEC311970).

The Anonym quarterly. Buffalo, N.Y., Anonym Press.   1432717
    Beg. date: 1968
    WU   UWM (RBR) V.1 no.1 (1968); unnumbered, undated issue; Fall 1968; no.4-6 (1969-1970).

Another poetry magazine. Toronto.   143272A
    Beg. date: 1970
    WU   UWM (RBR) No.1-3 (JUN1970-SUM1971).

Antaeus. New York.   0067124
    ISSN: 0003-5319 LCCN: 70-612646 Beg. date: 1970
    Indexes: nos. 6-10, 1972-1973, with nos. 6-10; nos. 11-16, 1973-1975, with nos. 11-16.
    Author index: nos. 1-20, 1970-1975, in nos. 21-22.
    WU   UWM (RBR) No.1-27 (SUM1970-1977).

Ante. Los Angeles, Echo Press.   1432732
    ISSN: 0570-2860 Beg. date: 1964 End date: 1968
    Ceased publication with vol. 4 no. 2/3, Summer/Fall 1968.
    WU   UWM (RBR) V.1-v.4 no.3 (SUM1964-SUM/FAL1968).

Anthill. London, The Sarum Press.   1528310
    Beg. date: 1977
    WU   UWM (RBR) No.1-2 (JAN-APR1977).

Anthos. Dublin, Whitehall Musical and Dramatic Society.   1432745
    Beg. date: 1972
    WU   UWM (RBR) No.2-3 (DEC1972-1973).

Anthropos; the quarterly of humanist poetry. Toledo, Humanist Education Press, Inc.   1432760
    ISSN: 0518-004X Beg. date: 1959
    WU   UWM (RBR) V.1 no.1 (SPR1959).

Anti-Philistine; a monthly magazine and review of belles-lettres; also a periodical of protest. London, J. and H. Cowley.   006761A
    LCCN: 17-14452
    WU   UWM (RBR) No.1-4 (JUN15-SEP151897).

The Antidote. London.   0067754
    Beg. date: 1912 End date: 1915
    WU   UWM (RBR) V.1 no.1 (DEC211912).

The Antigonish review. Antigonish, N.S., Dept. of English, St. Francis Xavier University.   1438075
    ISSN: 0003-5661 LCCN: 73-641763 Beg. date: 1970
    WU   UWM (RBR) No.1-30 (SPR1970-1977).

Antinarcissus; surrealist conquest. San Francisco.   1432773
    Beg. date: 1969
    WU   UWM (RBR) No.1 (SUM1969).

Antioch College. Appalachia. What's a nice hillbilly like you..? See What's a nice hillbilly like you..? Beckley, W.Va., Southern Appalachian Circuit of Antioch College.   1518750

Antioch College. Southern Appalachian Circuit. What's a nice hillbilly like you..? See What's a nice hillbilly like you..? Beckley, W.Va., Southern Appalachian Circuit of Antioch College.   1518763

Antioch International Writing Seminars. Atlantic review. See Atlantic review. London.   1528349

The Antioch review. Yellow Springs, Ohio, Cleveland World Pub. Co.   0067873
    ISSN: 0003-5769 LCCN: 44-660 Beg. date: 1941
    Frequency varies, 1972- .
    Indexed by Humanities index, Public affairs information service, and Social sciences and humanities index.
    WU   UWM (RBR) V.6 no.1; v.18 no.2; v.27-32; v.33 no.1 (SPR1946-SPR1975).

Antipiugiú. Torino.   1432786
    WU   UWM (RBR) 1964.

Anubis. Arlington, Va., Golden Goblin Press.   1432799
    ISSN: 0003-6196 Beg. date: 1966
    WU   UWM (RBR) V.1 no.1-4 (AUT1966-AUT1968).

Anvil; life and the arts. London, Meridian Books.   1438090
    Beg. date: 1947 End date: 1947
    Ceased publication with Book 1, 1947.
    WU   UWM (RBR) Book 1 (1947).

Anvil, a student socialist magazine. [New York].   143810A
    LCCN: 58-23596 Beg. date: 1950
    Title varies: Spring 1950-Fall 1953, Anvil and student partisan, ISSN 0402-6772.
    Other slight variations in title.
    Issued -Summer/Fall 1954 by the New York Student Federation Against War and other student organizations.
    WU   UMW (RBR) V.2 no.1-3; v.3 no.1-2; v.4 no.1-3; v.5 no.1-2; v.6 no.1; v.7 no.1-4; v.8 no.1; v.9 no.1; v.10 no.1 (WIN1950-WIN1959).

Anvil, the proletarian fiction magazine. Moberly, Montana.   0068787
    ISSN: 0003-6226 LCCN: 42-47022
    Supersedes Rebel poet.
    United with Partisan Review to form Partisan Review and Anvil, later Partisan Review.
    WU   UWM (RBR) No.1-10; v.2 no.11-13 (MAY1933-OCT/NOV1935).

Anvil and student partisan. See Anvil, a student socialist magazine. [New York].   1438112

The Apalachee quarterly. Tallahassee, Fla., Dixie Dung Beetle Press.   1432810
    WU   UWM (RBR) Summer 1973; no.2-9 (WIN1974-1977).

Apex one. [n.p.].   1432823
    Beg. date: 1973
    WU   UWM (RBR) No.1-5 (SEP1973-n.d.).

Aplomb zero. Sherborne, Dorset, Eng., South Street Publications.   1432836
    WU   UWM (RBR) No.1-2 (1969).

Apocalypse. Purchase, N.Y.   1441276
    Beg. date: 1975
    WU   UWM (RBR V.1 no.1 (SPR1975).)

Apollo. Bigfork, Minn., Northwoods Press.   1432849
    Beg. date: 1973
    WU   UWM (RBR) V.1 no.1-2; v.2 no.1 (SPR1973-SPR1974).

Appalachian heritage; a magazine of Appalachian life and culture. Pippa Passes, Kentucky.   1086340
    Beg. date: 1973
    WU   UWM (RBR) V.1 no.1-4; v.2-3; v.4 no.2-4; v.5 no.1-3 (WIN1973-1977).

Appalachian review. Morgantown, W. Va., West Virginia University.   1438140
    ISSN: 0570-4766 LCCN: 66-9941 Beg. date: 1966 End date: 1968
    Ceased publication with vol. 3 no. 1, Fall 1968.
    WU   UWM (RBR) V.1-v.3 no.1 (SUM1966-FAL1968).

Appalachian south. Charleston, W. Va., Appalachian Associates, Inc.   1432851
    ISSN: 0003-6633 LCCN: 66-9890 Beg. date: 1965
    WU   UWM (RBR) V.2 no.2 (FAL/WIN1967).

Apple. Springfield, Ill.   0069283
    ISSN: 0003-6765 LCCN: 76-641441 Beg. date: 1967
    WU   UWM (RBR) No.1-12 (SUM1967-1976).

Apple (of beauty and discord). London, Colour publishing company.   0069296
    LCCN: 23-14990 Beg. date: 1920 End date: 1922
    Ceased publication with vol. 2 no. 2, 1922.
    WU   UWM (RBR) V.1 no.1-4 (1920).

Applegarth's folly. London, Ont.   1432877
    Beg. date: 1973
    WU   UWM (RBR) No.1-2 (1973-1975).

Apprentice. New York, New York University, Washington Square College.   1438166
    ISSN: 0402-7280 Beg. date: 1960
    WU   UWM (RBR) Feb. 1960.

Approach. Wallingford, Pa. [etc.].   143288A
    LCCN: 52-21026 Beg. date: 1947 End date: 1967
    Ceased publication with no. 64, Summer 1967.
    WU   UWM (RBR) No.1-64 (SPR1947-SUM1967).

Approach magazine. Oxford, St. Peter's College.   1468660
    ISSN: 0003-7125 Beg. date: 1967
    WU   UWM (RBR) No.1-2 (JUN1967-n.d.).

Approaches. See Kentucky poetry review. [Elizabethtown, Ky.?].   1493861

Approaches; a periodical of poems by Kentuckians. 1438181
Elizabethtown, Ky.
ISSN: 0003-7133 Beg. date: 1964
Continued by Kentucky poetry review.
WU   UWM (RBR) V.5-11 (NOV1968-SUM1975).

Aquarius; poetry magazine. *London.* 1432892
ISSN: 0003-7303 Beg. date: 1969
WU   UWM (RBR) No.1-6 (1969-1973).

Aquila. *Petersburg, Pa., Bob Quarteroni.* 1528323
Beg. date: 1976
WU   UWM (RBR) V.2 no.1 (SPR1977).

Arachne, a literary journal. *Wellington, N.Z., Crocus Pub. Co.* 1438194
ISSN: 0518-1984 LCCN: 57-58218 Beg. date: 1950 End date: 1951
Publication of Victoria University.
Ceased publication with vol. 1 no. 3, Dec. 1951.
"Published on behalf of the Literary Society of Victoria College, Wellington."
WU   UWM (RBR) No.2-3 (FEB-DEC1951).

Ararat. *New York, Armenian General Benevolent Union of America.* 1432901
ISSN: 0003-7583 LCCN: 63-51224 Beg. date: 1960
WU   UWM (RBR) V.7-v.9 no.3; v.11 no.3; v.15-16; v.17 no.3-4; v.18 no.1-3 (WIN1966-1977).

Arbiter. *London.* 1432927
ISSN: 0402-8449 Beg. date: 1952 End date: 1953
Ceased publication with no. 2, Spring 1953.
WU   UWM (RBR) No.1-2 (WIN1952-SPR1953).

Arbitrarium. *Washington, Pa., Washington and Jefferson College.* 143293A
Beg. date: 1973
WU   UWM (RBR) V.1 no.1 (SPR1973).

Arcade. *London.* 1432955
ISSN: 0570-6017 Beg. date: 1964
WU   UWM (RBR) No.1-2 (1964).

The Archer. *[North Hollywood, Calif.].* 1432968
ISSN: 0003-8237 LCCN: 58-22453 Beg. date: 1951
WU   UWM (RBR) V.1-6; v.7 no.1-3; v.9 no.1; v.10 no.1; v.11-13; v.14 no.1-2; v.15; v.16 no.1,3; v.17 no.1-3; v.18-20; v.21 no.1-2,4; v.22; v.23 no.1-2 (AUT1951-SUM1975).

The Archive. *Durham, N.C., Duke University Pub. Board.* 1438216
LCCN: 44-35322
Title varies: 18 -   The Trinity archive.
WU   UWM (RBR) V.77 no.1 (NOV1964).

Archives de la Danse.   En avant. **See** En avant. Auckland, N.Z., Les Archives de la Danse. 1432143

Archives de la Danse (Auckland). News-sheet. *[n.p.].* 1507488
WU   UWM (RBR) Aug., Dec. 1958; Mar./Apr. 1959.

Arden Club, Madison.   Rocking horse. **See** Rocking horse. Madison, Wisc., The Arden Club, University of Wisconsin, Madison. 1504772

Arena. *Coolgreany, Ire.* 1430103
ISSN: 0570-7404 Beg. date: 1963 End date: 1965
Ceased publication with no. 4, Spring 1965.
WU   UWM (RBR) No.1-4 (SPR1963-SPR1965).

Arena. *[London, P.E.N. Centre for Writers in Exile].* 1441198
ISSN: 0570-7439 LCCN: 65-77115 Beg. date: 1961
In English, French or German.
WU   UWM (RBR) No.1,3-4,6-26 (1961-MAR1967).

Arena; a literary magazine. *Wellington, N.Z., Handcraft Press.* 1438257
ISSN: 0004-0959 Beg. date: 1943 End date: 1975
Title varies: nos. 1-7, June 1943-Jan. 1945, Letters; quarterly; nos. 8-10, April-Dec. 1945, Letters magazine; nos. 11-   , March 1946-   , Arena; a quarterly of New Zealand international writing.
Other subtitle variations.
Absorbed New triad with July 1947.
Ceased publication with 1975.
WU   UWM (RBR) No.12-13,15-81 (JUN1946-FEB1975).

Arena; a magazine of modern literature. *London.* 007652A
Beg. date: 1949 End date: 1951
Subtitle varies.
Ceased publication with vol. 2 (no. 8), June/July 1951.
WU   UWM (RBR) No.1-8 (1949-1951).

Arena; a quarterly of New Zealand international writing. **See** Arena; a literary magazine. Wellington, N.Z., Handcraft Press. 1438285

Arete. *San Francisco.* 1438833
ISSN: 0363-2903 LCCN: 76-645854 Beg. date: 1976
WU   UWM (RBR) V.1 no.1-2 (1976).

Argo; an individual review. *Princeton, N.J.* 1430116
Beg. date: 1930 End date: 1930
Ceased publication with vol. 1 no. 2, Dec. 1930.
WU   UWM (RBR) V.1 no.2 (DEC1930).

Argot, a literary magazine. *Wellington, N.Z.* 1430129
ISSN: 0004-1130 Beg. date: 1961 End date: 1972
Ceased publication with no. 29, Dec. 1972.
Superseded by New argot with July 1973.
WU   UWM (RBR) V.2 no.2-3; v.3 no.10-12; no.13-29 (MAY1963-DEC1972).

Arion's dolphin. *Cambridge, Mass.* 0077420
ISSN: 0044-8834 LCCN: 72-620107 Beg. date: 1971
WU   UWM (RBR) V.1-3 (AUT1971-1974); no.14 (1975).

Arizona. University. Poetry Center. Grilled flowers. **See** Grilled flowers. Tucson, Ariz., Poetry Center, University of Arizona. 1442333

The Ark. *San Francisco.* 144121A
Beg. date: 1947 End date: 1947
Ceased publication with 1947.
Superseded by Ark II, Moby I with 1956.
WU   UWM (RBR) Spring 1947.

Ark; a journal of the Royal College of Art. *London, W.S. Cowell Ltd.* 1430131
ISSN: 0004-1688 Beg. date: 1950
WU   UWM (RBR) No.21-48,50-52 (SPR1958-SPR1972).

Ark II, Moby I. *San Francisco.* 1441222
ISSN: 0403-1148 Beg. date: 1956 End date: 1957
Supersedes The Ark.
On cover: Poetry. Cross section.
Ceased publication with 1957.
WU   UWM (RBR) 1956-Winter 1957.

Ark River review. *Philadelphia, Jonathan Katz.* 1362927
ISSN: 0044-8885 LCCN: 77-645130 Beg. date: 1971
WU   UWM (RBR) V.1 no.1-4; v.2 no.1-2,4; v.3-v.4 no.1 (APR1971-1977).

Armadillo. *Sarasota, Fla., Periplus Press.* 143016A
Beg. date: 1970
WU   UWM (RBR) Unnumbered 1970 issue; no.2 (FAL1971).

Armenian General Benevolent Union of America.   Ararat. **See** Ararat. New York, Armenian General Benevolent Union of America. 1432914

Arnold Bocklin. *Birmingham, Eng., Flat Earth Press.* 1429388
ISSN: 0307-6148
WU   UWM (RBR) No.1-5 (n.d.-1975).

Arrows. *[Sheffield, Eng., Sheffield University, Union of Students].* 1430172
Beg. date: 1929
WU   UWM (RBR) No.92-96 ([1967-1968]).

Arsenal; surrealist subversion. *Chicago.* 1430198
Beg. date: 1970
WU   UWM (RBR) No.1 (1970).

Arson; an ardent review. Part one of a surrealist manifestation. *London.* 1430207
Beg. date: 1942 End date: 1942
Ceased publication with no. 1, March 1942.
WU   UWM (RBR) No.1 (1942).

Art and artists. *[London, Hansom Books].* 008039A
ISSN: 0004-3001 LCCN: 66-9880
Vol. 4 no. 12 dated March 1969. With April 1969 started renumbering vol. 4; therefore, April 1969 issue is vol. 4 no. 1.
WU   UWM (RBR) V.2 no.5-12 (AUG1967-MAR1968); v.3 no.1-10 (APR1968-JAN1969); v.4 no.11-12 (FEB-MAR1969); v.4 no.1-2,4 (APR-JUL1969).

Art and letters. *London.* 1087254
LCCN: 23-14075 Beg. date: 1917 End date: 1920
WU   UWM (RBR) Originals: v.1 no.1-2 (JUL-OCT1971); reprints: v.1 no.1-4; n. ser. v.2 no.1-4; v.3 no.1-2 (1917-SPR1920).

Art and literature. *Lausanne, Société anonyme d'éditions littéraires et artistiques; distributed by Eastern News Distributors [etc.] New York.* 0080437
LCCN: 64-9401 Beg. date: 1964 End date: 1967
Quarterly.
Ceased with no. 12 (1967).
WU   UWM (RBR) No.1-12 (MAR1964-SPR1967).

The Art bulletin. [New York, etc.], College Art Association of America. 0080530
ISSN: 0004-3079 LCCN: 29-12891 rev Beg. date: 1913
Title varies: Jan.? 1913, College Art Association. Bulletin; Feb.? 1913-Sept. 1918, College Art Association of America. Bulletin.
Indexed by Art index.
Index: vols. 1-30, 1913-1948, 1 vol.
WU   UWM (RBR) V.11-14 (MAR1929-1932).

Art front. New York. 143021A
LCCN: 43-41268 Beg. date: 1934 End date: 1937
Official publication of the Artists' Union.
Ceased publication with vol. 3 no. 8, 1937.
WU   UWM (RBR) V.1 no.3-4,6 (FEB-JUL1935).

Art press. Spokane. 1432563
Sponsored by the English Dept. at Eastern Washington College of Education, Cheney, Washington.
WU   UWM (RBR) V.8 (SUM1959).

Art Young quarterly. New York. 0081128
Beg. date: 1922 End date: 1922
Supersedes Good morning.
Ceased publication with vol. 1 no. 1, 1922.
WU   UWM (RBR) V.1 no.1 (1922).

Artesian. [Ann Arbor, Mich., Great Lakes Publishers]. 1430235
ISSN: 0518-7915 LCCN: 62-65826 Beg. date: 1955
Frequency varies.
Subtitle varies.
WU   UWM (RBR) V.4 no.1-3; v.5 no.1-2; v.6 no.1-2; v.7 no.1-2 (WIN1958/1959-AUT1962).

Artisan. London, etc., Heron Press, etc. 1430248
ISSN: 0403-3574 Beg. date: 1952
Subtitle varies.
WU   UWM (RBR) Autumn 1952; Spring 1953; no.5-6 (SUM-AUT1954).

The Artist's miscellany. Montezuma, N.M., Gallinas Press. 1430250
ISSN: 0403-3671 Beg. date: 1958
WU   UWM (RBR) No.2-10 (OCT1958-1960); no.2 was preceded by an unnumbered, undated issue.

Artists' Union, New York. Art front. See Art front. New York. 1430222

The Artist's view. San Francisco. 1430263
ISSN: 0403-368X Beg. date: 1952
WU   UWM (RBR) No.1-7 (JUL1952-MAR1954).

The Arts. London, Lund Humphries and Co. Ltd. 1430276
Beg. date: 1946 End date: 1947
Ceased publication with no. 2, 1947.
WU   UWM (RBR) No.1-2 (1946-1947).

The Arts and philosophy. London. 1430289
ISSN: 0518-8199 Beg. date: 1950 End date: 1951
Ceased publication with no. 2, Autumn 1951.
WU   UWM (RBR) No.1 (SUM1950).

Arts and sciences in China. London. 1430291
ISSN: 0571-2181 Beg. date: 1963 End date: 1964
Ceased publication with vol. 2 no. 1, April/May 1964.
WU   UWM (RBR) V.1 no.1-4; v.2 no.1 (1963-MAY1964).

Arts in Society. Madison, University of Wisconsin Extension Division. 0081864
ISSN: 0004-4024 LCCN: 67-115032 Beg. date: 1958 End date: 1976
Frequency varies.
Ceased publication with vol. 13 no. 2, Summer/Fall 1976.
Indexed by Humanities index and Music article guide.
Indexes: Vols. 1-3, Jan. 1958-summer 1966, in v. 3:4.
WU   UWM (RBR) V.1 no.1-3,5; v.2 no.1-4; v.3-v.13 no.2 (1958-1976).

Arts Together. And. See And. London, Writers Forum. 1438047

Arx. Austin, Tex., Arx Foundation. 1440964
ISSN: 0004-4148 Beg. date: 1967
WU   UWM (RBR) No.1-12; v.2-3; v.4 no.1-2 (1967-JUN1970).

Ascent. Urbana, Ill. 1430300
ISSN: 0098-9363 LCCN: 75-646186 Beg. date: 1975
WU   UMW (RBR) V.1 no.2-3; v.2 no.1-3; v.3 no.1 (1975-1977).

Askance. Pullman, Wash. 1430313
ISSN: 0518-9055 Beg. date: 1962 End date: 1964
Ceased publication with no. 7, April 1964.
WU   UWM (RBR) No.1-7 (OCT1962-APR1964).

Aspect. Somerville, Mass., New View Publishing Association. 1430326
Beg. date: 1969
WU   UWM (RBR) No.1-68 (MAR1969-1977).

Aspects. Eugene, Ore. 1430339
ISSN: 0518-987X Beg. date: 1964
WU   UWM (RBR) No.1-13 (1964-SPR1971).

Aspen. New York, Roaring Fork Press, etc. 0083352
ISSN: 0004-4938 Beg. date: 1965
Title varies: , Aspen; the magazine in a box; Aspen magazine.
WU   UWM (RBR) V.1 no.1-4; no.5-6,6a,7,9-10 (1965-SUM1971).

Aspen; the magazine in a box. See Aspen. New York, 1343582

Aspen anthology. Aspen, Colo., Aspen Leaves Literary Foundation. 1430341
ISSN: 0362-9554 LCCN: 76-644446 Beg. date: 1976
Supersedes Aspen leaves; a literary magazine.
WU   UWM (RBR) No.1-3 (WIN1976-1977).

Aspen leaves; a literary magazine. [Aspen, Colo., Aspen Magazine]. 1311637
Beg. date: 1973 End date: 1975
Ceased publication with vol. 2 no. 2, Summer 1975.
Superseded by Aspen anthology with Winter 1976.
WU   UWM (RBR) V.1 no.1-2; v.2 no.1-2 (1973-1975).

Aspen Leaves Literary Foundation. Aspen anthology. See Aspen anthology. Aspen, Colo., Aspen Leaves Literary Foundation. 1430354

Aspen magazine. See Aspen. New York, 1343595

Assassinators' broadsheet. See Broadsheet. Sutton, Surrey, Eng. 1441313

Assay. Seattle, Department of English, University of Washington. 1440977
ISSN: 0004-5004 Beg. date: 1945
Continues Month's best.
WU   UWM (RBR) V.13 no.1-2; v.14 no.2; v.15 no.1; v.16 no.1-2; v.17 no.1-2; v.18-27; v.28 no.2-3; v.29-v.32 no.1 (WIN1955/1956-1977).

Assegai. Hornchurch, Essex, Eng., Poetry One. 144100A
Beg. date: 1974
WU   UWM (RBR) No.1-2 ([1974-1976]).

Assembling. Brooklyn, N.Y., Assembling Press. 1430367
Beg. date: 1970
"A collection of otherwise unpublishable manuscripts."
WU   UWM (RBR) No.1-5 (1970-1974).

Associated Council of the Arts. See Cultural affairs. New York, Associated Council of the Arts. 0083681

Asterisk II. Brooklyn, N.Y., Pratt Institute. 1432970
WU   UWM (RBR) Spring 1961.

Asylum. Bootle, Lancs., Eng. 1438298
ISSN: 0004-6426 Beg. date: 1967
Ceased publication.
Superseded by Driftwood; booklets of poems.
WU   UWM (RBR) No.3-6 (JAN-OCT1968).

Athanor. Clarkson, N.Y., etc., Athanor Press. 143037A
ISSN: 0044-9857 Beg. date: 1971
WU   UWM (RBR) V.1 no.1; no.2-6 (WIN/SPR1971-SPR1975).

Athanor. New York, Winepress. 1430382
ISSN: 0571-7469 Beg. date: 1967
Subtitle varies.
WU   UWM (RBR) V.1 no.1-2 (SPR-SUM1967).

Atlanta Poetry Collective. Daimon. See Daimon. Atlanta, Atlanta Poetry Collective, Inc. 1528665

The Atlantic review. London. 1528336
Beg. date: 1976
Edited and published by the Antioch International Writing Seminars.
WU   UWM (RBR) V.1 no.1-[3] (WIN1975/1976-SUM1976).

Atlantis. Dublin. 0088929
ISSN: 0004-6884
WU   UWM (RBR) No.1-6 (MAR1970-WIN1973/1974).

Atlas; the magazine of world press. *New York.* 1146988
ISSN: 0004-6930 LCCN: 63-24771 Beg. date: 1961 End date: 1972
Suspended publication with vol. 21 no. 3, April 1972.
Continued by Atlas world press review with vol. 21 no. 4, May 1974.
Indexed by Public affairs information service.
WU   UWM (RBR) V.1 no.1 (MAR1961).

Atom mind. *Syracuse, N.Y., Atom Mind Publications.* 1430395
Beg. date: 1968
WU   UWM (RBR) V.1 no.1-4; v.2 no.5-7 (SUM1968-1970).

Attack. Magazine for new art and new poetry. *Tokyo, Onion Press.* 1430404
ISSN: 0519-3680 Beg. date: 1956
In English and Japanese.
WU   UWM (RBR) No.4,6 (APR-NOV1957).

Attention please. *Broderick, Calif., Hearthstone Press.* 1429390
WU   UWM (RBR) V.1 no.1-3; v.2 no.1-2 (OCT1975-1977).

Auburncrest Library, Cincinnati. Imprimatur. *See* 1442621
Imprimatur; a folio of personalities, impressions and observations; an adventure in expression. Cincinnati.

Auckland, New Zealand. University. Literary Society. One: the word is freed. *See* One: the word is freed. Auckland, N.Z. 1499332

Audience. *Cambridge, Mass.* 0089598
Beg. date: 1955 End date: 1963
Ceased publication with vol. 8, 1963.
WU   UWM (RBR) V.3 no.1,4-5,8; v.4 no.2,3/4; v.5-v.8 no.4 (FEB101956-FEB1963).

Audit. *See* Audit/poetry. Buffalo, N.Y. 1430432

Audit-action. *See* Audit/poetry. Buffalo, N.Y. 143042A

Audit/poetry. *Buffalo, N.Y.* 1430417
ISSN: 0004-7643 LCCN: 68-130687 Beg. date: 1960
Title varies: 1960-1963, Audit.
Supplements, with title Audit-action, accompany some issues.
WU   UWM (RBR) V.1-8 (FEB1960-1976).

Auguries, a continuing anthology of the arts. *Ottawa, Commoners' Publishing Society, Inc.* 1528351
ISSN: 0702-715X
Title varies: Early evening pieces, ISSN 0703-2676.
WU   UWM (RBR) [1975].

Aura. *Birmingham, Ala.* 1438307
Beg. date: 1975
"The University of Alabama in Birmingham literary/arts review."
WU   UWM (RBR) V.1 no.2; v.2 no.1-2; no.5 (SPR1975-1976).

Austin College, Sherman, Texas. Harlequin. *See* 1441564
Harlequin. Sherman, Tex., Austin College.

Austin Peay State University, Clarksville, Tennessee. English Department. Tower. *See* Tower. Clarksville, Tenn. 1512831

Australasian small press review. *Manly, N.S.W., Second Back Row Press.* 1430445
ISSN: 0312-0112 Beg. date: 1975
WU   UWM (RBR) No.1-4 (1975-1976).

Australia. *See* Bookfellow, The Australasian review and journal of the Australasian book trade. *Sydney.* 0090774

Australian Amateur Press Association. Coo-ee. *See* Coo-ee. [n.p.]. 1429111

Australian National University, Canberra. Canberra poetry. *See* Canberra poetry. Canberra, Australian National University. Poetry Society. 1441928

Australian new writing. *Sydney, Mastercraft Printing and Pub. Co.,etc.* 1430458
Beg. date: 1943 End date: 1946
Ceased publication with no. 4, 1946.
WU   UWM (RBR) No.4 ([1946]).

Author/poet. *Birmingham, Ala., Thom Henricks Associates.* 142940A
"Combined with 'Bama writer."
WU   UWM (RBR) No.61-63,79-80 (JAN1967-n.d.).

Autograph collectors' journal. *See* Manuscripts. *New York.* 0094183

The Avalanche. *Berkeley, Calif., Undermine Press.* 1430460
ISSN: 0005-187X Beg. date: 1966
WU   UWM (RBR) No.2-5 (FAL1966-WIN1968/1969).

Avalon. Different; a voice of the atomic age. *See* Different; a voice of the atomic age. Floral Park, N.Y. [etc.], Avalon. 1434729

Avalon dispatch. *See* Cyclo-flame. San Angelo, Tex. 1431831

Avalon National Poetry Shrine. Different. *See* Different; a voice of the atomic age. Floral Park, N.Y. [etc.], Avalon. 1434731

Avalon National Poetry Shrine. Raven. *See* Raven. San Antonio, Tex. [etc.]. 1504142

Avalon news. *Alpine, Tex.* 1430473
ISSN: 0404-388X Beg. date: 1955 End date: 1957
Each issue includes current list of poetry markets.
Ceased publication with vol. 3 no. 1, Spring 1957.
Absorbed by The Flame.
WU   UWM (RBR) V.3 no.1 (SPR1957).

Avalon news digest. *Alpine, Tex.* 1429412
Beg. date: 1961
WU   UWM (RBR) V.1 no.1; v.2 no.1 (JUN1961-SPR1962).

Avalon World Arts Academy. Different. *See* Different; a voice of the atomic age. Floral Park, N.Y. [etc.], Avalon. 1434744

Avant garde. *New York, Avant-garde Media, Inc.* 0094588
ISSN: 0005-1918
WU   UWM (RBR) No.1-14 (1968-SUM1971).

Avante. *Tegucigalpa, Honduras.* 1430486
ISSN: 0404-3960 Beg. date: 1951
In English and Spanish.
WU   UWM (RBR) V.1 no.1-8; v.2 no.1-11 (NOV1951-SEP1954).

Awwrrrr. *See* Or oar ore. Monterey, Calif. 1499596

Axis. *New York Arno Press.* 0095030
LCCN: 68-9236
"Review of contemporary 'abstract' painting and sculpture."
Photo-offset of a periodical published quarterly (irregular) in London and edited by M. Evans.
WU   UWM (RBR) No.1-3,8 (1935-WIN1937).

Aylesford review. *Aylesford, Eng., St. Albert's Press.* 1430499
ISSN: 0572-2756 Beg. date: 1955
Subtitle varies.
sponsored by the English Carmelites.
WU   UWM (RBR) V.1 no.1-8; v.2 no.1,3; v.3 no.2-3; v.4 no.3,8; v.5 no.1-2; v.6 no.2,4; v.7 no.1-4; v.8 no.1-4; v.9 no.1; n. ser. v.1 (AUT1955-SUM1968).

Azimuth. *Portland, Ore.* 1430510
End date: 1973
Ceased publication with vol. 1 no. 6, Jan. 1973.
WU   UWM (RBR) V.1 no.2-3; no.4-6 (n.d.-1973).

Azu; bilingual poetry review. *New York.* 1430523
Beg. date: 1970
WU   UWM (RBR) No.1,7 (NOV1970-1972).

B

Babel. Lynbrook, N.Y., Babel Press. 1430536
ISSN: 0404-5785 Beg. date: 1959
WU   UWM (RBR) V.1 no.1 (OCT1959).

Babel; a multi-lingual critical review. Cambridge, Eng., Bowes and Bowes. 1430549
LCCN: 43-33052 Beg. date: 1940
WU   UWM (RBR) V.1 no.1-3 (JAN-SUM1940).

Baby John gets shot on his way to the west; a magazine of fiction and poetry. West Lafayette, Ind. 1430551
Beg. date: 1970
WU   UWM (RBR) No.1-5 (MAY1970-NOV1972).

Bachaet. Bloomfield, N.J., Hamlet Publications. 1468686
ISSN: 0005-3619 Beg. date: 1969
WU   UWM (RBR) V.2 no.6; v.3 no.1-3 (FEB-JUN1972).

Bachy. [W. Los Angeles, Calif., Papa Bach Bookstore]. 1430564
ISSN: 0091-1488 LCCN: 73-643234 Beg. date: 1972
WU   UWM (RBR) V.1 no.1; v.2 no.1; v.3-9 (JUL1972-1977).

The Back door. Athens, Ohio [etc.], The Back Door Press [etc.]. 1430577
Beg. date: 1970
WU   UWM (RBR) V.1 no.1-3; no.4-8 (1970-SPR1975).

Back roads; a magazine of the written and graphic arts. Cotati, Calif. 143058A
Beg. date: 1974
Continues Paper pudding with no. 6, Summer 1974.
WU   UWM (RBR) No.6-8 (SUM1974-1977).

Bag balm. Sugar Run, Pa., Plunkett Press. 1430592
Beg. date: 1975
Supersedes The Outer Circle and The Accumulation.
WU   UWM (RBR) No.1 (MAR1975).

The Baker Street journal, an irregular quarterly of Sherlockiana. New York, B. Abramson. 0096195
ISSN: 0005-4070 LCCN: 49-17066 Beg. date: 1946
Indexes: vols. 1-n.s. v. 19, 1946-1969, with v. 20.
WU   UWM (RBR) V.1 no.1-4; v.2 no.1-4 (1946-OCT1947).

Balanced living. Brookville, Ohio, School of Living. 1430614
ISSN: 0404-6749 Beg. date: 1958 End date: 1962
Continues The Interpreter with vol. 14, 1958.
Subtitle varies.
Official journal of the School of Living.
Continued by Way out with vol. 18 no. 7, July/Aug. 1962.
WU   UWM (RBR) V.14 no.9; v.15 no.1-3,5-8; v.16 no.6; v.17 no.4 (SEP1958-SPR1961).

Balcony; the Sydney review. Sydney, Dept. of English, University of Sydney. 143063A
ISSN: 0522-0572
WU   UWM (RBR) No.4-6 (SUM1966-SUM1967).

Ballsout; a magazine of unpleasant verse and impolite prose. Vancouver, B.C., The Pendejo Press. 1430668
ISSN: 0005-4399 Beg. date: 1969
WU   UWM (RBR) V.1 no.1-2 (MAR/JUN-SUM1969).

Bananas. London, Bananas Ltd. 1430670
Beg. date: 1975
WU   UWM (RBR) No.1-8 (1975-1977).

Bananas: a thatch of creativity. Shawnee, Okla., Kickapoo Spur Press. 1430683
Beg. date: 1974
Continued by Faust: a litany of the ants with no. 3, 1975.
WU   UWM (RBR) No.1-2 (1974-n.d.).

Barat College of the Sacred Heart. Barat faculty review. *See* Barat review. [Lake Forest, Ill., Barat College]. 1430720

Barat College of the Sacred Heart. Barat review. *See* Barat review. [Lake Forest, Ill., Barat College]. 1430705

Barat faculty review. *See* Barat review. [Lake Forest, Ill., Barat College]. 1430718

The Barat review. [Lake Forest, Ill., Barat College]. 1430696
ISSN: 0005-5859 LCCN: 66-9858 Beg. date: 1966 End date: 1971
Title varies: Jan. 1966, Barat faculty review.
Ceased publication with vol. 6, 1971.
WU   UWM (RBR) V.1-6 (1966-1971).

The Barataria review. New Orleans. 1430733
Beg. date: 1974
WU   UWM (RBR) V.1 no.1 (1974).

Barbeque planet. Nashville, Project House Publications. 1430746
ISSN: 0364-2194 LCCN: 76-641984 Beg. date: 1975
WU   UWM (RBR) No.1-7 (FAL1975-1977).

The Bard. Minneapolis, University High School, University of Minnesota. 1430759
Beg. date: 1958
WU   UWM (RBR) No.1 (1958).

The Bard. West Lafayette, Ind., Purdue University. 1430774
ISSN: 0408-5620 Beg. date: 1960
WU   UWM (RBR) Fall 1966.

Bard College. Lampeter muse. *See* Lampeter muse. Annandale-on-Hudson, N.Y., Bard College. 1493755

Bard College, Annandale-on-Hudson, New York. Muse. *See* Muse. Annandale-on-Hudson, N.Y., Bard College. 1497387

Bard review. Annandale-on-Hudson, N.Y. 0098454
Ceased publication.
WU   UWM (RBR) V.1-3 (WIN1946-1950).

Bardic echoes. Grand Rapids, Mich., Bards of Grand Rapids. 143079A
ISSN: 0005-5948 Beg. date: 1960
WU   UWM (RBR) V.2 no.2,4; v.3 no.2; v.5 no.2; v.6 no.3-4; v.8 no.4; v.12 no.1-4; v.13 no.1-2,4 (JUN1961-DEC1972); extra issue no.1 (FEB1971).

Bards of Grand Rapids, Michigan. Bardic echoes. *See* Bardic echoes. Grand Rapids, Mich., Bards of Grand Rapids. 1430809

Barefoot. Memphis. 1430811
Beg. date: 1965
WU   UWM (RBR) No.1-2 (SPR-SUM1965).

Barefoot, barefoot, barefoot. London, Oyster Publications. 1430824
WU   UWM (RBR) Winter 1968; Summer 1969; January 1971.

The Barker brigade. Delavan, Wis. [etc.]. 1430837
Beg. date: 1974
WU   UWM (RBR) V.3 no.1-3 (SPR-SUM1975).

Bartleby's. Olmstead Falls, Ohio, Rathskeller Press. 143084A
ISSN: 0522-4373 Beg. date: 1967
WU   UWM (RBR) V.1 no.3 (JUL1967).

Bartleby's review. Machias, Maine. 1430852
Beg. date: 1972
WU   UWM (RBR) V.1 no.1-4; no.5 (FAL1972-1975).

Baseball. Oshkosh, Wis., River Bottom Press. 1430865
Beg. date: 1974
WU   UWM (RBR) No.1-5 (MAY1974-1977).

Bastard angel. San Francisco. 1430878
Beg. date: 1972
WU   UWM (RBR) No.1-3 (SPR1972-FAL1974).

The Bawl street journal. New York, The Bond Club of New York. 1430880
WU   WUM (RBR) V.30 no.1 (JUN071957).

The Bay quarterly. Berkeley, Calif. 1430893
Beg. date: 1945
WU   UWM (RBR) V.1 no.1 (1945).

Bay shore breeze. Tujunga, Calif. [etc.]. 1430902
WU   UWM (RBR) Mar./Apr. 1965; Dec. 1965/Jan. 1966.

Beacon. Dorchester, N.B. 1430915
Beg. date: 1951
"A Dorchester Penitentiary inmate publication."
Suspended publication Aug. 1969-April 1970.
WU   UWM (RBR) Oct./Nov. 1970-Dec. 1970/Jan. 1971.

The Beacon; Chicago's liberal magazine. Chicago, Beacon Pub. Co. 1430928
Beg. date: 1937
WU   UWM (RBR) V.1 no.3-10 (JUL1937-MAR1938).

Bean train express. [n.p.]. 1430930
WU   UWM (RBR) V.3 no.1 (NOV1963).

Beatitude. [San Francisco], City Lights Books. 1430943
ISSN: 0408-7461 Beg. date: 1959
WU   UWM (RBR) No.1,3,15-18,20 (MAY091959-MAR1968).

Beatitude/east. New York, Beatitude Press, Inc. 1430956
ISSN: 0522-5515
WU   UWM (RBR) No.16-17 (SEP/OCT1960-FEB061961).

Beethoven Memorial Foundation, Incorporated. Gadfly; an occasional review. *See* Gadfly; an occasional review. Milwaukee, Wis., Beethoven Memorial Foundation, Inc.   1439719

The Beginning. *Cleveland, Promise Press.*   1430969
Beg. date: 1966
WU   UWM (RBR) No.1 (1966).

The Bell; [a survey of Irish life]. *Dublin.*   1430971
LCCN: 43-38345 Beg. date: 1940 End date: 1954
Suspended publication May 1948-Oct. 1950.
Ceased publication with vol. 19, 1954.
WU   UWM (RBR) V.8 no.1-6; v.9 no.1-6; v.10-15; v.16 no.2-6; v.17 no.1-4,9,11; v.18 no.3-5,8,10-11 (APR1944-SUM1953).

The Bellingham review. *Bellingham, Wash., The Signpost Press.*   1528377
Beg. date: 1977
WU   UWM (RBR) V.1 no.1-2 (JAN-SPR1977).

Bellow, Saul, ed. *See* Noble savage. New York, Meridian Books.   0102586

Belmont Abbey College, Belmont, North Carolina. Agora. *See* Agora. Belmont, N.C., Belmont Abbey College.   143251A

the Beloit poetry journal. *Beloit, Wisconsin.*   0102608
ISSN: 0005-8661 LCCN: 62-59685 Beg. date: 1950
Author index: vols. 1-25, 1950-1975, with vol. 25.
WU   UWM (RBR) V.1-v.27 no.4 (1950-1977).

Beltaine; an occasional publication. The organ of the Irish literary theatre. *London.*   0102636
Beg. date: 1899 End date: 1900
A re-issue of the first year's numbers in one volume.
No more published.
WU   UWM (RBR) No.1-3 (MAY1899-APR1900).

Bennington College, Bennington, Vermont. Bennington review. *See* Bennington review. Bennington, Vt., Bennington College.   1432535

Bennington College, Bennington, Vermont. Silo. *See* Silo. Bennington, Vt., Bennington College.   1505028

The Bennington review. *Bennington, Vt., Bennington College.*   1432522
ISSN: 0522-8999 Beg. date: 1966 End date: 1970
Vol. 1 no. 4; vol. 2 nos. 3-4 not published.
Ceased publication with vol. 4 no. 1, Summer 1970.
WU   UWM (RBR) V.1 no.1-3; v.2 no.1-2; v.3 no.1-4; v.4 no.1 (FAL1966-SUM1970).

Berkeley poets cooperative. *Berkeley, Calif., Berkeley Poets' Workshop and Press [etc.].*   1438322
LCCN: 77-615501 Beg. date: 1970
WU   UWM (RBR) No.1-11 (1970-1977).

The Berkeley review. *[Berkeley, Calif.], Barlow, Huppert and Tong.*   1432996
ISSN: 0405-4644 LCCN: 65-50057 Beg. date: 1956 End date: 1957
Ceased publication with vol. 1 no. 3, 1957.
WU   UWM (RBR) V.1 no.1-3 (WIN1956-1957).

Berkeley samisdat review. *See* Samisdat. Berkeley, Calif.   1438805

Berkshire review. *Williamstown, Mass., Department of English, Williams College.*   1070649
ISSN: 0005-920X Beg. date: 1965
WU   UWM (RBR) V.1-v.10 no.1; v.11-v.13 no.1 (SPR1965-1977).

Bermondsey book; a quarterly review of life and literature. *London, C. Palmer, etc.*   0104951
LCCN: 31-9578 rev Beg. date: 1923 End date: 1930
V. 3-7 published by William Heinemann.
Includes the section "The Bookshelf".
Ceased publication with vol. 7 no. 2, May 1930.
WU   UWM (RBR) V.3 no.2 (MAR1926).

Best articles & stories. *[Spencer, Ind.].*   1433003
ISSN: 0409-252X LCCN: 63-27053 Beg. date: 1957 End date: 1961
Ceased publication with vol. 5 no. 5, May 1961.
WU   UWM (RBR) V.2 no.1-2 (JAN-FEB1958).

Best friends; poems and drawings by women from Albuquerque. *[Albuquerque, N.M.], The Best Friends Poetry Collective.*   1433016
Beg. date: 1971
Subtitle varies.
WU   UWM (RBR) No.2-5 (SUM1972-JAN1976).

The Best in poetry for [1968]. *Deerpark, N.Y.*   1438335
Title includes date of issue.
WU   UWM (RBR) No.3 (1968).

Bethune-Cookman College of Daytona Beach, Florida. Volusia review. *See* Volusia review. Aliandale, Fla.   1517505

Better verse. *St. Paul, Minn. [etc.].*   1433029
Beg. date: 1932 End date: 1938
Ceased publication with vol. 6 no. 3, 1938.
WU   UWM (RBR) V.3 no.3 (APR1935).

Between worlds. *[Denver, A. Swallow].*   1438348
ISSN: 0523-1116 LCCN: 68-7216 Beg. date: 1960 End date: 1962
Chiefly in English; some French, German, Italian or Spanish.
Issues for 1960- published for Inter American University.
Ceased publication with vol. 2 no. 1, Fall/Winter 1962.
WU   UWM (RBR) V.1 no.1-2; v.2 no.1 (SUM1960-FAL/WIN1962).

Beyond Baroque. *Venice, Calif., Beyond Baroque Foundation.*   0105969
ISSN: 0006-0445 Beg. date: 1968
WU   UWM (RBR) V.1 no.1-4; v.2 no.1-2; v.3 no.1-2; v.4 no.1-6; v.6 no.1-4; v.7 no.1,3-6; v.8 no.1-6 (DEC1968-1977).

Bezoar. *Gloucester, Mass.*   152838A
Beg. date: 1975
WU   UWM (RBR) V.1-v.10 no.1 (APR1975-OCT1977).

Bibelot, a reprint of poetry and prose for booklovers, chosen in part from scarce editions and sources not generally known. *New York, W. H. Wise and company.*   0106110
Beg. date: 1895
Index: 1-20.
WU   UWM (RBR) V.1 no.1; v.9 no.9-11; v.15 no.9; v.18 no.10 (JAN1895-OCT1912).

Bibliognost; the book collector's little magazine. *New York, Three Mountains Press.*   1433031
Beg. date: 1975
WU   UWM (RBR) V.1 no.1,3-4; v.2 no.1-2 (FEB1975-MAY1976).

Bibliography III. Supplement. *See* Descant. Toronto, Graduate English Assn., University of Toronto.   1434638

The Bibliophile, a magazine and review for the collector, student and general reader. *London, The Bibliophile Office.*   0898050
LCCN: 9-18978 rev
WU   UWM (RBR) V.1-4 (no.1-19) (APR/AUG1908-SEP1909).

Big boulevard. *Long Beach, Calif.*   1433044
Beg. date: 1973
WU   UWM (RBR) V.1 no.1-6; v.2 no.1-3; v.3 no.1-2 (1973-1975).

Big deal. *New York.*   1433057
WU   UWM (RBR) No.2-4 (SPR1974-1976).

Big moon. *Oakdale, Calif.*   143306A
Beg. date: 1975
WU   UWM (RBR) V.1; v.2 no.3-4; v.3 no.1 ([1975]-1977).

Big scream. *Wyoming, Mich. [etc.], Nada Press.*   1433072
Beg. date: 1974
WU   UWM (RBR) No.[1]-2,4-5,7 ([1974]-1976).

Big sky. *Bolinas, Calif.*   1433085
Beg. date: 1971
WU   UWM (RBR) No.1-10 (1971-1976).

Big table. *[Chicago], Big Table, Inc.*   1433098
ISSN: 0523-5286 LCCN: 59-9754 Beg. date: 1959 End date: 1960
No. 1 contains "the complete contents of the suppressed Winter 1959 Chicago review."
Ceased publication with vol. 2 no. 5, Fall 1960.
WU   UWM (RBR) V.1 (no.1-4); v.2 (no.5) (SPR1959-FAL1960).

Big venus. *London.*   1433107
Beg. date: 1969
WU   UWM (RBR) No.1-4 (1969-1970).

Big yellow bust. *Green Bay, Wis.*   143311A
WU   UWM (RBR) V.1 no.2 (1970).

Bim. *[St. Michael, Barbados, Young Men's Progressive Club].*   1433122
ISSN: 0006-2766 LCCN: 59-27799 Beg. date: 1942
WU   UWM (RBR) V.1 (no.4); v.2 (no.5); v.4 (no.13-14); v.5 (no.18-20,22); v.6 (no.23-24); v.7 (no.25); v.8 (no.32); v.10 (no.40-41); v.11 (no.42-43); v.13 (no.50-52); v.14 (no.54-56); v.15 (no.57-60) (APR1944-1976).

Bird effort. *East Hampton, L.I.* 1528392
Beg. date: 1975
WU   UWM (RBR) No.1/2 (1975).

Birmingham, England. University. Alta. *See* Alta. 1429858
Birmingham, Eng., University of Birmingham.

Birmingham, England. University. Left. *See* Left. 1492540
[Birmingham, Eng.], University of Birmingham Socialist Union.

Birmingham central literary association. *See* Central literary 0112629
magazine. *Birmingham [etc.]*.

Birmingham Poetry Centre. Muse. *See* Muse. [n.p.], 1497409
Birmingham Poetry Centre.

Birth. *New York.* 1433148
ISSN: 0520-2183 Beg. date: 1958
WU   UWM (RBR) No.1-3 (AUT1958-AUT1960);
bibliography no.1 (1959).

Birthstone. *San Francisco, Calif.* 1528401
"Quarterly publication of poetry, photography and graphic art."
WU   UWM (RBR) No.2 (FAL1976).

Bit. *Milan.* 1433150
Beg. date: 1967
In English and Italian.
WU   UWM (RBR) No.1-6 (MAR/APR-DEC1967); v.2 no.1-3
(MAR/APR-JUN1968).

Bits. *Cleveland, Case Western Reserve University,* 1438376
Department of English.
Beg. date: 1975
WU   UWM (RBR) No.1-6 (1975-1977).

The Bitter oleander. *Syracuse, The Bitter Oleander Press.* 1433163
WU   UWM (RBR) V.1 no.2; v.2 no.1-2
(1975-1977).

Bitterroot; international poetry quarterly. *Brooklyn, N.Y.* 1433176
ISSN: 0006-3908 Beg. date: 1962
WU   UWM (RBR) V.1-15 (no.1-31,33,35-37,39-61)
(FAL1962-1977).

Black and red. *Kalamazoo, Mich.* 0113021
WU   UWM (RBR) No.2-6 1/2 (OCT1968-1969).

Black Bart brigade; the outlaw magazine. *Canyon, Calif.* 1433189
Beg. date: 1971
WU   UWM (RBR) No.1,4-7 (NOV1971-MAY1974).

Black book. *Bowling Green, Ohio.* 1438391
Beg. date: 1975
WU   UWM (RBR) No.1-2 (WIN1975-1976).

Black box. *Washington, D.C.* 1071000
Beg. date: 1972
A periodical of poetry and music in cassette form.
WU   UWM (RBR) No.1-11 (1972-1976).

Black cat review. *San Bernardino, Calif.* 1438413
ISSN: 0520-2493 Beg. date: 1962
WU   UWM (RBR) No.1,3 (JUN1962-JUN1965).

Black creation. *New York, Institute of Afro-American Affairs.* 0113125
ISSN: 0045-2149
WU   UWM (RBR) V.1 no.1-2; v.2 no.2-3; v.3; v.4 no.1-3;
v.5 no.1; v.6 (APR1970-1975).

Black dialogue magazine. *San Francisco, New York.* 1433191
ISSN: 0523-7181 Beg. date: 1965
WU   UWM (RBR) V.1 no.[1]-3; v.4 no.1-2
([1965]-SUM1970).

Black eggs. *[Winchester, Hants., Eng., Blue Dog* 1468699
Publications].
Beg. date: 1971
WU   UWM (RBR) No.1-3 (1971-SEP1972).

Black graphics international. *San Francisco.* 1433200
ISSN: 0045-2165 Beg. date: 1970
WU   UWM (RBR) Unnumbered issue (1969); no.3,9,18
(1969-1974).

Black jack. *Riverdale, Calif. [etc.]*. 1433213
WU   UWM (RBR) No.2 (1973).

Black Maria. *Chicago [etc.]*. 1433226
Beg. date: 1971
WU   UWM (RBR) V.1 no.4; v.2 no.1-4; v.3 no.1-2
(SPR/SUM1973-1976).

Black mask. *New York.* 1433239
Beg. date: 1966
WU   UWM (RBR) No.1-10 (NOV1966-APR/MAY1968).

Black moss. *Windsor, Ont., Bandit Press Productions.* 1433241
ISSN: 0067-9097 Beg. date: 1969
WU   UWM (RBR) V.1 no.2-3; v.2 no.1 (SPR1969-1970); n.
ser. no.1-3 (1976-1977).

Black Mountain College, Black Mountain, North Carolina. 1429438
Black mountain college review. *See* Black mountain college review.
Black Mountain, N.C., Black Mountain College.

The Black mountain college review. *Black Mountain, N.C.,* 1429425
Black Mountain College.
Beg. date: 1951 End date: 1951
Ceased publication with vol. 1 no. 1, June 1951.
WU   UWM (RBR) V.1 no.1 (JUN1951).

Black Mountain College review. *See* Black mountain review. 0113229
Black Mountain, N.C.

Black mountain review. *Black Mountain, N.C.* 0113231
ISSN: 0523-7211 Beg. date: 1954 End date: 1957
Ceased publication with no. 7, Autumn 1957.
WU   UWM (RBR) V.1 no.1-4; no.5-7 (SPR1954-AUT1957).

Black music in evolution. *See* Cricket; black music in 1431584
evolution. Newark, N.J.

Black Orpheus; a journal of African and Afro-American 0113257
literature. *Ikeja [etc.], Nigeria, Longman [etc.]*.
ISSN: 0067-9100 LCCN: 65-81645 Beg. date: 1957 End date: 1967
Volumes for 1957-1962 issued by the General Publications Section,
Western Nigeria Ministry of Education; 1963-   by the Mbari
Club (called 1963-   Mbari Ibadan).
Ceased publication with no. 22, 1967.
WU   UWM (RBR) No.1-22; v.2 no.1-3,5-7; v.3 no.1-4
(SEP1957-1976).

Black sun. *Brooklyn, N.Y.* 1433254
ISSN: 0523-7262 Beg. date: 1965
WU   UWM (RBR) V.1 no.1-4 (1965).

Black swamp review. *Bowling Green, Ohio, Bowling Green* 1438426
State University, English Department.
ISSN: 0006-4629 Beg. date: 1970
Supersedes Brown paper bag.
WU   UWM (RBR) V.1 no.1-6 (1970-1972).

The Black tear. *Milwaukee, Wis., Goliards Press Inc.* 1433267
ISSN: 0523-7270 Beg. date: 1966
WU   UWM (RBR) No.1 (1966).

Black theatre. *New York, New Lafayette Theatre.* 0926714
ISSN: 0006-4270 Beg. date: 1968
WU   UWM (RBR) No.1-6 (1968-1972).

The Black warrior review. *University, Ala., University of* 143327A
Alabama.
Beg. date: 1974
WU   UWM (RBR) V.2 no.2; v.3 no.1-2 (SPR1976-1977).

Blackberry. *Albuquerque, N.M.* 1433295
Beg. date: 1975
WU   UWM (RBR) No.1-6 (SUM1975-1977).

Blackberry. *Brunswick, Maine.* 1433304
Beg. date: 1974
WU   UWM (RBR) No.1-15 (1974-1977).

Blackberry reader. *[n.p.]*. 1528414
Beg. date: 1977
WU   UWM (RBR) No.1 (1977).

Blackbird. *Chicago.* 1433317
ISSN: 0520-2523 Beg. date: 1963
WU   UWM (RBR) V.1 no.1-3 (1963-1966).

The Blackbird circle. *Jeffersontown, Ky. [etc.], The* 143332A
Blackbird Press, Inc.
Beg. date: 1971
WU   UWM (RBR) No.1-7 (SPR1971-SPR1975).

Blackfish. *Burnaby, B.C., Blackfish Press.* 1433332
ISSN: 0045-2270 Beg. date: 1971
WU   UWM (RBR) No.1-5 (SPR1971-SPR1973).

Blank tape. *Brooklyn, N.Y., Permanent Press.* 1528427
Beg. date: 1977
WU   UWM (RBR) No.1 (1977).

Blast; a magazine of proletarian short stories. *New York.* 0113714
WU   UWM (RBR) V.1 no.1-3
(SEP/OCT1933-JAN/FEB1934).

Blast; review of the great English vortex. *London, New York,* 0113727
John Lane.
Beg. date: 1914
WU   UWM (RBR) No.1-2 (JUN261914-JUL1915).

Bleb. *New York.*   1433345
    ISSN: 0006-467X   Beg. date: 1970
    WU   UWM (RBR) No.1-11 (1970-1976).

Blew ointment. *See* Blew ointment press. Vancouver, B.C.,   1438454
Blew Ointment Press.

Blew ointment press. *Vancouver, B.C., Blew Ointment*   1438441
Press.
    ISSN: 0520-2728   Beg. date: 1963
    Title varies: , Blew ointment.
    WU   UWM (RBR) V.9 no.1 (JUN1967); Aug., Sept. 1967; Aug. 1968.

Blitz. *Lagrande, Ore.*   1433358
    ISSN: 0523-7483   Beg. date: 1965
    WU   UWM (RBR) No.1-3 ([1965]-FAL1966).

Bloodroot. *Madison, Wis., Dept. of English, Univ. of*   1438467
Wisconsin, and Memorial Union Directorate.
    Beg. date: 1974
    WU   UWM (RBR) No.1-[3] (1974-APR1975).

The Bloody horse. *Montreal.*   1433360
    Beg. date: 1963
    WU   UWM (RBR) V.1 no.1 (JAN1963).

Blue beat. *See* Bluebeat. New York, Bluebeat Publications.   143348A

Blue bus. *Newton Square, Pa.*   0114067
    WU   UWM (RBR) V.1 no.1-3 (SEP1967-APR1968).

Blue cloud quarterly. *Marvin, S. Dakota.*   011407A
    ISSN: 0006-5064   Beg. date: 1955
    WU   UWM (RBR) V.14; v.15 no.1-2; v.16-22; v.23 no.1-3 (1968-1977).

Blue grass. *Georgetown, Ky. [etc.].*   1433386
    ISSN: 0523-7661   Beg. date: 1962   End date: 1964
    Ceased publication with no. 3, 1964.
    WU   UWM (RBR) Oct. 1962; no.2-3 (WIN1963-1964).

Blue guitar. *[Long Beach, Calif.].*   1433399
    ISSN: 0523-767X   Beg. date: 1952   End date: 1962
    Title varies slightly: nos. 1-5, The Blue guitar.
    Subtitle varies.
    Nos. 15-   also include Pacific explicator, vol. 1 no. 1-
    Spring 1959-
    Ceased publication with no. 20, Fall 1962.
    WU   UWM (RBR) No.2-10 (v.1 no.2-10); no.11-14 (V.2 no.1-4); no.15-20 (AUG1952-FAL1962).

Blue horse. *See* (Redivivus) Blue horse. Augusta, Ga., Blue   1529371
Horse Publishers.

Blue horse (Redivivus). *See* (Redivivus) Blue horse.   1529369
Augusta, Ga., Blue Horse Publishers.

Blue lick review. *Louisville.*   1433410
    Beg. date: 1970
    WU   UWM (RBR) V.1 no.1 (SPR1970).

Blue pig. *Northampton, Mass.*   1441289
    Beg. date: 1968
    WU   UWM (RBR) No.1-4,9-10,22 (n.d.-n.d.).

The Blue print. *Delaware, Ohio.*   1433423
    Beg. date: 1966
    WU   UWM (RBR) No.1,3-6 (WIN1966-AUT1968).

Blue review; literature, drama, art, music. *London, M.*   0114264
Secker.
    LCCN: 14-13061
    Ceased publication.
    Reprint: London, Franklin Cass and Company, 1968.
    WU   UWM (RBR) V.1 no.1-3 (MAY-JUL1913).

The Blue river anthology. *Shelbyville, Ind., The Blue River*   1438482
Press.
    WU   UWM (RBR) V.25 (n.d.).

The Blue river poetry magazine. *Shelbyville, Ind., The Blue*   1433436
River Press.
    Beg. date: 1934
    Title varies: , Hoosier poetry magazine;
    Midland poetry review.
    WU   UWM (RBR) V.25 no.92-94; v.26 no.96-98; v.28 no.104-105 (SUM1956-SUM1959).

Blue suede shoes. *Monterey, Calif. [etc.].*   1433464
    Beg. date: 1970
    WU   UWM (RBR) No.1-15 (1971-n.d.); no. .5 (n.d.); no. .314159265 (n.d.).

Blue vulture; a voice of Florida published in the land of   1468708
sunshine and rain and mosquitoes. *Miami.*
    ISSN: 0406-4569   Beg. date: 1953
    WU   UWM (RBR) V.1 no.1-3 (1953).

Bluebeat. *New York, Bluebeat Publications.*   1433477
    ISSN: 0520-2884   Beg. date: 1964
    WU   UWM (RBR) No.1 (1964).

Blues. *New York, Johnson Reprint.*   011433A
    LCCN: 34-30568
    Originally published Columbus, Miss.
    Ceased with v. 2 no. 9 (Fall 1930).
    WU   UWM (RBR) V.1 no.1-9 (FEB1929-FAL1930).

Bluestone; the literary quarterly. *Woodstock, N.Y.*   1433492
    ISSN: 0006-5188   Beg. date: 1964
    WU   UWM (RBR) V.1 no.1-3 (1964-n.d.); 1 issue in 1970.

Bo heem e um. *Sherborne, Dorset, Eng.*   1433501
    ISSN: 0523-7726   Beg. date: 1967
    WU   UWM (RBR) No.3-5 (JAN1968-DEC1968).

Bogg. *Leeds, Eng., Fiasco Publications.*   1433514
    Beg. date: 1968
    WU   UWM (RBR) No.2-5 (1969-1970).

Boise College, Boise, Idaho. Impulse. *See* Impulse. Boise,   144265A
Idaho, Boise College.

Bolero; a magazine of poetry. *Oxford, Eng.*   1433527
    Beg. date: 1938
    WU   UWM (RBR) No.1-3 (SUM1938-SPR1939).

Bombast. *Modesto, Calif.*   152843A
    Beg. date: 1977
    WU   UWM (RBR) No.1 (1977).

Bondage and discipline. *Chicago, Never Again Press.*   1499646
    Beg. date: 1976
    "A magazine of shortworks."
    WU   UWM (RBR) V.1 no.1-3 (1976).

Bones. *New York, White Bones Press.*   143353A
    ISSN: 0006-7105   Beg. date: 1967
    WU   UWM (RBR) No.1-3 (FAL1967-SPR1971).

Bonsai; a quarterly of haiku. *Phoenix.*   1433542
    ISSN: 0362-4447   Beg. date: 1976
    WU   UWM (RBR) V.1; v.2 no.1,3 (1976-1977).

Book collector. *London, Queen Anne Press.*   0116341
    ISSN: 0006-7237   LCCN: 54-27405   Beg. date: 1952
    Supersedes the Book handbook.
    Indexes: vols. 1-10, 1952-1961. 1 v.
    WU   UWM (RBR) V.2 no.3 (AUT1953).

Book collector's packet; a monthly review of fine books,   0116367
bibliography, typography, and kindred literary matters. *Meriden,*
Conneticut, Woodstock, New York, Chicago, Crow's nest, Virginia
Fitzwater, Black Cat Press.
    LCCN: 35-25988
    V. 1-2 also as no. 1-20.
    Suspended publication Aug.-Nov. 1933, 1934-Mar. 1938, 1940-Aug. 1945.
    Ceased with V. 4, no. 10 (1946).
    WU   UWM (RBR) V.1 no.1-12; v.2 no.17-20; v.3 no.3,5-8, 10 (MAR1932-OCT1939).

Book magazine. *San Francisco.*   0950598
    Title varies: nos. - , San Francisco's openings; nos. 11-18, Book review; nos. 19-26, San Francisco book review.
    WU   UWM (RBR) No.13-28 (AUG1970-1972).

Book review. *See* Book magazine. *San Francisco.*   1450474

Bookfellow, The Australasian review and journal of the   0116811
Australasian book trade. *Sydney.*
    Title varies: v. 1, no. 1-17, Jan. 3-Apr. 25, 1907: The Bookfellow (variation in subtitle); v. 1, no.18-21, May 2-23, 1907: Australia and the Bookfellow; v. 1, no. 22-v. 2, no. 7, May 30-Aug. 15, 1907:Australia; Ser. 3, v. 1, 1913: The Bookfellow.
    WU   UWM (RBR) No.2-5 (FEB18-MAY311899).

Bookman. *London, Hodder and Stoughton.*   0116880
    LCCN: 7-23749   Beg. date: 1891   End date: 1934
    Absorbed by London mercury with 1935.
    Ceased publication with vol. 87 no. 519, Dec. 1934.
    WU   UWM (RBR) V.47 no.279; v.49 no.291; v.73 no.435; v.75 no.447; v.77 no.459; v.79 no.471; v.81 no.483; v.83 no.495-498; v.84 no.499 (DEC1914-APR1933).

Border. *Fort Smith, Ark., Border Press, Inc.*   1433555
    ISSN: 0520-6162   Beg. date: 1965
    WU   UWM (RBR) V.1 no.1-3 (JAN-JUL1965).

Boss. *New York.* 1433568
ISSN: 0006-792X Beg. date: 1966
WU   UWM (RBR) No.1-2,4 (SUM1966-1970).

The Boston review. *Cambridge, Mass.* 1433570
ISSN: 0045-2610 LCCN: 66-9977 Beg. date: 1966
WU   UWM (RBR) V.1 no.1 (FAL1966).

Boston University. Alcheringa. *See* Alcheringa; 1410745
ethnopoetics. *Boston,*

Bottega review. *Minneapolis, Bottega Gallery.* 0118901
WU   UWM (RBR) V.1 no.1 (1964).

Bottom fish. *See* Bottomfish. *Cupertino, Calif., DeAnza* 1438859
College.

Bottomfish. *Cupertino, Calif., DeAnza College.* 1438846
Beg. date: 1976
WU   UWM (RBR) V.1 [no.1-3] (SPR1976-Dec011977).

Boundary 2. *Binghamton, N.Y., [Dept. of English, State* 0118983
University of New York at Binghamton].
LCCN: 72-626433 Beg. date: 1972
"A journal of postmodern literature; a symposium."
WU   UWM (RBR) V.1-V.5 no.3 (FAL1972-SPR1977).

Boundary two. *See* Boundary 2. *Binghamton, N.Y., [Dept. of* 1182126
English, State University of New York at Binghamton].

Box 749. *New York, Printable Arts Society, Inc.* 1433583
Beg. date: 1972
"A quarterly magazine of the printable arts."
WU   UWM (RBR) V.1 no.1-4; v.2 no.1 (FAL1972-1975).

Box seven forty nine. *See* Box 749. *New York,* 1463718

Box spring. *See* Boxspring. *Amherst, Mass., Hampshire* 1433618
College.

Boxspring. *Amherst, Mass., Hampshire College.* 1433596
WU   UWM (RBR) No.1-5 ([197?]-1977).

Bozart-Westminster. *See* Westminster magazine. *Atlanta.* 0119568

Bradley: his book. *Springfield, Mass.* 1433633
Beg. date: 1896 End date: 1897
An unauthorized and spurious number was issued as vol. 2 no. 4, Feb. 1897.
Ceased publication with vol. 2 no. 3, Jan. 1897.
WU   UWM (RBR) V.1 no.1-4; v.2 no.1-3 (MAY1896-JAN1897).

Brain of Pooh newsletter. *San Francisco, Poets Press.* 1433620
Beg. date: 1969
WU   UWM (RBR) No.1 (JUN211969).

Brainchild. *Springfield, Ill., Brainchild Collective.* 1528442
WU   UWM (RBR) No.2-4 (1975-1977).

The Brambler. *Sweet Briar, Va., Sweet Briar College.* 1528455
WU   UWM (RBR) V.45 no.2-3; v.46 no.1-2 (MAY1968-APR1969); Spring 1974.

The Brand new testament. *Monterey, Calif., Monterey* 1492118
Peninsula College.
WU   UWM (RBR) 1 issue (1969).

Brand "X." *New York, 7 Poets Press.* 1433646
WU   UWM (RBR) No.2,6-12 (FEB-DEC1962).

Brandeis University. Folio. *See* Folio; the Brandeis literary 1437356
review. *Waltham, Mass., Brandeis University.*

The Brass ring: contemporary poetry, art, photography. 1433659
Milwaukee.
WU   UWM (RBR) V.1 no.2-4; v.2 no.1-4 (SUM1967-FAL1971).

Bravado. *Jackson Heights, N.Y.* 1433661
Beg. date: 1974
WU   UWM (RBR) V.1 no.1 (SUM1974).

Bread. *Wallingford, Pa.* 1433674
WU   UWM (RBR) May 1971-1972; no.1 (1972).

Bread &. *New York.* 1433687
ISSN: 0520-8823 Beg. date: 1960 End date: 1962
Ceased publication with no. 2, 1962.
WU   UWM (RBR) No.1 (1960).

Bread and. *See* Bread &. *New York.* 143369A

Bread and puppet newspaper. *[n.p.]* 1528468
WU   UWM (RBR) No.3-6 (JAN1967).

Breakthru. *See* Challenge. *[Reseda, Calif., etc.], Conference* 1434428
on Science and Religion.

Breakthru. *[New Delhi, K. Saxena]* 0912134
LCCN: 79-921465 Beg. date: 1971
WU   UWM (RBR) No.1 (MAR1971).

Breakthru; international poetry magazine. *Haywards Heath,* 1441291
Sussex, Eng., Breakthru Pub.
ISSN: 0006-9531 Beg. date: 1962
WU   UWM (RBR) V.2 no.8-v.8 no.48; no.49-54 (1963-n.d.).

Brecht times. *Wilwyn, Herts, Eng., Brecht Times Press.* 1433709
Beg. date: 1972
WU   UWM (RBR) No.1-4 ([1972-1973]).

Briarcliff quarterly. *Briarcliff Manor, N.Y., etc.* 0121175
Beg. date: 1945 End date: 1947
Continues Maryland quarterly with vol. 1 no. 4, Jan. 1945.
Ceased publication with vol. 3 no. 12, Jan. 1947.
Superseded by Golden goose.
WU   UWM (RBR) V.1 no.4; v.2 no.5-8; v.3 no.9-12 (JAN1945-JAN1947).

Bricoleur. *San Francisco.* 1433711
ISSN: 0068-0966 Beg. date: 1969
WU   UWM (RBR) No.1 (SEP1969).

The Bridge. *Eagle Creek, Ore., [etc.] Glen Coffield.* 1528470
Beg. date: 1947
"Le petit journal."
Ceased publication.
WU   UWM (RBR) v.1 no.4-5; v.2 no.1-4,6-9,11-12; v.3 no.7,9; v.4 no.1,6-11; v.5 no.1-9; v.6 no.1-2; v.7 no.1-8; v.8 no.1-2,5-6; v.9 no.3; v.10 no.6; v.11 no.5-6 (SEP021947-JUN1957).

The Bridge. *Los Angeles.* 1433737
ISSN: 0524-4641 Beg. date: 1968
WU   UWM (RBR) No.1-2 (1968).

Bridge; a poetry folio. *Coconut Grove, Fla., H. Martin Pitts* 1433724
Co.
Beg. date: 1972
Subtitle varies.
WU   UWM (RBR) V.1 no.2-4; no.5 (WIN1972-[1974]).

The Bright Medusa. *Berkeley, Calif., The Bright Medusa* 1528483
Press.
Beg. date: 1976
"A feminist journal."
WU   UWM (RBR) V.1 no.1-2 (FAL1976-SPR1977).

Brilliant corners; a magazine of the arts. *Chicago.* 143374A
Beg. date: 1975
WU   UWM (RBR) V.1 no.1; no.2-3,5-6 (1975-1977).

Brisbane editorial review. *New York, Albertson Pub. Co.* 1433752
Beg. date: 1922
WU   UWM (RBR) V.1 no.1 (APR1922).

Britain to-day. *London, The British Council.* 0121686
Beg. date: 1939 End date: 1954
Ceased publication with no. 224.
Index last no.
WU   UWM (RBR) No.170-171,174-177,179-194,196-198 (JUN1950-OCT1952).

British School of Archeology in Jerusalem. *See* Levant. 012554A
London.

Broadsheet. *Sutton, Surrey, Eng.* 1441300
ISSN: 0007-2044 Beg. date: 1967
Supersedes in part Origins/diversions.
Title varies: , Assassinators' broadsheet.
WU   UWM (RBR) No.1-4 (MAR1967-SEP1970); one issue in 1971; no.10 (n.d.).

The Broadside annual. *Detroit, Broadside Press.* 1433765
LCCN: 72-624192 Beg. date: 1972
"Introducing new black poets."
WU   UWM (RBR) 1972-1973.

Brooklyn College. Graduate English Student Association. 1439041
Junction. *See* Junction. *Brooklyn, N.Y., Brooklyn College, Graduate English Student Association.*

Broom street magazine. *Madison, Wis., Broom Street* 1441354
Theater Press.
Beg. date: 1972
Continues The Camel, the lion, and the child with vol. 1 no. 3, Jan. 1972.
WU   UWM (RBR) V.1 no.3 (JAN1972).

Brown paper; an occasional magazine of poetry. *Long Island City, N.Y.* 1433778
ISSN: 0007-2508 LCCN: 79-475430
WU   UWM (RBR) 1965.

Brown paper bag. *Bowling Green, Ohio.* 1434023
Beg. date: 1970
Ceased publication.
Superseded by Black swamp review.
WU   UWM (RBR) V.1 no.1 (WIN1970).

The Brown river revue. *Madison, Wis.* 1434036
WU   UWM (RBR) V.4 no.1 (1972).

Brown's window. *Ithaca, N.Y.* 1430984
WU   UWM (RBR) 1 issue (1973).

The Brownstone. *New York.* 1434049
Beg. date: 1963
WU   UWM (RBR) No.1-24; v.2 no.1 (no.25); v.2 no.2 (MAR051963-MAR081965).

Brunidor portfolio. *See* Instead. [New York]. 1440908

Bruno chap books. *New York.* 1434051
Beg. date: 1915 End date: 1916
Ceased publication with vol. 3 no. 5, May 1916.
WU   UWM (RBR) V.1 no.3; special series no.3-5; v.1 no.4-5,7-8; v.2 no.2-9; v.3 no.1 (FEB1915-JAN1916).

Bruno's review of two worlds. *New York.* 1434064
Beg. date: 1920 End date: 1922
Ceased publication with vol. 4 no. 3, Nov. 1922.
WU   UWM (RBR) V.1 no.1-2,4-6; v.2 no.1-2 (NOV1920-JUL1921).

Bruno's weekly. *New York.* 0127809
Superseded by Bruno's.
WU   UWM (RBR) V.1 no.14,22-23; v.2 no.1-4,7-9,11-16, 18-20,23-24; v.3 no.21 (OCT1915-NOV081916).

Brupa. *Sacramento, Calif.* 1434077
Beg. date: 1969
WU   UWM (RBR) V.1 no.1 (1969).

Brushfire. *Reno, University of Nevada, Dept. of English.* 143408A
ISSN: 0407-5048
WU   UWM (RBR) No.7-10 (1956-1959); May 1967; May 1969.

Buckle. *Buffalo, N.Y.* 151056A
Beg. date: 1977
WU   UWM (RBR) V.1 no.1 (1977).

Buffalo. *Bowling Green, Ky., Buffalo Press.* 1434101
Beg. date: 1973
WU   UWM (RBR) No.1 (FEB1973).

Bulletin from nothing. *San Francisco.* 1434114
ISSN: 0525-1303 Beg. date: 1965 End date: 1965
Ceased publication with no. 2, 1965.
WU   UWM (RBR) No.2 (1965).

The Bummer. *Milwaukee.* 1434127
Beg. date: 1969
WU   UWM RBR V.1 no.1-4 (JUN1969-1971).

The Burning bush. *Eton, Eng.* 143413A
Beg. date: 1928
WU   UWM (RBR) No.1-3 (JUN041928-JUN041929).

The Burning bush. *[San Francisco], The Inter-Hillel Council of Northern California.* 1438495
ISSN: 0525-2431 Beg. date: 1963
Title also in Hebrew: Ha-seneh ha-boer.
WU   UWM (RBR) No.1-3 (SUM1963-SUM1965).

Burning deck. *Ann Arbor.* 0134419
WU   UWM (RBR) No.1-4 (FAL1962-SPR1965).

Burning water. *Princeton, N.J.* 1434142
ISSN: 0525-2466 Beg. date: 1963
WU   UWM (RBR) No.1-5 (FAL1963-WIN1965).

Busara. *Nairobi, University College, Dept. of English.* 1441824
ISSN: 0007-6376 LCCN: 72-620460 Beg. date: 1968
Supersedes Nexus.
WU   UWM (RBR) V.1-4 (1968-1972).

Bust. *Toronto, Bust Press.* 1434155
ISSN: 0045-3676 Beg. date: 1968
WU   UWM (RBR) No.1-3 (SPR-SUM1968).

The Busy bee review. *Amsterdam, De Bezige Bij, New York, Morton Seif Associates.* 1434168
ISSN: 0525-3012 Beg. date: 1964
WU   UWM (RBR) No.1 (1964).

Butler University, Indianapolis. English Department. 1507999
Manuscripts. *See* Manuscripts. Indianapolis, English Dept., Butler University.

Butt. *Watertown, Mass.* 1434170
Beg. date: 1975
WU   UWM (RBR) V.1 no.2 (1975).

The Butterfly quarterly. *Philadelphia.* 1468710
LCCN: 11-14391 Beg. date: 1907 End date: 1909
Ceased publication with vol. 2, 1909.
WU   UWM (RBR) No.1-4 (AUT1907-SUM1908).

Byways. *London.* 1434183
Beg. date: 1971
Supersedes Haiku byways.
WU   UWM (RBR) No.5-6 (n.d.-1972).

C

C; a journal of poetry. *New York, Lorenz Gude.*   1265742
    ISSN: 0574-9115   Beg. date: 1963
    WU   UWM (RBR) V.1 no.1-10; v.2 no.11,13 (MAY1963-MAY1966).

C O S M E P newsletter. *See* Committee of Small Magazine   1442060
Editors and Publishers. C O S M E P newsletter. San Francisco.

C Q. *[Los Angeles.]*   1528496
    Beg. date: 1976
    "Quarterly journal of California poetry and art."
    WU   UWM (RBR) V.1-v.2 no.1 (WIN1976-SPR1977).

C V 2. *See* C V II. Contemporary verse/two. Winnipeg.   1431004

C V II. Contemporary verse/two. *Winnipeg.*   1430997
    ISSN: 0319-6879   LCCN: 75-649007   Beg. date: 1975
    "A quarterly of Canadian poetry criticism."
    WU   UWM (RBR) V.1 no.1-2; v.2-v.3 no.2 (SPR1975-1977).

Cacophony. *Bromsgrove, Eng.*   1434196
    ISSN: 0574-9921   Beg. date: 1967   End date: 1970
    Ceased publication with no. 9, May 1970.
    WU   UWM (RBR) No.2-9 (DEC1967-MAY1970).

Cafe solo. *Albuquerque, Solo Press.*   0137230
    ISSN: 0007-9537
    WU   UWM (RBR) No.1-9 (1969-SUM1975).

Cafeteria; a magazine of poetry. *San Diego.*   1434205
    WU   UWM (RBR) V.1 no.5; v.4 no.6; no.8 (1973-1976).

Caim. *Baltimore.*   1434218
    Beg. date: 1973
    WU   UWM (RBR) V.1 no.1; v.2 no.1-2 (SUM1973-FAL1975).

Calamus. A journal for those who like to write, and those who like to read. *Kulpsville, Pa.*   144184A
    ISSN: 0409-9311
    WU   UWM (RBR) Feb., July, Oct. 1954; Jan.-Mar. 1955; Feb. 1956; Oct., Dec. 1958; Feb., Mar., May, July, Sept., Nov., Dec. 1960; Jan.-July, Sept., Nov. 1961; Jan. 1962; Feb. 1963.

Calendar. *See* The Calendar; a quarterly review. London.   1434246

The Calendar; a quarterly review. *London.*   1434220
    Beg. date: 1925   End date: 1927
    Title varies: vol. nos. 1-2, March 1925-Feb. 1926, Calendar of modern letters; vol. 3 nos. 1-3, April-Oct. 1926, The Calendar. Ceased publication wiht vol. 4 no. 2, July 1927.
    WU   UWM (RBR) V.1 no.1-4; v.2 no.7-12; v.3 no.2-4; v.4 no.1-2 (MAR1925-JUL1927).

Calendar of modern letters. *See* The Calendar; a quarterly review. London.   1434233

Caliban. *Winchester, Hamps., Eng., Winchester College.*   1441852
    ISSN: 0008-0780   Beg. date: 1963
    WU   UWM (RBR) June, Dec. 1967; July 1968; Feb., June 1969; Dec. 1970; Summer, Winter 1971.

California. Labor School, San Francisco. Writers' Workshop.   1502288
San Francisco Writers' Workshop magazine. *See* San Francisco Writers' Workshop magazine. San Francisco, Writers' Workshop, California Labor School.

California. State College, Los Angeles. Associated Students.   1529644
Statement. *See* Statement. Los Angeles.

California. State College, San Francisco. Transfer. *See*   1512935
Transfer. San Francisco, Associated Students, San Francisco State College.

California. State University, Long Beach. General Honors   1494145
Program. Lunar adios. *See* Lunar retorno. Long Beach, Calif., General Honors Program, California State University, Long Beach.

California. State University, Long Beach. General Honors   149412A
Program. Lunar retorno. *See* Lunar retorno. Long Beach, Calif., General Honors Program, California State University, Long Beach.

California. State University, Long Beach. General Honors   1494894
Program. New moon. *See* New moon. Long Beach, Calif., General Honors Program, California State University, Long Beach.

California. State University, Sacramento. Department of   1511185
English. Squeeze. *See* Squeeze. Sacramento, Dept. of English, Calif. State University.

California. University. Occident. *See* Occident. Berkeley,   1509879
Calif., Associated Students of the University of California.

California. University. University at Los Angeles. Board of   151871A
Communications. Westwind. *See* Westwind. Los Angeles, ASUCLA Board of Communications.

California. University, Riverside. English Department.   1094557
Pucred. *See* Pucred. San Francisco; University of California at Riverside, English Dept.

California. University, San Diego. Communications Board.   1442151
Crawl out of your window. *See* Crawl out your window. San Diego, University of California Communications Board.

California. University, Santa Barbara. Spectrum. *See*   151098A
Spectrum. Goleta, Calif., Associated Students of the University of California, Santa Barbara.

California. University, Santa Cruz. College V. Quarry. *See*   150792A
Quarry. Santa Cruz, Calif., College V, University of California, Santa Cruz.

California. University, Santa Cruz. College V. Quarry west.   1507945
See Quarry west. Santa Cruz, Calif., College V, University of California, Santa Cruz.

California chromatones. *See* Chromatones. [Long Beach,   1428509
Calif.].

California liberal. *See* American liberal. San Francisco.   1430038

California poet. *Marina, Calif., Realities.*   1508216
    Beg. date: 1975
    WU   UWM (RBR) V.1 no.1-2 (1975).

California quarterly. *See* C Q. [Los Angeles.]   1528505

The California quarterly. *Los Angeles, The California Quarterly, Inc.*   1434259
    ISSN: 0527-298X   LCCN: 54-32339   Beg. date: 1951   End date: 1956
    Ceased publication with vol. 4 no. 1, 1956.
    Absorbed by Coastlines.
    WU   UWM (RBR) V.1-v.4 no.1 (FAL1951-1956).

California review. *Santa Barbara, Calif.*   1434261
    Beg. date: 1967
    WU   UWM (RBR) No.1-3 (SPR1967-SPR1970).

Californian. *See* American liberal. San Francisco.   1430040

The Calithump; prose, poetry, art. *[Austin, Tex., etc.].*   1434274
    LCCN: 42-4270   Beg. date: 1934   End date: 1934
    Subtitle varies slightly.
    Ceased publication with vol. 2 no. 7, Sept. 1934?
    WU   UWM (RBR) V.1 no.4 (1934).

Calumet review. *Hammond, Ind.*   1441878
    ISSN: 0575-6456   Beg. date: 1967
    WU   UWM (RBR) V.2 no.1-3; v.3 no.1-2 (OCT1967-FAL1969).

Calyx; a northwest feminist review. *Corvallis, Ore.*   1438874
    Beg. date: 1976
    WU   UWM (RBR) V.1-v.2 no.1 (JUN1976-1977).

Cambridge. University. Trinity College. Experiment. *See*   1442227
Experiment. Cambridge, Eng., Trinity College.

The Cambridge quarterly. *Cambridge, England.*   0143240
    ISSN: 0008-199X   Beg. date: 1965
    WU   UWM (RBR) V.2-v.5 no.1 (WIN1966/1967-SPR/SUM1970).

Cambridge verse. *Cambridge, Eng.*   1434287
    WU   UWM (RBR) No.1 (n.d.).

Cambridge writing. *Cambridge, Eng., Young Writers' Group.*   143429A
    Beg. date: 1949   End date: 1951
    Ceased publication with no. 8, 1951.
    WU   UWM (RBR) No.4 (1950).

The Camel, the lion, and the child. *Madison, Wis., Broom Street Theatre.*   1441367
    Beg. date: 1970   End date: 1971
    Continued by Broom street magazine with vol. 1 no. 3, Jan. 1972.
    WU   UWM (RBR) V.1 no.1-2 (NOV1970-1971).

Camels coming. *See* I think I hear camels coming. Reno, Nev.   1439199

Camels coming. Second series. *See* Camels coming   1519874
newsletter. *San Francisco,*

Camels coming newsletter. *San Francisco, Camels Coming Press.* 1441880
Beg. date: 1972
Supersedes I think I hear camels coming.
Also called Camels coming, second series.
WU   UWM (RBR) No.1-7 (MAY1972-1977).

The Camel's hump. *Reno, Nev. [etc.].* 1434311
ISSN: 0575-6901   Beg. date: 1966
WU   UWM (RBR) No.1-5 (1966).

Cameo. *London, Cameo Publications Ltd.* 1434324
WU   UWM (RBR) No.2 (1954).

Camera work; a photographic quarterly. *New York, A. Stieglitz.* 0143476
LCCN: 35-31392   Beg. date: 1903
No more published.
WU   UWM (RBR) No.1-19,21-47 (1903-JUL1914); special no.: Aug. 1912; special no.: June 1913.

The Canada goose; a Canadian poetry magazine. *Lethbridge, Alta., Colloquium Study, University of Lethbridge.* 1441893
Beg. date: 1973
WU   UWM (RBR) V.1 no.1-4; v.2 no.1 (FAL1973-1976).

Canadian Authors' Association. Poetry Group. Victoria and Islands Branch. Victoria poetry chapbook. *See* Victoria poetry chapbook. Victoria, B.C. 151717A

Canadian fiction magazine. *Vancouver, B.C.* 1364205
ISSN: 0045-477X   Beg. date: 1971
Mainly in English, occasionally in French.
WU   UWM (RBR) No.1-6,8-20,20a,21,23,24-25 (WIN1971-1977).

Canadian review. *Ottawa.* 143434A
ISSN: 0315-1190   LCCN: 75-642538   Beg. date: 1974
WU   UWM (RBR) V.1 no.1 (FEB1974); Apr. 1974; v.3 no.2-6; v.4 no.1-4 (1976-1977).

Canberra poetry. *Canberra, Australian National University. Poetry Society.* 1441915
WU   UWM (RBR) [No.2-3]; v.1 no.4; v.2 no.4; v.2? no.2 (SPR1973-WIN1975); another unnumbered issue in 1975.

Candelabrum; a magazine of poetry. *London, The Red Candle Press [etc.].* 1434352
Beg. date: 1972
WU   UWM (RBR) V.1 no.2-6; v.2 no.1-6; v.3 no.1-2 (OCT1970-1976).

Candor magazine. *[Puxico, Mo., etc.].* 1434365
LCCN: 43-36984   Beg. date: 1936   End date: 1964
Title varies: 1936-Nov. 1939, Candor.
Subtitle varies.
Suspended publication Oct. 1941-June 1944.
Ceased publication with vol. 25 no. 4, 1964.
WU   UWM (RBR) V.14 no.4; v.15 no.2,4; v.16 no.1-2; v.17 no.4; v.18 no.1-2,4; v.20 no.4; v.21 no.1-4; v.22 no.1-2; v.25 no.1 (APR1953-JUL1963).

Cannock Chase Literary Society. Chase. *See* Chase. Hednesford, Staffs, Eng., Cannock Chase Literary Society. 1428368

Cantaloupe. *Bloomington, Ind., Woodhix Press.* 1434380
Beg. date: 1970
WU   UWM (RBR) No.1 (FAL1970).

Canto. *Andover, Mass., Realforms Co., Inc.* 1510572
ISSN: 0146-8995   LCCN: 77-647843   Beg. date: 1977
"Review of the arts."
WU   UWM (RBR) V.1 no.1 (SPR1977).

Canto. *Swoyersville, Pa., Mitchell Books.* 1434393
WU   UWM (RBR) No.2 (SEP1973).

Canto; a literary quarterly. *Los Angeles, Delphic Press.* 1434378
ISSN: 0528-032X   Beg. date: 1959   End date: 1962
Ceased publication with vol. 1 no. 3, Winter 1962.
WU   UWM (RBR) V.1 no.1-3 (1959-WIN1961).

The Cape rock. *Cape Girardeau, Mo., Southeast Missouri State University.* 1441930
ISSN: 0008-5812   Beg. date: 1964
Title varies: vols. 1-4, Spring 1964-Spring 1967, Cape rock quarterly; vol. 5, 1967, Cape rock journal.
Issued   by the University under its earlier name: Southeast Missouri State College.
WU   UWM (RBR) V.1-2; v.3 no.1; v.4 no.1; v.5 no.1; v.6-v.12 no.2 (SPR1964-1977).

Cape rock journal. *See* Cape rock. Cape Girardeau, Mo., Southeast Missouri State University. 1441969

Cape rock quarterly. *See* Cape rock. Cape Girardeau, Mo., Southeast Missouri State University. 1441956

Cape Town, South Africa. University. Students' Representative Council. Groot schuur. *See* Groote schuur. Cape Town, Students' Representative Council, University of Cape Town. 1442359

Capella. *Dublin, Tara Telephone.* 1427846
WU   UWM (RBR) No.4,5/6 (APR1970-n.d.).

Capilano College. Capilano review. *See* Capilano review. West Vancouver, B.C., Capilano College. 1427861

Capilano review. *West Vancouver, B.C., Capilano College.* 1427859
ISSN: 0315-3754   Beg. date: 1972
WU   UWM (RBR) No.1-10 (SPR1972-1976).

Captain Farley's ragweed review. *Topeka, Kan., Groad Press.* 1427874
Beg. date: 1960
WU   UWM (RBR) Dec. 1968; Mar. 1969.

captain may i. *Marshalltown, Iowa.* 1528518
Beg. date: 1969
WU   UWM (RBR) V.1 no.1 (SPR1969).

Caravan; Hawkeye poetry magazine. *Lamoni, Iowa.* 142789A
ISSN: 0528-094X   Beg. date: 1954   End date: 1965
Cover title, 1954-   : The Poetry caravan.
Subtitle varies.
Ceased publication with vol. 10 no. 3, May/June 1965.
WU   UWM (RBR) V.1-v.3 no.2; v.3 no.4-v.10 no.3 (1954-MAY/JUN1964).

Caravel; a magazine of verse. *See* Caravel; an American magazine published in Majorca. San Antonio, Spain. 1450580

Caravel; an American magazine published in Majorca. *San Antonio, Spain.* 0153469
Beg. date: 1934   End date: 1936
Ceased publication with no. 5, March 1936.
WU   UWM (RBR) No.3-5 (SUM1935-MAR1936).

Caravel magazine. *Thief River Falls, Minn.* 0153471
ISSN: 0008-6207   Beg. date: 1958
Published 1958-   in Palo Alto, California.
Title varies: 1958-1967, Caravel; a magazine of verse.
WU   UWM (RBR) No.1-23 (1958-WIN1974/1975).

Carcanet. *Oxford, Eng.* 1262686
ISSN: 0008-624X   Beg. date: 1969
WU   UWM (RBR) Winter 1967/1968-Summer 1970.

The Cardinal. *Middletown, Conn., Wesleyan University.* 143102A
ISSN: 0528-1067   Beg. date: 1925
"The literary magazine of Wesleyan University."
Frequency varies.
WU   UWM (RBR) Fall 1965; Spring 1970.

Cardinal; poetry quarterly. *Cicero, Ill., Eda Casciani.* 1427911
ISSN: 0528-1059   Beg. date: 1965
WU   UWM (RBR) V.1-v.6 no.4; v.7 no.2 (JUL1965-DEC1972).

Caret. *Coleraine, N. Ireland, Cambridge, Eng.* 1427924
Beg. date: 1972
WU   UWM (RBR) No.1-8/9 (AUT1972-SPR/SUM1975).

Caricatour. *New York, Contemporary Publications, Inc.* 1427937
ISSN: 0576-7679   LCCN: 68-130996   Beg. date: 1968
"The new monthly of contemporary satire."
At head of cover page title: An international report on youth-cartoons-satire.
WU   UWM (RBR) May-July 1968.

Carleton College, Northfield, Minnesota. *See* Carleton miscellany. Northfield, Minnesota, Carleton College. 0154121

Carleton miscellany. *Northfield, Minnesota, Carleton College.* 0154162
ISSN: 0008-6649   LCCN: 61-41870   Beg. date: 1960
WU   UWM (RBR) V.1-v.16 no.2 (WIN1970-1977).

Carolina quarterly. *Chapel Hill.* 0154814
ISSN: 0008-6797   LCCN: 52-19435
Began publication Fall 1948.
Issued by the Students of the University of North Carolina.
1948-62: New York, Kraus Reprint 1967.
WU   UWM (RBR) V.1-2; v.3 no.1,3; v.4 no.2-3; v.5 no.3; v.6 no.2-3; v.7 no.2-3; v.8-13; v.14 no.3; v.15-v.29 no.2 (FEB1948-SPR1977).

Carrots and peas. *Madison, Wis., Ire Schneider.* 142794A
Beg. date: 1964
WU   UWM (RBR) No.1-3 (MAY1964-1964).

Caryatid. New Orleans, La. [etc.]. 1427952
ISSN: 0008-7106 Beg. date: 1969
"Upholding the best traditions in poetry and the arts."
WU   UWM (RBR) V.1 no.1; v.1 no.3-v.2 no.3 (1969-1971).

Casaba. Bellingham, Wash., Tyler Fleeson. 1427965
WU   UWM (RBR) No.3 (JUN1973); 1975.

Casanova Jr's tales. New York, Two Worlds Publishing Co. 1427978
Beg. date: 1926 End date: 1929
Vol. 2 has title: Secret memoirs of gallant men and fair women.
Ceased publication with vol. 3 (no. 12), Jan. 1929.
WU   UWM (RBR) V.1 no.1-4 (APR1926-JAN1927).

Case Western Reserve University. Department of English. 1438389
Bits. *See* Bits. Cleveland, Case Western Reserve University, Department of English.

Cassiopeia. San Francisco, Lewis Ellingham. 1427993
WU   UWM (RBR) No.1 (n.d.).

The Cat and the Moon. Arthur, N.D., The Cat's Paw Press. 1528520
Beg. date: 1976
WU   UWM (RBR) No.1 (1976).

The Cat mousam journal. Gorham, Me. 1468723
Beg. date: 1971
"A journal of the people of Maine."
WU   UWM (RBR) V.1 no.1-3 (1971).

The Catacomb. London, The Forty-Five Press. 1428000
LCCN: 59-40431 Beg. date: 1949
WU   UWM (RBR) No.4,8,11,14 (1949-MAY1950); n. ser. v.1 no.1-3; v.2 no.1-4 (SUM1950/1951-WIN1951/1952).

Catalyst. Brantford, Ont., Prison Arts Foundation. 1428013
ISSN: 0381-5005 Beg. date: 1975
WU   UWM (RBR) V.1 no.2-5 (AUG151975-APR1976).

Catalyst. Evanston, Ill., Chicago International Manuscripts. 1428039
ISSN: 0528-2616 Beg. date: 1963
"Magazine of art, science, and philosophy."
WU   UWM (RBR) V.1 no.1 (1963).

Catalyst. Peterborough, Ont. [etc.]. 0156161
ISSN: 0008-7661 Beg. date: 1965
Issued 1965-   by the State University of New York at Buffalo; 1972-   by Trent University.
WU   UWM (RBR) No.1 (SUM1965).

Catapult. Montreal. 1428041
ISSN: 0576-9221 Beg. date: 1964
Supersedes Cataract?
WU   UWM (RBR) No.2 (SUM1964).

Cataract. Montreal. 1428054
ISSN: 0576-923X Beg. date: 1961
WU   UWM (RBR) V.2 no.1,3 (SPR/SUM1961-JUL1962).

Caterpillar. New York, Clayton Eshleman. 0156252
ISSN: 0008-784X LCCN: 68-130926 Beg. date: 1967 End date: 1973
Ceased publication with no. 20 (vol. 5 no. 4), June 1973.
WU   UWM (RBR) No.1-20 (v.1-v.5 no.4) (OCT1967-JUN1973).

The Cathartic. Ft. Lauderdale, Fla. [etc.]. 1528533
Beg. date: 1974 End date: 1976
Ceased publication with vol. 3 no. 3, Fall 1976.
WU   UWM (RBR) V.2-3 (JAN1975-FAL1976).

Catholic Poetry Society of America. *See* Spirit: a magazine of poetry. New York, [etc.]. 0157047

The Catonsville roadrunner. London. 1428067
ISSN: 0008-8536 Beg. date: 196
"Revolutionary Christian monthly."
WU   UWM (RBR) May-Oct. 1969.

Causeway. Toronto, Inform. 1428082
ISSN: 0576-9655 Beg. date: 1966
WU   UWM (RBR) No.1 (1966).

Cave. Hamilton, N.Z., Outrigger Publishers, Inc. 1428095
Beg. date: 1972 End date: 1976
"An international review of arts and ideas."
Continued by The New quarterly cave with no. 9, n. ser. vol. 1 no. 1, 1976.
Has irregular supplement: Outrigger.
WU   UWM (RBR) No.1-8 (APR1972-1975).

Cave. Supplement. *See* Outrigger. Hamilton, New Zealand, Outrigger Publishers Ltd. 1497976

Caw! New York, Students for a Democratic Society. 1197243
ISSN: 0576-9698 Beg. date: 1968
WU   UWM (RBR) No.1-4 (FEB1968-JAN1969).

Caxton poetry review. Cincinnati, Caxton Press. 1428104
ISSN: 0411-3039 LCCN: 58-22541 Beg. date: 1956 End date: 1958
"A national quarterly magazine."
Ceased publication with no. 5, Winter 1958.
WU   UWM (RBR) Summer 1957; Winter 1958.

Cedar rock. New Braunfels, Tex., David C. Yates. 1428117
Beg. date: 1976
"A poetry quarterly."
WU   UWM (RBR) V.1-v.2 no.4 (WIN1976-1977).

Celebrate. Los Angeles, Celebrity Centre International. 142812A
Beg. date: 1970
"The revitalization of the arts."
WU   UWM (RBR) V.2 no.1 (JUL1970).

Celebration. Baltimore, Md., William J. Sullivan. 1528546
Beg. date: 1975
WU   UWM (RBR) No.1 (SUM1975).

Celebrity Centre. Celebrity Centre poets. *See* Celebrity Centre poets. Los Angeles, Celebrity Centre. 1428158

Celebrity Centre International. Celebrate. *See* Celebrate. Los Angeles, Celebrity Centre International. 1428132

Celebrity Centre poets. Los Angeles, Celebrity Centre. 1428145
Beg. date: 1970
WU   UWM (RBR) V.1 no.1-2 (1970-1971).

The Cellar door. Los Altos Hills, Calif. 1428160
Beg. date: 1970
WU   UWM (RBR) V.1 no.1 (SPR1970).

Censorship. London, Congress for Cultural Freedom. 0158117
ISSN: 0577-0009 LCCN: 74-235487 Beg. date: 1964 End date: 1967
Quarterly report on censorship of ideas and the arts.
Ceased publication with no. 9 (Winter 1967).
WU   UWM (RBR) No.2,4-7,9 (SPR1965-WIN1967).

Centaur. Chicago, K. Antoinette Graham. 1428173
WU   UWM (RBR) One unnumbered, undated issue.

Center. *See* Origin. Series 3. Kyoto, Origin Press. 1529146

Center. Woodstock, N.Y., Carol Berge. 1428186
Beg. date: 1970
WU   UWM (RBR) No.1-6 (1970-JUL1974).

Center for Religion and the Arts, San Francisco. Intersection newsletter. *See* Intersection newsletter. San Francisco, A Center for Religion and the Arts. 1442885

Centering: a magazine of poetry. East Lansing, Mich., Dept. of American Thought and Language, Michigan State University. 1428199
Beg. date: 1973
WU   UWM (RBR) No.1-3 (1973-1977).

Centigrade. London, Kings College. 1433780
Beg. date: 196
WU   UWM (RBR) No.7 (OCT1967).

Central issues. Marietta, Ohio, Acorn Pub. Co. 1428210
Beg. date: 1967 End date: 1974
"A journal of cooperative adult learning."
Cover title, May 1968?-   : Central issues in cooperative adult learning.
Title varies: vol. 1 no.1-   , Nov. 1967-   , National call, ISSN 0547-4744.
Ceased publication with vol. 7, 1974.
WU   UWM (RBR) V.1 no.7-12; v.2 no.1-9; v.3 no.1-4 (MAY1968-MAY/JUN1970).

Central issues in cooperative adult learning. *See* Central issues. Marietta, Ohio, Acorn Pub. Co. 1428223

The Central literary magazine. Birmingham [etc.]. 0159033
ISSN: 0069-164X Beg. date: 1873
"Issued...by the Birmingham central literary association."
WU   UWM (RBR) V.40 no.4-6 (SPR1969-1971).

Centre 17. Thaxted, Esses, Eng. [etc.]. 1428249
Beg. date: 1971
WU   UWM (RBR) No.1-6 (SUM1971-n.d.).

Century guild hobby horse. *See* Hobby horse. London, K. Paul, Tranch and Co. [etc.]. 1439446

Český boj za svobodu a demokracii. Czech struggle for freedom and democracy. London. 1441971
ISSN: 0411-6305 Beg. date: 1957
Supersedes Ceske listy. Czech news.
In English and Czech.
WU   UWM (RBR) No.1,4-5,7-8,10-12 (SEP281957-DEC1958).

Chalk circle. *New York.*   1428251
   ISSN: 0577-5051 Beg. date: 1966
   WU   UWM (RBR) V.1 no.1 (APR/MAY1966).

Challenge. *[Reseda, Calif., etc.], Conference on Science and*   1434402
Religion.
   Beg. date: 1958
   Supersedes Universal viewpoint.
   Title varies: nos. 1-17, 1958-1964, Breakthru.
   1962-1964 issued by the Conference under its earlier name, Peace
   Centers Foundation.
   WU   UWM (RBR) Summer-Fall 1959; Spring 1960; Fall-
   Winter 1960; no.9-30 (1960?-1970).

Champlain College, Lennoxville, Quebec.   Matrix. **See**   1509249
Matrix. Lennoxville, Quebec, Champlain College. Department of
English.

Chance; new writing and art. *London.*   1428264
   ISSN: 0528-8363 Beg. date: 1952 End date: 1953
   Ceased publication with vol. 4, Autumn 1953.
   WU   UWM (RBR) V.1-4 (OCT1952-AUG1953).

Change. *Detroit, Artists' Workshop Press.*   142828A
   ISSN: 0590-6180 Beg. date: 1965 End date: 1966
   Ceased publication with no. 2, Spring/Summer 1966.
   WU   UWM (RBR) No.2 (SPR/SUM1966).

Change. *San Francisco.*   1428277
   ISSN: 0528-8428 Beg. date: 1963
   WU   UWM (RBR) No.1-2 (1963-1965).

Changing world; a quarterly review. *London.*   0162773
   Ceased publication no. 7.
   WU   UWM (RBR) No.1-6 (SUM1947-JAN1949).

Chanticleer. *London.*   1428292
   Beg. date: 1952 End date: 1954
   Ceased publication with vol. 1 no. 4, Spring 1954.
   WU   UWM (RBR) V.1 no.2-4 (SPR1953-SPR1954).

Chaos fertilizer; the insight poetry magazine. *Harrison, N.J.*   1428301
   Beg. date: 1968
   Ceased publication with vol. 1 no. 1, 1968.
   WU   UWM (RBR) V.1 no.1 (1968).

Chap-book; semi-monthly. A miscellany and review of belles   0162836
lettres. *Chicago, Stone and Kimball.*
   LCCN: 7-7497 Beg. date: 1894
   Merged into Dial.
   WU   UWM (RBR) V.1-v.9 no.4 (MAY151894-JUL011898).

Chapbook. *London.*   0162849
   Beg. date: 1919 End date: 1925
   "A monthly miscellany" (nos. 39-40: "A yearly miscellany").
   Supersedes Poetry and Drama.
   Title varies: nos. 1-6, July-Dec. 1919, Monthly chapbook.
   Ceased with no. 40 (1925).
   WU   UWM (RBR) No.1-40 (JUL1919-1925).

Chapman. *Hamilton, Lanarkshire, Scotland [etc.].*   1428314
   Beg. date: 1970
   WU   UWM (RBR) No.3-6; v.2 no.1-5/6; v.3 no.1-6; v.4
   no.1,3-6 (NOV1970-1977).

Charas. *Tacoma, Wash.*   1428327
   Beg. date: 1971 End date: 1973
   Ceased publication with vol. 3 no. 3, 1973.
   WU   UWM (RBR) V.1 no.1; v.2 no.1; v.2 no.2-3 (no.3-4);
   v.3 no.1-3 (no.5-7) (1971-1973).

The Charioteer; a review of modern Greek literature. *New*   0162970
York, Parnassos, Greek Cultural Society.
   LCCN: 63-32647 Beg. date: 1960
   Subtitle varies.
   WU   UWM (RBR) No.1-18 (SUM1960-1976).

Chariton review. *Kirksville, Mo., Northeast Missouri State*   1431086
University.
   ISSN: 0098-9452 LCCN: 75-645643 Beg. date: 1975
   WU   UWM (RBR) V.1 no.1-2; v.2 no.1-2; v.3 no.1
   (SPR1975-1977).

Charlatan. *[Iowa City, Charlatan Publications.].*   142833A
   ISSN: 0009-1731 LCCN: 64-9497 Beg. date: 1964
   Title varies: no. 1, What can this charlatan be trying to say?
   WU   UWM (RBR) No.1-5 (SPR1964-1968).

Chase. *Hednesford, Staffs, Eng., Cannock Chase Literary*   1428355
Society.
   ISSN: 0577-5701 Beg. date: 1963 End date: 1965
   Ceased publication with no. 5, Nov. 1965.
   WU   UWM (RBR) No.1-5 (JUN1963-NOV1965).

Chasm. *Huntsville, Ala.*   1428370
   WU   UWM (RBR) May 1973.

The Chat noir review. *Chicago.*   1428383
   ISSN: 0577-5744 Beg. date: 1961 End date: 1964
   Ceased publication with vol. 2 no. 3, 1964?
   WU   UWM (RBR) V.1 no.1-4; v.2 no.1-3 (DEC1961-1964).

Chawed rawzin. *Lubbock, Tex.*   1528559
   Beg. date: 1974
   No. 3, Fall 1974, special issue with Mouse River review.
   WU   UWM (RBR) No.1,3 (SPR1974,FAL1974).

Chelsea. *New York.*   0163752
   ISSN: 0009-2185 Beg. date: 1958
   Title varies: nos. 1-5, Summer 1968-Summer 1969, Chelsea
   review.
   WU   UWM (RBR) No.1-35 (SUM1958-1976).   Nos. 8, 12-
   13 are reprints.

Chelsea College. Humanities Society.   New leaf. **See** New   1494838
leaf. London, The Humanities Society, Chelsea College.

Chelsea review. **See** Chelsea. New York.   0163778

Chernozem. *Sutton [etc.] Neb., Big Deal Press.*   1428396
   Beg. date: 1973
   WU   UWM (RBR) No.1-9 (1973-1976).

Cheshire. *Milwaukee, University of Wisconsin.*   1441997
   WU   UWM (RBR) V.23 no.3/4; v.30 no.1-2;
   v.31 no.1-2; v.32 no.1-2; v.33 no.1-2; v.34 no.3-4;
   v.35 no.1-2; v.36 no.1-2; v.37 no.1/2
   (JUN1954-SUM1968).

Chesil; the magazine of chesil poets. *Dorset, Eng., Word and*   1428405
Action.
   Beg. date: 1973
   WU   UWM (RBR) No.1-6 (FEB1973-MAY1975).

Chez limbo. **See** Limbo. Vancouver, B.C.   1492800

Chiaroscura. *Madison, Wis.*   1438887
   Beg. date: 1976
   WU   UWM (RBR) V.1 no.1 (SPR1976).

Chiaroscuro. *Ithaca, N.Y., Chiaroscuro Press.*   1528561
   Beg. date: 1976
   WU   UWM (RBR) No.1 (1976).

Chiaroscuro. *Waterloo, Ont., Student Board of Publications,*   1433815
Waterloo Lutheran University.
   ISSN: 0069-3200 Beg. date: 1957
   WU   UWM (RBR) V.9 (1965-1966).

Chicago. *Chicago., Contemporary Publications, Inc.*   1439459
   Beg. date: 1954
   WU   UWM (RBR) V.1 no.1 (MAR1954).

Chicago. *Chicago, Ill.*   1468736
   Beg. date: 1972
   WU   UWM (RBR) V.1 no.1; v.2 no.2/3; v.3 no.4/5; v.4
   no.6; v.5 no.1; v.6 (FEB1972-MAR1973).

Chicago. European edition. *Wivenhoe, Esses, Eng., Chicago*   1468749
Press.
   Beg. date: 1973
   WU   UWM (RBR) No.1-3 (OCT1973-1974).

Chicago. City College. Loop Campus.   Garland Court   143771A
review. **See** Garland Court review. Chicago, Loop College.

Chicago. University.   Phoenix. **See** Phoenix. Chicago.   1499990

Chicago. University.   University observer. **See** University   1516814
observer. Chicago.

Chicago. University. Poetry Club.   Forge. **See** Forge; a   1437447
Midwestern review. Chicago.

Chicago choice. **See** Choice. Chicago, Poetry Seminar.   0167265

Chicago literary times. **See** Literary times. Chicago, Literary   1508911
Communication Co.

Chicory. *Baltimore, Enoch Pratt Free Library Community*   1431108
Action Program [etc.].
   ISSN: 0009-3793 Beg. date: 1966
   WU   UWM (RBR) Jan., June/July, Nov.-Dec. 1972; Feb.,
   Apr.-Dec. 1973; 1974-1976; Feb-Mar. 1977.

Le Chien d'or. The Golden dog. *Montreal, Ottawa.*   1428418
   Beg. date: 1973
   Supersedes Yes.
   WU   UWM (RBR) No.1-4 (1973-NOV1974).

Child development monographs. *New York, Teachers College, Columbia University.* 0168179
ISSN: 0037-976X
WU   UWM (RBR) V.38 no.6-   (1973-   ).

Child's hat. *San Francisco.* 1428433
Beg. date: 1966 End date: 1966
Ceased publication with no. 1, 1966.
WU   UWM (RBR) No.1 (1966).

Chimera. *New York.* 0169368
LCCN: 45-17470 Beg. date: 1942 End date: 1947
Suspended publication with v. 5.
WU   UWM (RBR) V.1-5 (SPR1942-SUM1947).

Chimes; a quarterly. *Notre Dame, Ind., St. Mary's College.* 1433830
ISSN: 0009-4285
WU   UWM (RBR) Fall 1965; 1966-Winter/Fall 1968.

China reconstructs. *Peking, China Welfare Institute.* 0169998
ISSN: 0009-4447 Beg. date: 1952
WU   UWM (RBR) V.9 no.11-12; v.10-v.12 no.10 (NOV1960-OCT1963); suppl.: May, Sept. 1961; suppl.: Jan. 1962.

China today. *New York, Greenwood Reprint, 1968.* 0170152
Beg. date: 1934 End date: 1942
Originally published by the American Friends of the Chinese.
Ceased publication with ser. 2 vol. 8 no. 3, March 1942.
Superseded by Amerasia.
WU   UWM (RBR) V.1-4; v.5 no.2-12; v.6-v.8 no.3 (OCT1934-MAR1942).

China Welfare Institute. China reconstructs. *See* China reconstructs. *Peking,* 1164817

Chirimo. *Salisbury, Rhodesia, Berry Trust Co.* 1428446
ISSN: 0009-4684 LCCN: 70-445704 Beg. date: 1968 End date: 1970
"A thrice yearly review of Rhodesian and international poetry."
Ceased publication with vol. 2, Sept. 1970.
WU   UWM (RBR) V.1 no.1-3; v.2 no.1 (JUN1968-SEP1969); 1970 Festival leaflet.

Choice. *Chicago, Poetry Seminar.* 0171172
ISSN: 0009-4986 Beg. date: 1961
Title varies: no.1, Chicago choice.
WU   UWM (RBR) V.1 no.1; no.2-6 (SPR1961-1970).

Choice. *Madison, Wis., Bantling Press.* 1428459
ISSN: 0577-9464 Beg. date: 1960
WU   UWM (RBR) No.1-3 (1960-1962).

Choice; a magazine of poetry and photography. *See* Choice. *Chicago.* 1260780

Chomo-uri. *Amherst, Mass., Feminist Arts Program, Everywoman's Center, University of Massachusetts.* 1431123
Beg. date: 1974
WU   UWM (RBR) V.1-v.4 no.1 (SPR1974-1977).

Choomia. *Framingham, Mass., Yarrow Press.* 1428461
Beg. date: 1975
WU   UWM (RBR) No.1-3 (1975-1976); v.2 (1977).

Chouteau review. *Kansas City, Mo.* 1428474
Beg. date: 1975
WU   UWM (RBR) V.1-v.2 no.1 (FAL1975-1977).

The Chowder review. *Quincy, Mass.* 1428487
Beg. date: 1973
First issue unnumbered.
WU   UWM (RBR) V.1-v.2 no.1 (WIN1973-SPR/SUM1975); no.5-8 (FAL/WIN1975-1977).

Christian Frontier Council. Frontier. *See* Frontier. *Oxford, Christian Frontier Council.* 1439602

Chromatones. *[Long Beach, Calif.].* 142849A
LCCN: 50-55598 Beg. date: 1946 End date: 1958
Subtitle varies.
Title varies: 1946, California chromatones.
The first number issued as a brochure in 1946 was printed by the Candor Press, Dexter, Mo.
Ceased publication with vol. 13 no. 1/2, Jan./Apr. 1958?
WU   UWM (RBR) V.7 no.4; v.8 no.3-4; v.10 no.2; v.11 no.2-3/4; v.12 no.1-4; v.13 no.1/2 (OCT1952-JAN/APR1958).

Chrysalis; the pocket revue of the arts. *Boston [etc.].* 1428511
Beg. date: 1948 End date: 1961
Subtitle varies.
Some issues lack numbering and dates.
Ceased publication with vol. 14, 1961.
WU   UWM (RBR) V.1-6 (1948-1953); v.7-10 (no.1-12) (1954-1957); v.11 no.3-4; v.12 no.1-4; v.13 no.1-4 (1958-1960).

Chrysalis review. *San Francisco.* 1528574
ISSN: 0529-5009 Beg. date: 1961 End date: 1962
Ceased publication with vol. 1 no. 2, Spring 1962.
WU   UWM (RBR) V.1 no.2 (SPR1962).

Chrysalis West Foundation. *See* Genesis West. *Burlingame, California, Chrysalis West Foundation.* 0173080

Cimarron Review. *Stillwater, Okla. Published at Oklahoma State University.* 017513A
ISSN: 0009-6849 Beg. date: 1967
Indexes: Vols. 1-8, 1967-1969, with v. 8.
Author index. nos. 25-32, Oct. 1973-July 1975, with nos. 30-37.
WU   UWM (RBR) No.1-40 (1967-1977).

Cincinnati. University. Little man. *See* Little man. *Cincinnati, Ohio, University of Cincinnati.* 1493231

Cincinnati. University. Department of English. Cincinnati poetry review. *See* Cincinnati Poetry review. *Cincinnati, Department of English, University of Cincinnati.* 1431151

Cincinnati Poetry review. *Cincinnati, Department of English, University of Cincinnati.* 1431149
Beg. date: 1973
WU   UWM (RBR) V.1 no.1,3-4; v.2 no.1-2; no.2-3 (1973-1976).

Cinque foil. *See* Cinquefoil. *Allen Park, Mich.* 1431177

Cinquefoil. *Allen Park, Mich.* 1431164
ISSN: 0009-7225 Beg. date: 1968
Supersedes Trypod.
WU   UWM (RBR) No.1-3 (1968-1969).

Circle. *Berkeley.* 0175638
LCCN: 49-20741
Publication suspended during 1947.
WU   UWM (RBR) V.1 no.1-4 (1944); no.5-10 (1945-SUM1948); special circle edition (1947).

The Circle. *Chicago, Maroon Publications.* 1428524
Beg. date: 1922 End date: 1925
"A magazine of the arts, issued monthly by Maroon Publications at the University of Chicago."
Ceased publication with vol. 3 no. 5, April 1925.
Absorbed by Phoenix with Feb. 1926.
WU   UWM (RBR) V.1 no.2 (JAN1923); Apr. 1923.

The Circle; a journal of verse. *Baltimore, Md. etc., [Baltimore Poetry Circle].* 1428537
LCCN: 26-7379 Beg. date: 1924 End date: 1938
Subtitle varies.
Ceased publication with vol. 15 no. 4, Dec. 1938.
WU   UWM (RBR) V.4 no.5 (MAY/JUN1927).

Circle; a periodical of reversible poetry. *Portland, Ore., Circle Forum.* 142854A
Beg. date: 1973
WU   UWM (RBR) V.1 no.1,3-4; v.2 no.1-2 (SUM1973-AUT/WIN1974).

Circuit. *Cambridge, Eng.* 1428552
ISSN: 0578-3127 Beg. date: 1965
No. 8, Summer 1969, special issue called Language.
WU   UWM (RBR) No.1-5,7-9 (SUM1965-1969).

Circular causation. *Vancouver, B.C.* 1428565
Beg. date: 1969
WU   UWM (RBR) V.1 no.1-4 (1969-n.d.).

Circus; the pocket review of our times. *London.* 1428578
Beg. date: 1950 End date: 1950
Ceased publication with vol. 1 no. 3, June 1950.
WU   UWM (RBR) V.1 no.1-3 (APR-JUN1950).

The Circus compendium; the way of higher evolution. *Carmel, Calif.* 1428580
WU   UWM (RBR) V.4 no.1-2; v.5 no.1 (SEP1968-APR1969).

Circus maximus; a quarterly of contemporary poetry and poetics. *York, Pa.* 1428593
Beg. date: 1975
WU   UWM (RBR) V.1 no.1-3; v.2 no.1-4 (DEC1975-1977).

Citadel. *Los Angeles, Los Angeles City College.* 1442017
ISSN: 0578-3232 Beg. date: 1962
Wu   UWM (RBR) V.2 no.1-2; v.4 no.2; v.6 no.2 (FAL1963-SPR1968).

City. *New York.* 1428602
WU   UWM (RBR) No.2-5 (1967-1970).

City. *New York, Creative Writing Program, City College.* 1528587
Also called City magazine.
WU   UWM (RBR) No.4-6 (WIN1975/1976-FAL1977).

City lights. *San Francisco, Calif.* 1334237
ISSN: 0529-8334 Beg. date: 1952 End date: 1955
Ceased publication with no. 5, Spring 1955.
WU   UWM (RBR) No.1-5 (JUL1952-SPR1955).

City lights journal. *San Francisco, City Lights Books.* 1150462
ISSN: 0578-3607 LCCN: 63-3405 Beg. date: 1963 End date: 1966
Ceased publication with no. 3, 1966.
WU   UWM (RBR) No.1-3 (1963-1966).

City magazine. *See* City. New York, Creative Writing Program, City College. 1528609

Civ/n. *Montreal.* 1428615
ISSN: 0412-6602 Beg. date: 1953 End date: 1954
Ceased publication with 1954?
WU   UWM (RBR) No.2-7 (1953-1954).

The Clack Book. *Lansing, Mich., Wells and Hudson.* 143118A
LCCN: CA 11-2773 Beg. date: 1896 End date: 1897
Ceased publication with vol. 3 no. 3, 1897?
WU   UWM (RBR) V.1 no.1 (1896).

Clark University, Worcester, Massachusetts. English Department. Gob. *See* Gob. Worcester, Mass., Clark University, Dept. of English. 1438006

The Classic. *[Johannesburg].* 1431192
ISSN: 0009-8302 LCCN: 67-6830 Beg. date: 1963 End date: 1971
Subtitle: 1963-   , Johannesburg quarterly.
Ceased publication with vol. 3, 1971.
WU   UWM (RBR) V.1 no.3-4; v.2 no.1-4; v.3 no.1-4 (1964-1971).

Classic. *See* New classic. Johannesburg, South Africa, New Classic Publications. 1494615

Classic; Johannesburg quarterly. *See* Classic. [Johannesburg]. 1431201

The Clearing. *Auburn, Wash., Green River Community College.* 1431227
WU   UWM (RBR) 1968-1972, 1975-1976.

Cleft; a university quarterly. *Edinburgh.* 1428628
ISSN: 0529-9330 Beg. date: 1963
WU   UWM (RBR) V.1 no.2 (MAY1964).

Clemson University. South Carolina review. *See* South Carolina review. Clemson, S.C., Dept. of English, Clemson University. 1529594

Clenched horizon. *Sarasota, Fla., New Collage Press.* 1528611
WU   UWM (RBR) V.8 no.2 (1977).

Climax. *New Orleans, The Climax Jazz, Art and Pleasure Society of Lower Bourbon Street.* 1431242
ISSN: 0578-5103 Beg. date: 1955 End date: 1956
"A creative review in the jazz spirit."
Ceased publication with no. 2, Summer 1956.
WU   UWM (RBR) No.1-2 (1955-SUM1956).

Climax Jazz, Art and Pleasure Society of Lower Bourbon Street. Climax. *See* Climax. New Orleans, The Climax Jazz, Art and Pleasure Society of Lower Bourbon Street. 1431255

Clio; a literary magazine. *London.* 1428630
Beg. date: 1954
WU   UWM (RBR) V.1 no.1 (1954).

Clipper. *Hollywood, Calif., Hollywood Chapter of the League of American Writers.* 0178657
ISSN: 0009-9406 LCCN: 44-15737
Supersedes Black and white.
V. 1 has subtitle: A western review.
WU   UWM (RBR) V.1 no.3-5; v.2 no.1-9 (OCT1940-NOV1941).

Cloud marauder. *Berkeley, Calif.* 1428643
ISSN: 0009-9481 Beg. date: 1968
WU   UWM (RBR) V.1 no.1-6 (MAY1968-1970).

Cloven hoof. *University Center, Mich., Saginaw Valley College.* 1428656
Beg. date: 1969
WU   UWM (RBR) V.1 no.1-4 (1969-1970).

Coast; a magazine of western writing. *[San Francisco].* 1428671
Beg. date: 1937 End date: 1942
"An unofficial co-operative publication of writers on the San Francisco Writers Project."
Ceased publication with July 1942.
WU   UWM (RBR) V.1 no.1 (SPR1937).

Coastlines. *Hollywood, California.* 0179335
Beg. date: 1955 End date: 1964
Ceased with v. 6 no. 22 (1964).
WU   UWM (RBR) V.1-v.6 no.1/2 (no.1-21/22) (SPR1955-1964).

Coe College, Cedar Falls, Iowa. Student Senate. Coe review. *See* Coe review. Cedar Falls, Iowa, Coe College Student Senate. 1431270

The Coe review. *Cedar Falls, Iowa, Coe College Student Senate.* 1431268
Beg. date: 1972
Supersedes Caravan.
WU   UWM (RBR) No.1-4 (SPR1972-SPR1974).

Coercion. *Omaha.* 1428697
WU   UWM (RBR) No.4-5 (WIN1965-SUM1966).

The Coercion review. *Chicago.* 1428706
ISSN: 0530-024X Beg. date: 1958 End date: 1959
Ceased publication with no. 2, Spring 1959.
WU   UWM (RBR) No.1-2 (SUM1958-SPR1959).

The Coffeehouse; contemporary Greek arts and letters. *San Francisco.* 1431283
Beg. date: 1975
WU   WUM (RBR) No.1-3 (FAL1975-1976).

Coffin. *Eureka, Calif., Hearse Press.* 1431296
ISSN: 0530-0312 Beg. date: 1965
WU   UWM (RBR) No.1 (1965?).

Colchester, England. University of Essex. Flame. *See* Flame. Colchester, Essex, Eng., Societies' Pigeons' Holes, University of Essex. 1437105

Cold spring journal. *See* Coldspring journal. Cherry Valley, N.Y., Cherry Valley Editions. 1428721

The Coldspring journal. *Cherry Valley, N.Y., Cherry Valley Editions.* 1428719
ISSN: 0098-7093 Beg. date: 1974
WU   UWM (RBR) No.1-10 (SEP1974-APR1976).

Collection. *London [etc.].* 1428734
Beg. date: 1968
WU   UWM (RBR) No.1-5,7 (MAR1968-AUT1970); no.7 suppl. no.1-5 (n.d.-n.d.).

College Art Association. Bulletin. *See* The Art bulletin. [New York, etc.], 1164899

College Art Association of America. *See* Art bulletin. [New York, etc.], College Art Association of America. 0180825

College Art Association of America. Bulletin. *See* The Art bulletin. [New York, etc.], 1164908

College of the Mainland, Texas City, Texas. Division of Humanities. Poetry Texas. *See* Poetry Texas. Texas City, Tex., Division of Humanities, College of the Mainland. 1498955

Colombo special. *Colombo, Ceylon.* 1428747
WU   UWM (RBR) V.9 no.229; v.10 no.237,247 (OCT251957-JUL041958).

Colonial freedom news. *London, The Movement for Colonial Freedom.* 1431305
ISSN: 0531-108X
Ceased publication.
Superseded by Liberation.
WU   UWM (RBR) Nov./Dec. 1963-Apr./May 1966.

Colonnade. *London.* 1431320
Beg. date: 1952 End date: 1952
Ceased publication with vol. 1 no. 2, 1952.
Continued as a section of Adam international review.
WU   UWM (RBR) V.1 no.1-2 (SPR-WIN1952).

Colorado. University. Experimental Cinema Group. Koan. *See* Koan. Boulder, Colo., Experimental Cinema Group, University of Colorado. 1494013

Colorado review. *Fort Collins, Colo.* 142875A
ISSN: 0588-5027 Beg. date: 1956 End date: 1959
Ceased publication with vol. 3, Winter 1958/1959.
WU   UWM (RBR) V.1 no.1-2; v.2-3 (WIN1956/1957-WIN1958/1959).

Colorado state review. *Fort Collins, Colo., Colorado State University.* 1442032
ISSN: 0588-5043 Beg. date: 1966
WU   UWM (RBR) V.1 no.1; v.2 no.1-4; v.3 no.1-3; v.4 no.1-2 (SPR1966-1969).

Colorado State   Little Magazine Collection—University of Wisconsin

Colorado State University. Colorado state review. *See*   1442045
    Colorado state review. Fort Collins, Colo., Colorado State University.

Columbia University. School of General Studies. Quarto.   1501803
    See Quarto. New York.

Comment in motion. *Los Angeles, The Variegation Pub. Co.*   1508861
    LCCN: 68-7650. Beg. date: 1966 End date: 1968
    Continued by Translations with no. 6, 1968?
    Supplements accompany some numbers.
    WU   UWM RBR No.1-5 (1966-1968).

Committee for Nonviolent Action. Win. *See* Win. New York,   1112171

Committee of Small Magazine Editors and Publishers. C O S M E P newsletter. *San Francisco.*   1442058
    ISSN: 0007-8832 Beg. date: 1969
    WU   UWM (RBR) V.1 no.1-3,5-12; v.2 and 2 special issues; v.3 and 2 special issues; v.4 and 3 special issues; v.5 and 4 special issues; v.7-8 (1969-1977).

Committee of Small Magazine Editors and Publishers.   1442073
    Newsletter. *See* Committee of Small Magazine Editors and Publishers. C O S M E P newsletter. San Francisco.

Common Council for American Unity. Common ground.   1017453
    See Common ground. New York,

Common ground. *New York, Common council for American unity.*   0186876
    LCCN: 44-42804 Beg. date: 1940 End date: 1949
    Ceased publication v. 10 no. 1 (Aut. 1949).
    WU   UWM (RBR) V.1 no.1 (AUT1940).

Commonwealth College, Mena, Arkansas. Windsor   1519021
    quarterly. *See* Windsor quarterly. Mena, Ark., etc., Commonwealth College, etc.

The Communicator. *Springhill, N.S.*   1428762
    WU   UWM (RBR) V.4 no.2-6; v.5-v.6 no.3 (FEB1975-1977).

Communique. *Trevose, Pa.*   1428775
    Beg. date: 1963
    WU   UWM (RBR) V.1 no.1,3,10 (MAY061963-JAN1964); no.28,31 (JUL1965-MAR/MAY1966).

Community. *Colombo, Ceylon.*   1431333
    ISSN: 0588-8352 Beg. date: 1954
    Ceased publication.
    Superseded by a series of the same name issued by the Community Institute with 1962.
    WU   UWM (RBR) V.1 no.1-4; v.2 no.1-3; v.3 no.1 (APR1954-APR1958).

Community of friends. *Campbell, Calif.*   1428788
    Beg. date: 1973
    WU   UWM (RBR) V.1 no.1-4; v.2 no.1-4; v.3 no.1-4; v.4 no.1 (MAR211973-MAR211976).

Company of Free Men. Full cry. *See* Full cry. London,   1439656
    Company of Free Men.

The Compass. *Kutztown, Pa., Kutztown State College.*   1431346
    Beg. date: 1971
    Cover title varies.
    Supersedes The New century.
    WU   UWM (RBR) No.1-2 (AUT1971-SPR1972).

Compass. *Los Angeles.*   1428790
    Beg. date: 1939
    WU   UWM (RBR) V.1 no.1-2 (WIN1939-SPR1939).

Compass; a quarterly of contemporary verse. *Prairie City, Ill., Decker Press.*   1428825
    Beg. date: 1938
    Subtitle varies.
    Title varies: vol. 1 nos. 1-3, Upward; a quarterly magazine of verse.
    Suspended publication April 1941-Summer 1948.
    WU   UWM (RBR) V.2 no.1 (no.5) (SUM1939); v.2 (no.6,10,13) (FEB1940-SPR1950).

The Compass; an instrument of direction. *West Campton, N.H. [etc.].*   1431361
    Beg. date: 1942
    Vol. 1 nos. 1-3, Nov. 1942-Spring 1943, covers lack subtitle.
    Vol. 1 nos. 1-3, Nov. 1942-Spring 1943, published at West Campton, N.H.; by Civilian Public Service Camp no. 32; vol. 1 nos. 4/5- , May 1944- , published at Ames, Iowa "by men in civilian public service."
    WU   UWM (RBR) V.1 no.2-6; v.2 no.1/2-5/6 (FEB1943-SPR1946).

Compass; the student cultural review. *New York.*   142880A
    Beg. date: 1947 End date: 1949
    Suspended publication Nov. 1947-Jan. 1949.
    Subtitle varies.
    Title also as: Compass review.
    Ceased publication with vol. 3 no. 4, Oct./Nov. 1949.
    WU   UWM (RBR) V.3 no.4 (OCT/NOV1949).

Compass review. *See* Compass; the student cultural review.   1428812
    New York.

Compass review. *St. Louis.*   1428840
    ISSN: 0573-1763 Beg. date: 1958 End date: 1959
    Ceased publication with no. 6, Summer 1959.
    WU   UWM (RBR) No.1-6 (1958-SUM1959).

Compleat Neurotica. *See* Neurotica. St. Louis, Mo.   0189540
    Reprinted by Hacker Art Books, New York, 1963.

Complex. *Saugatuck, Conn., New York.*   1442086
    ISSN: 0414-2292 Beg. date: 1950
    Subtitle varies.
    WU   UWM (RBR) No.1-9 (SPR1950-WIN1953/1954).

Compositional culture. *New York.*   1428853
    ISSN: 0414-2306 Beg. date: 1957
    WU   UWM (RBR) V.1 no.1 (MAR1957).

Comprehension. *San Francisco.*   1428866
    ISSN: 0414-2330 Beg. date: 1950 End date: 1951
    Ceased publication with vol. 1 no. 3, Winter 1950/1951.
    WU   UWM (RBR) V.1 no.1-3 (SPR1950-1951).

Con Safos. *Los Angeles, Calif.*   0190285
    ISSN: 0010-5164 Beg. date: 1968
    In English and Spanish.
    WU   UWM (RBR) V.1 no.2-4; v.2 no.5 (FAL1968-1970); no.6-7 (SUM1970-WIN1971).

Concentrate. *Altrincham, Cheshire, Eng., Mwangaza Enterprises.*   1431374
    Beg. date: 1968
    Ceased publication.
    Superseded by Corridor with 1971.
    WU   UWM (RBR) No.1 (1968).

Conception: a young writer's magazine. *Chariton, Iowa.*   1428879
    ISSN: 0573-2263 Beg. date: 1962 End date: 1963
    Ceased publication with vol. 2 no. 1, Fall 1963.
    WU   UWM (RBR) V.1 no.2-4; v.2 no.1 (WIN1962/1963-FAL1963).

Concern. *Los Angeles.*   1428881
    "Newsletter of the Southern California Council on Religion and the Homophile."
    WU   UWM (RBR) No.3-6 (OCT1966-APR1967).

Concern; a literary magazine. *Cambridge, Eng.*   1428903
    ISSN: 0414-2551 Beg. date: 1951
    WU   UWM (RBR) No.1 (APR1951).

Concerning poetry. *Bellingham, Washington, English Department, Western Washington State College.*   0190376
    ISSN: 0010-5201
    WU   UWM (RBR) V.1-v.10 no.1 (SPR1968-SPR1977).

Concordia College, Moorhead, Minnesota. Discourse. *See*   1108628
    Discourse; a review of the liberal arts. Moorhead, Minn.,

Conditions. *[Brooklyn, N.Y., Conditions.]*   1528624
    ISSN: 0147-8311 LCCN: 77-641895 Beg. date: 1977
    "A magazine of writing by women with an emphasis on writing by lesbians."
    WU   UWM (RBR) V.1 no.1 (APR1977).

Conference on Jewish social studies. *See* Jewish social   0191903
    studies, a quarterly journal devoted to contemporary and historical aspects of Jewish life. New York.

Conference on Science and Religion. Challenge. *See*   1434415
    Challenge. [Reseda, Calif., etc.], Conference on Science and Religion.

Configuration. *Lake Forest, Ill., Lake Forest College.*   1442099
    WU   UWM (RBR) 1965.

Confluence; an international forum. *Cambridge, Harvard University Printing Office.*   0192425
    LCCN: 55-357 Beg. date: 1952 End date: 1958
    "Published under the auspices of Summer School of Arts and Sciences and of Education of Harvard University."
    Ceased with v. 7 (1958).
    WU   UWM (RBR) V.1 no.4 (DEC1952).

Confrontation. *Greenvale, N.Y.* 1433856
ISSN: 0010-5716 Beg. date: 1968
Spring 1968-   issued as literary supplements to the Long Island University, Brooklyn. Journal.
WU   UWM (RBR) No.1-14 (SPR1968-1977).

Congress. *New York.* 1428916
ISSN: 0010-5864 Beg. date: 1967
WU   UWM (RBR) No.1-4 (1967).

Congress for Cultural Freedom. *See* Censorship. *London, Congress for Cultural Freedom.* 0192923

Connecticut. University. Fine arts magazine. *See* Fine arts magazine. Storrs, Conn., Student Union Board of Governors, University of Connecticut. 1436979

The Connecticut critic. *Cheshire, Conn.* 1428929
Beg. date: 1973
Continues New England review with no. 7, March 1973.
WU   UWM (RBR) No.7-8 (1973).

Connecticut fireside. *Hamden, Conn.* 1431387
ISSN: 0300-8258 Beg. date: 1972
Also called Fireside.
WU   UWM (RBR) V.1 no.1; v.2 no.2; v.3 no.1; v.4 no.1-2 (APR1972-1976).

The Connecticut literary review. *Waterbury, Conn.* 1508874
Beg. date: 1955
Continued by New review.
WU   UWM (RBR) V.1 no.1 (SPR1955).

Connections. *Brooklyn, Print Center, Inc.* 1428931
Beg. date: 1972
WU   UWM (RBR) No.1-4 (WIN1972/1973-WIN1976).

Connotation. *Madison, N. J., Fairleigh Dickinson University.* 0194493
Beg. date: 1962 End date: 1963
"A magazine of the arts."
Ceased publication with vol. 2, no. 1, Spring 1963.
WU   UWM (RBR) V.1 no.1; v.1 pt.2; v.2 pt.1 (SPR1962-SPR1963).

Conseil pour le Developpement du Français en Louisiane. 1529419
Revue de Louisiane. *See* Revue de Louisiane. Louisiana review. Lafayette, La., Conseil pour le Développement du Français en Louisiane.

Consumption. *Seattle, San Vito Press.* 1428944
ISSN: 0001-7204 Beg. date: 1967
WU   UWM (RBR) V.1 no.1-4; v.2 no.1-4; v.3 no.1/2 (FAL1967-MAR1970).

Contac. *Near Doncaster, Yorks, Eng.* 1428957
Beg. date: 1971
"A magazine of modern poetry."
Continued by Contac arts magazine.
WU   UWM (RBR) No.1-6 (SEP1971-SUM1974).

Contact. *Antwerp.* 142896A
Beg. date: 1956
WU   UWM (RBR) No.1,3-4 (OCT16-DEC011956).

Contact; an American quarterly review. *New York, Moss and Kamin.* 0196003
LCCN: 35-9611 Beg. date: 1932
Editor: February 1932-October 1932, William Carlos Williams.
Ceased publication October 1932.
WU   UWM (RBR) V.1 no.1-3 (FEB-OCT1932).

Contact; the San Francisco journal of new writing, art and ideas. *Sausalito, Calif., Bayberry Corporation.* 0195996
ISSN: 0589-5049 LCCN: 64-6115 Beg. date: 1958 End date: 1965
Ceased publication with vol. 5 no. 1, March 1965.
Absorbed Western review in 1959.
WU   UWM (RBR) V.1 no.1-4; v.2 no.5-8; v.3 no.1-6; v.4 no.1-6; v.5 no.1 (1958-FEB/MAR1965).

Contact, an international magazine of modern poetry. *Toronto.* 1431409
ISSN: 0573-7818 Beg. date: 1952 End date: 1954
Ceased publication with no. 10, March 1954.
WU   UWM (RBR) V.1 no.2-4; v.2 no.1,3 (no.2-5,7) (MAR1952-AUG1953); no.8-10 (SEP/DEC1953-MAR1954).

Contact II. *New York, Contact II Publications.* 1528637
Beg. date: 1976
"The best of American Poetry."
WU   UWM (RBR) V.1 no.1-5 (NOV/DEC1976-JUL/AUG1977).

Contempa. *Armadale, Victoria, Australia.* 1428985
ISSN: 0310-2017
WU   UWM (RBR) No.10 (n.d.); ser. 2 no. 1 (1975).

Contempo. *Chapel Hill.* 0196072
LCCN: 38-29814
Ceased publication with volume 3 no. 13 (1934).
WU   UWM (RBR) V.1 no.17,19-22; v.2 no.1-7; v.3 no.1-13; v.4 no.1-2 (FEB011932-MAY151933).

Contempora; a literary magazine. *Atlanta, Ga., Contempora, Inc.* 0196085
Beg. date: 1970
WU   UWM (RBR) V.1 no.1-6; v.2 no.1-5 (MAR1970-SUM1973).

Contemporary. *Detroit.* 0196107
WU   UWM (RBR) V.1 no.1 (WIN1946).

Contemporary. *San Francisco, San Francisco Contemporary Dancer's Foundation.* 1428998
ISSN: 0573-7958 Beg. date: 1960 End date: 1962
Ceased publication with vol. 2 no. 10, Juen 1962.
WU   UWM (RBR) V.1 no.1-3,6-12; v.2 no.1-4 (1960-DEC1961).

Contemporary fiction. *Milwaukee.* 1429018
ISSN: 0573-8016 Beg. date: 1958 End date: 1959
Ceased publication with vol. 1 no. 3, May 1959.
WU   UWM (RBR) V.1 no.1-3 (AUT1958-1959).

Contemporary issues; a magazine for a democracy of content. *[London].* 1429020
LCCN: 54-37329 Beg. date: 1948 End date: 1966
Ceased publication with no. 52, Spring 1966.
WU   UWM (RBR) V.8 no.28; v.9 no.35 (AUG/SEP1956-OCT/NOV1958); no.51 (SUM1965).

Contemporary literature in translation. *Vancouver.* 019627A
ISSN: 0010-7492 LCCN: 72-17504 Beg. date: 1968
Began with spring 1968 issue.
WU   UWM (RBR) No.1-20 (n.d.-FAL/WIN1974).

Contemporary poetry. *Baltimore.* 0196332
LCCN: 44-44134 End date: 1970
Title varies: Spring-Summer 1941, The Poetry forum; Autumn 1941-   , Contemporary poetry.
Ceased publication with vol. 29, 1970.
WU   UWM (RBR) Spring 1941; v.1 no.3-4; v.2-15 (AUT1941-1955).

Contemporary poetry and prose. *Nendeln, Liechsterstein, Kraus Reprint.* 0196345
Originally published in London.
WU   UWM (RBR) No.1-10 (MAY1936-AUT1937).

The Contemporary reader. *New York, Contemporary Reader, Inc.* 1442110
ISSN: 0414-7812 Beg. date: 1953 End date: 1955
Ceased publication with vol. 1 no. 4, Jan. 1955.
WU   UWM (RBR) V.1 no.1-4 (MAR1953-JAN1955).

The Contemporary review. *London, A. Strahan [etc.].* 0196408
ISSN: 0010-7565 LCCN: 7-8871 Beg. date: 1866
Indexed by Humanities index, International index, Poole's index to periodical literature, Reader's guide to periodical literature, and Social sciences and humanities index.
WU   UWM (RBR) No.899 (NOV1940).

Contemporary verse; a Canadian quarterly. *Victoria, B.C. [etc.].* 1429033
ISSN: 0383-2902 Beg. date: 1941 End date: 1952
Ceased publication with no. 39, Fall/Winter 1952.
WU   UWM (RBR) V.1 no.1; v.2 no.5 (SEP1941-SEP1942); no.6-8,11,15,20,27,31-36,38-39 (SEP1941-FAL/WIN1952).

Contemporary verse/two. *See* C V II. Contemporary verse/two. Winnipeg. 1431017

Context. *Westgate on Sea, Kent, Eng., Context International Poetry Publications.* 1429046
WU   UWM (RBR) Winter 1970; Autumn 1971.

Continuum. *Bailrigg, Lancaster, Eng., Bowland College, University of Lancaster.* 1431411
WU   UWM (RBR) No.3 (n.d.).

Contour. *Berkeley, California.* 0196620
Discontinued publication with no. 3 (1948).
Title varies: no.1-2, Contour quarterly.
WU   UWM (RBR) V.1 no.1-3 (APR1947-SUM1948).

Contour quarterly. *See* Contour. Berkeley, California. 0196633

Contra. *[New Delhi, Hem Chandra].* 1429059
ISSN: 0589-5553 LCCN: S A 67-2778 Beg. date: 1966
Title also includes numerals indicating the year of issue.
WU   UWM (RBR) No.1-6 (OCT1966-1967).

Contraband; a magazine of poems and prose. Portland, Maine, Contraband Press. 1429061
Beg. date: 1971
WU   UWM (RBR) No.1-12 (OCT311971-FEB1976).

Contrasts. Liverpool, Eng. 1429074
WU   UWM (RBR) No.1-5 (n.d.-n.d.).

Converse. [n.p.], Leicester University. 1433871
Beg. date: 1968
WU   UWM (RBR) No.1 (1968).

Convoy. [London]. 1429087
LCCN: 46-2066 rev Beg. date: 1944
Title varies: no. 2, The Convoy File.
WU   UWM (RBR) No.1,3,5 (1944-1947).

Convoy file. *See* Convoy. [London]. 142909A

Coo-ee. [n.p.]. 1429109
Beg. date: 1948
"Official magazine of the Australian Amateur Press Association."
WU   UWM (RBR) V.1 no.1-3 (JUL1948-APR1952).

Cop killer. *See* Copkiller. New Orleans. 1429137

Copkiller. New Orleans. 1429124
ISSN: 0589-6797 Beg. date: 1968
WU   UWM (RBR) No.1 (1968).

Copperfield. Hamilton, Ont., McMaster University. 1433897
Beg. date: 1969
"An independent Canadian literary magazine of the land and the north."
WU   UWM (RBR) V.2,4-5 (SPR1970-1974).

Copy; todays better fiction. Beverly Hills, Calif., The Bards. 142914A
ISSN: 0574-0096 Beg. date: 1950 End date: 1950
Ceased publication with vol. 1 no. 1, 1950.
WU   UWM (RBR) V.1 no.1 (1950).

Corduroy. Bristol, Tenn. [etc.], Corduroy Publications. 1429152
ISSN: 0010-8707 Beg. date: 1968
WU   UWM (RBR) V.1 no.1-3 (1968-1970); no.4-9/10 (1972-1976).

Cornell College, Mount Vernon, Iowa. English Club. Husk. 1440412
See Husk. [Mount Vernon, Iowa].

Cornhill booklet. Boston, A. Bartlett. 0199299
LCCN: 18-19410
Publication suspended 1906-1913, inclusive.
WU   UWM (RBR) V.1 no.1-2; v.2 no.1-6; v.3 no.1-6 (JUL1900-WIN1905).

Cornish magazine. Truro, London, J. Pollard. 0199336
LCCN: 1-3025
WU   UWM (RBR) V.1 (JUL-DEC1898).

The Cornish review. Penzance, Cornwall [etc.]. 1429165
Beg. date: 1949 End date: 1952
Ceased publication with no. 10, Summer 1952.
WU   UWM (RBR) No.1-2 (SPR-SUM1949).

El Corno emplumado. The Plumed horn. México. 0199349
ISSN: 0010-8928 LCCN: 63-32200 Beg. date: 1962
WU   UWM (RBR) No.1-31 (1962-1969).

The Cornucopia. Indianapolis. 1442123
ISSN: 0525-7808
"Poetry magazine of the Poets' Corner, Incorporated."
WU   UWM (RBR) V.6 no.4,7; v.7 no.3,6,8; v.8 no.3,5-6; v.9 no.2; v.10 no.1; v.11; v.12 no.3-4; v.13-19; v.20 no.1; v.22 no.1 (1953-SPR1968).

Correspondence. Detroit. 1431437
WU   UWM (RBR) V.3 no.5,7,9-20; v.4 no.1-7,9-10,12-16,18-25 (MAY231959-DEC101960).

Corridor. Radcliffe, Manchester, Eng., M. Butterworth Publications. 1429178
ISSN: 0010-9142 Beg. date: 1971
Supersedes Concentrate.
Ceased publication.
Superseded by Wordworks; new writings quarterly with 1975.
WU   UWM (RBR) No.[1]-5 (1971-1974).

Cosmopolitan contact. Los Angeles, Planetary Legion for Peace. 1429180
ISSN: 0010-955X Beg. date: 1962
Several subtitles.
WU   UWM (RBR) V.6 no.16-18; v.7 no.19-20; v.10 no.21; v.11 no.22; v.12 no.23,25; v.13 no.24,26 (n.d.-n.d.).

Cosmopolitan review. *See* Cuddon's cosmopolitan review. London. 1431766

Cosmos. Mickelgate, York, Eng. 1429202
Beg. date: 1969
WU   UWM (RBR) No.1-[3] (1969-1970).

Cosmos; science-fantasy review. Ilford, Essex, Eng. 1429215
ISSN: 0010-9576 Beg. date: 1969
WU   UWM (RBR) No.1-3 (APR-JUN/JUL1969).

Coterie. London, Hendersons. 0200373
LCCN: 26-1017 Beg. date: 1919
WU   UWM (RBR) No.1-6/7 (MAY1919-WIN1920/1921).

Cottonwood review. [n.p.]. 143144A
ISSN: 0589-8986 Beg. date: 1965
Supersedes Cottonwood.
WU   UWM (RBR) V.1 no.1-3 (SPR1965-NOV1966); 1968; Spring, Fall 1969; Winter 1969/1970; Fall 1970; Winter 1971/1972; Fall 1972; Spring 1973; Winter 1973/1974; Summer 1974; Winter 1974/1975; Fall 1975; No.18 (1976).

Council for the Development of French in Louisiana. 1529406
Louisiana review. *See* Revue de Louisiane. Louisiana review. Lafayette, La., Conseil pour le Développement du Français en Louisiane.

Counter/measures; a magazine of rime, meter and song. Bedford, Mass. 0202175
ISSN: 0070-1246 LCCN: 71-618069 Beg. date: 1972 End date: 1974
Ceased publication with no. 3, 1974.
WU   UWM (RBR) No.1-3 (1972-1974).

Counterpoint. Kingston upon Thames, Surrey, Eng. 152864A
ISSN: 0309-3328
WU   UWM (RBR) No.2 (SUM1977).

Counterpoint. Oxford, Alden Press Limited. 020220A
WU   UWM (RBR) V.1 ([1944]).

Counterpoint. West New York, N.J. 1429228
ISSN: 0525-9665 Beg. date: 1958
Ceased publication with vol. 1 no. 1, Jan./March 1958.
WU   UWM (RBR) V.1 no.1 (JAN/MAR1958).

Counterpoise series. Nashville. 1429230
Beg. date: 1948
Issued by Counterpoise Cohort, Fisk University.
WU   UWM (RBR) No.1 (1948).

Country bard. *See* American bard. Madison, N.J., Los Angeles, R. Sharp. 0202240

COW. *See* COWard. San Francisco. 1429269

COWard. San Francisco. 1429256
Beg. date: 1965
WU   UWM (RBR) No.1-3 (1965-n.d.).

Cowskin review. Wichita, Kan. 1429271
WU   UWM (RBR) No.1-2 (1974?-n.d.).

Coyote's journal. [Berkeley, Calif. etc.]. 1429284
ISSN: 0011-0736 LCCN: 76-649256 Beg. date: 1964
WU   UWM (RBR) No.1-10 (1964-1974).

Crab grass; poetical sonatas. Belfast. 1429297
WU   UWM (RBR) No.4 (1970?).

Cracked looking glass. London. 1429306
Beg. date: 1975
WU   UWM (RBR) No.1-2 (JUL-NOV1975).

Crafts review. Tring, Eng., Action Movement for the Crafts. 1429319
ISSN: 0574-3761 Beg. date: 1959
WU   UWM (RBR) No.3-6 (1960).

The Crank; an unconventional magazine. London, C.W. Daniel. 1429334
WU   UWM (RBR) V.4 no.12 (DEC1906).

Crawl out your window. San Diego, University of California Communications Board. 1442149
Beg. date: 1975
WU   UWM (RBR) No.1-2 (1975-1976).

Crazy horse. New York, Mandrill Press. 1429347
ISSN: 0574-3885 Beg. date: 1962
WU   UWM (RBR) No.1-3,5-17 (1962-1977).

The Creative advertiser. Portland, Ore. 142935A
ISSN: 0574-3923 Beg. date: 1954
WU   UWM (RBR) V.1 no.1,4; v.2 no.2 (SPR1954-SUM1956).

Creative arts '67. [Madison, Wisc.]. 1442164
"University of Wisconsin Award Winners - The Wisconsin Union Creative Arts Competitions."
WU   UWM (RBR) Spring 1967.

Creative campus. *Winnipeg, Students' Union, University of Manitoba.* 1429362
ISSN: 0590-062X
WU   UWM (RBR) 1962.

Creative moment. *Sumter, S.C., Poetry Eastwest Publications.* 1431452
ISSN: 0045-897X Beg. date: 1972
"A journal of creative writing and criticism."
WU   UWM (RBR) V.1-9 (SPR1972-n.d.).

Creative review. *Carthage, Mo. [etc.].* 1431465
ISSN: 0011-0914 Beg. date: 1960
Supersedes Golden Gate.
WU   UWM (RBR) V.1-v.3 no.3; v.4 no.2-4; v.5 no.2-4; v.6-v.11 no.1 (WIN1960/1961-WIN1970/1971).

Creative Wisconsin. *Birnamwood, Wis. [etc.].* 1431478
ISSN: 0574-3974 LCCN: 58-26456 Beg. date: 1954 End date: 1961
Published by the Wisconsin Regional Writers Association (1954-1955, as the Wisconsin Rural Writers Association).
Ceased publication with vol. 8 no. 2, Summer 1961.
WU   UWM (RBR) V.1 no.2-3; v.2 no.1-2,4; v.3 no.1; v.4 no.1-2; v.5 no.2,4; v.6 no.1-4; v.7 no.2-4; v.8 no.1 (APR1954-SPR1961).

Creative writing. *Los Angeles, National Poetry Association.* 1210112
ISSN: 0011-0930 Beg. date: 1950
WU   UWM (RBR) V.9 no.? (OCT1958).

Creative writing. *See* New horizons. *Chicago, Ill.* 0203310

Creative youth. *Wauwatosa, Wis., American Literary Association.* 1431502
Beg. date: 1934 End date: 1935
Ceased publication with vol. 1 no. 4, June 1934.
WU   UWM (RBR) V.1 no.1-2 (NOV1934-FEB1935).

Creativity; a monthly newsletter for freelancers in the creative arts. *Brooklyn, N.Y.* 1431528
WU   UWM (RBR) V.1 no.3-4,6-8 (JUL-DEC1965).

Credences. *Kent, Ohio, The Credences Press.* 1431530
Beg. date: 1974
WU   UWM (RBR) No.1-3 (1974-1976); v.2 no.1 (1977).

Crescendo. *New Orleans [etc.].* 1431543
Beg. date: 1942 End date: 1944
Subtitle varies.
Absorbed Iconograph, Winter 1943.
Ceased publication with vol. 3. Autumn 1944.
WU   UWM (RBR) V.1 no.1-5; v.2 no.1,3/4; v.3 (SEP1941-AUT1944).

Crescendo poetry series. *Saint Ives, Eng., Latin Press.* 1431556
ISSN: 0574-4180 Beg. date: 1951 End date: 1952
Ceased publication with no. 8, June 1, 1952.
WU   UWM (RBR) No.1-8 (SEP011951-JUN011952).

Crescent. *Leicester, Eng.* 1431569
Beg. date: 1959
"A magazine devoted to the arts and matters of topical interest."
WU   UWM (RBR) V.1 no.1-3 (NOV1959-SUM1960).

Cricket; black music in evolution. *Newark, N.J.* 1431571
ISSN: 0011-1244 LCCN: 71-60020 Beg. date: 1969
Caption title.
WU   UWM (RBR) 1969.

The Criterion. *Springfield, Mass., Literary Club, American International College.* 1431597
WU   UWM (RBR) V.16-17 (1961-1962).

Criterion miscellany. *London, Faber and Faber Ltd.* 1431619
Beg. date: 1929 End date: 1936
Ceased publication with no. 43, 1936.
WU   UWM (RBR) No.1-43 (1929-1936).

The Critic; a quarterly review of criticism. *London, the Critic press limited.* 0204159
Absorbed by Politics and letters with Winter 1947
WU   UWM (RBR) V.1 no.1 (SPR1947).

Critical. *Boston, Stuart Publications.* 1431621
ISSN: 0526-1368 Beg. date: 1959
"A review of art and criticism."
WU   UWM (RBR) Oct. 1959-Jan. 1960; no.4-6 (APR1960-n.d.).

Critique. A critical review of theatre arts and literature. *See* Drama critique; a critical review of theatre arts and literature. *Lancaster, N.Y., National Catholic Theatre Conference.* 0204406

Critique; a review of contemporary art. *New York.* 0204419
Beg. date: 1946
Ceased publication with vol. 1 no.3, Jan./Feb. 1947.
WU   UWM (RBR) V.1 no.1-3 (OCT1946-JAN/FEB1947).

The Crocodile. *Gainesville, Fla.* 0204540
WU   UWM (RBR) V.3 no.1 (OCT1967?).

Crocodile review. *New York.* 1431634
ISSN: 0574-4652 Beg. date: 1961
WU   UWM (RBR) No.3-4 (MAY/JUN-SUM1961).

Cronopios. *Madison [etc.] Wis.* 1431647
ISSN: 0590-1200 Beg. date: 1966
WU   UWM (RBR) No.1-7 (NOV1966-MAY1970).

Cronos. *Columbus, Ohio, Ohio State University.* 143165A
Beg. date: 1947 End date: 1948
"An international quarterly review."
Subtitle varies.
Ceased publication with vol. 2 no. 4, March 1948.
Superseded by Golden goose with Summer 1948.
WU   UWM (RBR) V.1 no.1-3; v.2 no.4 (SPR1947-MAR1948).

Cross country. *Montreal, Woodhaven, N.Y., Cross Country Press.* 1431675
Beg. date: 1975
"A magazine of Canadian-U.S. poetry."
WU   UWM (RBR) No.1-7 (WIN1975-1977).

Cross section, a collection of new American writing. *New York, L. B. Fischer.* 0834649
LCCN: 44-5533 Beg. date: 1944
None published 1946.
WU   UWM (RBR) V.1-4 (1944-1948).

Crosscountry. *See* Cross country. *Montreal, Woodhaven, N.Y., Cross Country Press.* 1431688

The Croupier. *Seattle, The Croupier Press.* 1431690
ISSN: 0590-1316 Beg. date: 1965
WU   UWM (RBR) No.1 (SPR1965).

Crow's nest. *Millbrae, Calif., Scarecrow Books.* 143170A
Beg. date: 1975
WU   UWM (RBR) No.1 (1975).

Crucible. *Auckland, N.Z.* 1431712
Beg. date: 1965
Ceased publication.
WU   UWM (RBR) No.1-[2] (SUM1966/1967-AUT1967); Summer 1969.

Crucible. *Cass Lake, Minn., America's Cavalier Poet, Garry de Young.* 0205088
WU   UWM (RBR) Mar.-July/Aug. 1968.

Crux. *Oxford, Union of Catholic Students of Great Britain.* 1431725
WU   UWM (RBR) V.7 no.3; v.8 no.1 (SUM-AUT1953).

Csakazértis. *Georgetown, Guyana.* 1439160
Beg. date: 1971
Title page in Hungarian and English.
English title: Just for all that.
WU   UWM (RBR) No.1-2 (1971-n.d.).

Cubicle. *[Mahonoy City, Pa.].* 1431740
LCCN: 44-42920 Beg. date: 1935 End date: 1972
Ceased publication with 1972?
WU   UWM (RBR) No.1-4 (NOV1935-APR1936); v.1 no.5; v.2 no.1-4; v.3 no.2-4; v.4 no.1-2 (SEP1936-JUN1939); no.17-34,36-40,42-49 (WIN1939-1972).

Cuddon's cosmopolitan review. *London.* 1431753
ISSN: 0590-3025
WU   UWM (RBR) No.6,10-11 (NOV1965-JUL1967).

Cuervo international. *Hollywood, Calif.* 0205651
WU   UWM (RBR) No.6-10 (1968-OCT1969); suppl. 1969.

Cultural affairs. *New York, Associated Council of the Arts.* 0205742
ISSN: 0011-2828
WU   UWM (RBR) No.1-2,4-11 (1967-1970).

Cultural Worker's Front of Our America. Left curve, art and revolution. *See* Left Curve, art and revolution. *San Francisco, Cultural Workers' Front of Our America.* 1277656

The Curiously strong. *Cambridge, Eng.* 1431779
ISSN: 0011-3077 Beg. date: 1969
WU   UWM (RBR) V.1 no.1-10 (FEB24-MAY251969).

Curled wire chronicle. *St. Louis.*   1431781
    ISSN: 0526-4316 Beg. date: 1954
    Continues Curled wire dispatches.
    WU   UWM (RBR) V.2 no.1,5-7 (SEP1954-JAN/JUL1955).

Curled wire dispatches. *[n.p.].*   1431794
    Continued by Curled wire chronicle.
    WU   UWM (RBR) V.1 no.3-10 (SEP1953-JUN1954).

Curlew. *Harrogate, Eng., The Curlew Press.*   1431803
    End date: 1975
    Continued by Poet quarterly with no. 11, Spring 1976.
    WU   UWM (RBR) [No.] 9-15 (OCT/NOV1975-1977).

Curtains. *Yorkshire [etc.] Eng., Pressed Curtains.*   1431816
    Beg. date: 1971
    WU   UWM (RBR) No.1-6/7 (1971-1974); 1975; no.14-17 (1977); suppl. no.3 (1972).

Cut bank. *Missoula, Dept. of English, University of Montana.*   137116A
    Beg. date: 1973
    WU   UWM (RBR) 1973-Spring 1975; no.6-8 (1976-1977).

Cutbank. *See* Cut bank. Missoula, Dept. of English, University of Montana.   1371172

Cutely. *See* Mainly. Brecon, Wales.   149577A

Cuyahoga Community College, Cleveland. Everyman. *See* Everyman. Cleveland, Cuyahoga Community College.   1433988

Cyclo-flame. *San Angelo, Tex.*   1431829
    ISSN: 0011-4359 Beg. date: 1966
    Formed by the union of Cyclotron and Flame; Avalon annual.
    Numbering computed from the beginning date of Flame (Alpine, Tex.).
    Includes supplement: Avalon dispatch.
    WU   UWM (RBR) V.14-22 (1966-1976); suppl. Nov. 1974; Feb., Oct. 1975; Mar., June, Sept. 1976.

Cyclops. *Scarborough, Ont.*   1431844
    Beg. date: 1968
    Ceased publication.
    Absorbed by the Catalyst.
    WU   UWM (RBR) No.1-5 (NOV1968-SPR1970).

Cyclotron. *San Angelo, Tex.*   146901A
    ISSN: 0590-4668 Beg. date: 1963 End date: 1965
    Supplement to Flame; Avalon annual.
    Ceased publication with vol. 3 no. 4, Winter 1965.
    United with Flame; Avalon annual to form Cyclo-flame with Spring 1966.
    WU   UWM (RBR) V.1; v.2 no.2-3; v.3 (SPR1963-WIN1965).

Cypher. *Salisbury, Wilts., Eng.*   1439461
    WU   UWM (RBR) No.8-10,12 (SEP1972-NOV1974).

Cyphers. *Dublin.*   1431857
    Beg. date: 1975
    WU   UWM (RBR) No.1-6 (JUN1975-1977).

Czech struggle for freedom and democracy. *See* Český boj za svobodu a demokracii. Czech struggle for freedom and democracy. London.   1441984

D

Da Vinci. *Montreal.* 1371235
ISSN: 0315-9914 LCCN: 75-30763 Beg. date: 1973
WU   UWM (RBR) V.1 no.1-3 (WIN1973-AUT1974).

Dacotah territory. *Moorhead, Minn.* 0209073
ISSN: 0084-9529 LCCN: 75-617271 Beg. date: 1971
WU   UWM (RBR) No.1-13 (1971-1976).

Daedalian monthly. *See* Daedalian quarterly. Denton, Tex. 1431885

Daedalian quarterly. *Denton, Tex.* 143186A
"Published by the students of the Texas State College for Women, Denton, Texas."
Title varies: -1924, Daedalian monthly.
WU   UWM (RBR) V.60 no.1; v.63 no.2; v.65 no.1; v.67 no.1 (SPR1968-1973).

Daimon. *Atlanta, Atlanta Poetry Collective, Inc.* 1528652
Beg. date: 1976
WU   UWM (RBR) No.1-6 (SUM1976-AUT1977).

Dallas review. *Irving, Tex.* 1431907
ISSN: 0416-6574 Beg. date: 1962
WU   UWM (RBR) V.1 no.1-2 (OCT1962-FEB1963).

Daimo'ma. *Port Townsend, Wash.* 143889A
Beg. date: 1976
WU   UWM (RBR) V.1 no.1 (JUL1976).

Damascus road. *Allentown, Penn.* 0210338
Beg. date: 1961
WU   UWM (RBR) No.1-5 (1961-1975).

Damn you; a magazine of the arts. *Allahabad, India.* 143191A
ISSN: 0011-5940 Beg. date: 1965
WU   UWM (RBR) No.4-6 (n.d.-n.d.).

Danse macabre. *Manhattan Beach, Calif.* 1431922
ISSN: 0415-0015 Beg. date: 1957
WU   UWM (RBR) V.1 no.1 ([1957]).

Dar es Salaam. University. Literature Department. Umma. 1516686
See Umma. Dar es Salaam, Literature Dept., University of Dar es Salaam.

Dare. *[Cleveland, Ohio, Cashing Publishing Company].* 1431935
ISSN: 0418-3789 LCCN: 78-13335 Beg. date: 1963
WU   UWM (RBR) V.5 no.4-7; v.6 no.1-3 (SUM1967-FAL1968).

Dark horse. *Cambridge, Mass., Dark Horse Poets Co-op.* 1431948
Beg. date: 1974
"Boston's first poetry and fiction newspaper."
WU   UWM (RBR) V.1 no.1-4; v.2 no.1,6-12 (FAL1974-1977).

Dark Horse Poets Co-op. Dark horse. *See* Dark horse. 1431950
Cambridge, Mass., Dark Horse Poets Co-op.

Dark tower. *Cleveland.* 1431963
WU   UWM (RBR) V.3 no.2; v.5 no.1-2; v.6 no.1 (SPR1974-1977).

Dark waters. *Seattle, United Black Artists Guild.* 1431976
Beg. date: 1973
WU   UWM (RBR) V.1 no.1-3/4; v.2 no.2 (1973-1976).

Dasein. *New York, etc.* 1431991
ISSN: 0011-6807 Beg. date: 1961
Subtitle varies.
Nos. 1-2/3 issued by the Dasein Literary Society of Howard University, Washington, D.C.
WU   UWM (RBR) V.1 no.1-9; v.10 no.1 (MAR1961-WIN1973/1974).

Datr. *Brighton, Sussex, Eng.* 1432011
WU   UWM (RBR) No.1-3 (1971-1974).

Daughter of Ore. *See* Ore. Stevenage, Herts., Eng. [etc.]. 1497690

Daughters of Bilitis. Lesbian tide. *See* Lesbian tide. Santa Monica, Calif. [etc.], Tide Collective. 149266A

David. *See* David; a quarterly of the writing. New York. 1441025

David; a quarterly of the writing. *New York.* 1441012
ISSN: 0415-0686 Beg. date: 1955
Title varies: Spring 1955-   , The David.
WU   UWM (RBR) V.1 no.1 (APR1955).

Davinci. *See* Da Vinci. Montreal. 1371248

Dawn; young writers' magazine. *Lamoni, Iowa.* 1432024
ISSN: 0415-0821 Beg. date: 1955
WU   UWM (RBR) V.1 no.2,5-6; v.2 no.1-2,4-6; v.3 no.1-2 (JAN/FEB1956-JAN/FEB1958).

The Day after yesterday. *Hammond, Ind., Catalyst Press.* 1432037
Beg. date: 1971
WU   UWM (RBR) V.1 no.1 (1971).

The De Paul literary magazine. *Chicago, De Paul University.* 1434443
ISSN: 0418-4440 Beg. date: 1963 End date: 1964
Ceased publication with vol. 2 no. 2, Spring 1964.
WU   UWM (RBR) No.1; v.2 no.1 (SPR1963,WIN1963); Spring 1964.

De Paul University, Chicago. De Paul literary magazine. 1434456
See De Paul literary magazine. Chicago, De Paul University.

DeAnza College, Cupertino, California. Bottomfish. *See* 1438861
Bottomfish. Cupertino, Calif., DeAnza College.

Death; a literary quarterly. *New York, H. Herschkowitz.* 021281A
Beg. date: 1946 End date: 1946
Ceased publication with vol. 1 no. 1, Summer 1946.
WU   UWM (RBR) V.1 no.1 (SUM1946).

The Debunker. *Escondido, Calif.* 143204A
ISSN: 0418-4653 Beg. date: 1969
WU   UWM (RBR) V.1 pt.1 (MAR1969).

Debunker and the American parade. *Girard, Kan., The Haldeman-Julius company.* 0212926
LCCN: 32-8880 rev.
Title varies: vol. 1-vol. 8 no. 4, 1924/1925-1928, Haldeman-Julius monthly; vol. 8 no. 5-vol. 11 no. 6, Oct. 1928-May 1930, Debunker.
Absorbed American parade in May 1929.
Ceased publication with vol. 15 no. 5, Oct. 1931.
WU   UWM (RBR) V.2 no.2; v.4 no.3; v.6 no.3; v.8 no.4 (JUL1925-SEP1928).

The Decachord. *[London].* 1434469
Beg. date: 1924 End date: 194
"A magazine for poetry-lovers" (varies).
Publication suspended Aug. 1926-Jan. 1927, March-June 1931.
WU   UWM (RBR) V.14 no.63; v.18 no.88; v.22 no.109-115 (MAY/JUN1937-JAN/FEB1946).

Decade. *See* Decade of short stories. Chicago, Decade Magazine. 1434484

Decade magazine. *See* Decade of short stories. Chicago, Decade Magazine. 1434497

Decade of short stories. *Chicago, Decade Magazine.* 1434471
LCCN: 49-674 Beg. date: 1939
Also referred to as Decade and Decade magazine.
WU   UWM (RBR) V.1 no.1,4; v.2 no.1,3-4,6; v.4 no.1-6; v.5,7; v.8 no.1-6; v.9 no.1-4; v.10 no.1-6; v.11 no.1-4 (1939-1953).

Decal; poetry review. *Cardiff, Wales, Decal Press.* 1434506
Beg. date: 1972
Also called Decal review.
WU   UWM (RBR) No.1/2-3 (1972-WIN1972/1973).

Decal review. *See* Decal; poetry review. Cardiff, Wales, Decal Press. 1434519

Decision. *New York.* 0213030
LCCN: 43-5532 Beg. date: 1941 End date: 1942
V. 1 has subtitle: A review of free culture.
Ceased publication with vol. 3 no. 1/2, Jan./Feb. 1942.
WU   UWM (RBR) V.1 no.1-6; v.2 no.1-6; v.3 no.1/2 (JAN1941-JAN/FEB1942).

The Deer and dachshund. *Ranches of Taos, N.M.* 1434521
ISSN: 0418-4920 Beg. date: 1952 End date: 1954
Ceased publication with vol. 1 no. 6, 1954.
WU   UWM (RBR) V.1 no.3-6 (1952?-1954).

Defilee's offbeat. *See* Offbeat. Encino, Calif., Defilee Publications. 1509894

Definition. *New York, Definition Press.* 1434534
ISSN: 0011-7676 Beg. date: 1961 End date: 1967
"A journal of events and aesthetic realism."
Ceased publication with no. 21, 1967.
WU   UWM (RBR) No.1-20 (1961-1966); special issue 1965.

DeHart's courier. *See* American courier; dedicated to the mental and material improvement of man. Kansas City, Mo. 144179A

DeKalb College, Clarkston, Georgia. DeKalb literary arts journal. *See* DeKalb literary arts journal. Clarkston, Ga., DeKalb College. 1286042

DeKalb literary arts journal. *Clarkston, Ga., DeKalb College.* 128603A
ISSN: 0011-7714 Beg. date: 1966
WU   UWM (RBR) V.1 no.3-4; v.2 no.1-3; v.3 no.2-4; v.4 no.1,3-4; v.5 no.2-4; v.6-v.10 no.3 (SPR1967-1976).

Delirium. *Wataga, Ill., Jim McCurry.* 1434547
Beg. date: 197
WU   UWM (RBR) No.2-3 (FAL1975-1976).

Delos; a journal on and of translation. *Austin, National Translation Center.* 143455A
ISSN: 0011-7951 LCCN: 68-130669 Beg. date: 1968
WU   UWM (RBR) No.1-6 (1968-1971).

Delta. *Montreal, Louis Dudek.* 1434575
ISSN: 0382-9065 Beg. date: 1957 End date: 1966
"A magazine of poetry and criticism."
Ceased publication with no. 26, Oct. 1966.
WU   UWM (RBR) No.1-26 (1957-1966).

Delta; the Cambridge literary magazine. *See* Delta, a Literary review. Plymouth, Eng. 1450684

Delta, a Literary review. *Plymouth, Eng.* 0214693
ISSN: 0011-7986 Beg. date: 1954
Subtitle varies.
"Founded...by a group of Cambridge undergraduates."
Subtitle varies: The Cambridge literary magazine.
WU   UWM (RBR) No.18-56 (1958-1977).

The Denishawn magazine. *New York, Ruth St. Denis and Ted Shawn School of Dancing.* 1434588
LCCN: 29-20355 Beg. date: 1924 End date: 1925
Ceased publication with vol. 1 no. 4, Summer 1925.
WU   UWM (RBR) V.1 no.1-4 (1924-SUM1925).

Denishawn School of Dancing, New York. Denishawn magazine. *See* Denishawn magazine. New York, Ruth St. Denis and Ted Shawn School of Dancing. 1434590

Denison University, Granville, Ohio. Exile. *See* Exile. [Granville, Ohio], Denison University. 1435708

Dental floss. *West Branch, Ia., Toothpaste Press.* 143460A
Beg. date: 1975
WU   UWM (RBR) V.1 no.1 (MAR1975); no.2 (1976).

Denver. University. Denver quarterly. *See* Denver Quarterly. Denver, 1338341

Denver Quarterly. *Denver, University of Denver.* 0216651
ISSN: 0011-8869 Beg. date: 1966
Cover title: The University of Denver Quarterly.
WU   UWM (RBR) V.1-v.12 no.1 (SPR1966-SPR1977).

Departure; a magazine of literature and the arts. *Oxford.* 021673A
ISSN: 0415-4444 Beg. date: 1952 End date: 1957
Ceased publication with vol. 4 (no.11), Jan. 1957.
Superseded by New departures, ISSN 0028-4580, with Summer 1959.
WU   UWM (RBR) V.1-4 (no.1-11) (1952-JAN1957).

Descant. *Fort Worth, Texas, Texas Christian University.*
ISSN: 0011-9210 Beg. date: 1956
"The Texas Christian University literary journal."
WU   UWM (RBR) V.1-13; v.14 no.2-3; v.15-21 (FAL1956-SPR1977).

Descant. *Toronto, Graduate English Assn., University of Toronto.* 1434612
ISSN: 0382-909X Beg. date: 1970
Nos. 1- published as a literary supplement to Bibliography III, the GEA newsletter, Toronto University.
WU   UWM (RBR) No.[1]-17 (1970-1977).

The Desert review. *Albuquerque, N.M., Desert Review Press.* 1434640
ISSN: 0418-7628 Beg. date: 1963
WU   UWM (RBR) Spring 1964; Spring 1965; Fall 1967; Summer/Fall 1970.

Desert tracks; literature and art magazine. *[n.p.].* 1434653
WU   UWM (RBR) 1968-1969.

Desperado. *San Francisco, Calif., Grande Ronde Press.* 1434666
Beg. date: 1969
WU   UWM (RBR) V.1 no.1 (1969); no.5 (JUN1971).

Despite everything. *Berkeley, Calif.* 0217251
ISSN: 0011-9482 LCCN: 70-25494 Beg. date: 1963
WU   UWM (RBR) V.1 no.1-2,4; v.3 no.1-4; v.4 no.1-2 (FEB1963-JAN1969); special issues: Jan. 1965, Apr. 1966, July 1966.

Detroit. University. Fresco. *See* Fresco. Detroit, University of Detroit. 1442283

Deuce. *Southall, Eng.* 1434679
ISSN: 0417-1268 Beg. date: 1958
WU   UWM (RBR) Aug. 1958; Jan., Mar., Nov. 1959; n. ser. no.1-9 (1960-1962); supplement.

Dew-line newsletter. *See* McLuhan dew-line. New York, Human Development Corp. 1494355

Dharma. *Prospect, South Australia.* 1434681
WU   UWM (RBR) No.11 (1974).

Dial; an annual of fiction. *New York Dial Press.* 0221836
ISSN: 0419-0580 LCCN: 65-29871 Beg. date: 1959 End date: 1962
First 3 issues quarterly.
Subtitle varies.
WU   UWM (RBR) V.1 no.1-3 (1959-1960); Annual 1962.

Dialogue Calcutta; poetry from India. *Calcutta.* 0913035
Beg. date: 1968 End date: 1971
Title varies: no. 1- , 1968- , Dialogue.
Ceased publication.
Superseded by Dialogue India.
WU   UWM (RBR) No.1-19 (1968-1971).

Dialogue India. *[Calcutta].* 1313244
LCCN: 76-923741 Beg. date: 1971
Supersedes Dialogue Calcutta.
WU   UWM (RBR) No.1-3,6-19 (1971-n.d.).

Diameter; a magazine of the arts. *Brooklyn, N.Y., Diameter, Inc.* 1434694
ISSN: 0415-7869 LCCN: 55-43738 Beg. date: 1951
WU   UWM (RBR) No.1-2 (FEB-APR1951).

Diana's bi-monthly. *Providence, R.I., Burning Deck Press.* 1434703
ISSN: 0046-0222 Beg. date: 1972
WU   UWM (RBR) V.1-v.5 no.3 (FEB1972-1977).

Dickinson review. *Dickinson, N.D., Dickinson State College.* 0222239
ISSN: 0419-1102 Beg. date: 1967
WU   UWM (RBR) V.1 no.1; v.3 no.1; v.4 no.1-2 (SPR1967-1976).

Different; a voice of the atomic age. *Floral Park, N.Y. [etc.], Avalon.* 1434716
Beg. date: 1945
Formed by the union of Now and Raven.
Subtitle varies: The voice of the cultural renaissance.
Name of issuing body varies: March/April 1945-April 1947, Avalon National Poetry Shrine; · , Avalon World Arts Academy.
WU   UWM (RBR) V.4 no.4; v.5 no.5-6; v.6 no.1,3-4; v.8 no.1-4 (MAY/JUN1948-WIN1954).

Dill Pickle Club. Dill pickler. *See* Dill pickler. Chicago, Dill Pickle Club. 143476A

The Dill pickler. *Chicago, Dill Pickle Club.* 1434757
WU   UWM (RBR) V.1 no.1-2 (n.d.).

Dimas. *Elmhurst, N.Y., Alan Jay Arikian.* 1434772
Beg. date: 196
WU   UWM (RBR) No.3 (n.d.).

Dime bag. *Toronto, Glendon College.* 1434785
Beg. date: 1970
WU   UWM (RBR) No.11-17 (MAR1974-1977).

Dimensions. *Bronxville, N.Y.* 1434807
LCCN: 52-66273 Beg. date: 1947
Running title: The Sarah Lawrence review.
Published by the students of Sarah Lawrence College.
WU   UWM (RBR) V.1 no.1; v.3 no.2 (WIN1947,SPR1949).

Diogenes. *Madison, Wis.* 1434835
LCCN: 45-45965 Beg. date: 1940 End date: 1941
Ceased publication with vol. 1 no. 3, Autumn 1941.
WU   UWM (RBR) V.1 no.1-3 (OCT/NOV1940-AUT1941).

Dion. *Inglewood, Calif., Wagon and Star Publishers.* 1434848
ISSN: 0012-3064 Beg. date: 1963
WU   UWM (RBR) No.1-8 (1963-1967).

Dionysus. *Bombay, S.V. Pradhan and A.S. Benjamin.* 1434850
ISSN: 0419-1668 LCCN: S A 67-4927 Beg. date: 1965
WU   UWM (RBR) V.1 no.1 (AUG1965).

Direction. *Darien, Connecticut.* 0223205
LCCN: 42-34640.
V. 1 no. 3 (Feb. 1938) is a special issue sponsored by the Guilds' committee for federal writers' publications, inc., with title "American stuff by workers of Federal writers' project; with eight prints by Federal art project."
Continued —

Continued —
Ceased with v. 8 no. 1 (Fall 1945).
Superseded by Pharos.
WU   UWM (RBR) V.1-3; v.4 no.1-5; v.5 no.3-4; v.6-v.8 no.1 (DEC1937-FAL1945).

Direction. *New York.* 1434876
LCCN: 48-14393 Beg. date: 1947
Supersedes Pharos.
WU   UWM (RBR) No.1-7 (1947-1948).

Direction. *Peoria, Ill., Kerker Quinn.* 1434863
LCCN: 44-44548 Beg. date: 1934 End date: 1935
"A quarterly of new literature."
Ceased publication with vol. 1 no. 3, April/June 1935.
WU   UWM (RBR) V.1 no.1,3 (AUT1934,APR/JUN1935).

Discourse; a review of the liberal arts. *Moorhead, Minn., Concordia College.* 0224632
ISSN: 0012-3609 LCCN: 59-37657 Beg. date: 1958 End date: 1970
Ceased with v. 13 no. 4 (1970).
WU   UWM (RBR) V.1 no.1 (JAN1958).

Discourses on poetry. *Fort Smith, Ark., South and West, Inc.* 1434889
ISSN: 0070-6671 LCCN: 75-613020 Beg. date: 1966
"A literary annual."
WU   UWM (RBR) V.1-6 (1966-1972).

Discovery. *New York, Pocket Books, Inc.* 1434900
ISSN: 0419-4098 LCCN: 55-8714 Beg. date: 1953 End date: 1955
Ceased publication with no. 6, Sept. 1955.
WU   UWM (RBR) No.1-6 (FEB1953-SEP1955).

The Disinherited. *Cheltenham, Eng.* 1434913
Beg. date: 1965
WU   UWM (RBR) No.1-3 (1965-1967).

Dispatch. *Venice, Calif.* 1434926
Beg. date: 1968
WU   UWM (RBR) V.1 no.2-8 (DEC1968-JUN1969).

Dissent; a quarterly of socialist opinion. *New York.* 0224777
ISSN: 0012-3846 LCCN: 57-2963 Beg. date: 1954
WU   UWM (RBR) V.1-3 (1954-1957); v.10 no.3 (SUM1963).

Diversion. *Louisville, Ky.* 1434939
ISSN: 0012-4176 Beg. date: 1952
WU   UWM (RBR) V.8 no.3-9 (MAR-SEP1959).

Diversion. *Reading, Eng., Milford Harrison.* 1434941
Beg. date: 1972
WU   UWM (RBR) No.1-6 (SPR1972-1977).

Do-it. *Cleveland, Ohio [etc.].* 1434954
ISSN: 0012-4362 Beg. date: 1966
WU   UWM (RBR) V.1 no.1-2,4 (1966-JUL/AUG1967).

Dock leaves. *See* Anglo-Welsh review. Pembroke Dock, Eng., Temby, Wales, [etc.]. 1185972

Dodo. *Manchester, Eng.* 1434967
WU   UWM (RBR) No.5-6 (1971).

Dog soldier. *See* Dogsoldier. Spokane, Wash., Dogsoldier Press. 1434995

Dogberry. *Huddersfield, W. Yorks., Eng.* 143497A
WU   UWM (RBR) V.1 no.2 (n.d.).

Dogsoldier. *Spokane, Wash., Dogsoldier Press.* 1434982
ISSN: 0094-3118 LCCN: 74-645087 Beg. date: 1974
WU   UWM (RBR) No.1-3 (1974-1975).

The Dolphin. a periodical for all people who find pleasure in fine books. *New York, The Limited Editions Club.* 022650A
LCCN: 33-33067 Beg. date: 1933 End date: 1941
Subtitle varies.
WU   UWM (RBR) No.4 pt.1 (FAL1940).

Dome; an illustrated magazine and review of literature, music, architecture, and the graphic arts. *London.* 0226553
LCCN: 44-12450 Beg. date: 1897 End date: 1900
Quarterly, Mar. 1897-May 1898; monthly, Oct. 1898-July 1900.
Subtitle varies: Mar. 1897-May 1898, a quarterly containing examples of all the arts.; Oct. 1898-July 1900, an illustrated magazine and review of literature, music, architecture, and the graphic arts.
Ceased publication with new ser. vol. 7 (no.19/21), May/July 1900.
WU   UWM (RBR) No.1-5 (MAR1897-MAY1898); n. ser. v.1-7 (OCT1898-JUL1900).

Don Freeman's newsstand. *New York, Associated American Artists, Inc.* 1435002
LCCN: 43-38246 Beg. date: 1936 End date: 1941
"Leaves from a Manhattan sketchbook" (varies).
Vol. 1 no. 1, called new series, has title: Newsstand.
Ceased publication with n. ser. vol. 1 no. 4, Fall 1941.
WU   UWM (RBR) N. ser. v.1 no.1-4 (WIN1941-FAL1941).

Don Quijote; revista panamericana. *Hollywood, Calif., Latin American Bureau of Journalism.* 1435028
LCCN: 59-56625 Beg. date: 1941 End date: 1941
Ceased publication with vol. 1 no. 3, April 1941.
WU   UWM (RBR) Año 1 no.3 (APR1941).

Doones. *Bowling Green, Ohio, Raymond diPalma.* 1441395
Beg. date: 1969
WU   UWM (RBR) V.1 no.1-4 (1969-1971).

Doors and windows. *Berkeley, Tom Barter.* 1435043
ISSN: 0420-1671 Beg. date: 1966
WU   UWM (RBR) No.1 (JUN1966).

Doris. *Norwich, Eng.* 1435056
Beg. date: 1974
Supersedes Norch, ISSN 0029-117X.
WU   UWM (RBR) No.1-8 (MAR1974-MAY1975).

Dot zero. *See* DotZero. New York. 1435071

DotZero. *New York.* 1435069
ISSN: 0012-5644 Beg. date: 196
Sponsored by Finch, Pruyn and Company.
WU   UWM (RBR) No.3-5 (1967-FAL1968).

The Double dealer. *New Orleans, Double Dealer Pub. Co.* 0227034
Beg. date: 1921 End date: 1926
June-Oct. 1923 not published.
None published June-October, 1923.
Frequency varies.
Ceased publication with vol. 8 (no. 48), May 1926.
WU   UWM (RBR) V.1 no.3,6; v.2 no.11-12; v.5 no.25 (MAR1921-JAN1923).

Doubt. *New York, Fortean Society.* 0227047
LCCN: 55-58505 Beg. date: 1937
Irregular.
Title varies: nos. 1-10, Sept. 1937-Autumn 1944, Fortean Society magazine.
WU   UWM (RBR) No.36,38-40,43-49,51-53,55-61 (v.2-3) (n.d.-n.d.).

Douglas College, New Westminster, British Columbia. 1432550
Department of English. Event. *See* Event. New Westminster, B.C., Douglas College, Department of English.

Down here. *New York, Tompkins Square Press, Ltd.* 1435084
ISSN: 0419-7003 Beg. date: 1966
"A magazine from the East Village."
WU   UWM (RBR) V.1 no.1; v.2 no.1 (1966,SPR1967).

Drafts; a magazine of short stories. *Minneapolis, Robert Wadsworth.* 0227244
Beg. date: 1940
WU   UWM (RBR) V.1 no.1 (OCT/NOV1940).

The Dragonfly. *Pocatello, Idaho, Idaho State University.* 1435097
ISSN: 0012-5903 Beg. date: 1969
WU   UWM (RBR) V.1; v.2 no.1,3/4; v.3 (1969-1972); no.13-14 (1973-1974).

Dragonfly. *Portland, Ore.* 1435119
ISSN: 0364-359X LCCN: 76-648183 Beg. date: 1973
Supersedes Haiku highlights, ISSN 0017-6664.
WU   UWM (RBR) V.1-5 (1973-1977).

Drama critique; a critical review of theatre arts and literature. *Lancaster, N.Y., National Catholic Theatre Conference.* 0227363
ISSN: 0419-7119 Beg. date: 1958 End date: 1968
Title varies: v. 1 no. 1-2, Feb. 1958-May 1958, Critique. A critical review of theatre arts and literature.
Ceased publication with vol. 11 no. 3, Fall 1968.
WU   UWM (RBR) V.1-11 (1958-1968).

Drama survey. *Minneapolis.* 0227426
ISSN: 0419-7127 Beg. date: 1961 End date: 1969
Ceased publication with vol. 7 no. 2, Winter 1968/1969.
Indexed by Social Sciences and humanities index.
Subject index: vols. 1-6, 1961-1968, with vols. 5-6.
WU   UWM (RBR) V.1-v.5 no.1 (MAY1961-SPR1966).

Dramatika. *New York.* 1435121
ISSN: 0012-5997 Beg. date: 1968
WU   UWM (RBR) V.1-11 (1968-1977).

Dream journal. *San Francisco.* 1435134
Beg. date: 1975
WU   UWM (RBR) V.1 no.1 (SPR1975).

Dreams. *See* Sueños: Dreams. Los Altos, Calif. 1511670

Dremples. *[Amsterdam.]* 1528678
Beg. date: 1975
"A cross between the arts."
WU   UWM (RBR) V.1 no.1-4 (SUM1975-SUM1976).

Dretch exsibilate magazine. *Huddersfield, Yorks., Eng., Huddersfield Polytechnic Students' Union.* 144218A
Beg. date: 1974
WU   UWM (RBR) No.[1]-2 (1974-n.d.).

Drift wind. *See* Driftwind. Winchendon, Mass. [etc.], Warman Press. 143515A

Driftwind. *Winchendon, Mass. [etc.], Warman Press.* 1435147
Beg. date: 1926
Title varies: April 1927-June 1933, Driftwind from the north hills.
WU   UWM (RBR) V.23-v.24 no.2 (JUL1948-SPR1950).

Driftwind from the north hills. *See* Driftwind. Winchendon, Mass. [etc.], Warman Press. 1435162

Driftwood; a literary magazine. *Woodburn, Ore. [etc.].* 1435175
ISSN: 0418-0674 Beg. date: 196
WU   UWM (RBR) V.2 no.3-4; v.3 no.3; v.4 no.1; v.5 no.1-2, 4; v.6; v.7 no.1,3-4; v.8 no.1-2; v.9 no.1,3; v.10 no.1; v.11 no.1, 3-4; v.12 no.2-4 (SUM1963-AUT1974).

Driftwood; booklets of poems. *Bootle, Lancs., Eng.* 1468751
Beg. date: 1968
Supersedes Asylum, ISSN 0004-6426
Title varies: 1968- , Driftwood quarterly.
WU   UWM (RBR) No.1 (1968).

Driftwood east. *See* Driftwood east quarterly. Pawtucket, R.I., Marjorie Look Drake. 1435190

Driftwood east quarterly. *Pawtucket, R.I., Marjorie Look Drake.* 1435188
Beg. date: 1973
Supersedes Poetry prevue.
Title varies: vol. 1 no. 1, Summer 1973, Driftwood east.
WU   UWM (RBR) V.1 no.1-2 (SUM-FAL1973).

Driftwood quarterly. *See* Driftwood; booklets of poems. Bootle, Lancs., Eng. 1468764

The Druid. *London, Druid Order.* 143520A
ISSN: 0012-6705 Beg. date: 1965
WU   UWM (RBR) No.1-3 (1965-1967).

Druid; a humanities magazine. *Knoxville, Tenn.* 1435225
WU   UWM (RBR) 1969.

Druid Order. Druid. *See* Druid. London, Druid Order. 1435212

Drum; sex in perspective. *Philadelphia, Janus Society.* 1435238
ISSN: 0418-0933 LCCN: 68-6149 Beg. date: 196
Called also Drum magazine.
WU   UWM (RBR) V.4 no.8-10; v.5-v.6 no.2 (no.1-17) (OCT1964-FEB1966); no.18-31 (SEP1966-JAN1969).

Drum magazine. *See* Drum; sex in perspective. Philadelphia, Janus Society. 1435253

Dryad. *[Washington, D.C., etc.].* 1435266
ISSN: 0012-6780 LCCN: 74-644702 Beg. date: 1968
WU   UWM (RBR) V.1 no.1-4 (WIN1968-WIN/SPR1969); no.5/6-16 (1969-1976).

Dublin. University. Icarus. *See* Icarus. Dublin, University of Dublin. 1440516

Dublin magazine. *Dublin.* 0228524
ISSN: 0012-687X LCCN: 68-141267 Beg. date: 1961
Title varies: 1961-1964, Dubliner.
WU   UWM (RBR) V.1-v.2 no.2; v.3; v.4 no.2-v.7 no.1; v.8 no.3-v.10 (1961-SPR/SUM1974).

The Dublin magazine; a quarterly review of literature, science and art. *Dublin.* 0228537
LCCN: 49-52551 Beg. date: 1923 End date: 1958
Originally published in Dublin.
Ceased publication with vol. 33 no. 2, April/June 1958.
WU   UWM (RBR) N. ser. v.15 no.3 (JUL/SEP1940).

Dubliner. *See* Dublin magazine. Dublin. 0228602

DuBois Clubs of America. Insurgent. *See* Insurgent. San Francisco, W E B DuBois Clubs of America. 1440936

Dubuque dial. *Dubuque, Ia.* 1435279
Beg. date: 1934 End date: 1935
Ceased publication with no. 4, Dec. 1935.
WU   UWM (RBR) No.1,3-4 (JUN/DEC1934-DEC1935).

Duck. *Wichita, Kansas.* 1435281
Beg. date: 1974
WU   UWM (RBR) V.1 no.1-3 (SEP021974-JAN021975).

Duel. *Montreal, Communications Board, Student Assn., Sir George Williams University.* 1435294
ISSN: 0420-0977 LCCN: 77-20465 Beg. date: 1969
WU   UWM (RBR) No.1 (WIN1969).

Duende. *Placitas, N.M., Larry Goodell.* 1435316
ISSN: 0012-6993 Beg. date: 1964
WU   UWM (RBR) No.1-14 (1964-OCT1966).

Duke University, Durham, North Carolina. Archive. *See* Archive. Durham, N.C., Duke University Pub. Board. 1438229

Duke University, Durham, North Carolina. Trinity archive. *See* Archive. Durham, N.C., Duke University Pub. Board. 1438244

Dune forum. *Oceano, Calif., The Dunes.* 1435329
Beg. date: 1934 End date: 1934
Ceased publication with no. 5, May 1934.
WU   UWM (RBR) V.1 no.1 (JAN151934).

Dust. *El Cerrito, Calif.* 0230300
ISSN: 0012-7302 LCCN: 68-53978 Beg. date: 1964 End date: 1971
Publication suspended with vol. 5 no. 1, 1971.
WU   UWM (RBR) V.1-v.5 no.1 (no.1-17) (SPR1964-1971).

Dyn, a review of art and literature. *Coyoacán, Mexico.* 0230508
LCCN: 49-37119 Beg. date: 1942 End date: 1944
In English or French.
Suspended publication between Fall 1942 and Dec. 1943.
Ceased publication with no. 6, Nov. 1944.
WU   UWM (RBR) No.1-6 (APR/MAY1942-NOV1944).

Dynamo; a journal of revolutionary poetry. *New York.* 1435331
Beg. date: 1934 End date: 1936
Ceased publication with vol. 3 no. 4, Sept./Dec. 1936.
WU   UWM (RBR) V.1 no.1-3; v.2 no.1 (JAN1934-MAY/JUN1935).

Dypstych; a magazine of prose. *Torrance, Calif., Hors Commerce Press.* 1435344
Beg. date: 1966
WU   UWM (RBR) No.1 (1966).

E

E L A M. *See* Elam. London, East London Arts Magazine Society. 1435660

E R. *See* Earlham review. Richmond, Ind., Earlham College. 143536A

The Ear in a wheatfield. *Hawthorn, Australia.* 1439474
Beg. date: 1973
Second series of Earth ship.
WU   UWM (RBR) No.1-3,5-6,12,16-17 (MAY1973-1976).

Earlham College, Richmond, Indiana. Earlham review. *See* Earlham review. Richmond, Ind., Earlham College. 1435372

The Earlham review. *Richmond, Ind., Earlham College.* 1435357
ISSN: 0012-8120 Beg. date: 1966 End date: 1972
Supersedes Earlham journal.
Above title on title page: E R.
Ceased publication with vol. 4 no. 1, Spring/Summer 1972.
WU   UWM (RBR) V.1 no.1-3; v.2 no.1; v.3 no.2/3; v.4 no.1 (SPR1966-SPR/SUM1972).

Early evening pieces. *See* Auguries, a continuing anthology of the arts. Ottawa, Commoners' Publishing Society, Inc. 1528364

Earth. *Santa Monica, Calif., Earth Books and Gallery.* 1435385
ISSN: 0012-8201 Beg. date: 1965
WU   UWM (RBR) No.1-2 (1965-1966).

Earth and you. *Toronto.* 1435398
ISSN: 0085-011X Beg. date: 1970
WU   UWM (RBR) V.1-7 (no.1-34) (1970-1976).

Earth poet series. *Santa Monica, Calif., Earth Books and Gallery.* 1435407
ISSN: 0424-0405 Beg. date: 1966
WU   UWM (RBR) No.1 (1966).

Earth ship. *Southampton, Eng. [etc.], Kris Hemensley.* 143949A
Beg. date: 1970 End date: 1972
Ceased publication with no. 13, Oct. 1972.
Second series continued as Ear in a wheatfield.
WU   UWM (RBR) No.1-4/5,7-13 (OCT1970-OCT1972).

Earth ship. Second series. *See* Ear in a wheatfield. Hawthorn, Australia. 1439487

Earthjoy. *Fort Wayne, Ind., Jim Jordan.* 1435422
Beg. date: 1971
WU   UWM (RBR) No.1 (1971).

Earth's daughters. *Buffalo, N.Y.* 1435435
Beg. date: 1971
WU   UWM (RBR) V.1 no.1-5/6 (FEB1971-FAL1975).

East and west. *Secunderabad, India.* 1435448
ISSN: 0420-3216 Beg. date: 1956
WU   UWM (RBR) V.1 no.1-2/3 (SPR1956-SUM/AUT1956).

East Carolina College, Greenville, North Carolina. Rebel magazine. *See* Rebel magazine. Greenville, N.C., East Carolina College. 1504218

East Harlem Writing Center. Uptown beat. *See* Uptown beat. New York, East Harlem Writing Center. 1516883

East London Arts Magazine Society. Elam. *See* Elam. London, East London Arts Magazine Society. 1435658

East Side review. *New York, East Side Press.* 1435450
ISSN: 0424-1436 Beg. date: 1966
"A magazine of contemporary culture."
WU   UWM (RBR) V.1 no.1 (JAN/FEB1966).

Eastern horizon. *Hong Kong, Eastern Horizon Press.* 0232613
ISSN: 0012-8813 LCCN: 63-48779 Beg. date: 1960
WU   UWM (RBR) V.1 no.1-15; v.2 no.4-15; v.3 no.1-2,4,7; v.4-9; v.10 no.1 (1960-1971).

Eastern Washington State College, Cheney. Organon. *See* Organon. Cheney, Wash., Eastern Washington State College. 1396659

Echanges. *Paris.* 1435463
Beg. date: 1929 End date: 1931
"Revue trimestrielle de littérature anglaise et française."
Ceased publication with no. 5, Dec. 1931.
WU   UWM (RBR) No.1-4 (DEC1929-MAR1931).

Echo. *Vancouver, B.C.* 1435476
Beg. date: 1975
WU   UWM (RBR) No.1-2 (FAL1975-1976).

Echo, the magazine of the Hudson valley. *See* Hudson river magazine. Hudson, N.Y., HUDSON river Publishers, Inc. 1440334

Echoes. *Danbury, Conn., Dora Tompkins.* 1435489
Beg. date: 1965
"A publication for reprints of published poets."
WU   UWM (RBR) V.1 no.1-3 (OCT1965-FEB/AUG1966).

Echoes of West Virginia. *Huntington, W. Va.* 1435491
LCCN: 53-37997 Beg. date: 1949 End date: 1955
"A magazine of representative verse to encourage and promote creative writing in West Virginia."
Official publication of the West Virginia Poetry Society, Winter 1951-
Ceased publication with vol. 6, 1955.
WU   UWM (RBR) V.1 no.1; v.2 no.5; v.3 no.1; v.4 no.2; v.5 no.1,3-4 (SUM1949-2ND QTR 1954).

Eclectic. *Philadelphia.* 1435513
ISSN: 0012-9399 Beg. date: 196
Some text occasionally in Spanish.
WU   UWM (RBR) No.3 (FAL1969).

Edge. *Christchurch, N.Z.* 1441404
ISSN: 0046-1253 Beg. date: 1971
WU   UWM (RBR) V.1-7 (AUG1971-1976).

Edge. *Melbourne, Australia.* 1435526
ISSN: 0422-4221 Beg. date: 1952 End date: 1957
Ceased publication with no. 8, Oct. 1957.
WU   UWM (RBR) No.1-8 (OCT1952-OCT1957).

Edge; an independent periodical. *Edmonton, Alta., H. Beissel.* 1435539
ISSN: 0424-3943 Beg. date: 1963 End date: 1969
Ceased publication with no. 9, Summer 1969.
WU   UWM (RBR) No.2-9 (SPR1963-SUM1969).

Edinburgh. University. Gambit. *See* Gambit; Edinburgh University review. Edinburgh. 1437629

Edinburgh. University. Jabberwock. *See* Jabberwock; Edinburgh University review. Edinburgh. 1443169

Edinburgh. University. Review. *See* Jabberwock; Edinburgh University review. Edinburgh. 1443156

Edinburgh University review. *See* Jabberwock; Edinburgh University review. Edinburgh. 1443171

Edition et. *Berlin, Christian Grützmacher Druckerei und Verlag.* 1435541
ISSN: 0424-4842 Beg. date: 1966
WU   UWM (RBR) No.1-4 (1966-SEP1967); no.13-15 (n.d.-n.d.).

Egg. *[n.p.].* 1435554
WU   UWM (RBR) V.1 no.4; v.2 no.2 (OCT141968,FEB101969).

Egg. *Surfside, Calif.* 1435567
Beg. date: 1972
"A literary quarterly."
WU   UWM (RBR) V.1 no.1-4 (WIN1972/1973-FAL1973).

Eggs. *Princeton, N.J.* 143557A
Beg. date: 1964
WU   UWM (RBR) V.1 no.1 (1964).

Ego. *Belfast, Botanic House Printers Ltd.* 1435582
Beg. date: 1971
WU   UWM (RBR) No.1-5 (1971).

Egoist; an individualist review. *London; New York, Kraus Reprint.* 0237986
LCCN: 16-7183. Beg. date: 1914 End date: 1919
Supersedes The New freewoman.
Frequency varies.
Ceased publication with Dec. 1919.
WU   UWM (RBR) V.1-6 (1914-1919).

Eidos; a journal of painting, sculpture and design. *London, N. Wolsey.* 0238350
ISSN: 0420-8676 LCCN: 58-26968 Beg. date: 1950 End date: 1950
Publication ceased with no. 3 (Dec. 1950).
WU   UWM (RBR) No.1-3 (MAY/JUN1950-NOV/DEC1950).

The Eight pager. *Niagara Falls, N.Y.* 1435595
ISSN: 0424-6918 Beg. date: 1966
WU   UWM (RBR) Ser. 1 pt.1-4 (1966).

Eikon. *Portsmouth, N.H.* 1435604
ISSN: 0013-2616 LCCN: 68-130929 Beg. date: 1967
WU   UWM (RBR) V.1 no.1-3 (1967-1971).

The Eildon tree. [n.p.]. 1435617
Beg. date: 1974
"A quarterly journal of fantasy."
WU   UWM (RBR) V.1 no.1-2 (1974-[1976]).

Eire-Ireland. St. Paul, Irish American Cultural Institute. 0238454
ISSN: 0013-2683 LCCN: 78-2498 Beg. date: 1966
WU   UWM (RBR) V.1-3 (1965/1966-1968).

Either/or. Wolfville, N.S., Acadia Students' Union. 143562A
ISSN: 0424-7124 Beg. date: 1965
Supersedes Amethyst, ISSN 0569-9290.
Irregular.
WU   UWM (RBR) No.1-5 (FAL1965-FAL1967); Spring/Summer 1972; Spring 1974; 1976.

Elam. London, East London Arts Magazine Society. 1435645
ISSN: 0013-4058 Beg. date: 1964
WU   UWM (RBR) V.5 no.1-6 (JAN/FEB1968-MAY1969).

Electra. Salisbury. 1441417
Beg. date: 1968
WU   UWM (RBR) No.1 (MAY1968).

Elegreba. [Albergele, N. Wales]. 1435673
ISSN: 0420-9834 Beg. date: 1958
WU   UWM (RBR) No.1-3 (SPR1958-SPR1959).

Element. Glendora, Calif. 1435686
ISSN: 0422-9584 Beg. date: 1960 End date: 1960
Ceased publication with vol. 1 no. 1, Jan. 1960.
WU   UWM (RBR) V.1 no.1 (1960).

Elephant. New York. 1432052
Beg. date: 1965
WU   UWM (RBR) No.1-2 (SUM-WIN1965).

Eleventh finger. Brighton, Eng. 1432065
ISSN: 0424-8864 Beg. date: 1965
WU   UWM (RBR) No.1-4 (1965-SPR1968).

The Elf; a little book. Ingrave, Essex [etc.]. 1432078
Beg. date: 1899 End date: 1905
Subtitle varies.
Ceased publication with ser. 3 no. 3, 1905.
WU   UWM (RBR) No.1-4 (AUT1899-AUG1900).

Elizabeth, a magazine of modern Elizabethan and metaphysical poetry. New Rochelle, N.Y. 0240215
ISSN: 0013-6247
Ceased with no. 18, Dec. 1971.
WU   UWM (RBR) No.1-18 (MAR1961-DEC1971).

Ellipse. Sherbrooke, Qué., Université de Sherbrooke, Faculté des Arts. 1441038
ISSN: 0046-1830 Beg. date: 1969
In French and English.
WU   UWM (RBR) No.1-20 (FAL1969-1977).

Elmira College, Elmira, New York. Sibyl. See Sibyl. Elmira, N.Y. 150745A

Embryo. [Louisville, Ky.]. 1432080
ISSN: 0423-0078 LCCN: 68-7538 Beg. date: 1954 End date: 1955
"A literary quarterly."
Ceased publication with vol. 2, 1955.
WU   UWM (RBR) V.1 no.1-4; v.2 no.1-2/3 (SPR1954-1955).

Embryo. Oundle, Northants, Eng. 1432093
WU   UWM (RBR) No.8-11 (1965-JUN1968).

Emergent. Gardena, Calif. 1432102
ISSN: 0421-0794 Beg. date: 1957
WU   UWM (RBR) V.1 no.1; no.2,4-5 (WIN1957-1958).

Emerson College, Boston. Department of English. Words. See Words. Boston. 1514828

Emerson College of Oratory, Boston. Emerson quarterly. See Emerson quarterly. Boston, Emerson College of Oratory. 1441066

The Emerson quarterly. Boston, Emerson College of Oratory. 1441053
Beg. date: 1920 End date: 1942
Supersedes Emerson College magazine.
Ceased publication with vol. 22 no. 4, June 1942.
WU   UWM (RBR) V.21 no.2 (FEB1941).

The Emerson review. Hollywood, Calif. 1432115
ISSN: 0424-9135 Beg. date: 1963
WU   UWM (RBR) V.1 no.1 (WIN1963).

Emmanuel College, Boston. Ethos. See Ethos. Boston, Emmanuel College. 1433962

Empty elevator shaft. San Francisco. 1432128
Beg. date: 1973
WU   UWM (RBR) No.1 ([1973]).

En avant. Auckland, N.Z., Les Archives de la Danse. 1432130
WU   UWM (RBR) No.7 (JUN1954); v.2 no.1,7, 11,14-15; v.3 no.1-2,4,6,11; v.4 no.2; v.5 no.1; v.6 no.3-4; v.7 no.2 (JUL1954-1956).

En garde. Detroit. 1432156
WU   UWM (RBR) No.4-6 (1968-1969); suppl. no.5 1/2 (JAN1969).

En passant poetry quarterly. Wilmington, Del. 1432169
ISSN: 0363-3780 LCCN: 76-645819 Beg. date: 1975
WU   UWM (RBR) No.1-5 (1975 4th qtr.-1977).

Encore; a quarterly of verse and poetic arts. Albuquerque, N.M. 1432171
ISSN: 0013-7057 Beg. date: 1966
WU   UWM (RBR) V.1 no.4-v.11 (SUM1967-1977).

The End, a magasin of verse. Oakland, Calif. 1442201
Beg. date: 1970
WU   UWM (RBR) V.1 no.1-2 (n.d.-1972).

Endymion. New York. 1432184
Beg. date: 1972
WU   UWM (RBR) No.1-4 (JUN1972-MAY1976).

The Enemy; a review of art and literature. London, The Arthur Press. 0241683
LCCN: 32-5087. Beg. date: 1927 End date: 1929
Publication suspended from Oct. 1927-Dec. 1928.
Ceased publication with vol. 1 no. 3, Jan. 1929.
WU   UWM (RBR) V.1 no.1-3 (1927-1929).

Enemy pamphlets. London, The Arthur Press. 1432197
Beg. date: 1930 End date: 1930
Ceased publication with 1930?
WU   UWM (RBR) No.1 (1930).

Energy west. Hollywood, Calif., Energy West Literary Works. 1432206
Beg. date: 1970
WU   UWM (RBR) V.1 no.1-2 (WIN1970-WIN1971).

English Association. Sydney Branch. See Southerly; a literary magazine. Sydney [New South Wales], Angus and Robertson. 0242619

English Carmelites. Aylesford review. See Aylesford review. Aylesford, Eng., St. Albert's Press. 1430508

The English intelligencer. Hastings, Sussex, Eng. 1432219
WU   UWM (RBR) Jan. 16, Oct. 26, Nov. 1966; Jan., Feb. 14, 1967.

English plug. Abilene, Tex. 1441079
ISSN: 0013-8347 Beg. date: 1969
Text mainly in English, occasionally in French and Spanish.
WU   UWM (RBR) No.1 (1969).

Enigma. [Leicester, Eng., Cog Press]. 1432221
ISSN: 0531-7975 LCCN: 70-13088 Beg. date: 1969
WU   UWM (RBR) No.1-4 (1969-1971).

Enigma. London. 1432234
ISSN: 0013-8428 Beg. date: 1968
WU   UWM (RBR) V.1 no.1-3; v.2 no.1-2 (1968-1970).

Enoch Pratt Free Library, Baltimore. Community Action Program. Chicory. See Chicory. Baltimore, Enoch Pratt Free Library Community Action Program [etc.]. 1431110

Enquiry. Nottingham, Eng., Nottingham University, Arts Faculty. 1432247
ISSN: 0423-1945 Beg. date: 1958 End date: 1960
Ceased publication with vol. 2 no. 1, June 1960.
WU   UWM (RBR) V.1 no.2-3; v.2 no.1 (JUN1958-JUN1960).

Entrails. New York, Whispershit Press. 1432262
ISSN: 0425-1148 Beg. date: 1966
WU   UWM (RBR) No.1-4 (JUL1966-JUL/AUG1967).

Envoi. Cheltenham, Eng. 1432275
ISSN: 0013-9394 Beg. date: 1957
"A quarterly review of new poetry."
WU   UWM (RBR) No.1-59 ([1957]-1977).

Envoy; an Irish review of literature and art. Dublin. 1432288
LCCN: 55-18095 Beg. date: 1949 End date: 1951
Subtitle varies.
Ceased publication with vol. 5 no. 20, July 1951.
WU   UWM (RBR) V.1 no.1-4; v.2 no.5-8; v.3 no.9-12; v.4 no.13-16; v.5 no.17-20 (1949-1951).

Ephemeris. *San Francisco, New York.* 1432290
Beg. date: 1968
WU   UWM (RBR) No.1-3 (1968-n.d.).

Epilark. *See* The Lark. *San Francisco.* 1465732

Epilogue; a critical summary. *Deyà Majorca, The Seizin press; London, Constable and co. ltd.* 0245218
LCCN: 37-6045.
WU   UWM (RBR) V.2 (SUM1936).

Epos, a quarterly of poetry. *Crescent City, Fla.* 0245365
ISSN: 0013-9734   LCCN: 73-642111   Beg. date: 1949
A quarterly of poetry, the work of American and British poets.
WU   UWM (RBR) V.3 no.1 (FAL1951).

Equality. *Frankfurt/Main.* 143230A
Beg. date: 1965
WU   UWM (RBR) No.7-19 (JUL1967-FEB1970).

Era. *Castleknock, Eng.], The Goldsmith Press.* 1441081
Beg. date: 1974
WU   UWM (RBR) No.1 (SPR1974).

Era. *Philadelphia, Pennsylvania. University. Philomathean Society.* 1468777
ISSN: 0013-9920   Beg. date: 1964
WU   UWM (RBR) V.3 no.2; v.5 no.2; v.6; v.7 no.1; v.8 no.1; v.9-10 (FAL1966-SPR1974).

Ern Malley's journal. *Melbourne.* 1432312
ISSN: 0421-3807   Beg. date: 1952
WU   UWM (RBR) V.1 no.2 (MAR1953).

Eros. *New York, Eros Magazine, Inc.* 1202157
ISSN: 0425-2357   LCCN: 62-3170   Beg. date: 1962   End date: 1962
Ceased publication with vol. 1 no. 4, Winter 1962.
WU   UWM (RBR) No.1-4 (SPR-WIN1962).

Erratica; a magazine of literature. *Milwaukee, Erratica Press.* 1432325
ISSN: 0046-2470   Beg. date: 1971
Ceased publication.
WU   UWM (RBR) No.1-4 (1971-1973).

Eschata. *Niagara Falls, Ont., Mount Carmel College.* 1432338
Beg. date: 1966
WU   UWM (RBR) No.1 (1966).

Escutcheon. *Columbus, Ohio, Department of English, Ohio State University.* 1432366
Beg. date: 1966
WU   WUM (RBR) V.1 no.1-2; v.2 no.1; v.3 no.1; v.5 no.1-2; v.6 no.1-2 (SPR1966-SPR1972); special edition: 1969.

Espontaneo. *Jamaica Plain, Mass., Hellric Publications.* 1432353
Beg. date: 1972
WU   UWM (RBR) No.1-3 (1972-1975).

Espresso. *Pacifica, Calif.* 1432381
Beg. date: 1973
WU   UWM (RBR) No.1 (1973).

Esprit. *Scranton, Pa., University of Scranton.* 1433919
ISSN: 0425-290X   Beg. date: 1958
WU   UWM (RBR) V.1 no.1; v.2 no.1; v.3 no.1-2; v.4 no.1-2; v.5 no.1-2; v.6 no.1; v.7 no.2; v.8 no.1; v.9 no.1-2; v.10 no.1-2; v.11 no.1-2; v.12 no.1-2; v.13 no.1-2 (SPR1958-1970).

Essays on Canadian writing. *Downsview, Ont., York University.* 1433934
ISSN: 0316-0300   Beg. date: 1974
WU   UWM (RBR) No.2-6 (SPR1975-1977).

Essence. *New Haven, Conn.* 1432394
ISSN: 0014-0872   LCCN: sc77-532   Beg. date: 1950
WU   UWM (RBR) No.1-2,4-17,19-47 (1950-1977).

Essex, England. University. Department of Literature. 151910A
Wivenhoe Park review. *See* Wivenhoe Park review. Colchester, Essex, Eng., Department of Literature, University of Essex.

Ethos. *Boston, Emmanuel College.* 143395A
WU   UWM (RBR) V.36 no.1,3; v.37 no.1-4; v.38 no.1-3; v.39 no.1-2; v.40 no.2-3; v.43 no.1 (1961-1969).

Euphoria. *Peterborough, Eng.* 1441094
Beg. date: 1967
Continues Target, ISSN 0082-1721, with no. 5, 1967.
WU   UWM (RBR) No.5 (1967).

Eureka. *Stockholm.* 1441116
WU   UWM (RBR) No.4-12 (OCT1973-1976).

Eureka review. *Willows [etc.] Calif., Orion Press.* 1432403
ISSN: 0363-1850   LCCN: 76-645368   Beg. date: 1975
"A journal of fiction, poetry and art."
WU   UWM (RBR) No.1-2 (WIN1975/1976-1977).

The European. *London.* 1432416
Beg. date: 1953   End date: 1959
Ceased publication with no. 72, Feb. 1959.
United with Action to form Action and the European.
WU   UWM (RBR) No.1-48 (1953-1957).

Event. *New Westminster, B.C., Douglas College, Department of English.* 1432548
ISSN: 0315-3770   Beg. date: 1971
WU   UWM (RBR) V.1-v.6 no.1 (SPR1971-1977).

The Eventorium muse. *New York.* 1432429
ISSN: 0531-4917   Beg. date: 1964   End date: 1967
Ceased publication with no. 5, Spring 1967.
WU   UWM (RBR) No.1-5 (SPR1964-SPR1967).

Every man. *See* Everyman. Cleveland, Cuyahoga Community College. 1433990

Everyman. *Cleveland, Cuyahoga Community College.* 1433975
ISSN: 0094-2367
WU   UWM (RBR) 1973; Summer 1974.

Evidence. *Toronto.* 0251137
ISSN: 0531-4968
WU   UWM (RBR) No.2-10 (1961-1967).

Ex umbra. *Durham, N.C., North Carolina Central University.* 1432444
ISSN: 0014-3944   Beg. date: 1963
Co-sponsored by the North Carolina Arts Council.
WU   UWM (RBR) V.4 no.2; v.5 no.2; v.6 no.1-2 (SPR1967-SPR1969); suppl. 1969.

Exe. *Exeter, Eng.* 1434008
Beg. date: 1947
Published by the Literary Society in the College of the South West of England.
WU   UWM (RBR) No.1 (WIN1947).

Exeter, England. University College of the Southwest of England. Literary Society. Exe. *See* Exe. Exeter, Eng. 1434010

Exile. *Chicago, etc.* 0252222
LCCN: 29-29190   Beg. date: 1927   End date: 1928
Edited by Ezra Pound.
Ceased publication with no. 4, Autumn 1928.
WU   UWM (RBR) No.1-4 (1927-1928).

Exile. *[Granville, Ohio], Denison University.* 1435699
ISSN: 0421-9090
WU   UWM (RBR) V.22 no.1 (AUT1975).

Exile; a literary quarterly. *Toronto, Atkinson College, York University.* 1140783
Beg. date: 1972
WU   UWM (RBR) V.1-2; v.3 no.1-2; v.4 no.1-4 (1972-1977).

Existaria. *Hermosa Beach, Calif.* 1435710
ISSN: 0423-9032   Beg. date: 1956   End date: 1957
"A journal of existential hysteria."
Ceased publication with no. 7, Sept./Oct. 1957.
WU   UWM (RBR) No.1-7 (SEP1956?-SEP/OCT1957).

Exit. *Risley, Eng.* 1435723
ISSN: 0531-5409   Beg. date: 1965
WU   UWM (RBR) No.1-5/6 (1965-1967).

Exit; urbi et orbi. *New York.* 1435736
Beg. date: 1965   End date: 1966
Ceased publication with no. 5, Sept. 1966.
WU   UWM (RBR) No.1-5 (JUL1965-SEP1966).

Exodus. *New York.* 1435749
ISSN: 0531-5417   Beg. date: 1959   End date: 1960
Ceased publication with no. 3, Spring/Summer 1960.
WU   UWM (RBR) No.1-3 (SPR1959-SPR/SUM1960).

The Expatriate review. *New York, London.* 1435751
ISSN: 0300-709X   LCCN: 75-617882   Beg. date: 1971
WU   UWM (RBR) No.1-4 (SUM1971-WIN/SPR1973/1974).

Experiment. *Cambridge, Eng., Trinity College.* 1442214
Beg. date: 1928   End date: 1931
Ceased publication with no. 7, Spring 1931.
WU   UWM (RBR) No.1-5 (1928-FEB1930).

Experiment. Kirkwood, Mo.   1435764
    Beg. date: 1967
    WU   UWM (RBR) V.1 no.3,6; v.2 no.1-2
    (DEC1967-AUG1969).

Experiment. *Seattle [etc.], Experiment Press.*   1435777
    ISSN: 0014-4770   LCCN: 49-17070   Beg. date: 1944
    "An international review of new poetry" (varies).
    Publication suspended Summer 1954 and Fall 1957 and Fall 1961-
      Summer 1976.
    WU   UWM (RBR) V.1 no.3-v.8 no.3/4
    (OCT1944-AUT/WIN1975/1976).

Experimental review. *Woodstock, N.Y.*   0252510
    LCCN: 45-25135   Beg. date: 1940   End date: 1941
    Title varies: no.1, Spring 1940, Ritual.
    Ceased publication with no. 3, 1941.
    WU   UWM (RBR) No.1-3 (1940-SEP1941); suppl. no.2,
    Jan. 1941.

Experimental typography series. *[Bloomington], Design*   143578A
    Program of the Dept. of Fine Arts, Indiana University.
    WU   UWM (RBR) No.2-3 (NOV1965).

The Experimentalist. *Geneseo, N.Y., State University*   1435801
    College at Geneseo.
    Published with the cooperation of the English Department.
    WU   UWM (RBR) Apr. 1968; May 1972.

The Explicator. *Fredricksburg, Va.*   0252642
    ISSN: 0014-4940   LCCN: 47-41241   Beg. date: 1942
    Caption title.
    Indexes: vols. 1-20, Oct. 1942-June 1962, in vol. 22; vols. 1-30, 1942-1972.
      1 vol.
    WU   UWM (RBR) V.1 no.1,3-4; v.2 no.1-8; v.3 no.3-8; v.4-
    v.7 no.2; v.8 no.2; v.11 no.4; v.12 no.5; v.13 no.2
    (OCT1942-NOV1954).

Explorations. *Berkeley, Calif., Explorations Publishing Co.*   1435827
    ISSN: 0014-4967   LCCN: SC 76-280   Beg. date: 1964   End date: 1970
    Continued by Personal growth, ISSN 0360-6511, with no. 18, June
      1973.
    WU   UWM (RBR) No.1-17
    (WIN1964/1965-WIN1969/1970).

Exposé. *See* Independent. New York, Exposé [etc.].   144270A

Express magazine. *Palatka, Fla., Gil Sheridan.*   143583A
    WU   UWM (RBR) No.12-13 (1969-1970).

Expression. *Adelaide.*   144142A
    The magazine of the Writers' Guild of Queensland (and
      the Guild Academy of Art).
    WU   UWM (RBR) V.3 no.4-11; v.4 no.1-5; v.4 no.7-v.10
    no.1; v.10 no.3-v.11 no.2 (MAY1964-SEP1972).

Expression. *See* Expression one. Twickenham, Eng.   1435896

Expression. *Kenton Harrow, Middlesex, Eng.*   1435842
    ISSN: 0014-5319   Beg. date: 1966
    WU   UWM (RBR) No.2-3,5-12 (1966-1970).

Expression. *New York.*   1435855
    Beg. date: 1946   End date: 1946
    Ceased publication with no. 1, Summer 1946.
    WU   UWM (RBR) No.1 (SUM1946).

Expression. *Turkeyen, Guyana, University of Guyana*   1435868
    Library.
    Beg. date: 196
    WU   UWM (RBR) No.6 (MAR1970).

Expression one. *Twickenham, Eng.*   1435883
    ISSN: 0014-536X   Beg. date: 196
    Quarterly journal of the New Richmond Poetry Group, 1965?-
    Title varies: Expression.
    WU   UWM (RBR) No.5-24 (JAN1966-n.d.).

Extantis. *San Francisco.*   1435918
    ISSN: 0423-9636   Beg. date: 1958   End date: 1959
    Ceased publication with no. 2, Summer 1959.
    WU   UWM (RBR) No.1 (WIN1958/1959).

Extensions. *New York.*   1435920
    ISSN: 0014-5416   LCCN: SC76-335   Beg. date: 1969
    WU   UWM (RBR) No.1-8 (1969-1974).

Extra verse. *Edinburgh [etc.].*   1435933
    ISSN: 0531-6243   Beg. date: 1959
    WU   UWM (RBR) No.6-18 (SPR1962-1966).

Eye. *See* Eye on the Denver scene. Denver.   1435959

Eye - on the Denver scene. *Denver.*   1435946
    ISSN: 0531-6294   Beg. date: 1963
    WU   UWM (RBR) V.1 no.2; v.2 no.1
    (NOV1963,FEB/MAR1964?).

Eye poems. *Eureka, Calif., Hearse Press.*   1508887
    WU   UWM (RBR) [No.1] ([1958]).

Ezra. *Allahabad, India, Ezra-Fakir Press.*   1435961
    "A magazine of neo imagiste poetry."
    WU   UWM (RBR) No.1-5 (n.d.-1966).

F

F D A R T S; a literary newsletter. *Rhu, Ullapool, Wales.* 1435974
Beg. date: 1950
WU   UWM (RBR) No.1-2,4-17,19-24 (APR1950-MAR1952).

Fact. *London.* 143599A
Beg. date: 1937 End date: 1939
Ceased publication with no. 27, June 1939.
Complete contents are listed on the covers of no. 27.
WU   UWM (RBR) No.1-27 (APR1937-JUN1939).

Fact. *New York, Ralph Ginsburg, Publisher.* 0254184
ISSN: 0429-9825 LCCN: 64-9363 Beg. date: 1964 End date: 1967
Ceased publication with vol. 4 no. 4, July/Aug. 1967.
WU   UWM (RBR) V.1-v.4 no.4 (1964-JUL/AUG1967).

Factotum. *Chapel Hill, N.C.* 0254290
LCCN: 59-40433 Beg. date: 1948 End date: 1949
Ceased publication with no. 3, May 1949.
WU   UWM (RBR) No.1-3 (MAY1948-MAY1949).

The Fair. *Terre Haute, Ind.* 1436007
ISSN: 0014-6900 LCCN: 70-29559 Beg. date: 1966
WU   UWM (RBR) V.1 no.1; v.2 no.1-3 (JAN1966-SUM1968).

Fairleigh Dickinson University. Connotation. *See* Connotation. *Madison, N. J.,* 1109046

Fairleigh Dickinson University. Now. *See* Now. Rutherford, N.J., Fairleigh Dickinson University. 1497452

Fairleigh Dickinson University. English Club. Lunch. *See* Lunch. Rutherford, N.J., The English Club, Fairleigh Dickinson University. 1494160

The Fairy stone. *Ashland, Ky., Miriam B. Campbell.* 1528680
WU   UWM (RBR) N. ser. no.2 (SPR1967).

Fakir. *Bombay, Arvind Krishna Mehrotra.* 143601A
WU   UMW (RBR) No.1 (n.d.).

The Falcon. *Mansfield, Pa., Mansfield State College.* 0940930
ISSN: 0014-7079 LCCN: 72-626742 Beg. date: 1970
WU   UWM (RBR) No.1-14 (AUG1970-1977).

Falmouth review of literature. *Falmouth, Mass.* 1436022
ISSN: 0430-0378 Beg. date: 1966 End date: 1967
Ceased publication with vol. 1 no. 2, Spring 1967.
WU   UWM (RBR) V.1 no.1-2 (WIN1966/1967-SPR1967).

Fantasia. *See* Fantasma. Worthing, Eng. 1436048

Fantasma. *Worthing, Eng.* 1436035
Beg. date: 1946
Title varies: no. 2, Jan./Feb. 1947, Fantasia.
WU   UWM (RBR) No.22 (1952).

Fantasma miscellany. *Worthing, Eng.* 1436050
WU   UWM (RBR) No.4,9 (n.d.-n.d.).

Fantasy. *Pittsburgh.* 0255620
LCCN: 44-48248 Beg. date: 1931 End date: 1943
"A literary quarterly with an emphasis on poetry" (varies).
Ceased publication with no. 27 (vol. 7 no. 3), 1943.
WU   UWM (RBR) V.1-6; v.7 no.1 (SUM1931-1941); no.26 (1942).

Fapto. *Margate, Kent, Eng.* 1436063
Beg. date: 1971
WU   UWM (RBR) No.[1]-9 (1971/1972).

Far afield. *Berkeley, Calif.* 1436076
Beg. date: 1949
WU   UWM (RBR) No.14-17 (SPR1959-SPR1963).

The Far point. *Winnipeg, University of Manitoba, Dept. of English.* 1436089
ISSN: 0014-7621 LCCN: 76-14144 Beg. date: 1968 End date: 1973
Ceased publication with no. 7/8, Fall 1972/Spring 1973.
Superseded by Northern light with Winter 1974.
WU   UWM (RBR) No.1-8 (FAL/WIN1968-SPR1973).

Fat abbot. *New Haven, Connecticut.* 0257710
ISSN: 0430-1129 Beg. date: 1960 End date: 1962
Ceased with Fall/Winter 1962.
WU   UWM (RBR) No.1-4 (FAL1960-FAL/WIN1962).

The Fat frog. *San Bruno, Calif.* 1436100
Beg. date: 196
WU   UWM (RBR) V.1 no.6,11,14 (NOV1965-n.d.); also 2 unnumbered, undated issues.

Fathar. *Bolinas, Calif., [etc.], Duncan McNaughton.* 1436113
Beg. date: 1970
WU   UWM (RBR) No.1-7 (JUN1970-MAR1975).

Faulkner Studies. *Minneapolis, Kraus Reprint.* 025783A
ISSN: 0430-1196 Beg. date: 1952 End date: 1954
Ceased publication with vol. 3 no. 4, Winter 1954.
Superseded by Critique. Studies in modern fiction, ISSN 0011-1619, with Winter 1965.
WU   UWM (RBR) V.1-v.3 no.2/3 (SPR1952-SUM/AUT1954).

The Fault. *Fremont, Calif.* 1436126
ISSN: 0146-5848 LCCN: 77-649443 Beg. date: 1972
WU   UWM (RBR) No.1-11 (SPR1972-1977).

Der Faust. *Shawnee, Okla., Kickapoo Press.* 1436139
Beg. date: 1975
Continues Bananas: a thatch of creativity with no. 3, 1975.
WU   UWM (RBR) No.3 (1975).

The Fawnlight. *Maywood, Ill., Marion Schoeberlein.* 1436141
ISSN: 0425-8010
WU   UWM (RBR) Jan. 1950; Spring 1952; Summer-Winter 1953; Spring 1954-Winter 1954/1955.

Fdarts. *See* F D A R T S; a literary newsletter. Rhu, Ullapool, Wales. 1435987

Features. *San Francisco, Bill Presson.* 1436154
Beg. date: 1970
WU   UWM (RBR) No.1,3 (1970,DEC1972).

Federal Union Club. *See* World review. [London, E. Hulton, etc.]. 0259419

Federal Writers' Project, San Francisco. Coast; a magazine of western writing. *See* Coast; a magazine of western writing. [San Francisco]. 1428684

Feedback. *Edinburgh, George Square Publishers Ltd.* 1436167
Beg. date: 196
WU   UWM (RBR) V.1 no.2 (SPR1967).

The Feet. *New York, Modern Organization for Dance Evolvement (M O D E).* 143617A
ISSN: 0046-3612 Beg. date: 196
"The monthly arts and dance maganews."
WU   UWM (RBR) V.3 no.6 (1970); no.23 (JUN1973).

Femora. *New York, George Montgomery.* 1436195
Beg. date: 1964
"A newsletter of female poets."
WU   UWM (RBR) No.1-2 (1964).

Fenn College, Cleveland. Writers' Club. Fenn literary omnibus. *See* Fenn literary omnibus. Cleveland, Fenn College Writers' Club for the Students of Fenn College. 1436217

The Fenn literary omnibus. *Cleveland, Fenn College Writers' Club for the Students of Fenn College.* 1436204
Beg. date: 1963 End date: 1964
WU   UWM (RBR) V.1-2 (1963-1964).

Ferment. *Canton, Mo. [etc.], Transient Press.* 1436743
Beg. date: 1963
"A quarterly of and about poetry" (varies).
WU   UWM (RBR) No.1-7 (JAN/MAR1963-APR/JUN1965).

Fern fire. *See* FernFire. Auckland, N.Z., FernFire Publications. 1436769

FernFire. *Auckland, N.Z., FernFire Publications.* 1436756
ISSN: 0428-2329 Beg. date: 1958
Cover title: Fern fire.
WU   UWM (RBR) No.12-14 (OCT1964-SEP1966).

Fervent valley. *Placitas, N.M.* 1436771
Beg. date: 1972
WU   UWM (RBR) No.1 (1972).

Fever. *Leicester, Eng.* 1436784
Beg. date: 1967
WU   UWM (RBR) No.1-2 ([1967]).

Fiction. *New York.* 1218344
ISSN: 0046-3736 LCCN: 73-63 Beg. date: 1972
WU   UWM (RBR) No.8-9 (1974-1976).

Fiction international. [Canton, N.Y., J.D. Bellamy]. 135501A
ISSN: 0092-1912 LCCN: 73-647017 Beg. date: 1973
WU   UWM (RBR) No.1-7 (FAL1973-1977).

Fiction west. Santa Rosa, Calif., R.F. Bruns. 1528693
Beg. date: 1976
WU   UWM (RBR) V.1 no.1 (1976).

The Fiddlehead. Fredericton, N.B., Departments of English, 1436797
University of New Brunswick and St. Thomas University.
ISSN: 0015-0630 LCCN: 61-37330 Beg. date: 1945
Published 1945-   by the Bliss Carman Society of Fredericton,
N.B. (called   the Bliss Carman Poetry Society of
Fredericton, N.B.).
Supplements accompany some issues.
WU   UWM (RBR) No.19-31,33-109 (1953-1976).

Field. Oberlin, Ohio, Oberlin College. 0261251
ISSN: 0015-0657 LCCN: 76-646532 Beg. date: 1969
"Contemporary poetry and poetics."
WU   UWM (RBR) No.1-16 (FAL1969-1977).

Fields. Mylor, South Australia. 1436821
Beg. date: 1971
WU   UWM (RBR) No.1-4 (1971-AUT1973).

Fifth floor window. New York City. 1436834
Beg. date: 1932 End date: 1932
Ceased publication with vol. 1 no. 4, May 1932.
WU   UWM (RBR) V.1 no.3 (FEB1932).

Fifth horseman. Fargo, N.D. 0261669
Beg. date: 1967
A magazine of poetry and occasional criticism.
WU   UWM (RBR) V.1 (1969).   A reprint of 8 issues
published 1967-1968.

The Fifth season. Berkeley, Calif. 1436847
ISSN: 0430-3830
WU   UWM (RBR) One unnumbered issue (1967).

The Fifties. [Pine Island, Minn.]. 1121746
LCCN: 72-621797 Beg. date: 1958 End date: 1959
Continued by The Sixties with no. 4, Fall 1960.
WU   UWM (RBR) No.1-3 (1958-1959).

The Figure in the carpet. New York, New School for Social 143685A
Research.
Beg. date: 1927 End date: 1929
Title varies: -May 1929, Salient.
Ceased publication with vol. 2, May 1929.
WU   UWM (RBR) No.2-3 (NOV1927-FEB1928).

Figures. Paris, New York. 1436890
ISSN: 0428-3201 Beg. date: 1961
English and French.
Edited by the Albert Loeb Gallery, New York.
WU   UWM (RBR) No.1 (1961).

Film culture. New York. 0262087
ISSN: 0015-1211 LCCN: 59-37118 Beg. date: 1955
Suspended publication Summer 1969-Jan. 1970.
Indexes: No. 1-46, 1955-1967, in no. 40-47.
WU   UWM (RBR) V.1-4 (no.1-18) (1955-APR1958); no.20,
30,40-41 (1959-SPR1966).

Film front. See Filmfront. New York, National Film and Photo 1436938
League.

Film makers' cooperative, New York. See Film culture. New 0262215
York.

Filmfront. New York, National Film and Photo League. 1436912
Beg. date: 1934 End date: 1935
Ceased publication with vol. 1 no. 5, March 15, 1935.
Absorbed by New theatre.
WU   UWM (RBR) V.1 no.1-5 (DEC241934-MAR151935);
special issue Mar. 1935.

Fine arts calendar. Shawnee Mission, Kansas, Little Gallery 1436940
Press.
WU   UWM (RBR) V.4 no.2 (NOV1962); Jan.-May, Summer
1963.

Fine arts discovery. Kansas City, Mo., Fine Arts Discovery 1436953
Press.
ISSN: 0015-2315 Beg. date: 1967
WU   UWM (RBR) V.1 no.2-4; v.2-v.5 no.2
(SUM1967-SPR/SUM1971).

Fine Arts Fellowship, Grand Rapids, Michigan. For the time 1437397
being. See For the time being. Grand Rapids, Mich., Fine Arts
Fellowship.

Fine arts magazine. Storrs, Conn., Student Union Board of 1436966
Governors, University of Connecticut.
ISSN: 0428-4194 Beg. date: 1956
WU   UWM (RBR) Apr. 1958; Apr. 1959; Apr. 1960; May
1961; Apr. 1962; 1963; May 1964.

Fine print. San Francisco. 1436981
ISSN: 0361-3801 LCCN: 76-640597 Beg. date: 1975
"A newsletter for the arts of the book."
WU   UWM (RBR) V.1-   (1975-   ).

Fire exit. Boston, New Poets' Theatre. 1436994
ISSN: 0430-5868 Beg. date: 1968
WU   UWM (RBR) V.1 no.1-4 (1968-1974).

Firebird. Manchester, Eng. 1437014
WU   UWM (RBR) No.4 (n.d.).

Firebird. Yellow Springs, Ohio. 1437001
WU   UWM (RBR) V.1 no.1 (n.d.).

Fireflower. Whitehorse, Yukon Territory, Yukoner Mimeo 1437027
Press.
WU   UWM (RBR) May-Dec. 1967; Jan.-Feb. 1968.

Firelands arts review. Huron, Ohio, Rudinger Foundation. 143703A
ISSN: 0094-8012 LCCN: 74-646319 Beg. date: 1974
Continues Mixer: Firelands arts review with vol. 3, 1974.
WU   UWM (RBR) V.3-4 (1974-1975); special issue 1976.

Fireside. See Connecticut fireside. Hamden, Conn. 143139A

Fireweed. Columbus, Ohio, Galen Green. 1437055
ISSN: 0364-5118 Beg. date: 1975
WU   UWM (RBR) V.1 no.1-5; v.2 no.2-4 (FAL1975-1977).

First dozen. See Gaberbocchus black series. London, 1441523
Gaberbocchus Press, Ltd.

First issue. New York, Bill Wertheim.
Beg. date: 1968
WU   UWM (RBR) No.3-9 (1969-FAL/WIN1975/1975).

First person. Rockport, Mass. 0264136
ISSN: 0430-5914 LCCN: 64-39565 Beg. date: 1960 End date: 1961
Ceased publication with vol. 1 no. 3, Spring/Summer 1961.
WU   UWM (RBR) Fall 1960, Winter 1961, Spring/Summer
1961.

First stage, a quarterly of new drama. Lafayette, Indiana, 0875225
Purdue University.
Beg. date: 1961 End date: 1968
Continued by Drama and theatre with vol. 7, Fall 1968.
WU   UWM (RBR) V.1; v.2 no.1,3-4; v.3 no.1; v.6 no.2-4
(WIN1961/1962-WIN1967/1968).

First statement. Montreal. 1437068
ISSN: 0381-0127 Beg. date: 1942 End date: 1945
"Canadian prose and poetry."
Ceased publication with vol. 3 no. 1, June/July 1945.
United with Preview to form Northern review; new writing in
Canada.
WU   UWM (RBR) V.2 no.2-12 (SEP1943-APR/MAY1945).

Fishpaste. Oxford [etc.], Pandora Press. 1437070
ISSN: 0015-3087 LCCN: 68-128600 Beg. date: 1967
"Postcard review of art and letters."
WU   UWM (RBR) No.1-22 (FEB1967-MAY1968); ser. 2
no.1-3 (MAY-AUG1968).

Fisk University, Nashville.   Counterpoise series. See 1429243
Counterpoise series. Nashville.

Fits. San Francisco, 7 Freds Press. 1437083
Beg. date: 1971
WU   UWM (RBR) No.1-2 (1971).

Fix. Middlesex, Eng. 1438909
Beg. date: 1974
WU   UWM (RBR) No.1-3 (MAY1974-SUM1976).

Flame. Alpine, Tex. 1441499
ISSN: 0428-545X Beg. date: 1954 End date: 1963
Absorbed Avalon news with June 1957.
Ceased publication with Winter 1962/Spring 1963.
Superseded by Flame; Avalon annual with 1964.
WU   UWM (RBR) V.1 no.3; v.2 no.2-4; v.3 no.1,3; v.5 no.4;
v.6-v.9 no.3 (n.d.-1962); Winter 1962/Spring 1963.

Flame. Colchester, Essex, Eng., Societies' Pigeons' Holes, 1437096
University of Essex.
Beg. date: 196
WU   UWM (RBR) No.3-5 (1967-1968).

Flame. Avalon annual. Supplement. See Cyclotron. San 1469022
Angelo, Tex.

Flame; Avalon annual. *Corpus Christi, Tex., Avalon World Arts Academy.* 1441486
ISSN: 0428-5468 Beg. date: 1964 End date: 1966
Supersedes the quarterly, Flame, and the annual, Avalon anthology.
Ceased publication with May 1966.
United with Cyclotron to form Cyclo-flame with Spring 1966.
WU   UWM (RBR) 1964-1966.

The Flamingo. *Winter Park, Fla., Rollins College, English Dept.* 1437118
Beg. date: 1927
"A literary magazine of the youngest generation."
Title varies: vol. 13, Dec. 1938-May 1939, Rollins flamingo.
WU   UWM (RBR) V.1 no.1 (MAR1927).

Flash. *Pasadena, Calif., David Laidig Pub. Co.* 1437146
WU   UWM (RBR) No.1-7 (1967).

Fleur de lis. *St. Louis, Mo., St. Louis University, Writers' Institute.* 1437159
ISSN: 0428-5654 Beg. date: 1959
WU   UWM (RBR) V.3 no.1; v.5 no.1; v.6 no.1 (SPR1961-SPR1964).

Floating. *[n.p.], River Bottom Press.* 1437174
Beg. date: 1974
WU   UWM (RBR) No.1-6 (NOV1974-1977).

Floating bear; a newsletter. *New York.* 0265080
ISSN: 0430-6570 Beg. date: 1961 End date: 1969
Ceased publication with no. 37, 1969.
Supplement issued in 1971: The Intrepid-Bear issue (Intrepid no. 20/ Floating bear no. 38).
WU   UWM (RBR) No.3-23,25-37 (1961-1969); special issue no.38 (1971).

Floating island. *Point Reyes Station, Calif., Floating Island Publications.* 1439509
ISSN: 0147-1686 LCCN: 76-6871 Beg. date: 1976
WU   UWM (RBR) No.1-2 (SPR1976-1977).

Florida. University, Gainesville. Florida quarterly. See Florida quarterly. *Gainesville, Fla.,* 1450825

Florida. University, Gainesville. Florida review. See Florida review. Gainesville. 1437209

Florida. University of South Florida, Tampa. Gryphon. See Gryphon. Tampa, University of South Florida. 1442374

Florida. University of South Florida, Tampa. i e. See i e; the University of South Florida Literary journal. Tampa. 1442543

Florida. University of South Florida, Tampa. South Florida poetry journal. See South Florida poetry journal. Tampa, Fla., University of South Florida. 1510425

Florida. University of South Florida, Tampa. South Florida review. See South Florida review. Tampa, Fla., University of South Florida, Tampa. 1510440

Florida magazine of verse. *Winter Park, Fla., Helen Aubrey Pratt.* 1437187
Beg. date: 1940
WU   UWM (RBR) V.10 no.1; v.12 no.1; v.13-v.14 no.1 (AUT1949-AUT1953).

Florida quarterly. *Gainesville, Fla., University of Florida.* 0929551
ISSN: 0015-4253 LCCN: 74-644627 Beg. date: 1967 End date: 1976
"Official student-edited literary magazine of the University of Florida."
Ceased publication with vol. 6 no. 4, July 1976.
WU   UWM (RBR) V.1; v.2 no.1-3; v.3 no.1-3; v.4 no.1-3; v.5 no.1,2/3; v.6 no.1,2-4 (1967-JUL1976).

The Florida review. *Gainesville.* 143719A
ISSN: 0426-5939 LCCN: A 58-1130 Beg. date: 1957 End date: 1958
Issued by students at the University of Florida.
Supersedes an earlier publication with the same title.
Ceased publication with no. 2, Spring 1958.
WU   UWM (RBR) No.2 (SPR1958).

Flow. *Kathmandu.* 026669A
ISSN: 0046-4201 LCCN: 77-917627 Beg. date: 1970
WU   UWM (RBR) V.1 no.2 (1970).

Floyd Junior College, Rome, Georgia. Old red kimono. See Old red kimono. Rome, Georgia. 1509775

A Flute song. *Quincy, Ill.* 1528715
Beg. date: 1976
WU   UWM (RBR) One unnumbered issue (1976).

Fluxus. *[n.p.].* 1437211
WU   UWM (RBR) Jan.-June 1964.

Fly leaf, a pamphlet periodical of the new-the new man, new woman, new ideas, whimsies and things. Conducted by Walter Blackbury Harte. *Boston, Fly leaf publishing co.* 0266869
LCCN: 7-17129. Beg. date: 1895 End date: 1896
Title varies slightly.
Ceased publication with vol. 5 no. 1, April 1896.
Merged into the Philistine.
WU   UWM (RBR) V.1 no.1-5 (DEC1895-APR1896).

The Flying horse. *London.* 1437224
Beg. date: 1923 End date: 1931
Ceased publication with n. ser. no. 17, Feb. 1931.
WU   UWM (RBR) No.1 (1923).

The Fly's eye. *Houston, New English Club, University of Houston.* 1437237
Beg. date: 196   End date: 1967
Ceased publication with June 1967.
WU   UWM (RBR) V.2 no.1-3 (SEP1965-MAY1966); one unnumbered, undated issue (JAN1966?).

Focus/Midwest. *Saint Louis, Mo.* 1090875
ISSN: 0015-508X LCCN: 68-51059 Beg. date: 1962
WU   UWM (RBR) V.1-4 (JUN1962-1965); v.5 no.33-v.7 no.45 (1966-JAN/FEB1969); v.8 no.54-v.12 no.72 (MAY/JUN1970-1977).

Fog dogs. See Fogdogs. Waterville, Me. 1437265

Fogdogs. *Waterville, Me.* 1437252
WU   UWM (RBR) No.1-3 (n.d.).

Folder. *New York, The Tiber Press.* 1441705
ISSN: 0428-8181 Beg. date: 1953 End date: 1956
Ceased publication with no.4, 1956.
Superseded by New folder with 1959.
WU   UWM (RBR) V.1 no.1-2; v.2 no.1 (no.1-3) (WIN1953-1954/1955); no.4 (1956).

Folio. *Birmingham, Ala.* 1437278
ISSN: 0015-5756 Beg. date: 1965
"The booksellers sheet, published occasionally by Adele de la Barre Robinson and Charlotte Kelly Gafford."
WU   UWM (RBR) V.1-10 (1965-1974).

Folio. *Bloomington, Ind., English Dept., Indiana University.* 1437280
LCCN: 44-14777 Beg. date: 1936 End date: 1960
Various subtitles.
Ceased publication with vol. 25 no. 3, Summer 1960.
WU   UWM (RBR) V.4-5 (FAL1938-1940); v.20,23-25 (1954-1960).

Folio. *LaPorte, Ind.* 1437302
LCCN: 47-41242 Beg. date: 1943
Title varies: Autumn 1943-Spring 1946, Living poetry quarterly.
WU   UWM (RBR) V.3 no.4 (SUM1946).

The Folio. *London, Folio Society.* 1437328
ISSN: 0015-5772 LCCN: 56-35735 Beg. date: 1947
WU   UWM (RBR) V.5 no.2-3,5 (NOV/DEC1951-MAY/JUN1952).

Folio; the Brandeis literary review. *Waltham, Mass., Brandeis University.* 1437343
ISSN: 0015-5780
Published by the students of Brandeis University, sponsored by the University, the English Department and the Student Senate.
WU   UWM (RBR) V.1 no.2; v.2,5-8,12 (SUM1963-1974).

Folio Society, Limited, London. Folio. See Folio. London, Folio Society. 1437330

Folios of new writing. *London, The Hogarth Press.* 0267822
LCCN: 37-11079 rev Beg. date: 1936 End date: 1941
Title varies: Spring 1936-Christmas 1939, New writing (London).
Ceased publication with ser. 3, no. 4, Autumn 1941.
United with Daylight to form New writing and daylight.
WU   UWM (RBR) No.1 (SPR1940).

Foot. *Berkeley, Calif.* 1437369
ISSN: 0429-0135
WU   UWM (RBR) No.2 (1962).

Foot magazine. See Foot. Berkeley, Calif. 1437371

For now. *New York, AMS Press.* 0269875
ISSN: 0429-0224
WU   UWM (RBR) No.5,7,9 (n.d.).

For the time being. *Grand Rapids, Mich., Fine Arts Fellowship.* 1437384
WU   UWM (RBR) V.3 no.3; v.4-v.5 no.3 (SPR1975-1977).

Foreground; a creative and literary quarterly. *Cambridge, Mass.*   1437406
   LCCN: 51-25697   Beg. date: 1946   End date: 1946
   Ceased publication with vol. 1 no. 2, Spring/Summer 1946.
   WU   UWM (RBR) V.1 no.1-2 (1946).

Forever. *Pontrefact, Yorks., Eng. [etc.].*   1528728
   ISSN: 0140-3141   Beg. date: 1976
   "Poetry and prose."
   WU   UWM (RBR) No.1-4 (1976-AUT1977).

Forge. *Wolverhampton, Eng., Polytechnic Wolverhampton.*   1437419
   Beg. date: 1970
   "A literary periodical from the Polytechnic, Wolverhampton."
   WU   UWM (RBR) No.2-6 (1971-FEB1976).

The Forge; a Midwestern review. *Chicago.*   1437434
   Beg. date: 1924   End date: 1929
   Founded and published May 1924-   by the Poetry Club of the University of Chicago.
   Subtitle varies.
   Ceased publication with vol. 5 no. 1, Winter 1929.
   WU   UWM (RBR) V.1-3; v.4 no.4 (MAY1924-1929).

Form. *Cambridge, England; Philip Steadman.*   0271846
   ISSN: 0532-1697   LCCN: 66-9950   Beg. date: 1966   End date: 1969
   Ceased publication with no. 10, 1969.
   WU   UWM (RBR) No.1-9 (SUM1966-APR1969).

Form; a monthly magazine containing poetry, sketches, essays of literary and critical interest. *London, The Morland Press, Ltd.*   0271861
   LCCN: 25-13817   Beg. date: 1916   End date: 1922
   Ceased publication with n. ser. no. 3, Jan. 1922.
   WU   UWM (RBR) N. ser. no.1-3 (OCT1921-JAN1922).

The Formalist. *Oakland, Calif.*   143745A
   Beg. date: 1949   End date: 1949
   Ceased publication with vol. 1 no. 3, Winter 1949.
   WU   UWM (RBR) V.1 no.1-3 (SUM-WIN1949).

Format. *Stroud, Gloucestershire, Eng.*   1437462
   ISSN: 0015-7740   Beg. date: 1966
   WU   UWM (RBR) No.1-4 (JAN1966-SEP1967).

Fortean Society. *See* Doubt. New York, Fortean Society.   0272684

Forum. *Houston, University of Houston.*   1313833
   ISSN: 0015-8410   Beg. date: 1956
   WU   UWM (RBR) V.3 no.1,3,8; v.4 no.1,3-4,9 (SPR1959-SPR1966).

Forum stories and poems. *London.*   1437475
   Beg. date: 1949
   WU   UWM (RBR) Summer 1949.

The Fountain. *Orlando, Fla.*   1439511
   WU   UWM (RBR) V.1 no.2 (1976).

Four elements. *See* 4 elements. St. Simons Island, Ga.   1427805

Four winds. *Gloucester, Mass.*   1437488
   ISSN: 0427-1033   Beg. date: 1952   End date: 1953
   Ceased publication with vol. 1 no. 4, Winter 1953.
   WU   UWM (RBR) V.1 no.1-4 (SUM1952-WIN1953).

The Four zoas. *Ware, Mass.*   1437490
   ISSN: 0362-0247   LCCN: SC 76-193   Beg. date: 1974
   "A journal of poetry and letters."
   WU   UWM (RBR) No.1/2-3,6 (1974-1977).

Foxfire: *Rabun Gap, Georgia, Rabun Gap-Nacoochee School.*   0273782
   ISSN: 0015-9220   LCCN: 71-291286   Beg. date: 1967
   WU   UWM (RBR) V.1-v.11 no.2 (SPR1967-1977).

Fragments. *New York, Neil Greenberg.*   143750A
   ISSN: 0015-9328   Beg. date: 1968
   WU   UWM (RBR) No.1-6 (FAL1968-1973).

Fragments. *Seattle, Dept. of English, Seattle University.*   1437512
   ISSN: 0015-9344   Beg. date: 196
   WU   UWM (RBR) Spring, Winter 1966; 1967; Winter 1969; v.12-17 (SPR1970-1976).

Freak. *San Francisco, T. Hawkins, Alab Press.*   1437538
   WU   UWM (RBR) Feb. 1964-Jan. 1965.

The Freark brownelbeck review. *Manhattan Beach, Calif.*   1437540
   ISSN: 0016-027X   Beg. date: 1969
   WU   UWM (RBR) No.7 (WIN1971).

The Free lance. *Cleveland, Free Lance Poets and Prose Workshop, Inc.*   1437553
   ISSN: 0016-0369   Beg. date: 1953
   WU   UWM (RBR) V.1 no.1; v.2 no.1; v.3-v.10 no.1; v.11-18 (1953-1977).

Free lance. *See* Free lance; the magazine of the student mind. St. Louis, Washington University.   1442268

Free lance; the magazine of the student mind. *St. Louis, Washington University.*   144223A
   ISSN: 0429-6206
   WU   UWM (RBR) V.5 no.4; v.6 no.1-2; v.7 no.1-3; v.8 no.1 (MAY1967-1969).

Free Lance Poets and Prose Workshop. Free lance. *See* Free lance. Cleveland, Free Lance Poets and Prose Workshop, Inc.   1437566

Free love periodically. *Cleveland.*   1437579
   WU   UWM (RBR) No.1-2 (1967).

Free passage. *Fargo, N.D.*   1528730
   Beg. date: 1976
   "A journal of prose and poetry."
   WU   UWM (RBR) V.1 no.1-3 (SUM1976-FAL1977).

Free poems/among friends. *Detroit [etc.]., Artists Workshop Press [etc.].*   1439524
   Beg. date: 1965
   WY   UWM (RBR) No.2-4 (WIN1966-NOV1967).

Free poetry. *East Balmain, N.S.W.*   1439537
   Beg. date: 1968
   WU   UWM (RBR) No.6-7 (1969).

Free unions. Unions libres. *London.*   1441720
   Beg. date: 1946
   In English, Grench or German.
   WU   UWM (RBR) No.1 (JUL1946).

Freed. *See* One: the word is freed. Auckland, N.Z.   1499345

Freedomways. *New York, Freedomways Associates.*   0277150
   ISSN: 0016-061X   LCCN: 68-3518   Beg. date: 1961
   Began with Spring 1961 issue.
   WU   UWM (RBR) V.1 no.3; v.2-6; v.7 no.1-3; v.9-14; v.15 no.1; v.16 no.1-3; v.17 no.1-2 (FAL1961-1977).

Freelance. *See* Free lance; the magazine of the student mind. St. Louis, Washington University.   1442255

Freelance writer's newsletter. *Appalachia, Va., Young Publications.*   143954A
   Beg. date: 1975
   WU   UWM (RBR) V.1 no.1-5,7-8,10-12; v.2 no.1-5 (1975-1977).

Freeman. *New York.*   0277189
   Beg. date: 1920   End date: 1924
   Ceased publication with vol. 8 (no. 208), March 5, 1924.
   WU   UWM (RBR) V.1-8 (1920-1924).

Fremantle Arts Centre. Patterns. *See* Patterns. Fremantle, Western Australia, Fremantle Arts Centre.   1498498

Fresco. *Detroit, University of Detroit.*   1442270
   ISSN: 0429-7113   Beg. date: 1951   End date: 1961
   Ceased publication with new series vol. 1 no. 3, Spring 1961.
   WU   UWM (RBR) V.8 no.3; v.9-10 (SPR1958-SUM1960); n. ser. v.1 (1960-SPR1961).

Friday market. *Thames Ditton, Surrey, Eng.*   1468814
   ISSN: 0429-7210   Beg. date: 1956   End date: 1961
   1957- , also have title, Vrijdagmarkt.
   Ceased publication with no. 15, Oct. 1961.
   WU   UWM (RBR) No.1-15 (APR1956-OCT1961).

Friendly local press. *New York.*   1439552
   ISSN: 0016-1306   Beg. date: 1968
   WU   UWM (RBR) V.1 no.1-7 (1968-1970).

Frog sandwich. *[n.p.].*   1439565
   WU   UWM (RBR) No.3 (SEP1975).

From a window. *Tucson, Ariz.*   1439578
   ISSN: 0532-7318   Beg. date: 1965   End date: 1966
   Ceased publication with no. 5, Nov. 1966.
   WU   UWM (RBR) No.1-5 (APR1965-NOV1966).

Front. *The Hague.*   0278863
   WU   UWM (RBR) V.1 no.1-2,4 (DEC1930-1931).

Front door. *[n.p.].*   1439580
   Beg. date: 1964
   WU   UWM (RBR) No.1 (SPR1964).

The Frontier. *Oxford, Christian Frontier Council.*   1439593
   ISSN: 0429-7679   Beg. date: 1950   End date: 1952
   Supersedes The Christian news-letter, published 1939-1949.
   Ceased publication with vol. 3, 1952.
   Superseded by Christian news-letter with 1953.
   WU   UWM (RBR) V.1 no.1 (JAN1950).

Frontiers; a magazine of the arts. *Christchurch, N.Z., Frontiers Publishers.*   1439615
   ISSN: 0016-2140 Beg. date: 1968
   WU   UWM (RBR) V.1 no.1-4; v.2 no.1-2 (MAR1968-1970).

Frostbite: a journal of thought. *Saco, Maine.*   1439628
   ISSN: 0532-7512 Beg. date: 1965
   WU   UWM (RBR) V.1 no.1; v.2 no.1 (1965-JAN1966).

Fubbalo. *Buffalo, N.Y., Fubbalo Press.*   1439630
   ISSN: 0016-2337 Beg. date: 1964
   WU   UWM (RBR) V.1 no.1-2 (SUM1964-SUM1965).

Fuck you/ a magazine of the arts. *New York.*   1441508
   WU   UWM (RBR) No.1-4 (n.d.-AUG1962; v.1-9 (DEC1962-JUN1965).

The Fugitive. *[Nashville, The Fugitive Publishing Company].*   0279489
   LCCN: 35-16113 Beg. date: 1922 End date: 1925
   Ceased publication with vol. 4, Dec. 1925.
   WU   UWM (RBR) V.1 no.1-4; v.2 no.5-10; v.3 no.1-3,5/6; v.4 no.1,3-4 (APR1922-DEC1925).

Full cry. *London, Company of Free Men.*   1439643
   ISSN: 0427-7430 Beg. date: 1958
   WU   UWM (RBR) No.1-8 (MAR1958-FEB1959).

Full house. *Hemel Hempstead, Herts., Eng.*   1439669
   WU   UWM (RBR) No.1-3 (n.d.-SPR1975).

Furioso. *New Haven, Conn.*   0280050
   Beg. date: 1939
   Publication suspended from 1944 to summer 1946, inclusive.
   Ceased pub. with v. 8:1.
   WU   UWM (RBR) V.1-8 (1939-1953).

Furman University, Greenville, South Carolina. South Carolina review. *See* South Carolina review. Clemson, S.C., Dept. of English, Clemson University.   1529603

Fuse. *San Diego.*   1439671
   Beg. date: 1971
   WU   UWM (RBR) No.1-3 (1971-1972).

Futura. *[n.p.], Edition Hansjoerg Mayer.*   1442296
   ISSN: 0532-9019 Beg. date: 1965
   WU   UWM (RBR) No.1-4,7-23 (1965-1967).

Fux magascean! *San Francisco.*   1439684
   ISSN: 0532-9094 Beg. date: 1965
   WU   UWM (RBR) No.1 (1965).

G

Gaberbocchus black series. London, Gaberbocchus Press, Ltd. 1441510
ISSN: 0430-912X Beg. date: 1954
Nos. 1-12 also published in one volume with title First dozen.
WU　　　UWM (RBR) No.1-12 (1954-1958).

Gadfly. Cambridge, Mass. 1439697
ISSN: 0433-0927 Beg. date: 1959 End date: 1959
Ceased publication with Dec. 1959.
WU　　　UWM (RBR) May, Dec. 1959.

The Gadfly; an occasional review. Milwaukee, Wis., Beethoven Memorial Foundation, Inc. 1439706
ISSN: 0433-0935
WU　　　UWM (RBR) No.3 (1963).

Gaga. London, Gaga Bureau. 1439721
Beg. date: 1969
WU　　　UWM (RBR) No.1-3 (1969-APR/JUN1970).

Gale. Arroyo Hondo, N.M. 1439734
Beg. date: 1949 End date: 1950
Ceased publication with vol. 2 no.5, July/aug. 1950.
WU　　　UWM (RBR) V.1 no.10; v.2 no.2-4 (no.15-17); v.2 no.15 (NOV1949-JUL/AUG1950).

Galleon. See Golden galleon. Kansas City, Missouri, A. Fowler. 0281070

Gallery. Lincoln, Neb., Row Charter Associates. 1439747
ISSN: 0433-1303 Beg. date: 1963 End date: 1964
Ceased publication with vol. 1 no. 2, April 1964?
WU　　　UWM (RBR) V.1 no.1-2 (APR1963-APR1964).

Gallery. Newark, N.J. 143975A
Beg. date: 1969
WU　　　UWM (RBR) Spring 1969; 1970.

Gallery; an illustrated poetry magazine. London. 1439762
ISSN: 0306-1256 Beg. date: 1974
WU　　　UWM (RBR) No.1-2 (AUT/WIN1974-SUM1975).

Gallery series: Poets. Chicago. 0281118
ISSN: 0072-0097
WU　　　UWM (RBR) Series 1-4 (1967-1973).

Galley, the little magazine for little magazine publishers. Hollywood. 0281120
LCCN: 66-50214 Beg. date: 1949 End date: 1953
Suspended between Spring 1951 and Spring 1953.
Subtitle varies.
Ceased publication with vol. 4 no. 2, Summer 1953.
Each issue within a volume is devoted to a special aspect of little magazine publishing: no. 1, Little magazine directory; no. 2, Advertising rates and data; no. 3, Who's who in little magazine publishing; no. 4, Little magazine presses.
WU　　　UWM (RBR) V.1-v.4 no.2 (SPR1949-SUM1953).

The Galley sail review. San Francisco. 1439775
ISSN: 0016-4100 Beg. date: 1958
Ceased publication.
WU　　　UWM (RBR) V.1 no.1-4; v.2 no.1-3/4 (no.5-7); v.3 no.1-3 (no.8-10); v.4 no.1 (no.11); no.12-19 (WIN1958-1967).

Gallimaufry. San Francisco. 1439788
Beg. date: 1973
WU　　　UWM (RBR) No.1-9 (SUM1973-1976).

Gallows. Eureka, Calif. 1439790
ISSN: 0433-1397 Beg. date: 1959
Pilot number issued in 1959.
WU　　　UWM (RBR) V.1 no.1; v.2 no.1 (1962).

Gambit. Hammond, La., Dept. of English, Southeastern Louisiana College. 1437581
Beg. date: 1960
Supersedes Pick of the patch.
WU　　　UWM (RBR) Spring 1962.

Gambit. New York, Gambit Associates. 1437603
ISSN: 0433-1494 LCCN: 58-1994 Beg. date: 1952 End date: 1952
Ceased publication with vol. 1 no. 4, Nov./Dec. 1952.
WU　　　UWM (RBR) V.1 no.1-4 (MAY/JUN-NOV/DEC1952).

Gambit; Edinburgh University review. Edinburgh. 1437616
WU　　　UWM (RBR) Summer 1965.

Gamut. Pullman, Wash., Washington State University. 1437631
ISSN: 0433-1540
"Washington State University Literary magazine."
WU　　　UWM (RBR) Mar., May 1963; no.4-9 (1963-1968).

Gandalf's garden. London. 0281356
Beg. date: 1968
WU　　　UWM (RBR) No.1-5 (MAY1968-1969).

Ganglia. Toronto. 1441696
ISSN: 0435-1142 Beg. date: 1966
WU　　　UWM (RBR) No.1-6,7-8 (1966-1972).

Gangrel. London. 1437657
Beg. date: 1945 End date: 1946
Ceased publication with no. 4, [1946].
WU　　　UWM (RBR) No.1-4 (1945-1946).

Garfield Lake review. Olivet, Mich., Olivet College. 143766A
Beg. date: 1971
WU　　　UWM (RBR) No.1-3 (1971-1973).

Gargantua. Birmingham, Eng. 1437685
WU　　　UWM (RBR) No.1-2 (n.d.-1971).

Gargoyle. [n.p.]. 1437698
Published in England.
WU　　　UWM (RBR) Oct. 1952.

Garland Court review. Chicago, Loop College. 1437707
Beg. date: 1969
WU　　　UWM (RBR) No.1-3 (1969).

Gate; international review of literature and art in English and German. London. 028210A
Beg. date: 1947 End date: 1949
German title: Tor.
Ceased publication with vol. 3 no. 1, 1949.
WU　　　UWM (RBR) V.1 no.2,4; v.2 no.1 (1947-MAR/MAY1948).

Gato. Los Gatos, Calif. 1437722
Beg. date: 1966
WU　　　UWM (RBR) V.1 no.1; v.2 no.1,3 (AUT1966-1968); May, July 1969; Jan., June 1970; one undated issue 1970.

Gay sunshine. San Francisco. 1437735
ISSN: 0046-550X Beg. date: 1970
"Published by a gay men's collective."
WU　　　UWM (RBR) No.2,4-34 (1970-1977).

Gazebo. Wichita, Kan., Student Government Association, Wichita State University. 1437748
Beg. date: 1975
WU　　　UWM (RBR) V.1 no.1-2 (APR-AUG1975); Fall 1975; v.2 no.2 (1976).

The Gegenschein quarterly. Whitestone, N.Y., [etc.], Philip Raymond Smith. 1437763
LCCN: 76-649136 Beg. date: 1972
WU　　　UWM (RBR) No.1-15 (1972-n.d.).

Gemini; the Oxford and Cambridge magazine. Cambridge, Eng. 1437776
ISSN: 0433-2989 Beg. date: 1957 End date: 1960
Jan. 1960- every 4th issue called Gemini/Dialogue, due to union of Gemini and Dialogue.
Ceased publication with vol. 3 no. 3, Summer 1960.
WU　　　UWM (RBR) V.1; v.2 no.1,6,8; v.3 no.2 (1957-SPR1960).

Gemini/Dialogue. See Gemini; the Oxford and Cambridge magazine. Cambridge, Eng. 1437789

Generation; the inter-arts magazine. Ann Arbor, University of Michigan, Board in Control of Student Publications. 1437791
ISSN: 0016-6626 Beg. date: 1950
WU　　　UWM (RBR) V.16 no.2; v.17-v.21 no.3 (1964-SPR1970).

Genesis: grasp. [New York]. 1437813
ISSN: 0016-6650 LCCN: 68-7001 Beg. date: 1968
WU　　　UWM (RBR) V.1 no.1-4; v.2 no.1/2 (no.5/6) (1968-1971).

Genesis West. Burlingame, California, Chrysalis West Foundation. 0283788
ISSN: 0435-2807 LCCN: 63-23336 Beg. date: 1962 End date: 1965
"Incorporating Coastlines" fall 1963.
Ceased publication with vol. 3 no. 1/2, Winter 1965.
With supplements.
WU　　　UWM (RBR) V.1 no.1-4; v.2 no.1,2/3; v.3 no.1/2 (SEP1962-WIN1965); suppl. Aug. 1964.

The Genre of silence. [n.p.], Joel Oppenheimer. 1437826
Beg. date: 1967 End date: 1967
"A one-shot review."
"This then will be the first and last issue of The Genre of silence."
WU   UWM (RBR) June 1967.

Gentry. New York, Reporter Publications. 1437839
ISSN: 0433-4124 LCCN: 54-34588 Beg. date: 1951 End date: 1957
Ceased publication with no. 22, Spring 1957.
WU   UWM (RBR) No.2-4,7-8 (SPR1952-FAL1953).

George Mason University, Fairfax, Virginia. Phoebe. *See* 1499906
Phoebe. Fairfax, Va.

Georgia. University. *See* Georgia review. Athens, Georgia, 0286781
University of Georgia.

The Georgia review. Athens, Georgia, University of Georgia. 028730A
ISSN: 0016-8386 LCCN: 48-10729 Beg. date: 1947
WU   UWM (RBR) V.1-25 (1947-1971).

The Germ; thoughts towards nature in poetry, literature and 1200251
art. London, Pre-Raphaelite Brotherhood.
Beg. date: 1850 End date: 1850
Introduction by William Michael Rossetti.
Ceased publication with no. 4, May 1850.
WU   UWM (RBR) No.1-4 (1850).

Germination. [Guelph, Ont., etc.] 1528743
Beg. date: 1976
WU   UWM (RBR) No.1-3 (SPR1976-MAY1977).

The Ghost. [n.p.] 1437841
Beg. date: 1943 End date: 1947
"Issued for his own amusement and that of his friends, by W. Paul Cook."
Ceased publication with no. 5, July 1947.
WU   UWM (RBR) No.4 (JUL1946).

Ghost dance. *See* Ghostdance. Lansing, Mich., University 143787A
College, Dept. of American Thought and Language, Michigan State
University.

Ghostdance. Lansing, Mich., University College, Dept. of 1437854
American Thought and Language, Michigan State University.
ISSN: 0016-9633 Beg. date: 1968
Title varies: Ghost dance; Ghost-dance.
WU   UWM (RBR) No.1-28 (1968-1976).

The Ghourki. Morgantown, W. Va. 1437895
LCCN: 7-15356 Beg. date: 1901 End date: 1909
Ceased publication with vol. 6 no. 2, April 1909.
WU   UWM (RBR) V.1-4 (1901/1902-1905).

Gilt edge. *See* GiltEdge. Missoula, Mont., Women's 1528771
Resource Center, University of Montana.

GiltEdge. Missoula, Mont., Women's Resource Center, 1528756
University of Montana.
Beg. date: 1975
WU   UWM (RBR) No.1-3 (JUN011975-MAR1977).

The Glass. Lowestoft, Suffolk, Eng. 1437904
Beg. date: 1948 End date: 1954
Ceased publication with no. 11, [Summer 1954].
WU   UWM (RBR) No.1-11 (SEP1948-1954).

Glass hill. Buffalo, N.Y. 1437917
Beg. date: 1949 End date: 1950
Ceased publication with no. 5, Nov. 1950.
WU   UWM (RBR) No.1-5 (OCT1949-NOV1950).

Glass onion. Glamorgan, Wales, Together Publications. 143792A
Beg. date: 197
WU   UWM (RBR) No.1-2 (1971?-n.d.).

Glassworks. Staten Island, N.Y. 1437932
ISSN: 0145-6792 Beg. date: 1975
WU   UWM (RBR) V.1-v.2 no.3 (FAL1975-1977).

Gleam. *See* Saplings. Peekskill, N.Y., Oak Lane, Pa. 1502353

The glebe. New York, Kraus Reprint Corp. 0291624
Beg. date: 1913 End date: 1914
Ceased publication with vol. 2 no. 4, 1914.
WU   UWM (RBR) V.1 no.1,6 (SEP1913,MAR1914).

Glendon College, Toronto. Dime bag. *See* Dime bag. 1434798
Toronto, Glendon College.

Global tapestry. Salesbury, Lancs., Eng. 1437945
Beg. date: 197
WU   UWM (RBR) Five unnumbered issues (1970-1974).

Gnaoua. Tangier, Morocco, Ira Cohen. 1437958
ISSN: 0436-0761 Beg. date: 1964 End date: 1964
Ceased publication with no. 1, Spring 1964.
WU   UWM (RBR) No.1 (SPR1964).

Gnomon. Lexington, Ky. [etc.], Jonathan Greene. 1437960
ISSN: 0436-077X Beg. date: 1965
WU   UWM (RBR) No.1-2 (FAL1965-SPR1967).

Gnosis. Brooklyn, N.Y. 1437973
ISSN: 0017-1425
WU   UWM (RBR) Fall 1968; Spring, Winter 1969; Fall-Winter 1970; no. 7 (1972).

Goad. Sausalito, Calif. [etc.], Horace Schwartz. 1437986
ISSN: 0432-0050 Beg. date: 1951 End date: 1953
Ceased publication with vol. 2 no. 1, Jan. 1953.
WU   UWM (RBR) V.1 no.1-3; v.2 no.1 (SUM1951-JAN1953).

Gob. Worcester, Mass., Clark University, Dept. of English. 1437999
Beg. date: 1972
WU   UWM (RBR) V.1; v.2 no.1/2; v.3 no.1/2-3 (FEB1972-1977).

Goddard College, Plainfield, Vermont. Goddard journal. 1436232
See Goddard journal. Plainfield, Vt., Goddard College.

The Goddard journal. Plainfield, Vt., Goddard College. 143622A
ISSN: 0030-7812 Beg. date: 1967
WU   UWM (RBR) V.1 no.1,4; v.5 no.1-2 (OCT1967-1976).

Gogebic review. *See* Lake Superior review. Ironwood, Mich., 1493714
Gogebic Press.

Gold rush. Morrisville, N.Y., State University of New York, A 1436245
and T College.
Beg. date: 1967
WU   UWM (RBR) V.1 no.1 (MAY1967).

Golden dog. *See* Chien d'or. The Golden dog. Montreal, 1428420
Ottawa.

Golden galleon. Kansas City, Missouri, A. Fowler. 0292707
LCCN: 28-1158 Beg. date: 1924 End date: 1925
Supersedes Miscellanea.
Title varies: vol. 1 nos. 1-3, Jan.-July 1924, The Galleon.
Ceased publication with vol. 2 no. 3, Summer 1925.
WU   UWM (RBR) V.1-v.2 no.3 (1924-SUM1925).

Golden gate. Carthage, Mo. [etc.], Glen Coffield. 1436260
ISSN: 0434-1678 Beg. date: 1958 End date: 1959
Ceased publication.
Superseded by Creative review with Winter 1960/1961.
WU   UWM (RBR) V.1-v.2 no.6 (MAR1958-AUG1959).

The Golden goose. Columbus, Ohio [etc.], Cronos Editions. 150889A
Beg. date: 1948
Supersedes Cronos, Sibylline and Briarcliff quarterly with same issue.
Publication suspended between June 1949 and Jan. 1951, during which time Golden goose chap book was published.
WU   UWM (RBR) No.1-3 (SUM1948-JUN1949); ser. 3 no.1,4 (1951-1952); v.4 no.5-7 OCT1952-APR1954).

Golden hind; a quarterly magazine of art and literature. 0292722
London.
LCCN: 38-11282 Beg. date: 1922 End date: 1924
Ceased publication with vol. 2 (no. 8), July 1924.
WU   UWM (RBR) V.1-2 (no.1-8) (OCT1922-JUL1924).

The Goliards. San Francisco [etc.], Jerry H. Burns. 1436273
ISSN: 0017-193X Beg. date: 1964
WU   UWM (RBR) No.1-7 (FEB291964-JUN1969).

Gone soft. Salem, Mass., Salem State College. 1436286
ISSN: 0362-1219 LCCN: SC 76-196 Beg. date: 1973
"A national literary magazine published bi-annually [sic] by the students of Salem State College."
WU   UWM (RBR) No.1-3 (SPR1973-SPR1974).

Gong. Nottingham, Eng., Student Union, Nottingham 1436308
University.
ISSN: 0017-1972 Beg. date: 1895
Includes special editions entitled New age.
WU   UWM (RBR) Feb., May 1970; Jan., June, Dec. 1971; Nov. 1972; Fall 1972; New age: no. 1 ([1973]).

Good cheer. A monthly magazine for cheerful thinkers. 0293006
Boston, Massachusetts, Forbes and co.
LCCN: 2-4275 Beg. date: 1900 End date: 1901
Ceased publication with vol. 2 no. 3, July 1901.
Absorbed by National magazine.
WU   UWM (RBR) V.1 no.1-6; v.2 no.1-3 (NOV1900-JUL1901).

Good elf. London, Lawrence Upton. 1436323
Beg. date: 1970
WU UWM (RBR) No.1-5 (SEP1970-1971).

Good morning. New York. 0293138
LCCN: 23-14073 Beg. date: 1919 End date: 1921
Ceased publication with vol. 3, 1921.
Superseded by Art Young quarterly with 1922.
WU UWM (RBR) V.1 no.1-14,16; v.2 no.1-9/10; v.3 no.1-12 (MAY081919-1921).

The Goodly co. Camas, Wash. [etc.], G. Russell Morgan. 1436336
Beg. date: 1964
WU UWM (RBR) No.1-15 (DEC1964-APR1970).

The Goose-quill. Chicago. 1436349
Beg. date: 1900 End date: 1904
Ceased publication with new series vol. 3 no. 3, March 1904.
WU UWM (RBR) Mar. 15, 1900; Dec. 1901.

Gooseberry. Point Pleasant, Pa. 1436351
Beg. date: 1964 End date: 1965
Ceased publication with vol. 1 no. 2, 1965.
WU UWM (RBR) V.1 no.1-2 (SPR1964-1965).

Graduate student of English. Minneapolis. 0294734
ISSN: 0436-2721 LCCN: 63-38784 rev Beg. date: 1957 End date: 1960
Ceased publication with vol. 3 no. 4, Summer 1960.
WU UWM (RBR) V.1 no.4-v.3 no.4 (SUM1958-SUM1960).

Graffiti. New York, R.S.V.P. (Redeeming Social Value Publisher). 1436364
ISSN: 0017-2855
WU UWM (RBR) V.1 no.8 (n.d.).

Graffiti. Washington, D.C., Steve Stern. 1436377
ISSN: 0436-2764 Beg. date: 1965
WU UWM (RBR) No.1-2 (1965).

Grafiktrakt. Rolla, Mo. 143638A
Beg. date: 1974
WU UWM (RBR) No.1-2 (1974).

Grain. Honolulu, American Studies Dept., University of Hawaii. 1436392
Beg. date: 1967
WU UWM (RBR) V.1 no.1 (OCT1967).

Grain. Saskatoon, Saskatchewan Writers' Guild. 1436414
LCCN: 74-641050 Beg. date: 1973
"Magazine of stories and poems."
Published with the assistance of the Saskatchewan Arts Board.
WU UWM (RBR) V.1-v.4 no.3; v.5 no.1-2 (JUN1973-1977).

Grain of sand. Omaha, University of Omaha. 1436442
ISSN: 0432-1987 Beg. date: 195
"A selection of the work of students of creative writing at the University of Omaha."
WU UWM (RBR) V.6 no.2; v.7 no.1; v.8-11; v.12 no.2; v.13-14 (DEC1957-DEC1965).

The Grande ronde review. Folsom, Calif. [etc.]. 1436468
ISSN: 0017-3150 Beg. date: 1964
WU UWM (RBR) No.1-6 (FAL1964-1966); v.2 no.1-2 ([1968]); no.10-14 (1968-1975).

Granite. Hanover, N.H., Granite Publications. 1436470
ISSN: 0046-6298 LCCN: SC 76-230 Beg. date: 1971
"A journal of poetry, fiction, poetics and thought."
WU UWM (RBR) No.1-9/10 (SPR1971-WIN1974/1975).

Grapeshot. [Wagga Wagga, N.S.W.], Riverina College of Advanced Education. 1436483
Beg. date: 1974
WU UWM (RBR) No.1-6 (OCT241974-1977).

Graphomania. See Graphomania et pierian. Santa Ana, Calif. 1436518

Graphomania et pierian. Santa Ana, Calif. 1436505
Beg. date: 1967
Title varies: , Graphomania.
WU UWM (RBR) V.1 no.2-3; v.2 no.1-4 (APR1967-OCT1968).

Grass roots. San Angelo, Tex. [etc.]. 1436520
ISSN: 0434-3808 Beg. date: 1953
"An independent monthly journal dedicated to a scientific study of the trends."
WU UWM (RBR) V.15 no.173-179; v.16 no.188; v.17 no.193,195-197 (APR1967-OCT1968).

The Grasshopper broadsheets. Derby, England. 0295663
Beg. date: 1942 End date: 1945
Ceased publication with the issue for Dec. 1945.
Includes supplementary nos. issued Mar. and Sept. 1943.
WU UWM (RBR) Ser. 3 no.1-7,9-12; ser. 4 no.1-12 (JAN1944-DEC1945).

Gravida. Hartsdale, N.Y. 1436533
Beg. date: 1974
Published Spring 1974- by the Women's Poetry Collective; by a collective of poets.
WU UWM (RBR) V.1-2; v.3 no.1,3-4 (SPR1974-1977).

Gray day magazine. Macon, Georgia, Garland Press. 1436559
ISSN: 0146-0188 Beg. date: 1975
WU UWM (RBR) No.1-4 (SUM1975-1976).

The Great auk. Gruyere, Victoria, Aust., Charles Buckmaster. 1436561
Beg. date: 1968
WU UWM (RBR) No.1-4,6-11 (SEP1968-JAN/FEB1970).

The Great blafigria IS. Santa Fe, N.M. 1436574
Beg. date: 1975
WU UWM (RBR) No.1-3 (1975-1976).

The Great circumpolar bear cult. Ashland, Wis., The Bear Cult Press. 1528784
Beg. date: 1976
WU UWM (RBR) No.1 (1976).

The Great Lakes review. Chicago, Northeastern Illinois University, College of Arts and Sciences, Departments of English and History. 1122528
ISSN: 0360-1846 LCCN: 75-648049 Beg. date: 1974
"A journal of Midwest culture."
WU UWM (RBR) V.1-v.3 no.2 (SUM1974-1977).

The Great society. New York. 1436587
ISSN: 0533-2028 Beg. date: 1966 End date: 1967
Ceased publication with no. 2, 1967.
WU UWM (RBR) One unnumbered issue (1966).

Great works. Hanley, Stoke-on-Trent, Eng. 143659A
Beg. date: 1973
WU UWM (RBR) No.1-6 (APR1973-1976).

The Grecourt review. Northampton, Mass., Smith College. 1436609
ISSN: 0017-3827 LCCN: 59-37875 Beg. date: 1958
Edited and published by the students at Smith College.
WU UWM (RBR) V.1-3; v.4 no.1-3; v.5 no.2-3; v.6; v.7 no.1-3; v.8 no.1-3; v.9 no.2-3; v.10 no.1-3; v.11 no.2; v.14 no.1; v.15 no.1; v.16 no.1 (1958-1973).

Greek Cultural Society of New York. See Charioteer; a review of modern Greek literature. New York, Parnassos, Greek Cultural Society. 0300144

Greek horizons. Athens, Icaros Pub. Co. 1436624
Beg. date: 1946 End date: 1946
"A quarterly review."
Ceased publication with no. 1, Summer 1946.
WU UWM (RBR) No.1 (SUM1946).

Green apple; a review of the arts. Cleveland, Green Apple Enterprises. 1436637
ISSN: 0533-2494 Beg. date: 1969
WU UWM (RBR) V.1 no.1-3 (1969).

The Green fuse. Broderick, Calif. 143664A
Beg. date: 1976
WU UWM (RBR) V.1-2 (1976-1977).

Green groad. Topeka, Kan. 1436652
ISSN: 0017-3959 Beg. date: 1968
WU UWM (RBR) V.1 no.1-11 (1968-JUL1970).

The Green horse for poetry. Bowling Green, Ohio, Creative Writing Program, Bowling Green State University. 1436665
WU UWM (RBR) V.1 no.1-4 (1973-1975).

Green island. Runcorn, Cheshire, Eng., David Kilburn. 1436680
ISSN: 0017-3967 Beg. date: 197
WU UWM (RBR) Five undated issues (197?-1975/1976?).

Green River Community College, Auburn, Washington. Clearing. See Clearing. Auburn, Wash., Green River Community College. 143123A

Green river review. Owensboro, Ky., Green River Press. 1436693
ISSN: 0017-4009 LCCN: 73-646947 Beg. date: 1968
WU UWM (RBR) V.1-v.7 no.1 (FAL1968-1976).

The Green world. *Baton Rouge, La.* 1436702
ISSN: 0017-4025 Beg. date: 1963 End date: 1966
Ceased publication with vol. 4, 1966.
WU   UWM (RBR) V.1-v.4 no.2 (SPR1963-1966).

Greenfeel. *Barre, Vt.* 0300382
WU   UWM (RBR) One unnumbered issue (1969).

The Greenfield review. *Greenfield Center, N.Y.* 1436715
ISSN: 0017-4041 LCCN: 72-622837 Beg. date: 1970
WU   UWM (RBR) V.1-5 (SPR1970-1977).

Greenhouse review. *Santa Cruz, Calif.* 1436728
Beg. date: 1975
WU   UWM (RBR) No.1-3 (SUM1975-1977).

Green's magazine. *Detroit, Green's Magazine, Inc.* 1436730
Beg. date: 1972
"Fiction for the family."
WU   UWM (RBR) V.1-v.5 no.1 (FAL1972-1977).

Greensboro review. *Greensboro, University of North Carolina at Greensboro.* 1218987
ISSN: 0017-4084 Beg. date: 1966
WU   UWM (RBR) V.1 no.1; v.2 no.1; v.3 no.1,4; v.4 no.1-2 (MAY1966-SPR1969); no.7-22 (SUM/FAL1969-1977).

Greenwich village. *New York.* 0300473
Beg. date: 1915
Began publication with the Jan. 20, 1915 issue.
Merged into Bruno's weekly.
WU   UWM (RBR) V.2 no.1-6 (JUN20-OCT301915).

Greenwich Village guardian quill. *New York.* 0300486
Title varies: Village guardian; G-V-G; Greenwich Village guardian; Guardian-quill; Greenwich Village guardian quill; etc.
Absorbed Contemporary quill, and New G. V. quill.
WU   UWM (RBR) V.19 no.4 (OCT1926).

The Griffin. *New York, Readers' Subscription, Inc.* 143980A
ISSN: 0434-670X Beg. date: 1951 End date: 1963
Ceased publication with vol. 12 no. 5, May 1963.
WU   UWM (RBR) V.2 no.3; v.9 no.1 (1953,JAN1960).

The Griffon. *Athens, Greece, American School of Classical Studies at Athens. Gennadius Library.* 1442305
ISSN: 0017-4246 Beg. date: 1965
WU   UWM (RBR) No.1-6 (APR1965-SUM1970).

Grilled flowers. *Tucson, Ariz., Poetry Center, University of Arizona.* 1442320
Beg. date: 1976
"Poetry and poetry in translation."
WU   UWM (RBR) V.1 no.1-2; v.2 no.1 (SPR1976-1977); special issue no.1 (SUM1976).

Grinnell College, Grinnell, Iowa. Tanager. *See* Tanager. 1510713
Grinnell, Iowa, English and Journalism Depts., Grinnell College.

Grist. *Cambridge, Mass., Grist Press.* 1439825
Beg. date: 1975
WU   UWM (RBR) V.1-3 (SPR1975-1977).

Grist. *Lawrence, Kan.* 1439812
ISSN: 0533-2923 Beg. date: 1964
WU   UWM (RBR) V.1 no.3-12 (OCT1964-1966).

Grist west. *Berkeley, Calif.* 1439838
ISSN: 0533-2931 Beg. date: 1964
At head of title: G W.
WU   UWM (RBR) No.2 (1965).

El Grito. *Berkeley, California.* 0300809
ISSN: 0017-4300 Beg. date: 1967 End date: 1974
Quarterly.
A journal of Contemporary Mexican-American thought.
Ceased publication with vol. 7, 1974.
WU   UWM (RBR) V.1-v.5 no.3 (FAL1967-SPR1972).

Grok. *San Francisco.* 1439840
WU   UWM (RBR) No.3 (n.d.).

Gronk. *Toronto, Ganglia Press.* 1441683
ISSN: 0017-453X Beg. date: 1967
Constitutes no. 6 of Ganglia.
WU   UWM (RBR) Ser. 2 no.1/2-3,6-7/8; ser. 3 no.1-2,5; ser. 4 no.2,4; ser. 5 no.1-2,7; ser. 6 no.5,8; ser. 7 no.2-3,5,7; ser. 8 no.3,5,7-8 (OCT1968-1972?).

Groote schuur. *Cape Town, Students' Representative Council, University of Cape Town.* 1442346
Beg. date: 1946
Continues South African college magazine and U C T quarterly.
Subtitle varies.
Some articles in Afrikaans, some in English.
WU   UWM (RBR) 1946, 1948, 1950, 1953, 1957-1962/1963.

Grope. *[n.p.].* 1439853
WU   UWM (RBR) No.2-6 (1972-1976).

Grosseteste review. *Lincoln, Eng., Grosseteste Press.* 1439866
ISSN: 0017-4637 Beg. date: 1968
WU   UWM (RBR) V.1-8 (SPR1968-1976).

Grove: contemporary poetry and translation. *Claremont, Calif., Pitzer College.* 1439879
Beg. date: 1975
WU   UWM (RBR) No.1-3 (SUM1975-1977).

Grub Street. *Bronx, Alan Ball.* 1528797
ISSN: 0149-4228 Beg. date: 1969
WU   UWM (RBR) V.1-6 (1969-1977).

Grump. *New York.* 1439894
ISSN: 0533-3342 Beg. date: 1964
WU   UWM (RBR) V.1 no.1-2 (MAY-JUL1965); Oct. 1965; Feb./Mar. 1967; no.5-12 (APR/MAY1966-1967).

The Grundtvig review. *Portland, Ore. [etc.].* 1439903
ISSN: 0432-7527 Beg. date: 1950
Title varies: nos. 1-2, Spring 1950-Sept. 1950, The Grundtvig review and almanac.
WU   UWM (RBR) No.1-3,6-7 (SPR1950-MAY1957).

Grundtvig review and almanac. *See* Grundtvig review. 1439916
Portland, Ore. [etc.].

Gryphon. *St. Louis, Mo. [etc.].* 1439929
ISSN: 0432-7659 Beg. date: 1950 End date: 1951
Ceased publication with Spring 1951.
WU   UWM (RBR) Spring, Fall 1950; Spring 1951.

Gryphon. *Tampa, University of South Florida.* 1442361
Beg. date: 1974
WU   UWM (RBR) V.1-2; v.3 no.1-2; v.4 no.3 (MAY1974-1977).

Guabi. *Santa Cruz, Calif., Merrill College, University of California, Santa Cruz.* 1442387
Beg. date: 1969
WU   UWM (RBR) V.1 no.1-2 (1969-1970).

The Guardian; a literary monthly published in Philadelphia. *Philadelphia.* 1439931
Beg. date: 1924 End date: 1925
Subtitle varies.
Ceased publication with vol. 2 no. 3, Oct. 1925.
WU   UWM (RBR) V.1 no.1-4 (NOV1924-FEB1925).

Guardino's gazette. *New York.* 1439944
Continues Writer's voice.
Ceased publication.
Absorbed by Spafaswap.
WU   UWM (RBR) V.16 no.10 (OCT1974).

The Guild. *Idaho Falls, Idaho, Idaho Poets' and Writers' Guild.* 143996A
ISSN: 0434-9172
WU   UWM (RBR) V.4 no.4; v.5-7; v.8 no.1-3 (1963-1966/1967).

Guild Academy of Arts. Expression. *See* Expression. 1441445
Adelaide.

Guild of handicraft, Birmingham, England. *See* Quest. 0302379
Birmingham, Printed at the press of the Guild of handicraft in Birmingham and published by Cornish brothers etc.

Gulf stream. *See* Gulfstream. Port Allen [etc.] La. 1439998

Gulfstream. *Port Allen [etc.] La.* 1439985
Beg. date: 1972
WU   UWM (RBR) No.1-3 (1972-1973).

Gum. *Iowa City, Iowa.* 1440005
Beg. date: 1970
WU   UWM (RBR) No.1/2-9 (MAR1970-JAN1973).

The Guppy fancier's quarterly. *Buffalo, N.Y.* 1440018
Beg. date: 1965
WU   UWM (RBR) V.1 no.1 (1967).

Guyana. University. Library. Expression. *See* Expression. 1435870
Turkeyen, Guyana, University of Guyana Library.

The Gypsy. *London, The Pomegranate Press.*   1440020
    LCCN: 16-12048. Beg. date: 1915 End date: 1916
    Ceased publication with vol. 1 no. 2, May 1916.
    WU   UWM (RBR) V.1 no.1-2 (MAY1915-MAY1916.).

Gypsy table. *San Francisco.*   1440033
    Beg. date: 1972
    WU   UWM (RBR) No.1-8/9 (1972-1975).

The Gyroscope. *Palo Alto, Calif., Yvor Winters.*   1528806
    LCCN: 40-38228 Beg. date: 1929 End date: 1930
    "A quarterly magazine."
    Ceased publication with Feb. 1930.
    WU   UWM (RBR) Aug. 1929, Feb. 1930.

H

H O P E. *See* Hallamshire and osgoldcross poetry express. 144009A
New Malden, Surrey, Eng.

Haiku byways. *London.* 1440046
ISSN: 0046-6719 Beg. date: 1970 End date: 1971
Ceased publication with 1971.
Superseded by Byways with 1971.
WU   UWM (RBR) No.1-3/4 (1970-1971).

Haiku highlights. *Kanona, N.Y., J & C Transcripts.* 1441592
ISSN: 0017-6664 Beg. date: 1965 End date: 1972
Ceased publication with vol. 8a no. 6, Nov./Dec. 1972.
Superseded by Dragonfly; a quarterly of haiku highlights with 1973.
WU   UWM (RBR) V.1-v.8a (DEC1965-DEC1972).

Haiku Magazine. *Toronto.* 1440059
ISSN: 0017-6656 Beg. date: 1967
WU   UWM (RBR) V.2-5 (1967-WIN1971/1972).

Haiku spotlight. *Matsuyama Shi, Japan.* 1440061
Beg. date: 1968
WU   UWM (RBR) No.1-70 (SEP1968-APR041970).

Haiku West. *Forest Hills, New York.* 0303828
ISSN: 0017-6672 Beg. date: 1967
WU   UWM (RBR) V.1-7; v.8 no.2 (JUN1967-JAN1975).

Halcyon. *Cambridge, Mass.* 1440109
Beg. date: 1947 End date: 1948
Ceased publication with Spring 1948.
WU   UWM (RBR) Winter, Spring 1948.

Haldeman-Julius monthly. *See* Debunker and the American 0303947
parade. Girard, Kan., The Haldeman-Julius company.

Haldeman-Julius quarterly. *See* American parade. Girard, 030395A
Kansas, Haldeman-Julius Company.

Halderman-Julius, Emanuel, 1889-, ed. *See* American 0303962
parade. Girard, Kansas, Haldeman-Julius Company.

The Half moon. *New York.* 1440074
ISSN: 0438-4288 Beg. date: 1959 End date: 1960
Ceased publication with no. 4, Summer 1960.
WU   UWM (RBR) No.1-4 (SUM1959-SUM1960).

The Hallamshire and osgoldcross poetry express. *New* 1440087
Malden, Surrey, Eng.
Beg. date: 1972
Also called H O P E.
WU   UWM (RBR) V.1 no.6; v.2 no.7-8; v.3 no.9
(JAN1974-SEP1975).

The Hampden-Sydney poetry review. *Hampden-Sydney, Va.* 1438911
Beg. date: 1976
Supersedes Maryland review.
WU   UWM (RBR) No.1-2 (WIN-SUM1976); Winter/
Summer 1977.

Hampshire College, Amherst, Massachusetts. Boxspring. 1433605
See Boxspring. Amherst, Mass., Hampshire College.

Hampshire poets. *Lee-on-the-Solent, Hants., Eng.* 1440111
Beg. date: 1969
WU   UWM (RBR) No.1-16 (1969-SEP1975).

Handsel. *Lexington, Ky.* 1440124
Beg. date: 1970
WU   UWM (RBR) No.2-4; v.2 no.1-2 (1971-1973).

Hanging loose. *New York.* 1440137
ISSN: 0440-2316 LCCN: sc77-735 Beg. date: 1966
Supersedes Things.
WU   UWM (RBR) No.1-18,20-29 (FAL1966-1977).

Happiness holding tank. *Okemos, Mich., Stone Press.* 144014A
ISSN: 0046-6832 Beg. date: 1970
WU   UWM (RBR) No.1-15/16
(OCT1970-WIN1975/1976).

Hapt. *Gloucester, England.* 0305617
WU   UWM (RBR) No.6-10,17-18,20
(n.d.-1969).

Haravec. *Lima, Peru.* 1440152
ISSN: 0017-7598 Beg. date: 1966
WU   UWM (RBR) No.1-5 (NOV1966-SEP1968).

Harbinger. *Providence, R.I.* 1440165
WU   UWM (RBR) V.1 no.4-5; v.2 no.1-2; v.3
no.1 (1974-1977).

Harbor lights. *Shoreview, Minn.* 1440178
Beg. date: 1962
WU   UWM (RBR) No.66,91 (APR1968,JAN/FEB1973).

Hard cider. *Columbus, Ohio, The Cider Press.* 1440180
Beg. date: 1974
WU   UWM (RBR) V.1 no.1 (1974).

Hard pressed. *Sacramento, Calif.* 1438924
Beg. date: 1975
WU   UWM (RBR) No.1-3 (1975-1977).

The Hardware poets occasional. *New York, Hardware Poets* 146883A
Playhouse.
ISSN: 0440-307X Beg. date: 1964
WU   UWM (RBR) V.1 no.1; v.2; no.3-4 (FEB-OCT1964);
special issue: 1965.

Haringey Arts Council. Ambience. *See* Ambience; the arts 1429936
in North London. [London], Haringey Arts Council.

The Harkness hoot. *New Haven, Conn.* 1441536
Beg. date: 1930
WU   UWM (RBR) V.1 no.5-6 (APR-MAY1931).

Harlem quarterly. *New York.* 0305896
WU   UWM (RBR) V.1 no.1-2
(WIN1949/1950-SPR1950).

Harlequin. *Hermosa Beach [etc.] Calif.* 144239A
ISSN: 0438-6132 Beg. date: 1956 End date: 1959
Ceased publication with vol. 3, 1959.
WU   UWM (RBR) V.1 no.1; v.2 no.1; v.3 no.1 (1956-1959).

Harlequin. *Oxford, Eng.* 1441549
Beg. date: 1950 End date: 1950
Ceased publication with no. 2, 1950.
Absorbed by Panorama with 1951.
WU   UWM (RBR) No.1-2 (1950).

Harlequin. *Sherman, Tex., Austin College.* 1441551
Beg. date: 1964
WU   UWM (RBR) V.1 no.1-2; v.2 no.1
(SPR1964-SPR1965).

Harlequin press. *Ashland, Ore.* 1441577
Beg. date: 1968
WU   UWM (RBR) V.1 no.1,4-7/8; v.2 no.1-3,10/12
(1968-FEB1970).

Harpoon. *Milwaukee, Harpoon Press.* 144158A
Beg. date: 1972
WU   UWM (RBR) V.1 no.1 (DEC1972).

The Harris review. *New York.* 1468842
WU   UWM (RBR) [1971].

Harrison street review. *Kansas City, Mo.* 1439208
WU   UWM (RBR) No.3 (1971).

Hartwick review. *Oneonta, N.Y.* 1439210
ISSN: 0440-3371 Beg. date: 1965
WU   UWM (RBR) V.1 no.1; v.2-5 (OCT1967-1969).

Harvard University. Summer School of Arts and Sciences 0307763
and of Education. *See* Confluence; an international forum.
Cambridge, Harvard University Printing Office.

Harvard wake. *See* Wake, the creative magazine. *New York,* 1484111

The Harvest; anthology of student writing at the University 1442409
of Houston. *Houston, University of Houston, Writers Club.*
Beg. date: 1936
WU   UWM (RBR) V.18-24,27; v.31 no.2; v.32; v.34 no.1;
v.35 no.2; v.36-40 (1954-1976).

Hawaii. University, Honolulu. American Studies 1436401
Department. Grain. *See* Grain. Honolulu, American Studies Dept.,
University of Hawaii.

Hawaii. University, Honolulu. Associated Students. Hawaii 1442452
literary review. *See* Hawaii review. [Honolulu, Board of Publications,
Associated Students of the University of Hawaii].

Hawaii. University, Honolulu. Associated Students. Hawaii 1442437
review. *See* Hawaii review. [Honolulu, Board of Publications,
Associated Students of the University of Hawaii].

Hawaii literary review. *See* Hawaii review. [Honolulu, Board 144244A
of Publications, Associated Students of the University of Hawaii].

Hawaii review. [Honolulu, Board of Publications, Associated Students of the University of Hawaii]. 1442424
ISSN: 0093-9625   LCCN: 73-644462   Beg. date: 1973
Title varies: vol. 1 no. 1, Winter 1973, Hawaii literary review, ISSN 0090-8274.
WU   UWM (RBR) V.1 no.1-2; v.2 no.2,5-7 (WIN1973-1977).

Hawk Oxford, Eng. 1439223
ISSN: 0437-0678   Beg. date: 1955
WU   UWM (RBR) V.1 no.1 (NOV1955).

Hawk and whippoorwill; poems of man and nature. London. 1439236
ISSN: 0438-8313   Beg. date: 1960   End date: 1963
Ceased publication with vol. 4 no. 3, Autumn 1963.
WU   UWM (RBR) V.1 no.1-2; v.2 no.1-3; v.3 no.1-2; v.4 no.1-3 (SPR1960-AUT1963).

Hawk and whippoorwill recalled. Madison, Wis., Wisconsin Fellowship of Poets. 1439249
Beg. date: 1973
WU   UWM (RBR) V.1-2 (SUM1973-SPR1975).

Head. Staatsburg, N.Y. 1439264
ISSN: 0440-5374   Beg. date: 1964   End date: 1966
Ceased publication with no. 6, 1966.
WU   UWM (RBR) No.1-6 (1964-1966).

Head and freak mag. Brighton, Eng.? 1441458
WU   UWM (RBR) No.6 (n.d.).

Headland. See New Headland. Sheffield, Eng. 143928A

Headland poetry. See New Headland. Sheffield, Eng. 1439292

Heads up; a journal of the new literature. Philadelphia. 1439301
ISSN: 0017-8799   Beg. date: 1967
WU   UWM (RBR) No.1-5 (SPR1967-FAL1970).

Hearse; a Vehicle used to convey the dead. Eureka, Calif. 1439314
ISSN: 0017-9213   Beg. date: 1957
Publication suspended between no. 9, 1961, and no. 10, 1969.
WU   UWM (RBR) No.1-17 (1957-1972).

Hebrew Union College-Jewish Institute of Religion. Variant. See Variant. Cincinnati. 151699A

Heirs. San Francisco. 1439327
ISSN: 0017-9884   Beg. date: 1968
WU   UWM (RBR) V.1 no.1-[4?]; v.4 no.6/7-9; v.6 no.1 (MAR1968-1975/1976).

Hemispheres; revue franco-américaine de poesie; French-American quarterly of poetry. Brooklyn, New York. 0311341
WU   UWM (RBR) No.1-4 (SUM1943-1944); v.2 no.5-6 (SPR1945-n.d.).

Hemlock. Berkeley, Calif. 1441670
WU   UWM (RBR) Winter 1970.

Hendon Arts Together. And. See And. London, Writers Forum. 1438034

Henry Miller Literary Society. Newsletter. Minneapolis. 0311865
Ceased publication.
WU   UWM (RBR) No.1-11 (FAL1958-1962).

The Herb o'grace, a monthly miscellany. Fairseat, Wrotham, Kent, Printed by E. F. Gascoine. 0312017
WU   UWM (RBR) No.1-18 (1901-1902).

Here and now. Toronto. 0312151
Ceased publication with v. 2 no. 4.
WU   UWM (RBR) V.1 no.1-3; v.2 no.4 (DEC1947-JUN1949).

Here now; the South Tyneside arts quarterly. Hebbrun, Durham, Eng. 143933A
ISSN: 0046-7294   Beg. date: 1972
WU   UWM (RBR) V.1-2; v.3 no.1-2 (SPR1973-1975).

Heritage. Amherst, Mass. 1439342
Beg. date: 1931   End date: 1932
Ceased publication with vol. 1 no.2, July/Aug. 1932.
WU   UWM (RBR) V.1 no.1 (MAY1932).

The Her(m)etic press. Arnold, Notts., Eng. 1439355
Beg. date: 1968
WU   UWM (RBR) No.1 (1968).

Hey lady. Milwaukee, Morgan Press. 1439368
ISSN: 0018-1188   Beg. date: 1969
WU   UWM (RBR) No.1-8 (1969-1974); suppl. no.1-11, 13-18 (1969-1973).

Hiatus. London, Oasis Books. 1439370
Beg. date: 1970
WU   UWM (RBR) No.1-2 (1970-1972).

Hierophant. Los Angeles, Hierophant Press. 0312935
ISSN: 0018-1366   Beg. date: 1969
WU   UWM (RBR) No.[1-6] (1969-1970).

The High country. [Temecula, Calif., High Country Associates, etc.]. 1439383
ISSN: 0018-1420   LCCN: 68-55653   Beg. date: 1967
WU   UWM (RBR) No.1-12 (SUM1967-SPR1970).

Hika. [Gambier, Ohio], Kenyon College. 1442465
ISSN: 0018-179X   Beg. date: 1935
Title varies: , Hika magazine.
WU   UWM (RBR) Fall 1949; Winter 1950; Winter 1956; [n. ser.] no.1-3 (FAL1973-SPR1974).

Hika magazine. See Hika. [Gambier, Ohio], Kenyon College. 1442480

Hill School, Pottstown, Pennsylvania. Record. See Record. Pottstown, Pa., The Hill School. 1504259

Hill trails. Burlington, Vt. 1468855
Beg. date: 1936
WU   UWM (RBR) V.1-9 (1936-1944).

Hinterland. Cedar Rapids, Iowa.
Beg. date: 1934   End date: 1936
Ceased publication with no. 4, Jan. 1936.
Superseded by a publication with the same title published by the midwest Literary League with Sept. 1936.
WU   UWM (RBR) No.1-4 (NOV/DEC1934-JAN1936).

Hinterland. Des Moines, Midwest Literary League. 0313955
Beg. date: 1936   End date: 1939
Reprint title page calls this "New Series" but first issue says "The Midwest Literary League has named its magazine Hinterland, A title formerly used by a now defunct 'little magazine..."
Vol. 2, No. 4-8 are numbered 9-13 (whole numbered series beginning with no. 1 of v. 1).
WU   UWM (RBR) V.1 no.1-6; v.2 no.1-2; v.2 no.3 (no.9); no.10-11,13 (SEP1936-1939).

Hippocrene: a collection of new poetry. Houston. 1441460
Beg. date: 1970
WU   UWM (RBR) V.1 no.1; v.2; no.3-4 (SPR1970-1973).

Hippocrene; a quarterly of poetry. [New York]. 1468868
LCCN: 51-32678   Beg. date: 1945   End date: 1947
Ceased publication with vol. 3 no. 1, Fall 1947.
WU   UWM (RBR) V.1-2; v.3 no.1 (FAL1945-FAL1947).

Hiram Poetry Review. Hiram, Ohio, Hiram College. 0313983
ISSN: 0018-2036   Beg. date: 1966
Indexes: Author index. Vols. 1-10, 1966-1971, in vol. 10.
WU   UWM (RBR) No.1-21 (FAL/WIN1966-1976); suppl. no.2-4 (1971-1972).

Hob-nob quarterly. Lancaster, Pa. 1439405
WU   UWM (RBR) No.26-32 (FAL1975-1977).

The Hobby horse. London, K. Paul, Tranch and Co. [etc.]. 1439433
LCCN: 13-3907   Beg. date: 1886   End date: 1893
Title varies: 1886-1892, The Century guild hobby horse.
Ceased publication with new series no. 3, 1893.
WU   UWM (RBR) No.7-8 (JUL-OCT1887); n. ser. no. 1-3 (1893).

Hobnob. See Hob-nob quarterly. Lancaster, Pa. 1439418

Hofstra College, Hempstead, New York. Word. See Word. Hempstead, N.Y., Hofstra College. 151926A

Hollins critic. Hollins, Virginia, Hollins College. 0316883
ISSN: 0018-3644   Beg. date: 1964
WU   UWM (RBR) V.1-v.12 no.3 (APR1964-1975).

Hollow orange. San Francisco. 1439420
ISSN: 0441-0971   Beg. date: 1966   End date: 1970
Ceased publication with no. 6, 1970.
WU   UWM (RBR) No.2-6 (1966-1970).

The Hollow spring review. Berkshire, Mass., The Hollow Spring Review Press. 1438937
Beg. date: 1975
WU   UWM (RBR) V.1 no.1-2 (1975-1976).

The Holy door. Dublin. 1440193
ISSN: 0441-1013   Beg. date: 1965
WU   UWM (RBR) No.2/3/6 (WIN1965).

Home and empire. See New English review. London. 1523255

Home and empire. See New English review. London, Eng. 1529014

Home news magazine. New York, Home News Co. 1440202
ISSN: 0428-6227   Beg. date: 1969
Title varies: , Matador; , Matador home news.
WU   UWM (RBR) No.1 (1969); June, Dec. 1970; June 1971.

Homophile studies. See One Institute quarterly. Los Angeles. One Institute of Homophile Studies. 1499399

The Honest Ulsterman. *Belfast [etc.].* 1440230
ISSN: 0018-4543 LCCN: 68-129774 Beg. date: 1968
"A magazine of revolution."
WU UWM (RBR) No.1-54 (MAY1968-1977).

Honey jar; a receptacle for literary preserves. *Columbus,* 0317940
Ohio; Champlin Press.
LCCN: 3-29654rev.
From May 1908-Sept. 1910 cover titles read: Ye Honey jar; filled with bits of discourse meant to sweeten life.
Publication suspended from Nov. 1910-Jan. 1905, inclusive.
No nos. were issued for Aug. 1906 and Mar. 1910.
WU UWM (RBR) V.1-4 (NOV1898-OCT151900).

Hoo-doo. *DeRidder, La., Energy BlackSouth Press.* 1440243
Beg. date: 1972
WU UWM (RBR) No.1-4 (1972-1976).

The Hoosier challenger. *Cincinnati.* 1440256
Beg. date: 1956
WU UWM (RBR) Jan., Mar. 1957; July 1958; May, Aug. 1959; n. ser. v.1 no.1,4; v.2 no.2, 4 (JAN/FEB1965-JUL/AUG1967).

Hoosier poetry magazine. *See* Blue river poetry magazine. 1433449
Shelbyville, Ind., The Blue River Press.

The Hopkins review. *Baltimore, Johns Hopkins University.* 0318356
LCCN: 50-56422
Ceased publication with vol. 6 no. 4, 1953.
WU UWM (RBR) V.3 no.4; v.4 no.2-3; v.5 no.2 (SUM1950-WIN1952).

The Horbly gnome. *Edinburg, Tex., Funch Press.* 1440269
Beg. date: 1970
WULbUWM (RBR) No.1,3 (DEC1970/JAN1971-1973).

Horde. *London.* 1440271
ISSN: 0439-5522 Beg. date: 1964
WU UWM (RBR) No.1 (DEC1964).

Horizon; a review of literature and art. *London.* 031850A
Beg. date: 1940 End date: 1950
Ceased publication with vol. 20 (no. 120/121), Dec. 1949/Jan. 1950.
Index for v. 1-18 nos. 1-108 in v. 18 (Jan. 1940-Dec. 1948).
WU UWM (RBR) V.1-20 (1940-1950).

Horseshit. *[Hermosa Beach, Calif.], Scum Pub. Co. [etc.].* 1440284
ISSN: 0439-5794 LCCN: 73-618100 Beg. date: 1965
WU UWM (RBR) No.1-3 (1965-1968).

Hound and horn. *Portland, Me., The Hound and Horn,* 0319677
Incorporated.
LCCN: 31-10598 Beg. date: 1927 End date: 1934
Vol. 1-2 have title: The hound and horn; a Harvard miscellany.
Ceased publication with vol. 7 no. 4, 1934.
WU UWM (RBR) V.1-7 (1927-1934).

Houston, Texas. University. Forum. *See* Forum. Houston, 1313846
University of Houston.

Houston, Texas. University. New English Club. Fly's eye. 143724A
See Fly's eye. Houston, New English Club, University of Houston.

Houston, Texas. University. Writers Club. Harvest. *See* 1442411
Harvest; anthology of student writing at the University of Houston. Houston, University of Houston, Writers Club.

Houyhnhnm's scrapbook. *New Orleans.* 0930753
"Affiliated with the New Orleans poetry journal."
WU UWM (RBR) V.1 no.1-4 (AUT1956/WIN1957-DEC1958).

How. *London.* 1440297
WU UWM (RBR) No.3-7 (1965-1966).

Howard University, Washington. Dasein Literary Society. 1432009
Dasein. *See* Dasein. New York, etc.

However. *Cincinnati.* 1440306
ISSN: 0438-0177 Beg. date: 1959
WU UWM (RBR) No.2-3; v.2 no.1 (1962-WIN1962/1973).

However. *See* Mount Adams review. Cincinnati. 1497192

Huddersfield Polytechnic. Students' Union. Dretch 1442192
exsibilate magazine. *See* Dretch exsibilate magazine. Huddersfield, Yorks., Eng., Huddersfield Polytechnic Students' Union.

The Hudson review. *New York, The Hudson review, inc.* 0320957
ISSN: 0018-702X LCCN: 50-2532 Beg. date: 1948
Indexed by Social sciences and humanities index.
WU UWM (RBR) V.1-23 (1948-1971).

Hudson river anthology. *[Poughkeepsie, N.Y.].* 1468870
ISSN: 0362-8604 LCCN: 72-624337 Beg. date: 1972
WU UWM (RBR) V.3 (SPR1974).

Hudson river magazine. *Hudson, N.Y., HUDSON river* 1440319
Publishers, Inc.
Beg. date: 1938 End date: 1941
Suspended March-April 1941.
Title varies: vol. 1 no. 1, May 1938, Magazine of the Hudson valley; vol. 1 nos. 2-5, ·   , Echo, the magazine of the hudson valley.
Ceased publication with vol. 4 no.3, May 1941.
WU UWM (RBR) V.1 no.1; v.3 no.1 (MAY1938-1940).

Huerfano; a literary orphanage. *Flagstaff, Ariz., Daran Inc.* 1440347
Beg. date: 1973
WU UWM (RBR) V.1-v.4 no.2; v.5 no.1-2 (1973-1977).

La Huerta. *Livonia [etc.], N.Y., Brador Publications.* 144035A
Beg. date: 1971
WU UWM (RBR) V.1 no.1-3 (1971-1973).

Hull House Theater, Chicago. Intermission. *See* 1442753
Intermission. Chicago, Hull House Theater.

The Human handkerchief. *Colchester, Essex, Eng.* 1440362
WU UWM (RBR) No.1-5 (n.d.-SUM1975).

The Human voice. *Homestead, Florida, Olivant Press.* 0321531
ISSN: 0018-7305 LCCN: 68-44775 Beg. date: 1965 End date: 197
Began with Feb. 1965 issue.
Title varies: 1965-Spring 1967, Human voice quarterly.
Vols. for Sum/Fal 1967-   with, as issued, Village post, v. 13, no. 7-
Continued by Weid, ISSN 0145-983X.
WU UWM (RBR) V.1-3; v.4-7 (no.13/14-32) (FEB1965-1971).

The Humanist way. *Calcutta, Renaissance Publishers.* 1440375
LCCN: 52-42677 Beg. date: 1945 End date: 1962
Title varies: vol. 1-3, The Marxian way.
Ceased publication with vol. 5 no. 1, Spring 1952.
WU UWM (RBR) V.4 no.2-4; v.5 no.1 (1949/1950-SPR1952).

Huntsville Literary Association. Poem. *See* Poem. 1501270
Huntsville, Alabama, Huntsville Literary Association.

Huron review. *Flint, Mich.* 1440390
WU UWM (RBR) Spring, Winter 1974; Spring, Winter 1975; Spring 1976; Spring 1977.

The Husk. *[Mount Vernon, Iowa].* 144040A
LCCN: 46-42094 Beg. date: 1922
Published by the English Club of Cornell College.
Ceased publication with vol. 46 no. 4, May 1967.
Superseded by Cornellian.
WU UWM (RBR) V.35 no.3-4; v.36 no.1-3; v.37 no.4; v.38-v.44 no.1 (1955-1964/1965).

Hustler. *Cambridge, Eng.* 1440425
Beg. date: 1975
WU UWM (RBR) [No.1 (1975)].

Hyacinths and biscuits. *Brea, Calif.* 1440438
Beg. date: 1969
WU UWM (RBR) No.1-22 ([1969]-1977).

Hyn. *New York.* 1442502
Beg. date: 1969
Title varies: , Hyn anthology and New York Muse - a yellow journal of the arts.
Cover title: ·   , Hyn anthology.
WU UWM (RBR) V.2-3 (1970-1972).

Hyn anthology. *See* Hyn. New York. 1442528

Hyn anthology and New York muse a yellow journal of the 1442515
arts. *See* Hyn. New York.

Hyperion; a poetry journal. *Berkeley.* 1440440
ISSN: 0018-8328 Beg. date: 1970
WU UWM (RBR) V.2-5 (SUM1970-SPR/SUM1971); [n. ser.] v.2 no.2; v.2 no.3/4-v.3 (no.7-11); v.4 no.1/2; v.5 (no.12-13) (FAL1971-1976).

Hypermodern. *Santiago, D.R.* 1440453
Beg. date: 1968
WU UWM (RBR) No.1-21 (APR201968-NOV1973).

Hyphid. *Toronto.* 1440466
ISSN: 0441-6631 Beg. date: 1968
WU UWM (RBR) No.1-4 (1968).

I

i e. *New York.* 1440481
WU UWM (RBR) V.1 no.2 (1961).

i e; The Cambridge review. *Cambridge, Mass.* 1440479
ISSN: 0441-8603 LCCN: 60-39855 Beg. date: 1954 End date: 1956
Includes an unnumbered issue called Harvard 1956.
Ceased publication with no. 6, Dec. 1956.
Indexes: nos. 1-6 in no. 6.
WU UWM (RBR) V.1-v.2 no.2 (FAL1954-JUN1956); Dec 1956.

,i e; the University of South Florida Literary journal. *Tampa.* 1442530
Beg. date: 1962
WU UWM (RBR) V.1 no.1; v.3 no.1; v.4 no.1 (SPR1962-FAL1964).

I-kon. *New York.* 1442556
ISSN: 0579-4315 Beg. date: 1967 End date: 1969
Ceased publication with no. 7, Jan./Feb. 1969.
WU UWM (RBR) V.1 no.1-7 (FEB1967-JAN/FEB1969).

I o. *See* Io. Plainfield, Vt. [etc.]. 1442989

I think I hear camels coming. *Reno, Nev.* 1439186
ISSN: 0536-2172 Beg. date: 1965 End date: 1968
Cover title: Camels coming.
Ceased publication with 1968.
Superseded by Camels coming newsletter with 1972.
WU UWM (RBR) No.1-9 (AUG1965-1968).

Icarus. *Dublin, University of Dublin.* 1440503
ISSN: 0019-1027 Beg. date: 1950
WU UWM (RBR) No.28,30-34,36-47,49-55 (1959-1968/1969).

Icarus. *London.* 0937965
Beg. date: 1962 End date: 1962
WU UWM (RBR) No.1-3 (MAY1962-JAN1963).

Icarus; a poetry quarterly. *Baltimore [etc.].* 1440494
Beg. date: 1973
WU UWM (RBR) V.1-v.4 no.3; v.5 no.1 (SUM1973-1977).

Ice; a one shot magazine. *Brightlingsea, Essex, Eng.* 1440529
WU UWM (RBR) V.1 no.1 (n.d.).

Iconograph. *See* New iconograph. New York. 1482649

Iconograph. *New Orleans.* 1440531
LCCN: 45-43750 Beg. date: 1940 End date: 1043
Reproduced from type-written copy.
Title varies: no.3, Iconograph press pamphlet.
Absorbed Motive with March 1941.
Ceased publication with no. 8, May 1943.
WU UWM (RBR) No.1-8 (FAL1940-MAR1943); special issue 1950.

Iconograph press pamphlet. *See* Iconograph. New Orleans. 1440544

Iconolatre. *County Durham, Eng.* 1440557
ISSN: 0019-1140 Beg. date: 1963
Subtitle varies.
WU UWM (RBR) No.12-24a (1965-1969).

Id. *Belfast.* 1468883
Beg. date: 1971
WU UWM (RBR) No.1-4 (1971).

Idaho. State College, Pocatello. Department of English. L A 201. *See* L A 201. Pocatello, Id., Department of English, Idaho State College. 1493623

Idaho. State University, Pocatello. Dragonfly. *See* Dragonfly. Pocatello, Idaho, Idaho State University. 1435106

Idaho. State University, Pocatello. Rendezvous. *See* Rendezvous. Pocatello, Idaho, Idaho State University. 1222000

Idaho. State University, Pocatello. Department of English. Iota. *See* Iota. [Pocatello, Id.], English Department, Idaho State University. 1468946

Idaho Poets' and Writers' Guild. Guild. *See* Guild. Idaho Falls, Idaho, Idaho Poets' and Writers' Guild. 1439972

Idea and image. *New York.* 144056A
ISSN: 0536-3187 Beg. date: 1967
First issue, called charter issue, unnumbered but constitutes vol. 1 no. 1.
WU UWM (RBR) V.1 no.1-2 (1967-1968).

Identity magazine. *Cambridge, Mass.* 0325317
ISSN: 0019-1469
WU UWM (RBR) No.13,22 (1960-1966).

Idiom. *Passaic, N.J.* 1440585
ISSN: 0445-2321 Beg. date: 1953
"Experimental writing of unusual direction and interest."
WU UWM (RBR) V.1 no.1-2 (SPR-SUM1953).

The Idiot. *San Francisco, Michaeljohn Publications.* 1440598
WU UWM (RBR) No.2-4 (SEP-DEC1965).

Ikon. *See* I-kon. New York. 1442569

Ikon. *Leeds, Eng., Leeds University Union.* 1442571
WU UWM (RBR) Autumn 1964; Spring 1965; v.1 no.3-4 (1966).

Illinois. Northeastern Illinois University, Chicago. College of Arts and Sciences. Department of English. *See* Great Lakes review. Chicago, Northeastern Illinois University, College of Arts and Sciences, Departments of English and History. 1122530

Illinois. Northeastern Illinois University, Chicago. College of Arts and Sciences. Department of History. Great Lakes review. *See* Great Lakes review. Chicago, Northeastern Illinois University, College of Arts and Sciences, Departments of English and History. 1122543

Illinois. Northeastern Illinois University, Chicago. Department of English. Great Lakes review. *See* Great Lakes review. Chicago, Northeastern Illinois University, College of Arts and Sciences, Departments of English and History. 1122556

Illinois. Northeastern Illinois University, Chicago. Department of History. Great Lakes review. *See* Great Lakes review. Chicago, Northeastern Illinois University, College of Arts and Sciences, Departments of English and History. 1122569

Illinois. Southern Illinois University, Carbondale. English Club. Search. *See* Search. Carbondale, Ill., Southern Illinois University Press. 1529525

Illinois. State University, Normal. English Department. Triangle. *See* Triangle. Normal, Ill. 1513065

Illinois. Western Illinois University, Macomb. Mississippi Valley review. *See* Mississippi Valley review of creative writing. Macomb, Ill., Western Illinois University. 1508112

Illinois. Western Illinois University, Macomb. Mississippi Valley review of creative writing. *See* Mississippi Valley review of creative writing. Macomb, Ill., Western Illinois University. 1508090

The Illiterati. *Waldport, Ore., etc.* 0938160
Beg. date: 1943
WU UWM (RBR) No.3-6 (SUM1944-1955).

Illuminations. *San Francisco.* 1440607
ISSN: 0019-2368 Beg. date: 1965
Ceased publication.
Absorbed by Gar.
WU UWM (RBR) No.3-10 (SUM1967-SUM1975).

Illustrated paper. *Mendocino, Calif.* 0328784
WU UWM (RBR) One unnumbered, undated issue.

Image. *Castor Bay, Auckland, N.Z.* 144061A
ISSN: 0445-4464 Beg. date: 1958 End date: 1961
Subtitle varies.
Ceased publication with no.8, Aug. 1961.
WU UWM (RBR) No.1-8 (1958-AUG1961).

Images. *Dayton, Ohio.* 1440622
Beg. date: 1974
WU UWM (RBR) V.1-v.4 no.1 (1974-1977).

Images and information (sort of an art magazine). *Calgary, Alta., Art Catalyst.* 143894A
WU UWM (RBR) V.2 no.1-2 (SUM1976-1977).

Imagi. *[Allentown, Pa., etc.].* 1440635
LCCN: 64-30873 Beg. date: 1945
WU UWM (RBR) V.3 no.2/3-4; v.4; v.5-v.7 no.1 (no.12-20) (SUM/FAL1947-1956).

Imago. *Montreal [etc.].* 1440648
ISSN: 0085-1744 Beg. date: 1964 End date: 1974
Ceased publication with no. 20, 1974.
WU UWM (RBR) No.1-20 ([SEP[1964-1974).

Impact. *Sunnyvale, Calif., The Commentators' Press.* 1528819
Beg. date: 1977
"An international quarterly of contemporary poetry."
WU UWM (RBR) V.1 no.1-3 (MAR-SEP1977).

Impetus. *Deland, Fla.* 1440650
Beg. date: 1958 End date: 1964
Issued in cooperation with the Creative Writing Workshop at Stetson University, Deland, Florida.
Continued by Southern poetry review with Fall 1964.
WU   UWM (RBR) No.3-8 (WIN1959-SPR1964).

Impetus. Chapbook; southern poetry today. *Deland, Fla.* 1442597
ISSN: 0445-4847 Beg. date: 1960
WU   UWM (RBR) No.2 (1962).

Imprimatur; a folio of personalities, impressions and observations; an adventure in expression. *Cincinnati.* 1442619
Beg. date: 1941
Published by the Auburncrest Library.
WU   UWM (RBR) Summer 1942 v.1 no.8-10 (SUM1944-AUT1945).

Imprimatur; a literary quarterly for bibliophiles. *Cincinnati [etc.].* 0938461
LCCN: 52-34969 Beg. date: 1947 End date: 1947
Ceased publication with vol. 1 no. 2/3, April/July 1947.
WU   UWM (RBR) V.1 no.1-2/3 (JAN-APR/JUL1947).

Imprint; poetry quarterly. *Brislington, Bristol, Eng.* 1440676
ISSN: 0019-3038 Beg. date: 1967
WU   UWM (RBR) No.1-5 (1967-1969).

Imprints quarterly. *Kanona, N.Y.* 1440689
ISSN: 0019-3070 Beg. date: 1967
WU   UWM (RBR) V.1-v.7 no.1 (WIN1967-WIN1973).

Impromptu. *New York.* 1440691
Beg. date: 1931
WU   UWM (RBR) V.1 no.1-2 (JAN-APR1931).

Improving Poets Arriving at Critical Thought. Wisconsin's 1519088
impact! *See* Wisconsin's impact! [n.p.].

Impulse. *Boise, Idaho, Boise College.* 1442647
Beg. date: 1966
WU   UWM (RBR) Winter 1966/1967.

Impulse. *Toronto, Erindale College, University of Toronto.* 1442662
ISSN: 0315-3649 LCCN: 73-640450 Beg. date: 1971
WU   UWM (RBR) V.1-v.6 no.1 (FAL1971-1977).

In a nutshell. *Sacramento, Hibiscus Press.* 1440700
ISSN: 0146-0129 LCCN: sc77-59 Beg. date: 1975
WU   UWM (RBR) V.1; v.2 no.1-3; v.3 (WIN1975-1977).

In particular. *Oxford, Eng.* 1440713
ISSN: 0019-3216 Beg. date: 1967
WU   UWM (RBR) Summer 1967.

In the light. *[Iowa City, Iowa, etc.]* 1528821
Beg. date: 1975
WU   UWM (RBR) No.1-3 (AUG1975-MAR1977).

In transit. *Bronx, N.Y., Van Cortlandt Workmen's Circle* 1442688
Community House (teen age writer's workshop).
WU   UWM (RBR) V.1 no.1-2 (n.d.-n.d.).

In transit. *See* Intransit. Eugene, Ore., 1482677

Incept. *Shalford, Surrey, Eng.* 1440726
WU   UWM (RBR) No.1-2 (n.d.-n.d.).

The Independent. *New York, Exposé [etc.].* 1442690
ISSN: 0019-364X Beg. date: 1951
Title varies: nos. 1-52, Nov. 1951-March 1956, Exposé; The Independent and the Californian.
WU   UWM (RBR) No.32-86,93-200 (1955/1956-1973).

Independent and the Californian. *See* Independent. New 1442712
York, Exposé [etc.].

Indian Committee for Cultural Freedom. *See* Quest. 0334032
[Bombay, S. Singh, etc. for the Indian Committee for Cultural Freedom].

Indian scrapbook. *Palo Alto, Calif.* 1468905
ISSN: 0537-2496
WU   UWM (RBR) Autumn 1965; Autumn 1966; Winter 1966/1967.

Indiana. University. Department of English. Pegasus. *See* 1498626
Pegasus. Bloomington, Ind., Department of English, University of Indiana.

Indiana. University. Department of Fine Arts. Design 1435792
Program. Experimental typography series. *See* Experimental typography series. [Bloomington], Design Program of the Dept. of Fine Arts, Indiana University.

Indiana. University. English Department. Folio. *See* Folio. 1437293
Bloomington, Ind., English Dept., Indiana University.

Indiana writes. *Bloomington, Ind.* 1440739
Beg. date: 1976
WU   UWM (RBR) V.1-v.2 no.1 (WIN1976-1977).

Indiana Writes. Writer's newsletter. *See* Writer's 1529904
newsletter. Bloomington, Ind., Indiana Writes.

Indigo; the voice of American poets. *New York.* 1440741
Beg. date: 1974
WU   UWM (RBR) V.1 no.1-11; v.2 no.1-8 (FEB1974-AUG1975).

Individual action; an anarchist publication. *New York.* 1440767
ISSN: 0445-9113 Beg. date: 1952
WU   UWM (RBR) V.1 no.1-17; v.2 no.1-18; v.3 no.1-12 (OCT311952-NOV1955).

Inferno. *San Francisco, Inferno Press.* 144077A
ISSN: 0446-138X Beg. date: 1950 End date: 1966
Ceased publication with no. 11, 1966.
WU   UWM (RBR) No.1-11 (1950-1966).

The Informer; a literary magazine. *Oxford [etc.] Eng., Circle* 1440754
Books.
ISSN: 0020-0840 Beg. date: 1966
WU   UWM (RBR) No.1-7 (JUN1966-n.d.).

Ingluvin. *Montreal.* 1440782
Beg. date: 1970
WU   UWM (RBR) No.1-2 (1970-JAN/MAR1971).

Inherited. *London.* 1440795
ISSN: 0021-1332.
WU   UWM (RBR) No.6-7 ([1969]).

Inland. *Salt Lake City, Inscriptors.* 1440804
ISSN: 0020-1456 Beg. date: 1957 End date: 1962
"Incorporating Interim."
Ceased publication with vol. 4 no. 3, Spring 1962?
WU   UWM (RBR) V.1-3; v.4 no.1,3 (SUM1957-SPR1962).

Inlet. *Norfolk, Va.* 1468918
WU   UWM (RBR) No.2-4 (1973-1975).

Inner City Cultural Center, Los Angeles. Neworld. *See* 1495228
Neworld. Los Angeles.

Inner space. *New York [etc.].* 1442725
ISSN: 0537-717X Beg. date: 1966
Subtitle varies.
WU   UWM (RBR) No.1-2 (1966).

The Inner well. *Marion, Ind., Harris Publications.* 144082A
ISSN: 0537-7153 Beg. date: 1967
WU   UWM (RBR) V.1 no.1-4 (JUL1967-JAN/FEB1968).

Inprint. *Dobbs Ferry, N.Y.* 1438952
Beg. date: 1975
WU   UWM (RBR) No.1-8 (JUN1975-1977).

Input. *[Valley Stream, N.Y.].* 1440845
ISSN: 0446-2866 Beg. date: 1963 End date: 1965
Ceased publication with vol. 2 no. 1 (no. 5), Spring 1965.
WU   UWM (RBR) V.1 no.1-4; v.2 no.1 (no.5) (DEC1963-SPR1965).

Inscape. *Albuquerque.* 1440858
ISSN: 0446-2904 Beg. date: 1959 End date: 1962
Ceased publication with no. 8 (vol. 3 no. 2), 1962.
WU   UWM (RBR) No.1-6 (1959-WIN1960/1961); no.7-8 (v.3 no.1-2) (n.d.-1962).

Inscape. *Ottawa, Univ. of Ottawa. Dept. of English. Faculty* 0931197
of Arts.
ISSN: 0020-1782 Beg. date: 1959
"Assembled by the Hopkin's Club."
WU   UWM (RBR) V.4 no.1; v.5 no.1-2; v.6 no.1-3; v.7 no.1-4; v.8 no.2; v.9 no.1; v.10 no.1-2; v.11 no.2-3 (SUM1965-FAL1974); 1977.

Inscape. *Phoenix, Baleen Press.* 1440832
ISSN: 0020-1774 Beg. date: 1970
New Series of a publication with the same title published in Albuquerque, 1959-1962.
WU   UWM (RBR) V.1-3; v.4 no.1-3; v.5 no.1 (SPR1970-1976).

Inscape; Sarah Lawrence literary review. *See* Sarah 1508021
Lawrence literary review. Bronxville, N.Y., Sarah Lawrence College.

Inscriptors, Salt Lake City. Inland. *See* Inland. Salt Lake 1440817
City, Inscriptors.

The Insect trust gazette. *Berkeley.* 1440860
ISSN: 0573-3774 Beg. date: 1964
WU   UWM (RBR) No.1-3 (SUM1964-SUM1965).

Insert. *Portland, Ore.* 1440873
ISSN: 0446-2963 Beg. date: 1955
WU   UWM (RBR) V.1 no.1-4 (SEP1955-1962).

Inside. *New York.* 1440886
ISSN: 0446-2971 Beg. date: 1962 End date: 1963
Supersedes Inside science fiction.
Ceased publication with 1963.
WU   UWM (RBR) No.1-2 (OCT1962-JUN1963).

Inside and science fiction advertiser. *See* Inside science fiction. New York [etc.]. 1441614

Inside science fiction. *New York [etc.].* 1441601
ISSN: 0046-303X
Title varies: nos. 1-17,   -March 1957, Inside and science fiction advertiser.
Ceased publication.
Superseded by Inside with Oct. 1962.
WU   UWM (RBR) No.14-18 (MAR1956-OCT1957).

Instead. *[New York].* 1440899
Beg. date: 1948
Some issues lack numbering and date.
No. 1 lacks title.
No. 2 also called Brunidor portfolio no. 1.
WU   UWM (RBR) No.1-7 (1948-n.d.).

Institute for Research in Art and Technology. Amazing grace. *See* Amazing grace. London, Institute for Research in Art and Technology. 1429908

Institute of Afro-American Affairs.   Black creation. *See* Black creation. New York, Institute of Afro-American Affairs. 0344103

Institute of Contemporary Arts, London.   Magazine of the Institute of Contemporary Arts. *See* Magazine of the Institute of Contemporary Arts. [London]. 1495663

Insurgent. *San Francisco, W E B DuBois Clubs of America.* 1440910
ISSN: 0538-2653 Beg. date: 1965
WU   UWM (RBR) V.1 no.1 (MAR/APR1965).

Intak'. *Sheffield, Eng.?* 1440949
Beg. date: 1971
"The journal of the Yorkshire Poets' Association."
WU   UWM (RBR) V.1 pt.1-2 (1971-1972); 1973; no.4 (1974/1975); 1976.

Inter-American University of Puerto Rico. Between worlds. *See* Between worlds. [Denver, A. Swallow]. 1438363

Inter-Hillel Council of Northern California. Burning bush. *See* Burning bush. [San Francisco], The Inter-Hillel Council of Northern California. 143852A

Inter-Hillel Council of Northern California. Seneh ha-boer. *See* Burning bush. [San Francisco], The Inter-Hillel Council of Northern California. 1438517

Intercourse. *Berkeley, Calif.* 144163A
WU   UWM (RBR) No.3-5b (1966-JAN1970).

Intercourse. *Montreal, Poverty Press.* 1441627
ISSN: 0020-5311 Beg. date: 1966
WU   UWM (RBR) No.1-16 (1966-1970).

Interim. *Los Angeles [etc.], Mattachine Society, Inc.* 1441642
ISSN: 0534-6282
WU   UWM (RBR) June, Oct. 1956; Jan., May, Aug., Dec. 1957; Nov. 1958; Mar., June, Sept., Dec. 1959; no.1-4 (1960); May, Aug, 1961; Feb. 1962; Jan. 1963.

Interim. *Seattle, Gateway Print Company.* 0350665
ISSN: 0020-5478 LCCN: 49-20472 Beg. date: 1944 End date: 1958
WU   UWM (RBR) V.1-v.4 no.1/2 (SUM1944-1954).

Interim pad. *San Francisco, City Lights.* 1468920
Beg. date: 1967
WU   UWM (RBR) No.1 (SEP1967).

Interlace. *Lima, Peru.* 1442738
Beg. date: 1968
In English and Spanish.
WU   UWM (RBR) V.1 no.1 (1968).

Intermedia. *Los Angeles, Century City Educational Arts Project.* 1441668
ISSN: 0147-5754 LCCN: 76-649539 Beg. date: 1974
WU   UWM (RBR) V.1 no.1-4 (1974-1976).

Intermission. *Chicago, Hull House Theater.* 1442740
WU   UWM (RBR) V.2 no.26,28-29,31-33,35-36 (JAN231966-JUN261966); Sept.-Oct. 1966; v.3 no.2-7,11/12; v.4 no.1 (1967).

The International arts. *New York.* 1442766
Beg. date: 1925 End date: 1925
Ceased publication with vol. 1 no. 2, August 1925?.
WU   UWM (RBR) V.1 no.2 (AUG1925).

The International Henry Miller letter. *Nijmegen, Netherlands.* 1442779
ISSN: 0535-0786 Beg. date: 1961
WU   UWM (RBR) No.1-5,7 (JUN1961-MAR1966).

International Olympiad of the Revolutionary Non-Professional Theatres.   Bulletin. *See* International theatre. Moscow. 1442844

International poetry review. *Greensboro, N.C., Green River Press.* 1442794
ISSN: 0145-0786 LCCN: 76-647056 Beg. date: 1975
French, German, Spanish and/or English.
WU   UWM (RBR) V.1; v.2 no.1-2; v.3 no.1 (SPR1975-1977).

International poetry review. *Hollywood, Calif. [etc.].* 1442781
ISSN: 0020-8329 Beg. date: 1960
WU   UWM (RBR) V.3 no.2-3/4; v.8 no.2-3 (SPR1964-JUN1971).

International socialist journal. *Rome.* 0361925
LCCN: 67-93336
Ceased with vol. 5, no. 26/27, 1968.
Index last no.
WU   UWM (RBR) Year 1 no.1-2 (JAN/FEB-APR1964).

The international theatre. *Moscow.* 1442816
Beg. date: 1932 End date: 1935
Irregular, 1932-1933; bimonthly (irreg.), 1934 (complete in 4 issues); 1935, complete in one issue?
Published by the International Union of the Revolutionary Theatre (no. 1, Oct. 1932, under its former name: International Workers' Dramatic Union).
Nos. 1-5, [Oct.] 1932-1933, also called Bulletin of the International Olympiad of the Revolutionary Non-Professional Theatres (with variations: no. 1, Oct. 1932, lacks title International theatre.
Issued also in Russian, French and German.
Ceased publication with no. 10, 1935.
WU   UWM (RBR) No.1 (1934).

International theatre. *New York.* 1442803
ISSN: 0444-2172 Beg. date: 1951 End date: 1955
Ceased publication with vol. 1 no.1, 1955.
WU   UWM (RBR) 1955.

International Union of the Revolutionary Theatre. International theatre. *See* International theatre. Moscow. 1442829

International Workers' Dramatic Union.   International theatre. *See* International theatre. Moscow. 1442831

International writers fellowship. *Los Angeles, Spearman Publications.* 1442857
WU   UWM (RBR) No.2 (SEP1966).

Intersection; a magazine of new writing. *Cleveland, Ohio, Literary Arts Association, Inc.* 144286A
ISSN: 0444-3489 Beg. date: 1953 End date: 1953
Ceased publication with vol. 1 no.2, Winter 1953.
WU   UWM (RBR) V.1 no.1-2 (SPR-WIN1953).

Intersection newsletter. *San Francisco, A Center for Religion and the Arts.* 1442872
Beg. date: 1969
WU   UWM (RBR) V.7 no.2; v.8 no.1-3; v.9 no.1-2 (SPR1975-1977).

Interstate. *Austin, Tex.* 1442898
Beg. date: 1974
WU   UWM (RBR) No.1-4 (SPR1974-SUM1975); no.5-6/7 (v.2 no.1-2/3) (1976); v.2 no.4; v.3 no.1 (1977).

Intransit. *Eugene, Ore., Toad's Press.* 1442907
WU   UWM (RBR) Summer, Fall 1965; 1966-1969.

Intrepid. *New York.* 0365215
ISSN: 0020-9864 Beg. date: 1964
Indexes: No. 1-20 in no. 23-24.
WU   UWM (RBR) No.1-35 (MAR1964-1976).

Intro. *[New York].* 144291A
ISSN: 0444-3705 LCCN: 54-19732 Beg. date: 1950 End date: 1953
Ceased publication with vol. 2 no. 2, June 1953.
Superseded by Intro bulletin; a literary newspaper of the arts with Oct. 1955.
WU   UWM (RBR) V.1 no.1-3/4; v.2 no.1-2 (AUT1950-1953).

Intro bulletin; a literary newspaper of the arts. *New York.* 1442922
ISSN: 0535-4947   Beg. date: 1955   End date: 1957
Supersedes Intro.
Ceased publication with vol. 2 no.3, Dec. 1957?
WU   UWM (RBR) V.1 no.1-11/12; v.2 no.1-2 (OCT1955-DEC1957).

Introductions from an island. *Victoria, B.C., University of Victoria.* 1442935
ISSN: 0318-3270   Beg. date: 1969
WU   UWM (RBR) 1973-1976.

Invictus; contemporary and traditional writings. *Phoenix [etc.], J & A Publications.* 1442950
Subtitle varies slightly.
WU   UWM (RBR) Spring 1974-Spring 1976.

Invisible city. *Fairfax, Calif., Red Hill Press.* 1442963
ISSN: 0147-4936   LCCN: 77-649984   Beg. date: 1971
Supersedes Red Hill Press, ISSN 0034-2009.
WU   UWM (RBR) No.1-20 (FEB1971-1976).

Invitation to learning. *See* Invitation to learning reader. *New York.* 0365754

Invitation to learning reader. *New York.* 0365767
ISSN: 0535-5397   Beg. date: 1951   End date: 1957
Ceased publication with v. 6, no. 4 (Mar.? 1957).
Title varies: v. 1-2, Invitation to learning.
WU   UWM (RBR) V.1-v.4 no.1 (SPR1951-1954).

Io. *Plainfield, Vt. [etc.].* 1442976
ISSN: 0021-0331   Beg. date: 1964
WU   UWM (RBR) No.1-23 (1964-1976).

Iota. *[Pocatello, Id.], English Department, Idaho State University.* 1468933
ISSN: 0578-5960   Beg. date: 1966
Title printed in Greek letters.
WU   UWM (RBR) V.1 no.1-3; v.2 no.1-2 ([1966]-SPR1968).

Iowa. University. *See* American prefaces; a journal of critical and imaginative writing. *[Iowa City, University of Iowa Press].* 0366746

Iowa. University. Graduate College.   Iowa review. *See* Iowa review. Iowa City, University of Iowa, School of Letters and the Graduate College. 1338696

Iowa. University. School of Letters.   Iowa review. *See* Iowa review. Iowa City, University of Iowa, School of Letters and the Graduate College. 1338683

Iowa review. *Iowa City, University of Iowa, School of Letters and the Graduate College.* 0367530
ISSN: 0021-065X   LCCN: 76-294841   Beg. date: 1970
WU   UWM (RBR) V.1-3 (WIN1970-FAL1972).

Iowa Workshop poets/1963. *See* Statements. *Rochester, N.Y.* 1009799

Ireland to-day. *Dublin.* 1442991
Beg. date: 1936   End date: 1938
Ceased publication with vol. 3 no. 3, March 1938.
WU   UWM (RBR) V.1 no.1 (JUN1936).

Ireland today. *See* Ireland to-day. Dublin. 1443009

Irish American Cultural Institute. *See* Eire-Ireland. *St. Paul, Irish American Cultural Institute.* 036867A

Iron. *Cullercoats, Northumberland, Eng.* 1443011
Beg. date: 1973
Cover title: Iron magazine.
WU   UWM (RBR) No.2-17 (SUM1973-1977).

Iron. *Port Moody, B.C. [etc.], English Department, Simon Fraser University.* 1443037
Beg. date: 1966
WU   UWM (RBR) No.1-7 ([1966]-1969).

The Iron flute. *London, The Iron Flute Publications.* 1443052
WU   UWM (RBR) No.1 (n.d.).

Iron magazine. *See* Iron. Cullercoats, Northumberland, Eng. 1443024

Ironwood. *[Tucson, Ariz.], Ironwood Press.* 1443065
ISSN: 0047-150X   LCCN: 72-623029   Beg. date: 1972
WU   UWM (RBR) No.1-4 (SPR1972-1974); no.5-7/8 (v.3-v.4 no.1/2) (1975-1976); no.9 (1977).

Is. *Clarksville, Tenn., The Transient Press.* 1443080
Beg. date: 1973
WU   UWM (RBR) 1973.

Is. *Lakemont, Ga., Fan Press.* 1443078
Beg. date: 1971
WU   UWM (RBR) 1972.

Is. *Toronto.* 1443093
ISSN: 0047-1526   Beg. date: 1966
WU   UWM (RBR) No.1-2,4,6-7,9-15 (n.d.-SPR1973).

Ishmael. *San Francisco.* 1468959
ISSN: 0578-7939
WU   UWM (RBR) No.1 (n.d.).

Isinglass review. *Cambridge, Mass. [etc.].* 1468961
Beg. date: 1965
WU   UWM (RBR) V.1-7 (SPR1965-1975).

Island. *Toronto.* 1443102
ISSN: 0578-8099   Beg. date: 1964
WU   UWM (RBR) No.1-3 (SEP1964-MAR1965); no.6-7/8 (n.d.-n.d.).

Islands. *[Torbay, N.Z., s.n.].* 1468974
ISSN: 0110-0858   LCCN: 75-641542   Beg. date: 1972
"A New Zealand quarterly of arts and letters."
WU   UWM (RBR) V.1 no.1-2; v.2-v.5 no.1 (SPR1972-AUT1976).

Isthmus. *San Francisco.* 1443115
Beg. date: 1972
WU   UWM (RBR) No.1-5 ([1972]-1976).

It. *Platteville, Wisc. [etc.].* 1443128
ISSN: 0021-2695   Beg. date: 1965
Special issue, entitled Every significant and major anthology of contemporary American poetry since 1945, was published in lieu of nos. 17-21.
Subtitle varies.
Ceased publications.
WU   UWM (RBR) No.1-16 (SEP1967-MAR1968); special issue (1969).

It is; a magazine for abstract art. *New York.* 0371896
WU   UWM (RBR) No.1-5 (SPR1958-SPR1960).

J

J. [n.p.]. 1443130
WU UWM (RBR) No.1-5 (n.d.-n.d.).

Jabberwock; Edinburgh University review. *Edinburgh.* 1443143
WU UWM (RBR) V.4 no.1-2; v.5 no.1; v.6 no.1 (FEB1952-n.d.).

Jacaranda *Canton, Mo., Transient Press.* 1443184
Beg. date: 1964
WU UWM (RBR) No.1-8 (SEP1964-APR1966).

Jam to-day. *Northfield, Vt.* 1443197
ISSN: 0362-8302 LCCN: 76-644489 Beg. date: 1973
WU UWM (RBR) No.1-5 (1973-1977).

James Cook University of North Queensland. Department of English. LiNQ. *See* LiNQ. Townsville, Australia, Department of English, James Cook University of North Queensland. 149287A

Jana, Kesho, Leo. *Madison, Wisc.* 1443206
WU UWM (RBR) No.2 (1974).

Janus. *London.* 1468987
Beg. date: 1936
WU UWM (RBR) May 1936.

Janus. *London, Balliol College.* 1443219
WU UWM (RBR) Summer 1953.

Janus. *Seaside Park, N.J., Media consultants and publications.* 1528834
Beg. date: 1970
Also called Janus magazine.
Wu UWM (RBR) V.1 no.1; v.3 no.1-2 (SPR1970-SEP1972).

Janus; a quarterly review of letters, thought, and the new mythology. *Washington, D.C.* 1443234
Beg. date: 1929 End date: 1929
Ceased publication with vol. 1 no. 1, Nov. 1929.
WU UWM (RBR) V.1 no.1 (NOV1929).

Janus, cahiers mensuels bilingues de la jeune poésie française et américaine. *Paris.* 1443247
ISSN: 0447-3477 Beg. date: 1950
In English and French.
WU UWM (RBR) No.1-5 (MAR1950-AUT1951).

Janus & S C T H. *Venice, Calif. [etc.].* 144325A
ISSN: 0021-4272 Beg. date: 1969
Supersedes S C T H.
WU UWM (RBR) V.1-v.9 no.1 (JUL1969-1977).

Janus magazine. *See* Janus. Seaside Park, N.J., Media consultants and publications. 1528847

Janus Society of America. Drum. *See* Drum; sex in perspective. Philadelphia, Janus Society. 1435240

Japan forum. *Tokyo.* 1438532
ISSN: 0024-127X Beg. date: 1962
WU UWM (RBR) V.10-15; v.16 no.2-3 (WIN1971-1977).

Japan quarterly. *Tokyo, Asahi Shimbun-Shai.* 0376557
ISSN: 0021-4590 LCCN: 56-34321 Beg. date: 1954
WU UWM (RBR) V.1-4; v.5 no.3 (OCT/DEC1954-JUL/SEP1958).

Japanese poetry in English. *Kobe, Japan.* 1438545
ISSN: 0021-535X Beg. date: 1961
WU UWM (RBR) No.3-4 (JUN1963-AUG1965).

Jason. *[Salem, Ore.], Willamette University.* 1438558
WU UWM (RBR) Spring 1966; Spring 1967.

Jaw. *Detroit, Dept. of English, Wayne State University.* 1438573
WU UWM (RBR) Summer 1972.

Jawbone. *Seattle.* 1438599
Beg. date: 1975
WU UWM (RBR) V.1 no.1 (FAL1975).

Jazz; a quarterly of American music. *[Albany, Calif. etc.].* 1438608
ISSN: 0447-6204 LCCN: 67-33137/MN Beg. date: 1958 End date: 1960
Ceased publication with no. 5, Winter 1960.
WU UWM (RBR) No.1-5 (OCT1958-WIN1960).

Jazz forum; quarterly review of jazz and literature. *[Fordingbridge, Hants., Eng., Delphic Press].* 1438610
LCCN: 51-17469 Beg. date: 1946 End date: 1947
Ceased publication with no. 5, Autumn 1947.
WU UWM (RBR) No.1-5 ([1946]-AUT1947).

Jean's journal. *See* Jean's journal of poems. Kanona, N.Y., J & C Transcripts. 1438636

Jean's journal of poems. *Kanona, N.Y., J & C Transcripts.* 1438623
ISSN: 0021-5767 Beg. date: 1963
Cover title: Jean's journal.
WU UWM (RBR) V.2 no.4-v.6 no.3 (WIN1964-AUT1968).

The Jeffersonian review. *Charlottesville, Va., [F. Conneen III, Productions Ltd.].* 1438649
ISSN: 0094-1360 LCCN: 74-76728 Beg. date: 1973
WU UWM (RBR) V.2 no.1 (SPR1974).

Jeopardy. *Bellingham, Wash., Associated Student Body of Western Washington State College.* 1438651
ISSN: 0021-5880 Beg. date: 1966
WU UWM (RBR) No.1,3-12 (1966-SPR1976).

Jesse Stuart Exchenge. W-Hollow harvest. *See* W-Hollow harvest. Cincinnati, The Kentucky Writers' Guild, Inc., Jesse Stuart Exchange. 1518252

Jewish social studies, a quarterly journal devoted to contemporary and historical aspects of Jewish life. *New York.* 0378766
"Edited for the conference on Jewish Social Studies" (1939-January 1955, under its earlier name: Conference on Jewish Relations).
Indexes: volumes 1-25 (1939-1964) 1 volume.
WU UWM (RBR) V.1-5; v.6 no.1,3 (1939-1944).

Joglars. *Providence, R.I.* 1438677
ISSN: 0449-0622 Beg. date: 1964
WU UWM (RBR) V.1 no.1-2; no.3 (SPR1964-1966).

Johannesburg quarterly. *See* Classic. [Johannesburg]. 1431214

John Berryman studies. *Derry, Pa.* 1220027
ISSN: 0098-2199 LCCN: 75-643270 Beg. date: 1975
WU UWM (RBR) V.1-v.3 no.2 (1975-1977).

John Reed Club, Philadelphia. Left review. *See* Left review. Philadelphia, John Reed Club of Philadelphia. 1528890

John Reed Club, Philadelphia. Red pen. *See* Red pen. Philadelphia, John Reed Club. 1504309

John Reed Club of Chicago. Left front. *See* Left front. Chicago, John Reed Clubs of the Middle West, a section of the International Union of Revolutionary Writers and Artists. 1492581

John Reed Clubs of the Middle West. Left front. *See* Left front. Chicago, John Reed Clubs of the Middle West, a section of the International Union of Revolutionary Writers and Artists. 1492579

Johns Hopkins University. *See* Hopkins review. Baltimore, Johns Hopkins University. 0379654

Johns Hopkins University. Department of English. Strivers' row. *See* Strivers' row. Baltimore, Dept. of English, The Johns Hopkins University. 1132395

Joint conference; magazine of inmate writings and art. *Washington, D.C.* 143868A
ISSN: 0145-8795 LCCN: sc77-404 Beg. date: 1974
WU UWM (RBR) V.1-v.2 no.3 (FAL1974-1977).

The Jongleur; a magazine of verse. *Frizinghall, Bradford, Eng.* 1438692
Beg. date: 1927
Subtitle varies.
WU UWM (RBR) No.30 (AUT1934).

The Journal. *Detroit, Wayne State University. Monteith College.* 1438701
Beg. date: 1967
WU UWM (RBR) Summer 1967.

The Journal. *Keene, N.H.* 1438768
Published by the members of Sigma Pi Epsilon, Keene State College, Keene, New Hampshire.
WU UWM (RBR) V.2 no.2-4 (DEC1966-1967); Winter, Spring 1968; Spring 1969; Winter, Spring 1970; Winter 1971.

Journal 31. *San Francisco.* 1438727
ISSN: 0047-2921 Beg. date: 1972
WU UWM (RBR) V.1 no.1-2 (1972).

Journal for the protection of all beings. *San Francisco, City Lights Books.* 143873A
ISSN: 0075-4099 LCCN: 62-51635 Beg. date: 1961
WU UWM (RBR) No.1-3 (1961-1969).

Journal of Black poetry. *San Francisco.* 0383665
ISSN: 0021-9339 Beg. date: 1966 End date: 1974
Continued by Kitabu cha jua with vol. 1 no. 18, Summer 1974.
WU   UWM (RBR) V.1 no.2-3,5-17 (SUM1966-SUM1973).

Journal of the new African literature. *New York.* 1438742
ISSN: 0022-5118 Beg. date: 1966
Title varies slightly.
Text mainly in English; occasionally in African languages, French and Portuguese.
WU   UWM (RBR) No.1-13/14 (SPR1966-SEP1973).

The Journals of Pierre Menard. *Oxford, Eng.* 1438755
ISSN: 0449-4768 Beg. date: 1970
"A magazine devoted to poetry in translation and theory of translation."
WU   UWM (RBR) No.1 (1970).

The Joy bearer. *Poynette, Wis.* 1438965
Beg. date: 1922
WU   UWM (RBR) V.21 no.10,12; v.22 no.1-5,7-10 (OCT1958-OCT1959).

Jubilee. *Wingham [etc.], Ont., Jubilee Press.* 1438978
ISSN: 0316-8417 Beg. date: 1974
WU   UWM (RBR) No.1-3 (n.d.-n.d.).

The Judson review. *[New York, Hesperidian Press].* 1438980
ISSN: 0447-9971 LCCN: 63-13510 Beg. date: 1963
WU   UWM (RBR) V.1 (1963).

Juggler. *Notre Dame, Ind.* 1438993
Beg. date: 1947
Supersedes the periodical with the same title, published Dec. 1919-May 1934.
Published by and for the members of the Notre Dame-St. Mary's community.
Title varies: April 1947-   , Juggler of Notre Dame.
WU   UWM (RBR) V.8 no.3; v.16 no.2; v.17 no.3; v.18; v.19 no.1,3; v.20; v.21 no.1; v.22 no.3; v.23,26-30; v.31 no.1; v.32 no.2 (SPR1954-1977).

Juggler of Notre Dame. **See** Juggler. Notre Dame, Ind. 1439000

Juice. *Oakland, Calif.* 1439013
Beg. date: 1975
WU   UWM (RBR) No.1-5 (1975-1977).

Juillard. *Leeds, Eng.* 1439026
WU   UWM (RBR) Spring 1968; Spring 1968 suppl.; Dec. 1968 suppl.; Winter 1968/1969; Pinecone suppl. (1968/1969); Summer 1970; no.7-9 FAL1970-SPR1972).

Junction. *Brooklyn, N.Y., Brooklyn College, Graduate English Student Association.* 1439039
Beg. date: 1972
"A creative and critical review."
WU   UWM (RBR) V.1 no.3 (SPR1973).

The Junk; a periodical of thoughts and things. *Ogdensburg, N.Y.* 1439054
Beg. date: 1901 End date: 1902
Subtitle varies slightly.
Ceased publication with vol. 3 no. 1, April 1902?
WU   UWM (RBR) V.1-v.2 no.6 (APR1901-MAR1902).

Junkmail oracle. *Cleveland, Angry City Press.* 152885A
End date: 1969
Ceased publication with no. 5, May 1969.
WU   UWM (RBR) No.4-5 (MAY-JUN1969).

Just for all that. **See** Csakazértis. Georgetown, Guyana. 1439173

K I W C. *See* King Ida's watch chain. Newcastle upon Tyne, Eng.   1493937

K P R. *See* Kentucky poetry review. [Elizabethtown, Ky.?].   1493859

Kaleidoscope. *See* Kaleidoscope: Melbourne. Melbourne.   1482909

Kaleidoscope. *London.*   143907A
WU   UWM (RBR) No.5 (1975).

Kaleidoscope: Melbourne. *Melbourne.*   1439067
ISSN: 0449-6442 Beg. date: 1959
"A literary quarterly with a certain preference for poetry."
WU   UWM (RBR) V.2 no.1 (SUM1961/1962-AUT1962).

Kamadhenu. *Pullman, Wash. [etc.].*   1439082
ISSN: 0022-8044 LCCN: 72-622981 Beg. date: 1970
WU   UWM (RBR) V.1 no.1-2; v.3 no.1-2; v.4-5; no.6/7 (MAR1970-APR1975).

Kansas. Fort Hays State College, Hays. Sheaf. *See* Sheaf. Hays, Kan., Fort Hays State College.   1507369

Kansas. State College, Fort Hays. Division of Language, Literature, and Speech. Smoky Hill review. *See* Smoky Hill review. Hays, Kansas, Division of Language, Literature, and Speech, Fort Hays Kansas State College.   1510074

Kansas. State University, Wichita. Department of English. Mikrokosmos. *See* Mikrokosmos. Wichita, Kan., Department of English, Wichita State University.   1496536

Kansas. State University, Wichita. Student Government Association. Gazebo. *See* Gazebo. Wichita, Kan., Student Government Association, Wichita State University.   1437750

Kansas City courier. *See* American courier; dedicated to the mental and material improvement of man. Kansas City, Mo.   1441809

Kapustka Literary Foundation. Kapustkan; an American journal of dynamic democracy. *See* Kapustkan; an American journal of dynamic democracy. Chicago, The Kapustka Literary Foundation.   1439104

The Kapustkan; an American journal of dynamic democracy. *Chicago, The Kapustka Literary Foundation.*   1439095
LCCN: 45-53038 Beg. date: 1940
Subtitle varies.
Began publication with May 1940.
Reproduced from typewritten copy.
Absorbed Vers libre.
Vol. 1 nos. -4 lack subtitle.
WU   UWM (RBR) V.1 no.11/12; v.6 no.10 (FEB1941-MAY1946).

Karaki. *Victoria, B.C., English Department, University of Victoria.*   1439117
WU   UWM (RBR) No.2-3,5-6 (FEB1972-1977).

Karamu. *Charleston, Ill.*   1439132
WU   UWM (RBR) No.3-4 (MAY1967-JUN1968); v.2 no.1-2; v.3 no.1-3; v.4 no.1-3; v.5 no.1 (SPR1967-1977).

Karuba; a synthesis of verse, image and typography. *[Norman, Okla.], Karuba Press.*   1439145
ISSN: 0449-9018 Beg. date: 1957
WU   UWM (RBR) No.1 (1957).

Karyn. *Los Angeles.*   1439158
WU   UWM (RBR) V.1 no.1; no.4 (n.d.-1966).

Kast. *Tokyo, Club Kast.*   1493768
"International art and poetry."
Title varies: Olivant.
WU   UWM (RBR) No.4-5 (JUL1955-APR1956).

Kauri. *Washington, D.C. [etc.], Will Inman.*   1493783
ISSN: 0453-4050 Beg. date: 1964 End date: 1971
"An American Congress of Poets."
Ceased publication with no. 33, Dec. 1970/Jan. 1971.
WU   UWM (RBR) No.1-33 (APR/MAY1964-DEC1970/JAN1971); Book no.1-2 (1964-n.d.).

Kavita. *Calcutta, Buddhadeva Bose.*   1493805
WU   UWM (RBR) V.16 no.1 (serial no.67); v.17 no.4 (serial no.74) (DEC1950-JUN1953).

Kayak. *Santa Cruz, Calif.*   0397931
ISSN: 0022-9555 LCCN: 75-644631 Beg. date: 1964
Began publication in 1964.
WU   UWM (RBR) No.1-   (AUT1964-).

Keepsake poems. *Richmond, Surrey, Eng., Keepsake Press.*   1493818
Beg. date: 1972
Each vol. has a distinctive title.
WU   UWM (RBR) No.1-2,5-29 (1972-1976).

The Kelsey review. *Trenton, N.J., Trenton Junior College.*   1493820
ISSN: 0451-6338 LCCN: 67-5463 Beg. date: 1962
WU   UWM (RBR) V.1-5 (AUT1962-SPR1967).

Kent and Sussex Poetry Society. Poetry folio. *See* Poetry folio. Horsmonden, Kent, Eng., Kent and Sussex Poetry Society.   1501465

Kentucky poetry review. *[Elizabethtown, Ky.?].*   1493846
Beg. date: 1976
"Poems by Kentuckians and others."
Title varies: vols. 1-11, 1964-1976, Approaches.
Also called K P R.
WU   UWM (RBR) V.12 no.1-3; v.13 no.1-2 (WIN1976-1977).

Kenyon College, Gambier, Ohio. Hika. *See* Hika. [Gambier, Ohio], Kenyon College.   1442478

Kenyon College, Gambier, Ohio. Hika magazine. *See* Hika. [Gambier, Ohio], Kenyon College.   1442493

Keryx. *Stamford, Conn., St. Basil's College.*   1493874
WU   UWM (RBR) V.3 no.3-4; v.4 no.1-2,4; v.5 no.1 (SUM1950-SUM1953).

Key poets. *Denver, A. Swallow.*   149389A
ISSN: 0451-7849 Beg. date: 1950
Each vol. has also a distinctive title.
WU   UWM (RBR) No.2-10 (1950).

Khasmik quarterly. *Annandale-Sydney, Australia, Khasmik Enterprises.*   1493909
Beg. date: 1974
Two issues published in 1974 prior to vol. 1 no. 1, Jan. 1975.
WU   UWM (RBR) Ed.1 (1974); no.1 (1974); v.1 no.1 (JAN1975).

Kinesis. *Milford, Pa., Virginia Kidd.*   1493978
Beg. date: 1969
WU   UWM (RBR) No.1-3 (FEB1969-DEC1970).

King Ida's watch chain. *Newcastle upon Tyne, Eng.*   1493911
Also called KIWC.
WU   UWM (RBR) One unnumbered, undated issue.

King James* version. *See* King James review. Wilkes-Barre, Pa.   1493952

King James review. *Wilkes-Barre, Pa.*   149394A
Beg. date: 1973
Title varies: vol. 1 nos. 1-2, Winter-Spring 1973, King James* version.
WU   UWM (RBR) V.1 no.1-3 (WIN1973-AUT/WIN1973).

Kingdom come. *Oxford [etc.].*   1493965
LCCN: 44-48249 Beg. date: 1939
"The magazine of war-time Oxford" (varies).
Absorbed Bolero with Spring 1940, Light and dark with Summer 1940.
WU   UWM (RBR) V.1-2; v.3 no.9 (NOV1939-NOV/DEC1941).

Kings College, London. Centigrade. *See* Centigrade. London, Kings College.   1433793

The Kinsman. *Bethpage, N.Y., Kinsman Press, Inc.*   1493980
ISSN: 0451-9744 LCCN: 67-122852 Beg. date: 1961
WU   UWM (RBR) V.2 no.3 (FAL1962).

Kitabu cha jua. *San Francisco.*   1266916
Beg. date: 1974
Continues Journal of Black poetry with vol. 1 no. 18, Summer 1974.
WU   UWM (RBR) V.1 no.18-19 (SUM1974-SUM1975).

KIWC. *See* King Ida's watch chain. Newcastle upon Tyne, Eng.   1493924

Klactoveedsedsteen. *Heidelberg, Panic Press.*   1505175
WU   UWM (RBR) No.0,4,23 (n.d.-SEP1967).

The Knocker. *Philadelphia, Knocker Co.*   1493993
LCCN: 2-19431 Beg. date: 1901 End date: 1901
Ceased publication with vol. 1 no. 6, Oct. 1901.
WU   UWM (RBR) V.1 no.1-6 (MAY1901-OCT1901).

Koan. *Boulder, Colo., Experimental Cinema Group,* 1494000
University of Colorado.
   ISSN: 0454-0964 Beg. date: 1966
   WU   UWM (RBR) V.2 no.1 (WIN1967/1968).

Kolokon. *Durham, Eng., Peter Lattin.* 1494026
   ISSN: 0454-238x Beg. date: 1966
   WU   UWM (RBR) V.2 no.1 (SPR1967).

Konglomerati. *Gulfport, Fla., Konglomerati Press.* 1494039
   ISSN: 0146-2377
   "A magazine of visual poetry."
   WU   UWM (RBR) Four unnumbered, undated issues.

The Kontakion. *[n.p.].* 1494041
   WU   UWM (RBR) One unnumbered, undated issue.

Kontexts. *Whimple, Exeter, Devon, Eng. [etc.], Michael* 1494054
Gibbs.
   "An occasional review of concrete/visual/experimental poetry."
   WU   UWM (RBR) No.2-10 (SUM1970-1977).

Koolinda. *East Gordon, New South Wales, Wayside Press.* 1494067
   Beg. date: 1943
   WU   UWM (RBR) No.1-10 (OCT1943-DEC1955).

Kosmos. *New Milford, N.J., Milky Way Press.* 1493495
   Beg. date: 1975
   "Milky way quarterly."
   Editor: Kosrof Chantikian.
   WU   UWM (RBR) No.1-2 (1975).

Kosmos. *Philadelphia.* 1493504
   Beg. date: 1933 End date: 1935
   "Dynamic stories of today."
   Ceased publication with vol. 4 no. 2, Aug. 1935.
   WU   UWM (RBR) V.3 no.1,3 (AUG/SEP1934-FEB/MAR1935).

Krax. *Leeds, Yorkshire, Eng.* 149352A
   WU   UWM (RBR) No.2-11 ([1972]-1977).

Ktaadn. *Houghton, N.Y., John Leax and Lionel Basney.* 1493532
   ISSN: 0023-3536 Beg. date: 1970
   WU   UWM (RBR) V.1 no.1-2 (1970-1974?).

Kudzu. *Cayce, S.C.* 1528862
   Beg. date: 1977
   WU   UWM (RBR) No.1,3 (1977,NOV/DEC1977).

Kuksu. *Nevada City, Calif., Kuksu Press.* 1493545
   "Journal of backcountry writing."
   Title varies: nos. 1-2,   -Spring 1973, Kyoi; no. 3, Spring 1974, Kyoi/Kuksu.
   WU   UWM (RBR) No.2-6 (SPR1973-1977).

Kulchur. *New York.* 0404411
   ISSN: 0454-7852 Beg. date: 1960 End date: 1965
   Ceased publication with vol. 5, Winter 1965.
   Indexes: vols. 1-5, Spring 1960-Winter 1965/1966 (included in Whe're, no. 1, Summer 1966).
   WU   UWM (RBR) V.1-5 (no.1-20) (SPR1960-WIN1965/1966).

Kumquat. *Montclair, N.J., The Kumquat Press.* 1493573
   ISSN: 0454-6253 Beg. date: 1967
   WU   UWM (RBR) No.1-3 L1967-1971).

Kyoi. *See* Kuksu. *Nevada City, Calif., Kuksu Press.* 1493558

Kyoi/Kuksu. *See* Kuksu. *Nevada City, Calif., Kuksu Press.* 1493560

L

L A. *Claremont, Calif., D and R Pub. Co.* 1493586
ISSN: 0456-9407 Beg. date: 1958 End date: 1961
Ceased publication with vol. 2 no. 2, Dec. 1960/Jan. 1961.
WU   UWM (RBR) V.1-v.2 no.2 (OCT1958-DEC1960/JAN1961).

L A 201. *Pocatello, Id., Department of English, Idaho State College.* 1493610
Beg. date: 1962
WU   UWM (RBR) No.1-2 (MAY1962-MAY1963).

L A journal of sound. *[Los Angeles?].* 1493636
Beg. date: 1972
WU   UWM (RBR) One unnumbered issue in 1972?

L A magazine. *See* L A. Claremont, Calif., D and R Pub. Co. 1493608

L magazine. *Berkeley, Calif.* 1493651
Beg. date: 1972
Curtis Faville, editor.
WU   UWM (RBR) V.1 no.1-2/3; v.2 no.1/2 (1972-SPR1974).

Là-Bas. *College Park, Md.* 1507475
Beg. date: 1976
WU   UWM (RBR) No.1-8 (1976-1977).

La Salle College, Philadelphia. Weber-English Club. Tricon. 1513093
See Tricon. Philadelphia, Weber-English Club, La Salle College.

Labris. *Lier, Belgium.* 1505147
ISSN: 0023-7043
Editor: Max Kazan.
WU   UWM (RBR) V.3 no.4; v.4 no.3-4; v.6 no.4; v.7 no.3 (JUL1965-SUM1969).

Lace. *See* Lace review. Newark, N.J., The Joycian Court Publishers. 1493677

The Lace review. *Newark, N.J., The Joycian Court Publishers.* 1493664
ISSN: 0458-6115 Beg. date: 1967
Also called Lace.
Ceased publication with vol. 1 no. 4, 1969.
WU   UWM (RBR) V.1 no.1-4 (1967-1969).

Ladies' delight magazine. *Houston, LDM Publications.* 149368A
ISSN: 0458-6131 Beg. date: 1967
WU   UWM (RBR) V.1 no.1-3; v.2 no.4 (JUL/AUG1967-JAN/FEB1968).

Laissez faire. *Epping, Essex, Eng., Ember Press.* 1493692
Beg. date: 1971 End date: 1975
Ceased publication with no. 6, March 1975.
"A broadsheet of little magazine reviews" (varies).
WU   UWM (RBR) No.1-6 (1971-MAR1975).

Lake Forest College, Lake Forest, Illinois. Configuration. 1442108
See Configuration. Lake Forest, Ill., Lake Forest College.

The Lake Superior review. *Ironwood, Mich., Gogebic Press.* 1493701
ISSN: 0364-720X Beg. date: 1970
Title varies: vol. 1-vol. 2 no. 1, Summer 1970-Spring 1971, The Gogebic review.
"A magazine of the arts."
WU   UWM (RBR) V.1-v.8 no.2 (SUM1970-1977).

Lake Superior State College, Sault Sainte Marie, Michigan. 1519203
Woods-runner. *See* Woods-runner. Sault Ste. Marie, Mich., Lake Superior State College, Publications Committee.

Lakes and prairies. *Chicago, etc., E.R. Haggard.* 1493727
Beg. date: 1974
"A journal of writings."
WU   UWM (RBR) No.1-3 (FAL1974-1977).

Laminas. *Los Angeles.* 149373A
Beg. date: 1968
Published under the direction of Communications Board, Associated Students, University of California, Los Angeles.
WU   UWM (RBR) No.1 (MAY1968).

The Lamp in the spine. *Iowa City, Ia.* 0409336
Beg. date: 1971
WU   UWM (RBR) No.1-9 (1971-1974).

The Lampeter muse. *Annandale-on-Hudson, N.Y., Bard College.* 1493742
ISSN: 0023-7434 Beg. date: 1966
WU   UWM (RBR) V.2 no.2-3; v.3 no.1-3; v.4 no.1; Spring 1970; v.5 no.1; v.6 no.1; v.7 no.1; v.8 no.1 (DEC1966-n.d.).

Lancaster, England. University. Bowland College. 1431424
Continuum. *See* Continuum. Bailrigg, Lancaster, Eng., Bowland College, University of Lancaster.

Landfall; a New Zealand quarterly. *Christchurch, Caxton Press.* 0409875
ISSN: 0023-7930 LCCN: 50-21200 Beg. date: 1947
Indexes: Vols. 1-5, 1947-1951, with vol. 5; vols. 6-10, 1952-1956, with vol. 10; v. 11-15, 1957-1961, with vol. 15; vols. 16-20, 1962-1966, with vol. 20; vols. 21-25, 1967-1971, with vol. 25.
WU   UWM (RBR) V.4 no.1 (no.13); v.26 no.4 (no.104) (MAR1950-DEC1972).

The Lantern. *Brooklyn, N.Y.* 1507644
Beg. date: 1926
Official organ of the American Literary League, 1926-1935.
Ceased publication.
Superseded by Seven.
WU   UWM (RBR) V.1 no.3; v.3 no.1,4; v.4 no.2; v.12 no.3; v.26 no.3-v.28 no.1; v.28 no.3-v.29 no.2 (MAY1927-APR/JUN1955).

Laomedon review. *Mississaugo, Ontario, Erindale College, Univ. of Toronto.* 1492384
ISSN: 0382-8824 Beg. date: 1975
WU   UWM (RBR) V.1-v.2 no.1; v.3 no.1 (DEC1974/JAN1975-1976).

Lapis lazuli. *Corvallis, Ore.* 1528875
Beg. date: 1977
WU   UWM (RBR) V.1 no.1-2 (1977).

The Lark. *San Francisco.* 0410698
LCCN: 7-21067 Beg. date: 1895 End date: 1897
Vol. 2 contains the "Epi-lark; no. 25", published May 1, 1897.
Ceased publication with vol. 2 (no. 25), May 1, 1897.
WU   UWM (RBR) No.1-25 (MAY1895-APR1897); Lark almanack: 1899.

Larus, The celestial visitor. *Lynn, Press of the Lone Gull.* 0410735
LCCN: 32-31984 Beg. date: 1927 End date: 1928
With which has been combined Tempo.
Ceased publication with vol. 1 no. 7, June 1928.
WU   UWM (RBR) V.1 no.1-5/7 (FEB1927-APR/JUN1928).

Larvae du Golden Gate. *San Francisco.* 1492406
ISSN: 0023-8511 Beg. date: 1968
WU   UWM (RBR) No.1-3 (1968).

LaSalle College, Philadelphia. Weber-English Club. Tricon. 1513102
See Tricon. Philadelphia, Weber-English Club, La Salle College.

The Last call. *Houston.* 1492419
WU   UWM (RBR) V.2 no.3,5-11 (FEB-OCT1951).

The Last cookie. *San Francisco.* 1492421
Beg. date: 1972
WU   UWM (RBR) V.1 no.1 (1972).

The Last times. *San Francisco, Vortex Printers.* 1492434
WU   UWM (RBR) One unnumbered issue in 1967.

Latin American Bureau of Journalism. Don Quijote. *See* 1435030
Don Quijote; revista panamericana. Hollywood, Calif., Latin American Bureau of Journalism.

The Latin quarter-ly. *New York, Parnassus Press, [etc.].* 1492447
LCCN: 54-50787 Beg. date: 1933 End date: 1934
Ceased publication with vol. 1 no. 3, Autumn 1934.
WU   UWM (RBR) V.1 no.1-3 (SEP1933-AUT1934).

Latin quarterly. *See* Latin quarter-ly. New York, Parnassus Press, [etc.]. 149245A

Latitudes. *Houston, Latitudes Press.* 1492462
ISSN: 0458-8207 Beg. date: 1967 End date: 1972
Ceased publication with vol. 2 no. 4, Spring 1972.
WU   UWM (RBR) V.1-2 (FEB1967-SPR1972).

Laugh literary and man the humping guns. *Los Angeles.* 1492475
ISSN: 0023-8953 Beg. date: 1969
Editors: Charles Bukowski and Neeli Cherry.
WU   UWM (RBR) V.1 no.1-3 (1969-1971).

Laughing bear. *Woodinville, Wash., Laughing Bear Press.* 1492488
ISSN: 0363-2164 Beg. date: 1976
Vol. 1 no. 1 subtitled The Special experimental issue.
WU   UWM (RBR) V.1 no.1; v.2 no.2 (no.5) (SUM1976-1977).

Laughing bear newsletter. *Woodinville, Wash., Laughing Bear Press.* 1492490
Beg. date: 1976
WU   UWM (RBR) No.2-4 (MAR061976-1977).

Laughing horse. *Berkeley.* 0411125
Also New York, Kraus Reprint, 1967.
Supplement to no. 1-2.
WU   UWM (RBR) No.9 (DEC1923).

Laurel review. *Buckhannon, W. Va., West Virginia Wesleyan College.* 1450054
ISSN: 0023-9003 Beg. date: 1961 End date: 1970
Ceased publication with vol. 10 no. 2, Fall 1970.
Superseded by New laurel review with 1971.
WU   UWM (RBR) V.3 no.3; v.5-10 (1962/1963-1970).

Lazarus. *East Lansing, Mich., David Highsmith.* 1492525
Beg. date: 1974
"A review of the arts."
WU   UWM (RBR) No.1 (OCT/NOV1974).

League of American Writers. Hollywood Chapter. Clipper. 0413951
See Clipper. Hollywood, Calif., Hollywood Chapter of the League of American Writers.

League of Militant Poets. Pa'lante. *See* Pa'lante. New York, The League of Militant Poets. 1498197

League of Workers Theatres. New theatre. *See* New theatre. New York. 1529042

League to support poetry. *See* New quarterly of poetry. New York, League to support poetry. 041442A

Leeds, England. University. Ikon. *See* Ikon. Leeds, Eng., Leeds University Union. 1442584

Leeds, England. University. Union. M O M A. *See* M O M A; magazine of modern arts. Leeds, Eng., Leeds University Union. 1323581

Left. *[Birmingham, Eng.], University of Birmingham Socialist Union.* 1492538
WU   UWM (RBR) No.3-4 (1966).

The Left. *Davenport, Ia., George Redfield and Jay du Von.* 1492553
Beg. date: 1931 End date: 1931
"A quarterly review of radical and experimental art."
Ceased publication with vol. 1 no. 2, Autumn 1931.
WU   UWM (RBR) V.1 no.1-2 (APR1931-SUM/AUT1931).

Left Curve, art and revolution. *San Francisco, Cultural Workers' Front of Our America.* 1277643
Beg. date: 1974
WU   UWM (RBR) No.1-6 (SPR1974-SUM/FAL1976).

Left front. *Chicago, John Reed Clubs of the Middle West, a section of the International Union of Revolutionary Writers and Artists.* 1492566
Beg. date: 1933 End date: 1934
"Revolutionary art of the Midwest."
No. 1 issued by the John Reed Club of Chicago.
Ceased publication with vol. 1 no. 4, June 1934.
WU   UWM (RBR) V.1 no.3-4 (JAN/FEB-MAY/JUN1934).

The Left review. *London, Writers International, British Section.* 150515A
Beg. date: 1934 End date: 1938
Absorbed Viewpoint.
Editor: Randall Swingler.
Ceased publication with vol. 3 no. 16, May 1938.
Reprint edition, London, 1968, issued in the series, English little magazines, no. 3.
WU   UWM (RBR) V.1-3 (OCT1934-MAY1938).

Left review. *Philadelphia, John Reed Club of Philadelphia.* 1528888
Beg. date: 1934 End date: 1934
Continues Red pen with vol. 1 no. 2, Feb. 1934.
"Organ of the Philadelphia John Reed Club."
WU   UWM (RBR) V.1 no.2-3 (FEB-MAR1934).

Legend. *Westland, Mich., J.L. Parker.* 1492594
WU   UWM (RBR) V.2 no.1 (WIN1973).

Leicester, England. University. Converse. *See* Converse. [n.p.], Leicester University. 1433884

Lemming. *San Diego, San Diego Council for Poetry.* 1492603
ISSN: 0047-4398 Beg. date: 1971
Formed by the union of Lemming review, Mandelia, and Showcase.
WU   UWM (RBR) No.1-8 (WIN1971-1975).

Leopardess. *[London], Queen Mary College, [London School of Economics and Political Science].* 1492616
Beg. date: 1967
WU   UWM (RBR) No.1 (1967).

The Leprechaun review. *New York, Neil T. Curran.* 1492631
ISSN: 0024-0990 Beg. date: 1968
WU   UWM (RBR) V.1 no.1-2 (WIN1967/1968-SUM1968).

The Lesbian tide. *Santa Monica, Calif. [etc.], Tide Collective.* 1492644
Early issues published by Daughters of Bilitis.
WU   UWM (RBR) V.2 no.5,7-12; v.3 no.2-6,9,11; v.4 no.1-6; v.5 no.2 (DEC1972-NOV/DEC1975).

Lethbridge, Alberta. University. Colloquium Study. 1441902
Canada goose. *See* Canada goose; a Canadian poetry magazine. Lethbridge, Alta., Colloquium Study, University of Lethbridge.

Let's have a chat. *Tokyo, Shigeo Urabe.* 1492672
WU   UWM (RBR) V.3 no.2; v.4 no.2; v.5 no.1-2, 4; v.6-9 (SPR1964-AUT1970).

A Letter. *Pasadena, Calif.* 1492685
WU   UWM (RBR) V.1 no.2 (SEP/OCT1967).

Letters. *Saratoga Springs, N.Y., The Country Press.* 152890A
Beg. date: 1974
WU   UWM V.1-v.2 no.3 (SUM1974-SUM1977).

Letters; quarterly. *See* Arena; a literary magazine. Wellington, N.Z., Handcraft Press. 143826A

Letters magazine. *See* Arena; a literary magazine. Wellington, N.Z., Handcraft Press. 1438272

Levant. *London.* 0417897
ISSN: 0075-8914 LCCN: 76-13723
Journal of the British School of Archeology in Jerusalem.
WU   UWM (RBR) V.6-7 (JUL-DEC1967).

Leveller. *London.* 1492698
"Leveller is produced in conjunction with Synic, a monthly broadsheet with comprehensive dairy [sic], news and information on Left activities."
WU   UWM (RBR) No.1 (1969).

Levels. *Syracuse, N.Y.* 1492707
Beg. date: 1966
Editor: Walt Shepperd.
WU   UWM (RBR) V.1 no.1 (APR1966).

Leviathan. *New York, V. R.-Leviathan Publications, Inc.* 0417934
ISSN: 0024-1563 Beg. date: 1966 End date: 1970
Supersedes Viet-report.
Absorbed May with June 1969.
Includes an unnumbered broadside published as a farewell issue and distributed to subscribers in Spring 1971.
Ceased publication with vol. 2 no. 4, Fall 1970.
WU   UWM (RBR) V.2 no.2 (JUN1970).

Libera. *Berkeley?, Libera.* 1492722
Beg. date: 1972
Sponsored by the Associated Students of the University of California and the Berkeley Women's Collective.
"A new woman's journal."
WU   UWM (RBR) No.1-6 (WIN1972-SPR1975).

Liberation. *New York.* 0418393
ISSN: 0024-189X Beg. date: 1956
Indexed by Public affairs information service.
WU   UWM (RBR) V.1-v.9 no.10; v.13 no.7; v.16 no.4; v.17 no.1 (MAR1956-APR1972).

Liberator. *New York, The Liberator publishing co. inc.* 0418469
LCCN: 22-10275 Beg. date: 1918 End date: 1924
Supersedes Masses.
Ceased publication with vol. 7 no. 10, Oct. 1924.
United with Labor herald and Soviet Russia pictorial to form Workers monthly, continuing volume numbering of Labor herald, Nov. 1924.
WU   UWM (RBR) V.1-5; v.6 no.3-6,11-12; v.7 no.1-10 (MAR1918-OCT1924).

Libertarian League. Views & comments. *See* Views & comments. New York, The Libertarian League. 1517245

Life and letters. *Girard, Kan.* 1492748
Beg. date: 1922 End date: 1925
Editor: E. Haldeman-Julius.
Ceased publication with vol. 3 no. 11, July 1925.
Absorbed by Haldeman-Julius weekly (later Debunker and the American parade).
WU   UWM (RBR) V.3 no.6 (FEB1925).

Light. *New York.* 1492750
ISSN: 0147-121X LCCN: 76-648460 Beg. date: 1973
"A poetry review."
Editor: Roberta C. Gould.
WU   UWM (RBR) V.1 no.1-4 (FAL1973-1977).

The Light year. *San Diego, Calif.* 1492763
ISSN: 0457-8767 Beg. date: 1958
WU   UWM (RBR) Autumn 1958; Autumn 1961.

Lili. *St. Louis, Mo., Ronald Voigt.* 1492776
ISSN: 0457-8899 Beg. date: 1963 End date: 1963
"A poetry quarterly."
Ceased publication with vol. 1 no. 3, July 1963.
WU   UWM (RBR) V.1 no.1-3 (JAN-JUL1963).

Lillabulero. *Chapel Hill, N.C.* 095495A
ISSN: 0024-3485 Beg. date: 1967
WU   UWM (RBR) V.1; v.2 no.1,6-7; n. ser. no.8-14 (WIN1967-1974).

Limbo. *Vancouver, B.C.* 1492789
ISSN: 0024-3531 Beg. date: 1964
Cover title, Feb. 1964: Chez limbo.
Vols. for Feb.-Mar. 1964 published by the Neo-Surrealist Research Foundation; Apr. 1964- by the Limbo Literary Society.
WU   UWM (RBR) V.1-v.2 no.7/8 (FEB1964-NOV1967).

Limbo Literary Society. Limbo. *See* Limbo. Vancouver, B.C. 1492791

Limestone. *London, Limestone Publications.* 1492826
Beg. date: 1974
"Literary magazine."
WU   UWM (RBR) No.1-6 (JUN1974-1977).

Limited Editions Club. Dolphin. *See* Dolphin. a periodical for all people who find pleasure in fine books. *New York, The Limited Editions Club.* 0420966

Lincolnshire and South Humberside Arts. Proof. *See* Proof. Beaumont Fee, Lincoln., Eng., Lincolnshire and South Humberside Arts. 150912A

Lincolnshire Association. Proof. *See* Proof. Appleby, Lincoln., Eng. 1507722

Lincolnshire Association. Written and Spoken Word Panel. Lincolnshire writers. *See* Lincolnshire writers. New Waltham, Grimsby, Eng.?, The Written and Spoken Word Panel of The Lincolnshire Association. 1507707

Lincolnshire writers. *New Waltham, Grimsby, Eng.?, The Written and Spoken Word Panel of The Lincolnshire Association.* 1507698
Beg. date: 1966
Continued Proof with no. 2, Summer 1966.
"A magazine of new writing."
WU   UWM (RBR) No.2-9 (SUM1966-WIN1969-SPR1970).

Line. *Los Angeles, Line.* 1492839
Beg. date: 1948 End date: 1949
Ceased publication with vol. 1 no. 3, May 1949.
WU   UWM (RBR) V.1 no.1-3 (APR/MAY1948-MAY1949).

Lines. *New York.* 1492841
ISSN: 0459-4533 Beg. date: 1964 End date: 1965
Editor: Aram Saroyan.
Ceased publication with no. 6, Nov. 1965.
WU   UWM (RBR) No.1-6 (SEP1964-NOV1965).

Lines. *North Shields, Northumberland, Eng., Elpar Poem Productions.* 1492854
Editor: Geoff Holland.
Absorbed P/S (Poetry Section) and Leaves with no. 12.
WU   UWM (RBR) No.5,7-12 (AUG1970-JUN1972).

Lines review. *Edinburgh.* 094766A
ISSN: 0459-4541 Beg. date: 1952
WU   UWM (RBR) No.3-6,8-10/11,14-15,17,19-55/56 (SUM1953-JAN1976).

LiNQ. *Townsville, Australia, Department of English, James Cook University of North Queensland.* 1492867
WU   UWM (RBR) V.1-v.5 no.1 (1971-1976).

The Lion and crown. *New York, The Lion and Crown.* 1492882
Beg. date: 1932
WU   UWM (RBR) V.1 no.1 (FAL1932).

The Lion and unicorn. *New York, The Lion and Unicorn Press.* 1492895
Beg. date: 1934 End date: 1934
"An American review of the arts."
Ceased publication with vol. 1 no. 1, Oct./Nov. 1934.
WU   UWM (RBR) V.1 no.1 (OCT/NOV1934).

Lip magazine. *Philadelphia, Middle Earth Books, Inc.* 1492904
Beg. date: 1972
WU   UWM (RBR) No.1 (1972).

Listen. *Hessle, Eng.* 0422322
Ceased publication with vol. 4, 1962.
WU   UWM (RBR) V.1-2; v.3 no.2 (1954-SPR1959).

Lit. *Notre Dame, Ind.* 1492917
Beg. date: 1967
WU   UWM (RBR) V.1 no.1-7,9/10-11 (OCT071967-MAY1969).

Literary amateur. *Morristown, Ind., Kenneth L. Rhodes and L.G. Merrell, Publishers.* 149292A
ISSN: 0456-2313 Beg. date: 1951 End date: 1951
Ceased publication with vol. 1, 1951.
WU   UWM (RBR) V.1 no.1-4 (JAN-OCT1951).

Literary America. *New York, The Galleon Press, Inc.* 1492932
Beg. date: 1934 End date: 1936
"Devoted to the American Scene."
Ceased publication with vol. 4 no. 2, Winter 1936.
WU   UWM (RBR) V.1 no.7-8; v.2 no.1-5,11 (NOV1934-DEC1935).

Literary artpress. *Cheney, Wash.* 1492945
ISSN: 0459-522X Beg. date: 1959 End date: 1961
"Published under the auspices of the English Department of Eastern Washington College of Education, Cheney, Washington."
Ceased publication with vol. 2 no. 2, April 1961.
WU   UWM (RBR) V.1 no.1-2; v.2 no.1-2 (FAL1959-SPR1961).

Literary calender. *Shreveport, La., Estelle Trust.* 1492960
ISSN: 0456-233x
WU   UWM (RBR) March, Summer 1956; March, Summer 1958; Spring, Summer, Dec. 1959.

The Literary digest. *London, Dublin.* 1492973
Beg. date: 1946
"A monthly magazine of popular literary interest."
WU   UWM (RBR) V.1 no.2-v.4 no.3 (JUL1946-AUT1949).

Literary guide. *London.* 1505134
Beg. date: 1954 End date: 1956
Continues Literary guide and rationalist review with vol. 69 no. 4, April 1954.
Continued by The Humanist with vol. 71 no. 9, Oct. 1956.
WU   UWM (RBR) V.67 no.4,6,8-v.68 no.1; v.68 no.3-v.69 no.2; v.69 no.4-7,9-v.71 no.8 (APR1954-SEP1956).

The Literary guide and rationalist review. *London.* 1505119
Beg. date: 1885 End date: 1954
Title varies: 1885-July 1894, Watts literary guide.
Continued by Literary guide with vol. 69 no. 4 [?], April 1954.
WU   UWM (RBR) V.64 no.7-11; v.65-66; v.67 no.1-4,6,8-12; v.68 no.1,3-12; v.69 no.1-2 (JUL1949-MAR1954).

Literary half-yearly. *Mysore, Mysore University, Dept. of Post-graduate Studies in English.* 0895191
ISSN: 0024-4554 LCCN: sa62-210 Beg. date: 1960
Began publication with Jan. 1960 issue.
WU   UWM (RBR) V.1 no.1; v.3-v.18 no.1 (1960-1977).

The Literary magazine of Tufts University. *Medford, Mass., Tufts University.* 1492986
ISSN: 0459-5246 Beg. date: 1966
Cover title: Tufts literary magazine.
WU   UWM (RBR) V.1 no.2-v.2 no.2 (1966-SPR1967).

Literary observer. *Hartford, Conn.* 0423199
Bimonthly.
WU   UWM (RBR) No.1,4 (APR/MAY-OCT/NOV1934).

The Literary preview. *Madison, Wis., Univ. of Wisconsin.* 1493021
Beg. date: 1946
"The University of Wisconsin literary magazine."
WU   UWM (RBR) V.1 no.1,3 (DEC1946-MAR1947).

Literary sketches. *Williamsburg, Va.* 1493047
ISSN: 0024-4597 Beg. date: 1961
"A magazine of interviews, reviews, and memorabilia."
WU   UWM (RBR) V.4 no.9; v.5 no.10-v.13; v.14 no.1-6,9-12; v.15-v.17 no.5 (SEP1964-MAY1977).

The Literary tabloid. *Bergenfield, N.J., H. Prim Co., Inc.* 149305A
Beg. date: 1975
WU   UWM (RBR) V.1 no.1-5 (FEB1975-OCT1975).

Literary times. *Chicago, Literary Communication Co.* 1508909
ISSN: 0024-4619 Beg. date: 1961
Title varies: Nov. 1961-Oct. 1962, Chicago literary times.
WU   UWM (RBR) V.1 no.1-4; v.2 no.1-7; v.3 no.1-2,4-5,7; v.4 no.1-6; v.5 no.1 (NOV1961-DEC1971).

The Literary world. *Montreal, Lane Publications.* 1493062
Beg. date: 1963
"An International newsletter."
WU   UWM (RBR) V.1 no.1-2 (1963-NOV1964).

The Literary world. *New York, Froben Press.* 1493075
Beg. date: 1934 End date: 1935
"A monthly survey of international letters."
Suspended publication Jan.-May 1935.
Ceased publication with no. 9, June 1935.
WU   UWM (RBR) No.1-2,4-9 (MAY1934-JUN1935).

Litmus. *Berkeley, Calif. [etc.].* 1493088
ISSN: 0024-4953 Beg. date: 1967
"The poetry paper."
WU   UWM (RBR) No.1-12 (1967-[1971]).

Littack. *Epping, Surrey, Eng., Ember Press.* 1493090
Beg. date: 1972 End date: 1976
Ceased publication with vol. 4 no. 3 (no. 12), May 1976.
Absorbed by Littack supplement with May 1976.
WU   UWM (RBR) V.1-v.4 no.3 (no.1-12) (1972-MAY1976).

The Littack supplement. *Brixham, South Devon, Eng., Ember Press.* 149310A
Beg. date: 1976
Absorbed Littack.
"Reviews and poetry."
WU   UWM (RBR) No.1-2 (OCT1976-1977).

Little Caesar. *Monrovia, Calif.* 1528912
Beg. date: 1976
WU   UWM (RBR) No.1-3 (1976-AUG1977).

The Little mag. *Niagara Falls, N.Y.* 1493112
Beg. date: 1968
WU   UWM (RBR) V.1 no.1-2 (1968).

The Little magazine. *New York.* 0424020
ISSN: 0033-6300 LCCN: 74-648863 Beg. date: 1970
Continues The Quest with vol. 4, Spring 1970.
Includes supplements.
WU   UWM (RBR) V.4-10 (SPR1970-FAL/WIN1976); suppl.

The Little man. *Cincinnati, Ohio, University of Cincinnati.* 1493229
Beg. date: 1938
"...the official quarterly of the University of Cincinnati."
WU   UWM (RBR) No.1-4 (SPR1938-1940).

The Little newspaper. *New York.* 1493125
ISSN: 0024-5046 Beg. date: 1969 End date: 1969
"An Independent American fortnightly."
Ceased publication with vol. 1 no. 3, Feb. 21, 1969.
WU   UWM (RBR) V.1 no.1-3 (JAN20-FEB211969).

The Little review. *Huntington, W. Va., Little Review Press.* 1493138
ISSN: 0024-5054 Beg. date: 1969
Vol. 4 no. 2 (issue no. 8) is a special issue entitled Snerd magazine.
WU   UWM (RBR) V.1-2; v.3 no.2-v.5 no.1 (SPR1969-1974).

The Little review of the Pacific Northwest. *Portland, Ore.* 1493153
ISSN: 0459-5920 Beg. date: 1965
Ceased publication.
Superseded by Journeybook.
WU   UWM (RBR) V.1 no.1 (FAL1965).

The Little square review. *Santa Barbara, Calif.* 1493166
ISSN: 0024-5070 Beg. date: 1966 End date: 1967
Ceased publication with no. 9/10, Spring/Summer 1972.
WU   UWM (RBR) No.1-9/10 (FAL1966-SPR/SUM1972).

The Little word machine. *Moseley, Birmingham, Eng., l.w.m. Publications.* 1493179
Beg. date: 1972
WU   UWM (RBR) No.1-7 (1972-1975).

Littletown. *Lancaster, Wisc.* 1493181
Beg. date: 1939 End date: 1940
"A magazine written by the people of Littletowns."
Ceased publication with vol. 1 no. 8, Nov. 1940.
WU   UWM (RBR) V.1 no.1-2,6-7 (DEC1939-OCT1940).

Live oak. *Asheville, N.C., etc., Neti Neti Publications, etc.* 1493194
Beg. date: 1968
WU   UWM (RBR) V.1 no.1 (NOV1968).

Living hand. *Paris, Chicago, Paul Auster.* 1493203
LCCN: 75-68 Beg. date: 1973
WU   UWM (RBR) No.1-4 (FAL1973-WIN1975).

Living poetry quarterly. *See* Folio. LaPorte, Ind. 1437315

Living poetry quarterly. *[La Porte, Ind., Dierkes Press].* 1493216
Beg. date: 1943
Suspended publication Spring 1947-Spring 1949.
Continued by Folio.
WU   UWM (RBR) V.3 no.2 (WIN1946).

Local tenderness. *East Lansing, Mich?* 1493244
Editor: Terry Henry.
WU   UWM (RBR) V.1 no.1-2 (1974).

Location. *New York, Longview Foundation, Inc.* 1493257
ISSN: 0459-6706 Beg. date: 1963
WU   UWM (RBR) V.1 no.1-2 (SPR1963-SUM1964).

Lock Haven bulletin. *See* Lock Haven review. *Lock Haven, Pennsylvania. State Teachers College.* 0425131

Lock Haven review. *Lock Haven, Pennsylvania. State Teachers College.* 0425144
Title varies: Ser. 1 no. 1-4 (1959-1962), Lock Haven bulletin.
WU   UWM (RBR) No.13-15 (1972-1974).

Locus solus. *Lans-en-Vercors (Isère), France.* 0425326
LCCN: 66-86595
Ceased publication with no. 5, 1962.
Nos. 1-5 published by Kraus Reprints, 1971.
WU   UWM (RBR) No.1-5 (1960-1962).

Loeb (Albert) Gallery, New York.   Figures. *See* Figures. Paris, New York. 143690A

Logos. *Charlotte, N.C., The Student Government Association of Queens College.* 149326A
WU   UWM (RBR) V.1 no.2; v.2 no.1; v.3 no.1-2; v.4 no.1-2; v.5 no.1 (SPR1960-WIN1963); Spring 1964.

London. Royal College of Art.   Ark. *See* Ark; a journal of the Royal College of Art. London, W.S. Cowell Ltd. 1430144

London. University. Goldsmiths' College.   Prism. *See* Prism. London, England, Goldsmiths' College, University of London. 1508980

London. University. King's College.   Centigrade. *See* Centigrade. London, Kings College. 1433802

London. University. Literary Society.   Thames. *See* Thames. London, University of London Literary Society. 1512110

The London Aphrodite [a literary periodical]. *London, Fanfrolico press.* 0426844
Beg. date: 1928 End date: 1929
WU   UWM (RBR) No.1-6 (AUG1928-JUL1929).

The London broadsheet. *London, Kenneth Coutts-Smith.* 1493272
ISSN: 0456-4898 Beg. date: 1955
WU   UWM (RBR) No.1-4 (n.d.-APR1955).

London forum. *London, Falcon Press, Ltd.* 1493285
Beg. date: 1946 End date: 1947
"A quarterly review of literature, art and current affairs."
Editors: 1946-   , P. Baker and R. Gant.
Ceased publication with vol. 1 no. 4, Dec. 1947.
WU   UWM (RBR) V.1 (WIN1946-DEC1947).

London Mercury... *London, The field press ltd.* 0427206
LCCN: 20-23882. Beg. date: 1919 End date: 1939
Absorbed the Bookman, Jan. 1935.
Ceased publication with vol 39 (no. 234), April 1939.
Absorbed by Life and letters with May 1939.
General index. v. 1-20, Nov. 1919-Oct. 1929.
WU   UWM (RBR) V.1-39 (no.1-234) (NOV1919-APR1936).

London School of Economics and Political Science. Queen Mary College.   Leopardess. *See* Leopardess. [London], Queen Mary College, [London School of Economics and Political Science]. 1492629

London Writer Circle.   Within the circle. *See* Within the circle. London. 1514802

Long hair. *London, New York, Lovebooks Ltd.* 1493298
ISSN: 0459-7613 Beg. date: 1965 End date: 1965
Ceased publication with vol. 1 no. 1, 1965.
WU   UWM (RBR) V.1 no.1 (1965).

The Long Island Poetry Collective. Newsletter. *[n.p.].* 1493307
WU   UWM (RBR) V.3 no.1-8 (1976-MAR/APR1977).

Long Island Poetry Collective. Process magazine. *See* 1509039
Process magazine. South Hempstead, N.Y., Long Island Poetry Collective.

Long Island Poetry Collective. Xanadu. *See* Xanadu. 1515218
Wantagh, N.Y., Long Island Poetry Collective.

Long Island review. *Cambria Heights, N.Y.?* 149331A
Beg. date: 1973
Editors: Edward Faranda and Stephen Sossaman.
Also called Long Island review of poetry, fiction, and criticism.
WU   UWM (RBR) No.1-3/4 (SPR1973-WIN1976/SPR1977).

Long Island review of poetry, fiction, and criticism. *See* Long 1493322
Island review. Cambria Heights, N.Y.?

Long Island University, Brooklyn. Journal. Supplement. 1433869
See Confrontation. Greenvale, N.Y.

Long pond review. *Selden, N.Y., English Dept., Suffolk Community College.* 1493335
WU   UWM (RBR) Jan. 1976.

Longhouse. *Green River, Vt.* 1493348
WU   UWM (RBR) Spring 1976.

Look quick. *Boulder, Colo., H. Hutson Printery.* 1493350
"A magazine of poetry and prose."
WU   UWM (RBR) V.1 no.1-6 (1975-1977).

Loon. *Santa Rosa, Calif., DeBlois/Henderson.* 1493363
ISSN: 0360-5612 LCCN: 75-649150 Beg. date: 1973
"A journal of poetry."
WU   UWM (RBR) No.1-8 (OCT311973-1977).

Loose lips sink ships. *Oakland, Calif.* 1493376
WU   UWM (RBR) V.2 no.1 (FAL1976).

Loras College, Dubuque, Iowa. Spokesman. *See* 1511144
Spokesman. Dubuque, Iowa, Loras College.

Los. *Providence, R.I., Heilcoal Press.* 1493389
Beg. date: 1967
"A magazine of poetry."
WU   UWM (RBR) V.1 no.1-5; v.2 no.1-3 (MAR1967-SPR1970).

Los Angeles. *See* L A. Claremont, Calif., D and R Pub. Co. 1493599

Los Angeles. City College. Citadel. *See* Citadel. Los 144202A
Angeles, Los Angeles City College.

Los Angeles journal of sound. *See* L A journal of sound. [Los 1493649
Angeles?].

Lost and found times. *Columbus, Ohio.* 1493391
Beg. date: 1975
WU   UWM (RBR) No.1-4 (AUG1975-1977).

Lotus. *Athens, Ohio, Jonathan Hemley.* 1493400
ISSN: 0459-8261 LCCN: 75-649490
WU   UWM (RBR) No.1 (1968).

Lotus. *Cairo, Permanent Bureau of Afro-Asian Writers.* 1323475
ISSN: 0002-0665 Beg. date: 1967
"Afro-Asian writings. Oeuvres afro-asiatiques."
Title varies: vol. 1 (nos. 1-5), 1967-   , Afro-Asian writings.
Added title,   : Lutus.
WU   UWM (RBR) V.1 no.1-3 (MAR1967-SUM1968); Jan., Apr., Oct. 1970; Jan., Apr., July, Oct. 1971.

Loudspeaker. *London.* 1493441
WU   UWM (RBR) One unnumbered issue: 1968.

Louisiana. Southeastern Louisiana College, Hammond. 1437594
Gambit. *See* Gambit. Hammond, La., Dept. of English, Southeastern Louisiana College.

Louisiana review. *See* Revue de Louisiane. Louisiana review. 1529397
Lafayette, La., Conseil pour le Développement du Français en Louisiane.

Louisville. University. Views. *See* Views. Louisville, Views 1517217
Associates.

Lovat Dickson's magazine. *London.* 0429848
New York, Kraus Reprint, 1967.
WU   UWM (RBR) V.4 no.1 (JAN1935).

Love. *See* Love (incorporating Hate). Berkeley, Calif. 149347A

Love (incorporating Hate). *Berkeley, Calif.* 1493467
ISSN: 0459-9241 Beg. date: 1966
Editor: Al Young.
Ceased publication.
Absorbed by Loveletter.
WU   UWM (RBR) [No.1]; v.2 no.3 [1966].

Love/woman. *Milwaukee, Wis.* 1493454
Beg. date: 1970
Editor: Michael Joseph Phillips.
WU   UWM (RBR) V.1 no.1-4 (FAL1970-SUM1971).

Loveletter. *Palo Alto, Calif.* 1493482
Editor: Al Young.
Absorbed Love (incorporating Hate).
WU   UWM (RBR) No.3-4/6 (1967-1968).

The Low down. *New York, The Bozo Pub. Co., Inc.* 149407A
Beg. date: 1925
"A magazine for hypocrites."
WU   UWM (RBR) V.1 no.1 (MAY1925).

The Lower Stumpf Lake review. *Collegeville, Minn., St. John's University.* 1352709
Ceased publication.
WU   UWM (RBR) Winter 1970-Spring 1971.

Lowlands review. *Lake Charles, La.* 1494082
Beg. date: 1975
WU   UWM (RBR) No.1-4 (1975-1977).

Loyola University, New Orleans. New Orleans review. *See* 1421115
New Orleans review. New Orleans.

Lucille. *Austin, Tex., Poems-While-U-Wait Pub.* 1494095
Beg. date: 1973
WU   UWM (RBR) No.1-8 (WIN1973-WIN/SPR1977).

Ludd's mill. *Huddersfield, Eng.* 1528925
ISSN: 0047-5157 Beg. date: 1971
WU   UWM (RBR) No.11 (1971).

Luna. *Victoria, Australia.* 1494104
Beg. date: 1975
"A literary publication edited by women."
WU   UWM (RBR) V.1 no.1-3; v.2 no.1 (1975-1977).

Lunar adios. *See* Lunar retorno. Long Beach, Calif., General 1494132
Honors Program, California State University, Long Beach.

Lunar retorno. *Long Beach, Calif., General Honors Program,* 1494117
California State University, Long Beach.
Beg. date: 1973
Title varies: vol. 1 no. 1, 1973, Lunar adios.
"A magazine of the arts."
WU   UWM (RBR) 1973; Fall-Winter 1974; 1975.

Lunch. *Rutherford, N.J., The English Club, Fairleigh Dickinson University.* 1494158
WU   UWM (RBR) Seven unnumbered, undated issues.

Lune. *Bellmore, N.Y.* 1494173
Beg. date: 1973
WU   UWM (RBR) No.1 (SUM1973).

Lutus. *See* Lotus. Cairo, 1519887

Luv. *Toronto, Fleye Press.* 1494186
ISSN: 0460-0363 Beg. date: 1967
WU   UWM (RBR) No.1-3,5-6 (1967).

Lynx. *Amherst, Mass., Lynx House Press.* 1494199
Beg. date: 1972
WU   UWM (RBR) V.1-v.2 no.1 (1972-FAL/WIN1973); special issues 1-2 (1976-FAL1975): not in chronological order.

Lynx. *Plainview, Tex.* 1494208
ISSN: 0458-5461 Beg. date: 1962 End date: 1964
Editors: Paul Levine and Margaret Lee Johnson.
Ceased publication with no. 6, July 1964.
WU   UWM (RBR) V.1 no.1-6 (1962-JUL1964).

Lyric. *Norfolk, Va., Roanoke, Va.* 0432397
ISSN: 0024-7820 Beg. date: 1921
WU   UWM (RBR) V.14 no.1-3; v.15 no.2-4; v.21 no.2-4; v.22 no.1,3; v.23 no.2; v.24 no.2-3; v.25 no.2,4; v.30 no.1-2; v.33 no.3-4; v.34-35; v.36 no.2-4; v.37-v.57 no.2 (SPR1934-SPR1977).

Lyric west, a magazine of verse. *Los Angeles.* 0432421
WU   UWM (RBR) V.5 no.1-2 (OCT-NOV1925).

M

"M". *San Francisco.* 1528938
WU   UWM (RBR) One unnumbered, undated issue.

M A M A. Madison area magazine of the arts. *See* Madison 1495598 area magazine of the arts. Madison, Wisc., Madison Area Movement of the Arts (MAMA) and the Wisconsin Institute for Intermedia Studies.

M C 502. *[n.p.].* 1528940
Beg. date: 1969
WU   UWM (RBR) No.1 (WIN1969).

M O M A; magazine of modern arts. *Leeds, Eng., Leeds University Union.* 1323579
ISSN: 0580-4493   Beg. date: 1969
WU   UWM (RBR) V.1 no.2 (1969).

M S G. *See* Magdalene syndrome gazette. San Francisco. 1495691

Mabon. *Bangor, Wales, North Wales Association for the Arts.* 1505188
ISSN: 0024-886X   LCCN: 79-268861   Beg. date: 1969
WU   UWM (RBR) V.1 no.1-6 (SPR1969-SPR/SUM1976).

Macabre. *New Haven, Conn., Joseph Payne Brennan.* 1494223
ISSN: 0024-8886
WU   UWM (RBR) No.1-23 (1957-1976).

Madison area magazine of the arts. *Madison, Wisc., Madison Area Movement of the Arts (MAMA) and the Wisconsin Institute for Intermedia Studies.* 1495585
Beg. date: 1976
"An interart portfolio of original prints and offset reproductions by artists from the four corners of Madison."
WU   UWM (RBR) No.[1]-3 (1976-1977).

Madison Area Movement of the Arts. Madison area magazine of the arts. *See* Madison area magazine of the arts. Madison, Wisc., Madison Area Movement of the Arts (MAMA) and the Wisconsin Institute for Intermedia Studies. 149561A

Madison review. *[Madison, Wisc.], Department of English, University of Wisconsin.* 1494236
Beg. date: 1972
WU   UWM (RBR) No.1 (SPR1972).

Madrona. *Seattle, Gemini Press.* 1494251
ISSN: 0047-5432   LCCN: sc77-1139   Beg. date: 1971
WU   UWM (RBR) No.1-12,15-16 (SUM1971-1978).

Madrugada. *Westport, Calif., Madrugada Press.* 1494264
Beg. date: 1970
WU   UWM (RBR) No.1 (1970).

Maelstrom. *Blacksburg, Va., Student Publications Board, Virginia Polytechnic Institute.* 1494277
Beg. date: 1966
WU   UWM (RBR) V.1 no.1-3; v.2 no.1-3; v.3 no.1-2 (SPR1966-SPR1969).

Mafkikker. *Allentown, Pa.* 1494292
WU   UWM (RBR) 1975-1976.

Mag. *Long Beach, Calif.* 1494301
Beg. date: 1971
WU   UWM (RBR) No.1-5 (FAL1971-1973).

Magazine. *New York.* 1494327
LCCN: 77-643042   Beg. date: 1965
WU   UWM (RBR) No.1-6 (SEP1965-MAR061966).

Magazine. *New York, Crank Books.* 1495635
Beg. date: 1964
WU   UWM (RBR) No.1-5 (1964-1972).

The Magazine; a journal of contemporary writing. *Beverly Hills, Calif., The Magazine Corp.* 0434931
Beg. date: 1933   End date: 1935
Subtitle varies.
Ceased publication with vol. 2 no. 6, May/June 1935.
WU   UWM (RBR) V.1 no.1-6; v.2 no.1-6 (DEC1933-MAY/JUN1935).

The Magazine of fantasy and fiction science. *[v.p.].* 1528953
"Published once by Quicksilver Press."
Also called The Magazine of science fantasy and fiction. Appears to be a parody.
WU   UWM (RBR) V.1 no.1 (no.87) (APR1958). Also called v.12, May.

The Magazine of further studies. *[n.p.].* 1495648
WU   UWM (RBR) No.4-6 (1967-1969).

Magazine of modern arts. *See* M O M A; magazine of modern arts. Leeds, Eng., Leeds University Union. 1323603

Magazine of science fantasy and fiction. *See* Magazine of fantasy and fiction science. [v.p.]. 1528966

Magazine of the Hudson valley. *See* Hudson river magazine. Hudson, N.Y., HUDSON river Publishers, Inc. 1440321

The Magazine of the Institute of Contemporary Arts. *[London].* 1495650
WU   UWM (RBR) V.1 no.2/3-8 (MAY/JUN-NOV1968).

The Magazine world. *[Columbus, Ohio, American Education Press, Inc., etc.].* 1495676
LCCN: 29-22182 rev   Beg. date: 1925   End date: 1931
"A miscellany of the best in current periodical literature for the English class."
Editor: D.B. Snyder.
Ceased publication with vol. 7 no. 2, Nov. 1931.
Absorbed by Scholastic with Nov. 28, 1931.
WU   UWM (RBR) V.1 no.3 (DEC1925).

The Magdalene syndrome gazette. *San Francisco.* 1495689
ISSN: 0024-9882   Beg. date: 1966
"An irregular sheath of verse."
Also called M S G.
WU   UWM (RBR) No.2-5 (n.d.-n.d.).

The Magenta frog. *Vancouver, B.C.* 1495700
ISSN: 0381-0607   Beg. date: 1970
"Published in conjunction with Talonbooks."
Title varies: no. 1, March 1970, The Magenta frog magasine.
WU   UWM (RBR) No.1-2 (MAR1970-NOV1972).

Magenta frog magasine. *See* Magenta frog. Vancouver, B.C. 1495713

Magic Sam. *Sydney.* 1495726
WU   UWM (RBR) No.1-2 (n.d.-n.d.).

The Magpie. *[Charlottesville, Virginia].* 1495739
LCCN: 10-8246   Beg. date: 1896   End date: 1896
"One of the ephemerals."
Ceased publication with vol. 1 no. 5, Oct. 1896.
WU   UWM (RBR) V.1 no.1-5 (JUN-OCT1896).

Maguey. *El Cerrito, Calif.* 1495741
ISSN: 0025-0031   Beg. date: 1968   End date: 1972
In English and Spanish.
Ceased publication with no. 6/7/8, Winter 1972.
WU   UWM (RBR) No.1-6/7/8 (MAY1968-WIN1972).

Mahfil; a quarterly magazine of South Asian literature. *Chicago.* 0436549
Beg. date: 1963   End date: 1972
Continued by Journal of South Asian literature with vol. 9, 1973.
WU   UWM (RBR) V.1 no.3; v.3 no.4; v.5-6 (1964-WIN1970).

Mail. *New York.* 150520A
ISSN: 0025-0546   Beg. date: 1969   End date: 1971
Ceased publication with no. 4, Spring 1971.
Superseded by Red crow with Winter/Spring 1972.
WU   UWM (RBR) No.1-4 (1969-SPR1971).

Mainline. *Windsor, Ont.* 1495754
ISSN: 0025-0821   Beg. date: 1968   End date: 1974
Ceased publication with no. 13/14, [1974].
WU   UWM (RBR) No.1-13/14 (1968-[1974]).

Mainly. *Brecon, Wales.* 1495767
ISSN: 0025-0848   Beg. date: 1965
Includes a special issue called cutely.
"A mainly publication."
WU   UWM (RBR) No.3-4 (MAY-SEP1966).

Mainstream. *New York.* 0437374
Beg. date: 1956   End date: 1963
Continues Masses and mainstream with vol. 9 no. 8, Sept. 1956.
Not published Dec. 1957.
Ceased publication with vol. 16 no. 8, 1963.
WU   UWM (RBR) V.9 no.11; v.10 no.8; v.13 no.7-8 (DEC1956-AUG1960).

Mainstream. Palatine, Ill. 1495782
ISSN: 0460-7104 End date: 1958
"A quarterly journal of poetry, the arts and contemporary comment."
Ceased publication with vol. 2 no. 3, Winter 1958.
WU   UWM (RBR) V.2 no.1-3 (SPR1957-WIN1958).

Mainstream, A literary quarterly. New York. 0437387
LCCN: 54-39518
Ceased with vol. 1, Fall 1947.
Superseded by Masses and mainstream.
WU   UWM (RBR) V.1 (1947).

The Mainstreeter. Grand Forks, Scopecraeft Press. 1229513
Beg. date: 1971
WU   UWM (RBR) No.1-8 (NOV171971-1977).

Maitreya. Berkeley, Calif., Shambala Publications. 1495817
ISSN: 0025-1011 Beg. date: 1970
Available on microfilm from Xerox University Microfilms.
WU   UWM (RBR) No.1-6 (1970-1977).

Makar. St. Lucia, Queensland, Dept. of English, University of Queensland. 1495795
WU   UWM (RBR) V.10-v.12 no.2 (SEP1974-1976).

Makerere College, Kampala. School of Art. Roho. See 1504848
Roho. Kampala, Uganda, School of Art, Makerere College.

Makerere University College, Kampala, Uganda. English Department. Penpoint. See Penpoint. Kampala, Uganda, English Department. Makerere University College. 1499752

Malaspina College. Pugn. See Pugn. [n.p.], Malaspina College. 1529328

Malenka. [n.p.]. 149582A
Editors: Brian Moses and Jeffrey S. Bleakley.
WU   UWM (RBR) No.2-6 (AUT1972-n.d.).

Mallorn. Liverpool. 1495832
WU   UWM (RBR) Fourth issue (n.d.); an additional unnumbered, undated issue.

MAMA. Madison area magazine of the arts. See Madison area magazine of the arts. Madison, Wisc., Madison Area Movement of the Arts (MAMA) and the Wisconsin Institute for Intermedia Studies. 1495607

Man! London. 1495845
ISSN: 0460-878X Beg. date: 1955
"The measure of all things. An Anglo-American anarchist publication."
Revival of an earlier periodical published in California: Man. A journal of the anarchist ideal and movement. Issued by the Man. Group (London) in association with the Man. Group (Los Angeles).
WU   UWM (RBR) V.1 no.1-6 (MAY1955-MAR/APR1957).

Man-root. San Francisco. 1495873
Beg. date: 1969
Editors: Paul Mariah and Richard Tagett.
WU   UWM (RBR) No.1-11 (AUG1969-1977).

Mandala. Iowa City, Ia., Madison, Wisc. 1495858
ISSN: 0025-2050 Beg. date: 1968
"A magazine of satire, speculation, and supereality" (varies).
WU   UWM (RBR) No.1-6 (1968-1971).

Mandala. Philadelphia, National Advertising Manufacturing Co. 1495860
ISSN: 0460-9158 LCCN: 59-3160
WU   UWM (RBR) V.1 no.1 (n.d.).

Mandella. San Diego, Calif., Mandella Press. 1495899
Beg. date: 1969
Ceased publication.
Superseded by Lemming.
WU   UWM (RBR) No.1 (1969).

Mandrake. London. 1495908
Beg. date: 1945
Editors: Arthur Boyars and Audrey M. Arnold.
WU   UWM (RBR) V.1 no.2-6; v.2 no.7-11 (FEB1946-AUT1955/WIN1956).

Mango. San Jose, Calif. 1528979
Beg. date: 1976
"Literature chicana."
English or Spanish.
WU   UWM (RBR) V.1 no.1-2 (FAL1976-1977).

Manhattan review. New York, Eric F. Oatman. 1495910
ISSN: 0025-2123 Beg. date: 1966 End date: 1967
"A little magazine of emerging poetry and fiction."
Ceased publication with vol. 1 no. 3, 1967.
WU   UWM (RBR) V.1 no.1-3 (1966-1967).

Manifold. London. 1495923
ISSN: 0025-2166 Beg. date: 1962
"A quarterly of new verse" (varies).
Editor: Vera Rich.
WU   UWM (RBR) No.1-9,11-28 (1962-SUM1969).

Manitoba. University. Department of English. Far point. 1436091
See Far point. Winnipeg, University of Manitoba, Dept. of English.

Manitoba. University. Students' Union. Creative campus. 1429375
See Creative campus. Winnipeg, Students' Union, University of Manitoba.

Manna. Toronto [etc.]. 1495936
Beg. date: 1972
"A review of contemporary poetry."
WU   UWM (RBR) No.1-5 (MAR1972-1974).

Mano-mano. Denver, Bowery Press. 1495949
Beg. date: 1968
WU   UWM (RBR) No.[1]-2 ([1968]-JUL1971).

Manroot. See Man-root. San Francisco. 1495886

Mansfield State College. Falcon. See The Falcon. Mansfield, Pa., 145109A

Manuscript. Athens, Ohio, The Lawhead Press. 1495951
Beg. date: 1934 End date: 1936
Ceased publication with vol. 3 no. 6, Nov./Dec. 1936.
Editors: John Rood and Mary Lawhead.
WU   UWM (RBR) V.1; v.2 no.1-5; v.3 no.2-6 (1934-NOV/DEC1936).

Manuscript. Dagenham, Essex, Eng., West Essex Writers' Club. 1495964
Beg. date: 1967
"Manuscript is to be published quarterly by and as the journal of the West Essex Writers' Club."
WU   UWM (RBR) No.1-6 (JUL1967-OCT1968/JAN1969).

Manuscript lab. New York, Margaret Howard. 149598A
ISSN: 0461-0334 Beg. date: 1956
"The writer's workshop magazine."
WU   UWM (RBR) V.1 no.1-3 (1956).

Manuscript Society. See Manuscripts. New York. 0440848

Manuscripts. Indianapolis. 1507631
LCCN: 34-16559 Beg. date: 1929 End date: 1929
"A magazine for and from the universities" (varies).
Ceased publication with vol. 1 no.3, Dec. 1929.
WU   UWM (RBR) V.1 no.1 (OCT1929).

Manuscripts. Indianapolis, English Dept., Butler University. 1507986
Continues MSS.
WU   UWM (RBR) V.41 no.2; v.42 no.1 (DEC1973-MAY1974).

Manuscripts. New York. 0440876
ISSN: 0025-262X LCCN: 52-67050 Beg. date: 1948
Title varies: Oct. 1948-spring 1953, Autograph collectors' journal.
Published by the Manuscript Society (called Oct. 1948-Spring 1953, National Society of Autograph Collectors).
Indexes: v. 1-11, 1948-1959, bound with v. 10-11.
WU   UWM (RBR) V.24 no.2; v.27 no.3; (SPR1972,SUM1975).

Manuscripts. New York, N.Y. 0955519
Beg. date: 1922 End date: 1923
WU   UWM (RBR) No.1-5 (FEB1922-MAR1923).

Many smokes. Reno, Nevada. 0440941
ISSN: 0025-2670 Beg. date: 1966
WU   UWM (RBR) V.6-v.10 no.3 (SPR1972-FAL1976).

Maps. [n.p.] and etc., Syracuse University Press, etc. 150750A
ISSN: 0542-626X Beg. date: 1966
Editor: John Taggart.
WU   UWM (RBR) No.1-6 (1966-1974).

Marchand's magazine. New York, Werner Marchand. 1496012
WU   UWM (RBR) V.2 no.10; v.3 no.1,6 (AUG201929-FEB1930).

The Margarine maypole orangoutang express. Albuquerque, N.M., The Anonymous Owl Press. 1496025
Beg. date: 1973
WU   UWM (RBR) No.1-27 (1973-1977).

Margins. *Milwaukee.* 1265335
ISSN: 0300-7553 Beg. date: 1972
"A review of little magazines and small press books."
Includes supplement: Sources.
WU   UWM (RBR) No.1-28/30 (AUG1972-JAN/MAR1976).

Marilyn. *Claremont, Calif.* 1496053
Beg. date: 1975
"A magazine of new poetry."
WU   UWM (RBR) V.1-2 (AUT1975-SPR1976); no.4 (1977).

Mark Twain Association of America. *See* The Twainian. 0441710
Perry, Mo., Mark Twain Research Foundation.

Mark Twain Research Foundation.   Twainian. *See* The 151989A
Twainian. *Perry, Mo.,*

Mark Twain Society of Chicago.   Twainian. *See* The 1519909
Twainian. *Perry, Mo.,*

Marketwise. *Kingsland, Herefordshire, Eng.* 1496066
WU   UWM (RBR) No.3,5-12,15
(SPR1967-SUM/AUT1970).

The Marrahwanna quarterly. *Cleveland, Ohio, Renegade* 1496079
Press.
ISSN: 0465-0301 Beg. date: 1964 End date: 1968
Ceased publication with vol. 4 no. 2, 1968.
WU   UWM (RBR) V.1 no.1-4; v.2 no.1-2; v.3 no.2-4; v.4
no.1-2 (1964-1967/1968).

Marsyas. *New York, Institute of Fine Arts, New York* 1496081
University.
Beg. date: 1941   End date: 1946
Ceased publication with no. 8, Jan. 1946.
WU   UWM (RBR) No.1-[2],7-8 (1944-JAN1946).

Maryland. University.   Maryland quarterly. *See* Maryland 1496116
quarterly. College Park, Md., University of Maryland.

Maryland. University.   Old line. *See* Old line. College Park, 1505526
Md., University of Maryland.

Maryland quarterly. *College Park, Md., University of* 1496103
Maryland.
Beg. date: 1943
WU   UWM (RBR) No.1-2 (DEC1943-1944).

Marzian way. *See* Humanist way. Calcutta, Renaissance 1440388
Publishers.

Mask. A quarterly journal of the art of the theatre. *Florence.* 044345A
LCCN: 11-2108 Beg. date: 1908 End date: 1929
Subtitle varies.
Suspended May 1915-Mar. 25 1918, 1919-1922.
Ceased publication with vol. 15 no. 4, March 1929.
WU   UWM (RBR) V.1-6; v.7inc.; v.9-15
(MAR1908-OCT1929).

Masque. *Leicestershire, Eng., Masque Enterprises.* 1515547
ISSN: 0025-4703 Beg. date: 1968
WU   UWM (RBR) V.1 no.1,3 (NOV1968-OCT1969).

The Masque. *London, Curtain Press.* 1509199
LCCN: 58-16664 Beg. date: 1946 End date: 1949
Ceased publication with no. 9, 1949.
WU   UWM (RBR) No.1-8 (DEC1946-1948).

Masque. *Sydney, Australia, Masque Publications.* 1509208
ISSN: 0025-469X LCCN: 70-205183 Beg. date: 1967
"Magazine of the performing arts."
WU   UWM (RBR) No.15 (AUG1970).

Massachusetts. University. Everywoman's Center. Feminist 1431136
Arts Program. Chomo-uri. *See* Chomo-uri. Amherst, Mass.,
Feminist Arts Program, Everywoman's Center, University of
Massachusetts.

Matador. *See* Home news magazine. New York, Home News 1440215
Co.

Matador home news. *See* Home news magazine. New York, 1440228
Home News Co.

Mate. *Auckland, N.Z.* 1509210
ISSN: 0025-5130 Beg. date: 1957
WU   UWM (RBR) No.2-26 (NOV1958-JUL1976).

Mati. *Chicago.* 1509223
Beg. date: 1975
WU   UWM (RBR) No.1-5 (1975-1977).

Matrix. *Bootle, Lancs., Eng.* 1508140
WU   UWM (RBR) No.1-2 (SEP-NOV1967).

Matrix. *Lennoxville, Quebec, Champlain College.* 1509236
Department of English.
ISSN: 0318-3610 Beg. date: 1975
"New Canadian writing."
WU   UWM (RBR) V.1-v.3 no.1 (SPR1975-1977).

Matrix. *Los Angeles, Charmian.* 1509251
Beg. date: 1970
"A collection of works by and/or for women."
WU   UWM (RBR) V.1-3 (SPR1970-1973).

Matrix. *Philadelphia, Matrix Association.* 1509264
Beg. date: 1938 End date: 1952
"A magazine of creative writing."
Ceased publication with vol. 14 no. 34, Spring/Summer 1952.
WU   UWM (RBR) V.2-3; v.4 no.1 (OCT1939-SPR1942);
Winter 1942-1943; Little book No.1-4 (FAL1943-SPR1945);
Summer, Nov. 1945, Spring 1946; v.9 no.2-4
(SUM1946-WIN1946/1947); Spring-Summer 1947; v.10; v.11
no.1/2-3; v.12 no.1-3; v.13 no.2 (FAL-WIN1947-[1950?]); no.32-
34 ([1951]-SPR/SUM1952).

Mattachine review. *San Francisco [etc], Mattachine Society.* 1509277
ISSN: 0465-3874 LCCN: 59-28623 Beg. date: 1955
WU   UWM (RBR) No.1,3-6; v.1-10; v.11 no.1; v.12 no.1
(1955-JUL1966).

Mattachine Society.   Mattachine review. *See* Mattachine 150928A
review. San Francisco [etc], Mattachine Society.

Mattachine Society, Incorporated.   Interim. *See* Interim. 1441655
Los Angeles [etc.], Mattachine Society, Inc.

Matter. *Annandale-on-Hudson, N.Y.* 1509314
ISSN: 0025-6005 Beg. date: 1963
WU   UWM (RBR) No.1,3-4 ([1964?-1968?]).

Mbari Club. *See* Black Orpheus; a journal of African and 0446741
Afro-American literature. Ikeja [etc.], Nigeria, Longman [etc.].

McLean County poetry review. *Normal, Ill., The Worn-Out* 149433A
Press.
Beg. date: 1975
WU   UWM (RBR) V.1 no.2 (WIN1975/SPR1976).

The McLuhan dew-line. *New York, Human Development* 1494342
Corp.
Beg. date: 1968
Some issues called The Dewline newsletter.
WU   UWM (RBR) V.1 no.1-12; v.2 no.1-5; v.3 no.1-2
(JUL1968-SEP/OCT1970).

McMaster University, Hamilton, Ontario.   Copperfield. *See* 1433906
Copperfield. Hamilton, Ont., McMaster University.

McMaster University, Hamilton, Ontario.   Waterloo review. 1518421
See Waterloo review. Waterloo, Ont.

Me too. *Iowa City, Iowa.* 1509292
WU   UWM (RBR) No.2-3 (FEB1975-APR1976).

Measure. *Bowling Green, Ohio [etc.].* 1509301
Beg. date: 1971
WU   UWM (RBR) No.1-11 (1971-1976); suppl. 1972,
1974.

Measure. *San Francisco [etc.].* 1509327
ISSN: 0465-434X Beg. date: 1957 End date: 1962
Ceased publication with no. 3, Summer 1962.
WU   UWM (RBR) No.1-3 (1957-1962).

Measure. a journal of poetry. *New York, Kraus Reprint.* 044742A
WU   UWM (RBR) No.2-10,28-29,37,40-41,47,
51-52,63 (APR1921-MAY1926).

Measure; a critical journal. *Chicago, H. Regnery Co.* 0447432
LCCN: 51-8347 rev Beg. date: 1950 End date: 1951
Supersedes Human affairs pamphlets.
Ceased publication with vol. 2, 1951.
WU   UWM (RBR) V.1-2 (1950-1951).

Meatball! *Cambridge, Mass., etc., The Lone Ranger Biology* 150933A
Press.
Beg. date: 1969 End date: 1971
Ceased publication with no. 8, Nov. 1971.
WU   UWM (RBR) No.1-4,6-8 (1968-NOV1971).

Mediterranean review. *Oakdale, N.Y., Dowling College.* 0904608
ISSN: 0025-8288 LCCN: 73-212615 Beg. date: 1970 End date: 1973
Some selections also in French, Portuguese or Spanish.
Ceased publication with vol. 3 no. 1/2, Fall/Winter, 1972/1973.
WU   UWM (RBR) V.1-v.3 no.1/2
(FAL1970-FAL1972/WIN1973).

The Medusa. [Amherst, Mass.]   1509342
   Beg. date: 1946   End date: 1946
   Ceased publication with vol. 1 no. 1, Fall 1946.
   WU   UWM (RBR) V.1 no.1 (FAL1946).

Mele. *Honolulu.*   1509355
   ISSN: 0025-8954   Beg. date: 1965
   "Carta internacional de poesia/International poetry letter."
   In English and Spanish.
   WU   UWM (RBR) No.2,4-18,20-21 (MAR1966-MAR1972); suppl.

Mendicant. *Boston, San Francisco.*   0451324
   WU   UWM (RBR) No.1 (AUT1961).

El Mensaje. *Los Angeles, Benjamin Press.*   1509368
   WU   UWM (RBR) Spring 1970.

Meridian. *Chicago, Harold Bordwell.*   1505225
   Beg. date: 1964
   WU   UWM (RBR) No.1-2 (1964-1965).

Meridian poetry magazine. *Liverpool, Rondo Publications.*   1505238
   LCCN: 74-645772   Beg. date: 1973
   WU   UWM (RBR) V.1 no.1-8 (AUT1973-SPR1976).

Merlin. *Paris.*   1229567
   ISSN: 0543-5277   Beg. date: 1952   End date: 1955
   Ceased publication with vol. 3 no.1, Spring/Summer 1955?
   WU   UWM (RBR) V.1 no.1-3; v.2 no.1-3; v.3 no.1 (SPR1952-SPR/SUM1955).

Merlin's magic. *Brooklyn, M.F. Teed.*   1496326
   "Distributed monthly to members of the American Amateur Press Association."
   WU   UWM (RBR) V.1 no.3,7,11; v.2 no.9-10; v.3; v.4 no.1-3,7-12; v.5-9; v.10 no.2-6; v.11 no.1-3,5-6; v.12 no.1-4 (NOV1959-MAR/APR1971).

Mesa. *Aurora, Wells College Press.*   0452539
   WU   UWM (RBR) No.1-5 (AUT1945-AUT1955).

Mesopotamia. *Oxford, Balliol College.*   1496339
   ISSN: 0539-4287
   WU   UWM (RBR) [No.1-2] ([1959]).

Message. *Paris.*   1496354
   "Bilingual poetry quarterly" (varies).
   In English and French.
   Title includes date of issue.
   WU   UWM (RBR) No.2-10 (WIN1965-AUT1968).

Metamorphosis. *Philadelphia, New York, Nashville, etc.*   0453561
   ISSN: 0543-5889   Beg. date: 1961   End date: 1964
   Ceased publication with no. 4, Summer/Fall 1964.
   WU   UWM (RBR) V.1 no.1-4 (SPR1961-SUM/FAL1964).

Metanoia. *Minneapolis.*   1496367
   WU   UWM (RBR) V.1 no.1-8 (1967-MAR1969).

Mexico quarterly review. *Mexico, D.F.*   149637A
   ISSN: 0026-1823   LCCN: 64-47184   Beg. date: 1962
   "An international cultural review."
   WU   UWM (RBR) V.2 no.4; v.3 no.2,4 (FAL1967-1969).

Mica. *Santa Barbara, Calif., Helmut Bonheim and Raymond Federman.*   1496382
   ISSN: 0543-8179   Beg. date: 1960   End date: 1962
   Ceased publication with no. 7, Nov. 1962.
   WU   UWM (RBR) No.1-7 (DEC1960-NOV1962).

Michigan. State University, East Lansing. Department of American Thought and Language. Centering. *See* Centering: a magazine of poetry. East Lansing, Mich., Dept. of American Thought and Language, Michigan State University.   1428208

Michigan. State University, East Lansing. Department of American Thought and Language. Ghostdance. *See* Ghostdance. Lansing, Mich., University College, Dept. of American Thought and Language, Michigan State University.   1437867

Michigan. University. Board in Control of Student Publications. Generation. *See* Generation; the inter-arts magazine. Ann Arbor, University of Michigan, Board in Control of Student Publications.   1437800

Michigan's voices; a literary quarterly magazine. *Saginaw, Mich.*   0956071
   Beg. date: 1960
   Title varies: Summer-Autumn 1960, Voices; a Michigan literary quarterly.
   WU   UWM (RBR) V.1 no.1-2; v.2-3 (SUM1960-SPR1964).

Micromegas. *Iowa City, Iowa.*   1496395
   ISSN: 0026-2773   Beg. date: 1965
   Editor: Frederic Will.
   WU   UWM (RBR) V.1-v.7 no.1 (1965-1977).

The Midatlantic review. *Mamaronek, N.Y., The Country Press.*   1496404
   ISSN: 0145-6229   Beg. date: 1975
   WU   UWM (RBR) V.1; v.2 no.5-7 (SUM1975-1977).

The Middle R. *La Grande, Ore.*   1496417
   Beg. date: 1950
   Publication suspended 1956-1960.
   WU   UWM (RBR) 1963-1968, 1970.

Midland poetry review. *See* Blue river poetry magazine. Shelbyville, Ind., The Blue River Press.   1433451

Midnightsun quarterly. *Whitehorse, Yukon.*   149642A
   ISSN: 0382-828X   Beg. date: 1965
   WU   UWM (RBR) V.1 no.1-2; v.2 no.1-3 (FAL1965-FAL1966).

Midstream, a quarterly Jewish review. *New York, Theodor Herzl Foundation.*   0459948
   ISSN: 0026-332X   LCCN: 58-32015   Beg. date: 1955
   WU   UWM (RBR) V.1 no.1; v.2; v.4 no.1 (AUT1955-WIN1958).

Midway, a magazine of discovery in the arts and sciences. *Chicago, University of Chicago Press.*   0459950
   ISSN: 0544-067X   Beg. date: 1960   End date: 1970
   Ceased publication with vol. 11 no. 1, Summer 1970.
   "All material in Midway has appeared, or will appear, in books and journals of the University of Chicago Press."
   Vol. 1-7 (1960-1966) also called no. 1-28.
   WU   UWM (RBR) V.1-v.11 no.1 (1960-SUM1970).

Midwest. *Minneapolis, The Midwest Federation of Arts and Professions.*   1496445
   Beg. date: 1936   End date: 1937
   "A review."
   Ceased publication with vol. 1 no. 3, Jan. 1937.
   WU   UWM (RBR) Aug., Nov.-Dec. 1936; Jan. 1937.

Midwest; a magazine of poetry and opinion. *Chicago.*   0459976
   ISSN: 0544-0688   Beg. date: 1961   End date: 1966
   Ceased publication with no. 8, Winter 1965/1966?
   Special issue 1963 as "Statements no. 6.".
   WU   UWM (RBR) No.1-8 (SPR1961-WIN1965/1966).

Midwest chaparral. *Iowa City [etc.].*   1496460
   ISSN: 0026-3346
   Founded by M. Ball Dickson and edited by her until 1968.
   WU   UWM (RBR) Summer 1953, Spring 1955, Summer 1955, Spring 1956, Fall 1956/Winter 1957, Spring/Summer 1959, Spring/Summer 1960, Winter 1960-Summer 1961, Summer/Fall 1961, Summer/Fall 1962, Spring 1970.

Midwest Federation of Arts and Professions. Midwest. *See* Midwest. Minneapolis, The Midwest Federation of Arts and Professions.   1496458

Midwest Literary League. *See* Hinterland. Des Moines, Midwest Literary League.   0460156

Midwest monographs. Series 1 (Drama). *Urbana, Ill., The Depot Press.*   1496499
   ISSN: 0076-8596   Beg. date: 1967
   WU   UWM (RBR) No.1-2 (SEP-OCT1967).

Midwest monographs. Series 2 (Poetry). *Urbana, Ill., The Depot Press.*   1496508
   ISSN: 0076-860X   Beg. date: 1968
   WU   UWM (RBR) No.1 (MAR1968).

The Midwest quarterly. *Pittsburg, Kansas, Kansas State College of Pittsburg.*   0460275
   ISSN: 0026-3451   LCCN: 61-41898   Beg. date: 1959
   Supersedes Educational leader.
   WU   UWM (RBR) V.2 no.2-4; v.3-7,9-11 (1961-JUL1970).

The Midwest review. *Wayne, Neb., Nebraska State Teachers College.*   1496473
   ISSN: 0544-0823   LCCN: 64-35459   Beg. date: 1959   End date: 1963
   Ceased publication with 1963.
   WU   UWM (RBR) Spring 1960.

Midwestern University, Wichita Falls, Tex. Department of English. *See* Midwestern University quarterly. Wichita Falls, Department of English, Midwestern University.   0460563

Midwestern University quarterly. *Wichita Falls, Department of English, Midwestern University.* 0460576
Ceased with v. 2 (1966).
WU UWM (RBR) V.1-v.2 no.3 (1965-1967).

Migrant. *Ventura, Calif., Worcester, Eng.* 1496510
ISSN: 0540-004X Beg. date: 1959 End date: 1960
Editor: Gael Turnbull.
Ceased publication with no. 8, Sept. 1960.
Superseded by Mica.
WU UWM (RBR) No.1-8 (JUL1959-SEP1960).

Mikrokosmos. *Wichita, Kan., Department of English, Wichita State University.* 1496523
ISSN: 0540-018X
WU UWM (RBR) No.1-7,9-14,20 (SPR1958-1975).

Mile high underground. *Denver.* 0461098
ISSN: 0544-1714 Beg. date: 1966 End date: 1967
Ceased publication with vol. 1 no. 6, Fall 1967.
WU UWM (RBR) No.1-6 (DEC1966-FAL1967).

The Milk quarterly. *Chicago, The Yellow Press.* 1496549
LCCN: sc77-519 Beg. date: 1972
WU UWM (RBR) No.1-9/10 (1972-1976).

The Mill. *Adelphi, Md.* 1496551
Beg. date: 1976
WU UWM (RBR) No.1-2 (AUG1976-1977).

The Mill Mountain review. *Roanoke, Va.* 1496564
ISSN: 0026-4245 Beg. date: 1969
WU UWM (RBR) 1969-1971.

Million. *Glasgow, William MacLellan.* 1496577
WU UWM (RBR) No.1-3 (1943?-1944?).

Milwaukee arts monthly. *See* Prairie. Milwaukee. 1499226

Milwaukee literary times. *Milwaukee.* 149658A
ISSN: 0540-1119
WU UWM (RBR) V.1 no.2 (FEB1961).

Mimeo. *Cambridge, Mass.* 1496592
WU UWM (RBR) One unnumbered, undated issue; v.2 no.2-4 (1967).

Mind fucke. *Washington, D.C., War Babies Unlimited.* 0462365
WU UWM (RBR) No.4 (FAL1968).

Mindfucke. *See* Mind fucke. *Washington, D.C.,* 1483054

Minnesota. State College, Moorhead. Aegis. *See* Aegis. Moorhead, Minn., 1109795

Minnesota. State College, Saint Cloud. Minnesota poetry anthology. *See* Minnesota poets anthology. St. Cloud, Minn., St. Cloud State College. 149663A

Minnesota. State College, Saint Cloud. Minnesota poets anthology. *See* Minnesota poets anthology. St. Cloud, Minn., St. Cloud State College. 1496614

Minnesota. University. College of Liberal Arts. Honors Student Council. Academy. *See* Academy. Minneapolis, University of Minnesota, College of Liberal Arts, Honors Student Council. 1011036

Minnesota. University. Department of English. Tyro. *See* Tyro. Minneapolis, Dept. of English, University of Minnesota. 1516582

Minnesota. University. Duluth Branch. U M D humanist. *See* U M D humanist. *Duluth,* 1483082

Minnesota. University. Duluth branch. Division of humanities. *See* U M D humanist. Duluth, University of Minnesota. 0475728

Minnesota. University. University High School. Bard. *See* Bard. Minneapolis, University High School, University of Minnesota. 1430761

Minnesota poetry anthology. *See* Minnesota poets anthology. St. Cloud, Minn., St. Cloud State College. 1496627

Minnesota poets anthology. *St. Cloud, Minn., St. Cloud State College.* 1496601
Title varies: Spring 1972, Minnesota poetry anthology.
WU UWM (RBR) Spring 1972; v.2 no.1 (1973).

Minnesota quarterly. *Minneapolis.* 0482102
LCCN: 62-48996 Beg. date: 1923 End date: 1950
Publication suspended June 1932-Winter 1947.
Ceased publication with Spring 1950.
WU UWM (RBR) No.1-2 (1948); Fall 1949; Winter, Spring 1950.

Minnesota review (1971-). *Milwaukee, etc.* 1080211
ISSN: 0026-5667 Beg. date: 1971
Supersedes with Fall 1971 a publication with the same title published in Minneapolis Oct. 1960-1970.
WU UWM (RBR) N. ser. no.1 (FAL1973).

The Minority of one. *Richmond.* 0484196
ISSN: 0544-3725 Beg. date: 1959 End date: 1968
Ceased publication with v. 10 (1968).
WU UWM (RBR) V.1 no.1; v.2-7 (no.1-73) (DEC1959-1965).

Minotaur. *Eagle River, Alaska.* 1496655
Beg. date: 1975
Editor: Jim Gove.
WU UWM (RBR) V.1 no.1-2 (1975-1976).

Minotaur. *London, Robert Knight and Robert Lee.* 1496668
WU UWM (RBR) 1970.

Minus one. *London, S.E. Parker.* 1496670
ISSN: 0026-5721
"An individualist anarchist review" (varies slightly).
WU UWM (RBR) No.6-21 (1965-FEB1968).

Mirage. *Baltimore, Md., Jack L. Chalker.* 1496683
"The amateur magazine of fantasy."
WU UWM (RBR) V.1 no.5-6; v.2 no.1-2 (no.7-10) (1962-1971).

Mirror northwest. *Wenatchee, Wash., Mirror Northwest.* 1496696
Beg. date: 1971
WU UWM (RBR) V.1-5 (WIN1971-1974).

Mirror of taste and dramatic censor. *Philadelphia, Thomas Barton Zantzinger and Co.* 0484324
LCCN: 5-22009 Beg. date: 1810 End date: 1811
Included in American Periodical Series.
WU UWM (RBR) V.1-4 (1810-1811).

Miscellaneous man. *Berkeley, Calif., William J. Margolis.* 1496705
ISSN: 0540-3324 Beg. date: 1954 End date: 1959
Ceased publication with vol. 2 no.15, Spring 1959.
WU UWM (RBR) V.1-2 (no.1-15) (APR1954-SUM1959).

Miscellaneous man. Second series. *Los Angeles, Los Angeles Free Press.* 1496718
ISSN: 0544-4144 Beg. date: 1968
WU UWM (RBR) V.1 no.1 (SUM1968).

Miscellany. *Calcutta, Writers Workshop.* 095641A
ISSN: 0026-5896 LCCN: 76-640850 Beg. date: 1960
Title varies: - , Writers Workshop miscellany.
WU UWM (RBR) No.1,4,15,17-36 (AUG1960-1969).

The Miscellany. *Davidson, N.C., Davidson College.* 1496720
ISSN: 0026-590X Beg. date: 1966
"A Davidson review."
WU UWM (RBR) V.1 no.2; v.3-4; v.5 no.2; v.6-9,11; v.12 no.1 (MAY1966-1977).

The Miscellany. *New York.* 0484519
End date: 1931
A prospectus number was issued Dec. 1929.
Ceased publication with vol. 1 no. 6, March 1931.
WU UWM (RBR) V.1 no.1 (MAR1930).

Mississippi. University of Southern Mississippi, Hattiesburg. Center for Writers. Mississippi review. *See* Mississippi review. [Hattiesburg, Miss., Center for Writers, English Dept., University of Southern Mississippi]. 1445941

The Mississippi mud. *Portland, Ore.* 1496733
WU UWM (RBR) V.2 no.6-7; v.3 no.1-2,5; no.16 (n.d.-1977).

Mississippi review. *[Hattiesburg, Miss., Center for Writers, English Dept., University of Southern Mississippi].* 1445939
ISSN: 0047-7559 LCCN: 72-620236 Beg. date: 1972
WU UWM (RBR) V.1-v.6 no.2 (1972-1977).

Mississippi Valley review. *See* Mississippi Valley review of creative writing. Macomb, Ill., Western Illinois University. 150810A

The Mississippi Valley review of creative writing. *Macomb, Ill., Western Illinois University.* 1508088
Title varies: - , The Mississippi Valley review.
WU UWM (RBR) V.1 no.2-v.6 no.2 (SPR1972-1977).

Missouri. Northeast Missouri State University, Kirksville. Chariton review. *See* Chariton review. Kirksville, Mo., Northeast Missouri State University. 1431099

Missouri. Southeast Missouri State University, Cape Girardeau. Cape rock. *See* Cape rock. Cape Girardeau, Mo., Southeast Missouri State University. 1441943

Missouri. University, Kansas City. Number one. *See* Number one. Kansas City, Mo. 1497543

The Missouri poet. *Columbo, Mo.* 1496746
WU UWM (RBR) V.1 no.1-2; v.2 no.1 (1973-1974).

Mister Clean. *See* Mr. Little Magazine Collection—University of Wisconsin

Mister Clean. *See* Mr. Clean. New Orleans. — 1496774

Mister Cogito. *See* Mr. Cogito. Forest Grove, Ore. — 149679A

Mixer: Firelands arts review. *Huron, Ohio, Rudinger Foundation.* — 1432472
Beg. date: 1972 End date: 1973
Title varies: vol. 1, Spring 1972, Mixer magazine.
Continued by Firelands arts review with vol. 3, 1974.
WU UWM (RBR) V.1-2 (1972-1973).

Mixer magazine. *See* Mixer: Firelands arts review. Huron, Ohio, Rudinger Foundation. — 1432498

Modern haiku. *Los Angeles, Kay Titus Mormino.* — 1496759
ISSN: 0026-7821 Beg. date: 1969
WU UWM (RBR) V.1-v.8 no.2 (WIN1969-1977).

Modern images. *El Dorado, Ark.* — 1496809
ISSN: 0026-7848
Editor: Roy Douglass Burrow.
WU UWM (RBR) Ser. 4-14 (1969-1973); Winter 1973/1974-Spring/Summer 1976; special summer series 1970 and 1971.

Modern monthly. *See* Modern quarterly; a journal of radical opinion. New York. — 1483132

Modern occasions; a quarterly of literature and ideas of culture and politics. *Cambridge, Mass.* — 0488441
Beg. date: 1970 End date: 1972
Ceased with vol. 2 no. 2.
To be superseded by a hardbound annual edition.
WU UWM (RBR) V.1-v.2 no.2 (FAL1970-SPR1972).

Modern Organization for Dance Evolvement. Feet. *See* Feet. New York, Modern Organization for Dance Evolvement (M O D E). — 1436182

Modern poetry in translation. *London.* — 0488560
ISSN: 0026-8291 Beg. date: 1965
WU UWM (RBR) No.1-6,8-30 (1966-1977).

Modern Poetry studies. *Buffalo, New York.* — 0488573
ISSN: 0026-8305 Beg. date: 1970
WU UWM (RBR) V.1-v.8 no.2 (1970-1977).

Modern quarterly. *London.* — 0488649
Beg. date: 1938 End date: 1953
Ceased publication with new ser. vol. 8 no. 4, Autumn 1953.
Superseded by Marxist quarterly with Jan. 1954.
WU UWM (RBR) N. ser. v.1 no.3-4; v.2 no.1-3; v.3 no.1-2; v.4 no.4; v.5 no.2; v.6 no.2-4; v.7-v.8 no.2 (SUM1946-SPR1953).

Modern quarterly; a journal of radical opinion. *New York.* — 0488651
LCCN: 27-4464 rev Beg. date: 1923 End date: 1940
Title varies: 1923-Autumn 1932, Modern quarterly; 1933-June 1938, Modern monthly.
V. 6 no. 4 never published.
Ceased publication with vol. 11, 1940.
WU UWM (RBR) V.7 no.2 (MAR1933).

The Modern school. *Stelton, N.J., The Modern School Association of North America, Ferrer Colony.* — 1496811
LCCN: CA19-169 Beg. date: 1912 End date: 1922
"A monthly magazine devoted to liberatarian ideas in education."
Ceased publication with midwinter issue, 1922.
WU UWM (RBR) V.5 no.8,10-12; v.6 no.1,3-4/5; v.7 no.1/2/3 (AUG1918-JAN/MAR1920).

Modern School Association of North America. Ferrer Colony, Stelton, New Jersey. **Modern school.** *See* Modern school. Stelton, N.J., The Modern School Association of North America, Ferrer Colony. — 1496824

The Modern Scot. *St. Andres, Scotland, J.H. Whyte.* — 1496837
LCCN: 32-28906 Beg. date: 1930 End date: 1936
Ceased publication with vol. 6, Winter 1936.
United with Scottish standard to form Outlook.
WU UWM (RBR) V.3 no.3 (OCT1932).

Modern utopian. *Medford, Massachusetts, Tufts University.* — 0488980
ISSN: 0026-8534 Beg. date: 1966
Bimonthly. Richard I. Fairfield, P. O. Box 44, ZIP 02153.
WU UWM (RBR) V.1-5 (1967-1971); 1972 (special issue).

Modern verse. *Albuquerque, N.M.* — 149684A
LCCN: 45-47154 Beg. date: 1941 End date: 1941
Ceased publication with vol. 1, Oct. 1941.
Absorbed by New Mexico quarterly review.
WU UWM (RBR) V.1 (1941).

Modernalia. *Shreveport, La., Estelle Trust.* — 1496852
WU UWM (RBR) No.2 (SEP1960).

The Modernist. *New York, The Modernist Association.* — 1496865
Beg. date: 1919 End date: 1919
"A monthly magazine of modern arts and letters."
Ceased publication with vol. 1 no. 1, Nov. 1919.
WU UWM (RBR) V.1 no.1 (NOV1919).

Modernist Association. Modernist. *See* Modernist. New York, The Modernist Association. — 1496878

Modine gunch. *Madison, Wisc., Department of English, University of Wisconsin.* — 1496880
ISSN: 0026-8763 Beg. date: 1969
WU UWM (RBR) V.1 no.1-8 (1969-JAN1973).

The Modularist review. *Cambridge, Mass., Wooden Needle Press.* — 1496902
ISSN: 0360-2885 LCCN: 75-648304 Beg. date: 1975
WU UWM (RBR) No.1-2 (1975-1976).

Modus operandi. *Brookeville, Md., Andreas and Sheila Jensen.* — 1496915
ISSN: 0026-8828 Beg. date: 1974
Published for four years previous to 1974 as "a small paper in UAP bundles."
WU UWM (RBR) V.5 no.1; v.7-v.8 no.7 (JAN1974-JUL1977).

Mofussil. *Kettering, Eng.* — 1496928
ISSN: 0026-8860 Beg. date: 1968
"A quarterly of poetry."
WU UWM (RBR) No.1-4 (1968-1969).

Mojo navigator R and R news. *San Francisco.* — 1497584
WU UWM (RBR) V.1 no.11 (NOV221966).

Mojo navigator(e). *Oak Park, Ill. [etc.], Cat's Pajamas Press.* — 0489236
ISSN: 0026-8909
WU UWM (RBR) No.1-5 (1969-1976).

MOMA; magazine of modern arts. *See* M O M A; magazine of modern arts. Leeds, Eng., Leeds University Union. — 1323594

Momentum. *Los Angeles, Century City Educational Arts Project.* — 1497597
Beg. date: 1974
WU UWM (RBR) No.1-8 (MAR1974-1977).

Monarchist quarterly. *See* Nationalist quarterly. Boston, Mass. — 1492302

Monks pond. *Trappist, Ky., Thomas Merton.* — 1497606
ISSN: 0544-7925 LCCN: 70-1003 Beg. date: 1968 End date: 1968
Ceased publication with no. 4, Winter 1968.
WU UWM (RBR) No.1 (SPR1968).

Monmouth review. *West Long Branch, N.J., Monmouth College.* — 1497619
ISSN: 0085-3534 LCCN: 73-641823 Beg. date: 1972
"A journal of the literary arts."
WU UWM (RBR) V.1 no.1 (SPR1972).

Monocle. A leisurely quarterly of political satire. *New Haven.* — 0490202
ISSN: 0026-9824 Beg. date: 1957
"Founded by law and graduate students in and around Yale University."
WU UWM (RBR) V.1 no.2-v.6 no.5 (WIN1957/1958-1966); special issue: 1969.

Monsieur Dada. *Hounslow, Middlesex, Eng., De-Press.* — 1497621
WU UWM (RBR) 1974.

Montana. University. Women's Resource Center. GiltEdge. — 1528769
See GiltEdge. Missoula, Mont., Women's Resource Center, University of Montana.

Montana. University, Missoula. Department of English. — 1371185
Cutbank. *See* Cut bank. Missoula, Dept. of English, University of Montana.

Montana gothic. *Missoula, Mont.* — 1497634
Beg. date: 1974
WU UWM (RBR) No.1-5 (FAL1974-WIN1977).

Montana poetry quarterly. *Seeley Lake, Mont.* — 1497647
WU UWM (RBR) Jan./Mar., Oct./Dec. 1953; Jan./Mar.-July/Sept. 1954.

Montemora. *New York.* — 1496930
WU UWM (RBR) No.1-3 (FAL1975-1977).

Monterey Peninsula College, Monterey, California. Brand new testament. *See* Brand new testament. Monterey, Calif., Monterey Peninsula College. — 1492120

Montevallo review. *Montevallo, Ala., Montevallo Press, Alabama College.*   1496943
ISSN: 0463-3016   LCCN: 58-29554   Beg. date: 1950
WU   UWM (RBR) No.1-4 (SUM1950-SUM1953).

The Month. *London, Simpkin, Marshall and company.*   049179A
ISSN: 0027-0172   LCCN: 8-32184   Beg. date: 1882
Continues The Month and Catholic review with vol. 44, Jan. 1882.
Subtitle varies: 1882-1896, A Catholic magazine and review; 1897-May 1913, A Catholic magazine.
Indexed by Catholic periodical and literature index.
Indexes: vol. 44-112, 1882-1908. (Includes index for Month and Catholic review, vol. 20-43, 1874-1881; Month: a magazine and review, vol. 1-9, 1865-1873); vol. 113-138, 1909-1921.
WU   UWM (RBR) N. ser. v.1-2; v.3 no.1-5; v.4-7; v.8 no.1-2; v.9 no.2-6; v.10-v.11 no.1 (1949-JAN1954).

Monthly chapbook. *See* Chapbook. *London.*   1483158

Month's best. *Seattle, Department of English. University of Washington.*   1496969
WU   UWM (RBR) V.7 no.3; v.8 no.1; v.9 no.2; v.10 no.1; v.11 no.1; v.12 no.1 (MAY1950-WIN/SPR1955).

The Montparnasse review. *Paris, American Center for Students and Artists.*   1496984
ISSN: 0544-9626   Beg. date: 1965
Supersedes Parnassus with Winter 1964/1965.
"A magazine of creative writing."
WU   UWM (RBR) No.6 (WIN1964/1965); no.2 (SUM1966).

Monument. *See* Monument in cantos and essays. *Columbia, Mo.,*   1519911

Monument in cantos and essays. *Columbia, Mo., Monument Press.*   1497004
ISSN: 0027-0733   LCCN: sc77-533   Beg. date: 1968
WU   UWM (RBR) V.1 no.1-3; v.2 no.1 (no.4); v.2 no.5-6 (1968-1973).

Moon shine. *London, Tina Fulker.*   1497045
"A magazine of poetry."
WU   UWM (RBR) 1972?, 1974?, 1975.

Moondance. *Memphis, Moonbeam Publications.*   1497017
Beg. date: 1975
WU   UWM (RBR) V.1 no.1; v.2 no.1 (AUT1975-SPR1976).

Moongoose. *Montreal, Ralph Alfonso.*   149702A
WU   UWM (RBR) No.2-4 (MAR-NOV1972).

Moonlight review. *Brooklyn, N.Y.*   1497032
ISSN: 0545-0268   Beg. date: 1967
WU   UWM (RBR) V.1 no.1-3 (JUN1967-1968).

Moons and lion tailes. *Minneapolis, Permanent Press.*   1007601
ISSN: 0099-0264   LCCN: 77-648741   Beg. date: 1973
WU   UWM (RBR) No.1-4; v.2 no.1-3 (SPR1973-1977).

Moonshine. *See* Moon shine. *London, Tina Fulker.*   1497058

Moonstone. *St. Louis, Mo.*   1497060
Beg. date: 1971
WU   UWM (RBR) V.1 no.1-2 (JUN1971-FEB1974).

Moonstones. *Sacramento.*   1497073
End date: 1968
Ceased publication with no. 4, 1968.
Superseded by Runcible spoon.
WU   UWM (RBR) No.2-4 (1966-1968).

The Morada. *Albuquerque, N.M.*   1497086
LCCN: 59-56631   Beg. date: 1929   End date: 1931
"A tri-lingual quarterly."
In English, French and German.
Ceased publication with 1931.
WU   UWM (RBR) No.1-2 (1929); 1 unnumbered, undated issue (1931?).

Morehouse College, Atlanta. Phoenix. *See* Phoenix.   1499975
Atlanta, The Arts Club of Morehouse College.

Morning star; a quarto of poetry. *See* Morning star quarto.   1497108
Scottsdale, Ariz., Rampart Press.

Morning star quarto. *Scottsdale, Ariz., Rampart Press.*   1497099
ISSN: 0463-4128   Beg. date: 1956   End date: 1962
Title varies: no. 1-4, Oct. 1956-Autumn 1959, Morning star; a quarto of poetry.
Ceased publication with no. 7, 1962.
WU   UWM (RBR) No.1-4 (OCT1956-AUT1959).

Mosaic. *New York, Mosaic Pub. Co.*   1497110
Beg. date: 1934
Editors: S. and V. Koch and Alvin Schwartz.
"A critical quarterly."
WU   UWM (RBR) V.1 no.1 (NOV/DEC1934); Spring 1935.

Mosaic. *San Diego, Calif. [etc.]*   1497149
Beg. date: 1973
WU   UWM (RBR) No.1-7 (1973-WIN1974).

Mosaic. *Walnut, Calif., Associated Students of Mt. San Antonio College, Walnut.*   1497123
WU   UWM (RBR) V.1-5 (1960-WIN1964).

Mother. *Pittsburgh, Mother Press.*   1497151
ISSN: 0541-1645   Beg. date: 1963
WU   UWM (RBR) No.1-12 (n.d.-n.d.).

Mother; a journal of new literature. *Dallas, etc.*   0905719
Beg. date: 1964
Beginning with no. 9, issued in phonorecord form only.
WU   UWM (RBR) No.3-9 (NOV/DEC1964-1968).

Motion. *Vancouver, Villiers Publications Ltd.*   1497164
WU   UWM (RBR) No.1-6 (1962).

Mount Adams review. *Cincinnati.*   1497177
Title varies: vol. 1, no. 1, However.
WU   UWM (RBR) V.1 no.2-6; v.2-v.3 no.1 (MAR/APR1964-SPR1970).

Mount Carmel College, Niagara Falls, Ontario. Eschata.   1432340
See Eschata. Niagara Falls, Ont., Mount Carmel College.

Mount San Antonio College, Walnut, California. Mosaic.   1497136
See Mosaic. Walnut, Calif., Associated Students of Mt. San Antonio College, Walnut.

Mount Union College, Alliance, Ohio. Saga. *See* Saga.   1506784
Alliance, Ohio. Mt. Union College.

Mountain. *Hamilton, Ont.*   1497201
ISSN: 0541-1998   Beg. date: 1962
WU   UWM (RBR) No.1-4 (1962-1963).

Mountain summer. *Sewanee, Tenn., Ex Libris.*   1497214
ISSN: 0146-7689   LCCN: sc77-515   Beg. date: 1974
WU   UWM (RBR) No.1-3 (1974-1976).

The Mountain troubador. *Burlington, Vt., The Poetry Society of Vermont.*   1497227
ISSN: 0027-2604   Beg. date: 1956
WU   UWM (RBR) V.9 no.2; v.10-v.20 no.1 (FAL1964-SPR1975).

Mouth. *Buffalo, N.Y.*   1497242
Beg. date: 1972
WU   UWM (RBR) V.1-v.2 no.1 (MAY1972-WIN1974).

Mouth of the dragon. *New York.*   1497255
ISSN: 0145-0042   LCCN: 77-649541   Beg. date: 1974
"A poetry journal of male love."
WU   UWM (RBR) No.1-4 (MAY1974-MAR1975).

Move. *Preston, Eng.*   1497268
ISSN: 0580-0854   Beg. date: 1964   End date: 1968
Special issue called Thirteen American poets was issued Nov. 1966.
Ceased publication with no. 8, April 1968.
WU   UWM (RBR) No.1-8 (DEC1964-APR1968).

Movement. *New Delhi, Sudhir Balsaver.*   1497283
LCCN: 76-641788   Beg. date: 1968
WU   UWM (RBR) No.4-5 (1969-JUN1970).

Movement for Colonial Freedom. Colonial freedom news.   1431318
See Colonial freedom news. London, The Movement for Colonial Freedom.

Moving on. *Santa Monica, Calif. [etc.].*   1497296
ISSN: 0027-2825   Beg. date: 1968
"A slim quarterly to celebrate the human-Mystery-lived!"
Editor: George Hoyt.
WU   UWM (RBR) V.1 no.1-6 (SEP1968-[1971]).

Moving out. *Detroit.*   1497305
ISSN: 0047-830X
WU   UWM (RBR) V.1 no.2-v.7 no.1 (1971-1977).

Mr. Clean. *New Orleans.*   1496761
Beg. date: 1969
WU   UWM (RBR) No.1-3 (1969).

Mr. Cogito. *Forest Grove, Ore.*   1496787
WU   UWM (RBR) V.1-v.3 no.2 (FAL1973-SPR1977).

MS. *Los Angeles.*   1497318
    WU   UWM (RBR) V.1 no.3-7 (APR-SEP1941).

Mss. *Chico, Calif., John Gardner.*   1497320
    Beg. date: 1961
    WU   UWM (RBR) V.1-2 (SPR1961-1964).

MSS. *Claremont, Calif.*   1497333
    "Literary magazine of Pomona College."
    WU   UWM (RBR) Dec. 1951, May 1952, two unnumbered, undated issues.

Mt. Adams review. *See* Mount Adams review. Cincinnati.   149718A

Mulberry. *New Haven, Conn., Mulberry Press.*   1497359
    ISSN: 0090-4953   LCCN: 73-641374   Beg. date: 1972
    WU   UWM (RBR) Nov. 1972; Mar., May 1973.

Mulch. *New York.*   1497361
    ISSN: 0027-3112   LCCN: 79-617579   Beg. date: 1971
    WU   UWM (RBR) V.1-v.4 no.1 (no.1-9) (APR1971-SPR/SUM1976).

Mummy. *San Francisco.*   0497245
    WU   UWM (RBR) No.1-2 (1962-1963/1964).

Mummy's little mummy. *See* Mummy. San Francisco.   0497258

Mundus artium. *Athens, Ohio.*   0497323
    ISSN: 0027-3406   Beg. date: 1967
    "A journal of international literature and the arts".
    Published 1967-   by the department of English, Ohio University, Athens, Ohio.
    WU   UWM (RBR) V.1-9 (WIN1967-1976).

The Muse. *Annandale-on-Hudson, N.Y., Bard College.*   1497374
    WU   UWM (RBR) V.7 no.2 (FAL1972).

Muse. *[n.p.], Birmingham Poetry Centre.*   149739A
    Beg. date: 1971
    WU   UWM (RBR) V.1 no.1-8 (1971-MAY1976).

The Muse. *Newberg, Ore.*   1497411
    ISSN: 0580-2520   Beg. date: 1957
    "A poetry quarterly."
    WU   UWM (RBR) V.1 no.1,3-4; v.2 no.3-v.13 no.3 (FAL1957-SPR1970).

Mushrooom. *New York.*   1497424
    Beg. date: 1974
    WU   UWM (RBR) No.1-3 (APR1974-APR1975).

Music Center Operating Company of Los Angeles County.   1499802
    Performing arts. *See* Performing arts. Los Angeles, Music Center Operating Company of Los Angeles County.

Music vanguard. *New York.*   1494368
    Beg. date: 1935   End date: 1935
    "A critical review."
    Ceased publication with vol. 1 no. 2, Summer 1935.
    WU   UWM (RBR) V.1 no.1-2 (MAR/APR1935-SUM1935).

Muskrat magazine. *Brunswick, Maine.*   1494370
    Beg. date: 1974
    WU   UWM (RBR) V.1 no.1 (FAL1974).

Mustang review. *Denver, Colo., Karl Edd.*   1494383
    ISSN: 0027-4917   Beg. date: 1967
    WU   UWM (RBR) Aug. 1967; Feb., June, Dec. 1968; May, Dec. 1969; May, Dec. 1970; June, Dec. 1971; June 1972; Jan. 1973; Feb., Oct. 1975.

Mute. *Cass City, Mich., Mute Press.*   1494396
    ISSN: 0541-4571
    WU   UWM (RBR) 1961.

Mutiny. *New York, Mutiny press.*   0499755
    LCCN: 61-4410.
    Ceased pub. v. 4 no. 1.
    WU   UWM (RBR) No.1; v.1 no.2-v.4 no.1; no.12 (1956-1963).

My landlord must be really upset. *Sacramento, Runcible Spoon.*   1494405
    Beg. date: 1970
    "A quarterly workers magazine."
    WU   UWM (RBR) V.1 no.1-2 ([1969]-[1970?]).

My own mag. *Barnet, Herts., Eng.*   1494418
    ISSN: 0580-3799   Beg. date: 1964
    WU   UWM (RBR) Nov. 1964; Feb., May, Aug., Dec. 1965; April, July 1966; three unnumbered, undated special issues.

Mysore. University. Department of Postgraduate Studies in English. Literary half-yearly. *See* Literary half-yearly. Mysore, Mysore University, Dept. of Post-graduate Studies in English.   0895200

The Mysterious barricades. *New York.*   1494420
    Beg. date: 1972
    WU   UWM (RBR) No.1-4 (SPR1972-WIN1976).

N

N R G. *Pittsburgh.* 1494433
 Beg. date: 1976
 WU   UWM (RBR) No.1-3 (1976).

Nada review. *See* The Smith. New York, Horizon Press. 1159500

Nadada. *New York.* 1494459
 ISSN: 0547-1028 Beg. date: 1964 End date: 1965
 Ceased publication with no. 2, Oct. 1965.
 WU   UWM (RBR) No.2 (OCT1965).

Nairobi. University College. Department of English. 1441837
 Busara. *See* Busara. Nairobi, University College, Dept. of English.

Naissance. *Winchester, Eng.* 1494461
 Ceased publication with no. 5/6.
 WU   UWM (RBR) No.4-5/6 (n.d.-n.d.).

The Naked ear. *Taos, N.M.* 1494474
 ISSN: 0465-7888
 WU   UWM (RBR) No.1-2,4-5,7-8,10 (n.d.-n.d.).

The Nantucket review. *Nantucket, Mass.* 1494487
 ISSN: 0094-4114 LCCN: 74-655141 Beg. date: 1974
 WU   UWM (RBR) No.1-8 (SPR1974-1977).

Nassau Community College, Garden City, New York. 1494509
 Nassau review. *See* Nassau review. Garden City, N.Y., Nassau Community College.

The Nassau review. *Garden City, N.Y., Nassau Community College.* 149449A
 ISSN: 0077-2879 Beg. date: 1964
 "The faculty journal of Nassau Community college."
 WU   UWM (RBR) V.1-v.3 no.3 (SPR1964-1977).

The Nation. *London, Paisley, Alexander Gardner.* 1495557
 Beg. date: 1903 End date: 1903
 Ceased publication with no. 6, Oct. 1903.
 WU   UWM (RBR) No.1 (MAY1903).

National call. *See* Central issues. Marietta, Ohio, Acorn Pub. Co. 1428236

The National call. *Marietta, Ohio, C. Franklin Eicher.* 1494511
 ISSN: 0547-4744 Beg. date: 1967
 "For responsible citizenship."
 Continued by Central issues.
 WU   UWM (RBR) V.1 no.1-6 (NOV1967-APR1968).

National Catholic Theatre Conference. *See* Drama critique; a critical review of theatre arts and literature. Lancaster, N.Y., National Catholic Theatre Conference. 050658A

National Council of the Realist Writers' Groups. Realist. *See* Realist. Northbridge, Australia. 1504183

National Film and Photo League. Filmfront. *See* Filmfront. New York, National Film and Photo League. 1436925

National Film and Photo League. New theatre. *See* New theatre. New York. 1529055

National Poetry Association. Creative writing. *See* Creative writing. Los Angeles, National Poetry Association. 1210125

National Poetry Circle. New melody. *See* New melody. Chard, Somerset, Eng. 1494879

National Translation Center. Delos. *See* Delos; a journal on and of translation. Austin, National Translation Center. 1434562

Nationalist quarterly. *Boston, Mass.* 1492280
 Beg. date: 1935 End date: 1938
 Title varies: vol. 1 nos. 1-4, 1935-Jan./Mar. 1936, Anathema; vol. 2 nos. 1-2, April/June-July/Sept. 1936, Monarchist quarterly.
 WU   UWM (RBR) V.1 no.1; v.2 no.2 (APR/JUN1935,JUL/SEP1936).

Nativity. *Delaware, Ohio.* 1494524
 LCCN: 67-91646 Beg. date: 1930 End date: 1931
 "An American quarterly."
 Ceased publication with vol. 1 no. 2, Spring 1931.
 WU   UWM (RBR) No.1-2 (WIN1930-SPR1931).

Nausea. *Long Beach, Calif.* 1528981
 Beg. date: 1973
 Title varies: v.1-   (no.1-   ), Winter 1972/1973-   , Nausea one.
 WU   UWM (RBR) V.1-v.4 no.1 (no.1-11) (WIN1972/1973-SPR1977).

Nausea one. *See* Nausea. Long Beach, Calif. 1528994

Nebraska. State Teachers College, Wayne. Midwest review. *See* Midwest review. Wayne, Neb., Nebraska State Teachers College. 1496486

Nebula. *North Bay, Ont., Nebula Press.* 1494537
 ISSN: 0317-2104 Beg. date: 1975
 WU   UWM (RBR) No.1-5 (1975-1977).

Neo-Surrealist Research Foundation. Limbo. *See* Limbo. Vancouver, B.C. 1492813

Neurotica. *St. Louis, Mo. Reprinted by Hacker Art Books, New York, 1963.* 0524945
 LCCN: 51-22550 Beg. date: 1948 End date: 1951
 Lettered on spine the Compleat Neurotica.
 Ceased publication with no. 9, 1951.
 WU   UWM (RBR) V.1 no.1-9 (SPR1948-WIN1952).

Nevada. University. Department of English. Brushfire. *See* Brushfire. Reno, University of Nevada, Dept. of English. 1434092

New. *Trumansburg, N.Y., John Gill.* 1507540
 ISSN: 0028-4203 LCCN: 79-612513 Beg. date: 1966
 WU   UWM (RBR) No.1-27/28 (SEP1966-1976).

The New act. *New York.* 149454A
 Beg. date: 1933 End date: 1934
 "A literary review."
 Ceased publication with no. 3, May 1934.
 WU   UWM (RBR) No.1-3 (JAN1933-APR1934).

New age. *See* Gong. Nottingham, Eng., 1483208

New American caravan. *See* American caravan, a yearbook of American literature. New York, The Macaulay Company. 0525651

New American Library of World Literature, inc., New York. *See* New American review. New York, New American Library. 0525677

New American mercury. *See* The American Mercury, a monthly review. New York, 1168332

New American review. *New York, New American Library.* 0525692
 ISSN: 0028-4211 LCCN: 67-27377 Beg. date: 1967 End date: 1972
 Continued by American review; the magazine of new writing with no. 16, Feb. 1973.
 Index: nos. 9-15, included with index to nos. 16-24 of American review.
 WU   UWM (RBR) No.1-20 (SEP1967-APR1974).

The New anvil. *Chicago.* 1494552
 Beg. date: 1939 End date: 1940
 Editor: Jack Conroy.
 Ceased publication with vol. 1 no. 7, July/August 1940.
 WU   UWM (RBR) V.1 no.6 (MAY/JUN1940).

The New anvil. *Chicago, B.G. Haglund.* 1432808
 Beg. date: 1939 End date: 1940
 Ceased publication with vol. 1 no. 7, July/Aug. 1940.
 WU   UWM (RBR) V.1 no.1-7 (MAR1939-JUL/AUG1940).

New athenaeum. *Crescent City, Fla. [etc.].* 1494565
 Beg. date: 1948 End date: 1964
 Suspended between Winter 1952 and Summer 1953 issues; between Fall 1954 and Winter 1956 issues?
 Ceased publication with 1964.
 WU   UWM (RBR) Fall 1953; Winter 1956-Summer 1958; Summer 1959-Winter 1964.

New broom. *Glasgow.* 1494578
 ISSN: 0467-1759
 Ceased publication with no. 3, 1955?
 WU   UWM (RBR) No.2-3 (n.d.-1955?).

New campus review. *Denver.* 0526095
 WU   UWM (RBR) V.1-v.2 no.2 (MAY1966-SPR1969).

New Caravan. *See* American caravan, a yearbook of American literature. New York, The Macaulay Company. 0526117

The New castle. *Crystal Bay, Nevada, J.K. Bowen.* 1494580
 ISSN: 0545-087X
 WU   UWM (RBR) March 1961.

New chapter. *London.* 1494593
 ISSN: 0467-1945 Beg. date: 1957 End date: 1958
 "A magazine of literature."
 Ceased publication with vol. 1 no. 3, Sept. 1958.
 WU   UWM (RBR) V.1 no.2-3 (OCT1957-SEP1958).

New classic. Johannesburg, South Africa, New Classic Publications. 1494602
Beg. date: 1975
Title varies: The Classic.
In Afrikaans or English.
WU   UWM (RBR) No.2-4 (1975-1977).

New coin. Grahamstown, South Africa, South African Poetry Society. 1494628
ISSN: 0028-4459   Beg. date: 1965
Title varies: New coin poetry.
WU   UWM (RBR) V.1-v.4 no.2; v.5-v.12 no.1/2 (JAN1965-APR1976).

New coin poetry. *See* New coin. Grahamstown, South Africa, South African Poetry Society. 1494643

New collage. Sarasota, Fla. 1494656
ISSN: 0028-4467   Beg. date: 1970
WU   UWM (RBR) V.1-7; v.8 no.2 (1970-1977).

New Colophon: a book collector's quarterly. New York, [Ouschness, Crawford]. 0526249
LCCN: 48-816   Beg. date: 1948
Supersedes The Colophon.
Subtitle varies.
WU   UWM (RBR) V.1-2 (1948-1950).

New coterie; a quarterly of literature and art. London, E. Archer. 0526301
Beg. date: 1925
No more published.
WU   UWM (RBR) No.1-6 (NOV1925-SUM/AUT1927).

New Departures. London. 0526383
ISSN: 0028-4580
WU   UWM (RBR) Summer 1959; no.4,6-10/11 (1962-1975).

New dimensions. Whitewater, Wisc. 1507553
Beg. date: 1973
WU   UWM (RBR) V.1 no.1-3 (FEB-MAY/JUN1973).

The New earth review. Staten Island, N.Y. 1494669
Beg. date: 1976
WU   UWM (RBR) V.1 no.3 (1976).

New eclectic magazine. *See* Southern magazine. Baltimore, Turnbull and Murdoch [etc]. 0526474

New editions. San Francisco. 1494671
Beg. date: 1956
Editors: Byron R. Bryant and Michael Gvieg.
WU   UWM (RBR) V.1 no.1-2 (FAL1976-[196?]).

New England review. Hamden, Conn., John DeStefano. 1494684
End date: 1972
Continued by Connecticut critic with no. 7, March 1973.
WU   UWM (RBR) V.1 no.4-6 (JAN/FEB1970-1972).

A New England review. New Haven, Conn. 1494697
ISSN: 0545-1183   Beg. date: 1961
WU   UWM (RBR) Summer 1961; Spring 1962; Spring 1963.

The New English review. London, Eng. 1529001
End date: 1948
Title varies: Home and empire.
Ceased publication with vol. 17 no. 3, August 1948.
Superseded by English review magazine with Sept. 1948.
WU   UWM (RBR) V.11 no.2; v.14 no.1-2,5; v.15 no.2,4,6; v.16 no.1 (JUN1945-JAN1948).

New era. Leavenworth, Kan., Federal Prison Industries, Inc., Press. 1494706
Published by permission of the Bureau of Prisons, Dept. of Justice.
WU   UWM (RBR) V.16 no.1-2; v.17; v.18 no.1-2; v.19 no.1; v.20-21,54 (AUT1962-SUM1968); Winter 1970.

New expression. Oddingley, Eng., New Expression Publications. 1494719
Beg. date: 1971
Supersedes Vis viva.
WU   UWM (RBR) No.1,4 ([1971]).

New folder. New York. 1441718
Supersedes Folder.
WU   UWM (RBR) 1959.

New foundations. New York, Greenwood reprint, 1968. 0527228
V. 1 no. 2, Winter 1948 never published.
WU   UWM (RBR) V.1 no.1,3-4; v.2; v.3 no.2; v.4 no.1-2; v.7 no.1 (FAL1947-FAL1953).

New freewoman; an individualist review. New York, Kraus Reprint Corp., 1967. 0527243
Beg. date: 1913
Originally published in Oxford, Eng.
WU   UWM (RBR) V.1 no.1-13 (JUN15-DEC151913).

New frontiers. Fairfield, Conn. 1494721
ISSN: 0548-4553   Beg. date: 1955
Published by the students of Fairfield University.
WU   UWM (RBR) V.5 no.2 (SPR1960).

New Hampshire. State College, Keene. Sigma Pi Epsilon. Journal. *See* Journal. Keene, N.H. 1438770

New Haven, Connecticut. University. English Club. Noiseless spider. *See* Noiseless spider. New Haven, Conn., English Club of the University of New Haven. 1507672

New Haven Poetry Society. Orange Street poetry journal. *See* Orange Street poetry journal. New Haven, Conn., New Haven Poetry Society. 1497675

New Headland. Sheffield, Eng. 1439277
ISSN: 0017-8756   Beg. date: 1970
Title varies: · , Headland;   · , Headland poetry.
WU   UWM (RBR) No.1-8 (1970-1971); Jan. 1972.

New headland poetry magazine. Epping, Essex, Eng. 1494734
LCCN: 73-641221   Beg. date: 1972
WU   UWM (RBR) No.1/2-7 (AUG1972-OCT1974).

New helios. London. 1494747
ISSN: 0567-2860   Beg. date: 1956
WU   UWM (RBR) V.1 no.1-3 (OCT1956-SUM1958).

New horizons. Chicago, Ill. 0528081
Title varies: 1938-May/June 1940, Creative writing.
WU   UWM (RBR) V.2 no.4; v.3 no.1-2 (JUL/AUG1940-JAN/FEB1941).

New iconograph. New York. 0528129
Title varies: Spr. 1946-Win. 1946/1947 called Iconograph.
Includes Iconograph quarterly supplement of prejudice and opinion no. 1-4 (no. 4 as Iconograph news issue of the Iconograph quarterly supplement).
WU   UWM (RBR) No.2,4 (SUM-WIN1946); Fall 1947; suppl. no.1-2 (n.d.-n.d.).

The New idea. Madison, Wisc., The University of Wisconsin. 149475A
ISSN: 0467-2933
WU   UWM (RBR) V.1 no.1-8 (1956-MAR1959); Winter 1960-Winter 1963.

New improved zest. Chicago. 1494775
"Official organ of the New Realist Poetry School."
WU   UWM (RBR) V.1 no.1-2 (1964); Special issue 1964.

The New infinity review. South Point, Ohio, Infinity Publications. 1494790
WU   UWM (RBR) V.3 no.10-v.4 no.13 (SUM1976-1977).

New Jersey. State College, Trenton. Trenton review. *See* Trenton review. Trenton, N.J., Trenton State College. 1513024

The New laurel review. Pennington, N.J., The Pennington School. 149480A
ISSN: 0145-8388   LCCN: sc77-400   Beg. date: 1971
Supersedes Laurel review.
WU   UWM (RBR) V.1-v.2 no.1; v.3-v.7 no.1 (FAL1971-1977).

New leaf. London, The Humanities Society, Chelsea College. 1494825
WU   UWM (RBR) No.1-2 (1974?-1975?).

New magazine. Boston. 1494840
WU   UWM (RBR) V.1 no.1-2; v.2 no.1; v.3 no.1 (1968-1969).

New measure. Oxford, Donald Parsons and Co., Ltd. 1494853
ISSN: 0548-5940   LCCN: 66-9886   Beg. date: 1965   End date: 1968
"A quarterly magazine of poetry."
Ceased publication with no. 10, Oct. 1968.
WU   UWM (RBR) No.1-10 (AUT1965-1969).

New melody. *Chard, Somerset, Eng.* 1494866
ISSN: 0545-2872 Beg. date: 1962
Supersedes The Melody.
Issued by the National Poetry Circle.
WU UWM (RBR) V.1 no.4; v.2 no.5-7; v.3 no.9-12; v.4 no.13-15 (1965-WIN1968).

New Mexico. State University, Las Cruces. *Puerto del sol.* 150165A
See Puerto del sol. Las Cruces, New Mexico State University.

New Mexico. University. *Word.* See Word. Albuquerque, N.M., University of New Mexico. 1519229

New moon. *Long Beach, Calif., General Honors Program, California State University, Long Beach.* 1494881
Beg. date: 1975
"A magazine of the arts."
WU UWM (RBR) No.1 (NOV1975).

The New nation. *?, Australia.* 1494903
Beg. date: 1955
"An Australian review."
WU UWM (RBR) V.1 no.1,3-4; v.2 no.1/2 (SEP1955-JAN/FEB1956).

New numbers. *Ryton, Dymock, Gloucester, Eng.* 1494916
Beg. date: 1914 End date: 1914
Ceased publication with vol. 1 no. 4, Dec. 1914.
WU UWM (RBR) V.1 (1914).

New opinion. *Oxford.* 1494929
Beg. date: 1962
WU UWM (RBR) No.1-2 (NOV1962-FEB1963).

New Orleans poetry journal. *New Orleans.* 0530379
ISSN: 0467-5037 Beg. date: 1955 End date: 1958
Ceased publication with vol. 4 no. 4, 1958.
WU UWM (RBR) V.1-v.3 no.3; v.4 no.1-3 (1955-n.d.).

The New Orleans review. *New Orleans.* 1421102
ISSN: 0028-6400 LCCN: 71-3898 Beg. date: 1968
Vols. for 1968-   published by Loyola University for the New Orleans Consortium.
WU UWM (RBR) V.1 no.2-4; v.2-v.5 no.3 (WIN1969-1977).

New plays. *London, Los Angeles, T Q Publications.* 1510873
Beg. date: 1977
WU UWM (RBR) Ser. 1 no.1-   (1977-   ).

New poems. *Swinford, Eng., Fantasy Press.* 1494931
ISSN: 0467-5118 Beg. date: 1952 End date: 1953
Ceased publication with vol. 2 no. 2, Winter 1953.
WU UWM (RBR) V.1 no.2-3 (WIN1952-SPR1953).

New Poetry. *London, Workshop Press.* 1494944
LCCN: 76-645004 Beg. date: 1975
Continues Workshop new poetry with no. 28, 1975.
WU UWM (RBR) No.28-37 (1975-1977).

New poetry. *Sydney.* 1494957
ISSN: 0028-6478 LCCN: 70-649241 Beg. date: 1971
"Magazine of the Poetry Society of Australia."
Continues Poetry magazine with vol. 19, Feb. 1971.
WU UWM (RBR) V.19 no.1,3-6; v.20-23; v.24 no.1-2,4; v.25 no.1-2 (FEB1971-1977).

New politics. *New York.* 0530576
ISSN: 0028-6494 Beg. date: 1961
WU UWM (RBR) V.1-3 (FAL1961-FAL1964).

The New quarterly. *Rock Island, Ill., Jay du Von.* 1494972
Beg. date: 1934 End date: 1934
Ceased publication with vol. 1 no. 2, Summer 1934?
WU UWM (RBR) V.1 no.1-2 (SPR-SUM1934).

The New quarterly cave. *Hamilton, N.Z., Outrigger Publishers Ltd.* 1507581
LCCN: 76-647578 Beg. date: 1976
"An international review of arts and ideas."
Continues Cave with no. 9, n. ser. vol. 1 no.1, 1976.
Irregular supplement: Outrigger.
WU UWM (RBR) V.1; v.2 no.1,3 ([1976]-1977).

New quarterly of poetry. *New York, League to support poetry.* 0530654
LCCN: 52-26651 Beg. date: 1946
WU UWM (RBR) V.1 no.1-2 (FAL1946-WIN1946/1947).

New Realist Poetry School. *New improved zest.* See New improved zest. Chicago. 1494788

The New renaissance. *Arlington, Mass.* 1494985
ISSN: 0028-6575 LCCN: 76-643398 Beg. date: 1968
WU UWM (RBR) V.1-v.3 no.1 (no.1-9) (FAL1968-1977).

The New review. *Oxford.* 1093236
LCCN: 74-644964 Beg. date: 1974
Superseded The Review; a magazine of poetry and criticism.
WU UWM (RBR) V.1-3 (no.1-27) (APR1974-JUN1976).

The New review; an international notebook for the arts. *Paris.* 0530773
Beg. date: 1931
In English, with some articles in French.
WU UWM (RBR) V.1-v.2 no.5 (1931-APR1932).

New Richmond Poetry Group. *Expression.* See Expression one. Twickenham, Eng. 1435905

New river. *Dallas, Texas Bookman.* 1494998
ISSN: 0077-8648 Beg. date: 1969
WU UWM (RBR) No.3 (1970).

New river review. *Radford, Va., Highlands Press.* 1495005
ISSN: 0360-1455 LCCN: 75-647802 Beg. date: 1975
WU UWM (RBR) No.1-2 (FAL1975-SUM1976); v.2 no.1 (1977).

The New Salt Creek reader. *Lincoln, Neb., Windflower Press.* 1529027
Beg. date: 1972
Continues Salt Creek reader with vol. 5, Winter 1972.
WU UWM (RBR) V.5-v.7 no.1 (WIN1972-SPR1975).

New Saxon Pamphlets. See Albion. Oswestry, T. Owen and son, printers. 053088A

New Saxon Review. See Albion. Oswestry, T. Owen and son, printers. 0530892

New School for Social Research. *12th street.* See 12th street. New York, Students of the New School for Social Research. 151474A

New School for Social Research. *Figure in the carpet.* See Figure in the carpet. New York, New School for Social Research. 1436862

New School for Social Research. *Salient.* See Figure in the carpet. New York, New School for Social Research. 1436888

The New shetlander. *Lerwick, Shetland Islands.* 1495018
ISSN: 0047-987X
WU UWM (RBR) No.84-91 (SPR1968-WIN1969).

New smart set. See Smart set, a magazine of cleverness. New York, 1206010

The New sonnet sequences. *Paterson, N.J.* 1509957
Supersedes Sonnet sequences.
WU UWM (RBR) June 1959.

The New south quarterly. *Baton Rouge, La.* 1495020
Beg. date: 1967
"A journal of poetry, prose, and photography."
WU UWM (RBR) V.2 no.1-3/4 (WIN1968-1969).

The New south student. *Nashville, Tenn., Southern Student Organizing Committee.* 0531003
Title varies: May-OCT. 1964, New Rebel; Dec. 1964-May1965, Newsletter.
WU UWM (RBR) V.2 no.6-8; v.3 no.3,5-8; v.4 no.1-7; v.5-v.6 no.1 (NOV1965-JAN1969).

New stories. *Oxford.* 1495033
Beg. date: 1934 End date: 1936
Ceased publication with vol. 2 no. 8, April/May 1936.
WU UWM (RBR) V.1-v.2 no.8 (FEB/MAR1934-APR/MAY1936).

New story. *New York, Gargoyle Press.* 1495046
ISSN: 0548-6904 LCCN: 57-23444 Beg. date: 1951 End date: 1953
"A monthly magazine for the short story."
Editorial offices: Paris.
Ceased publication with vol. 3 no. 13, Feb. 1953.
WU UWM (RBR) No.1-13 (MAR1951-FEB1953).

New student review. *Buffalo, N.Y., Faculty-Student Association of the State University of New York at Buffalo.* 1495059
ISSN: 0028-6850
WU UWM (RBR) No.13-14,16,18-20 (1965-1968).

New theatre. *New York.* 152903A
Beg. date: 1934 End date: 1936
Supersedes Workers theatre.
"Official organ of the League of Workers Theatres and National Film and Photo League."
Continued by New theatre and film with vol. 4 no. 1, March 1937.
WU UWM (RBR) V.1-v.3 no.11 (JAN1934-NOV1936).

New theatre and film. *New York, Social Theatre Publications, Inc.* 1529068
Beg. date: 1937 End date: 1937
Continues New Theatre with vol. 4 no. 1, March 1937.
WU UWM (RBR) V.4 no.1-2 (MAR-APR1937).

New Thursday. *Red Deer, Alt., Red Deer College Press.* 1495074
Beg. date: 1974
Supersedes Thursday.
WU   UWM (RBR) No.[1]-2 (SPR1974-1975).

New university thought. *Chicago.* 0531897
ISSN: 0028-6931 Beg. date: 1961 End date: 1972
Continued by Journal of university studies with vol. 10, Spring 1974.
WU   UWM (RBR) V.5; v.6 no.2-4 (1967-SUM1968).

New ventures. *Philadelphia.* 1253917
ISSN: 0545-3941 LCCN: 58-26025 Beg. date: 1954 End date: 1954
"Contemporary writing."
Ceased publication with no. 1, 1954.
WU   UWM (RBR) No.1 (1954).

New verse. *London, G. Grigson.* 0531906
Ceased publication with n. ser. v. 1 no. 2 (1939).
WU   UWM (RBR) No.1-31/32 (1933-AUT1938); n. ser. v.1 no.1-2 (JAN-MAY1939).

New vision. *London, New Renascence.* 1507566
ISSN: 0467-5479 Beg. date: 1952
Supersedes Humanity now.
WU   UWM (RBR) No.1-19 (SUM1952-1964).

New voices. *New Paltz, N.Y., Don Fried.* 1495087
ISSN: 0094-4645 LCCN: 74-645140 Beg. date: 1972
WU   UWM (RBR) No.1-5 (WIN1972-1976).

New voices magazine. *Orange, N.J., Alexander Pazandak.* 149509A
Beg. date: 1964
"A magazine for writers to write in."
Absorbed Philae.
WU   UWM (RBR) V.1 no.1-10 (FAL1964-SPR1967).

New Wilderness Foundation. New wilderness letter. *See* 1495111
New wilderness letter. [n.p.], New Wilderness Foundation.

New wilderness letter. *[n.p.], New Wilderness Foundation.* 1495109
Beg. date: 1977
WU   UWM (RBR) V.1 no.1-2 (1977).

New world haiku. *San Fernando, Calif., The Heliopolis Press.* 1495124
Beg. date: 1973
WU   UWM (RBR) V.1 no.1-4 (SUM1973-1974).

New world monthly. *New York.* 1495137
LCCN: 32-32645 Beg. date: 1930 End date: 1930
Ceased publication with vol. 1 no. 2, Feb. 1930.
WU   UWM (RBR) V.1 no.1-2 (JAN-FEB1930).

New writers. *New York, Literary Workshop Publications, Inc.* 149514A
ISSN: 0092-6698 LCCN: 74-640231 Beg. date: 1973
"Devoted to the art of the short story and the recognition of gifted new writers."
WU   UWM (RBR) V.1 no.1-2; v.2-v.3 no.2 (FAL1973-MAR1976).

New writing. *See* Folios of new writing. *London, The Hogarth Press.* 0532101

New York. State University College, Oneonta. *See* Satire newsletter. *Oneonta, N.Y., State University College.* 0532393

New York arts journal. *New York, Manhattan Arts Review, Inc.* 1495152
WU   UWM (RBR) V.1 no.3/4 (DEC1975/MAR1976).

New York (City). City College. Promethean. *See* Promethean. New York, City College. 1509082

New York (City). City College. Creative Writing Program. City. *See* City. New York, Creative Writing Program, City College. 152859A

New York (City). City College. Evening Session. Pulse quarterly. *See* Pulse quarterly. New York, College of the City of New York. 1501690

New York (City). City College, Writing Organization for Women. 13th moon. *See* 13th moon. New York. 1512032

New York (City). New School for Social Research. Salient. *See* Salient. New York, New School for Social Research. 1502078

The New York culture review. *Brooklyn, N.Y.* 1495165
ISSN: 0094-0194
The New York culture review is published in book form in April, July, September and October, and in newsletter form 8 times a year.
WU   UWM (RBR) V.1 no.1-24; v.2 no.1-2/3/4 (APR1974-JUN291976).

New York poetry. *New York, Steven Roday.* 1495178
ISSN: 0028-744X Beg. date: 1969
WU   UWM (RBR) V.1 no.1 (1969).

New York quarterly. *New York.* 0534559
ISSN: 0028-7482 LCCN: 77-27099 Beg. date: 1970
WU   UWM (RBR) No.1-8 (1970-WIN1976).

New York review. *New York.* 1495193
ISSN: 0545-6320 Beg. date: 1958 End date: 1958
Ceased publication with Spring 1958.
WU   UWM (RBR) Spring 1958.

New York smith. *See* The Smith. New York, 1483249

New York (State). State University, Buffalo. New student review. *See* New student review. Buffalo, N.Y., Faculty-Student Association of the State University of New York at Buffalo. 1495061

New York (State). State University at Binghamton. Department of English. Boundary 2. *See* Boundary 2. Binghamton, N.Y., 1346181

New York (State). State University at Buffalo. Catalyst. *See* Catalyst. Peterborough, Ont. [etc.]. 1206036

New York (State). State University at Stony Brook. Soundings. *See* Soundings. Stony Brook, N.Y., State University of New York at Stony Brook. 1510362

New York (State). State University College at Geneseo. Experimentalist. *See* Experimentalist. Geneseo, N.Y., State University College at Geneseo. 1435814

New York Student Federation Against War. Anvil. *See* Anvil, a student socialist magazine. [New York]. 1438138

New York Student Federation Against War. Anvil and student partisan. *See* Anvil, a student socialist magazine. [New York]. 1438125

New York University. Institute of Fine Arts. Marsyas. *See* Marsyas. New York, Institute of Fine Arts, New York University. 1496094

New York University. Washington Square College. Apprentice. *See* Apprentice. New York, New York University, Washington Square College. 1438179

New York Workshop in Nonviolence. Win. *See* Win. New York, 1112942

The New Zealander. *Christchurch, New Zealand, Stuart McMillan.* 1495202
ISSN: 0549-0642 Beg. date: 1968
"A fortnightly magazine."
WU   UWM (RBR) No.1-8 (JUN04-NOV181968).

Neworld. *Los Angeles.* 1495215
Beg. date: 1974
"A quarterly of the Inner City Cultural Center."
WU   UWM (RBR) V.1-v.2 no.1 (FAL1974-FAL1975).

News from Golgonooza. *Millfield, Ohio, Church of the Blake Concert.* 1495230
Beg. date: 1973
WU   UWM (RBR) V.1 no.1-16; v.2 no.1 (n.d.-1974); Dec. 1974; [May 1975]; unnumbered, undated issue; May, Aug. 1976.

News-sheet. *See* Archives de la Danse (Auckland). News-sheet. [n.p.]. 1507490

Newsart. *New York, Generalist Association.* 1495243
"The New York smith."
Subseries of the Smith.
WU   UWM (RBR) V.1 no.1-3 (APR151975-JAN151977); Apr. 1977.

Newspaper. *New York.* 1495269
ISSN: 0545-879X Beg. date: 1957
WU   UWM (RBR) No.1-17 (n.d.-n.d.).

Newsstand. *See* Don Freeman's newsstand. New York, Associated American Artists, Inc. 1435015

Nexus. *Dayton, Ohio.* 1495271
WU   UWM (RBR) Spring-Fall 1970; Spring/Summer, Winter 1971; Fall/Winter-Spring 1972; Spring 1973-Summer 1976.

Nexus. *Nairobi, Kenya.* 1495284
Beg. date: 1966 End date: 1968
"Nexus is produced by students of English, at the English Department of the University College, Nairobi."
Ceased publication with vol. 2, 1968.
Superseded by Busara.
WU   UWM (RBR) V.1 no.1-3; v.2 no.1 ([1966]-JUL1968).

Nexus. *San Francisco.* 1495306
ISSN: 0549-1274 Beg. date: 1963 End date: 1967
Ceased publication with vol. 3 no. 2 (no. 15), April 1967.
WU   UWM (RBR) V.1-v.13 no.2 (no.1-15)
  (JUL1963-MAR/APR1967).

The Niagara frontier review. *Buffalo, N.Y., Frontier Press,* 1495319
Inc.
ISSN: 0549-138X Beg. date: 1964 End date: 1966
Ceased publication with 1966.
WU   UWM (RBR) Summer 1964; Spring/Summer-Fall
  1965; Spring 1966.

The Niagara Magazine. *Buffalo, N.Y.* 1495321
Beg. date: 1974
WU   UWM (RBR) No.1-7 (SUM1974-WIN1977).

Nice. *Brightingsea, Essex, Eng.* 1495334
"A one shot magazine."
WU   UWM (RBR) V.1 no.1 (n.d.).

Nickel and dime quarterly. *Minneapolis.* 1495347
Beg. date: 1968
"A publication connected with the Free University of Minnesota."
WU   UWM (RBR) No.1-2 (SPR1968-SPR1969).

Nickle times. *Oshkosh, Wis., River Bottom Press.* 149535A
WU   UWM (RBR) No.1-3,5 (1974?-1977).

Nicotine soup. *San Francisco, Sea of Storms Press.* 1495362
Beg. date: 1976
WU   UWM (RBR) No.1-5 (JUL1976-1977).

Night watchman. *South Wigston, Leicester, Eng.* 1495388
ISSN: 0468-2343 Beg. date: 195 End date: 1953
Ceased publication with no. 5, 1953?
WU   UWM (RBR) May 1952; no.5-6 ([1954]).

Nightshade. *[n.p.].* 1495375
"Devoted to fantasy and the macabre in poetry."
WU   UWM (RBR) V.2 no.2 (1967).

Nightwords. *Succasunna, N.J.* 1529070
Beg. date: 1977
"A cooperative venture in the arts."
WU   UWM (RBR) V.1 no.1 (1977).

Nimbus. *London, The Westminster Press.* 1495390
ISSN: 0549-4931 LCCN: 58-30860 Beg. date: 1951 End date: 1958
"A quarterly magazine."
Ceased publication with vol. 4 no. 2, Feb. 1958.
WU   UWM (RBR) V.1 no.1-3; v.2-v.4 no.2
  (1951-FEB1958).

Nimrod. *Tulsa, Okla.* 149540A
ISSN: 0029-053X Beg. date: 1956
"An individual review."
WU   UWM (RBR) V.1-2; v.3 no.3; v.4 no.1,3; v.9 no.3; v.14
  no.3; v.15 no.1; v.16 no.2; v.17-v.21 no.1
  (FAL1956-FAL/WIN1976).

Nine. *London, Peter Russell.* 1495412
Beg. date: 1949
"A magazine of poetry and criticism" (varies).
WU   UWM (RBR) V.1 no.1; v.2-v.4 no.2
  (OCT1949-APR1956).

Ninepence. *Bournemouth, Eng.* 1495425
ISSN: 0468-2696 Beg. date: 1951 End date: 1952
Ceased publication with no. 3, Autumn 1952.
WU   UWM (RBR) No.1 (SEP1951).

The Ninth circle. *University Park, N.M.* 1495438
Beg. date: 1966
WU   UWM (RBR) V.1 no.1-[3] (SUM1966-NOV1967).

Niobe. *Brooklyn Heights, N.Y.* 1495440
ISSN: 0549-4990 Beg. date: 1965
WU   UWM (RBR) No.2 (1966).

Nitty-gritty. *Pasco, Wash., Goldermood Rainbow Press.* 1496129
"A survival tool chest."
WU   UWM (RBR) V.1 no.1-3 (1975-1977).

Nix. *New York.* 1496131
WU   UWM (RBR) Dec. 1953.

Nkombo. *New Orleans, Nkombo Writing Workshop.* 1496144
WU   UWM (RBR) No.8-9 (AUG1972-JUN1974).

Nkombo Writing Workshop. Nkombo. *See* Nkombo. New 1496157
Orleans, Nkombo Writing Workshop.

The No-eyed monster. *Ortonville, Mich., M.M. Publication.* 149616A
ISSN: 0029-0807
WU   UWM (RBR) No.15-18 (SPR1969-SUM1970).

No walls broadsheet. *Cardiff, Wales, Second Aeon* 1496172
Publications.
WU   UWM (RBR) No.5-6,8-18 (1968-1969).

Noble savage. *New York, Meridian Books.* 0542200
ISSN: 0549-5601 LCCN: 60-9654
Ceased no. 5.
Editor: Saul Bellow.
WU   UWM (RBR) No.1-5 (MAR1960-OCT1962).

Noetics. *Syracuse, N.Y., Fugitive Press.* 1496185
ISSN: 0546-210X Beg. date: 1964
"The form of all possible methods."
WU   UWM (RBR) 1964.

The Noiseless spider. *New Haven, Conn., English Club of the* 150766A
University of New Haven.
LCCN: sc77-117
WU   UWM (RBR) V.1-2; v.3 no.2; v.4; v.5 no.1
  (FAL1971-FAL1975).

Nomad. *Culver City, Calif.* 0542501
ISSN: 0549-5946 Beg. date: 1959 End date: 1962
Ceased publication with no. 10/11, Autumn 1962.
"Published in London by Villiers Publications, Ltd., for
  Nomad...Culver City, Calif."
WU   UWM (RBR) No.1-10/11 (WIN1959-AUT1962).

None such. *Washington, D.C., SaviLane Press.* 1496198
WU   UWM (RBR) V.1 no.2 (AUT1970).

Noonday. *New York, Noonday Press.* 1496207
ISSN: 0549-6101 LCCN: 58-13190 Beg. date: 1958 End date: 1959
"Stories, articles, poetry."
Ceased publication with no. 3, Dec. 1959.
WU   UWM (RBR) No.1-3 (SEP1958-DEC1959).

Noose. *New York.* 1529083
Beg. date: 1968
WU   UWM (RBR) No.1-20 (MAR231968-1969).

Norch. *[n.p.].* 1507512
ISSN: 0029-117X Beg. date: 1969
Superseded by Doris.
WU   UWM (RBR) 1969-1970.

The Norman hackforth. *Cambridge, Eng.* 1529096
Beg. date: 1969
"A magazine."
WU   UWM (RBR) No.1 (1969).

North. *[Leeds, Eng.?].* 149621A
WU   UWM (RBR) No.3-4; v.2 no.1-2
  (AUT1965-SUM1971); Winter 1973/1974-Winter/
  Spring 1975.

The North American mentor. *Conesville, Iowa, John* 1496222
Westburg and Associates.
ISSN: 0549-7078 Beg. date: 1964
WU   UWM (RBR) V.1-v.15 no.2 (SPR1964-SUM1977);
  special poetry suppl. 1965.

North Carolina. Agricultural and Technical State University, 1441131
Greensboro.   A and T poetry review. *See* A and T poetry review.
Greensboro, N.C., A and T Register, N.C. Agric. and Tech. State
Univ. newspaper.

North Carolina. Agricultural and Technical State University, 1468617
Greensboro.   A and T register. Poetry supplement. *See* A and T
register. Poetry supplement. Greensboro, N.C., North Carolina
Agricultural and Technical State University.

North Carolina. Central University, Durham.   Ex umbra. 143246A
See Ex umbra. Durham, N.C., North Carolina Central University.

North Carolina. State University, Pembroke.   Pembroke 1498667
magazine. *See* Pembroke magazine. Pembroke, N.C., Pembroke
State University.

North Carolina. University, Greensboro.   Greensboro 121899A
review. *See* Greensboro review. Greensboro, University of North
Carolina at Greensboro.

North Carolina Arts Council.   Ex umbra. *See* Ex umbra. 1432457
Durham, N.C., North Carolina Central University.

The North Carolina review. *Raleigh, N.C., Carol Lynn* 1496235
Wilkinson.
WU   UWM (RBR) 1976.

North Coast poetry. *East Machias, Maine [etc.], North Coast* 1496248
Poetry Cooperative.
WU   UWM (RBR) No.2,5-8 (MAR1973-1976?).

North Coast Poetry Cooperative.   North Coast poetry. *See* 1496250
North Coast poetry. East Machias, Maine [etc.], North Coast Poetry
Cooperative.

North country. Grand Forks, University of North Dakota. 1259290
Beg. date: 1974
"Literary magazine of the University of North Dakota."
WU   UWM (RBR) V.1-2 (1974?-1975); one unnumbered issue (1976).

North country anvil. Millville, Minn., North Country Alternatives. 0546512
Beg. date: 1972
WU   UWM (RBR) No.1- (JUN1972-).

North Dakota. State University of Agriculture and Applied Science, Fargo. Department of English. Scopcraeft. *See* Scopcraeft. Fargo, 1168501

North Dakota. University. North country. *See* North country. Grand Forks, University of North Dakota. 125930A

North Devon snail. *See* Snail. Barnstaple, North Devon, England. 1510111

North-East. *See* Northeast. La Crosse, Wis. 1129965

North Stone review. Minneapolis, J. Naiden. 1060117
LCCN: 70-612926 Beg. date: 1971
Nos. 1-3 called vol. 1.
WU   UWM (RBR) V.1 no.3-7 (SUM/FAL1972-FAL/WIN1975/1976).

North Wales Association for the Arts. Mabon. *See* Mabon. Bangor, Wales, North Wales Association for the Arts. 1505190

North West Arts Association, Manchester, England. Phoenix. *See* Phoenix. Manchester, Eng. 149995A

Northeast. La Crosse, Wis. 1129952
WU   UWM (RBR) 1969.

Northeast. Waterville, Maine, Hammond Press. 1496263
ISSN: 0549-8880 Beg. date: 1963
"A new international literary journal."
WU   UWM (RBR) No.1-4 (1963-1966); 1967-Spring/Summer 1976; ser. 3 no. 2 (WIN1976/1977-SUM1977).

Northeast rising sun. Baltimore, Md., Cherry Valley Editions, etc. 1496276
Beg. date: 1976
"A magazine of small press reviews."
WU   UWM (RBR) V.1 no.1-4/5; v.2 no.6-7 (1976-1977).

Northern broadsheet. Edinburgh. 1496289
ISSN: 0468-6896 Beg. date: 1956
WU   UWM (RBR) No.1-6 (SUM1956-SPR1960).

Northern journey. Ottawa, Ont., Northern Journey Press. 1496291
ISSN: 0315-3630 Beg. date: 1971 End date: 1976
Ceased publication with no. 7/8, 1976.
WU   UWM (RBR) No1-7/8 (1971-1976).

Northern light. Winnipeg, The University of Manitoba Press. 1496300
Beg. date: 1974
Supersedes Far point.
WU   UWM (RBR) No.1-2 (WIN1974-SUM1975).

Northern Minnesota review. Bemidji, Bemidji State College. 0548812
ISSN: 0029-3180 Beg. date: 1970 End date: 1970
"A magazine of contemporary literature from the Upper Midwest Writers Conference."
Ceased publication with vol. 1 no. 1, Aug. 1970.
WU   UWM (RBR) V.1 no.1 (AUG1970).

Northern review. Toronto [etc.], Northern Review Press. 0548998
ISSN: 0381-0143 Beg. date: 1946 End date: 1956
Formed by the union of Preview and First statement.
Ceased publication with vol. 7, Summer 1956.
WU   UWM (RBR) V.1-v.7 no.4 (DEC1945/JAN1946-SUM1956).

The Northland magazine. Whangarei, New Zealand, Northland Magazine (Inc.). 1495453
ISSN: 0029-3261 Beg. date: 1958
"A regional magazine."
WU   UWM (RBR) No.1-16; v.5-14 (MAR1958-SUM1971).

Northwest challenge. Corvallis, Ore., Thomas A. Wilson. 1495466
WU   UWM (RBR) V.3 no.5; v.4 no.1,3 (AUT1960-SUM1961).

Northwest review. Eugene. 0549936
ISSN: 0029-3423 LCCN: 63-25021 Beg. date: 1957
Issued by the Student Publications Board of the University of Oregon.
WU   UWM (RBR) Fall 1957; v.16 no.1-3 (1977).

Northwestern University, Evanston, Illinois. Tri-quarterly. *See* Tri-quarterly. Evanston, 1295002

Northwestern University tri-quarterly. *See* Tri-quarterly. Evanston, 1295015

Northwoods journal. Meadows of Dan, Va. [etc.], Northwoods Press, Inc. 1495479
WU   UWM (RBR) V.3 no.3; v.4 no.1,4-7; v.5 no.1-5 (NOV1975-1977).

A Nosegay in black. St. Louis, Eastgate Press, Inc. 1495481
ISSN: 0550-0745 Beg. date: 1966
WU   UWM (RBR) V.1 no.1 (AUT1966).

Nostoc. Waban, Mass. 1495494
WU   UWM (RBR) No.1-5 (MAR1973-AUG1976).

Not guilty! New York, Not Guilty Press. 1495503
Beg. date: 1975
WU   UWM (RBR) V.1 no.1-2 (SEP1975-OCT1976); no.2 (1977).

The Notebook. Cleveland, Pegasus Studio. 1495516
Beg. date: 1934
"An international newsmagazine of the creative arts" (varies).
WU   UWM (RBR) V.4 no.3 (AUG/SEP1937).

Notes from the garage door. Cincinnati, United Christian Ministries at the University of Cincinnati. 1495529
ISSN: 0550-0966 Beg. date: 1965
WU   UWM (RBR) V.2 no.3; v.3 no.1-2; v.4 no.1; v.5 no.1 (JUN1966-n.d.); special issue 1967.

Notes from underground. San Francisco, Underground Press. 1495531
ISSN: 0550-0974 LCCN: 64-9471 Beg. date: 1964
"Incorporating Renaissance."
WU   UWM (RBR) No.1-2 (1964-1966); one unnumbered, undated issue.

Nothing doing in London. London. 1495544
ISSN: 0029-411X LCCN: 75-644684 Beg. date: 1966
In English, French or Portuguese.
WU   UWM (RBR) No.1-2 (NOV1966-JAN1968).

The Notion. London, Paisley, Alexander Gardner. 1529105
Beg. date: 1903 End date: 1903
Ceased publication with no. 6, Oct. 1903.
WU   UWM (RBR) No.1 (MAY1903).

Nottingham, England. University. Arts Faculty. Enquiry. *See* Enquiry. Nottingham, Eng., Nottingham University, Arts Faculty. 143225A

Nottingham, England. University. Student Union. Gong. *See* Gong. Nottingham, Eng., Student Union, Nottingham University. 1436310

Now. Jerusalem, "Ah'shav" Publishers. 149556A
ISSN: 0078-2572 LCCN: HE 66-1218 Beg. date: 1964
Added title page in Hebrew.
Publication suspended with no. 1, 1964 and resumed with no. 2, 1969.
WU   UWM (RBR) 1964, 1969.

Now. London, G. Woodcock [etc.]. 0553919
LCCN: 44-43230
Imprint varies: v. 1, London, Freedom press, 1943.
V. 1-7, 1940-1941: Nendeln, Liechtenstein, Kraus Reprint.
WU   UWM (RBR) V.1-9 (1943-JUL/AUG1947).

Now. New York. 1495572
Beg. date: 1941 End date: 1941
Ceased publication with vol. 1 no. 1, Aug. 1941.
WU   UWM (RBR) V.1 no.1 (AUG1941).

Now. *See* Now now now. San Francisco. 1497478

Now. Rutherford, N.J., Fairleigh Dickinson University. 149744A
"A literary magazine published by Fairleigh Dickinson University."
WU   UWM (RBR) V.3 no.1-2; v.5,7 (n.d.-WIN1966).

Now now. *See* Now now now. San Francisco. 1497480

Now now now. San Francisco. 1497465
ISSN: 0550-2934 Beg. date: 1965 End date: 1965
Title varies: no. 1, Now; no. 2, Now now.
Ceased publication with no. 3, 1965.
WU   UWM (RBR) 1963, 1965; unnumbered, undated supplement.

Now save the dead. Cambridge, Mass. 1497493
Beg. date: 1971
"American avant-garde poetry."
WU   UWM (RBR) No.1-3 (SEP/OCT1971-JAN/FEB1972).

NRG. *See* N R G. Pittsburgh. 1494446

Nucleus. *Crowborough, Sussex, Eng., PV Publications.* 1497502
"An annual poetry publication."
Title is followed by year of volume; i.e., Nucleus seventy-four.
WU   UWM (RBR) 1974.

Nucleus. *Providence, R.I.* 1497515
ISSN: 0469-1679 Beg. date: 1953
"A little magazine."
WU   UWM (RBR) V.1 no.1-3 (WIN1953-WIN1954).

Nucleus seventy-four. **See** Nucleus. *Crowborough, Sussex,* 1519924
  Eng.,

Number. *London.* 1497528
ISSN: 0546-9333 Beg. date: 1961
WU   UWM (RBR) No.1-6 (FEB1961-1964).

Number magazine; a quarterly of modern poetry. *San* 0554506
Francisco, Wobber Brothers.
ISSN: 0546-9341 Beg. date: 1950 End date: 1955
Subtitle Varies: no. 1-4, A magazine of Modern poetry.
Numbers 1-4 issued as v. 1 no. 1-4.
Ceased publication with no. 8, Autumn 1955.
WU   UWM (RBR) V.1 no.1-8 (SPR1950-AUT1955).

Number one. *Kansas City, Mo.* 1497530
"A student publication of the University of Missouri at Kansas
  City."
WU   UWM (RBR) V.22 no.1-3 (1968-SPR1969).

Numbers. *Wellington, N.Z.* 1497556
ISSN: 0546-935X Beg. date: 1954 End date: 1959
"A quarterly collection of New Zealand new writing."
Ceased publication with vol. 3 no. 2 (no. 10), Sept. 1959.
WU   UWM (RBR) V.1 no.1-v.3 no.2 (JUL1954-SEP1959).

Nutmegger. *Greenwich, Conn., Nutmegger Publishing Corp.* 1497569
ISSN: 0550-4015 Beg. date: 1968
WU   UWM (RBR) No.7-9; v.2 no.10-11; v.3 no.15-16,18;
  v.4 no.1-5 (SEP1965-MAY1958).

O

O P. *See* OP. Houston, Okra Press.   1508138

Oak leaves. *West Seneca, N.Y.*   1497571
   ISSN: 0472-3902 Beg. date: 1959
   "Seeking beauty and lyrical truth" (varies).
   WU   UWM (RBR) V.1-v.3 no.3; v.4 no.1 (1959-SUM1962).

Oar. *See* Or oar ore. Monterey, Calif.   1499605

Oasis. *Kingston-upon-Thames, Surrey, Eng., Oasis Books.*   1505316
   ISSN: 0029-7410 Beg. date: 1969
   Absorbed Expression magazine with no. 4.
   WU   UWM (RBR) No.1-4,6-16 (NOV1969-1976).

Oberlin College. Plum Creek review. *See* Plum Creek review. Oberlin, Ohio, Oberlin College.   1501201

The Oberlin quarterly. *Oberlin, Ohio.*   1505329
   ISSN: 0473-7040 Beg. date: 1963 End date: 1964
   Ceased publication with vol. 1 no. 2, Winter/Spring 1964.
   WU   UWM (RBR) V.1 no.1-2 (SPR1963-WIN/SPR1964).

Obscurologist papers. *Blue Mounds, Wis.*   1505331
   Beg. date: 1965
   WU   UWM (RBR) No.1-2 (WIN1965-SUM1967).

Obsidian: black literature in review. *Fredonia, N.Y.*   1231750
   Beg. date: 1975
   WU   UWM (RBR) V.1-v.3 no.1 (SPR1975-SPR1977).

Ocarina. *Madras.*   113012A
   Beg. date: 1972
   "A bimonthly journal of poetry and aesthetics."
   WU   UWM (RBR) V.1-v.5 no.1 (OCT/NOV1970-JAN/FEB1975).

The Occident. *Berkeley, Calif., Associated Students of the University of California.*   1509866
   ISSN: 0029-7879 LCCN: 55-40692 Beg. date: 1881 End date: 1975
   Ceased publication with n. ser. vol. 9, Spring 1975.
   WU   UWM (RBR) V.88 no.3; v.89 no.1; v.91 no.2-3 (NOV1930-APR1933); n. ser. v.1 no.1-5 (SEP1934-APR1935); Spring 1947; Fall 1948; Fall 1949; Spring 1950; Spring 1951; Fall 1952; Winter, Spring 1953; Spring 1954; Fall 1956; Spring 1957; Spring 1958; Spring 1959; Fall 1960; Fall 1963; Spring 1964; Spring, Fall 1965; n. ser. v.1-9 (SPR/SUM1967-SPR1975).

Occult. *Tampa, Fla.*   1505344
   Beg. date: 1971
   WU   UWM (RBR) No.1 (1971).

Occum Ridge review. *South Willington, Conn.*   1505357
   Beg. date: 1973
   WU   UWM (RBR) Fall/Winter 1973; Spring/Summer 1974.

Occurrence. *Philadelphia.*   150536A
   ISSN: 0146-9118 LCCN: 77-647667 Beg. date: 1973
   WU   UWM (RBR) No.1-7 (1973-1977).

Ocean freedom. *See* Ocean living. Los Angeles.   1505385

Ocean living. *Los Angeles.*   1505372
   ISSN: 0029-8034
   Formerly Ocean freedom.
   WU   UWM (RBR) V.1 no.4-10; v.2 no.2 (n.d.-1970).

Oculist witnesses. *Dorchester, Mass. [etc.].*   1529118
   Beg. date: 1975
   WU   UWM (RBR) No.1-3 (SUM1975-FAL1976).

The Odd volume. *London, Simpkin Marshall Hamilton Kent and Co. Ltd.*   0884737
   Publication suspended 1916.
   1909, 1912-1913 have title: The Odd volume, literary and artistic.
   WU   UWM (RBR) 1910.

Odda-tala. *Palo Alto, Calif. [etc.], D. Alexander.*   1505398
   ISSN: 0029-8352 Beg. date: 1968
   WU   UWM (RBR) No.1-3 (1968-1969).

Odysseus. *Gresham, Ore. [etc.], [Troubador Press].*   1505407
   LCCN: 72-626312 Beg. date: 1971
   "Magazine of the arts."
   Masthead title: Odysseus magazine.
   WU   UWM (RBR) V.1 no.1-5 (AUG/SEP1971-1972).

Odysseus magazine. *See* Odysseus. Gresham, Ore. [etc.], [Troubador Press].   150541A

Odyssey. *Chicago.*   1505422
   ISSN: 0473-7873 Beg. date: 1958 End date: 1959
   "Explorations in contemporary poetry and the arts."
   Ceased publication with vol. 2 no. 1, Dec. 1959.
   WU   UWM (RBR) V.1 no.1-4; v.2 no.1 (SPR1958-DEC1959).

Odyssey review. *Richmond, Virginia.*   0557330
   ISSN: 0473-789X LCCN: 64-5795 rev Beg. date: 1961 End date: 1963
   "A quarterly of modern Latin America and European literature in English translation."
   Ceased publication with vol. 3 no. 2, June 1963.
   WU   UWM (RBR) V.1 no.1; v.2-v.3 no.2 (DEC1961-JUN1963).

Offbeat. *Encino, Calif., Defilee Publications.*   1509881
   ISSN: 0415-1712 Beg. date: 1959
   Also called Defilee's offbeat.
   WU   UWM (RBR) V.1 no.1-3 (1959).

Ohio. State University, Bowling Green. Creative Writing Program. Green horse for poetry. *See* Green horse for poetry. Bowling Green, Ohio, Creative Writing Program, Bowling Green State University.   1436678

Ohio. State University, Bowling Green. Department of English. Black swamp review. *See* Black swamp review. Bowling Green, Ohio, Bowling Green State University, English Department.   1438439

Ohio. State University, Columbus. Cronos. *See* Cronos. Columbus, Ohio, Ohio State University.   1431662

Ohio. State University, Columbus. Department of English. Escutcheon. *See* Escutcheon. Columbus, Ohio, Department of English, Ohio State University.   1432379

Ohio. State University, Columbus, College of the Humanities. Ohio journal. *See* Ohio journal. Columbus, Ohio, College of the Humanities, Ohio State University.   1505463

The Ohio journal. *Columbus, Ohio, College of the Humanities, Ohio State University.*   1505450
   Beg. date: 1973
   "A magazine of literature and the arts."
   WU   UWM (RBR) V.1-v.2 no.2; v.3 no.3; v.4 no.1 (MAY1973-1977).

The Ohio poetry review. *Toledo, Ohio, Ohio Poetry Society.*   1505476
   ISSN: 0472-7282 Beg. date: 1958 End date: 1959
   Ceased publication with vol. 1 no. 3, Spring 1959.
   WU   UWM (RBR) V.1 no.2-3 (WIN1959-SPR1959).

Ohio Poetry Society. Ohio poetry review. *See* Ohio poetry review. Toledo, Ohio, Ohio Poetry Society.   1505489

Ohio University, Athens. Department of English. *See* Mundus artium. Athens, Ohio.   056077A

Oink! *Chicago, Paul Hoover.*   1505491
   Beg. date: 1971
   WU   UWM (RBR) No.1-2 (1971-1976).

Oklahoma. State University of Agriculture and Applied Science, Stillwater. *See* Cimarron Review. Stillwater, Okla. Published at Oklahoma State University.   056158A

Old friends. *Washington, D.C., The Company of Old Friends.*   1505500
   Beg. date: 1973
   WU   UWM (RBR) No.1-4 (SPR1973-1974).

The Old line. *College Park, Md., University of Maryland.*   1505513
   Beg. date: 1930 End date: 1943
   Ceased publication.
   Superseded by Maryland quarterly with Jan. 1944.
   WU   UWM (RBR) V.12 no.6 (APR1943).

The Old red kimono. *Rome, Georgia.*   1509762
   Beg. date: 1972
   "Compiled...under the auspices of the Humanities Division at Floyd Junior College."
   WU   UWM (RBR) V.3 no.2-4; v.4 no.1-2 (SPR1974-WIN1975); v.6 (SPR1977).

Old second. *Detroit.*   1509788
   "Sponsored by the Liberal Arts Student Board and the English Department of Wayne State University."
   WU   UWM (RBR) Fall 1969; Summer 1970.

Ole. *San Francisco [etc.].* 1509790
ISSN: 0474-0920 Beg. date: 1964 End date: 1967
"Dedicated to the cause of making poetry dangerous."
Ceased publication with no. 8.
Superseded by Open skull.
WU   UWM (RBR) No.1,3-8 (1964-1967).

Olivant. *Coral Gables, Fla. [etc.].* 1509840
Beg. date: 1957
WU   UWM (RBR) No.1-4,7 (1957-1960).

Olivant. *See* Kast. Tokyo, Club Kast. 1493770

Olivant quarterly. *Hollywood, Calif. [etc.], Olivant House.* 1509853
ISSN: 0474-0971 Beg. date: 1952 End date: 1955
Ceased publication with vol. 1 no. 4, 1955.
Superseded by Olivant with 1956.
WU   UWM (RBR) V.1 no.2,4 (1952-1955).

The Olive dachsund. *Oxford, Eng.* 150980A
Beg. date: 1966
Continues Nebulum?
WU   UWM (RBR) No.1 (SPR1966).

Olivet College, Olivet, Michigan. Garfield Lake review. *See* 1437672
Garfield Lake review. Olivet, Mich., Olivet College.

Olivet College, Olivet, Michigan. Olivet quarterly. *See* 1509825
Olivet quarterly. Olivet, Mich., Olivet College.

Olivet quarterly. *Olivet, Mich., Olivet College.* 1509812
ISSN: 0472-8866 Beg. date: 1951 End date: 1951
Ceased publication with vol. 1 no. 1, Summer 1951.
WU   UWM (RBR) V.1 no.1 (SUM1951).

Olympia. *Paris, Olympia Press.* 1509838
ISSN: 0474-1234 Beg. date: 1961 End date: 1963
"A monthly review from Paris."
Ceased publication with no. 4, April 1963.
WU   UWM (RBR) No.1-4 (DEC1961-1963).

Omaha. University, Omaha. Grain of sand. *See* Grain of 1436455
sand. Omaha, University of Omaha.

Omens. *Leicester, Eng.* 1499282
Beg. date: 1971
WU   UWM (RBR) V.1-v.2 no.1; v.3-5; v.6 no.2-3 (NOV1971-1977).

One. *London [etc.].* 1499295
Beg. date: 1971
WU   UWM (RBR) No.1-3 (SUM1971-SPR1976).

One. *Los Angeles, One, Inc.* 1499304
ISSN: 0472-9544 LCCN: 54-35001 Beg. date: 1953
"The homosexual magazine."
WU   UWM (RBR) V.1 no.1-2,5-12; v.2-6; v.7 no.1-5,8-9, 12; v.9 no.1-4,6-12; v.10-15 (1953-JUN1967).

One. *New Brunswick, N.J., Andarth Interrelated Projects.* 1499317
Beg. date: 1973
"A magazine of fiction."
WU   UWM (RBR) V.1 no.1-3; v.2 no.1,[5-7] (1973-1975).

One: the word is freed. *Auckland, N.Z.* 149932A
Title varies: Freed.
Published by Auckland University Students' Association for Auckland University Literary Society.
WU   UWM (RBR) July 1969.

The One act play magazine. *New York, Contemporary Play Publications.* 1499358
Beg. date: 1937 End date: 1939
Suspended publication April-Dec. 1939.
Continued by One act play magazine and theatre review with 1940.
WU   UWM (RBR) V.1 no.1-2,4-5,10; v.2 no.4-6,8-9 (MAY1937-MAR1939).

One confidential. *Los Angeles, One Institute of Homophile Studies.* 1499360
ISSN: 0475-0187 Beg. date: 1956
"An occasional newsletter."
WU   UWM (RBR) V.1; v.2 no.2; v.3 no.1-2,4; v.9 no.6,8, 12; v.11 no.3-4,7,9-10 (MAR1956-OCT1966).

One hundred. *See* 100. Chicago. 1505253

One hundred and twenty one. *See* 121. Little Neck, N.Y. 1505294

One hundred flowers. *See* 100 flowers. Stanford, Calif. 1505279

One hundred twenty one. *See* 121. Little Neck, N.Y. 1505303

One Institute of Homophile Studies. One confidential. *See* 1499373
One confidential. Los Angeles, One Institute of Homophile Studies.

One Institute of Homophile Studies. One Institute 1499408
quarterly. *See* One Institute quarterly. Los Angeles, One Institute of Homophile Studies.

One Institute quarterly. *Los Angeles, One Institute of Homophile Studies.* 1499386
ISSN: 0030-2538 LCCN: 63-32882 Beg. date: 1958
"Homophile studies."
Ceased publication.
WU   UWM (RBR) V.1 no.1-3; v.2-8 (SPR1958-n.d.).

One shot. *Sauk City, Wisc.* 1499410
Beg. date: 1973
"Magazine of literature and art."
WU   UWM (RBR) 1973.

Onslaught. *Pepper Pike, Ohio.* 1499423
WU   UWM (RBR) [No.1-2] (APR1967-n.d.).

Ontario review. *New York, Vanguard Press, Inc.* 1278334
ISSN: 0316-4055 LCCN: 75-642814 Beg. date: 1974
WU   UWM (RBR) No.1-6 (FAL1974-1977).

OP. *Houston, Okra Press.* 1508125
Beg. date: 1969
WU   UWM (RBR) No.1-3 (1969-1971).

Open arms. *Livermore, Calif.* 1499449
Beg. date: 1967
WU   UWM (RBR) No.1 ([1967?]).

Open cell. *Berkeley, Free University.* 0564542
ISSN: 0030-3380 Beg. date: 1969
WU   UWM (RBR) V.1-v.2 no.18 (AUG1969-1975).

Open house. *Lawrence, Kansas, Cottonwood Review, University of Kansas.* 1499451
Beg. date: 1975
WU   UWM (RBR) V.1 no.1-2 (OCT1975-[1976?]).

The Open letter. *Toronto [etc.].* 1499464
ISSN: 0048-1939 Beg. date: 1966
"A Canadian ... review of writing and sources."
WU   UWM (RBR) No.1-9 (1966-APR1969); ser. 2 no.1-9 (WIN1971/1972-FAL1974); ser. 3 no.1-6 (1976/1977).

Open places. *Columbia, Mo., etc., Stephens College.* 1499514
Beg. date: 1966
WU   UWM (RBR) No.1-24 (NOV1966-1977).

Open reading. *Rohnert Park, Calif.* 1499477
Beg. date: 1972
WU   UWM (RBR) Ser. 2 no.1-4/5 (MAR1972-WIN/SPR1974).

Open skull. *San Francisco, Open Skull Press.* 149948A
ISSN: 0474-2400 Beg. date: 1967
Supersedes Olé.
WU   UWM (RBR) No.1 (1967).

Open space. *San Francisco.* 149953A
Beg. date: 1963 End date: 1965
Ceased publication with no. 12, 1965.
WU   UWM (RBR) No.0-8,10-12 (1963?-1965).

Open spaces. *See* Openspaces. Los Angeles, The Laurel Press. 1499501

The Open window. *London.* 0564674
Beg. date: 1910
WU   UWM (RBR) V.1 no.1-6; v.2 no.7-12 (OCT1910-SEP1911).

Open Window Society. Voyeur. *See* Voyeur. Brooklyn, N.Y., 1517546
The Open Window Society.

Opening. *Woodchester, Gloucestershire, Eng.* 1499542
ISSN: 0030-350X Beg. date: 1965
WU   UWM (RBR) No.1-9 (1965-1967).

Openspaces. *Los Angeles, The Laurel Press.* 1499492
Beg. date: 1973
WU   UWM (RBR) V.1 no.1 (SPR1973).

Ophir. *Johannesburg, Ravan Press.* 1499555
LCCN: 75-646169 Beg. date: 1967 End date: 1976
Ceased publication with no. 23, Spring 1976.
WU   UWM (RBR) No.2-23 (AUG1967-SPR1976); special issue (AUG1972).

Opinion. *Evanston, Ill. [etc.].* 1499568
Beg. date: 1954
"A journal of thought."
WU   UWM (RBR) No.17,19,21-29,31,33-38 (1965-1970); Dec.I-II (1971); no.50-55 (1972).

The Optimist. Boone, Iowa, H.S. Kneedler, The Nevernod Press. 1499570
Beg. date: 1900 End date: 1901
"A little journal of criticism, review and inspiration."
Ceased publication with vol. 2 no. 3, May 1901.
WU UWM (RBR) V.1 no.1-3 (SEP-NOV1900).

Or oar ore. Monterey, Calif. 1499583
ISSN: 0474-3210 Beg. date: 1966
Title varies: Awwrrrr; Oar; Ore.
WU UWM (RBR) No.1-2 (APR1966-1966).

The Oracle. New York, Marie J. Sutera. 149765A
ISSN: 0471-7368 Beg. date: 1954 End date: 1954
"A literary magazine."
Ceased publication with vol. 1 no. 2, Summer 1954.
WU UWM (RBR) V.1 no.1-2 (SPR-SUM1954).

The Orange bear reader. Windsor, Ont. 1499620
WU UWM (RBR) [No.1-9] (n.d.-n.d.).

Orange Street poetry journal. New Haven, Conn., New Haven Poetry Society. 1497662
ISSN: 0473-128X Beg. date: 1958 End date: 1963
Ceased publication with vol. 4 no. 1, Spring 1963.
WU UWM (RBR) V.2-v.4 no.1 (SPR1960-SPR1963).

The Orchard. Sebastopol, Calif., The Orchard Press. 1529120
Beg. date: 1976
WU UWM (RBR) V.1 no.1 (1976).

Ore. *See* Or oar ore. Monterey, Calif. 1499618

Ore. Stevenage, Herts., Eng. [etc.]. 1497688
ISSN: 0030-459X Beg. date: 1954
Suspended publication with no. 10, 1959.
Resumed publication with no. 11, 1968.
Includes supplement: Daughter of Ore.
WU UWM (RBR) No.1-20 (1954-1976); Daughter of Ore supplement (1968).

Oregon. Eastern Oregon State College, La Grande. 1516764
Underpass. *See* Underpass. La Grande, Ore., ASBEOSC, Eastern Oregon State College.

Organon. Cheney, Wash., Eastern Washington State College. 1396633
ISSN: 0030-5154 Beg. date: 1969
"A journal of the arts and sciences."
WU UWM (RBR) V.1 no.1-3; v.2 no.1-3; v.3 no.1 (WIN1969-SPR1972).

Orient opinion. *See* Orient review and literary digest. Calcutta. 1497712

Orient review. *See* Orient review and literary digest. Calcutta. 1497725

The Orient review and literary digest. Calcutta. 149770A
ISSN: 0473-3878 LCCN: 59-43238 Beg. date: 1955 End date: 1959
Supersedes Orient book world.
Title varies: May-July 1958, The Orient review.
"Orient opinion" accompanies most issues either as a section, usually separately paged, or as a supplement.
Includes special numbers.
Ceased publication with vol. 5 no. 8, Aug. 1959.
WU UWM (RBR) V.2 no.3,7-9; v.3 no.3 (1956-MAR1957).

Oriental blue streak. Placitas, N.M. 1497738
WU UWM (RBR) No.1 (1968).

Origin. Series 2. Nendeln/Liechtenstein, Kraus Reprint. 0569545
ISSN: 0474-6759 Beg. date: 1961 End date: 1964
Also called "Second series: response" in continuation of Origin. Dorchester, Mass., 1951-1957.
Continued in 1966 by Origin. Third series. Kyoto.
Indexes: Nos. 1-13, 1961-1964, in vol. 2.
WU UWM (RBR) No.1-14 (APR1961-JUL1964).

Origin. Series 3. Kyoto, Origin Press. 1529133
ISSN: 0030-5901 Beg. date: 1966
Also called "Third Series: (Center)" in continuation of Origin, Second series: Response, 1961-1964.
WU UWM (RBR) No.1-20 (APR1966-JAN1971).

Origin. Third series: (Center). *See* Origin. Series 3. Kyoto, Origin Press. 1529159

Origin; a quarterly for the creative. Series 1. Dorchester, Mass. 0569558
ISSN: 0473-4068 Beg. date: 1951 End date: 1957
Continued —

Continued —
Reprint of the edition originally published in Dorchester, Massachusetts.
Continued by Origin. Kyoto. 1961-1964.
Indexes: Nos. 1-20, 1951-1957, in v. 3.
WU UWM (RBR) No.1-20 (SPR1951-WIN1957).

Original works. Eugene, Ore. [etc.]. 1497740
ISSN: 0474-6791 Beg. date: 1964 End date: 1972
"The quarterly foreign language journal."
Ceased publication with Jan. 1972.
WU UWM (RBR) V.1-v.8 no.2 (FEB1964-JUL1971); one author series (1970).

Origins. Hamilton, Ont. 1497753
ISSN: 0048-2234 Beg. date: 1967
"A magazine based on a collection of creative writings from young Canadians."
WU UWM (RBR) V.1-v.5 no.4; v.6 no.1-3; v.7 no.1-3 (1967-1977).

Origins/diversions. Carshalton, Surrey, Eng. 1497766
WU UWM (RBR) No.3-4,6/7-12 (1964-SUM/AUT1966).

Orpheus magazine. Phoenix, etc. 1497779
ISSN: 0474-7372 Beg. date: 1967
WU UWM (RBR) V.1 no.3-4; v.2 no.1-2 (1967-1969).

The Orphic lute. Kansas City, Mo., etc. 1497781
ISSN: 0030-5804
WU UWM (RBR) V.1-v.2 no.5; v.3 no.1-3; v.4 no.1-2 (JUN/JUL1958-JUN1962); Spring-Summer 1963; Summer 1966; Autumn 1968; Spring 1971.

Osiris. Schenectady, N.Y. 1497794
ISSN: 0095-019X
"A international journal."
In English, French and German.
WU UWM (RBR) No.1-4 (1972-SPR1977).

Ostrich. Whitely Bay, Northumberland, Eng., Erdesdun Pomes. 1497803
ISSN: 0307-0786 Beg. date: 1971
"Magazine of arts and politics" (varies).
WU UWM (RBR) No.6-18/19 (SEP1972-SEP/OCT1976).

The Other. Milwaukee. 1497816
WU UWM (RBR) No.1-3 (1964-FAL1965).

Other voices. London, Ont. 1497829
ISSN: 0030-6576 Beg. date: 1965
"An independent quarterly of poetry."
WU UWM (RBR) V.1-v.2 no.1; v.3-7; v.8 no.1-2,4 (SPR1965-FEB1973).

Others. Grantwood, New Jersey. 0571124
Ceased publication with v. 5.
V. 4-5, New York Kraus reprint.
WU UWM (RBR) V.1 no.2,4-6; v.2 no.1; v.5 no.2 (AUG1915-JAN1919).

Ottawa. University. Department of English. Faculty of Arts. 0931206
Inscape. *See* Inscape. Ottawa, Univ. of Ottawa. Dept. of English. Faculty of Arts.

Our poets workshop. Brattleboro, Vt. 1529161
WU UWM (RBR) No.22 (JUL051974).

Our time. London, Our Time Publications. 1497831
Beg. date: 1941
"Incorporating Poetry and the people."
WU UWM (RBR) V.1; v.2 no.1,3,7,10,12-13; v.3 no.2-5,7-9,11-12; v.4; v.5 no.1-8,10-12; v.6 no.1-7,9-12; v.7 no.1-11,14; v.8 no.1-3,5-6 (FEB1941-JUN1949).

Out of sight. San Francisco, Kamikaze Press. 1497844
Beg. date: 1966
WU UWM (RBR) V.1 no.1-2 (1966).

Out of sight. Wichita, Kan., Out of Sight Library. 1497857
WU UWM (RBR) No.1,12,31,34,49-59,63,67, 69-70,75-79,82,84-85,87-89,91,93,95,99; ser. 2 no.70,75-76,79-87,90-91,95-97,99-100; ser. 3 no.1-4 (1971-1974).

Out there. Chicago. Out There Press. 149786A
Beg. date: 1973
WU UWM (RBR) No.1-13 (1973-1977).

Outburst. London. 1497872
ISSN: 0474-9111 Beg. date: 1960
WU UWM (RBR) No.1-2 (1961-1963); two unnumbered, undated special issues.

Outcast. *Santa Fe, N.M.* 1497885
ISSN: 0474-912X Beg. date: 1966
WU   UWM (RBR) No.1-15 (1966-OCT1969).

Outcry. *Washington, D.C.* 1497898
ISSN: 0474-9138 Beg. date: 1962 End date: 1963
Ceased publication with vol. 1 no. 3, 1963.
WU   UWM (RBR) V.1 no.1-3 (1962-1963).

The Outer circle. *Monroeton, Pa.* 1497907
Beg. date: 1972
"A journal of communication written by and for residents of the Twin Tiers.
WU   UWM (RBR) V.1 no.1-4; v.2 no.1 (DEC1972-JAN1974).

Outerbridge. *Staten Island, N.Y.* 149791A
Beg. date: 1975
WU   UWM (RBR) V.1 no.1 (SPR1975).

The Outlander. *Portland, Ore.* 1497922
WU   UWM (RBR) No.3 (SUM1933).

Outlet. *Glasgow, The Spearhead Press.* 1497935
"A critical approach to contemporary culture" (varies).
WU   UWM (RBR) N. ser. no.1-2 (SUM1950-n.d.).

Outlet. *Manhattan, Kan.* 1497948
ISSN: 0474-9200 Beg. date: 1967
WU   UWM (RBR) V.1 no.1-3 (1968-FEB201969).

Outpost. *Newton, Mass., Outpost Publications.* 1510585
Beg. date: 1977
WU   UWM (RBR) V.1 no.1-2/3 (WIN-SPR/SUM1977).

Outposts. *Walton on Thames, Surrey, Eng., Outposts Publications.* 1497950
ISSN: 0030-7297 LCCN: 77-5308 Beg. date: 1944
WU   UWM (RBR) No.5-13,21,24-25,27-34,36-37,40-113 (1945-SUM1977).

Outrigger. *Hamilton, New Zealand, Outrigger Publishers Ltd.* 1497963
Beg. date: 1974
Supplements Cave.
WU   UWM (RBR) No.1-12 (1974-OCT1976); special issue Mar. 1976.

Outsider. *Caterham, Surrey, Eng.* 1497989
WU   UWM (RBR) No.2-4 (n.d.-n.d.).

Outsider. *Tucson [etc.], Loujon Press.* 0572079
Beg. date: 1961 End date: 1969
Distributed by DeBoer, Bloomfield, N. J.
Ceased with no. 4-5 (1969).
WU   UWM (RBR) V.1-v.2 no.4/5 (FAL1961-WIN1968/1969).

The Outsider's newsletter. *New York, Monocle Publications, Inc.* 1497991
ISSN: 0474-9308 Beg. date: 1962 End date: 1964
Ceased publication with vol. 2 no. 32, June 1964.
Absorbed by Monocle magazine.
WU   UWM (RBR) V.1 no.1-30,36-42; v.2 no.1-32 (1962-JUN261964).

Overflow. *Ann Arbor, Mich.* 1498009
ISSN: 0030-7408 Beg. date: 1967
"A magazine of poetry" (varies).
WU   UWM (RBR) V.1 no.1-3; v.2 no.1-3; v.3 no.1-3; v.4 no.1 (AUG1967-1971).

Overland. *Melbourne.* 0572144
ISSN: 0030-7416 LCCN: 67-117472 Beg. date: 1954
Indexes: No. 17-24, autumn 1960-spring 1962, in no. 24.
WU   UWM (RBR) No.3-66 (AUT1954?-1977).

Overspill. *Shalford, Surrey, Eng.* 1498011
WU   UWM (RBR) No.1-9 (SUM1972-OCT1974).

Owl, a miscellany. *London, M. Secker.* 0572601
LCCN: 20-6820
WU   UWM (RBR) No.1-3 (MAY1919-1923).

Oxford. University. Balliol College. Janus. *See* Janus. London, Balliol College. 1443221

Oxford. University. Balliol College. Mesopotamia. *See* Mesopotamia. Oxford, Balliol College. 1496341

Oxford. University. Keble College. Tomorrow. *See* Tomorrow. Oxford, Keble College, Oxford University. 1512738

Oxford. University. Saint Peter's College. Approach magazine. *See* Approach magazine. Oxford, St. Peter's College. 1468673

The Oxford viewpoint. *Oxford.* 1498024
Beg. date: 1947 End date: 1950
"A review of Oxford writing" (varies).
Ceased publication with vol. 4 no. 2, June 1950.
WU   UWM (RBR) V.1 no.3-6; v.2 no.1-6; v.3 no.1-3,5 (OCT311947-FEB1950).

Oyez magazine. *See* Oyez review. Chicago. 1507616

Oyez review. *Chicago.* 1507594
Beg. date: 1965
Title varies: vols. 1- , 1965- , Oyez magazine.
Published by the students of Roosevelt University.
WU   UWM (RBR) V.1-v.6 no.1; v.7-v.9 no.1; no.4-5 (FAL1965/1966-1977).

Oyster. *Llandaff, Cardiff, Eng.* 1498037
Supersedes Paperway.
WU   UWM (RBR) No.1-3 (NOV1968-AUT/WIN1969).

Oz. *London. Oz Publications Ink Ltd.* 0573227
WU   UWM (RBR) No.[1],6-27,29-33,35-43,45-46 (MAR1967-JAN/FEB1973); special issue (1968?).

P

P E N Centre for Writers in Exile. Arena. *See* Arena. 1441207
[London, P.E.N. Centre for Writers in Exile].

P L. *See* Poetry London. [London.] 1529211

P M. *Tallahassee, Fla., Florida Free Press.* 149804A
WU UWM (RBR) No.3,5 (1971-n.d.).

P M newsletter. *Blackburn, Lancs., Eng.* 1498052
ISSN: 0030-8145 End date: 1969
Ceased publication with no. 19, Summer 1969.
Absorbed by Global tapestry.
WU UWM (RBR) No.15-19 (WIN1967/1968-SUM1969).

P N 2 experiment. *See* P N 3 experiment. Scranton, Pa. 1498080

P N 3 experiment. *Scranton, Pa.* 1498078
Title varies: nos. 1-29?, 1968- , P N 2 experiment.
WU UWM (RBR) No.1-7,9-20,22-29 (1968-n.d.); 1a,2-4 (n.d.-n.d.).

P N review. *Manchester, Eng.* 1498065
ISSN: 0308-2636 Beg. date: 1976
Continues Poetry nation with vol. 4, 1976.
WU UWM (RBR) V.1-4 (no.1-4) (1976-1977).

P S. *Denver.* 1501606
Beg. date: 1953
"Poems and stories."
Ceased publication with no. 8, 1965.
WU UWM (RBR) No.1-8 (1953-1965).

P V P. *Philadelphia.* 1498093
Title varies: , Powelton village people.
WU UWM (RBR) V.1 no.4-6 (JUL/AUG-NOV/DEC1965).

Pacific. *[Oakland, Calif.], Mills College.* 0963831
Beg. date: 1945 End date: 1948
WU UWM (RBR) V.1-2 (NOV1945-JUN1947).

Pacific explicator. *See* Blue guitar. [Long Beach, Calif.]. 1433408

Pacific nation. *Vancouver, B.C., Pacific Nation for the* 1498115
Authors.
ISSN: 0030-8773 Beg. date: 1967
WU UWM (RBR) No.1-2 (1967-FEB1969).

Pacifica Foundation. Annual annual. *See* Annual annual. 1432695
Los Angeles, Pacifica Foundation.

Pagan. *New York, Pagan Publishing.* 0574914
Beg. date: 1916 End date: 1922
"A magazine for eudaemonists."
WU UWM (RBR) V.1 no.3-9; v.2 no.1-10; v.3 no.1-4/5,8-12; v.4 no.1-3/4,9-10,12; v.5 no.1-3/5,7/8-11/12; v.6 no.1-8/9 (JUL1916-DEC1921-JAN1922).

Pagany; a native quarterly. *Boston, R. Johns.* 057493A
LCCN: 35-20981 Beg. date: 1930
WU UWM (RBR) V.1-3 (1930-1933).

Pages. *Jamaica, N.Y.* 1498128
WU UWM (RBR) No.11/12-23/24 (v.1-3) (1965-1967).

Paideia. *Amherst, Mass., Amherst College.* 1498130
ISSN: 0479-1533 Beg. date: 1965
"The journal of the students of Amherst College."
WU UWM (RBR) V.1 no.4,7 (SPR1966-SPR1974).

Paintbrush. *Laramie, Wyo., Ishtar Publications, Inc.* 1498156
ISSN: 0094-1964 LCCN: 74-644923 Beg. date: 1974
"A journal of poetry, translations, and letters."
WU UWM (RBR) No.1-6 (SPR1974-AUT1976).

The Painted bride quarterly. *Philadelphia.* 1498169
ISSN: 0362-7969 LCCN: 76-642993 Beg. date: 1973
WU UWM (RBR) V.1-v.4 no.2 (FAL1973-1977).

The Painter and sculptor. *London, Painter and Sculptor* 1498171
Press.
ISSN: 0479-1606 LCCN: 63-340 Beg. date: 1958 End date: 1963
"A journal of the visual arts."
Ceased publication with vol. 5, Spring 1963.
Index: vols. 1-5, with vol. 5.
WU UWM (RBR) V.1-v.5 no.1 (SPR1958-SUM1962).

Pa'lante. *New York, The League of Militant Poets.* 1498184
ISSN: 0552-9409 Beg. date: 1962
WU UWM (RBR) Summer-Fall/Winter 1962.

Palantir. *Preston, Lancs., Eng.* 1498206
Beg. date: 1973
WU UWM (RBR) No.1-5 (WIN1973-MAR1977).

The Pale dog. *San Francisco.* 1498219
ISSN: 0479-2564 Beg. date: 1960
WU UWM (RBR) V.1 no.2 (1960).

Palinurus. *Orange, N.J.* 1498221
ISSN: 0479-2696 Beg. date: 1959
WU UWM (RBR) V.1 no.1 (APR1959).

Palms. *Guadalajara, Mexico [etc.].* 0576913
Beg. date: 1923
Publication suspended from June 1930-Oct. 1936.
"A magazine of poetry."
WU UWM (RBR) V.1 no.1 (1923).

La Paloma. *Paterson, N.J.* 1498234
"Official organ of the Pan American Poetry Society."
WU UWM (RBR) V.3 no.1 (SPR1939).

Pan. *New York.* 149825A
ISSN: 0479-3021 Beg. date: 1958 End date: 1958
"A quarterly of poetry."
Ceased publication with no. 2, 1958.
WU UWM (RBR) No.1-2 (1958).

Pan American Poetry Society. Paloma. *See* Paloma. 1498247
Paterson, N.J.

The Pan American review. *Edinburg, Texas, Funch Press.* 0577385
WU UWM (RBR) V.1 no.1 (WIN1970/1971).

Panache. *New York.* 1498262
ISSN: 0031-062X LCCN: 75-643313 Beg. date: 1965
WU UWM (RBR) No.1-18 (1965-1977).

Panama gold. *San Francisco.* 1498275
WU UWM (RBR) July 1969.

Pandora. *Los Angeles, Pandora, Inc.* 1529174
Beg. date: 1962
"A quarterly for women."
WU UWM (RBR) V.1 no.1-2 (SPR-SUM1962).

The Panic button. *Islington, Ont.* 1498288
End date: 1964
"Canada's magazine of cerebral flatulence."
Ceased publication with no. 16, 1964.
WU UWM (RBR) No.15-16 (1963-1964).

Panjandrum. *San Francisco, Panjandrum Press.* 1498290
ISSN: 0092-5535 LCCN: 73-647556 Beg. date: 1972
"A journal of contemporary poetry."
WU UWM (RBR) No.1-5 (1972-1977).

The Paper. *Chicago, The Paper Inc.* 149830A
ISSN: 0479-4613 Beg. date: 1960
"A Chicago weekly."
WU UWM (RBR) V.1 no.3-45; v.2 no.1-2 (JUN251960-JUL1961).

Paper air. *Philadelphia.* 1498312
Beg. date: 1976
WU UWM (RBR) No.1-2 (1976-1977).

Paper pudding. *Monte Rio, Calif.* 1498325
Beg. date: 1972 End date: 1973
"With EZ vocabulary builder" (varies).
Continued by Back roads with no. 6, Summer 1974.
WU UWM (RBR) Spring 1972; one unnumbered, undated issue; no.3-5 (FAL1972-AUT1973).

Paperway. *Llandaff, Cardiff, Eng.* 1498338
WU UWM (RBR) No.1-2 (JUN-AUG1968).

Papyrus; a magazine of individuality. *Mount Vernon, New* 0578771
York.
LCCN: 6-4333
No numbers issued for Apr. 1904-May 1904. Publication suspended Sept. 1906-June 1907, May 1910-Oct. 1910.
Absorbed the Whim Feb. 1905.
New ser. v. 1-6 called also "Old ser. v.8-14".
Superseded by Phoenix.
WU UWM (RBR) V.1; v.2 no.2-3,6; v.4 no.3,6 (1903-1905); n. ser. v.1; v.2 no.1; v.3 no.1/2-4; v.6 no.1/2 (JUL1903-JAN/FEB1910).

Parabalou. *Farmington, Conn.* 1498340
LCCN: 20-15479 rev Beg. date: 1920 End date: 1921
Ceased publication with no. 3, Feb. 1921.
WU UWM (RBR) No.1-3 (1920-1921).

Parallax. *Carbondale, F. H. Moreno.* 057885A
Beg. date: 1961
WU   UWM (RBR) No.1-7 (SUM1961-1963); suppl. (MAR1964).

Parenthèse. *New York, Parenthèse.* 1498353
WU   UWM (RBR) No.1-4 (1975).

The Park. *London, The Ferry Press.* 1498366
ISSN: 0031-210X
WU   UWM (RBR) No.1,4/5 (1968-SUM1969).

Parley. *Worthing, Eng.* 1498379
"Incorporating Fantasma, Papuri. Bullring."
WU   UWM (RBR) N. ser. no.1 (AUT1959).

Parnassus. *Green Bay, Wisc., University of Wisconsin.* 1498381
Green Bay Extension Center.
ISSN: 0479-625X
"The magazine of the University of Wisconsin Center System."
WU   UWM (RBR) V.8 no.2; v.9 no.1 (FAL1961-SPR1962).

Parnassus. *Memphis, Tenn., Neil Mermelstein.* 1498403
ISSN: 0475-8196   Beg. date: 1960
"The magazine of eloquent literature."
WU   UWM (RBR) V.1 no.1-3 (WIN1960-WIN1961).

Parnassus. *Paris, Parnassus Publications.* 1498429
ISSN: 0553-3244   Beg. date: 1961   End date: 1964
Sponsored by the American Students' and Artists' Center of Paris.
Ceased publication with no. 5, 1964.
Superseded by Montparnasse review.
WU   UWM (RBR) No.1-5 (SUM1961-WIN/SPR1964).

Parnassus: poetry in review. *New York, H. Leibowitz.* 0932780
ISSN: 0048-3028   LCCN: 76-645866   Beg. date: 1972
Indexes: Author index: vols. 1-2, Fall 1972-Summer 1974, in vol. 2.
WU   UWM (RBR) V.1-V.5 no.2 (FAL/WIN1972-SPR/SUM1977).

Pasque petals. *Sioux Falls, S.D., South Dakota State Poetry* 0581208
Society.
ISSN: 0031-2649   Beg. date: 1926
"A monthly magazine devoted to South Dakota writers and readers."
WU   UWM (RBR) V.33 no.1,3-6 (MAY-SEP1958).

The Pastime printer. *Front Royal, Va.* 1498444
ISSN: 0475-8919   Beg. date: 1956
WU   UWM (RBR) No.8-10,12 (MAR1958-DEC1959).

Pathways. *Vacaville, Calif., The Pen and Pencil Set.* 1498457
WU   UWM (RBR) V.2 no.4; v.3 no.1; v.4 no.1,4; v.5 no.1 (JUL/SEP1967-WIN1970/SPR1971).

Patterns. *Burlington, Vt. [etc.].* 149846A
ISSN: 0479-7086   Beg. date: 1954
WU   UWM (RBR) V.1-3 (1954-1962).

Patterns. *Denville, N.J.* 1498472
ISSN: 0031-3211   Beg. date: 1970   End date: 1973
"A magazine of art and poetry."
Ceased publication with vol. 2, 1973.
Superseded by Stone country.
WU   UWM (RBR) V.1 no.1-4; v.2 no.1-2 (FEB1970-n.d.).

Patterns. *Fremantle, Western Australia, Fremantle Arts* 1498485
Centre.
Beg. date: 1974
WU   UWM (RBR) V.1-v.3 no.1 (WIN1974-SPR197[7]).

Paunch. *Buffalo, N.Y.* 1498507
ISSN: 0031-3262   LCCN: 77-647819
WU   UWM (RBR) No.21-33,35-46/47 (OCT1964-DEC1976).

Pavement. *Brooklyn, N.Y., H. Zucker.* 149851A
ISSN: 0479-7140   Beg. date: 1952
"A quarterly of poetry."
WU   UWM (RBR) Summer 1952; Summer 1953.

The Pawn review. *Dallas, etc.* 1498522
Beg. date: 1976
WU   UWM (RBR) V.1 no.2; v.2 no.1 (JUL1976-SPR1977).

Pax. *New York, N.Y.* 1529187
ISSN: 0479-723X
"A magazine of poetry and art."
WU   UWM (RBR) No.1 (n.d.); one unnumbered, undated issue; no.4-5,12-18 (1957-1962).

Peace. *San Francisco, Nevada/Tatoo Press.* 1498548
WU   UWM (RBR) Two unnumbered issues (1969).

The Peace and pieces review. *San Francisco, Peace and* 1498550
Pieces Press.
Beg. date: 1973
"Not just another pretty quarterly."
WU   UWM (RBR) V.1-v.2 no.2 (1973-SPR/SUM1976).

Peace Centers Foundation. Breakthru. See Challenge. 1434430
[Reseda, Calif., etc.], Conference on Science and Religion.

Peace poems. *London.* 1498563
Beg. date: 1969
WU   UWM (RBR) No.1 (1969).

The Peacock reviewer. *Berkeley, Calif., Peacock Press.* 1498576
ISSN: 0553-433X   Beg. date: 1966   End date: 1966
Ceased publication with vol. 1 no. 3, March 1966.
WU   UWM (RBR) V.1 no.1-3 (JAN-MAR1966).

Pearl. *Fountain Valley, Calif., Joan Smith.* 1498589
WU   UWM (RBR) Winter 1974; Spring/Summer 1975.

Pebble. *Crete, Neb., etc.* 1498591
ISSN: 0031-3696   Beg. date: 1968
"A magazine of poetry."
WU   UWM (RBR) No.1-16 (Aut1968-1976/1977).

Pebble. *Omaha.* 0582453
Beg. date: 1900
No more published.
Two letters addressed to Richard B. Shepard, one signed by L. McPherson, and the other by both editors, are attached to end-papers of v. 1.
WU   UWM (RBR) V.1-v.3 no.1 (MAR1900-APR1901).

Pebble breeze. Stone Wind bootleg edition. *Chicago.* 1498600
WU   UWM (RBR) One unnumbered, undated issue.

Pegasus. *Bloomington, Ind., Department of English,* 1498613
University of Indiana.
ISSN: 0479-7973   Beg. date: 1972
WU   UWM (RBR) V.2-4 (WIN1963-1966).

Pegasus. *New York, Pegasus Poetry Society of Greenwich* 1498639
Village.
ISSN: 0476-0182   Beg. date: 1952   End date: 1960
"The poetry quarterly."
Ceased publication with vol. 5 no. 4 (no. 20), 1960.
WU   UWM (RBR) V.1-5 (WIN1952-1960).

Pegasus Poetry Society of Greenwich Village. Pegasus. 1498641
See Pegasus. New York, Pegasus Poetry Society of Greenwich Village.

Pembroke. State College, Pembroke. Pembroke magazine. 149867A
See Pembroke magazine. Pembroke, N.C., Pembroke State University.

The Pembroke magazine. *Pembroke, N.C., Pembroke State* 1498654
University.
ISSN: 0097-496X   LCCN: 75-646163   Beg. date: 1969
No. 1 issued by Pembroke State College.
WU   UWM (RBR) No.1,3,9 (1969-1977).

Pen. *Salt Lake City, University of Utah.* 1498682
WU   UWM (RBR) Spring 1955; Feb., Mar., May, Summer 1956; Spring, Winter 1957; Winter 1958; Winter 1959; Winter, Spring 1960; Winter, Spring, Autumn 1961; v.50-51; v.52 no.2-3; v.53-57 (AUT1961-SPR1969).

Pen, heart, and cross. *Fairbanks, Alaska.* 1498704
WU   UWM (RBR) V.1 no.3-5,7,9-11 (SEP291958-JUL1959).

Pen point. See Penpoint. Kampala, Uganda, English 1499765
Department. Makerere University College.

The Pendulum. *Spokane, Wash.* 1498717
WU   UWM (RBR) 3 issues (1957).

The Pendulum of time and the arts. *Glendale, N.Y.* 1499633
ISSN: 0031-4269
WU   UWM (RBR) No.13-69 (v.2-10) (MAY/AUG-JAN/FEB1967).

Penguin new writing. *Harmondsworth, Eng., Allen Lane.* 0583066
Quarterly (no. 1-12); monthly (irregular).
WU   UWM (RBR) V.1-40 (1940-1950).

Peninsula poets. *Lansing, Mich.*   1499659
ISSN: 0031-4307
"Organ of the Poetry Society of Michigan."
WU   UWM (RBR) V.22 no.2-4; v.23; v.24 no.1-2; v.32 no.1 (SPR1967-WIN1977).

Pennine platform. *Wetherby, West Yorkshire, Eng.*   1499674
"Supported by the Yorkshire Arts Association."
WU   UWM (RBR) Spring, Summer, Autumn 1973; Winter 1973/1974; Spring, Summer, Autumn 1974; Winter 1975/1976; 1976 no.1-2; 1977 no.1-2.

Pennington School, Pennington, New Jersey. New laurel review. *See* New laurel review. Pennington, N.J., The Pennington School.   1494812

Pennsylvania. State College, Kutztown. Compass. *See* Compass. Kutztown, Pa., Kutztown State College.   1431359

Pennsylvania. State University. Poetry Workshop. Pivot. *See* Pivot. University Park, Pa., Pennsylvania State University. Poetry workshop.   1254980

Pennsylvania. University. American quarterly. *See* American quarterly. Minneapolis, etc. University of Minnesota Philadelphia Univ. of Penn.   0584359

Pennsylvania. University. Philomathean Society. Era. *See* Era. Philadelphia, Pennsylvania. University. Philomathean Society.   146878A

Pennsylvania literary review. *Philadelphia.*   149969A
ISSN: 0476-210X Beg. date: 1951
WU   UWM (RBR) V.1 no.1-2; v.2-3; v.4 no.1-3; v.5-9; v.10 no.3; v.11 no.2; v.12 no.1-2; v.13 no.1 (SPR1951-1962).

The Penny dreadful. *Bowling Green, Ohio.*   1499709
"Being a periodical of fiction, poems, articles, reviews, interviews."
WU   UWM (RBR) V.3 no.3; v.4 no.1-2 (SPR1974-FAL/WIN1975).

Penny poems. *New Haven, Conn.*   1499711
ISSN: 0476-2282
WU   UWM (RBR) No.45-93 (1959?).

Penny poems from Amarillo College. *Amarillo, Tex.*   1499724
Beg. date: 1963
Ceased publication.
Superseded by Penny poems from Midwestern College.
WU   UWM (RBR) V.1-7 (MAY051963-MAY311964).

Penny poems from Midwestern University. *Wichita Falls.*   0584935
Beg. date: 1964 End date: 1967
Supersedes Penny poems from Amarillo College.
Ceased publication with vol. 8, no. 10, May 15, 1967.
WU   UWM (RBR) V.1-8 (OCT301964-MAY151967).

Penpoint. *Kampala, Uganda, English Department. Makerere University College.*   149974A
ISSN: 0079-0702 Beg. date: 1958
Ceased publication.
WU   UWM (RBR) No.10,17-22,24-25 (MAR1961-1968).

Penumbra. *New York etc., Kauri-Penumbra Press.*   1499778
ISSN: 0031-4943
WU   UWM (RBR) V.1 no.3/4-13 (1968-JUL1974).

Pequod. *Forest Knolls, Calif.*   1499780
LCCN: sc77-141 Beg. date: 1974
"A journal of contemporary literature and literary criticism."
WU   UWM (RBR) V.1-v.2 no.2 (SPR1974-1977).

Per/Se. *Stanford, California.*   0585290
LCCN: 66-9887
Quarterly.
Ceased publication with v. 3, 1968/1969.
WU   UWM (RBR) V.3 (1968-1969).

Performance. *New York.*   058546A
ISSN: 0006-1883 Beg. date: 1971
Vol. 1 no. 1- published by the New York Shakespeare Festival Public Theater; vol. 1 no. 6 (?)- published by New York Performance Foundation.
WU   UWM (RBR) V.1 no.1-6; v.2 no.1 (no.7) (DEC1971-FAL1973).

Performing arts. *Los Angeles, Music Center Operating Company of Los Angeles County.*   1499793
ISSN: 0031-5222 Beg. date: 1967
"The Music Center monthly."
Los Angeles edition of Playbill, the magazine for theatergoers.
WU   UWM (RBR) V.2 no.1 (JAN1968).

The Periodical lunch. *Ann Arbor, Mich., Street Fiction Press.*   1499828
Beg. date: 1973
WU   UWM (RBR) No.1-6 (1973-1975).

Periodical review. *Seattle, Periodical Review, Inc.*   1499830
ISSN: 0031-5354 Beg. date: 1968
Vol. 1 no. 1 preceded by a sample issue dated 1968 and called vol. 1 no. 0.
WU   UWM (RBR) V.1 no.1-10 (DEC061968-DEC121969).

Permanent Bureau of Afro-Asian Writers. Afro-Asian writings. *See* Lotus. Cairo, Permanent Bureau of Afro-Asian Writers.   132350A

Permanent Bureau of Afro-Asian Writers. Lotus. *See* Lotus. Cairo, Permanent Bureau of Afro-Asian Writers.   1323488

Personal injury magazine. *New York.*   1499843
Beg. date: 1975
WU   UWM (RBR) No.1-3 (MAY1975-NOV1976).

Perspective; a quarterly of modern literature. *St. Louis, Missouri, Perspective, Inc.*   0586449
ISSN: 0031-5893 LCCN: 51-23302 Beg. date: 1947
Subtitle varies.
WU   UWM (RBR) V.1-10; v.12 no.1,3; v.13 no.4; v.14 no.1-2,4; v.15-17 (AUT1947-SPR1975).

Perspectives. British edition. *London, Hamish Hamilton Ltd.*   1499856
ISSN: 0553-7495 Beg. date: 1952 End date: 1956
"Perspectives is published also in French, German, and Italian language editions."
Ceased publication with no. 16, 1956.
WU   UWM (RBR) No.2 (WIN195?).

Perspectives. *San Francisco.*   1499869
WU   UWM (RBR) V.1 no.3-4 (FEB/MAR-APR/JUN1966).

Perspectives U S A. *Brooklyn, Intercultural Publications.*   0586633
ISSN: 0553-7606 LCCN: 54-50887 rev Beg. date: 1952 End date: 1956
Ceased publication with no. 16, Summer 1956.
Index: nos. 1-16, in no. 16.
WU   UWM (RBR) No.1-16 (FAL1953-SUM1956).

Phantasm. *Chico, Calif., Heidelberg Graphics.*   1499871
ISSN: 0145-5303 LCCN: sc77-158 Beg. date: 1976
WU   UWM (RBR) V.1-v.2 no.4 (1976-1977).

Phantasmus. *Pittsburgh.*   0587889
Beg. date: 1924
Cover title.
No more published?
WU   UWM (RBR) V.1 no.1-3/4 (MAY-JUL/AUG1924).

Pharos; a magazine dedicated to creative writing. *Murray, Utah.*   0588294
LCCN: 48-13643 rev Beg. date: 1945 End date: 1947
Supersedes Direction (1937-1945).
Ceased publication with no.4, Winter 1947.
Superseded by Direction with 1947.
WU   UWM (RBR) No.1/2-4 (SPR1945-WIN1947).

Phat mama. *New York, PM, Inc.*   1499884
Beg. date: 1970
WU   UWM (RBR) V.1 no.1 (MAR1970).

Phi Beta Kappa. *See* American scholar. New York, Phi Beta Kappa, Concord, New Hampshire, Rumford Press, etc.   0588331

Philistine, a periodical of protest. *East Aurora, Society of the Philistines.*   0589862
LCCN: 10-3700 Beg. date: 1895 End date: 1915
Editors: 1895-1896 H.P.Taber; 1896?-1915 Elbert Hubbard.
Ceased pub. Jul. 1915.
Index v. 1-20.
WU   UWM (RBR) V.11 no.5; v.13 no.6; v.14 no.2; v.15 no.2; v.16 no.3-5; v.17 no.2; v.19 no.1-2,4-6; v.19-21; v.22 no.1-3,5-6; v.23 no.1,3-6; v.24 no.1-3,5-6; v.25 no.1-3,5-6; v.26; v.27 no.1-4,6; v.28-29; v.30 no.1-2,4-6; v.31-33; v.34 no.2-6; v.35 no.1,4 (OCT1900-1912).

Philomathean Society. Era. *See* Era. Philadelphia, Pennsylvania. University. Philomathean Society.   1468792

Phoebe. *Fairfax, Va.*   1499897
"Phoebe is a student edited periodical published quarterly at George Mason University."
WU   UWM (RBR) V.3-4; v.5 no.2; v.6 no.1-3 (1973-1977).

Phoenix. *Atlanta, The Arts Club of Morehouse College.*   1499962
ISSN: 0476-7179
"A magazine of creative art."
WU   UWM (RBR) V.1 no.2; v.2 no.1 (MAY1954-1955).

The Phoenix. *[Berkeley], St. Mary's College (Calif.).*   1507854
Beg. date: 1951
"Student literary magazine."
WU   UWM (RBR) V.1 no.1; v.2 no.1 (SPR1956-SPR1957).

Phoenix. *Berlin.* 150000A
ISSN: 0031-8345 Beg. date: 1968
"International literary communication magazine."
In English, French and German.
WU   UWM (RBR) Jan. 1970.

Phoenix. *Chicago.* 1499988
"University of Chicago."
WU   UWM (RBR) Spring 1965.

Phoenix. *Haydenville, Mass., Morning Star Press.* 0590629
ISSN: 0031-1776 LCCN: 42-47161 Beg. date: 1938
Suspended 1940-1969.
WU   UWM (RBR) V.1 no.1-3; v.2-5 (MAR/MAY1938-SPR1976).

Phoenix. *Lewes, Sussex, Eng., The Furze Press.* 1500012
WU   UWM (RBR) Spring, Autumn 1946.

Phoenix. *Liverpool.* 1499921
ISSN: 0554-0909
WU   UWM (RBR) No.9 (SUM1963).

Phoenix. *London.* 1499934
ISSN: 0031-8302
"A magazine for writers" (varies).
WU   UWM (RBR) No.17-34,36-65 (OCT1965-NOV/DEC1969).

Phoenix. *Manchester, Eng.* 1499947
ISSN: 0031-8337 LCCN: 70-617925 Beg. date: 1967
Sponsored by the North West Arts Association.
Early issues published in Belfast.
WU   UWM (RBR) No.1-13 (MAR1967-SPR1975).

The Phoenix. *Ridgefield Park, N.J.* 1500025
LCCN: 53-35672
"Official organ of the United Amateur Press Alumni Association."
WU   UWM (RBR) V.3 no.1; v.11 no.5; v.14 no.3-4; v.16 no.2-3; v.29 no.1 (SEP1943-JUN1959).

Phoenix, a magazine of individuality. *South Norwalk, M. Monahan.* 0590644
LCCN: 17-19800 Beg. date: 1914 End date: 1916
Supersedes the Papyrus (July 1903-May 1912).
Ceased publication with vol. 6 no. 1, Dec. 1916.
Absorbed by the International with Jan. 1917.
WU   UWM (RBR) V.1 no.1-2,4; v.2 no.2; v.3 no.4 (JUN1914-SEP1915).

Phoenix fires. *Grand Rapids, Mich.* 1500040
"Anthology of mosaic creativity."
WU   UWM (RBR) Autumn 1973/Winter 1974-Spring 1974.

Phoenix quarterly. *London, Jason Press.* 1500053
Beg. date: 1946 End date: 1948
"A journal directed towards the recovery of unity in religion, politics and art."
Ceased publication with vol. 1 no. 3, April 1948.
WU   UWM (RBR) V.1 no.1-2 (AUT1946-1947).

Phylis. *Los Angeles, Spearman Assoc.* 1500066
Title varies: no. 5, Phylis and Karin.
WU   UWM (RBR) No.2,4-5,7-9 (SEP/NOV1965-1968).

Phylis and Karin. *See* Phylis. Los Angeles, Spearman Assoc. 1500079

Pick. *London, Pick Publications.* 1500094
ISSN: 0305-652X Beg. date: 1974
"A magazine of contemporary poetry."
WU   UWM (RBR) No.1-8 (AUT1974-1977).

Pierian spring. *Greeley, Colo., Pierian Press.* 1500103
Beg. date: 1968
"A quarterly journal of poetry."
WU   UWM (RBR) V.1-v.2 no.3 (SPR1968-FAL1970).

Pig iron. *See* Pigiron. Youngstown, Ohio, Pigiron Press. 1500129

Pigiron. *Youngstown, Ohio, Pigiron Press.* 1500116
ISSN: 0362-5214
WU   UWM (RBR) No.1-3 (1975-1977).

Pink peace. *Folkestone, Kent, Eng., The Aten Press.* 1500131
Ceased publication with no. 9, Winter 1973/1974.
WU   UWM (RBR) No.2-9 (NOV1971-WIN1973/1974).

Pinnacle. *Toledo, Ohio.* 1500144
ISSN: 0480-5267
"Pinnacle of literature."
WU   UWM (RBR) Autumn 1960; Summer 1961; Summer/Autumn 1962.

Pitzer College, Claremont, California. Grove. *See* Grove: 1439881
contemporary poetry and translation. Claremont, Calif., Pitzer College.

Pivot. *University Park, Pa., Pennsylvania State University.* 1254978
Poetry workshop.
ISSN: 0554-2324 Beg. date: 1951
1951-1955 have subtitle: Student magazine of verse.
WU   UWM (RBR) No.1-28 (SPR1951-1977).

Pivot; student magazine of verse. *See* Pivot. University 1254993
Park, Pa., Pennsylvania State University. Poetry workshop.

Place. *Palo Alto, Calif., Natural Wonders Inc.* 1500157
LCCN: 72-623690 Beg. date: 1972
WU   UWM (RBR) V.1 no.1-2; v.2 no.1-2; v.3 no.1 (SPR1972-JUN1973).

Plainsong. *Minneapolis.* 059437A
ISSN: 0032-0455 Beg. date: 1967
WU   UWM (RBR) V.1 no.1-3 (1967).

Plaintiff. *Mankato, Mankato State College.* 0594382
ISSN: 0032-0463 Beg. date: 1965 End date: 1972
Ceased publication with vol. 8, no. 3, 1972.
WU   UWM (RBR) V.3 no.2; v.4 no.2; v.5 no.1-3; v.6 no.1-3 (FAL1967/WIN1968-SPR1970).

Plan for freedom and progress. *London.* 150016A
"Monthly journal of the Progressive League."
WU   UWM (RBR) V.18 no.7; v.19 no.4; v.21 no.6,8; v.28 no.6; v.29 no.6; v.30 no.6; v.31 no.6 (JUL1950-JUN1961).

Planet. *Llandysul, Wales, J.D. Lewis and Sons, Ltd.* 1500185
ISSN: 0048-4288 LCCN: 76-648930 Beg. date: 1970
Published with the financial support of the Welsh Arts Council.
WU   UWM (RBR) No.1-39 (AUG/SEP1970-1977).

Planetary Legion for Peace. Cosmopolitan contact. *See* 1429193
Cosmopolitan contact. Los Angeles, Planetary Legion for Peace.

The Plasmadena gazette. *Pasadena, Calif., Poetry.* 1500198
WU   UWM (RBR) V.1 no.2 (n.d.).

Platform. *London.* 1500207
ISSN: 0032-1389 Beg. date: 1953
WU   UWM (RBR) No.1-4 (n.d.-AUT1955).

Platform. *Luddenden Foot, Yorkshire, Eng.* 150021A
ISSN: 0032-1389
"The magazine of the Pennine Poets."
WU   UWM (RBR) Apr., July, Oct. 1967; Jan. 1968; 1970-Apr. 1972.

Platform. *Stockbridge, Hampshire, Eng.* 1500222
Beg. date: 1972
WU   UWM (RBR) No.1-4,6-7 (FEB1972-[1974]).

The Play-book. *Madison, Wisc., The Wisconsin Dramatic Society.* 1500248
LCCN: 16-7204 Beg. date: 1913 End date: 1915
Ceased publication with vol. 2 no. 12, May,1915.
WU   UWM (RBR) V.1 no.3-12; v.2 no.1 (JUN1913-JUN1914).

Playbill. Los Angeles. Performing arts. *See* Performing 1499815
arts. Los Angeles, Music Center Operating Company of Los Angeles County.

Playbook. *See* The Play-book. Madison, Wisc., 1519937

Playboy. *New York, Egmont Arens.* 1500235
LCCN: 27-6945 Beg. date: 1919 End date: 1924
"A portfolio of art and satire."
Suspended publication July 1, 1921-Feb. 1923.
Ceased publication with vol. 2 no. 2, June 1924.
WU   UWM (RBR) No.1-7; v.2 no.1,9 (1919-JUL1924).

Pliego. *Milwaukie, Ore., Prensa de Lagar/Wine Press.* 1500263
WU   UWM (RBR) No.1-35,37-41 (1966-1967).

Ploughshares. *Cambridge, Mass.* 1336327
ISSN: 0048-4474 LCCN: 76-643915 Beg. date: 1971
"An occasional of the arts."
WU   UWM (RBR) V.1-v.3 no.3/4 (SEP1971-1977).

The Plowshare. *[n.p.]* 1501151
"A newsletter of peace ideas and information from Maine."
WU   UWM (RBR) No.7-8,10 (AUG1964-APR1965).

The Plowshare. *Woodstock, N.Y., Maverick Press.* 1501164
LCCN: 21-114 Beg. date: 1912 End date: 1935
"A magazine of the literature, arts, and life evolving in Woodstock."
Continued —

Pluck.
Continued —
Title varies: vols. 1-5, 1912-Oct. 1916, Wild hawk.
Suspended publication Dec. 1920-Jan. 1934.
Ceased publication with vol. 10 no.12, Jan. 1935.
WU   UWM (RBR) V.1 no.11-12 (NOV-DEC1911); v.6 no.6; v.7 no.1,12; v.8 no.2-8/9,12; v.9 no.1,4-5,8-9/10,12; v.10 no.3, 5,9-12 (MAY1917-JAN1935).

Pluck. *Edmonton.* 150118A
ISSN: 0556-0438 Beg. date: 1968
WU   UWM (RBR) V.1 no.1-2; v.2 no.2 (WIN1967/1968-FAL1968).

The Plum Creek review. *Oberlin, Ohio, Oberlin College.* 1501192
WU   UWM (RBR) No.10,15/16,19-20 (SPR1964-SPR1974).

Plume and sword. *Charlottsville, Va., University of Virginia.* 1501214
ISSN: 0554-3193
WU   UWM (RBR) V.6-7 (FAL1965-SUM1967).

Pocket pal. *Oberlin, Ohio [etc.], Pocket Pal Press.* 150123A
Beg. date: 1975
WU   UWM (RBR) V.1 no.2-v.2 no.3 (1975-SPR1977).

Pocket poetry monthly. *Key West, Fla., Pocket Poetry Press.* 1501242
Beg. date: 1974
WU   UWM (RBR) V.1-v.2 no.3 (no.1-9) (JUN1974-MAR1977).

Podium. *Brooklyn Heights, Ohio [etc.], Poetry Seminar.* 1501255
ISSN: 0032-1850 Beg. date: 1965
WU   UWM (RBR) V.1 no.1-2,4; v.2 no.1-3 (JUL1965-APR1969).

Poem. *Huntsville, Alabama, Huntsville Literary Association.* 1501268
ISSN: 0032-1885 Beg. date: 1967
WU   UWM (RBR) No.1-30 (NOV1967-1977).

The Poem company. *Vancouver, Intermedia Press and The Poem Company.* 1501283
WU   UWM (RBR) No.1-2 (1972); Phase 3 no.1-3,5-7 (n.d.-n.d.).

Poems by blacks. *Fort Smith, Ark.* 1151859
ISSN: 0079-2454
WU   UWM (RBR) 1972.

Poems by poets. *Fort Smith, Ark., South and West, Inc.* 152919A
Beg. date: 1973
WU   UWM (RBR) V.1 (1973).

Poems collected at Les Deux Magots. *See* Poets at le Métro. New York. 1529265

Poems from the floating world. *[n.p.], Hawk's Well Press.* 1256390
ISSN: 0554-3606 Beg. date: 1959
WU   UWM (RBR) V.1-5 ([1959?]-1963).

The Poet. *Balerno, Midlothian, Scot., Celandine Pub. Co.* 1501305
Beg. date: 1936
WU   UWM (RBR) No.6 (MAY/JUN1937).

The Poet. *Glasgow.* 1501318
ISSN: 0477-0557 LCCN: 55-40654 Beg. date: 1952 End date: 1957
Ceased publication with no. 15, 1957.
WU   UWM (RBR) No.3-15 (SUM1952-1957).

Poet. *Madras, Krishna Srinivas.* 0595963
ISSN: 0032-194X Beg. date: 1960
"An international monthly."
WU   UWM (RBR) V.1 no.2-3; v.2 no.1; v.3 no.1; v.4 no.2-3/4,9-11; v.5 no.1-4; v.6 no.2-6; v.7 no.2-8; v.8 no.1,4/5-12; v.9-10; v.11 no.1-6,8,12; v.12 no.2-12; v.13-v.17 no.10 (JUN1960-OCT1976).

Poet and critic. *Ames, Ia., Iowa State University.* 0890697
ISSN: 0032-1958 Beg. date: 1964
"A magazine of verse/a workshop in print/a forum of opinion."
Supersedes Poet and critic. Lafayette, Ind.
WU   UWM (RBR) V.1-9 (FAL1964-1976).

Poet and critic. *Lafayette, Ind.* 1501320
ISSN: 0551-1518 LCCN: 74-111373 Beg. date: 1961 End date: 1962
"A folder of poetry and criticism."
Ceased publication with vol. 2 no. 6, July/Aug. 1962.
Superseded by Poet and critic (Ames, Iowa State University).
WU   UWM (RBR) File no.1-2 (SEP1961-JUL/AUG1962).

Poet of the month. *See* Poets of the year. Norfolk, Conn., New Directions. 113757A

Poet quarterly. *Harrogate, Eng., The Curlew Press.* 150787A
Beg. date: 1976
Continues Curlew with no. 11, Spring 1976.
WU   UWM (RBR) No.11-12 (SPR1976-SUM1976).

Poet tree centaur. *London, Oddments.* 1501333
"A Walthamstow Group anthology."
WU   UWM (RBR) 1973.

Poetaster. *Bakersfield, Calif., Lance Associates.* 1501346
WU   UWM (RBR) V.1 no.3-v.3 (SPR1965-SUM1967).

Poetmeat. *Blackburn, Eng., Screeches Publications.* 1501359
ISSN: 0554-3886 End date: 1967
"For peace before our time and social and literary revolt now."
Ceased publication with no. 13, Spring 1967.
Superseded by Poetmeat newsletter.
WU   UWM (RBR) No.4-13 (WIN1964-SPR1967).

Poetry. Cross section. *See* Ark II, Moby I. San Francisco. 1441235

Poetry: London. *See* Poetry London. [London.] 1529224

Poetry: people. *Menomonee Falls, Wisc., R.V.K. Pub. Co.* 149872A
WU   UWM (RBR) 1973; May 1975; May 1976.

Poetry; a one-man magazine of verse. *Brooklyn, N.Y.* 0596078
ISSN: 0554-3894 Beg. date: 1965
WU   UWM (RBR) No.1 (OCT011965).

Poetry, the Australian international quarterly of verse. *Adelaide.* 0596080
Beg. date: 1941 End date: 1947
Subtitle varies.
Ceased publication with no. 25, Dec. 1947.
WU   UWM (RBR) V.1 no.4; no.12-13,15-19,22-25 (1942-DEC101947).

Poetry, Windsor, poésie. *Windsor, Ontario, French Department, University of Windsor.* 1507776
ISSN: 0317-0764 Beg. date: 1974
In English and French.
WU   UWM (RBR) V.1-v.3 no.1 (DEC1974-1977).

Poetry and audience. *Leeds, Eng.* 1507882
ISSN: 0032-2040 Beg. date: 1954
WU   UWM (RBR) V.5 no.6,8,11,15,18,20; v.6 no.1-24-5; v.7 no.1-22; v.8 no.1-23; v.9 no.1-22; v.10 no.5-25; v.11 no.1-9; v.12 no.11-17; v.13 no.1-3,5-9,20-23; v.14 no.1-5,7-14; v.15 no.1-6,9-14,16,18-19; v.16 no.1-19; v.17 no.1-19; v.18 no.1-14; v.19 no.1-8; v.20 no.1-6 (NOV221957-OCT1974).

Poetry and drama. *London, The Poetry Bookshop.* 0596093
LCCN: 14-21178
Superseded by The Chapbook (a monthly miscellany).
V. 1-2 New York, Kraus reprint, 1967.
WU   UWM (RBR) V.1 no.3-v.2 no.1 (SEP1913-MAR1914).

The Poetry and drama magazine. *New York.* 1501361
Beg. date: 1956
"A literary magazine."
Continues Poetry book magazine with vol. 8, 1956.
WU   UWM (RBR) V.8-15 (1956-1965).

Poetry and poverty. *London.* 0932962
Beg. date: 1949 End date: 1954
WU   UWM (RBR) No.2-7 (n.d.-n.d.).

Poetry Australia. *Sydney, South Head Press.* 1501374
ISSN: 0032-2059 LCCN: 78-294871 Beg. date: 1964
WU   UWM (RBR) No.1-63 (DEC1964-1977).

The Poetry bag. *Columbia, Mo.* 1501387
ISSN: 0032-2067 Beg. date: 1966
WU   UWM (RBR) V.1 no.1-7; v.2 no.2 (FAL1966-SPR1969).

The Poetry book magazine. *Brooklyn, N.Y., Waldorf Book Club.* 150139A
Beg. date: 1948 End date: 1955
Continued by Poetry and drama magazine with vol. 8, 1956.
WU   UWM (RBR) V.1-7 (FAL1948-SUM1955).

Poetry broadsheets. *Wellingron, N.Z., The Handcraft Press.* 1507895
WU   UWM (RBR) Sept. 1970.

Poetry broadside. *New York, Contemporary Craftsmen, Inc.* 1501409
ISSN: 0551-1682 Beg. date: 1957
WU   UWM (RBR) V.1 no.1-3 (SPR-WIN1957/1958).

Poetry caravan. *See* Caravan; Hawkeye poetry magazine. Lamoni, Iowa. 1427909

Poetry chap-book. *New York.* 0596115
End date: 1953
Ceased publication v. 11 no. 4, Summer 1953.
WU   UWM (RBR) V.5 no.4; v.7 no.4 (SUM1947-SUM1949).

Poetry collector. *Lafayette, Ind.* 1501411
ISSN: 0554-3924 Beg. date: 1958
   WU   UWM (RBR) Oct. 1958; Mar., June 1959.

Poetry commonwealth. *London.* 1501424
Beg. date: 1948 End date: 1951
Ceased publication with no. 8, Spring 1951.
   WU   UWM (RBR) No.1,3-5 (SUM1948-SUM1949).

Poetry dial. *South Bend.* 0596128
ISSN: 0551-1720 Beg. date: 1961 End date: 1961
Ceased publication with vol. 1 no. 2, Spring 1961.
   WU   UWM (RBR) V.1 no.1-2 (1961).

Poetry digest. *Waterbury, Conn., John DeStefano.* 1501437
ISSN: 0477-0935 Beg. date: 1953
Continues Quatrain digest with vol. 1 no. 5, Dec. 1953.
   WU   UWM (RBR) V.1 no.5; v.2-v.3 no.1; v.4 no.2-4;6; v.5 no.3-v.6 no.2 (DEC1953-APR/MAY1967).

Poetry eastwest. *Sumter, S.C. [ect.], Syed Amanuddin.* 150144A
ISSN: 0079-2519 Beg. date: 1967
"An anthology of new poetry."
   WU   UWM (RBR) No.1-6 (1967-1973).

Poetry Florida and. *Deland, Fla.* 1255000
ISSN: 0554-3940 Beg. date: 1967 End date: 1969
Ceased publication with vol. 2 no. 6, Spring 1969.
   WU   UWM (RBR) V.1-v.2 no.2 (FAL1967-SPR1969).

Poetry folio. *Horsmonden, Kent, Eng., Kent and Sussex Poetry Society.* 1501452
   WU   UWM (RBR) V.3-5,7-8,10,13-18,20-30 (1949-1976).

Poetry folios. *London.* 1507904
LCCN: 52-15370 Beg. date: 1942
Editors: Alex Comfort and Peter Wells.
   WU   UWM (RBR) No.1,3-10 (1941/1942-1945); Summer 1951.

Poetry fund journal. *El Centro, Calif.* 1501478
ISSN: 0551-1763 Beg. date: 1960 End date: 1961
"An esthetic quarterly."
Ceased publication with vol. 1 no.4, Spring 1961.
   WU   UWM (RBR) V.1 no.1-4 (SPR1960-SPR1961).

Poetry Glasgow. *Glasgow.* 1501480
   WU   UWM (RBR) No.1-4 (n.d.-n.d.).

Poetry Guild. We offer. *See* We offer. Driffield, Yorkshire, Eng. 1518512

Poetry information. *London, Peter Hodgkiss.* 1501493
ISSN: 0048-4598 Beg. date: 1970
   WU   UWM (RBR) No.7-17 (MAY1973-1977).

Poetry Ireland. *Cork, Ireland, Trumpet Books.* 0596143
LCCN: 52-18293 Beg. date: 1948 End date: 1952
Ceased separate publication with no. 19, Oct. 1952.
No. 20- published in Irish writing as Poetry Ireland supplement.
   WU   UWM (RBR) No.1-19 (APR1948-OCT1952).

Poetry journal. *Boston.* 0596156
Beg. date: 1912
Ceased.
V.6-8, 1916-1918: Nendeln. Kraus Reprint 1969.
   WU   UWM (RBR) V.1; v.2 no.1,6; v.3 no.3,5; v.4 no.1,5; v.7 no.6 (DEC1912-SEP1917).

Poetry London. *[London.]* 1529209
LCCN: 45-32097 Beg. date: 1939 End date: 1951
Also called P L.
Ceased publication with no. 22, Summer 1951.
Superseded by Poetry London-New York with March/April 1956.
   WU   UWM (RBR) V.2 no.7,9-10 (OCT/NOV1942-DEC1944).

Poetry London-New York. *New York, Poetry Institute Inc.* 1501502
ISSN: 0551-178x Beg. date: 1956 End date: 1960
Ceased publication with vol. 1 no. 4, Summer 1960.
   WU   UWM (RBR) V.1 no.1-4 (MAR/APR1956-SUM1960).

Poetry Los Angeles. *London, Villiers Publications, Ltd.* 1501515
LCCN: 63-46600 Beg. date: 1958 End date: 1958
Ceased publication with no.1, Dec. 1958.
   WU   UWM (RBR) No.1 (DEC1958).

The Poetry magazine. *Sydney, Australia, The Poetry Society of Australia.* 1507735
ISSN: 0554-3967 Beg. date: 1961
Continues Prism with vol. 9, 1961.
   WU   UWM (RBR) V.9 no.1-3; v.10 no.1-5 (JUL1961-NOV1962); 1963; 1964inc.; 1965-1969; v.18 (1970).

Poetry Manchester. *Leigh, Lancashire, Eng.* 1498732
ISSN: 0477-0951 Beg. date: 1951 End date: 1953
Ceased publication with no. 5, 1953.
   WU   UWM (RBR) No.1-5 (AUT1951-n.d.).

Poetry market. *Nottingham, Eng., Aubrey Bush.* 1498745
ISSN: 0032-2083
   WU   UWM (RBR) No.1-3 (JUL1965-MAY1967).

The Poetry miscellany. *Williamstown, Mass.* 1498758
Beg. date: 1971
   WU   UWM (RBR) V.1 no.1-2; v.2 no.1 (no.3),4-5; v.6 (FAL1971-1976).

Poetry nation. *Manchester, Eng.* 1221348
Beg. date: 1973
Continued by P N review with vol. 4, 1976.
   WU   UWM (RBR) No.1-6 (1973-1976).

Poetry New York. *New York.* 0596169
LCCN: 51-38583 Beg. date: 1949
"A magazine of verse and criticism."
Supersedes Yale poetry review.
Ceased publication.
Index to Yale Poetry review, 1945-48 included in no. 1.
   WU   UWM (RBR) No.1-3 (1949-1950).

A Poetry newsletter. *Albuquerque, N.M., The Desert Review Press.* 1498760
Beg. date: 1964
   WU   UWM (RBR) No.1-2 (1964); one unnumbered, undated issue.

Poetry newsletter. *New York.* 1498773
ISSN: 0032-2091 Beg. date: 1964
   WU   UWM (RBR) No.1-2,4-13 (DEC1964-n.d.).

Poetry newsletter. *Philadelphia.* 1498786
Beg. date: 1971
   WU   UWM (RBR) No.1-12,14-15,17-40,42-43 (DEC1971-1977).

Poetry newsletter. *Sacramento.* 1498799
ISSN: 0032-2091
   WU   UWM (RBR) Special issue no.6-7,11; no.14,16,22,24, 27 (1970-n.d.).

Poetry nippon. *Nagoya, Japan, The Poetry Society of Japan.* 1498808
ISSN: 0032-2105
   WU   UWM (RBR) No.8-37/38 (AUT1969-MAR1977).

Poetry nippon newsletter. *Nagoya, Japan, The Poetry Society of Japan.* 1498823
Beg. date: 1974
   WU   UWM (RBR) No.1-6 (DEC1974-JUN1977).

Poetry northwest. *Seattle.* 0596171
ISSN: 0032-2113 Beg. date: 1959
   WU   UWM (RBR) V.1-v.18 no.2 (JUN1959-1977).

Poetry now. *Eureka, Calif., E.V. Griffith.* 1062172
Beg. date: 1974
"Promoting today's poets and poetry".
   WU   UWM (RBR) V.1 no.1-6; v.2 no.1-6 (7-12); v.3 no.1-2 (13-14) (1973-1976).

Poetry of the circle in the square. *Bristol, Eng., Bristol Arts Centre.* 1508924
Beg. date: 1966
   WU   UWM (RBR) V.1-20 (1966-MAR1976); special issue preceding v.20.

Poetry of the wheatfield. *Mount Pleasant, Mich., Wheatfield Press.* 1498849
Beg. date: 1975
   WU   UWM (RBR) No.1-2 (1975-1976).

Poetry of today. *London, E. Macdonald, ltd.* 0596184
LCCN: 21-6585 Beg. date: 1919 End date: 1947
Supplement to and 1921-1924 incorporated in Poetry review.
Subtitle varies.
   WU   UWM (RBR) No.59,61 (JAN-MAR1941).

Poetry one. *Harold Wood, Essex, Eng.* 1507750
End date: 1973
Title varies: , Poetry two.
Ceased publication with 1973.
   WU   UWM (RBR) 1967, 1969, 1970, 1970/1971, 1971, Winter 1971/1972, 1972, 1973.

Poetry pamphlet. *See* The Little magazine. New York. 151994A

Poetry parade. *North Hollywood, Calif., Spencer Book Co.* 1498851
ISSN: 0554-3975 Beg. date: 1966
   WU   UWM (RBR) V.1 no.1-13 (1966-1969).

Poetry periodical. *Cambridge, Eng.* 1498864
ISSN: 0477-0978 Beg. date: 1952 End date: 1953
Ceased publication with no. 3, Summer 1953.
WU   UWM (RBR) No.2-3 (SPR-SUM1953).

Poetry pilot. *New York, Academy of American Poets.* 1529237
ISSN: 0554-3983 LCCN: sc77-202 Beg. date: 1959
WU   UWM (RBR) Mar.-June, Nov. 1964; Jan., July, Dec. 1965; Jan.-July, Sept.-Oct. 1977.

Poetry post. *London Colney, Herts, Eng., Ver Poets.* 1498877
WU   UWM No.4-5 (n.d.-n.d.).

Poetry prevue. *Brooklyn, N.Y.* 149888A
Beg. date: 1968
Continues The Saint with Fall/Winter 1968?
Superseded by Driftwood east with Summer 1973.
WU   UWM (RBR) Winter, Fall 1968; Winter, Summer-Fall 1969; 1970-1971; Winter, Summer-Fall 1972; Spring 1973.

Poetry public. *Chadron, Neb., Poetry Public.* 1498892
ISSN: 0477-0986 Beg. date: 1953
WU   UWM (RBR) V.1 no.1-11; v.2-6 (1953-1958).

Poetry quarterly. *London [etc.], The Grey Walls Press.* 1498901
Beg. date: 1939
Supersedes Poetry studies.
Ceased publication with vol.15, 1953.
WU   UWM (RBR) V.1 no.1-2; v.6-14; v.15 no.5 (SPR1939-SPR/SUM1953).

Poetry quarterly. *New York.* 1498914
Beg. date: 1930 End date: 1931
Ceased publication with vol. 1 no. 3, Spring 1931.
WU   UWM (RBR) V.1 no.1 (FEB1930).

Poetry review. *Tampa, Fla., University of Tampa.* 1509158
ISSN: 0554-4009 Beg. date: 1964
WU   UWM (RBR) No.1-23 (MAY1964-1971).

Poetry review. Supplement. *See* Poetry of today. *London, E. Macdonald, ltd.* 0596221

Poetry Saint Ives. *Penzance, Eng.* 1509173
WU   UWM (RBR) May 1971.

Poetry score. *Monterey, Calif.* 0596247
ISSN: 0551-1801 Beg. date: 1960
No. 3 never published. Special issue in its place.
WU   UWM (RBR) No.1-2 (FAL1960-WIN1962); special issue 1966.

Poetry Scotland. *Glasgow, William Maclellan.* 149893A
Beg. date: 1943
WU   UWM No.2-4 (1945-1949).

Poetry Society, London. Voice of youth. *See* Voice of youth. London, Poetry Society. 1517401

Poetry Society of Australia. New poetry. *See* New poetry. Sydney. 149496A

Poetry Society of Australia. Poetry magazine. *See* Poetry magazine. Sydney, Australia, The Poetry Society of Australia. 1507748

Poetry Society of Australia. Prism. *See* Prism. Sydney, Australia, The Poetry Society of Australia. 1509013

Poetry Society of Japan. Poetry nippon. *See* Poetry nippon. Nagoya, Japan, The Poetry Society of Japan. 1498810

Poetry Society of Japan. Poetry nippon newsletter. *See* Poetry nippon newsletter. Nagoya, Japan, The Poetry Society of Japan. 1498836

Poetry Society of Michigan. Peninsula poets. *See* Peninsula poets. Lansing, Mich. 1499661

Poetry Society of Vermont. Mountain troubador. *See* Mountain troubador. Burlington, Vt., The Poetry Society of Vermont. 149723A

Poetry St. Ives. *See* Poetry Saint Ives. Penzance, Eng. 1509186

Poetry Taos. *Ranches of Taos, N.M.* 1498968
ISSN: 0477-1001 Beg. date: 1957
WU   UWM (RBR) No.1 (1957).

Poetry Texas. *Texas City, Tex., Division of Humanities, College of the Mainland.* 1498942
Beg. date: 1976
WU   UWM (RBR) V.1 no.1-2 (1976-1977).

Poetry Therapy Institute. Therapy 14. *See* Therapy 14. Los Angeles, Poetry Therapy Institute. 1512177

Poetry to-day. *London.* 1498970
Beg. date: 1946
WU   UWM (RBR) V.1 no.2-3 (APR-SUM1946).

Poetry Toronto newsletter. *Toronto.* 1498983
ISSN: 0381-6591
WU   UWM (RBR) No.9-11 (1976).

Poetry two. *See* Poetry one. Harold Wood, Essex, Eng. 1507763

Poetry venture. *St. Petersburg, Fla., Poetry Venture Inc.* 1498996
ISSN: 0032-2199 Beg. date: 1968
"An international poetry magazine."
WU   UWM (RBR) V.1-6 (no.1-12) (FAL1968-SPR1974).

Poetry Wales. *Glamorgan, Wales.* 1499003
ISSN: 0032-2202 Beg. date: 1965
"Cylchgrawn cenedlaethol o farddoniaeth newydd."
In English or Welsh.
WU   UWM (RBR) V.1 no.2; v.2 no.1-3; v.3 no.1-3; v.4 no.1-2; v.5 no.1-3; v.6-12 (AUT1965-SPR1977).

Poetry-Windsor-poésie. *See* Poetry, Windsor, poésie. Windsor, Ontario, French Department, University of Windsor. 1507789

Poetry workshop. *Wolverhampton, Eng., Department of Art History and Contemporary Studies, Wolverhampton College of Art.* 1499016
WU   UWM (RBR) V.1 no.2; v.2 no.1 (n.d.-SPR1969).

Poetry world. *New York.* 1499031
Beg. date: 1929
Continues Poetry world and contemporary vision.
WU   UWM (RBR) V.8 no.12; v.11 no.9-v.12 no.1 (1937-AUG1940).

Poets, yeggs and thirsties. *Boston, Caedmon Literature.* 1499135
Beg. date: 1975
WU   UWM (RBR) V.1 no.1 (SUM1975).

Poets at le Métro. *New York.* 1529252
ISSN: 0554-4041 Beg. date: 1962 End date: 1965
Title varies: nos. 1-2,   . Poems collected at Les Deux Magots.
Ceased publication with no. 20, Jan. 1965.
WU   UWM (RBR) No.1-20 (DEC1962-JAN1965).

Poets at the gate. *Cleveland, Free Love Press.* 1499057
WU   UWM (RBR) V.1 no.4 (JUL041966).

Poet's bulletin. *Denver.* 149906A
WU   UWM (RBR) Jan./Feb., July/Aug.-Nov./Dec. 1964; 1965; Jan.-Mar. 1966.

Poet's calliope. *Tucson, C.L. Windsor Publications.* 1499072
Beg. date: 1976
WU   UWM (RBR) Introductory issue (n.d.); v.1 no.1 (JUL1976).

Poets' Corner, Incorporated, Indianapolis. Cornucopia. *See* Cornucopia. Indianapolis. 1442136

Poet's friend. *See* Visions. Alpine, Calif. 1517377

Poet's nook. *Whittier, Calif., Journal Publications.* 1499085
WU   UWM (RBR) V.2 no.8 (FAL1975).

Poets of the year. *Norfolk, Conn., New Directions.* 1137567
Beg. date: 1941 End date: 1944
Title varies: 1941-1942, Poet of the month.
WU   UWM (RBR) 1941: 12 issues; 1942: 11 issues; 1943: 12 issues; 1944: 1 issue.

Poets on. *Chaplin, Conn.* 1499098
ISSN: 0146-3136 LCCN: sc77-715 Beg. date: 1977
WU   UWM (RBR) V.1 no.1-2 (1977).

Poets on parade. *El Centro, Calif.* 1499107
WU   UWM (RBR) Dec. 1972; July-Dec. 1973.

The Poet's packet. *Springfield, Mass.* 149911A
WU   UWM (RBR) V.1 no.3; v.2 (SPR1960-SUM1961).

Poets who sleep. *Brattleboro, Vt., etc.* 1499122
WU   UWM (RBR) No.1-4,6-11 (SPR1974-1977).

Pogamoggan. *New York.* 1499148
ISSN: 0554-4114 Beg. date: 1964 End date: 1964
Ceased publication with no. 1, 1964.
WU   UWM (RBR) No.1 (1964).

Poiesis. *Bellingham, Wa.* 1499150
Beg. date: 1974
WU   UWM (RBR) No.1 (JUN1974).

Points. *Paris.* 1499163
LCCN: 53-31446 Beg. date: 1949
Subtitle varies.
WU   UWM (RBR) No.1-19 (FEB/MAR1949-SPR1954).

Polemic. *Cleveland.* 1507813
ISSN: 0551-2972 LCCN: 68-126142 Beg. date: 1956
"A journal of contemporary ideas."
Vols. for   published by Western Reserve University;
  by the students of Flora Stone Mather College. Adelbert College
  and Cleveland College, Western Reserve University.
WU   UWM (RBR) V.5,8-9,11 (SPR1960-SPR1967).

Polemic. *London. Rodney Phillips & Co. Ltd.* 1507800
Beg. date: 1945 End date: 1947
"A magazine of philosophy, psychology and aesthetics."
Ceased publication with no. 8, [1947].
WU   UWM (RBR) No.1-8 (1945-[1947]).

Politics and letters, a review of literature and society, edited 0597555
by Clifford Collins, Raymond Williams and Wolf Mankowitz. *London,*
The Critic Press, Ltd.
Vol. 1 no. 1 has subtitle: A Quarterly survey of intellectual
  background.
The Critic, a companion quarterly to Politics and letters is
  incorporated in no. 2-4, WIN/SPR 1947-SUM 1948.
Ceased publication.
WU   UWM (RBR) V.1 no.1-4 (SPR1947-SUM1948).

Poltergeist. *East Lansing, Mich.* 1499176
ISSN: 0556-0667 Beg. date: 1968
WU   UWM (RBR) No.1-2 (OCT-NOV1968).

Pomona College, Claremont, California. Mss. *See* MSS. 1497346
Claremont, Calif.

Poor old tired horse. *Ardgay, Ross-Shire, Scotland; Wild* 0599814
Hawthorn Press.
Ceased.
Title varies: No. 22, P O T H; no. 23, Teapoth.
WU   UWM (RBR) No.1-25 (1962-1969).

Popular talisman bulletin. *Chicago.* 1509903
ISSN: 0032-4655 Beg. date: 1960
"Literary magazine."
WU   UWM (RBR) 1970.

Popular talisman bulletin. *See* Popular talisman bulletin. 1509916
Chicago.

Porch. *Seattle.* 1510598
Beg. date: 1977
WU   UWM (RBR) V.1 no.1-2 (1977).

The Port Townsend journal. *Port Townsend, Wash., The* 1499189
Woolman Press.
WU   UWM (RBR) V.1 no.2-4 (1973-WIN1975/SPR1976).

Portfolio. *Baltimore, [etc.], Portfolio Press.* 1499191
WU   UWM (RBR) No.1-4 (1970-1972).

Possibilities, an occasional review. *New York, Wittenborn,* 0601345
Schultz.
LCCN: 49-6039 Beg. date: 1947 End date: 1948
Series: Problems of contemporary art. no. 4.
No. 1 only no. published.
WU   UWM (RBR) No.1 (WIN1947/1948).

The Poster. *New York.* 0601477
Beg. date: 1896
WU   UWM (RBR) V.1 no.1-5 (JAN-MAY1896).

Pot-hooks & hangers. *New York.* 1499200
ISSN: 0091-7230 LCCN: 73-645313 Beg. date: 1973
WU   UWM (RBR) V.1 no.1-2 (SUM1973-SPR1974).

Potpourri. *Seattle.* 125640A
ISSN: 0556-2961 Beg. date: 1964
WU   UWM (RBR) No.1-17 (SPR1964-WIN1969).

Pound, Ezra Loomis, 1885-1972, ed. *See* Exile. *Chicago,* 0602077
etc.

Powelton village people. *See* P V P. *Philadelphia.* 1498102

Prairie. *Milwaukee.* 1499213
Beg. date: 1922 End date: 1923
Title varies: Sept. 1922-Dec. 1922, The Milwaukee arts monthly.
Ceased publication with vol. 1 no. 5, April 1923.
WU   UWM (RBR) V.1 no.2,4 (OCT1922-JAN/FEB1923).

The Prairie poet. *Charleston, Ill.* 1507839
ISSN: 0032-6658 Beg. date: 1954
Title varies: . Prairie poet magazine.
WU   UWM (RBR) Spring 1958-Fall 1960; Spring 1961;
  April 1966; July-Sept. 1969.

Prairie poet magazine. *See* Prairie poet. *Charleston, Ill.* 1507841

Prairie prose. *Aberdeen, S.D.* 1499239
LCCN: 49-57161 Beg. date: 1943 End date: 1943
Ceased publication with vol. 1 no. 4, Fall 1943.
WU   UWM (RBR) V.1 no.1 (WIN1943).

Pratt Institute, Brooklyn. Asterisk II. *See* Asterisk II. 1432983
Brooklyn, N.Y., Pratt Institute.

Pre-Raphaelite Brotherhood. Germ. *See* Germ; thoughts 1200264
towards nature in poetry, literature and art. London, Pre-Raphaelite
Brotherhood.

Premiere. *Lexington, Mass., Premiere Performance Co.* 1499241
ISSN: 0032-7395 Beg. date: 1966
"A literary review."
WU   UWM (RBR) V.1 no.1; v.2 no.1 (no.2-3); v.2 no.4-7
  (JUN1966-1969).

Premiere. *Mobile, Ala., Premiere Press.* 1499254
ISSN: 0555-0440 Beg. date: 1965
WU   UWM (RBR) No.1-3 (1965).

Presence. *Buffalo, N.Y.* 1499267
ISSN: 0555-0610 Beg. date: 1967
"A magazine of the revolution."
WU   UWM (RBR) No.1-4 (SUM1967-SPR1969).

The Preserver. *Brooklyn, N.Y., Francesco Bivona.* 149927A
End date: 1970
Ceased publication with Summer 1970.
WU   UWM (RBR) No.1-8 (1968-1969); Winter-Summer
  1970.

Priapus. *Berkhamsted, Hert,. Eng.* 1529278
ISSN: 0032-8146 Beg. date: 1962 End date: 1972
Ceased publication with no. 22, Spring 1972.
WU   UWM (RBR) No.3-22 (AUT1964-SPR1972).

Primer. *Indianapolis.* 1508952
WU   UWM (RBR) No.1-3 (DEC1975-1977).

Primipara. *Oconto, Wisc., impress.* 1508965
WU   UWM (RBR) Founders edition; v.1 no.1-2;
  v.2 no.1-2; v.3 no.1 (NOV1974-1977).

Printable Arts Society. Box 749. *See* Box 749. *New York,* 1464816

Prism. *London, England, Goldsmiths' College, University of* 1508978
London.
WU   UWM (RBR) No.5-10,12-13 (OCT191965-1967).

Prism. *New York, Prism Publications, Inc.* 1508993
ISSN: 0555-1773
WU   UWM (RBR) No.1-2 (1962-1964).

Prism. *Sydney, Australia, The Poetry Society of Australia.* 1509000
Beg. date: 1954 End date: 1960
Continued by The Poetry magazine with vol. 9 no. 1, July 1961.
WU   UWM (RBR) V.1 no.1-5; v.2-v.8 no.6
  (JUL1954-JUN1961).

Prism. Vancouver, B. C. *See* Prism international. 0605973
[Vancouver, B. C.].

Prism international. *[Vancouver, B. C.].* 0605986
ISSN: 0032-8790 LCCN: 62-50367
Title varies: v. 1-3, Prism.
WU   UWM (RBR) V.1-4; v.7 no.2-3; v.8-15
  (SEP1959-SUM/FAL1976).

Prism sixty six. *See* Prism. *London, England,* 1519952

Prison Arts Foundation. Catalyst. *See* Catalyst. Brantford, 1428026
Ont., Prison Arts Foundation.

Problems of contemporary art. No.4. *See* Possibilities. an 0606495
occasional review. *New York, Wittenborn, Schultz.*

Process magazine. *South Hempstead, N.Y., Long Island* 1509026
Poetry Collective.
WU   UWM (RBR) No.3 (1975).

Procession. *Ann Arbor, Mich.* 1509041
Beg. date: 1931 End date: 1932
Ceased publication with vol. 1 no.2, Fall 1932.
WU   UWM (RBR) V.1 no.2 (FEB1932).

Progressive League. Plan for freedom and progress. *See* 1500172
Plan for freedom and progress. London.

Prologue. *New York.* 1509054
ISSN: 0033-1015
WU   UWM (RBR) V.3 no.1-4; v.4 no.1-3 (1968-1970).

Promenade. *Cheltenham, Gloucester, Eng.* 1509067
WU   UWM (RBR) No.65-66 (1955).

Promethean. New York, City College. 150907A
ISSN: 0033-1074
"The literary magazine of the City College."
WU   UWM (RBR) V.15 no.2; v.20 no.1 (1967/1968-1972).

The Promethean lamp. Sacramento, Calif. 1529280
ISSN: 0555-4616 Beg. date: 1965
"International literary and fine arts quarterly" (varies).
WU   UWM (RBR) V.1 no.1-3; v.2 no.3
(1965-JUL/SEP1966); anthology (1966).

The Promethean review. New York, Liberty Book Club, Inc. 1509095
ISSN: 0552-3370 LCCN: 67-239 Beg. date: 1959 End date: 1960
Ceased publication with vol. 2 no. 1, Feb./Mar. 1960.
WU   UWM (RBR) V.1 no.1-4; v.2 no.1
(1959-FEB/MAR1960).

Promontory. West Kirby, Wirral, Merseyside, Eng., etc., 1509104
Headland Publication.
"A magazine of progressive poetry."
WU   UWM (RBR) No.1-3 (1974-1976).

Proof. Appleby, Lincoln., Eng. 150771A
Beg. date: 1974
"Subsidised by the Lincolnshire Association."
WU   UWM (RBR) No.1-10 (JUL1974-AUT1977).

Proof. Beaumont Fee, Lincoln., Eng., Lincolnshire and 1509117
South Humberside Arts.
"A magazine of new writing."
WU   UWM (RBR) No.1-8 (JUL1974-WIN1976).

Prosidia. Hermosa Beach, Calif. 1509132
ISSN: 0478-5843 Beg. date: 1958 End date: 1958
Ceased publication with no. 3, Aug. 1958.
WU   UWM (RBR) No.1-3 (MAY-AUG1958).

Prospect. Cambridge, Eng., etc., The Clarement Press. 1509145
"The voice of the younger generation."
WU   UWM (RBR) V.2 no.9-10 (WIN1959-SPR1960); no.5
(WIN1961).

Prospero's cell. Seattle, Prospero's Cell and Company. 1501528
ISSN: 0555-4780 LCCN: 73-29581 Beg. date: 1966
WU   UWM (RBR) V.1 no.2-v.2 no.2 (SUM1966-SUM1967).

Prospice. Breakish, Isle of Skye, Scot., Aquila Pub. Co., Ltd. 1501556
Beg. date: 1973
WU   UWM (RBR) No.1-7 (NOV1973-1977).

Proteus. Alexandria, Va. 1501530
ISSN: 0090-2071 LCCN: 73-640726 Beg. date: 1972
WU   UWM (RBR) No.1-7 (FAL1972-1977).

Proteus quarterly. Spring Valley, N.Y., Proteus Press. 1501543
LCCN: 56-37503 Beg. date: 1950 End date: 1952
Ceased publication with vol. 3 no.2, Summer 1952.
WU   UWM (RBR) V.1-v.3 no.2
(WIN1949/1950-SUM1952).

Protocol. St. John's, Newfoundland, H.Horwood. 1501569
ISSN: 0478-6157 Beg. date: 1945
Ceased publication with no. 7, 1951?
WU   UWM (RBR) No.6 (n.d.).

The Providence review. Providence, R.I. 1501571
Beg. date: 1973
WU   UWM (RBR) No.1-25 (FEB1973-JUN1976).

Provincetown. Provincetown, Mass., Paul Smith. 1501584
Beg. date: 1934 End date: 1934
"A magazine."
Ceased publication with vol. 1 no. 6, Sept. 1934.
WU   UWM (RBR) V.1 no.1-6 (APR1934-SEP1934).

Provincetown poets. [Provincetown, Mass., Total World 1529293
Services of Provincetown.]
ISSN: 0362-8396 LCCN: sc77-393 Beg. date: 1975
WU   UWM (RBR) V.1 no.2-3; v.2 no.1-2/3 (1975-1976).

Provincetown review. New York [etc.]. 0609508
ISSN: 0552-3947 Beg. date: 1938
Title varies: No. 1, 1958, Provincetown quarterly, No. 2, 1959, Provincetown annual.
WU   UWM (RBR) No.3-7 (1960-FAL1968).

The Provincial. Richmond, Va. 1529302
ISSN: 0478-6254 Beg. date: 1956 End date: 1957
Ceased publication with vol. 1 no.4, April 1957.
WU   UWM (RBR) V.1 no.1-2,4 (OCT1956-APR1957).

Prufrock. Quezon City, Philippines. 1501597
Beg. date: 1957
WU   UWM (RBR) No.1 (1957).

PS. See P S. Denver. 1501619

Psychedelic review. New Hyde Park, N.Y. [etc.]. 1501621
ISSN: 0033-2631 LCCN: 67-5795 Beg. date: 1963
Vol. 1 no.1 issued by International Federation for Internal Freedom.
WU   UWM (RBR) V.1 no.1-4; no.5-11
(SUM1963-WIN1970/1971).

Pucred. San Francisco; University of California at Riverside, 1094544
English Dept.
Beg. date: 1972
Absorbed by Scholia satyrica.
WU   UWM (RBR) V.1-2 (OCT151972-APR011974); 2 suppl.

Puddingstone. Knoxville, Tenn. [etc.]. 1501634
Beg. date: 1974
WU   UWM (RBR) V.1-2 (no.1-6) (SPR1974-SPR1977).

Puerto del sol. Las Cruces, New Mexico State University. 1501647
WU   UWM (RBR) V.12-14
(MAR1972-SUM1976).

Pugn. [n.p.], Malaspina College. 1529315
WU   UWM (RBR) V.1 no.2 (FAL1975).

Pulp. New York. 1501662
ISSN: 0145-8787 LCCN: sc77-401
WU   UWM RBR V.1 no.1; v.2 no.1-3; v.3 no.1 (1975-1977).

Pulse. Sante Fe, N.M. 1501675
WU   UWM (RBR) No.1-4
(NOV1968-SUM/FAL1971).

Pulse quarterly. New York, College of the City of New York. 1501688
WU   UWM (RBR) Oct. 1947.

Purdue University, Lafayette, Indiana. Bard. See Bard. 1430787
West Lafayette, Ind., Purdue University.

Purdue University, Lafayette, Indiana. First stage. See 1411107
First stage, a quarterly of new drama. Lafayette, Indiana,

The Purple renoster. Johannesburg. 150170A
ISSN: 0033-4634 Beg. date: 1956
"Johannesburg literary magazine."
WU   UWM (RBR) No.1,5,8-12 (SEP1956-WIN1972).

Purple smoke. Stockport, Cheshire, Eng. 1501725
WU   UWM (RBR) Oct., Dec. 1972; Feb., Summer 1973.

Purr. Phoenix [etc.]. 1501712
WU   UWM (RBR) No.2-5 (1975-1976).

Pursuit. See Pursuit and symposium magazine. Los 1501740
Angeses, James Kepner.

Pursuit and symposium magazine. Los Angeses, James 1501738
Kepner.
Beg. date: 1966
WU   UWM (RBR) V.1 no.1-2 (MAR/APR1966-JUN1967).

Pyramid. Belmont, Mass., Hellric Publications. 1501753
ISSN: 0033-4723 Beg. date: 1968
WU   UWM (RBR) No.1-14 (1968-1975).

Q

Quagga. Austin, Texas. 1501766
ISSN: 0480-9009 Beg. date: 1960
WU   UWM (RBR) V.1; v.2 no.1-3 (MAY1960-1963).

Quark. Reno. 1501779
ISSN: 0481-1313 Beg. date: 1967 End date: 1968
Ceased publication with vol. 3, 1968.
WU   UWM (RBR) No.1-3 (1967-1968).

Quarry. Kingston, Ont. 0614896
ISSN: 0033-5266 Beg. date: 1962
WU   UWM (RBR) V.14-v.26 no.3 (1965-1977).

Quarry. Santa Cruz, Calif., College V, University of California, Santa Cruz. 1507917
ISSN: 0033-5266 Beg. date: 1972 End date: 1974
Continued by Quarry west with no. 5, 1976.
WU   UWM (RBR) No.1-4 (WIN1971/1972-1974).

Quarry west. Santa Cruz, Calif., College V, University of California, Santa Cruz. 1507932
Beg. date: 1976
Continues Quarry with no. 5, 1976.
WU   UWM (RBR) No.5-8 (1976-1977).

Quartet. College Station, Texas [etc.]. 0979559
ISSN: 0481-2204 Beg. date: 1962
"A magazine of the arts."
Issues numbered consecutively.
WU   UWM (RBR) V.1-8 (no.1-57/58) (FAL1962-WIN/SPR1977).

Quartier Latin. London, Paris, New York, Iliffe and son. 0615981
LCCN: 2-22962 rev
Journal of the American art association of Paris.
No more published.
WU   UWM (RBR) V.1 no.1; v.5 no.23 (JUL1896-JUN/JUL1898).

Quarto. Edgware, Middlesex, Eng. 1501781
ISSN: 0481-2220 Beg. date: 1951 End date: 1952
"A quarterly broadsheet of new poetry."
Ceased publication with no. 8, Winter 1952.
WU   UWM (RBR) No.4 (WIN1951).

Quarto. New York. 1501794
LCCN: 52-19434 Beg. date: 1949
"A literary magazine."
Issued by the students of the School of General Studies, Columbia University.
WU   UWM (RBR) V. no.1,3-4; v.2 no.1-3; v.3-v.6 no.[1] (FAL1949-1954).

Quarto. Portland, Ore. 1501816
Beg. date: 1967
WU   UWM (RBR) Aug., Oct. 1967; Feb., Oct. 1968.

Quatrain digest. Waterbury, Conn., John De Stefano. 1501829
Beg. date: 1953 End date: 1953
"A bi-monthly magazine of poetic gems."
Continued by Poetry digest with vol. 1 no. 5, Dec. 1953.
WU   UWM (RBR) V.1 no.1-4 (APR-OCT1953).

Queen Stree T magazine. Toronto, Goathair Press. 1507958
ISSN: 0380-2000
Title varies: , Queen Street magazine.
WU   UWM (RBR) V.1 no.2-3; v.2-v.3 no.1 (no.[2]-9) (OCT1973-1975); no.10/13 (SPR/WIN1976/1977).

Queen Street magazine. *See* Queen Stree T magazine. 1507960
Toronto, Goathair Press.

Queens Council on the Arts. Literary Arts Division. Source. 1510390
See Source. Jamaica, N.Y., Literary Arts Division, Queens Council on the Arts.

Queensland. University. Department of English. Makar. 1495804
See Makar. St. Lucia, Queensland, Dept. of English, University of Queensland.

Quest. Birmingham, Printed at the press of the Guild of handicraft in Birmingham and published by Cornish brothers etc. 061747A
Beg. date: 1894
The illustrations are woodcuts.
"This edition is limited to 300 copies of which this is no. 155".
No more published.
WU   UWM (RBR) No.1-5 (NOV1894-MAR1896).

Quest. [Bombay, S. Singh, etc. for the Indian Committee for Cultural Freedom]. 0617482
ISSN: 0018-7437 LCCN: S A 62-656
"A quarterly of inquiry, criticism and ideas."
WU   UWM (RBR) V.1 no.1,3-6; v.2-3 (AUG1955-FEB/MAR1958); no.17-21,23-26,28-29 (APR/JUN1958-APR/JUN1961).

Quest. Green Bay, Wisc.?, Brown County Publishing Co. 1501831
WU   UWM (RBR) V.1 no.3-4 (1968?).

The Quest. New York. 1529330
LCCN: 66-9864 Beg. date: 1966 End date: 1969
Beginning with vol. 3 no. 1, Summer-Fall 1968, accompanied by supplement called Poetry pamphlet.
Continued by Little magazine with vol. 4, Spring 1970.
WU   UWM (RBR) V.1-v.3 no.2 (WIN1965/1966-SPR1969); Poetry pamphlets no.1-3 (1969).

The Question. Albuquerque, N.M. 1501844
Beg. date: 1965
WU   UWM (RBR) V.1 no.1 (MAY1965).

Quetzal. Lumbee, N.C. [etc.], Randall Ackley. 1501857
ISSN: 0033-6394 LCCN: 72-624928 Beg. date: 1970
WU   UWM (RBR) V.1 no.1-3; v.2 no.1/2 (SPR1970-WIN/SPR1972).

Quickenings. Seattle. 150186A
WU   UWM (RBR) No.16 (1975).

Quicksilver. Fort Worth, Texas, Taos, N.M., Grace Ross, Mabel Kuykendall. 1501872
LCCN: 52-41925 Beg. date: 1948
"A quarterly magazine of poetry."
WU   UWM (RBR) V.3 no.4-v.15 no.1 (WIN1950-SPR1962).

Quill. Welwyn, Herts., Eng. [etc.], Quill Books. 1507973
WU   UWM (RBR) No.24-25,27-40 (SEP/OCT1965-SUM1970).

Quill, with guide to Greenwich village, a magazine of art, letters and other nonsense. New York, R. Edwards. 0617846
Beg. date: 1917 End date: 1929
Subtitle varies.
Ceased publication May 1929.
WU   UWM (RBR) V.1 no.1; v.9 no.4 (JUN301917-OCT1926).

The Quince poetry magazine. Palo Alto, Calif., Malcolm McDonald. 1501885
ISSN: 0481-4134 Beg. date: 1967
WU   UWM (RBR) V.1 no.1-2 (SEP201967-1968).

Quintessence. Shreveport, La. 1501898
ISSN: 0033-6564
WU   UWM (RBR) Summer 1964; March 1965; Summer 1971; Feb. 1972; Sept./Oct. 1972; Winter 1974.

The Quire. Berkeley, Calif. 1501907
WU   UWM (RBR) V.2 (n.d.).

Quixote. Madison, Wisc., Dept. of Comparative Literature. 150191A
ISSN: 0033-6629 Beg. date: 1965
WU   UWM (RBR) V.1 no.1-9; v.2 no.2-6; v.3 no.1,3-4,9; v.4 no.1-2,4,9; v.5 no.1,4,8,11-15; v.6 no.1,4,6-11,14-15; v.7 no.2,4-5,8-10,12; v.8 no.1-3,5-7,10-12; v.9; v.10 no.1-4,6,8 (1965-1977).

Quixote. New York. 0617937
ISSN: 0033-6629 LCCN: 56-41547 Beg. date: 1954 End date: 1960
Ceased publication Spring 1960.
WU   UWM (RBR) No.1-25 (1954-WIN/SPR1960).

Quoin. Springfield, Mo. 1501935
ISSN: 0033-6653 Beg. date: 1966
WULbUWM   (RBR) V.1-v.9 no.1 (1966-1976).

Quoz? San Francisco, Trinity Press. 1501948
WU   UWM (RBR) V.3 no.11-12 (AUT1975-WIN1975/1976).

R

R C Lion. Berkeley, Calif., Rhymers Club, University of California. 1501950
ISSN: 0485-8042 Beg. date: 1966
WU　　UWM (RBR) No.2-3 (1966-1967).

R T: a journal of radical therapy. West Somerville, Mass., Radical Therapist, Inc. 1149007
ISSN: 0360-4713 LCCN: 75-647444 Beg. date: 1974 End date: 1976
Continues Rough times with vol. 4 no. 5, Dec. 1974.
Continued by State and mind with vol. 5 no.3, July/Sept. 1976.
WU　　UWM (RBR) V.4 no.5-8; v.5 no.1-2 (DEC1974-APR/JUN1976).

The R T L proxy. Elmhurst, Ill., Penman Pub. Co. 1504010
Beg. date: 1975
WU　　UWM (RBR) V.1 no.1-2 (JAN-MAY1975).

Raccoon. Memphis, Tenn. 1504023
ISSN: 0148-0162 LCCN: 77-642120 Beg. date: 1977
WU　　UWM (RBR) No.1 (MAY1977).

Radical America. Madison, Wis. 0618706
ISSN: 0033-7617 LCCN: 78-8310 Beg. date: 1967
Includes special issues.
Indexes: Vols. 1-4, 1967-1970, with vol. 4.
WU　　UWM (RBR) V.1 no.1; v.2 no.3-6; v.3 no.1-3,5; v.4 no.1-3,8-9; v.5 no.4-6; v.6-v.11 no.4 (1967-1977).

Radical therapist. Minot, N.D., Radical Therapist, Inc. 114901A
ISSN: 0033-7641 LCCN: 75-647445 Beg. date: 1970 End date: 1972
Continued by Rough times with vol. 2 no. 6, April 1972.
WU　　UWM (RBR) V.1 no.2,4,6 (JUN/JUL1970-FEB/MAR1971); suppl. June 1971.

Radix. Crowborough, Sussex, Eng., PV Publications. 1504036
WU　　UWM (RBR) No.2-6 (1973-1975).

Radix. Somerville, Mass. 1504049
ISSN: 0485-9006 LCCN: 73-296525 Beg. date: 1964 End date: 1965
Ceased publication with no. 4, Fall 1965.
WU　　UWM (RBR) No.1-4 (WIN1964-FAL1965).

Ragweed review. *See* Captain Farley's ragweed review. 1427887
Topeka, Kan., Groad Press.

Rainbow. London, Phoenix Publications. 1504051
ISSN: 0033-9059 Beg. date: 1965
"A quarterly of verse."
WU　　UWM (RBR) No.1-7 (AUT1965-SPR1967).

The Rambler. Boston, Mass., The Rambler Pub. Co., Inc. 1504064
Beg. date: 1916
WU　　UWM (RBR) V.1 no.1-10 (OCT1916-JUL1917).

Rann. Lisburn, Co. Antrim, Ireland. 1504077
Beg. date: 1948 End date: 1953
"An Ulster quarterly of poetry" (varies).
Ceased publication with no. 20, June 1953.
WU　　UWM (RBR) No.2,17 (AUT1948-AUT1952).

Rapport. Amherst, N.Y., The Slow Loris Press. 150408A
LCCN: 71-615292 Beg. date: 1971
"A Chapbook series."
WU　　UWM (RBR) V.1-v.4 no.1 (no.1-10) (1971-1977).

The Rational individualist. Silver Spring, Md., Society for Individual Liberty. 1504092
ISSN: 0486-0527 Beg. date: 1968
Issued　　by Society for Rational Individualism.
WU　　UWM (RBR) V.1 no.11-13; v.2 no.1 (SEP1969-JAN1970).

Raven. Anchorage, Alaska. 1504127
LCCN: 72-620194
WU　　UWM (RBR) V.1-v.3 no.1 (1971-1974).

The Raven. San Antonio, Tex. [etc.]. 150413A
Beg. date: 1943 End date: 1944
"Official quarterly of the Avalon National Poetry Shrine."
Ceased publication with vol. 2, Winter 1944.
United with Now to form Different.
WU　　UWM (RBR) V.1 no.2-4; v.2 no.1-3 (SUM1943-AUT1944).

Re: artes liberales. Nacogdoches, Tex., School of Liberal Arts, Stephen F. Austin State University. 1508166
ISSN: 0099-0760 LCCN: 75-645924 Beg. date: 1974
Supersedes Re: arts and letters.
WU　　UWM (RBR) V.1-v.3 no.1 (FAL1974-FAL1976).

Re: arts & letters. Nacogdoches, Tex., School of Liberal Arts, Stephen F. Austin State University. 1508181
ISSN: 0034-0286 Beg. date: 1968
Ceased publication.
Superseded by Re: artes liberales with Fall 1974.
WU　　UWM (RBR) V.1 no.1; v.2 no.1; v.3-4; v.5 no.1; v.6 (SPR1968-FAL1972).

Reading. Toronto. 1504155
Beg. date: 1946 End date: 1946
"A Canadian magazine."
Ceased publication with no. 3, May 1946.
WU　　UWM (RBR) V.1 no.1 (FEB1946).

Reading and collecting, a monthly review of rare and recent books. Chicago. 0621922
Beg. date: 1936 End date: 1938
WU　　UWM (RBR) V.1-v.2 no.5 (DEC1936-FEB/MAR1938).

The Realist. New York, Realist Association.
ISSN: 0034-091X Beg. date:　　End date: 1974
Ceased publication with no. 98, 1974.
WU　　UWM (RBR) No.1-39 (1958-NOV1962).

Realist. Northbridge, Australia. 1504170
ISSN: 0048-6884 Beg. date: 1958
"Journal of the National Council of the Realist Writers' Groups."
Title varies:　　, Realist writer.
WU　　UWM (RBR) No.7-23,25-35 (OCT1961-AUT1970).

Realist, a journal of scientific humanism. London, Macmillan and company ltd. for the Realist publishing co. 062230A
LCCN: 30-22098 Beg. date: 1929
WU　　UWM (RBR) V.1-v.3 no.1 (APR1929-JAN1930).

Reality. New York. 1504196
ISSN: 0481-8989 Beg. date: 1953 End date: 1955
"A journal of artists' opinions."
Ceased publication with no. 3, Summer 1955.
WU　　UWM (RBR) No.2-3 (SPR1954-SUM1955).

The Rebel magazine. Greenville, N.C., East Carolina College. 1504205
WU　　UWM (RBR) V.8 no.2; v.9 no.1 (WIN1965-1965/1966); Spring 1970.

The Rebel poet. Holt, Minn., B.C. Hagglund. 1504220
Beg. date: 1931 End date: 1932
"Official organ of Rebel Poets, the Internationale of Song."
Ceased publication with no. 17, Oct. 1932.
Superseded by the Anvil.
WU　　UWM (RBR) No.1-17 (1931-OCT1932).

Rebel Poets. Rebel poet. *See* Rebel poet. Holt, Minn., B.C. Hagglund. 1504233

Recall. Los Angeles, Jewish Heritage Foundation. 0622485
Ceased publication Winter 1963.
WU　　UWM (RBR) V.1 no.2-3 (NOV/DEC1959-1960).

The Record. Pottstown, Pa., The Hill School. 1504246
WU　　UWM (RBR) No.4-6/7 (DEC1970-JUN1971).

Recuerdo. Baltimore. 1504261
ISSN: 0484-1646 Beg. date: 1959 End date: 1959
"A quarterly of poems."
Ceased publication with vol. 1 no. 3, Summer 1959.
WU　　UWM (RBR) V.1 no.1-3 (WIN-SUM1959).

Recurrence. Los Angeles, Variegation Pub. Co. 1504274
ISSN: 0482-0053 Beg. date: 1950 End date: 1959
"A quarterly of rhyme."
Ceased publication with vol. 8 no. 28, Fall 1959.
WU　　UWM (RBR) V.1 no.1-2; v.2 no.2-3.7; v.3 no.9,11-12; v.4 no.13-14,16; v.5 no.17-18,20; v.6 no.25-26; v.7 no.27-28 (SUM1950-1959).

Red cedar review. East Lansing, Michigan State University. 0624010
ISSN: 0034-1967 Beg. date: 1963
WU　　UWM (RBR) V.1 no.1; v.2 no.1; v.3 no.1; v.4 no.1; v.5 no.1-2; v.6-7; v.8 no.2/3; v.9 no.1-3; v.10 no.1-2/3; v.11 no.1-2 (SPR1963-MAY1977).

Red clay books. Charlotte, N.C. 1529343
WU　　UWM (RBR) V.8 no.1-4; v.9 no.1; v.10 no.1-4 (1973?-1975).

Red clay reader. Charlotte, North Carolina, Southern Review. 0624023
ISSN: 0034-1975 LCCN: 65-138
WU　　UWM (RBR) No.1-7 (1964-1970).

Red crow. *Gloucester, Mass.*   1505212
  Beg. date: 1972
  Supersedes Mail.
  WU   UWM (RBR) No.1 (WIN-SPR1972).

Red fox review. *Norwich, Conn.*   1504287
  Beg. date: 1974
  WU   UWM (RBR) No.1-4 (1974-1977).

Red pen. *Philadelphia, John Reed Club.*   150429A
  Beg. date: 1934   End date: 1934
  "Organ of the Philadelphia John Reed Club."
  Continued by Left review with vol. 1 no. 2, Feb. 1934.
  WU   UWM (RBR) V.1 no.1 (JAN1934).

Red weather. *Eau Claire, Wisc., Red Weather Press.*   1504311
  Beg. date: 1976
  WU   UWM (RBR) V.1 no.1-2 (FAL1976-1977).

(Redivivus) Blue horse. *Augusta, Ga., Blue Horse Publishers.*   1529356
  Decennial.
  On spine: Blue horse (Redivivus).
  Title varies: vol. 1, 1969, Blue horse.
  "Auxiliary verse and prose in monograph and in chapbook will follow the Redivivus edition."
  WU   UWM (RBR) V.1-3 (1969-1977).

Redlands, California. University. Spectrum. *See*   151100A
Spectrum. Redlands, Calif., Associated Students, University of Redlands.

The Redneck review. *Houston, [etc.].*   1504324
  ISSN: 0034-2149 Beg. date: 1968
  WU   UWM (RBR) No.1-2 (1968); Spring 1970.

The Reed. *San Jose, Calif., San Jose State College.*   1504337
  WU   UWM (RBR) May 1948-1968, 1971, Spring/Summer 1974.

Reflections. *Chapel Hill, N.C.*   1504352
  ISSN: 0484-2669 Beg. date: 1961
  "The free south review."
  Title varies: June 1961-1963?, Reflections from Chapel Hill.
  WU   UWM (RBR) V.1 no.3; v.2 no.1; v.3 no.1 (NOV/DEC1961-SPR1964).

Reflections from Chapel Hill. *See* Reflections. Chapel Hill, N.C.   1504365

The Refugee journal of poetry. *Melita, Manitoba.*   1229959
  Beg. date: 1968
  WU   UWM (RBR) V.1 no.1 (MAR1968).

Region. *Minneapolis.*   1504378
  Beg. date: 1963
  "A new magazine of the arts & social analysis."
  WU   UWM (RBR) No.1-3 (SUM1963-SUM1964).

Remember our fire. *Berkeley, Calif. [etc.], Shameless Hussy Press.*   1504380
  Beg. date: 1969
  Continued by Shameless hussy review with no. [4], 1974.
  WU   UWM (RBR) No.2-3 (1970-[1971]).

The Remington review. *New York.*   1504393
  LCCN: sc77-534 Beg. date: 1973
  WU   UWM (RBR) V.1-4 (APR1973-NOV1976).

Renaissance. *Long Island, N.Y.*   1504402
  Beg. date: 1968
  WU   UWM (RBR) V.1 no.1-3 (AUT1968-SPR1969).

Renaissance. *San Francisco.*   0627070
  Ceased with no. 4.
  Incorporated by Notes From the Underground.
  WU   UWM (RBR) V.1 no.1-4 (JUL1961-1962).

Rendezvous. *Pocatello, Idaho, Idaho State University.*   1221993
  ISSN: 0034-4400 Beg. date: 1966
  "Idaho State University journal of arts and letters."
  WU   UWM (RBR) V.1 no.2; v.2-11 (WIN1966-FAL1976).

Repository. *Seven Persons, Alberta [etc.], Repository Press.*   1504415
  ISSN: 0315-7415
  Title varies: , Seven persons repository.
  WU   UWM (RBR) No.1,5-19/20 (n.d.-SUM/FAL1976).

Residu. *Athens, Ohio, Daniel Richter.*   1504430
  ISSN: 0486-5421 Beg. date: 1965
  WU   UWM (RBR) V.1 no.1-2 (1965-SPR1966).

Resistance. *New York.*   1504443
  LCCN: 52-34449 Beg. date: 1942 End date: 1954
  Title varies: vols. 1-5, April 1942-April 1947, Why?
  Ceased publication with vol. 12 no. 4, Dec. 1954.
  WU   UWM (RBR) V.1 no.1; v.6 no.7-9; v.7-v.9 no.3; v.10 no.1; v.11-12 (APR1942-1954).

Response. *Charlotte, N.C.*   1504469
  ISSN: 0484-5617 Beg. date: 1960 End date: 1962
  Ceased publication with vol. 2 no. 1 (no. 5), [1962].
  WU   UWM (RBR) V.1 no.4; v.2 no.1 ([1961-1962]).

Resurgence. *London.*   0630453
  ISSN: 0034-5970
  Vol. 2:12 also called New Departures, no. 5.
  WU   UWM (RBR) V.2 no.12 (SPR1970).

The Resuscitator. *Paulton, Somerset, Eng.*   1504471
  ISSN: 0486-5677 Beg. date: 1963 End date: 1969
  Ceased publication with ser. 2 no. 4, Feb. 1969.
  WU   UWM (RBR) V.1 no.1-7 (AUT1963-1966); ser. 2 no.1-3/4 (1968-FEB1969).

Retort, an anarchist quarterly of social philosophy and the arts. *Bearsville, N.Y.*   0630622
  LCCN: 50-19736 Beg. date: 1942 End date: 1951
  Subtitle varies.
  Ceased publication with vol. 5 no. 1, Autumn 1951.
  WU   UWM (RBR) V.1-v.5 no.1 (WIN1942-AUT1951).

Reveille; devoted to the disabled sailor and soldier. *London.*   1046204
  LCCN: 20-11139 Beg. date: 1918 End date: 1919
  Supersedes Recalled to life.
  Ceased publication with no. 3, 1919.
  WU   UWM (RBR) No.1-3 (AUG1918-FEB1919).

Review. *New Philadelphia, Ohio, Pale Horse Press.*   1504484
  Title includes year of issue.
  WU   UWM (RBR) 1974-1975.

Review; a magazine of poetry and criticism. *Oxford, England.*   0630832
  ISSN: 0034-6330 LCCN: 67-33259 Beg. date: 1962 End date: 1972
  Ceased publication with no. 29/30, Spring/Summer 1972.
  Superseded by New review with April 1974.
  WU   UWM (RBR) No.1-25,27/28-29/30 (APR/MAY1962-SPR/SUM1972).

Review fifty. *Stockport, Chesire, Eng. [etc.].*   1504521
  ISSN: 0482-4539 LCCN: 59-49931 Beg. date: 1950 End date: 1951
  Ceased publication with Summer/Autumn 1951.
  WU   UWM (RBR) Winter 1950-Summer/Autumn 1951.

The Review of research and reflection. *New York.*   1504497
  ISSN: 0484-6281 Beg. date: 1960 End date: 196
  Ceased publication with vol. 1 no. 3, 196?.
  WU   UWM (RBR) V.1 no.1-2 (WIN1960-196?).

The Reviewer. *Richmond, Va., Chapel Hill, N.C.*   1504534
  LCCN: 26-11623 rev Beg. date: 1921 End date: 1925
  Frequency varies.
  Ceased publication with vol. 5 no. 4, Oct. 1925.
  Absorbed by Southwest review.
  WU   UWM (RBR) V.2 no.4 (JAN1922).

Revolution. *Paris, etc.*   0634596
  Beg. date: 1963
  Title varies: volume 1 no. 1-2, May-June 1963, African revolution; volume 1 no. 3- , July 1963- , Africa, Latin America, Asia revolution.
  None published May-August 1964.
  WU   UWM (RBR) V.1 no.1-11 (MAY1963-1964).

Revue 2. *Vancouver, B.C.*   1504547
  Beg. date: 1976
  Supersedes Revue, ISSN 0701-1989.
  WU   UWM (RBR) No.1 (1976).

Revue de Louisiane. Louisiana review. *Lafayette, La., Conseil pour le Développement du Français en Louisiane.*   1529384
  LCCN: 72-626233 Beg. date: 1972
  French or English.
  WU   UWM (RBR) V.1-v.6 no.1 (SUM1972-1977).

Revue integration. *Arnhem, Neth., etc.*   1508937
  Beg. date: 1965
  In Dutch, English, French or German.
  WU   UWM (RBR) No.1-7/8 (1965-FEB1967).

Rewrite. *Lunenburg, Mass., Writers' Counsel Service.*   150455A
  "The magazine of effective writing."
  WU   UWM (RBR) V.14; v.15 no.1; v.16 no.4; v.17 no.4 (MAR1954-AUG1958).

Rhythm. *London, The St. Catherine Press.* 1504562
Beg. date: 1911 End date: 1913
"Art, music, literature quarterly."
Ceased publication with vol. 2 (no. 14), March 1913.
Superseded by Blue review.
WU   UWM (RBR) V.1-v.2 no.4 (SUM1911-MAR1913).

Rhythmus, a magazine of the new poetry. *New York.* 0642038
Beg. date: 1923 End date: 1924
Publication suspended from Aug. 1923-April 1924 inclusive.
Ceased publication with vol. 2 no. 2, June 1924.
Superseded by Parnassus.
WU   UWM (RBR) V.1-v.2 no.2 (1923-MAY/JUN1924).

Riata. *Austin, Tex., Texas Student Publications, Inc.* 1504575
ISSN: 0035-4945
WU   UWM (RBR) V.5 no.1-2 (WIN1965/1966-SPR1966).

Riding west. *Huddersfield, Yorkshire, Eng.* 1504588
WU   UWM (RBR) No.4,8 (1968).

The Right review. *London.* 1504590
Beg. date: 1936
"The official organ of the Royal House of Poland."
WU   UWM (RBR) No.1-17 (OCT1936-JUN1947).

Rigmarole of the hours. *Victoria, Australia.* 150460A
Beg. date: 1974
WU   UWM (RBR) No.1-7 (AUG1974-1976); suppl. to no.2-3, 1975.

The Rimrock poets magazine. *Grand Junction, Colo.* 1504612
ISSN: 0557-0271 Beg. date: 1967
WU   UWM (RBR) V.1 no.1-3 (DEC1967-JUN1968).

Ripples. *Ann Arbor, Mich., Shining Waters Press.* 1504625
Beg. date: 1972
WU   UWM (RBR) V.1-v.2 no.3; v.3 no.1 (FAL[1972]-SPR1975).

Ritual. *Annapolis, Md.* 1504638
Beg. date: 1940
WU   UWM (RBR) No.1 (APR1940).

Ritual. *See* Experimental review. Woodstock, N.Y. 0643480

River. *Memphis, Tenn.* 1504640
ISSN: 0485-2230 Beg. date: 1959 End date: 1960
Ceased publication with Spring 1960.
WU   UWM (RBR) Spring 1959, Spring 1960.

River. *Oxford, Miss.* 1504653
Beg. date: 1937 End date: 1937
"A magazine in the deep south."
Ceased publication with vol. 1 no. 3, June 1937.
WU   UWM (RBR) V.1 no.1-3 (MAR-JUN1937).

River bottom. *Oshkosh, Wisc., River Bottom Press.* 1504666
Beg. date: 1973
WU   UWM (RBR) V.1 no.1; v.2 no.1-2; v.3-v.4 no.2 ([1973]-1977).

Riverina College of Advanced Education, Wagga Wagga, 1436496
New South Wales. Grapeshot. *See* Grapeshot. [Wagga Wagga, N.S.W.], Riverina College of Advanced Education.

Riverrun. *New York.* 1504679
ISSN: 0557-1227 LCCN: 66-9980 Beg. date: 1966
WU   UWM (RBR) V.1 no.1-5 (OCT1966-1967).

Riverside quarterly. *Saskatoon, Sask.* 0643528
ISSN: 0035-5704 Beg. date: 1964
Supersedes Inside.
WU   UWM (RBR) V.1-v.3 no.3; v.4-v.6 no.3 (AUG1964-AUG1975).

The Rivoli review. *San Francisco.* 1504681
ISSN: 0557-1472 Beg. date: 1963 End date: 1964
Ceased publication with vol. 0 no. 2, 1964.
WU   UWM (RBR) V.0 no.1-2 (1963-1964).

Road apple review. *Albuquerque, N.M., Road Runner Press.* 0644472
ISSN: 0035-7200 Beg. date: 1969
WU   UWM (RBR) V.1-4 (WIN1968/1969-WIN1973); Fall 1974-Fall 1976.

Road/house. *Belvidere, Ill., Road/house Press.* 1504694
ISSN: 0148-3730 LCCN: 77-642344
WU   UWM (RBR) No.1-4 (FAL1975-1977).

Roadrunner. *See* Catonsville roadrunner. London. 142807A

Roanoke review. *Salem, Va.* 1504703
ISSN: 0035-7367 Beg. date: 1961
WU   UWM (RBR) V.1-v.6 no.1; v.7-8 (FAL1967-WIN1976).

Robin. *Colfax, Calif.* 1504716
WU   UWM (RBR) 1969: 4 issues.

Rock bottom. *See* Rockbottom. Santa Barbara, Calif., 1504744
Mudborn Press.

Rock River anthology. *Janesville, Wisc.* 1504729
Beg. date: 1969
WU   UWM (RBR) V.1 no.1-2; v.3-5 (1969-SUM1973).

Rockbottom. *Santa Barbara, Calif., Mudborn Press.* 1504731
ISSN: 0146-1419 LCCN: sc77-734 Beg. date: 1976
WU   UWM (RBR) No.1-4 (SUM1976-1977).

The Rocking horse. *Madison, Wisc., The Arden Club,* 1504757
University of Wisconsin, Madison.
Beg. date: 1933 End date: 1935
Ceased publication with vol. 2, Summer 1935.
WU   UWM (RBR) V.1-2 (SEP1933-SUM1935); Chapbooks no.1-2 (n.d.).

Rocky Mountain arts. *Denver, Rocky Mountain Arts Press.* 1504785
ISSN: 0483-2396 Beg. date: 1954 End date: 1955
"An independent journal of the creative arts."
Ceased publication with vol. 2 no. 1, Spring 1955.
WU   UWM (RBR) V.1 no.1-3; v.2 no.1 (APR1954-SPR1955).

Rocky Mountain creative arts journal. *Casper, Wyo.* 1504798
Beg. date: 1974
WU   UWM (RBR) No.1 (FAL1974).

Rocky Mountain review. *Durango, Colo., Atlatl Press.* 1504807
Beg. date: 1974
WU   UWM (RBR) No.1-7 (1974-1976).

Rogue. *New York, Rogue, Inc.* 150481A
Beg. date: 1915 End date: 1916
Ceased publication with vol. 2 no. 3, Oct. 1?, 1916.
WU   UWM (RBR) V.1 no.2-v.2 no.3 (APR011915-OCT011916).

Rogue River gorge. *Ashland, Ore.* 1504822
Beg. date: 1970
WU   UWM (RBR) No.1-2 (1970).

Roho. *Kampala, Uganda, School of Art, Makerere College.* 1504835
ISSN: 0557-2452 Beg. date: 1961 End date: 1962
"Journal of the visual arts in East Africa" (varies).
Ceased publication with no. 2, June 1962.
WU   UWM (RBR) No.2 (JUN1962).

Rollins College, Winter Park, Florida. Flamingo. *See* 1437120
Flamingo. Winter Park, Fla., Rollins College, English Dept.

Rollins flamingo. *See* Flamingo. Winter Park, Fla., Rollins 1437133
College, English Dept.

Ronald Reagan. *London.* 1504850
Beg. date: 1968
"The magazine of poetry."
WU   UWM (RBR) [No.1] ([1968]).

RongWrong. *New York, 7 Poets Press.* 1504863
ISSN: 0485-4357 Beg. date: 1961 End date: 1962
Ceased publication with no. 4, 1962.
WU   UWM (RBR) No.2-4 (1962).

Room of one's own. *Vancouver, B.C., Growing Room* 1504876
Collective.
ISSN: 0316-1609 Beg. date: 1975
WU   UWM (RBR) V.1-v.3 no.1 (SPR1975-1977).

Roon. *Stanford, Calif., Half Moon Press.* 1529421
"A chapbook of modern verse."
WU   UWM (RBR) V.2 no.2 (Twelfth Night 1931).

Roosevelt University, Chicago. Oyez magazine. *See* Oyez 1507629
review. Chicago.

Roosevelt University, Chicago. Oyez review. *See* Oyez 1507603
review. Chicago.

Roosevelt University, Chicago. Vigil. *See* Vigil. Chicago, 1517273
Roosevelt University.

Root and branch. *Berkeley, Calif., Root and Branch Press.* 1504889
ISSN: 0485-4381 Beg. date: 1962
WU   UWM (RBR) 1962.

Roots forming. *Monroe. Mich.* 1504891
Beg. date: 1969
WU   UWM (RBR) Summer 1969.

Roth's ark. *Chicago.* 1504900
WU   UWM (RBR) No.1-3 (n.d.-n.d.).

Rough times. *West Somerville, Mass., Radical Therapist, Inc.*   1149089
    ISSN: 0360-4705   LCCN: 75-647443   Beg. date: 1972   End date: 1974
    Continues Radical therapist with vol. 2 no. 6, April 1972.
    Imprint varies.
    Continued by R T: a journal of radical therapy with vol. 4 no. 5, Dec. 1974.
    WU   UWM (RBR) V.2 no.6-8; v.3; v.4 no.1-3 (APR1972-SEP1974).

Roundtable. *Portland, Maine.*   1504913
    WU   UWM (RBR) V.2 no.1 (FAL1967).

Roy Rogers. *New York. Horspitality House.*   150664A
    Beg. date: 1970
    WU   UWM (RBR) V.1 no.1 (1970).

Rudinger Foundation.   Firelands arts review. ***See*** Firelands   1437042
arts review. Huron, Ohio, Rudinger Foundation.

Rudinger Foundation.   Mixer: Firelands arts review. ***See***   1432485
Mixer: Firelands arts review. Huron, Ohio, Rudinger Foundation.

The Rufus. *Los Angeles, Gyst Publications.*   1506652
    ISSN: 0147-1163   LCCN: 77-643103
    Cover title: Rufus poetry.
    WU   UWM (RBR) V.1 no.2,4; v.2 no.1-3; v.3 no.1 (FAL1972-1977).

Rumpus. *Swansea, Wales.*   1506665
    ISSN: 0035-9858   Beg. date: 1968   End date: 1971
    Ceased publication with no. 6, Sept. 1971.
    WU   UWM (RBR) No.1-6 (1968-SEP1971).

The Runcible spoon. *Sacramento, Calif.*   1506678
    Beg. date: 1967
    WU   UWM (RBR) No.1,3,5 (1967-n.d.); 1970 issue.

Rune. *Durham, Calif., Norman C. Mallory and Dennis H. Ross.*   1506680
    Beg. date: 1970
    "A journal of contemporary poetry."
    WU   UWM (RBR) V.1 no.1 (1970).

Rune. *Toronto.*   1506693
    ISSN: 0316-2192   Beg. date: 1974
    Published at St. Michael's College, University of Toronto.
    WU   UWM (RBR) V.1 no.1-3 (SPR1974-SPR1976).

The Running man. *London, The Running Man Publications.*   1506702
    ISSN: 0557-4889   LCCN: 73-618099   Beg. date: 1968
    WU   UWM (RBR) V.1 no.1-3/4/5 (MAY/JUN1968-1969).

Rūpāmbarā. *Calcutta.*   0916630
    ISSN: 0035-9963   LCCN: 70-906970   Beg. date: 1966
    WU   UWM (RBR) V.2 no.6-11 (FEB/MAR-OCT1969); special issue: v.3 no.4 (OCT1970).

Russell Sage College.   Studies in the twentieth century. ***See***   0651433
Studies in the twentieth century. Troy, N.Y., Russell Sage College.

The Rutgers review. *New Brunswick, N.J., Rutgers University.*   1506715
    ISSN: 0557-546X   Beg. date: 1966
    WU   UWM (RBR) V.2 (SPR1967).

Rutgers University, New Brunswick, New Jersey. ***See***   1506728
Rutgers review. New Brunswick, N.J., Rutgers University.

S

S 4 N. *Northampton, Mass., The S4N Society.* 1506730
Beg. date: 1919 End date: 1925
Ceased publication with vol. 6 no. 1 (no. 33), July 1925.
United with Modern review to form Modern S4N review.
WU   UWM (RBR) Nov. 1922; v.4 no.23-24; v.5 no.32 (DEC1922-FEB1924).

S 4 N Society. S 4 N. *See* S 4 N. Northampton, Mass., The S4N Society. 1506743

S C T H. *El Rito, N.M., ‡dSangre de Cristo Press.* 1506806
ISSN: 0558-0129 Beg. date: 1964 End date: 1969
"Sonnet cinquain tanka haiku."
Ceased publication with vol. 5 no. 4, Spring 1969.
Superseded by Janus and S C T H with July 1969.
WU   UWM (RBR) V.1 no.2-4; v.2 no.1,3-4; v.3-5 (AUT1964-SPR1969).

S D S. *See* Activist. Oberlin, Ohio, Students for a Democratic Society. 0653012

S H Y. *San Francisco.* 1506769
"A literate quarterly."
WU   UWM (RBR) V.1-v.4 no.2 (SUM1974-1977).

S L literary review. *See* Sarah Lawrence literary review. Bronxville, N.Y., Sarah Lawrence College. 1508047

S M S; (Letter Edged in Black Press). *New York.* 065282A
Ceased publication with no. 6.
WU   UWM (RBR) No.1-6 (1968).

S4N Society. S 4 N. *See* S 4 N. Northampton, Mass., The S4N Society. 1506756

Saga. *Alliance, Ohio. Mt. Union College.* 1506771
WU   UWM (RBR) June 1929.

Sage. *Claremont, Calif., Webb School of California.* 1509931
Beg. date: 1958
"A literary Blue and gold issue."
WU   UWM (RBR) No.1-4 (1958-1960).

Sage. *Laramie, University of Wyoming.* 1224354
ISSN: 0581-2844 LCCN: 58-62599 rev Beg. date: 1951 End date: 1968
Title varies: 1951- , Writing at Wyoming.
Issued 1951-1964 by the Dept. of English, University of Wyoming; 1966- by the University.
Publication suspended 1954-1956, 1965.
Ceased publication with vol. 12 no. 1, Spring 1968.
Index: vols. 1-10, 1951-1964, in vol. 10 no. 2.
WU   UWM (RBR) No.1-5 (SPR1966-SPR1968).

The Sage leaf. *Boston.* 1529434
Beg. date: 1901 End date: 1901
Ceased publication with vol. 1 no. 5, Sept. 1901.
WU   UWM (RBR) V.1 no.1-5 (MAR-SEP1901).

Sagebrush philosophy. *Douglas, Wyo.* 1506797
LCCN: 31-9596 Beg. date: 1904 End date: 1910
Ceased publication with vol. 14, Nov. 1910.
WU   UWM (RBR) V.6 no.3 (SEP1906).

Saginaw Valley College, University Center, Michigan. Cloven hoof. *See* Cloven hoof. University Center, Mich., Saginaw Valley College. 1428669

Sailing the road clear. *Old Mystic, Conn. [etc.].* 1476221
Beg. date: 1973
"A poetry magazine."
WU   UWM (RBR) V.1-5 (AUG1973-SEP1976).

The Saint. *Brooklyn, N.Y.* 1501963
End date: 1968
Continued by Poetry prevue with Fall/Winter 1968?
WU   UWM (RBR) Winter 1966; 1967; Summer 1968.

Saint Andrews Presbyterian College, Laurinburg, North Carolina. Saint Andrews review. *See* Saint Andrews review. Laurinburg, N.C., St. Andrews Presbyterian College. 1501989

Saint Andrews review. *Laurinburg, N.C., St. Andrews Presbyterian College.* 1501976
Beg. date: 1971
"A twice yearly magazine of the arts and humanities."
WU   UWM (RBR) V.1-v.4 no.2 (FAL1970/WIN1971-SPR/SUM1977).

Saint Basil's College, Stamford, Connecticut. Keryx. *See* Keryx. Stamford, Conn., St. Basil's College. 1493887

Saint Edward's University, Austin, Texas. Vagaries. *See* Vagaries. Austin, Tex., St. Edward's University. 1516959

Saint Edward's University, Austin, Texas. Writing magazine. *See* Writing magazine. Austin, Tex., St. Edward's University. 1515114

Saint Francis Xavier University, Antigonish, Nova Scotia. Department of English. Antigonish review. *See* Antigonish review. Antigonish, N.S., Dept. of English, St. Francis Xavier University. 1438088

The Saint George review. *Staten Island, New York, Bert Schultz's Cominsane Press.* 1502009
Beg. date: 1975
WU   UWM (RBR) 1975.

Saint John's bread. *Venice, Calif. [etc.].* 1502024
WU   UWM (RBR) 1970; three unnumbered, undated issues.

Saint John's University, Collegeville, Minnesota. Lower Stumpf Lake review. *See* Lower Stumpf Lake review. Collegeville, Minn., St. John's University. 1352711

Saint Louis University. Writers' Institute. Fleur de lis. *See* Fleur de lis. St. Louis, Mo., St. Louis University, Writers' Institute. 1437161

Saint Marks Church-in-the-Bowery. Poetry Project. Z. *See* Z. New York, Z Press. 1515469

Saint Mary's College, Berkeley. Phoenix. *See* Phoenix. [Berkeley], St. Mary's College (Calif.). 1507867

Saint Mary's College, Notre Dame, Indiana. Chimes; a quarterly. *See* Chimes; a quarterly. Notre Dame, Ind., St. Mary's College. 1433843

Saint Thomas University, Fredericton, New Brunswick. Department of English. Fiddlehead. *See* Fiddlehead. Fredericton, N.B., Departments of English, University of New Brunswick and St. Thomas University. 1436806

Salad. *Detroit, Salad Press.* 150204A
Beg. date: 1969
WU   UWM (RBR) No.1 (1969).

Salem State College. Gone soft. *See* Gone soft. Salem, Mass., Salem State College. 1436299

Salient. *New York, New School for Social Research.* 1502065
Beg. date: 192 End date: 1929
Continues Figure in the carpet.
Ceased publication with vol. 2, May 1929.
WU   UWM (RBR) V.2 no.5 (APR1929).

Salient. *New York [etc.].* 1502052
Beg. date: 1943
WU   UWM (RBR) No.1-2 (APR1943-JAN1944).

Salmagundi. *Flushing, N. Y., Asyla, Inc.* 0658870
ISSN: 0036-3529 Beg. date: 1965
"A quarterly of the humanities and social sciences."
Issued   by Skidmore College, Sarasota Springs, N.Y.
Indexes: vols. 1-30, 1965-1975, in vols. 25-30.
WU   UWM (RBR) V.1-v.2 no.4 (FAL1965-FAL1968); no.9-39 (SPR1969-1977).

Salome. *Chicago.* 1502102
"A literary dance magazine."
WU   UWM (RBR) V.1 no.1/2 (FAL/WIN1976).

Salt. *Moose Jaw, Sask., Tegwar Press.* 1502115
ISSN: 0085-5863 Beg. date: 1969
"A little magazine of contemporary poetry."
WU   UWM (RBR) No.6-16 (SUM1971-1977).

The Salt Creek reader. *Lincoln, Ted Kooser.* 1502128
ISSN: 0036-3588 Beg. date: 1967
Continued by New Salt Creek reader with vol. 5, Winter 1972.
WU   UWM (RBR) V.1-v.4 no.6 (1967-MAR1971).

Salt house. *See* Salthouse. Bowling Green, Ohio. 1502156

Salt Lake City, Utah. Public Library. Spectrum. *See* Spectrum. Salt Lake City, Utah, Salt Lake City Public Library. 1511040

Salt lick. *Quincy, Ill.* 1502130
WU   UWM (RBR) Three unnumbered, undated issues; no.5-9/10; v.2 no.1/2 (APR1970-1972).

Salted feathers. *Portland, Ore. [etc.].* 1529447
ISSN: 0036-3626 Beg. date: 1964
WU   UWM (RBR) V.1 no.1-2; v.2 no.1-3; v.3 no.1-2 (no.6-7); v.4 no.1/2-3 (no.8/9-11) (APR1964-FEB1975).

Salted in the shell. *Brunswick, Maine.* 150805A
Beg. date: 1971
WU UWM (RBR) No.1-21 (1971-1976); special issue v.1 no.1 (n.d.).

Salthouse. *Bowling Green, Ohio.* 1502143
Beg. date: 1975
WU UWM (RBR) Spring, Autumn 1975; Autumn 1976.

Saltillo. *Lincoln, Nebr.* 1502169
Beg. date: 1972
Title varies: 1972, Saltillo review.
WU UWM (RBR) Mar., Summer/May, Fall/Oct. 1972; Spring, Summer/Fall 1973; Winter, Spring/Summer, Fall 1974; Spring/Summer 1975.

Saltillo review. *See* Saltillo. Lincoln, Nebr. 1502171

Saltire review. *See* Saltire review of arts, letters and life. Edinburgh, Saltire Society. 1529475

Saltire review of arts, letters and life. *Edinburgh, Saltire Society.* 152945A
ISSN: 0581-4065 Beg. date: 1954 End date: 1961
Title varies: · , Saltire review.
Ceased publication with vol. 6 (no. 23), Winter 1961.
Superseded by New saltire.
WU UWM (RBR) V.1-6 (no.1-15,21) (APR1954-SUM1960).

Saltire Society. Saltire review of arts, letters and life. *See* Saltire review of arts, letters and life. Edinburgh, Saltire Society. 1529462

The Sam Houston literary review. *Huntsville, Texas, English Dept., Sam Houston State University.* 1502184
Beg. date: 1976
WU UWM (RBR) V.1-v.2 no.1 (APR1976-1977).

Sam Houston State University. English Department. Sam Houston literary review. *See* Sam Houston literary review. Huntsville, Texas, English Dept., Sam Houston State University. 1502197

Samisdat. *Berkeley, Calif.* 1438783
Beg. date: 1973
Title varies: · , The Berkeley samisdat review.
"Samisdat chapbooks are released concurrently with quarterly magazine issues, under separate volume number, and are included with all subscriptions."
WU UWM (RBR) V.1-v.15 no.3 (JUN1973-1977); chapbooks.

Samisdat chapbooks. *See* Samisdat. Berkeley, Calif. 1438796

Samphire. *Ipswich, Eng.* 1502219
Beg. date: 1968
WU UWM (RBR) V.1 no.1-16; v.2 no.1-15 (1968-1977).

San Carlos, California. Fine Arts Commission. San Carlos poetry workshop anthology. *See* San Carlos poetry workshop anthology. San Carlos, Calif, San Carlos Fine Arts Commission. 1502234

San Carlos poetry workshop anthology. *San Carlos, Calif, San Carlos Fine Arts Commission.* 1502221
WU UWM (RBR) No.1-2 (1974-1975).

San Diego State College, Imperial Valley Campus. Word. *See* Word. Galexico, Calif., San Diego State College, Imperial Valley Campus. 1519244

San Francisco book review. *See* Book magazine. San Francisco. 1451412

San Francisco Contemporary Dancers Foundation. Contemporary. *See* Contemporary. San Francisco, San Francisco Contemporary Dancer's Foundation. 1429005

The San Francisco earthquake. *San Francisco.* 1502247
ISSN: 0036-4126 LCCN: 74-646954 Beg. date: 1967
WU UWM (RBR) V.1 no.1-5 (FAL1967-1969).

The San Francisco evening lamp. *San Francisco, Marvin Sanford.* 150225A
ISSN: 0487-1472
WU UWM (RBR) No.15,19 (JUL1956-WIN1959/1960).

The San Francisco keeper's voice. *Daly City [etc.], Calif., Alexander Weiss.* 1502262
ISSN: 0581-5029 Beg. date: 1965
WU UWM (RBR) V.1 no.1-4,6,8; v.2 no.1-3; v.3 no.1 (1965-1967/1968).

San Francisco review. *[San Francisco, J.O. Degnan, etc.].* 1350004
ISSN: 0558-4205 LCCN: 64-36334 Beg. date: 1958 End date: 1962
Called also vol. 1.
Ceased publication with no. 13, Sept. 1962.
Superseded by San Francisco review annual with 1963.
WU UWM (RBR) No.1-13 (1958-SEP1962).

San Francisco review annual. *[New York], New Directions-San Francisco Review.* 1508075
ISSN: 0558-4213 LCCN: 63-18633 Beg. date: 1963
Supersedes San Francisco review.
Nos. 1- also called nos. 14- in continuation of San Francisco review.
WU UWM (RBR) No.1 (1963).

San Francisco Writers' Workshop magazine. *San Francisco, Writers' Workshop, California Labor School.* 1502275
ISSN: 0487-1499 Beg. date: 1952
WU UWM (RBR) No.2 (SPR1953).

San Francisco's openings. *See* Book magazine. San Francisco. 1451425

San German, Puerto Rico. Inter-American University. Between worlds. *See* Between worlds. [Denver, A. Swallow]. 1438350

San Jose State College. Reed. *See* Reed. San Jose, Calif., San Jose State College. 150434A

San Jose State University. Women's Center. Xanthippe. *See* Xanthippe. San Jose, Calif., Xanthippe Collective and the San Jose State University Women's Center. 1515246

Sand castles. *Drexel, Mo.* 150230A
Beg. date: 1969
WU UWM (RBR) V.1 no.1-2 (JUN-SEP1969).

Sand script. *San Bruno, Calif., Fat Frog Press.* 1502312
Beg. date: 1968
Supersedes Fat frog.
WU UWM (RBR) No.1 (FEB1968).

Sandwiches. *Leeds, Yorkshire, Eng. [etc.].* 1502325
Beg. date: 1973
WU UWM (RBR) No.1-19 (1973-JUL1977).

The sans souci quill. *Denver.* 1529488
ISSN: 0558-4981 Beg. date: 1957 End date: 1963
Ceased publication with vol. 7 no. 2, July 1963.
WU UWM (RBR) V.1-v.3 no.7; v.4 no.1; v.5 no.1-7; v.6 no.1; v.7 no.1-2 (OCT1957-JUL1963).

Sanskaras. *Clark Township, N.J.* 1502338
Beg. date: 1968
"A quarterly of poetry."
WU UWM (RBR) V.1 no.1-4 (AUT1968-1969).

Saplings. *Peekskill, N.Y., Oak Lane, Pa.* 1502340
Beg. date: 1929 End date: 1930
Title varies: vol. 1 nos. 1-3, Dec. 1929-Nov. 1930, Gleam.
Ceased publication with vol. 1 no.4, Nov. 1930.
WU UWM (RBR) V.1 no.4 (NOV151930).

Sarah Lawrence College, Bronxville, New York. Dimensions. *See* Dimensions. Bronxville, N.Y. 143481A

Sarah Lawrence College, Bronxville, New York. Sarah Lawrence literary review. *See* Sarah Lawrence literary review. Bronxville, N.Y., Sarah Lawrence College. 1508019

Sarah Lawrence literary review. *Bronxville, N.Y., Sarah Lawrence College.* 1508006
ISSN: 0036-4746 Beg. date: 1955
Title varies: Spring 1955, Inscape; Sarah Lawrence literary review; 1956, Sarah Lawrence review; Fall 1957-Spring 1960, S L literary review.
WU UWM (RBR) Spring 1958.

Sarah Lawrence review. *See* Dimensions. Bronxville, N.Y. 1434822

Sarah Lawrence review. *See* Sarah Lawrence literary review. Bronxville, N.Y., Sarah Lawrence College. 1508034

Saskatchewan Arts Board. Grain. *See* Grain. Saskatoon, Saskatchewan Writers' Guild. 143643A

The Saskatchewan poetry book. *Regina, Sask., Saskatchewan Poetry Society.* 1502366
LCCN: 44-33688 Beg. date: 1935
Title varies: 1935-1935/1936, Saskatchewan poetry year book.
WU UWM (RBR) 1948/1949-1952/1953.

Saskatchewan Poetry Society. Saskatchewan poetry book. *See* Saskatchewan poetry book. Regina, Sask., Saskatchewan Poetry Society. 1502379

Saskatchewan poetry year book. *See* Saskatchewan poetry book. Regina, Sask., Saskatchewan Poetry Society. 1502381

Saskatchewan Writers' Guild. Grain. *See* Grain. Saskatoon, Saskatchewan Writers' Guild. 1436427

Saskatshewan Poetry Society. Saskatchewan poetry year book. *See* Saskatchewan poetry book. Regina, Sask., Saskatchewan Poetry Society. 1502394

Satire newsletter. *Oneonta, N.Y., State University College.*   0661482
    ISSN: 0036-4967   LCCN: 64-9355   Beg. date: 1963   End date: 1973
    Ceased publication with vol. 10 no. 2, Spring 1973.
    1973 includes supplement: Bibliography, vols. 1-10, 1963-1973.
    Indexes: Vols. 1-5, 1963-1968, with v. 5.
    WU   UWM (RBR)   V.1-v.10 no.2 (FAL1963-SPR1973); suppl. Spring 1973.

Satis. *Newcastle-upon-Tyne, Eng., Malcolm Rutherford.*   1502429
    ISSN: 0558-7107   Beg. date: 1960   End date: 1962
    Ceased publication with no. 5, Spring/Summer 1962.
    WU   UWM (RBR)   No.1-5 (AUT1960-SPR/SUM1962).

Sattvas review. *Cleveland, Sattvas Press.*   1502431
    WU   UWM (RBR)   V.1 no.1 (FAL1969).

The Saturday Club book of poetry. *Cammeray, N.S.W., Saturday Centre.*   1502444
    ISSN: 0310-4273   Beg. date: 1972
    WU   UWM (RBR)   V.1 no.1,3-4; v.2-4 (SPR1972-WIN1976).

Saturday morning. *London, Acorn Press.*   1502457
    Beg. date: 1976
    WU   UWM (RBR)   No.1-3 (SPR1976-1977).

Saucerian. *Clarksburg, W. Va.*   150246A
    ISSN: 0487-434x   Beg. date: 1953   End date: 1955
    Ceased publication with vol. 3 no.2, Spring 1955.
    Superseded by Saucerian bulletin with March 1, 1956.
    WU   UWM (RBR)   V.1 no.2; v.2 no.2; v.3 no.2 (NOV1953-SPR1955).

Saucerian bulletin. *Clarksburg, W. Va.*   1502472
    ISSN: 0558-7158   Beg. date: 1956
    Supersedes Saucerian.
    WU   UWM (RBR)   V.1-v.3 no.4 (MAR011956-OCT151958).

The Savage. *Chicago.*   1529490
    Beg. date: 1972
    WU   UWM (RBR)   No.1-3 (SPR/SUM1972-WIN1973).

The Savoy. *London, Leonard Smithers.*   1502485
    LCCN: 6-4332   Beg. date: 1896   End date: 1896
    "An illustrated monthly."
    Ceased publication with no. 8, Dec. 1896.
    WU   UWM (RBR)   No.1-8 (1896).

The Scarlet letter. *Madison, Wisc., The Scarlet Letter Collective.*   1506819
    Beg. date: 1971
    WU   UWM (RBR)   V.1 no.1-7 (MAY1971-SUM1972).

Schist. *Willimantic, Conn.*   1506821
    ISSN: 0092-9425   LCCN: 74-640587   Beg. date: 1973
    "A journal of poetry and graphics."
    WU   UWM (RBR)   No.1-3 (FAL1973-SPR1975).

Schmuck. *Cullompton, Devon, Eng., Beau Geste Press.*   1506834
    Text in various languages.
    WU   UWM (RBR)   No.1-8 (MAR1972-SPR1976).

Scholia satyrica. *Tampa, Fla., Dept. of English, University of South Florida.*
    Beg. date: 1975
    Absorbed Pucred.
    WU   UWM (RBR)   V.1-v.2 no.3 (WIN1975-AUT1976).

School of Living. Balanced living. *See* Balanced living. Brookville, Ohio, School of Living.   1430627

Sciamachy. *Winnetka, Ill.*   1506847
    ISSN: 0582-1924   Beg. date: 1960   End date: 1964
    Ceased publication with no. 6, 1964.
    WU   UWM (RBR)   No.1-6 (1960-1964).

Scimitar and song. *Edgewater, Md., etc., Scimitar and Song Publications, etc.*   1508244
    ISSN: 0036-8938   LCCN: 42-48186   Beg. date: 1938
    WU   UWM (RBR)   V.22 no.2-7,9-11; v.23 no.1,3-7; v.24 no.7,9,12; v.25 no.4-5; v.26 no.12; v.31 no.1; v.33 no.1; v.34 no.1 (OCT1959-DEC1971/FEB1972); Summer 1964.

Scintilla. *[Shreveport, La.].*   150685A
    WU   UWM (RBR)   Dec. 1962.

Scopcraeft. *Fargo, North Dakota State University. Department of English.*   0666836
    ISSN: 0036-8962   Beg. date: 1966
    WU   UWM (RBR)   V.5 no.4,6 (MAR,AUG1971).

Scope. *Bayonne, N.J.*   1506862
    Beg. date: 1934   End date: 1934
    "A magazine of proletarian literature."
    Ceased publication with vol. 1 no.1, Sept./Oct. 1934.
    WU   UWM (RBR)   V.1 no.1 (SEP/OCT1934).

Scope; a literary review. *San Francisco.*   0666864
    Title varies: _____, called Turntable and Hut.
    WU   UWM (RBR)   No.10,13-15 (1964-JUN1966).

Scorpio. *See* Scorpio broadside. Kings Lynn, Norfolk, Eng.   1506888

Scorpio broadside. *Kings Lynn, Norfolk, Eng.*   1506875
    Title varies: _____, Scorpio.
    WU   UWM (RBR)   No.1-4,6,8-11,22 (n.d.-n.d.).

Scotia review. *Wick, Caithness, Scot.*   1506890
    Beg. date: 1972
    Supersedes Scotia.
    WU   UWM (RBR)   No.3-5,7-8,10-13/14 (APR1973-AUG/NOV1976).

Scots writing. *Glasgow.*   150690A
    WU   UWM (RBR)   No.3 (n.d.).

Scottish international. *Edinburgh, Scotland, Scottish International Review Ltd.*   1506912
    ISSN: 0036-9268   LCCN: 72-623192   Beg. date: 1968
    Absorbed Feedback.
    Also called Scottish international review.
    WU   UWM (RBR)   No.1-14 (1968-MAY1971); Aug.-Dec. 1971; v.5 no.1-9; v.6-v.7 no. 2 (1972-MAR1974).

Scottish international review. *See* Scottish international. Edinburgh, Scotland, Scottish International Review Ltd.   1506925

Scranton. University. Esprit. *See* Esprit. Scranton, Pa., University of Scranton.   1433921

Scree. *[Missoula, Mont., Duck Down Press].*   1412380
    ISSN: 0360-2672   Beg. date: 1974
    WU   UWM (RBR)   No.1-8 (1974-1977).

Scree poetry. *King's Lynn, Norfolk, Eng., Scree Publications.*   1506938
    WU   UWM (RBR)   No.3-7 (AUT1975-1977).

Screeches for sounding. *[n.p.]*   152950A
    "Volume the first and last."
    WU   UWM (RBR)   V.1 (n.d.).

Screen door review. *Onondaga, Mich.*   1506940
    Beg. date: 1974
    WU   UWM (RBR)   No.1-4 (1974-1977).

Scribe. *Boston, Mass.*   1506953
    ISSN: 0487-9813   Beg. date: 1953
    "The Emerson College literary magazine."
    WU   UWM (RBR)   V.3 (NOV1955-MAY1956).

Scribe. *See* SSCribe. Sacramento.   151121A

Scrip. *Chesterfield, Derbyshire, Eng. [etc.].*   1506966
    ISSN: 0036-9659   Beg. date: 1962   End date: 1973
    "A quarterly selection of recent poetry" (varies).
    Ceased publication with no. 44, 1973.
    WU   UWM (RBR)   No.1-44 (1962-1973).

Scripts. *New York.*   0668456
    ISSN: 0006-5307   Beg. date: 1971   End date: 1972
    Published by the New York Shakespeare Festival Public Theater.
    Ceased publication in 1972.
    WU   UWM (RBR)   V.1 no.1-10 (NOV1971-OCT1972).

Scrivener, *Jackson Heights, N.Y., Poet's Press.*   1506979
    WU   UWM (RBR)   Mar./Apr. 1965.

Scrutiny, a quarterly review. *Cambridge, England, Deighton, Bell and Co.*   0668506
    LCCN: A40-582   Beg. date: 1932   End date: 1953
    Ceased publication with vol. 19 no. 4, Oct. 1953.
    V. 20 Retrospect and index, is issued as part of the 1963 photographic reprint edition.
    WU   UWM (RBR)   V.3,5-6,8-10; v.11 no.4; v.14 no.2; v.15-19 (JUN1934-OCT1953).

Scythe. *London.*   1512634
    LCCN: 45-49175 rev   Beg. date: 1938   End date: 1946
    Title varies: nos. 1-20, 1938-Feb. 1944, Townsman.
    Ceased publication with no. 28, April 1946.
    WU   UWM (RBR)   V.1-5 (no.1-8,10-11,14-16,18-20) (1938-SPR1944).

Seaplane. *New York.*   1506981
    Beg. date: 1969
    WU   UWM (RBR)   No.1 (1969).

The Search. *Carbondale, Ill., Southern Illinois University Press.*   1529512
    ISSN: 0085-6010   LCCN: 61-3998   Beg. date: 1961
    "Creative work written by students and sponsored by the English Club of Southern Illinois University."
    WU   UWM (RBR)   Ser. 1-13 (1961-1974).

Search for tomorrow. *Iowa City, Iowa, Blue Wind Press.* 1506994
Beg. date: 1970
WU   UWM (RBR) No.1-4/5 (1970-SPR1972).

Seared eye. *Sacramento, Calif., Grand Ronde/Island City Press.* 1507001
ISSN: 0586-9714   Beg. date: 1968
WU   UWM (RBR) No.1-   (1968-   ).

Seattle University. Fragments. *See* Fragments. Seattle, Dept. of English, Seattle University. 1437525

The Secant. *St. Louis, Mo. [etc.].* 1507014
ISSN: 0559-2577   Beg. date: 1963
WU   UWM (RBR) June/July 1963; Mar., Dec. 1964; Sept. 1965; June/July 1966.

Secession. *Vienna, New York, Kraus Reprint.* 0668982
Ceased publication with Apr. 1924.
WU   UWM (RBR) No.1-7 (SPR1922-WIN1924).

Second aeon. *Cardiff.* 1508153
ISSN: 0037-0525   Beg. date: 1967
Ceased publication with no. 19/21, 1974.
WU   UWM (RBR) No.1-19/21 (FEB1967-1974).

Second American caravan. *See* American caravan, a yearbook of American literature. New York, The Macaulay Company. 0669002

Second coming. *San Francisco, Second Coming Press.* 1507027
ISSN: 0048-9956   LCCN: sc76-338
WU   UWM (RBR) V.1-v.5 no.1 (n.d.-1977).

The Second coming magazine. *New York.* 150703A
ISSN: 0582-3684   Beg. date: 1961
WU   UWM (RBR) V.1 no.1-5 (1961-JAN1965).

Second growth. *San Francisco.* 1507042
Beg. date: 1975
"Literature of environmental concern."
WU   UWM (RBR) V.1 no.1 (AUT1975).

The Second wave. *Boston, Mass., Female liberation.* 1507055
ISSN: 0048-9980   LCCN: 76-25749   Beg. date: 1971
"A magazine of the new feminism."
WU   UWM (RBR) V.1-v.5 no.1 (SPR1971-1977).

Secret memoirs of galiant men and fair women. *See* Casanova Jr's tales. New York, Two Worlds Publishing Co. 1427980

Section 8. *Brooklyn, N.Y.* 1507068
ISSN: 0488-0498   Beg. date: 1951   End date: 1955
Also called Section eight.
Ceased publication with 1955.
WU   UWM (RBR) V.1 no.1-9 (1951-1953); Dec. 1953; Jan.-Mar., June, Oct., Dec. 1954; Jan.-Feb., Apr., July, Sept., Dec. 1955.

Section eight. *See* Section 8. Brooklyn, N.Y. 1507070

Seed. *Canton, Mo. [etc.], Transient Press.* 1507083
WU   UWM (RBR) No.12-57 (OCT311962-JUN201966).

Seed. *London.* 1507096
Beg. date: 1933   End date: 1933
Ceased publication with July 1933.
WU   UWM (RBR) Jan. 1933.

Seems. *Cedar Falls, Iowa, Springfield, Mo.* 1507105
ISSN: 0095-1730   LCCN: 74-648056   Beg. date: 1971
"Prose and poetry."
WU   UWM (RBR) No.1-8 (AUT1971-1977).

Seer ox. *Los Angeles.* 1507118
WU   UWM (RBR) V.1 no.1-5 (1975-1976).

Seizure magazine. *Gresham, Ore., etc.* 1507120
Beg. date: 1972
WU   UWM (RBR) V.1 no.1,4-5/6 (SPR/SUM1972-1975).

The Self-publishing writer. *San Francisco.* 1507146
ISSN: 0091-6226   LCCN: 73-642687   Beg. date: 1972
"Quarterly journal for writers."
WU   UWM (RBR) V.1-v.3 no.3; v.4 no.1 (OCT1972-APR1976).

Selfhood architecture poetry. *Imperial Beach, Calif.* 1507133
WU   UWM (RBR) V.3 no.5; v.4 no.1-2,4-5; v.5 no.1 (JUL291971-MAY061973).

Semantika. *St. Louis, Mo.* 1507159
ISSN: 0059-3956   Beg. date: 1955   End date: 1958
"For better brain hygiene."
Title varies: , American Semantic Society. Journal.
Ceased publication with vol. 4 no. 7, Oct. 1958.
WU   UWM (RBR) V.2 no.3-4 (MAR-APR1956).

Semi-colon. *New York, Tibor de Nagy Gallery.* 1507187
ISSN: 0559-3980   Beg. date: 1955
Ceased publication with vol. 2 no. 6, 19??.
WU   UWM (RBR) V.1-v.2 no.4 (n.d.-n.d.).

Semina. *Los Angeles.* 1507174
WU   UWM (RBR) No.1-6 (1956?-1960).

Seneca review. *Geneva, N.Y., Student Association of Hobart and William Smith Colleges.* 067085A
ISSN: 0037-2145   Beg. date: 1970
WU   UWM (RBR) V.1-v.7 no.1 (MAY1970-JUN1976).

Seneh ha-boer. *See* Burning bush. [San Francisco], The Inter-Hillel Council of Northern California. 1438504

Sepharim. *Moorpark, Calif.* 150719A
WU   UWM (RBR) [No.2-4] (1970-1972).

Sepia. *See* Sepia magazine. Millbook nr. Plymouth, Devon, Eng. 1529540

Sepia magazine. *Millbook nr. Plymouth, Devon, Eng.* 1529538
Also called Sepia.
WU   UWM (RBR) July 1977.

Sequoia. *San Francisco, The Littlefield Press.* 1507209
Ceased publication.
WU   UWM (RBR) [No.1] (1973).

Sequoia. *Stanford, Calif., Associated Students of Stanford University.* 1507211
ISSN: 0037-2420   LCCN: 61-40841   Beg. date: 1956
"Stanford literary magazine."
WU   UWM (RBR) V.1 no.2; v.7 no.1,3; v.10 no.1-2; v.12 no.1-2; v.14; v.15 no.1-2; v.16 no.1; v.17-v.20 no.1; v.21 no.1-2 (SPR1956-SPR1977).

Sesheta. *[Sutton, England].* 1507237
LCCN: 72-625172   Beg. date: 1971
Supersedes Broadsheet.
WU   UWM (RBR) No.1-6 (WIN1971-1974).

Set. *Gloucester, Mass. [etc.], Gerrit Lansing.* 150724A
ISSN: 0559-6424   Beg. date: 1961
WU   UWM (RBR) No.1-2 (WIN1961/1962-WIN1963/1964).

Seton Hall University, South Orange New Jersey. Department of English. Spirit. *See* Spirit: a magazine of poetry. New York, [etc.]. 0671488

Seven. *Oklahoma City.* 1507252
Beg. date: 1957
Supersedes The Lantern.
WU   UWM (RBR) V.1-v.2 no.1 (1957-1975).

Seven. *Poplars, Taunton, Eng., John Goodland and Nicholas Moore.* 1507265
Beg. date: 1938   End date: 1947
"Magazine of People's writing" (varies).
Suspended publication Spring 1940-
Ceased publication with vol. 7 no.2, 1947.
WU   UWM (RBR) No.1-4,6-7 (SUM1938-WIN1939).

Seven arts. *New York, The Seven arts pub. co.* 0671553
LCCN: 18-14940   Beg. date: 1916   End date: 1917
Ceased publication with vol. 2 no. 12, Oct. 1917.
Absorbed by Dial.
Includes supplement to Apr. 1917 issue: American independence and the war.
WU   UWM (RBR) Nov. 1916-Oct. 1917.

Seven persons repository. *See* Repository. Seven Persons, Alberta [etc.], Repository Press. 1504428

Seven stars poetry. *San Diego, etc., Realities.* 1508203
ISSN: 0146-695X   Beg. date: 1975
Vol. 1 no.2 also published as California poet vol. 1 no.2.
WU   UWM (RBR) V.1 no.1-8,10; v.2 no.12-26; v.3 no.27-34 (1975-1977).

The Seventh day review. *Washington, Pa., Washington and Jefferson College.* 1507278
Beg. date: 1974
WU   UWM (RBR) V.1 no.1; v.2 no.1 (SPR1974-SPR1975).

Seventh Street. *New York.* 0671603
"A literary quarterly."
WU   UWM (RBR) Spring-Fall/Winter 1962.

The Seventies. Madison, Minn., The Seventies Press, Odin House, Madison. 0671616
ISSN: 0037-5969 Beg. date: 1972
Frequency varies.
Supersedes The Sixties.
WU UWM (RBR) No.1 (SPR1972).

Seventy-nine cent spread. *See* 79 [cent] spread. Carmel, Calif. 1510860

Shaded room. Pittsburgh. 1507293
ISSN: 0037-3141 Beg. date: 1970
WU UWM (RBR) No.1 (MAR1970).

Shaman. Kennebunk, Maine. 1507302
ISSN: 0145-3769 LCCN: 77-640111
"A magazine of poetry."
WU UWM (RBR) Autumn 1973; v.2 no.1; v.3 no.1 (1973).

Shameless hussy review. San Lorenzo, Calif., Shameless Hussy Press. 1508229
Beg. date: 1974
Continues Remember our fire with no. [4], 1974.
WU UWM (RBR) No.[4]-5 (1974).

Shankpainter. Provincetown, Mass., Fine Arts Work Center. 1507315
WU UWM (RBR) No.5,9 (SEP1971-JAN1974).

Shantih. [New York]. 1400213
ISSN: 0037-329X LCCN: 76-617641 Beg. date: 1971
"A quarterly of international writing" (varies).
WU UWM (RBR) V.1-v.3 no.4 (WIN1971-1977).

Shards. Augusta, Ga. 1507330
Beg. date: 1933 End date: 1939
"The poetry quarterly."
Ceased publication with vol. 7 no. 4, Nov. 1939.
WU UWM RBR V.5 no.3; v.6 no.1,4 (AUG151937-NOV151938).

Sheaf. Eureka, Calif. 1507343
ISSN: 0582-9712 Beg. date: 1955
WU UWM (RBR) No.1-3 (1955-FEB1956).

The Sheaf. Hays, Kan., Fort Hays State College. 1507356
WU UWM (RBR) 1958-1965.

Sheet. Heidelberg West, Victoria, Australia. 1529553
Beg. date: 1969
"An occasional sheet of concrete poetry."
WU UWM (RBR) No.1 (MAR1969).

Sheffield, England. University. Union of Students. Arrows. *See* Arrows. [Sheffield, Eng., Sheffield University, Union of Students]. 1430185

Shell. Waban, Mass. 1507371
ISSN: 0146-3985 LCCN: 77-649237 Beg. date: 1976
WU UWM (RBR) No.1-3 (FAL/WIN1976-1977).

Shelter. [n.p.], Doones Press. 1529566
WU UWM (RBR) Feb. 1972.

Sherbrooke, Québec. Université. Faculté des Arts. Ellipse. *See* Ellipse. Sherbrooke, Qué., Université de Sherbrooke, Faculté des Arts. 1441040

Shig's review. San Francisco, Adler Press. 1507384
Beg. date: 1960
WU UWM (RBR) No.1-2 (1960).

Shocks. San Francisco, Momo's Press. 1507397
ISSN: 0360-912X LCCN: 75-649527 Beg. date: 1972
WU UWM (RBR) V.1 no.1-6 (NOV1972-1976).

The Shore review. Milwaukee, Wisc. 1507406
Beg. date: 1971
WU UWM (RBR) No.1-14 (1971-n.d.).

A Shout in the street. Flushing, N.Y., Queens College Press. 1507419
ISSN: 0363-079X LCCN: 76-26442
"A journal of literary and visual art."
WU UWM (RBR) No.1-3 (1976-1977).

Showcase. San Marcos, Calif. [etc.]. 1507421
Beg. date: 1965
WU UWM (RBR) No.1-5 (SEP/OCT1965-SUM1970).

Shuttle. [n.p.]. 1507434
Beg. date: 1972
WU UWM (RBR) No.1 (MAY1972).

Sibyl. Elmira, N.Y. 1507447
"A literary quarterly published by the students of Elmira College, Elmira, New York."
WU UWM (RBR) Winter 1959-1960.

Sibyl-child. Hyattsville, Md. 1507462
"A women's arts and culture journal."
WU UWM (RBR) V.1-v.2 no.2 (WIN1975-1977).

Sibylline. Watertown, Mass. 1529579
Beg. date: 1948 End date: 1948
"A magazine of ideaistic writing."
Ceased publication with vol. 1 no.2, April/June 1948.
Superseded by Golden Goose.
WU UWM (RBR) V.1 no.1-2 (JAN/APR-APR/JUN1948).

Sidewalk. Edinburgh. 1504926
ISSN: 0583-1903 Beg. date: 1960 End date: 1960
"Scotland's quarterly review."
Ceased publication with vol. 1 no. 2, 1960.
WU UWM (RBR) V.1 no.1-2 (1960).

Sierra College, Rocklin, California. Creative Writing Program. Viewpoint. *See* Viewpoint. Rocklin, Calif., Creative Writing Program, Sierra College. 1517195

Sigma portfolio. London. 1504939
WU UWM (RBR) No.1-7,10,12-19,21-23,25-30,36 (n.d.-n.d.).

Sign. Headington, Oxford, Eng., Breed Publications. 1504941
WU UWM (RBR) [No.1] (n.d.).

Signal. New York, The Brownstone Press. 1504954
ISSN: 0583-2535 Beg. date: 1963
"A quarterly review."
WU UWM (RBR) V.1 no.1-3 (FAL1963-1965).

The Signature. London. 1504967
Beg. date: 1915 End date: 1915
Ceased publication with no. 3, Nov. 1, 1915.
Editors: D.H. Lawrence, Katherine Mansfield, John Middleton Murry.
WU UWM (RBR) No.1-3 (OCT04-NOV011915).

Signatures, work in progress. Detroit, Michigan, J. H. Thompson. 0675129
Beg. date: 1936
WU UWM (RBR) V.1 no.1-3 (SPR1936-WIN1937/1938).

Signet. Alamo, Calif. 150497A
ISSN: 0560-026X Beg. date: 1959
WU UWM (RBR) Jan. 1960.

Signet. Charlotte, N.C., Observer Printing House. 1504982
WU UWM (RBR) Winter 1965; Winter-Spring 1966; Fall 1967; Spring, Fall 1968, Spring 1969.

Signet. Cincinnati. 1504995
"A newsletter devoted to helping the poets' muse make her mark in Greater Cincinnati.
WU UWM (RBR) V.1 no.2-6,8-9; v.2-v.5 no.6 (MAY1959-1963).

Silhouettes. Ontario, Calif. 1505002
LCCN: 37-21890 Beg. date: 1932 End date: 1938
"An international magazine of poetry."
Title varies slightly.
Absorbed Five with 1935.
Ceased publication with vol. 5 no. 2, 1938.
United with Poetry caravan to form Poetry caravan and silhouettes.
WU UWM (RBR) V.4 no.3 (1937).

Silo. Bennington, Vt., Bennington College. 1505015
ISSN: 0037-5306 Beg. date: 1962
WU UWM (RBR) No.1-17; v.18 no.1; v.19 no.1 (SPR1962-SPR1971); Spring 1972; 1973-1975.

The Silver bough. Los Angeles, Calif., Wagon and Star, Publishers. 1505030
Beg. date: 1941 End date: 1941
"A literary journal."
Ceased publication with vol. 1 no. 1, Summer 1941.
WU UWM (RBR) V.1 no.1 (SUM1941).

The Silver cesspool. Cleveland, Renegade Press. 1505043
ISSN: 0560-0588 Beg. date: 1963
"Contemporary American haikus and prints."
WU UWM (RBR) No.1-5 (1963-1964).

Simbolica. Tiburon, Calif., etc., Ignace M. Ingianni. 1505056
ISSN: 0488-8642 Beg. date: 1949
"Avant-garde poetry magazine" (varies).
Ceased publication with no. 33, 1969.
WU UWM (RBR) No.1-10,17-22,28-33 (1949-1969).

Simon Fraser University. West coast review. *See* West coast review. Burnaby, B.C., Simon Fraser University. 1518616

Simon Fraser University. Department of English. Iron. *See* 144304A
Iron. Port Moody, B.C. [etc.], English Department, Simon Fraser University.

Sinister wisdom. *Charlotte, N.C.* 1505069
Beg. date: 1976
WU   UWM (RBR) V.1 no.1-3 (JUL1976-SPR1977).

The Sinking bear. *New York.* 1505071
"A newsletter."
WU   UWM (RBR) No.3-4 (DEC1963).

Sinter. *Basel.* 1505084
Beg. date: 1973
WU   UWM (RBR) No.1-10 (FEB031973-JUL281977).

Sipapu. *Davis, Calif., Noel Peattie.* 0942927
ISSN: 0037-5837   Beg. date: 1970
WU   UWM (RBR) V.2-v.8 no.2 (1971-1977).

Sir George Williams University. Students Association. 1435303
Duel. *See* Duel. Montreal, Communications Board, Student Assn., Sir George Williams University.

Sisters. *San Francisco, Daughters of Bilitis, San Francisco chapter.*
ISSN: 0049-0644   Beg. date: 1970
WU   UWM (RBR) V.3 no.1; v.5 no.1-2; v.6 no.2 (1972-1975).

Sixpack. *Lake Toxaway, N.C., London.* 1505106
WU   UWM (RBR) No.1-9 (MAY1972-FAL1975).

The Sixties. *Madison, Minnesota.* 0676060
ISSN: 0583-4570   LCCN: 72-621799   Beg. date: 1960   End date: 1968
Continues The Fifties with no. 4, Fall 1960.
None published in 1963 or 1965.
Ceased publication with no. 10, 1968.
Superseded by The Seventies with 1972.
WU   UWM (RBR) No.4-10 (FAL1960-SUM1968).

Skidmore College, Sarasota Springs, New York. 1465927
Salmagundi. *See* Salmagundi. Flushing, N. Y.,

Skylight. *Didsbury, Manchester, Eng.* 150996A
Beg. date: 1971
WU   UWM (RBR) No.1-2 (SPR1971-WIN/SPR1972).

Skywriting. *Eugene, Ore.* 1509972
LCCN: 72-620469   Beg. date: 1971
WU   UWM (RBR) V.1-v.2 no.3 (no.1-6) (OCT1971-WIN1975/1976).

Slice. *Brightlingsea, Essex, Eng.* 1509985
WU   UWM (RBR) V.1 no.1-2 (n.d.-n.d.).

Slit wrist. *New York, Poetry Project, St. Mark's Church-in-the-Bowery.* 1509998
Beg. date: 1976
WU   UWM (RBR) V.1-3/4 (SPR1976-SPR1977).

The Slumgullion review. *Holyoke, Mass.* 1510005
ISSN: 0037-7066   Beg. date: 1966
"A nongrim literary magazine" (varies widely).
WU   UWM (RBR) V.1 no.1-2 (1966).

Small circle of friends. *San Francisco.* 1510018
Beg. date: 1969
WU   UWM (RBR) April 1969.

The Small farm. *Jefferson City, Tenn.* 1510020
Beg. date: 1975
WU   UWM (RBR) No.1-5 (MAR1975-1977).

The Small pond. *Stratford, Conn. [etc.].* 1510033
ISSN: 0037-721X   Beg. date: 1964
WU   UWM (RBR) V.1-v.14 no.2 (no.1-40) (FAL1964-SPR1977).

Small press review. *El Cerrito, Calif.* 0677431
ISSN: 0037-7228   Beg. date: 1967
"A quarterly review of small-press publications."
WU   UWM (RBR) V.1-v.9 no.8 (no.1-55) (SPR1967-AUG1977).

Smart set, a magazine of cleverness. *New York, Ess Ess publishing company.* 067746A
LCCN: 9-33139.   Beg. date: 1900   End date: 1930
Absorbed New McClure's with May 1929.
Title varies: vol. 86 nos. 3-5, May-July 1930, New smart set.
Ceased publication with vol. 86 no. 5, July 1930.
WU   UWM (RBR) V.1; v.2 no.3; v.3 no.4; v.5 no.1; v.7 no.2; v.14 no.2,4; v.15 no.2; v.17 no.2; v.41 no.1; v.70 no.2 (MAR1900-FEB1923).

The Smith. *New York, Horizon Press.* 0677472
ISSN: 0037-7309   LCCN: 64-9367   Beg. date: 1964
WU   UWM (RBR) V.1 no.1,3-4; v.2; v.3 no.8,10-15,17-19 (FEB1964-1977); special issues no. 1-11,14-30 (APR1969-NOV1974).

Smith. Newsart. *See* Newsart. New York, Generalist Association. 1495256

Smith College. Grecourt review. *See* Grecourt review. Northampton, Mass., Smith College. 1436611

Smoke. *Liverpool, England. 486 Productions.* 1510046
WU   UWM (RBR) No.3-6 (1976-1977).

Smoke. *Providence, R.I.* 1510059
Beg. date: 1931   End date: 1937
Ceased publication with vol. 6 no. 1, May/Aug. 1937.
WU   UWM (RBR) V.4 no.3-4; v.5 no.1; v.6 no.1 (SUM1935-MAY/AUG1937).

The Smoky Hill review. *Hays, Kansas, Division of Language, Literature, and Speech, Fort Hays Kansas State College.* 1510061
ISSN: 0583-662X   Beg. date: 1966   End date: 1967
Ceased publication with vol. 2, 1967.
WU   UWM (RBR) V.1-2 (WIN1966-1967).

Smorgasbrain. *Cleveland.* 1510087
WU   UWM (RBR) Jan., June 1967; Jan. 1968.

A Smudge on the window. *Livonia, Mich., M.E. Pegs and Associates.* 151009A
WU   UWM (RBR) [No.2] ([1974]).

The Snail. *Barnstaple, North Devon, England.* 1510109
Title varies: The North Devon snail.
WU   UWM (RBR) No.2-20 (MAY1971-SPR1973).

Snakeroots. *Brooklyn, N.Y., The Print Center, Inc.* 1510124
WU   UWM (RBR) Fall 1974-Fall 1975; Fall 1976.

Snap dragon. *Kitchener, Ont.* 1510137
ISSN: 0560-3528
WU   UWM (RBR) No.1-2 (n.d.-n.d.).

Snerd magazine. *See* Little review. Huntington, W. Va., Little Review Press. 1493140

Snowy egret. *Battle Creek, Mich.* 1510544
Beg. date: 1924
Title varies: Spring 1939, Animal world.
Indexes: 1951-1962, in vol. 26 no. 2; 1963-1972 in vol. 36 no. 2; 1973-1975 in vol. 40 no. 1.
WU   UWM (RBR) V.14 no.1; v.15; v.16 no.1; v.17-v.40 no.2 (SPR1934-1977); indexes: 1951-1962, 1963-1972, 1973-1975.

Society for Individual Liberty. Rational individualist. *See* 1504101
Rational individualist. Silver Spring, Md., Society for Individual Liberty.

Society for Rational Individualism. Rational individualist. 1504114
See Rational individualist. Silver Spring, Md., Society for Individual Liberty.

Society of Umbra. Umbra. *See* Umbra. Berkeley, Calif., Society of Umbra. 1514765

Soft need. *Bonn, etc., Expanded Media Editions.* 151014A
WU   UWM (RBR) No.8-9 (SEP1973-SPR1976).

Softball. *Cambridge, Mass. [etc.].* 1510152
Beg. date: 1971
WU   UWM (RBR) No.1-2 (1971).

Software. *New York.* 1510165
WU   UWM (RBR) No.2-3 (NOV-DEC1965).

Soho. *London, Night Scene Publications.* 1510178
Beg. date: 1964
Ceased publication with no. 1, Sept. 1964.
WU   UWM (RBR) No.1 (SEP1964).

Soil; a magazine of art. *New York.* 0688128
WU   UWM (RBR) V.1 no.1-5 (DEC1916-JUL1917).

Sojourner. *New York, The Print Center, Inc.* 1510180
Beg. date: 1974
WU   UWM (RBR) No.1 (1974).

Sol quarterly. *Westcliff-on-Sea, Essex, Eng.* 1510193
WU   UWM (RBR) No.1-2,4-12 ([1969]-1977).

Solana. *[n.p.], Androgyny Press.* 1510202
WU   UWM (RBR) 1976.

The Sole proprietor. *Miami.* 1510215
Beg. date: 1976
WU   UWM (RBR) No.1-4 (WIN1976-SUM1977).

Soliloquy. *New Delhi, Sarabjeet Seth.* 1510228
WU   UWM (RBR) Jan./Mar.-July/Sept. 1975.

Soliloquy. *Stillwater, Okla., Oklahoma State University.* 1510230
ISSN: 0038-1179
WU   UWM (RBR) V.9 no.1 (FAL1968).

Solstice. *Cambridge, Eng.* 1510243
ISSN: 0038-1225 Beg. date: 1966
WU   UWM (RBR) No.1-9 (1966-1969).

Soma. *London.* 1510256
Beg. date: 1931 End date: 1934
Ceased publication with no. 5, 1934.
WU   UWM (RBR) Sept. 1931.

Soma-haoma. *Dennis, Mass., Salt Works Press.* 1510269
WU   UWM (RBR) No.7 (1976).

Some. *New York, The Print Center, Inc., etc.* 1510271
Beg. date: 1972
WU   UWM (RBR) No.1-5/6 (SPR1972-WIN1975).

Some friends. *Tyler, Tex., Some Friends, Inc.* 1510284
"A literary magazine."
WU   UWM (RBR) No.3 (WIN/SPR1974).

Some/thing. *New York, Hawk's Well Press.* 1252609
ISSN: 0038-1284 Beg. date: 1965 End date: 1966
Reprint of a periodical published in New York.
Ceased publication with no. 3, 1966.
WU   UWM (RBR) V.1-v.2 no.1 (SPR1965-WIN1966).

Something. *See* Some/thing. New York, Hawk's Well Press. 1252611

Something else newsletter. *New York; Something Else Press, Inc.* 0688901
ISSN: 0038-1349
WU   UWM (RBR) V.1-v.2 no.6 (FEB1966-JAN1973).

Somethings magazine. *Edgbaston, Birmingham, Eng.* 1510319
Beg. date: 1967
WU   UWM (RBR) No.1-11 (1967-JAN1970).

Song. *Bowling Green, Ohio, Richard Behm.* 1510321
Beg. date: 1975
"A magazine of verse and essay."
WU   UWM (RBR) No.1-2 (1975-1977).

Sonnet sequences. *Bladensburg, Md. [etc.].* 0688970
LCCN: 37-11077. Beg. date: 1928 End date: 1959
Subtitle varies.
Ceased publication with vol. 31 (no. 369), Feb. 1959.
Superseded by The New sonnet sequences.
WU   UWM (RBR) No.343,367 (DEC1956-DEC1958).

The Sonneteer. *New York.* 1510334
Beg. date: 1943 End date: 1944
"A magazine devoted to the sonnet in all its forms."
Ceased publication with no. 3, Summer 1944.
WU   UWM (RBR) No.1 (WIN1943/1944).

Sortie. *Baldwin, N.Y., The Donna Crouse Workshop.* 1510347
ISSN: 0584-1356 Beg. date: 1965
WU   UWM (RBR) No.1-4 (FAL1965-1970).

Soulbook; the quarterly journal of revolutionary Afroamerica. *Berkeley, Calif.* 0689373
ISSN: 0038-1780
WU   UWM (RBR) V.2 no.3-4; v.3 no.1 (SUM/FAL1967-FAL/WIN1970).

Soundings. *Stony Brook, N.Y., State University of New York at Stony Brook.* 151035A
ISSN: 0584-1682 LCCN: 75-12364 Beg. date: 1964
WU   UWM (RBR) V.4-5 (SPR1967-SPR1968); 1970-1971.

Sounds on campus. *New York, Campus Communications.* 1510375
WU   UWM (RBR) No.3 (1967).

Source. *Jamaica, N.Y., Literary Arts Division, Queens Council on the Arts.* 1510388
Beg. date: 1976
WU   UWM (RBR) V.1 no.1 (1976).

South. *Deland, Fla., Stetson University.* 0689542
ISSN: 0038-1918 Beg. date: 1969 End date: 1973
Ceased publication with vol. 5 no. 2, Spr. 1973.
WU   UWM (RBR) No.1-5 (1969-SPR1973).

South African Poetry Society. New coin. *See* New coin. Grahamstown, South Africa, South African Poetry Society. 1494630

South and west. *Fort Smith, Ark., South and West, Inc.* 151040A
ISSN: 0038-2833 LCCN: 74-642392 Beg. date: 1962
"An international literary magazine."
WU   UWM (RBR) V.1-v.14 no.1 (SUM1962-SUM1976).

South and West, Incorporated. Discourses on poetry. *See* Discourses on poetry. Fort Smith, Ark., South and West, Inc. 1434891

The South Carolina review. *Clemson, S.C., Dept. of English, Clemson University.* 1529581
ISSN: 0038-3163 LCCN: 73-643713 Beg. date: 1968
Issued Nov. 1968-June 1973 by Furman University.
WU   UWM (RBR) V.2-v.9 no.2 (NOV1969-1977).

South Dakota. University. English Department. *See* South Dakota review. Vermillion, English Department, University of South Dakota. 0692559

The South Dakota review. *Vermillion, English Department, University of South Dakota.* 069290A
ISSN: 0038-3368 LCCN: 64-9366 Beg. date: 1963
WU   UWM (RBR) V.1 no.1-2; v.2 no.1-2; v.3 no.1; v.4-v.15 no.3 (DEC1963-1977).

South Dakota State Poetry Society. *See* Pasque petals. Sioux Falls, S.D., South Dakota State Poetry Society. 0692953

The South Florida poetry journal. *Tampa, Fla., University of South Florida.* 1510412
ISSN: 0586-6456 Beg. date: 1968
WU   UWM (RBR) No.1-4/5 (FAL1968-1970).

The South Florida review. *Tampa, Fla., University of South Florida, Tampa.* 1510438
ISSN: 0081-279X
WU   UWM (RBR) No.2,5-6 (APR1968-MAY1972).

Southampton. University College. Wessex. *See* Wessex. Southampton, Eng., University College. 1518581

Southerly; a literary magazine. *Sydney [New South Wales], Angus and Robertson.* 0693538
ISSN: 0038-3732 LCCN: 48-37343 Beg. date: 1939
"Magazine of the Sydney branch of the English Association." 1939-1946 include the Annual report of the branch.
WU   UWM (RBR) V.15 no.3; v.16 no.1; v.19 no.1 (1954-1958).

Southern California Council on Religion and the Homophile. Concern. *See* Concern. Los Angeles. 1428894

Southern California lit scene. *Long Beach, Calif.* 1510453
Beg. date: 1970 End date: 1971
"A regional literary magazine."
Ceased publication with vol. 1 no. 3, Feb./June 1971.
WU   UWM (RBR) V.1 no.1-3 (DEC9170-FEB/JUN1971).

Southern historical society. *See* Southern magazine. Baltimore, Turnbull and Murdoch [etc]. 0694019

Southern magazine. *Baltimore, Turnbull and Murdoch [etc].* 0694203
LCCN: 5-14025.
Supersedes Richmand eclectic.
Title changes: v. 1-3, New Eclectic; v. 4-7, New eclectic magazine; v. 8-17, Southern magazine.
Absorbed the Land we love in April 1869.
WU   UWM (RBR) Oct. 1892.

Southern poetry review. *Raleigh, N.C.* 1510466
ISSN: 0038-447X Beg. date: 1958
Continues Impetus with vol. 5 no. 1, Fall 1964.
"Published by the editors in cooperation with the School of Liberal Arts at North Carolina State of the University of North Carolina at Raleigh, North Carolina."
WU   UWM (RBR) V.5-v.17 no.2 (FAL1964-FAL1977).

Southern poetry today. *See* Impetus. Chapbook; southern poetry today. Deland, Fla. 1442606

The Southern review. *Jackson, Miss.* 1510479
Beg. date: 1934 End date: 1934
Ceased publication with no. 1, Winter 1934.
WU   UWM (RBR) No.1 (WIN1934).

Southern visions. *Cedar Park, Tex.* 1510481
WU   UWM (RBR) V.1 no.2-4 (SPR1975-WIN1976).

The Sow's ear. *Pittsburg, Calif., The Blue Collar Press.* 1529616
Beg. date: 1977
WU   UWM (RBR) V.1 no.1-2 (SUM-FAL1977).

Span. *New York.* 1510494
ISSN: 0490-3528
WU   UWM (RBR) No.1,3,5 (n.d.-n.d.).

The Span. *St. Louis, Mo., The Ralph Cheyney Memorial Association, Inc.* 1510503
Beg. date: 1941
WU   UWM (RBR) V.1 no.2; v.4 no.1; v.5 no.1,4; v.6 no.1-2/3 (JUN/JUL1941-1948).

Spanish fleye. *Toronto, Ont., Fleye Press.* 1510516
ISSN: 0584-8032 Beg. date: 1966
WU UWM (RBR) No.1 (1966).

Spanner. *London, Spanner.* 1510529
WU UWM (RBR) V.1 no.1-10 (FEB1975-FEB1977).

Sparrow. *West Lafayette, Inc. [etc.], Vagrom Chapbooks.* 1510531
ISSN: 0038-6588 LCCN: 76-648631 Beg. date: 1954
WU UWM (RBR) No.2-6,9-19,21-33 (1955-1977).

Sparrow magazine. Supplement. See Ancillary; being a casual literary appendix to each printed issue of The Sparrow magazine. Corona, N.Y. 1492105

Speak 2. *Greensboro, N.C.* 1510899
WU UWM (RBR) No.9 (1975); one unnumbered issue (1975).

Speak out. *Detroit.* 1510910
ISSN: 0584-8148 Beg. date: 1964
"Bulletin of the Facing Reality Publishing Committee."
WU UWM (RBR) V.1 no.1-3,5,7-8,11-12,14/15-21/22; v.2 no.1-10 (APR271964-FEB1970).

Speak out. *Wastport, Conn., Soap Box Pub. Co.* 1510923
WU UWM (RBR) Spring 1975-Winter 1975/1976.

Speak two. See Speak 2. Greensboro, N.C. 1510908

Special song. *Durham, Ct., etc.* 1510936
WU UWM (RBR) V.1 no.1-2; v.2-v.3 no.3 (WIN1971-SUM1974); special issue 1973.

Spectacular diseases. *Peterborough, Eng.* 1510949
WU UWM (RBR) No.1 (1976?).

The Spectator. *Los Angeles.* 1510951
Beg. date: 1969
WU UWM (RBR) V.1 no.1; v.2 no.1-3 (NOV/DEC1969-JUN/SEP1970).

Spectroscope. *Fort Smith, Ark., Border Press, Inc.* 1510964
Beg. date: 1966
"A journal devoted to poetry and poetic freedom."
WU UWM (RBR) V.1 no.1 (APR1966).

Spectrum. *Goleta, Calif., Associated Students of the University of California, Santa Barbara.* 1510977
ISSN: 0038-7045 LCCN: 62-68128 Beg. date: 1957
WU UWM (RBR) V.2 no.2; v.3 no.2; v.4 no.2; v.8 no.1-2; v.10 no.1 (SPR/SUM1958-SPR1968).

The Spectrum. *Redlands, Calif., Associated Students, University of Redlands.* 1510992
ISSN: 0561-5895 Beg. date: 1962
"University of Redlands quarterly."
WU UWM (RBR) V.1 no.1 (JUN1962).

Spectrum. *Richmond, Va., Virginia Commonwealth University.* 1511012
"The Richmond tri-annual review."
WU UWM (RBR) V.5 no.2-3; v.6 no.1 (WIN1969/1970-FAL/WIN1970).

Spectrum. *Salt Lake City, Utah, Salt Lake City Public Library.* 1511038
WU UWM (RBR) V.2 no.1-6; v.3 no.1 (1969-SEP1970).

Spectrum. *Washington, D.C.* 1511053
WU UWM (RBR) V.1 no.1-11 (JUL15-SEP301967).

The Spero. *Flint, Mich., etc., The Fenian Head Centre Press.* 1511066
ISSN: 0038-7363
WU UWM (RBR) V.1 no.1-2 (1965-1966).

Spider. See Spider magazine. Oakland, Calif. 1511081

Spider magazine. *Oakland, Calif.* 1511079
ISSN: 0561-6166 Beg. date: 1965
Also called Spider.
WU UWM (RBR) V.1 no.3-5,7 (APR15-OCT131965).

The Spinners. *New York.* 1511094
Beg. date: 1934 End date: 1936
"A bi-monthly of women's verse."
Ceased publication with vol. 2 no. 4, Jan./Feb. 1936.
Absorbed by Poetry world.
WU UWM (RBR) V.2 no.2 (MAY/JUN1935).

Spirit: a magazine of poetry. *New York, [etc.].* 0698452
ISSN: 0038-7584 Beg. date: 1934
Indexed by Catholic periodical and literature index.
WU UWM (RBR) V.1 no.6; v.4 no.4-5; v.5 no.2-4; v.12 no.2; v.27 no.1; v.28 no.6 (1935-JAN1962).

The Spirit that moves us magazine. *Iowa City, Ia., Emmess Press.* 1511103
Beg. date: 1975
WU UWM (RBR) V.1 no.1-3; v.2 no.1 (SEP1975-FAL1976).

Spit in the ocean. *Pleasant Hill, Ore., Intrepid Trips Information Service.* 1511116
ISSN: 0095-0459 LCCN: 74-646278 Beg. date: 1974
WU UWM (RBR) V.1 no.1-2 (1974-1976).

Split level. *Winnipeg, Split Level Publishing House.* 1511129
WU UWM (RBR) V.1 no.1-2; v.2 no.1 (1974-1975).

The Spokesman. *Dubuque, Iowa, Loras College.* 1511131
WU UWM (RBR) V.56 no.4; v.57 no.1-3; v.58-67 (1959-SPR1970).

The Spoon River quarterly. *Mt. Sterling, Ill., The Spoon River Poetry Press.* 1511157
Beg. date: 1976
WU UWM (RBR) V.1 no.1-2; v.2 no.1-3 (WIN1976-1977).

Spring rain. *Seattle, Spring Rain Press.* 151116A
Beg. date: 1971
WU UWM (RBR) No.1-[11],13-14 (1971-1975).

Squeeze. *Sacramento, Dept. of English, Calif. State University.* 1511172
Beg. date: 1972
WU UWM (RBR) V.1 no.1-2; v.2 no.1; v.3 no.1 (1972-WIN1973/1974).

Squeezebox. *Wichita, Kan., Paper Tiger Press.* 1511198
"A magazine of pressing sounds."
Includes special issues.
WU UWM (RBR) V.2 no.1-2,5/6 (SUM1975-FAL/WIN1977); special issue Jan. 1975.

The SScribe. *Sacramento.* 1511207
Published at Sacramento State College.
WU UWM (RBR) V.1-v.2 no.1 (1952-WIN1954).

St. Andrews review. See Saint Andrews review. Laurinburg, N.C., St. Andrews Presbyterian College. 1501991

St. George review. See Saint George review. Staten Island, New York, Bert Schultz's Cominsane Press. 1502011

St. John's bread. See Saint John's bread. Venice, Calif. [etc.]. 1502037

Stable. *Sudbury, Suffolk, Eng., The Stable Press.* 1511222
Beg. date: 1975
WU UWM (RBR) No.1-3 (1975-1977).

Stand. *Leeds, Eng.* 1511235
ISSN: 0038-9366 LCCN: 65-56192 Beg. date: 1952
"A quarterly review of literature and the arts."
Absorbed The Three arts quarterly.
WU UWM (RBR) No.2-12 (1952-WIN1956/1957); v.4-v.18 no.4 (1960-1977).

Stanford University. Sequoia. See Sequoia. Stanford, Calif., Associated Students of Stanford University. 1507224

Star * west. *Sausalito, Calif.* 1529629
Beg. date: 1970
WU UWM (RBR) V.1 no.3 (1970).

Star dancer. See Stardancer. Oxford, Ohio, Stardance Publications. 1511263

Star-web paper. *Las Cruces, N.M., All This & Less Publishers.* 1511248
ISSN: 0146-2105 Beg. date: 1973
WU UWM (RBR) No.1-6 (SPR1973-1977).

Stardancer. *Oxford, Ohio, Stardance Publications.* 1511250
ISSN: 0363-8278 Beg. date: 1976
WU UWM (RBR) No.1-2 (SPR-AUT1976).

Starianes. *Ferndale, Mich.* 1511276
ISSN: 0561-8568 Beg. date: 1950 End date: 1960
"The international quarterly of science fiction poetry" (varies).
Ceased publication with no. 40, [Oct. 1960].
WU UWM (RBR) 1954-Apr. 1956; no.23-40 ([May 1956-OCT1960]).

State and mind. *West Somerville, Mass., Radical Therapist, Inc.* 1467731
Beg. date: 1976
Continues RT; a journal of radical therapy with vol. 5 no. 3, July/Sept. 1976.
WU UWM (RBR) V.5 no.3-v.6 no.1 (JUL/SEP1976-1977).

Statement. *Los Angeles.* 1529631
ISSN: 0039-0224 LCCN: 67-33260 Beg. date: 1950
"A journal of creative and critical expression."
Issued by Associated Students of California State College at Los Angeles.
WU   UWM (RBR) V.1 no.1-8; v.9-25 (SPR1950-1969).

Statements. *Rochester, N.Y.* 0702480
Beg. date: 1959   End date: 1963
Ceased with no. 6.
No. 6 also called Midwest, special issue.
No. 6 has also special title, Iowa Workshop poets/1963.
WU   UWM (RBR) No.1-6 (SPR1959-1963).

Stateside. *New York, Stateside, Inc.* 1511289
Beg. date: 1946   End date: 1948
"A preview of new authors."
Ceased publication with vol. 1 no. 3, 1948.
WU   UWM (RBR) V.1 no.1-3 (1946).

Stations. *Milwaukee, Wisc., Membrane Press.* 1511291
ISSN: 0090-4171 LCCN: 73-641351 Beg. date: 1971
WU   UWM (RBR) No.1-3/4 (FAL1972-1976).

Steelhead. *Duluth, Minn.* 0888707
Beg. date: 1971
Ceased publication with no. 6, 1975.
WU   UWM (RBR) No.1-6 (DEC1971-1975).

Stem. *Tampa, Fla.* 1511300
ISSN: 0562-0007 Beg. date: 1961
"A magazine of poetry, prose, philosophy and religion."
WU   UWM (RBR) No.1-7 (DEC9161-AUG/OCT1963).

Stephens College, Columbia, Missouri. Open places. *See* 1499527
Open places. Columbia, Mo., etc., Stephens College.

Steppenwolf. *Omaha, Neb.* 1511313
ISSN: 0081-5462 LCCN: 66-9866 Beg. date: 1966
"A journal of poetry and opinion."
WU   UWM (RBR) No.1-5
(WIN1965/1966-WIN1973/1974).

Stereo headphones. *Kersey, Eng.* 1511326
ISSN: 0039-1212 Beg. date: 1969
"An occasional magazine of the new poetries" (varies).
WU   UWM (RBR) V.1 no.1-7 (SPR1969-SPR1976).

Stetson University, Deland, Florida. Creative Writing 1440663
Workshop.   Impetus. *See* Impetus. Deland, Fla.

Stile. *Hinckley, Ohio [etc.].* 1511339
Beg. date: 1975
WU   UWM (RBR) No.1-3 (SPR1975-OCT1976).

The Stiletto. *New York, The Stiletto Pub. Co.* 1511341
Beg. date: 1900   End date: 1901
"A magazine with no fads."
Ceased publication with vol. 1 no. 6, Feb. 1901.
WU   UWM (RBR) V.1 no.1-6 (AUG1900-FEB1901).

Sting. *Folkestone, Kent, Eng.* 1511354
WU   UWM (RBR) No.3 (1971).

Stinktree. *Memphis, Stinktree Press.* 1511367
Beg. date: 1972
WU   UWM (RBR) No.1-3 (FEB1972-JUL1973).

Stolen paper review. *Tempe, Ariz.* 151137A
ISSN: 0585-3664 LCCN: 73-1994 Beg. date: 1963   End date: 1965
Ceased publication with no. 3, Spring 1965.
WU   UWM (RBR) No.1-3 (SPR1963-SPR1965).

The Stone. *San Francisco.* 1511382
Beg. date: 1967
WU   UWM (RBR) V.1-v.5 no.1 (1967-1975).

Stone cloud. *See* Stonecloud. Berkeley, etc. 1511417

Stone country. *Madison, N.J., Stone Country Press.* 1511395
Beg. date: 1974
Supersedes Patterns, ISSN 0031-3211, with 1974.
WU   UWM (RBR) V.74-v.77 no.2 (1974-1977).

Stone drum. *Huntsville, Tex., Stone Drum Press.* 151142A
Beg. date: 1972
WU   UWM (RBR) V.1 no.1-3 (SPR1972-1974).

Stone soup poetry. *Boston, Mass.* 1511432
Beg. date: 1971
WU   UWM (RBR) No.1-29 (JUL1971-1976).

Stone wind. *Chicago, Stone Wind Publications.* 1511445
WU   UWM (RBR) No.1-4,9 (APR1971-1975).

Stonecloud. *Berkeley, etc.* 1511404
Beg. date: 1972
A joint effort of staffs at Stanford, the University of Southern California, and the University of California at Berkeley and Santa Cruz.
WU   UWM (RBR) No.1-6 (1972-1976).

Stonehenge. *Birmingham, Ala., Little Mule Press.* 1529657
Beg. date: 1974
"A non political, non partisan, non weather broadside."
WU   UWM (RBR) No.1 (MAY1974).

Stoney lonesome. *Bloomington, Ind., Nosferatu Press.* 1511458
Beg. date: 1969
WU   UWM (RBR) No.1-6 (1969-1976).

Stony Brook. *Stony Brook, N.Y., The Stony Brook Poetics Foundation.* 1511460
ISSN: 0039-1794 LCCN: 78-12764 Beg. date: 1968
WU   UWM (RBR) No.1/2-3/4 (FAL1968-FAL1969).

Stony Brook Poetics Foundation. Stony Brook. *See* Stony 1511473
Brook. Stony Brook, N.Y., The Stony Brook Poetics Foundation.

Stooge. *Albuquerque, N.M. [etc.].* 1511486
Beg. date: 1967
WU   UWM (RBR) No.1-14 (1967-1975?).

Story quarterly. *See* StoryQuarterly. *Chicago,* 1519965

StoryQuarterly. *Chicago, Story Quarterly, Inc.* 1511499
LCCN: sc77-139 Beg. date: 1975
WU   UWM (RBR) No.1-5 (1975-1977).

Strange faeces. *London [etc.], The Strange Faeces Press.* 1511508
Beg. date: 1971
WU   UWM (RBR) No.1-12/13,16-18 (1971-NOV1975).

The Stratford magazine. *Boston, The Stratford Co.* 1511510
LCCN: 36-22295 Beg. date: 1926   End date: 1932
"A periodical for creative readers."
Supersedes Stratford monthly.
Ceased publication with vol. 7 no. 3, April 1932.
WU   UWM (RBR) V.1 no.1,3 (FEB-APR1926).

Strath. *Bletchley, Buckinghamshire, Eng.* 1511523
Beg. date: 1972
WU   UWM (RBR) No.1-8 (AUT1972-APR1975).

Street cries. *Old Westbury, N.Y.* 1511536
Beg. date: 1973
Title varies: no. 1, 1973, Street cries and whispers.
WU   UWM (RBR) No.1-4 (1973-1975).

Street cries and whispers. *See* Street cries. Old Westbury, 1511549
N.Y.

Street magazine. *New York.* 1511551
WU   UWM (RBR) V.1 no.2-v.2 no.2
(1974-1976).

Strivers' row. *Baltimore, Dept. of English, The Johns Hopkins University.* 1132382
ISSN: 0094-0674 LCCN: 74-644113 Beg. date: 1974   End date: 1974
Ceased publication with no. 1, Spring 1974.
WU   UWM (RBR) No.1 (SPR1974).

Stroker. *New York.* 1511564
Beg. date: 1974
WU   UWM (RBR) V.1-v.2 no.2 (no.1-5)
(JUL1974-WIN1976/1977).

The Struggle. *Newark, N.J.* 1511577
Beg. date: 1954
WU   UWM (RBR) V.1 no.1-6 (FEB-JUL1954).

Students for a Democratic Society. *See* Activist. Oberlin, 0707715
Ohio, Students for a Democratic Society.

Students for a Democratic Society.   Caw. *See* Caw! New 1197256
York, Students for a Democratic Society.

Studies in the 20th century. *See* Studies in the twentieth 1483697
century. Troy, N.Y.,

Studies in the twentieth century. *Troy, N.Y., Russell Sage College.* 0710264
ISSN: 0039-3835 LCCN: 78-11069 Beg. date: 1968   End date: 1975
Ceased publication with no. 16, 1975.
WU   UWM (RBR) No.1-2,4-6 (SPR1968-FAL1970).

Studies on the Left; a journal of research, social theory and review. *Madison.* 0710396
ISSN: 0585-7449 Beg. date: 1959   End date: 1967
Continued —

Continued —
Ceased publication with vol. 7 no.2, March/April 1967. Superseded by Socialist revolution with Jan./Feb. 1970.
WU   UWM (RBR) V.1 no.2-4; v.2 no.2-3; v.3-6 (WIN1960-JUL/AUG1966).

Studio news. *Friend, Neb.* 152966A
LCCN: 47-41026   Beg. date: 1942
Some issues include songs with piano accompaniment.
WU   UWM (RBR) Winter 1942-Dec. 1943; v.2-21 (1944-JUN1963).

Stuffed crocodile. *London, Ont., Killaly Press.* 1511592
ISSN: 0315-0496   Beg. date: 1972
WU   UWM (RBR) V.1-v.4 no.4 (FEB1972-1977).

Stump. *Athens, Ohio.* 1511601
WU   UWM (RBR) One issue in 1973.

The Stylus. *Granite City, Ill.* 1511614
ISSN: 0491-3744   LCCN: 63-26908   Beg. date: 1950   End date: 1956
"A magazine for young writers."
Ceased publication with vol. 7 no. 4, Oct. 1956.
WU   UWM (RBR) V.1 no.2-v.7 (APR1950-OCT1956).

Subterraneans. *Tokyo.* 1529672
Each number also has a distinctive title.
WU   UWM (RBR) No.5-6 (1969).

Subvers. *Ijmuiden, Netherlands.* 1511627
Beg. date: 1970
"Tijdschrift voor [onder meer] konkrete poëzie."
WU   UWM (RBR) No.[1]-11 (OCT1970-JUL1973).

Success. *Dorchester, Dorset, Eng.* 151163A
ISSN: 0049-2442   Beg. date: 1968
WU   UWM (RBR) No.1-9 (AUG/SEP1968-DEC1969/JAN1970).

Suck-egg mule. *Taos, N.M.* 1511642
ISSN: 0562-4827   Beg. date: 1951   End date: 1952
"A recalcitrant beast."
Ceased publication with no. 5, [1952].
WU   UWM (RBR) No.1-5 ([1951-1952]).

Suction. *Iowa City, Ia.* 1511655
Beg. date: 1969
WU   UWM (RBR) No.1-2 (MAY1969-n.d.).

Sueños: Dreams. *Los Altos, Calif.* 1511668
Beg. date: 1963
WU   UWM (RBR) No.1-3 (1963-1971).

The Sullivan slough review. *Edmonds, Wash., The Sullivan Slough Press.* 1511683
Beg. date: 1969
WU   UWM (RBR) No.1 (SPR1969).

Sum. *Buffalo, N.Y. [etc.].* 1511696
ISSN: 0562-5718   Beg. date: 1963   End date: 1965
Ceased publication with no. 7, April 1965.
WU   UWM (RBR) No.1-7 (DEC1963-APR1965).

Sumac. *Fremont, Mich., The Sumac Press.* 1511705
ISSN: 0039-4939   LCCN: 78-2254   Beg. date: 1968
WU   UWM (RBR) V.1-v.4 no.1 (FAL1968-FAL1971).

Sumus. *Chapel Hill, N.C.* 1511718
Beg. date: 1970
WU   UWM (RBR) No.1 (DEC1970).

Sun. *New York, Sun Press.* 1511720
Beg. date: 1971
Continues Sundial with vol. 3 nos. 2/3, Summer 1971.
WU   UWM (RBR) V.3 no.2/3-v.4 no.2 (SUM1971-SPR1975).

Sun. *San Francisco.* 1511733
ISSN: 0562-5920   Beg. date: 1961
"A monthly poetry journal."
WU   UWM (RBR) No.1-9 (1961-1962).

Sun and moon. *[College Park, Md., s.n.].* 146781A
ISSN: 0362-3742   LCCN: 76-643126   Beg. date: 1976
"A quarterly of literature and art."
WU   UWM (RBR) No.1-3 (WIN-SUM1976).

Sun-lotus haiku. *Manchester, N.H.* 1511761
Beg. date: 1976
WU   UWM (RBR) No.1-3 (SPR1976-1977).

Sunbury. *Bronx, N.Y.* 1511774
Beg. date: 1974
WU   UWM (RBR) V.1 no.1-3; v.2 no.1-2 (no.4-5) (APR1974-SUM1976).

Sunday clothes. *Hermosa, S.D.* 0711886
ISSN: 0090-4961   LCCN: 73-641607   Beg. date: 1972
"A magazine of fine arts."
WU   UWM (RBR) V.1 no.2-v.5 (SPR/SUM1972-WIN1976).

Sundial. *New York.* 1511787
Issued by the students of Columbia University and Barnard College.
WU   UWM (RBR) V.2 no.3; v.3 no.1 (1969).

The Sunset palms hotel. *Santa Monica, Calif.* 151179A
ISSN: 0145-9015
WU   UWM (RBR) V.1-v.3 no.2 (SPR1973-SUM1975).

Sunsprout. *Houston, The Poet's Workshop.* 1511809
WU   UWM (RBR) V.1 no.3 (1975).

The Sunstone review. *Sante Fe, N.M., Ellis Research Associates.* 1511811
LCCN: 74-617741   Beg. date: 1971
WU   UWM (RBR) V.1-v.6 no.2 (FAL1971-1977).

Suntemples. *La Jolla, Calif., Inca Press.* 1511824
WU   UWM (RBR) V.1 (FEB-NOV1974).

The Surfside poetry review. *Surfside, Calif.* 1511837
WU   UWM (RBR) V.2-v.3 no.1 (no.5-7) (WIN1974-SPR/SUM1975).

Surrealist transformaction. *Sidmouth, Devon, Eng., Transformaction.* 151184A
ISSN: 0039-6168
In English and French.
WU   UWM (RBR) No.1-7 (n.d.-1976).

Surrealist transformation. See Surrealist transformaction. 1511852
Sidmouth, Devon, Eng., Transformaction.

Survival. *Berkeley, Calif.* 1511865
Beg. date: 1970
WU   UWM (RBR) V.1 no.1 (APR1970).

Survival. *New York.* 1511878
ISSN: 0491-6328   Beg. date: 1950   End date: 1950
Ceased publication with vol. 1 no. 1, Autumn 1950.
WU   UWM (RBR) No.1 (1950).

Swing. *New York, A Birth Press Publication.* 1511880
ISSN: 0562-9012   Beg. date: 1960   End date: 1961
Ceased publication with no. 4, Fall 1961.
WU   UWM (RBR) No.1-4 (WIN1960-FAL1961).

The Swordsman review. *Los Angeles, Swordsman Pub. Co.* 1511893
Beg. date: 1966
WU   UWM (RBR) V.1 no.2-4 (OCT/DEC1966-APR/JUN1967).

Sydney. University. Department of English.   Balcony; the 1430642
Sydney review. See Balcony; the Sydney review. Sydney, Dept. of English, University of Sydney.

Sydney review. See Balcony; the Sydney review. Sydney, 1430655
Dept. of English, University of Sydney.

Symbol. *Shildon, Durham, Eng.* 1511902
WU   UWM (RBR) Nov. 1968-Oct. 1969.

Symposium. *Colombo.* 1511915
"A magazine of literature, art and film."
WU   UWM (RBR) V.2 no.3/4 (1950).

Symposium; a critical review. *Concord, The Symposium press, incorporated.* 0718730
LCCN: 32-3459
V. 4: New York, Kraus Reprint.
WU   UWM (RBR) V.1-4 (1930-1933).

Symptom. *Las Cruces, N.M., Hut Publications.* 1511928
ISSN: 0586-3147
WU   UWM (RBR) V.1 no.1-2 (DEC1965-1966); Apr. 1966.

Synapse. *Berkeley, Calif.* 1511930
Beg. date: 1964
Suspended publication   -Summer 1972.
Resumed publication with Fall 1972.
WU   UWM (RBR) No.1-4 (SPR1964-MAY1965); Autumn 1967; Spring 1968; Fall 1972.

Synapsis. *Toronto, Ganglia Press.* 1529685
WU   UWM (RBR) No.1 (n.d.).

Syracuse. *Syracuse, N.Y.* 1511943
Issued by the undergraduates of Syracuse University.
WU   UWM (RBR) V.1 no.2-4; v.2 no.2-3; v.3 no.1-2 (DEC1958-DEC1960/JAN1961).

Syracuse University. Department of English.   Thoth. See 1512359
Thoth. Syracuse, N.Y., Department of English, Syracuse University.

Syzygy. *Cincinnati, Cincinnati Women's Press, Inc.* 1511956
"Short fiction and sketches."
WU   UWM (RBR) 1976.

T

T R. *See* Transatlantic review. *Rome, N. Y.* 0736550

T R A. *See* Toward revolutionary art. *San Francisco.* 1512816

Tagus. *Oxford.* 1510607
ISSN: 0039-8950 Beg. date: 1970
WU   UWM (RBR) V.1 no.1 (WIN1970).

Talaria. *Cincinnati.* 151061A
Beg. date: 1936 End date: 1950
"A quarterly of poetry."
Ceased publication with vol. 15 no. 2, Summer 1950.
WU   UWM (RBR) V.2 no.3-4; v.3 no.1; v.4 no.1; v.5 no.1; v.14 no.1 (AUT1937-WIN1949).

Tales. *St. Louis, Mo., Tales Pub. Co.* 1348992
WU   UWM (RBR) Summer 1976; v.3 no.1; v.4 no.2 (FAL1976-WIN1976/1977).

Taliesin. *Providence, R.I., Evanescent Pub. Co.* 1510635
Beg. date: 1967
WU   UWM (RBR) No.1-2 (1967-1969).

Talisman. *Denver.* 1510648
ISSN: 0492-1860 Beg. date: 1952 End date: 1959
Ceased publication with no. 13, Winter/Spring 1959.
WU   UWM (RBR) No.1-13 (SUM1952-WIN/SPR1959).

Talisman. *Lincoln, Neb.* 1510650
WU   UWM (RBR) No.1-10 (1973-1976).

Talisman bulletin. *See* Popular talisman bulletin. *Chicago.* 1509929

Talon. *La Crosse, Wisc.* 1510663
Issued by the students of the University of Wisconsin, La Crosse.
WU   UWM (RBR) No.1-2 (SPR-SUM1973); v.2 no.1 (1973).

Talon. *Vancouver, B.C.* 1510676
ISSN: 0082-1543 Beg. date: 1963
WU   UWM (RBR) Spring 1964-Fall 1965; v.3 no.2-v.5 no.1 (1966-1968).

Tamarack review. *Toronto.* 0721277
ISSN: 0039-9256
Indexes: Vols. 1-20, with v. 21.
WU   UWM (RBR) No.1-49,53-71 (1956-1977).

Tamarisk. *Erith, Kent, Eng.* 1510689
Beg. date: 1968
"Quarterly poetry magazine."
WU   UWM (RBR) No.1-2 (MAR-JUN1968).

Tambour. *Paris.* 072128A
LCCN: 32-15556
WU   UWM (RBR) [V.1-8 (1929-1930)].

Tamesis. *Reading, Berkshire, Eng.* 1510691
ISSN: 0494-6073
"A literary magazine."
Issued by the Students Union of Reading University.
WU   UWM (RBR) 1973.

Tampa, Florida. University. Poetry review. *See* Poetry review. *Tampa, Fla., University of Tampa.* 1509160

Tampa, Florida. University. U T review. *See* U T review. *Tampa, Fla., University of Tampa.* 1516617

The Tanager. *Grinnell, Iowa, English and Journalism Depts., Grinnell College.* 1510700
"A bi-monthly review."
WU   UWM (RBR) V.15 no.4-5; v.17 no.1; v.21 no.4; v.22 no.1-2; v.23 no.1 (APR1940-OCT1947).

Tangent. *New Malden, Surrey, Eng., Tangent Books.* 1510726
Beg. date: 1976
WU   UWM (RBR) No.1 (WIN1975/1976).

Tangent. *Wadsworth, Ohio, Estuary Press.* 1510739
ISSN: 0039-9388 Beg. date: 1966
WU   UWM (RBR) V.1-v.4 no.1 (SPR1966-SUM1972).

Tangents. *Hollywood.* 072149A
ISSN: 0039-9396 Beg. date: 1965 End date: 1970
Ceased publication with vol. 4 no. 6, 1970.
WU   UWM (RBR) V.1-v.2 no.7; v.3-v.4 no.4/5/6 (OCT1965-JAN/MAR1970).

Tansy. *Lawrence, Kan., Tansy Publications.* 1529698
Beg. date: 1976
Nos. 1-3, 1976, are monographs.
WU   UWM (RBR) No.1-8 (SPR1970-1974); no.1-3 (1976).

Tantalus. *Honolulu.* 1510741
Beg. date: 1974
WU   UWM (RBR) No.1-2 (SPR-SUM1974).

Tarasque. *Cotgrave, Nottingham, Eng., Tarasque Press.* 1510754
ISSN: 0039-9647 Beg. date: 1966
WU   UWM (RBR) No.1-10 (1966-SUM1969).

Target. *Peterborough, Eng.* 1510767
ISSN: 0082-1721 Beg. date: 1965 End date: 1966
Continued by Euphoria with no. 5, 1967.
WU   UWM (RBR) No.1,4 ([1966]).

Targets, a quarterly of poetry. *Sandia Park, New Mexico.* 0721684
Ceased with no. 15.
WU   UWM (RBR) No.1-15 (DEC1959-SEP1963).

Teamwork. *Edinburgh, Scot.* 151077A
ISSN: 0497-0098
WU   UWM (RBR) V.1 no.2-6 (SEP/OCT1964-MAY/JUN1965).

Teangadoir. A magazine of current Canadian poetry. *Toronto.* 0723759
Beg. date: 1953
WU   UWM (RBR) Ser. 2: v.1 no.5 (no.41) (MAY151963).

Tejas. *Barry, Tex.* 1510782
ISSN: 0040-2214
WU   UWM (RBR) Jan., Apr., July 1967; no.5-8,13 (OCT1967-OCT1969).

Telephone. *New York.* 1510795
ISSN: 0147-5452 Beg. date: 1970
WU   UWM (RBR) No.1-11 (1970-1975).

Telescope. *Kingston, Ont.* 1510804
WU   UWM (RBR) Aug., Sept. 1961; Jan.-Sept., Nov.-Dec. 1962; Jan.-June, Aug.-Dec. 1963; Jan.-May, July/Aug.-Nov./Dec. 1964; 1965; Jan./Feb.-Aug. 1966.

Tempest. *London.* 1510817
Beg. date: 1943 End date: 1943
Ceased publication with ser. 1, Oct. 1943.
WU   UWM (RBR) Ser. 1 (OCT1943).

Tempest. *Milwaukee, University of Wisconsin, Milwaukee.* 151082A
Beg. date: 1969
WU   UWM (RBR) V.1 no.1 (SPR1969).

Tempo. *Tecumseh, Ont., Snowfield Publications.* 1510845
"For young poets of all ages" (varies).
WU   UWM (RBR) V.1 no.6; v.2 no.1-2 (SEP1969-JAN/FEB1970).

Ten point five. *See* 10 point 5. *Eugene, Ore., Oz Publications, Inc.* 1512004

Tennessee poetry journal. *Martin, Tenn., University of Tennessee.* 0725983
ISSN: 0040-3369 Beg. date: 1967
Ceased with vol. 4 no. 3, Spring 1971.
WU   UWM (RBR) V.1-v.4 no.3 (FAL1967-SPR1971).

Texas. State College for Women, Denton. Daedalian monthly. *See* Daedalian quarterly. *Denton, Tex.* 1431898

Texas. State College for Women, Denton. Daedalian quarterly. *See* Daedalian quarterly. *Denton, Tex.* 1431872

Texas. Stephen F. Austin State University, Nacogdoches. Re: artes liberales. *See* Re: artes liberales. *Nacogdoches, Tex., School of Liberal Arts, Stephen F. Austin State University.* 1508179

Texas. Stephen F. Austin State University, Nacogdoches. Re: arts & letters. *See* Re: arts & letters. *Nacogdoches, Tex., School of Liberal Arts, Stephen F. Austin State University.* 1508194

The Texas slough. *El Paso, Tex., Altruistic Enterprises.* 1512099
Beg. date: 1975
WU   UWM (RBR) No.1 (1975); 1976.

Thames. *London, University of London Literary Society.* 1512108
ISSN: 0493-0495 Beg. date: 1953
"Literary magazine - University of London" (varies).
WU   UWM (RBR) 1959, 1962.

The. *Boulder, Colo.* 1512123
WU   UWM (RBR) No.2-10,12-13 (1967-n.d.).

Theatre and cinema symposium. [n.p.]. 1512136
    Beg. date: 1969
    WU   UWM (RBR) V.1 no.1 (SUM1969).

Theo. Utica, N.Y., etc. 1512149
    ISSN: 0495-4416 Beg. date: 1964
    WU   UWM (RBR) V.1 no.1-3 (1964-1965).

Theodor Herzl Foundation. *See* Midstream, a quarterly Jewish review. New York, Theodor Herzl Foundation. 0729730

Therapy 14. Los Angeles, Poetry Therapy Institute. 1512151
    Beg. date: 1975
    "Poems from a workshop."
    WU   UWM (RBR) No.1 (1975).

Therapy fourteen. *See* Therapy 14. Los Angeles, Poetry Therapy Institute. 1512164

Thin line. Ann Arbor, Mich., The Thin Line Press. 151218A
    ISSN: 0495-4777 Beg. date: 1962
    WU   UWM (RBR) No.1 (1962).

Things. New York. 1512192
    ISSN: 0563-4660 LCCN: 64-9476 Beg. date: 1964 End date: 1966
    Ceased publication with no. 3, Spring 1966.
    Superseded by Hanging loose with Fall 1966.
    WU   UWM (RBR) No.1-3 (FAL1964-SPR1966).

The Third coast archives. Milwaukee. 1512201
    Beg. date: 1976
    WU   UWM (RBR) No.1-9 (FEB1976-1977).

Third rail. Los Angeles. 1512214
    Beg. date: 1975
    WU   UWM (RBR) No.1-2 (1975-1976).

Third rail. México, D.F. 1512227
    ISSN: 0495-4831 Beg. date: 1961
    WU   UWM (RBR) No.1-2 (1961).

Third thing. *See* 3rd thing. Edgewater, N.J. 1512086

Thirteen American poets. *See* Move. Preston, Eng. 1497270

Thirteenth moon. *See* 13th moon. New York. 151202A

This. Franconia, N.H. [etc.]. 151223A
    Beg. date: 1971
    Also called This magazine.
    WU   UWM (RBR) No.1-6,8 (WIN1971-SPR1977).

This and... New York [etc.]. 1512255
    WU   UWM (RBR) No.4-12 (1966-1969).

This issue. Atlanta, The McKee Pub. Co. 1512268
    Beg. date: 1970
    "The magazine book for stories."
    WU   UWM (RBR) No.2-3 (1971).

This magazine. *See* This. Franconia, N.H. [etc.]. 1512242

This morning the sea and our island. Reading, Pa. 1512270
    Beg. date: 1971
    WU   UWM (RBR) No.1 (1971).

This quarter. Paris. 1512283
    Beg. date: 1925 End date: 1932
    Publication suspended Summer 1927-June 1929.
    Ceased publication with vol. 5 no. 2, Oct./Dec. 1932.
    WU   UWM (RBR) V.1-v.5 no.1 (1925-SEP1932).

This trend. Philadelphia. 151265A
    Beg. date: 1948 End date: 1948
    Ceased publication with vol. 1 no. 2, Summer 1948.
    WU   UWM (RBR) V.1 no.1-2 (WIN-SUM1948).

This unrest. Oxford, Eng., Kemp Hall Press Limited. 1512296
    WU   UWM (RBR) 1934.

Thistle. Derry, Pa., The Rock Society, Inc. 1512305
    Beg. date: 1976
    WU   UWM (RBR) V.1-v.2 no.1 (1976-1977).

Thistle. Glasgow. 1512318
    ISSN: 0495-503X
    WU   UWM (RBR) No.2,4 (n.d.-n.d.).

The Thistle. New Rochelle, N.Y., Croscup & Sterling Co. 1512320
    LCCN: 10-21447 Beg. date: 1902 End date: 1903
    Ceased publication with vol. 1 no. 11, Jan. 1903.
    WU   UWM (RBR) V.1 no.8 (OCT1902).

Thoth. Madison, Wisc. 1512333
    Beg. date: 1966
    WU   UWM (RBR) V.1 no.1-2 (1966).

Thoth. Syracuse, N.Y., Department of English, Syracuse University. 1512346
    ISSN: 0040-6430 LCCN: 66-7906 Beg. date: 1959
    "Journal of the English Graduate Group."
    None published 1960.
    WU   UWM (RBR) V.3 no.1-2; v.7 no.2 (WIN1962-SPR1966).

Thought and action. Amityville, N.Y. 1512361
    ISSN: 0493-1440 Beg. date: 1951
    WU   UWM (RBR) V.1 no.1 (1951).

Thoughts on blackness. Trenton, N.J., The Black Cultural Center, Inc. 1512374
    Beg. date: 1970
    WU   UWM (RBR) V.1 no.1 (WIN1970).

Three arts quarterly. *See* 3 arts quarterly. London, Woodstock Gallery. 1528299

Three cent pulp. *See* 3 (cent) pulp. Vancouver, B.C., Pulp Press. 1511971

Three hands. Washington, D.C. 1512387
    ISSN: 0493-1491 LCCN: 62-42985 Beg. date: 1951
    WU   UWM (RBR) No.1-7 (1951-1954).

Three hundred and sixty five days of the year. *See* 365 days of the year. Warndon, Worcester, Eng. 1512058

Three hundred sixty five days of the year. *See* 365 days of the year. Warndon, Worcester, Eng. 1512060

Three Rivers poetry journal. Pittsburgh, Three Rivers Press. 151239A
    ISSN: 0362-4846 LCCN: 77-648979 Beg. date: 1973
    WU   UWM (RBR) No.1-9 (1973-1977).

Threshold. Belfast, Lyric Players. 0730986
    ISSN: 0040-6562 Beg. date: 1957
    WU   UWM (RBR) V.2 no.2; v.3 no.4 (SUM1958,WIN1959/1960).

Threshold. New York, International Student Service. 1512411
    Beg. date: 1941 End date: 1943
    Ceased publication with vol. 3 no. 3, Feb. 1943.
    WU   UWM (RBR) V.1 no.1 (OCT1941).

Throb. Manhattan Beach, Calif., The Horsehead Nebula Press. 1512424
    Beg. date: 1971
    WU   UWM (RBR) No.1-2 (SPR-FAL1971).

Thrush. London. 0731019
    V. 1, no. 2, v. 2, no. 2 contain a list of contents of preceding volumes.
    WU   UWM (RBR) V.1-2 (no.1-6) (DEC1909-MAY1910).

Thrush, a periodical for the publication of original poetry; edited by T. Mullett Ellis. London. 0731021
    WU   UWM (RBR) 1901-Jan. 1902.

Thrust. Summerland, Calif. 1512437
    ISSN: 0040-6627
    WU   UWM (RBR) No.25 (NOV241966).

Thumb. Athens, Ohio. 151244A
    Beg. date: 1959
    WU   UWM (RBR) No.1-3 (1959).

The Thunder City press broadside series. Birmingham, Ala. 1512452
    Beg. date: 1975
    WU   UWM (RBR) No.1-6,8,10,12 (SEP1975-APR1976).

Tide. Montreal, The Wandering Albatross Press. 1512465
    WU   UWM (RBR) No.4-7 (AUT1970-1971).

Tide Collective. Lesbian tide. *See* Lesbian tide. Santa Monica, Calif. [etc.], Tide Collective. 1492657

The Tiger's eye. New York, etc., Tiger's Eye Pub. Co. 1512478
    LCCN: 54-29272 Beg. date: 1947 End date: 1949
    "On arts and letters."
    Ceased publication with no. 9, Oct. 1949.
    WU   UWM (RBR) No.1-9 (OCT1947-OCT1949).

Tight rope. *See* Tightrope. Oneonta, N.Y., Swamp Press. 1512493

Tightrope. Oneonta, N.Y., Swamp Press. 1512480
    Beg. date: 1975
    WU   UWM (RBR) V.1 no.1-5 (1975-1977).

Time & tide. Lorton, Va. 1512502
    WU   UWM (RBR) V.22 no.4-10; v.23 no.1-4 (APR1968-SEP/OCT1969).

Time and tide. *See* Time & tide. Lorton, Va. 1512515

The Time machine. London. 1512530
ISSN: date: 1970
"A magazine devoted to literature and the arts."
WU   UWM (RBR) No.1 (SPR1970).

Time stream. *See* Timestream. Strathfield, Eng. 1512556

Time to pause. Nampa, Idaho. 1512528
WU   UWM (RBR) Autumn/Winter 1969-Autumn/Winter 1971.

Timestream. Strathfield, Eng. 1512543
"Poetry magazine."
WU   UWM (RBR) Three unnumbered, undated issues.

Ting pa magazine. Kathmandu, Nepal, Dreamweapon Press. 1512569
WU   UWM (RBR) No.3 (WIN1973).

The Tiresian. New Orleans, Tulane University. 1512571
ISSN: 0495-6516   Beg. date: 1965
WU   UWM (RBR) V.1-v.2 no.1 (SPR1965-FAL1966).

Tish. Vancouver, B.C. 1512597
ISSN: 0040-8158   Beg. date: 1961
"A magazine of Vancouver poetry" (varies).
WU   UWM (RBR) No.2-41,43 (OCT071961-1968?).

Titmouse review. Vancouver, B.C. 1512606
ISSN: 0315-0720   Beg. date: 1972
WU   UWM (RBR) No.1-6 (1972-1976).

Tlaloc. London. 1512662
ISSN: 0563-6086   Beg. date: 1964   End date: 1970
Ceased publication with no. 22, 1970.
WU   UWM (RBR) No.1-13,15-22 (DEC1964-1970).

To-day. London, Eng. 0957496
LCCN: 19-19003   Beg. date: 1917   End date: 1923
Supersedes To-day (Weekly).
Ceased publication with vol. 10 (no. 58), March 1923.
United with Life and letters to form Life and letters incorporating To-day.
WU   UWM (RBR) V.1-6 (no.1-36) (MAR1917-FEB1920).

Together. Maidstone, Kent, Eng. 1512688
WU   UWM (RBR) Summer 1971.

The Token. Birmingham, Ala. 1512690
ISSN: 0495-7555   Beg. date: 1962
WU   UWM (RBR) V.1 no.2-3; v.2 no.1 (FAL1962-SPR1963).

The Tolar Creek syndicate. Tucumcari [etc.], N.M. 151270A
ISSN: 0040-9030   Beg. date: 1968
WU   UWM (RBR) V.1 no.1-13 (1968-1975).

Tolkien Society. Bulletin. *See* Anduril, magazine of fantasy. Bushey, Eng. 1432639

Tom Veitch magazine. San Francisco. 1512712
Beg. date: 1970
WU   UWM (RBR) No.1-4 (1970-1971).

Tomorrow. New York. 0734787
LCCN: 45-49176 rev   End date: 1951
Ceased publication with vol. 10, Aug. 1951.
Superseded by Tomorrow: quarterly review of psychical research with Autumn 1952.
Index last no.
WU   UWM (RBR) V.1 no.1; v.2 no.8 (SEP1941-APR1943).

Tomorrow. Oxford, Keble College, Oxford University. 1512725
ISSN: 0495-8349   Beg. date: 1959   End date: 1960
"A review of literature."
Ceased publication with no. 4, 1960.
WU   UWM (RBR) No.2-4 (OCT/NOV1959-1960).

Tone. Buffalo, N.Y. 1529707
Beg. date: 1933   End date: 1935
"Modern poetry."
Ceased publication with Jan. 1935.
WU   UWM (RBR) No.2-3 (DEC1933-MAR1934).

Toothpaste. Iowa City, Iowa, Toothpaste Press. 1512740
Beg. date: 1971
WU   UWM (RBR) No.1-7 (1971-1972).

Toothpick, Lisbon & the Orca Islands. Seattle. 1512753
WU   UWM (RBR) V.2-v.3 no.1 (no.3-5) (FAL1972-1973).

Tor. *See* Gate; international review of literature and art in English and German. London. 0735214

Tornado. Bombay. 1512766
ISSN: 0040-9499   Beg. date: 1967
"The mag of geniuses."
WU   UWM (RBR) No.5 (AUG1969).

Toronto. University. Erindale College. Impulse. *See* Impulse. Toronto, Erindale College, University of Toronto. 1442675

Toronto. University. Erindale College. Laomedon review. 1492397
See Laomedon review. Mississaugo, Ontario, Erindale College, Univ. of Toronto.

Toronto. University. Graduate English Association. 1434625
Descant. *See* Descant. Toronto, Graduate English Assn., University of Toronto.

Toronto. University. Innis College. Writ. *See* Writ. Toronto, 151495A
Writing Lab, Innis College, University of Toronto.

Totem. Pasadena, Calif., Division of the Humanities and 1512779
Social Sciences, California Institute of Technology, Pasadena.
ISSN: 0495-9329   Beg. date: 1951
WU   UWM (RBR) V.1 no.3; v.2 no.1-3; v.3 no.1; v.4 no.1-2; Mar. 1968; 1969: one issue; v.5 no.1-2; v.6 no.1 (FAL1958-APR1972).

Tottel's. San Francisco. 1512781
WU   UWM (RBR) No.7-10,13-16 (DEC1971-n.d.).

Toucan. Kent, Ohio. 1512794
Beg. date: 1967
WU   UWM (RBR) V.1 no.1-2; v.2 no.1-2/3; v.3 no.1-3 (SPR1967-1972).

Touchstone. [n.p.], Office of Information Services. 152971A
WU   UWM (RBR) V.4 (n.d.).

Touchstone. Newport, Tenn., Jim Stokely. 1529722
Beg. date: 1977
WU   UWM (RBR) No.1-3 (SUM1977-AUT1977).

Touchstone. Toronto, Peter Cameron. 1529735
ISSN: 0564-7681   Beg. date: 1965
WU   UWM (RBR) No.2 (SEP1965).

Touchstone; the creative literary monthly. New York. 0735976
Ceased publication with vol. 1 no. 3, 1947.
WU   UWM (RBR) V.1 no.1-2 (NOV-DEC1947).

Toward revolutionary art. San Francisco. 1512803
Beg. date: 1971
Also called T R A.
WU   UWM (RBR) No.6-7 (v.2 no.2-v.3 no.1) (1975-1976).

The Tower. Clarksville, Tenn. 1512829
"A literary anthology."
"Sponsored by the English Department of Austin Peay State University, Clarksville, Tenn."
WU   UWM (RBR) 1969, 1973, 1975.

The Tower. Hamilton, Ont., Robert Duncan & Co. Ltd. 1512844
ISSN: 0495-9701   Beg. date: 1952
"Poems by friends and associates of McMaster University."
WU   UWM (RBR) No.3-12 (1953-1963).

Tower smiling. Los Angeles, Zen Cimarron Center of Rinzai-ji. 1512857
ISSN: 0040-991X   Beg. date: 1961
WU   UWM (RBR) Jan. 1969; Winter 1975/1976-Fall 1976.

Town talk. San Francisco, Pan-Graphic Press. 1529748
WU   UWM (RBR) V.2 no.1-2,4 (AUG-DEC1965).

Townsman. *See* Scythe. London. 1512647

Trace; a chronicle of living literature. Hollywood [etc.]. 0736576
ISSN: 0564-0350   Beg. date: 1952   End date: 1970
Comprising annual directories of (English language) poetry and small literary magazines appearing throughout the world.
Ceased publication with no. 72/73, Autumn 1970.
WU   UWM (RBR) No.1-64 (JUN1952-SPR1967).

Track. Bristol, Eng. 151286A
"New poetry and prose quarterly."
WU   UWM (RBR) No.2 (FEB1967).

Tracks. Conventry, Eng., University of Warwick. 1512872
ISSN: 0041-0349   Beg. date: 1967
WU   UWM (RBR) No.1-8 (SUM1967-SUM1970).

Tractor. San Francisco, etc. 1512885
Beg. date: 1971
WU   UWM (RBR) No.1-6 (1971-1975).

The Tramp. [Anacortes, Wash.], etc. 1512898
Beg. date: 1939
WU   UWM (RBR) V.1-v.2 no.2 (SUM1939-WIN1941).

Trans/formation. New York, Wittenborn, Schultz, Inc. 1512907
ISSN: 0564-1063   Beg. date: 1950   End date: 1952
"Arts, communication, environment; a world review."
Ceased publication with no. 3, 1952.
WU   UWM (RBR) No.1-3 (1950-1952).

Transatlantic review. New York, TT. Seltzer. 0737464
LCCN: 37-6041   Beg. date: 1924   End date: 1924
Edited by F. M. Ford.
In English and French.
Ceased publication with vol. 2 no. 6, Dec. 1924.
WU   UWM (RBR) V.1-v.2 no.6 (1924).

The Transatlantic review. Rome, N. Y. 0737477
ISSN: 0041-1078   LCCN: 59-15690   Beg. date: 1959   End date: 1977
Ceased publication with no. 60, June 1977.
WU   UWM (RBR) No.1-60 (SUM1959-JUN1977).

Transfer. San Francisco, Associated Students, San Francisco State College. 1512922
ISSN: 0496-0742   Beg. date: 1956
WU   UWM (RBR) No.1-11,13-21 (1956-SPR1966).

Transformation. London, Lindsay Drummond Ltd., etc. 1512950
LCCN: A44-364   Beg. date: 1943
WU   UWM (RBR) No.1-4 (1943-1945).

Transformation. *See* Trans/formation. New York, Wittenborn, Schultz, Inc. 151291A

Transformations. Bellingham, Wash., The Bellingham Free Press. 1512963
Beg. date: 1970
WU   UWM (RBR) V.1 no.1 (1970).

The Transient. Albuquerque, N.M., The Transient Press. 1512976
Beg. date: 1974
WU   UWM (RBR) No.1-4,6 (MAY1974-1977).

Transition. Paris. 0737633
LCCN: 51-3066   Beg. date: 1948   End date: 1950
Supersedes another periodical having the same title published 1927-1938.
Publication suspended with v. 6, 1950.
WU   UWM (RBR) No.1-6 (1948-1949).

Transition. Paris; The Hague. 0737646
Suspended July 1930-Feb. 1932.
Ceased publication with Spr. 1938 issue; superseded by Vertical.
Subtitle varies.
WU   UWM (RBR) No.1-27 (SPR1927-APR/MAY1938).

Translations. Los Angeles, The Variegation Pub. Co. 150894A
ISSN: 0041-1248
Continues Comment in motion with no. 6, 1968?
WU   UWM (RBR) No.6-7 (1968?-?).

TransPacific. Yellow Springs, Ohio. 0909130
WU   UWM (RBR) V.1 no.1-4; v.2 no.5-8; v.3 no.9-10 (1969-1974).

Tree. Santa Barbara, Calif., Christopher Books. 1512989
Beg. date: 1970
WU   UWM (RBR) No.1-4 (WIN1970-WIN1974).

Trellis. Morgantown, W. Va., Trellis Press Assoc. 1512991
Beg. date: 1973
"A poetry publication for use" (varies).
WU   UWM (RBR) V.1 no.1-2 (1973-1975); suppl. Summer 1974.

Trend. New York, The Society of Teachers and Composers, Inc. 1513009
LCCN: 38-3486   Beg. date: 1932   End date: 1935
"An illustrated bi-monthly of the arts" (varies).
Suspended publication July 1933-Feb. 1934.
Ceased publication with vol. 3 no. 1, March/April 1935.
WU   UWM (RBR) V.1-v.3 no.1 (MAR/MAY1932-MAR/APR1935).

Trend. *See* This trend. Philadelphia. 1519978

Trend; a literary magazine published at the University of Chicago. Chicago. 0738653
ISSN: 0041-2309
Ceased publication with vol. 1 no. 4, Apr. 1942.
WU   UWM (RBR) V.1 no.1-2,4 (1942).

Trent University. Catalyst. *See* Catalyst. Peterborough, Ont. [etc.]. 1207175

Trenton Junior College, Trenton, New Jersey. Kelsey review. *See* Kelsey review. Trenton, N.J., Trenton Junior College. 1493833

The Trenton review. Trenton, N.J., Trenton State College. 1513011
ISSN: 0564-2027   Beg. date: 1966
"A journal of the arts, letters and contemporary life."
WU   UWM (RBR) Fall 1966.

Tri-quarterly. Evanston, Northwestern University. 0738900
ISSN: 0041-3097   LCCN: 65-3811   Beg. date: 1958
Title varies: v. 1-4 no. 2, Fall 1958-Winter 1962, Northwestern University tri-quarterly.
Includes supplements.
Indexes: No. 4-10, Fall 1965-Fall 1967, with no. 8-10.
WU   UWM (RBR) V.1-6; no.[1]-33 (FAL1958-SPR1975).

Triad. Austin, Tex., Triad Publications, Inc. 1513037
ISSN: 0564-2078   Beg. date: 1963   End date: 1964
Ceased publication with no. 3, 1964.
WU   UWM (RBR) No.1-3 (1963-1964).

Triad. New Haven, Conn. 151304A
ISSN: 0496-1897   LCCN: 59-53240   Beg. date: 1957   End date: 1959
"Poetry, art, music."
Ceased publication with no. 3, 1959.
WU   UWM (RBR) No.1-3 (9157-1959).

The Triangle. Normal, Ill. 1513052
"A student literary magazine of Illinois State University."
A publication of the Illinois State University English Dept. and the Lambda Delta Chapter of Sigma Tau Delta.
WU   UWM (RBR) V.7 (SEP1968).

Tricolor. New York, Labarthe Pub. Co., Inc. 1513078
LCCN: 47-19678   Beg. date: 1944   End date: 1945
"Tricolor is the American affiliate of La France libre."
Ceased publication with vol. 3 no. 17, Sept. 1945.
WU   UWM (RBR) V.1-v.3 no.17 (APR1944-SEP1945).

Tricon. Philadelphia, Weber-English Club, La Salle College. 1513080
WU   UWM (RBR) V.1 no.2 (SPR1958); Fall 1958.

Trident. London, Fore Publications Ltd. 1513115
WU   UWM (RBR) Mar. 1944.

Trinity archive. *See* Archive. Durham, N.C., Duke University Pub. Board. 1438231

Trinity College, Hartford. Trinity review. *See* Trinity review. Hartford, Conn. 1529763

Trinity College, Washington, D.C. Trinity College record. *See* Trinity College record. Washington, D.C., Trinity College. 1504519

Trinity College record. Washington, D.C., Trinity College. 1504506
ISSN: 0041-3054
WU   UWM (RBR) Fall 1962; Winter-Summer 1963; 1964-Summer 1967.

The Trinity review. Hartford, Conn. 1529750
"Published by the undergraduate students of Trinity College."
WU   UWM (RBR) V.8 no.3 (MAY1954).

Trio. Oxford. 1230308
ISSN: 0493-9883   Beg. date: 1952
WU   UWM (RBR) No.1-5 ([1952]-1954).

Triptych. New York, Prologue Magazine. 1513128
Beg. date: 1969
WU   UWM (RBR) [No.1] (1969).

Trobar. Brooklyn, N.Y. 1513130
ISSN: 0496-2826   Beg. date: 1960   End date: 1964
"A magazine of the new poetry."
Ceased publication with no. 5, 1964.
WU   UWM (RBR) No.1-5 (1960-1964).

Troubadour. Ross-on-Wye, Eng., etc., The Guild House. 1529776
Beg. date: 1949
"A Writers' Guild publication."
WU   UWM (RBR) No.3 (n.d.).

Troubadour, [A magazine of verse]. San Diego. 0739961
Publication suspended with volume 4.
WU   UWM (RBR) V.2 no.8 (MAY1930).

Truck. Carrboro, N.C., Truck Press. 1476626
Beg. date: 1970
WU   UWM (RBR) No.1-17 (1970-SPR1976).

True Thomas. Nacton, Suffolk, Eng., The Willow Kate Book Co. 1513156
WU   UWM (RBR) No.1-6 (n.d.-n.d.).

Trumpet. Dallas, Tom Reamy. 1513169
WU   UWM (RBR) No.3-10 (DEC1965-1969).

Tuatara. *Victoria, B.C.* 1513171
Beg. date: 1969
WU   UWM (RBR) No.1-12 (FAL1969-SUM1974).

Tufts literary magazine. *See* Literary magazine of Tufts 1493006
University. Medford, Mass., Tufts University.

Tufts University. Literary magazine of Tufts University. 1492999
See Literary magazine of Tufts University. Medford, Mass., Tufts
University.

Tufts University. Tufts literary magazine. *See* Literary 1493019
magazine of Tufts University. Medford, Mass., Tufts University.

Tulane University of Louisiana. Tiresian. *See* Tiresian. 1512584
New Orleans, Tulane University.

The Tulsa poetry quarterly. *Tulsa, Okla., South and West,* 1513184
Inc.
ISSN: 0564-4445   Beg. date: 1968
WU   UWM (RBR) V.1 no.1-4 (SPR1968-WIN1969).

Turntable and Hut. *See* Scope; a literary review. *San* 0742034
Francisco.

The Twainian. *Perry, Mo., Mark Twain Research* 0742112
Foundation.
ISSN: 0041-4573   LCCN: 45-27196   Beg. date: 1939
Began publication with the Jan. 1939 issue; publication suspended
from Jan.-May, Oct.-Dec. 1941; new ser.began publication with
the Jan. 1942 issue.
Published 1939-1941 by the Mark Twain Society of Chicago; 1942-
by the Mark Twain Association of America.
WU   UWM (RBR) O. ser. v.1-v.3 no.1
(JAN1939-JUN1941); n. ser. v.1-v.37 no.2 (JAN1942-1978).

Tweed. *Murwillumbah, N.S.W.* 1513197
Beg. date: 1972
WU   UWM (RBR) V.1-v.5 no.2 (SEP1972-1977).

Twelfth key. *London, Ont.* 1513206
ISSN: 0380-9919
Each number also has a distinctive title.
WU   UWM (RBR) June 1977.

Twelfth street. *See* 12th street. New York, Students of the 1514737
New School for Social Research.

Twelve poems. *Port Townsend, Wash., Graywolf Press.* 1513219
Beg. date: 1974
WU   UWM (RBR) V.1 no.1-3 (1974-SPR1975).

Twentieth century literature, a scholarly and critical journal. 0742229
Denver.
ISSN: 0041-462X   Beg. date: 1955
Began publication 1955.
1955-62: Kraus reprint, 1965.
WU   UWM (RBR) V.1-3 (APR1955-JAN1958).

Twentieth century verse. *[London].* 1529789
Beg. date: 1937   End date: 1939
Ceased publication with no. 18, June/July 1939.
WU   UWM (RBR) No.9 (MAR1938).

Twenty-first century. *See* 21st century. Sydney. 1512621

Twice a year; a semi-annual journal of literature, the arts, 0742307
and civil liberties. *New York.*
LCCN: 40-8785
1948, called tenth anniversary issue, has special title: Art and
action.
WU   UWM (RBR) No.1-16/17 (FAL/WIN1938-1948).

Twigs. *Floral Park, N.Y., Floral Park Manuscript Clinic.* 1513221
ISSN: 0496-6120   Beg. date: 1961
WU   UWM (RBR) V.1 no.4-6,9; v.2 no.1-2,4/5,7-9; v.3
no.1 (JUL1961-APR1964).

Twigs. *Pikeville, Ky., Pikeville College Press.* 1516513
ISSN: 0496-6120   LCCN: 79-618742   Beg. date: 1965
"Hilltop editions."
WU   UWM (RBR) No.1-7 (SUM1965-SPR1971); v.8-13
(FAL1971-SPR1977).

Two Charlies magazine. *Alameda, N.M., Scappose, Ore.* 1516526
WU   UWM (RBR) No.2 (1973).

Two cities. *Paris.* 1516539
ISSN: 0564-5743   Beg. date: 1959   End date: 1964
"La revue bilingue de Paris."
In English and French.
Publication suspended 1963-1964.
Ceased publication with no. 9, Autumn 1964.
WU   UWM (RBR) No.1-9 (APR151959-AUT1964).

Two rivers. *London, Two Rivers.* 1516541
Beg. date: 1969
"A literary quarterly."
WU   UWM (RBR) V.1 no.1-2 (WIN1969-SPR1970).

Two tone. *Salisbury, Rhodesia.* 1516554
ISSN: 0049-4917   LCCN: 74-649139
"A quarterly of Rhodesian poetry."
WU   UWM (RBR) Mar., June, Sept. 1965; v.2-v.4 no.3; v.5
no.1-3; v.6 no.1-3; v.7 no.4; v.8-v.13 no.2 (DEC1965-JUN1977).

Two worlds, a literary quarterly devoted to the increase of 0743054
the gaiety of nations. *New York.*
LCCN: 27-2748   Beg. date: 1925   End date: 1927
Title varies slightly.
Contributing editors: Arthur Symons, Ezra Pound, Ford Madox
Hueffer.
Ceased publication with vol. 3 no. 4, Oct. 1927.
WU   UWM (RBR) V.1-v.3 no.3 (1926-1927).

Typewriter. *Iowa City, Iowa.* 1516567
Beg. date: 1971
WU   UWM (RBR) No.1-7 (1971-1976).

Typographica. *London, Lund Humphries.* 0743277
ISSN: 0564-5891   Beg. date: 1949   End date: 1967
Summaries in French.
Ceased publication with ser. 2 no. 16, Dec. 1967.
WU   UWM (RBR) Ser. 2 no.8,11-16 (DEC1963-1967).

Tyro. *Minneapolis, Dept. of English, University of* 151657A
Minnesota.
ISSN: 0494-3678   Beg. date: 1952
"A collection of freshman writings."
WU   UWM (RBR) V.1-v.2 no.1 (WIN1952-WIN1953).

The Tyro; a review of the arts of painting, sculpture and 087186A
design. *London, Frank Cass [1970].*
Beg. date: 1921   End date: 1922
English Little Magazines No. 5.
Originally published by the Egoist Press, London.
WU   UWM (RBR) No.2 (n.d.).

Tzarad. *London.* 1516595
Beg. date: 1965
WU   UWM (RBR) No.1-2 (AUG1965-OCT1966).

U

U C L poetry. London, Poetry Workshop Seminar, London University, University College.
Title varies: University College poetry.
Name of seminar varies: Poetry Seminar/Workshop.
WU   UWM (RBR) 1967, 1969.

U M D humanist. Duluth, University of Minnesota.   0744741
WU   UWM (RBR) V.9-18 (WIN1961-SPR1970).

U S 1 worksheets. Princeton, N.J., U S 1 Poet's Cooperative.   1529791
ISSN: 0362-7012 LCCN: 76-644236 Beg. date: 1973
WU   UWM (RBR) No.1-8 (OCT1973-FAL1976).

U T review. Tampa, Fla., University of Tampa.   1516604
Beg. date: 1972
"A continuing anthology of poetry."
WU   UWM (RBR) V.1-3; v.4 no.1,3; v.5 no.1-2 (1972-1977).

Ubris. Orono, Me.   151662A
Published by the students of the University of Maine.
WU   UWM (RBR) Spring 1968.

Ubulum. Oxford.   1516632
Beg. date: 1966
WU   UWM (RBR) No.1 (1966).

Ugly duckling. High Wycombe, Bucks, Eng.   1516645
WU   UWM (RBR) No.2/3 (1975).

Umbra. Berkeley, Calif., Society of Umbra.   1514752
ISSN: 0016-6618 Beg. date: 1963
WU   UWM (RBR) V.1 no.1-2 (WIN-DEC1963); no.[3]-5 (1967/1968-1974).

Umbrella. Coventry, Eng., The Umbrella Club.   1516658
ISSN: 0501-0772 Beg. date: 1958
WU   UWM (RBR) V.1-v.2 no.8 (OCT1958-SUM1962).

Umbrella Club, Coventry. Umbrella. *See* Umbrella.   1516660
Coventry, Eng., The Umbrella Club.

Umma. Dar es Salaam, Literature Dept., University of Dar es Salaam.   1516673
LCCN: 73-617651 Beg. date: 1970
"A magazine of original writing from the University of Dar es Salaam."
Supersedes Darlite.
English and Kiswahili.
WU   UWM (RBR) V.1 no.1 (1970).

Unconventional. Seine-et-Marne, France.   1516699
Beg. date: 1928
WU   UWM (RBR) 1928.

Underdog. Liverpool, Eng., Citybird Press.   1516708
ISSN: 0503-1656
WU   UWM (RBR) No.8 (1966).

Undergrad. Minneapolis.   1516710
Beg. date: 1947
"Undergrad is a student publication of the University of Minnesota sponsored by the advanced writing staff of the Department of English."
WU   UWM (RBR) V.1 no.1-3 (MAY-NOV1947).

Underground. Oxford.   1516723
ISSN: 0503-1680 Beg. date: 1967
WU   UWM (RBR) No.1 ([1967]).

Underground digest. New York.   0744923
WU   UWM (RBR) V.1 no.1-2 (1967).

Underground telegram. [n.p.].   1516736
"Bulletin from nothing."
WU   UWM (RBR) No.1 (n.d.).

The Underhound. San Francisco.   1516749
WU   UWM (RBR) V.1 no.4 (1960).

Underpass. La Grande, Ore., ASBEOSC, Eastern Oregon State College.   1516751
WU   UWM (RBR) Unnumbered, undated issue; v.3-5 (1972/1973-1974/1975).

Unfold. Folsom, Calif., Zetetic Press.   1516777
Beg. date: 1972
WU   UWM (RBR) V.1 no.1-4; v.2 no.1-3 (MAY1972-[1973]).

Unicorn. Baltimore, Md.   1516792
"A quarterly of literature and art."
Published by the students of Loyola College, Baltimore.
WU   UWM (RBR) V.5 no.1-3; v.6 (FAL1965-SUM1977).

Unicorn. Brooklyn, N.Y., Karen Rockow.   151678A
ISSN: 0041-6673 Beg. date: 1967
WU   UWM (RBR) V.1 no.1-4; v.2 no.1-5; v.3 no.1-3 (MAY1967-SUM1976).

Unicorn journal. Santa Barbara, Calif., Unicorn Press.   0745354
ISSN: 0041-669X LCCN: 75-647142 Beg. date: 1968
WU   UWM (RBR) No.1-4 (1968-1972).

Unilit. Secunderabad, Andhra Viswa Sahiti.   0824894
LCCN: S A 64-675 Beg. date: 1961
WU   UWM (RBR) No.2 (DEC1961).

Union of Catholic Students of Great Britain. Crux. *See* Crux. Oxford, Union of Catholic Students of Great Britain.   1431738

Unions libres. *See* Free unions. Unions libres. London.   1441733

United Amateur Press Alumni Association. Phoenix. *See* Phoenix. Ridgefield Park, N.J.   1500038

United Black Artists Guild. Dark waters. *See* Dark waters. Seattle, United Black Artists Guild.   1431989

United States one worksheets. *See* U S 1 worksheets. Princeton, N.J., U S 1 Poet's Cooperative.   1529800

University College, Nairobi. English Department. Nexus. *See* Nexus. Nairobi, Kenya.   1495297

University observer. Chicago.   1516801
LCCN: 50-32049 Beg. date: 1947 End date: 1947
"A journal of politics published at the University of Chicago" (varies).
Ceased publication with vol. 1 no. 2, Spring/Summer 1947.
WU   UWM (RBR) V.1 no.1 (WIN1947).

University of Birmingham review. *See* Alta. Birmingham, Eng., University of Birmingham.   1429845

University of Denver quarterly. *See* Denver Quarterly. Denver,   1020849

University of Houston forum. *See* Forum. Houston, University of Houston.   1313859

University of New Brunswick. Department of English. Fiddlehead. *See* Fiddlehead. Fredericton, N.B., Departments of English, University of New Brunswick and St. Thomas University.   1436819

University of New Haven. English Club. Noiseless spider. *See* Noiseless spider. New Haven, Conn., English Club of the University of New Haven.   1507685

University of Portland review. Portland, Ore.   0892354
ISSN: 0041-9923 Beg. date: 1948
Frequency varies.
WU   UWM (RBR) V.13-v.29 no.1 (MAY1961-SPR1977).

Unmuzzled ox. New York.   1468294
ISSN: 0049-5557 LCCN: 72-621023 Beg. date: 1971
WU   UWM (RBR) V.1-v.4 no.2 (1971-1976).

Unshackled. [n.p.], Whispershit Press.   1529813
WU   UWM (RBR) No.1 (n.d.).

The Unspeakable visions of the individual. California, Pa.   1227737
ISSN: 0049-0549 Beg. date: 1971
Each volume has also a distinctive title.
WU   UWM (RBR) V.1-5 (FEB1971-1977).

Unusual. New York.   1516827
ISSN: 0500-6597 LCCN: 70-200609 Beg. date: 1955 End date: 1955
Vol. 1 no. 1 published by Script Delivery Service.
Ceased publication with vol. 1 no. 3, 1955.
WU   UWM (RBR) V.1 no.1-3 (1955).

Upriver. Philadelphia.   151683A
ISSN: 0566-3180 Beg. date: 1965
"Currents of poetry."
WU   UWM (RBR) V.1 no.2-5 (SUM1964-1966).

Upstream. Northallerton, North Yorkshire, Eng.   1516842
Beg. date: 1975
WU   UWM (RBR) No.1-2 (OCT1975-OCT1976).

Upsurge. Tacoma, Wash.   1516855
Beg. date: 1946 End date: 1949
"The Pacific Coast's progressive quarterly."
Title varies: no. 3, Upsurge in Washington.
Ceased publication with no. 10, 1949.
WU   UWM (RBR) No.1-10 (1946-[1949]).

Upsurge in Washington. *See* Upsurge. Tacoma, Wash.   1516868

Uptown beat. *New York, East Harlem Writing Center.*   1516870
  Beg. date: 1968
  WU   UWM (RBR) Spring 1968-Winter 1969; v.2-v.3 no.3 (SPR1969-1970).

Upward; a quarterly magazine of verse. *See* Compass; a   1428838
quarterly of contemporary verse. Prairie City, Ill., Decker Press.

Uroboros. *Olean, N.Y., Allegany Mountain Press.*   1516896
  ISSN: 0146-8510   LCCN: sc77-1296   Beg. date: 1977
  WU   UWM (RBR) V.2 no.1 (1977).

Utah. University.   Pen. *See* Pen. Salt Lake City, University   1498695
of Utah.

Utah. University.   Wasatch front. *See* Wasatch front. Salt   1518356
Lake City, University of Utah.

The Utopian papers. *Oakland, Calif., Utopians for Political*   1516905
Action.
  WU   UWM (RBR) Two unnumbered, undated issues.

Utopians for Political Action.   Utopian Papers. *See* Utopian   1516918
papers. Oakland, Calif., Utopians for Political Action.

Uzzano. *Mount Carroll, Ill.*   1516920
  Beg. date: 1975
  WU   UWM (RBR) No.1-7 (WIN1975-1977).

V

V. San Francisco, Vanguard, Inc. 0773195
"The magazine of the tenderloin."
WY   UWM (RBR) V.1 no.2-3 (OCT-NOV1966).

V V V, [poetry, plastic arts, anthropology, sociology, psychology]. New York. 077241A
LCCN: 45-27206
In English and French.
Ceased publication with no. 4 (Feb. 1944).
WU   UWM (RBR) No.2/3-4 (MAR1943-FEB1944).

Vagabond. Ellensburg, Wash., etc., J. Bennett. 1516933
ISSN: 0042-2193   LCCN: 66-9946   Beg. date: 1966
WU   UWM (RBR) No.1-25 (1966-JAN/MAR1977); suppl no. 25 (1977).

Vagaries. Austin, Tex., St. Edward's University. 1516946
"The student literary-art magazine."
WU   UWM (RBR) V.2 no.1 (SPR1970).

Valhalla. Birmingham, Ala. [etc.], Ragnarok Press. 1529826
WU   UWM (RBR) No.4 (1977).

Vanessa poetry magazine. London, The Many Press. 1516961
WU   UWM (RBR) No.1-3 (1976?-1977).

Vangard. Cincinnati. 1516974
Beg. date: 1965
WU   UWM (RBR) No.1-8 (OCT041965-SEP201966).

Vanguard. See V. San Francisco, 148435A

Variant. Cincinnati. 1516987
ISSN: 0505-0251   Beg. date: 1961
Issued by the student body of the Hebrew Union College, Jewish Institute of Religion.
WU   UWM (RBR) V.2 no.1-3 (FAL1961-1962).

Variegation. Los Angeles, Variegation Pub. Co. 1517007
LCCN: 52-36281   Beg. date: 1946   End date: 1959
"A free verse quarterly."
Suspended publication between Spring 1957 and Feb. 1959.
Ceased publication with vol. 12 (no. 46) Feb. 1959.
WU   UWM (RBR) Jan., Apr. 1946; v.1 no.3-v.11 (JUL1946-WIN1956) issues missing.

The Vehicle. Charleston, Ill. 151701A
ISSN: 0503-7638   Beg. date: 1959
WU   UWM (RBR) V.1-v.2 no.3 (APR1959-1960).

Veins. Ripton, Vt., St. Mawr Jazz Poetry Project. 1517022
WU   UWM (RBR) V.2 no.1-3 (DEC151975-1976).

Velvet glove. Livermore, Calif. 1358355
ISSN: 0042-3270   Beg. date: 1971
WU   UWM (RBR) No.6 (FEB/MAR1972).

Velvet wings. Berkeley, Calif., Paradoxical Press. 1517035
ISSN: 0148-8635   Beg. date: 1976
WU   UWM (RBR) No.1-2 (1976-1977).

Venture. New York, Venture Publications, Inc. 1517048
ISSN: 0505-2149   LCCN: 64-9444   Beg. date: 1954   End date: 1961
Vol. 1 published by the Writers' Workshops of the New York Council of Arts, Sciences and Professions.
Ceased publication with vol. 4 no. 1, 1961.
WU   UWM (RBR) V.1-v.4 no.1 (1954-1961).

Venture; an annual of art and literature. London. 0935076
Beg. date: 1903
WU   UWM (RBR) 1903-1905.

Ver poets voices. London Colney, Herts., Eng., Ver Poets. 1517050
WU   UWM (RBR) No.1,6 (n.d.-MAR1974).

Verb. Denver. 1517063
ISSN: 0506-6530   Beg. date: 1962
WU   UWM (RBR) V.1 no.5; v.2 no.1-5; v.3 no.1-3 (NOV1963-1966).

Verdure. Oyster Bay, N.Y., Verdure Publications. 1517076
Beg. date: 1969
"The grass roots of America."
WU   UWM (RBR) V.1 no.1; v.2 no.1; v.3 no.2; v.4 no.1 (SPR1969-SPR1972).

Verge. Ann Arbor, Mich. 1517089
Beg. date: 1956
WU   UWM (RBR) No.1 (1956?).

The Verist. Bristol, Eng. 1517091
End date: 1947
Ceased publication with vol. 2 no. 1, Spring 1947.
WU   UWM (RBR) V.2 no.1 (SPR1947).

Versantics. St. Louis, Mo., Acrostic Press. 1517100
WU   UWM (RBR) One unnumbered, undated issue.

Verse. London. 1517126
Beg. date: 1947   End date: 1947
Ceased publication with no. 1, Winter 1947?
WU   UWM (RBR) No.1 (WIN1947).

Versus. Montreal. 1517113
ISSN: 0384-868X   Beg. date: 1976
WU   UWM (RBR) No.1-3 (SUM1976-1977).

Vertigo newsextra. Cardiff, Wales. 1517139
Beg. date: 1969
WU   UWM (RBR) No.1 (AUT1969).

Verve. Kent, Eng. 1517141
WU   UWM (RBR) No.5,8-9 (1964-1966).

Vespers. New York. 1514778
"A magazine of beautiful poetry."
WU   UWM (RBR) V.16 no.2-6,9-10; v.17 no.2 (FEB1959-FEB1960); Winter 1961-Summer/Autumn 1962.

Vice. Brightlingsea, Essex, Eng. 1517154
"A one shot magazine."
WU   UWM (RBR) V.1 no.1 ([1966?]).

Vice versa. New York. 077714A
Beg. date: 1940
WU   UWM (RBR) V.1 no.1-3/4/5 (NOV/DEC1940-JAN1942).

Victoria, British Columbia. University. Introductions from an island. See Introductions from an island. Victoria, B.C., University of Victoria. 1442948

Victoria, British Columbia. University. English Department. Karaki. See Karaki. Victoria, B.C., English Department, University of Victoria. 143912A

Victoria poetry chapbook. Victoria, B.C. 1517167
ISSN: 0702-2298
A year book of the Canadian Authors' Association. Poetry Group. Victoria and Islands Branch.
WU   UWM (RBR) 1934-1941/1942.

Victoria University College, Wellington, New Zealand. Literary Society. Arachne, a literary journal. See Arachne, a literary journal. Wellington, N.Z., Crocus Pub. Co. 1438203

View. New York, View Inc. 0778683
LCCN: 45-31664   Beg. date: 1940   End date: 1947
Vols. 2- called ser. 2.
Title varies: 1940-1942, View "through the eyes of poets."
Ceased publication with vol. 7 no. 3, Spring 1947?
Includes unpaged supplements.
WU   UWM (RBR) V.1 no.1-3,6-11/12; v.2-v.7 no.3 (SEP1940-MAR1947).

View through the eyes of poets. See View. New York, 1484362

Viewpoint. Rocklin, Calif., Creative Writing Program, Sierra College. 1517182
WU   UWM (RBR) Jan., June 1965.

Viewpoints. Manchester, Lancaster, Eng. 1519298
WU   UWM (RBR) No.42-64 (AUG1965-JUN1969).

Views. Louisville, Views Associates. 1517204
ISSN: 0506-9947   Beg. date: 1952   End date: 1959
Some issues have subtitle: "The official magazine of the University of Louisville."
Ceased publication with vol. 5 no. 2, 1959.
WU   UWM (RBR) V.2 no.1-2; v.3 no.1-3; v.4 no.1-3; v.5 no.1-2 (1954-1958).

Views & comments. New York, The Libertarian League. 151722A
Beg. date: 1955
Continued by Towards anarchism, ISSN 0563-9999, with no. 50.
WU   UWM (RBR) No.2,5-9,11-16,18-34,36-40 (APR1955-JAN/FEB1961).

Views and comments. See Views & comments. New York, The Libertarian League. 1517232

Vigil. *Chicago, Roosevelt University.* 1517260
Beg. date: 1959
"New writing by new writers."
WU　　UWM (RBR) V.1 no.1-2 (SPR-AUT1959).

Vigilante. *Calgary, Alt.* 1517258
Beg. date: 1970
WU　　UWM (RBR) No.1-3 (MAY1970-APR1971).

Vile. *San Francisco, Banana Productions.* 1517286
WU　　UWM (RBR) No.4 (SEP1974).

The Village green. *New York, Greenwich Avenue Committee, Inc.* 1529839
LCCN: 45-28109 Beg. date: 1936 End date: 1937
Ceased publication with vol. 2 no. 7, Aug. 1937.
WU　　UWM (RBR) Mar. 1, 1936.

The Village review. *Newport, Essex, Eng.* 1517299
Beg. date: 1972
WU　　UWM (RBR) V.1 no.1-4 (SPR1972-WIN1973).

Vincent. *New York.* 1517308
Beg. date: 1966
"The mad brother of Theo."
WU　　UWM (RBR) No.1-2 (1966-1968).

Virgin. *New York.* 1517310
ISSN: 0507-0287 Beg. date: 1967
WU　　UWM (RBR) No.1 (1967).

Virginia. University. *Plume and sword. See* Plume and sword. Charlottsville, Va., University of Virginia. 1501227

Virginia Commonwealth University, Richmond, Virginia. Spectrum. *See* Spectrum. Richmond, Va., Virginia Commonwealth University. 1511025

Virginia Polytechnic Institute, Blacksburg. Maelstrom. *See* Maelstrom. Blacksburg, Va., Student Publications Board, Virginia Polytechnic Institute. 149428A

Virginia verse. *University, Va.* 1517323
LCCN: 43-34268 Beg. date: 1938 End date: 1938
Ceased publication with vol. 1 no. 5, June 1, 1938.
WU　　UWM (RBR) V.1 no.5 (JUN011938).

Vis viva. *Droitwich, Worcester, Eng., New Expression Publications.* 1517336
Beg. date: 1970
Ceased publication.
Superseded by New expression.
WU　　UWM (RBR) No.1-2 (1970-1971).

Vision. *Sydney, Adelphi Students' Library.* 1517349
ISSN: 0042-689X Beg. date: 1963
"A magazine of the arts, science and Australiana."
WU　　UWM (RBR) V.1 no.1; v.3 no.1; v.4 no.1; v.8-20,22 (JUN1963-1970),

Visions. *Alpine, Calif.* 1517364
Beg. date: 1930
"Book of verse."
"The poet's friend from the garden of the sun."
Title varies: vol. 1-vol. 8 no. 3, 1930-March 1938, Poet's friend.
WU　　UWM (RBR) Mar. 1939.

Visual dialog. *Los Altos, Calif.* 151738A
ISSN: 0360-4225 LCCN: 75-648825 Beg. date: 1975
WU　　UWM (RBR) V.1-v.3 no.1 (DEC1975-JAN/FEB1976-1977).

The Voice of youth. *London, Poetry Society.* 1517392
ISSN: 0504-6211 Beg. date: 1951 End date: 1963
"The Poetry Society's junior quarterly."
Ceased publication with vol. 7 no. 11, Autumn 1963.
WU　　UWM (RBR) V.1 no.1-8; v.2 no.1-8; v.3 no.1-2,7; v.4 no.1; v.5 no.4; v.6 no.1-4; v.7 no.1-11 (SPR1951-AUT1963).

Voices. *Wigginton, Herts., Eng., The Opus Press.* 1517427
LCCN: 44-44209 Beg. date: 1943 End date: 1947
Supersedes Opus.
"An anthology of individualist writings."
Ceased publication with n. ser. no. 1, 1946/1947?
WU　　UWM (RBR) No.1,3-5 (1943-1944); n. ser. no.1 (1946/1947).

Voices. A journal of poetry. *Brattleboro, Vt.* 078195A
End date: 1965
Ceased publication with 1965.
WU　　UWM (RBR) No.94,96-111,113-184 (SUM1938-1964).

Voices; a Michigan literary quarterly. *See* Michigan's voices; a literary quarterly magazine. Saginaw, Mich. 0956084

Voices. *London.* 1517442
Beg. date: 1919 End date: 1921
Ceased publication with vol. 5 no. 4, 1921.
WU　　UWM (RBR) No.1,4-5; v.2 no.2-6; v.3 no.3-4; v.4 no.1,5-6 (1919-1920).

Voices international. *Fort Smith, Ark., South and West, Inc.* 151743A
ISSN: 0042-8280 Beg. date: 1966
"An international literary quarterly."
WU　　UWM (RBR) V.1 no.2-v.3 no.2; v.4-v.12 no.2 (SUM1966-SUM1977).

Vole. *Hitchin, Herts., Eng.* 1517442
"Bi monthly magazine of poems, stories, pictures, pieces, articles, reviews, etc."
WU　　UWM (RBR) No.2-3 (1972).

Volt. *Luddenden Foot, York., Eng., Pennine Poets.* 1517455
Beg. date: 1972
Supersedes Platform.
"Poetry magazine."
Produced with the help of the Yorkshire Arts Association.
WU　　UWM (RBR) No.1-2 (1972).

Volume 63. *Waterloo, Ont., Board of Publications, University of Waterloo.* 1517470
ISSN: 0701-3485 Beg. date: 1963 End date: 1967
Ceased publication with no. 6, 1967.
WU　　UWM (RBR) No.1-5 (DEC1963-SUM1966).

The Volusia review. *Allandale, Fla.* 1517496
ISSN: 0504-7196 Beg. date: 1954
Published at Bethune-Cookman College of Daytona Beach, Florida.
WU　　UWM (RBR) V.1 no.1 (1954).

Vort. *Silver Spring, Md.* 1517518
Beg. date: 1972
WU　　UWM (RBR) V.1 no.1-6; v.3 no.1-3 (FAL1972-1976).

Voyages. *Washington, D.C., Voyages: A National Literary Magazine, Inc.* 1517520
ISSN: 0042-9031 LCCN: 68-7689 Beg. date: 1967
WU　　UWM (RBR) V.1 no.1; v.2-5 (AUT1967-1973).

The Voyeur. *Brooklyn, N.Y., The Open Window Society.* 1517533
Beg. date: 1974
WU　　UWM (RBR) V.1-v.3 no.6 (DEC1974-JUN1977).

Vrijdagmarkt. *See* Friday market. Thames Ditton, Surrey, Eng. 1468827

W

W E B DuBois Clubs of America. Insurgent. *See* Insurgent. San Francisco, W E B DuBois Clubs of America.   1440923

W-Hollow harvest. *Cincinnati, The Kentucky Writers' Guild, Inc., Jesse Stuart Exchange.*   151824A
ISSN: 0042-9708   Beg. date: 1967
WU   UWM (RBR) V.1 no.7/8; v.2 no.1/2,5-10 (JUL/AUG1967-OCT1968).

W I N; workshop in nonviolence. *See* Win. New York,   1113687

W W. *See* Wwhimsy. St. Louis.   1515183

Wagner College, Staten Island, New York. Wagner literary magazine. *See* Wagner literary magazine. Staten Island, N.Y., The Student Association of Wagner College.   1518278

Wagner literary magazine. *Staten Island, N.Y., The Student Association of Wagner College.*   1518265
ISSN: 0509-576X   Beg. date: 1959   End date: 1964
Supersedes Nimbus.
Ceased publication with 1963/1964.
WU   UWM (RBR) Spring 1959-1963/1964.

Wagtail. *Sarnia, Ont.*   1518280
Beg. date: 1970
WU   UWM (RBR) No.1-3 (APR1970-WIN1970/1971).

Wake, the creative magazine. *New York, Wake Editions.*   0784048
Beg. date: 1943   End date: 1953
Suspended publication Spring 1946-Spring 1948.
Ceased publication with no. 12, 1953.
Vol. 1 nos. 1-3, 5 have caption and running title, no. 4 cover and caption title: Harvard wake.
WU   UWM (RBR) V.1 no.3,5-12 (MAR1945-1953).

Wakra. *Boston, Wakra Publishing Group.*   1518293
Beg. date: 1971
WU   UWM (RBR) No.1 (WIN1971).

Wales. *Newton, Montgomeryshire. Wales, Montgomeryshire Printing Co. Ltd.*   1518302
ISSN: 0043-0056   LCCN: 59-34289   Beg. date: 1937
Suspended publication between Winter 1939/1940 and July 1943; Oct. 1949 and Sept. 1958.
WU   UWM (RBR) No.1-4,6/7-11 (SUM1937-WIN1939/1940).

Wallpaper. *London, New Paltz, N.Y.*   1518315
ISSN: 0307-5834   Beg. date: 1974
WU   UWM (RBR) No.1-5/6 (SEP1974-JUN1976).

The Walrus. *Chesham, Bucks, Eng.*   1518328
Beg. date: 1957
WU   UWM (RBR) No.1-18 (MAR1957-OCT1962).

Wanderlust magazine. *Metairie, La.*   1518330
ISSN: 0509-6146   Beg. date: 1958
WU   UWM (RBR) V.1-2; no.9-11 (APR1958-JUL1961).

War Resisters' League. Win. *See* Win. New York, Win Publishing Empire.   0784938

Wasatch front. *Salt Lake City, University of Utah.*   1518343
WU   UWM (RBR) V.58 no.1-2; v.60 (WIN1971-1972).

Wascana review. *Regina, Saskatchewan.*   0785330
ISSN: 0043-0412   Beg. date: 1966
Indexes: volumes 1-4, 1966-1969, with volumes 3-4.
WU   UWM (RBR) V.1-10 (1966-FAL1975).

Washington and Jefferson College, Washington, Pennsylvania. Arbitrarium. *See* Arbitrarium. Washington, Pa., Washington and Jefferson College.   1432942

Washington and Jefferson College, Washington. Pennsylvania. Seventh day review. *See* Seventh day review. Washington, Pa., Washington and Jefferson College.   1507280

Washington and Jefferson College, Washington, Pennsylvania. Washington and Jefferson literary journal. *See* Washington and Jefferson literary journal. Washington, Pa., Washington and Jefferson College.   1518371

Washington and Jefferson literary journal. *Washington, Pa., Washington and Jefferson College.*   1518369
ISSN: 0043-0455   Beg. date: 1966
WU   UWM (RBR) V.1 no.2; v.2 no.1; v.3 no.1; v.4 no.1; v.5 no.1; v.6 no.1 (1967-SPR1972).

Washington (State). Eastern Washington College of Education, Cheney. Literary artpress. *See* Literary artpress. Cheney, Wash.   1492958

Washington (State). Eastern Washington State College, Cheney. Art press. *See* Art press. Spokane.   1432576

Washington (State). Eastern Washington State College, Cheney. Organon. *See* Organon. Cheney, Wash., Eastern Washington State College.   1396646

Washington (State). State University, Pullman. Gamut. *See* Gamut. Pullman, Wash., Washington State University.   1437644

Washington (State). University. Department of English. Assay. *See* Assay. Seattle, Department of English, University of Washington.   144098A

Washington (State). University. Department of English. Month's best. *See* Month's best. Seattle, Department of English. University of Washington.   1496971

Washington (State). Western Washington State College, Bellingham. Jeopardy. *See* Jeopardy. Bellingham, Wash., Associated Student Body of Western Washington State College.   1438664

Washington University, Saint Louis. Free lance. *See* Free lance; the magazine of the student mind. St. Louis, Washington University.   1442242

Washout review. *Schenectady, N.Y., Washout Pub. Co.*   1518384
Beg. date: 1975
WU   UWM (RBR) V.1-v.2 no.2 (OCT1975-WIN1977).

Waste paper. *Shibpur, Howrah, India.*   1518397
Beg. date: 1967
"An irregular Hungry Generation newsletter."
WU   UWM (RBR) No.1-4 (1967-SEP1969).

Waterloo, Ontario. University. Waterloo review. *See* Waterloo review. Waterloo, Ont.   1518419

Waterloo, Ontario. University. Board of Publications. Volume. *See* Volume 63. Waterloo, Ont., Board of Publications, University of Waterloo.   1517483

Waterloo Lutheran University, Waterloo, Ontario. Student Board of Publications. Chiaroscuro. *See* Chiaroscuro. Waterloo, Ont., Student Board of Publications, Waterloo Lutheran University.   1433828

Waterloo review. *Waterloo, Ont.*   1518406
ISSN: 0511-3792   Beg. date: 1958   End date: 1961
Issued by faculty members at Waterloo College and McMaster University.
Ceased publication with vol. 3 (no. 6), Winter 1961.
Absorbed by Alphabet.
WU   UWM (RBR) V.1-2; no.5-6 (SPR1958-WIN1961).

Waters. *Cincinnati.*   1518434
Beg. date: 1975
WU   UWM (RBR) No.1-4 (1975-FAL1976).

Watts literary guide. *See* Literary guide and rationalist review. London.   1505121

Wave. *Copenhagen, Chicago, New York.*   1228101
Beg. date: 1922   End date: 1924
Ceased publication with vol. 2 no. 2, Oct. 1924.
WU   UWM (RBR) V.1 no.1-2,5-6; v.2 no.1-2 (1922-OCT1924).

Waves. *Downsview, Ont., York University.*   1518447
ISSN: 0315-3932   LCCN: 72-622957   Beg. date: 1972
"A tri-annual York University magazine."
WU   UWM (RBR) V.1-v.5 no.3; v.6 no.1 (SPR1972-AUT1977).

Wayne review. *Detroit.*   1518462
"Sponsored by Liberal Arts Student Board and English Department of Wayne State University."
WU   UWM (RBR) No.13 (SPR1963); Fall/Winter 1964/1965; Winter, Summer 1969; Spring 1974.

Wayne State University, Detroit. Wayne review. *See* Wayne review. Detroit.   1518475

Wayne State University, Detroit. Department of English. Jaw. *See* Jaw. Detroit, Dept. of English, Wayne State University.   1438586

Wayne State University, Detroit. Monteith College. Journal. *See* Journal. Detroit, Wayne State University. Monteith College.   1438714

Waysgoose. *Coulsdon, Surrey, Eng.* 1518488
ISSN: 0509-9331 Beg. date: 1963
WU   UWM (RBR) No.2 (1963).

We magazine. *New Paltz, N.Y.* 1518490
Beg. date: 1964
WU   UWM (RBR) V.1 ed.1-2 (DEC1964-APR1965).

We offer. *Driffield, Yorkshire, Eng.* 151850A
ISSN: 0508-1858 Beg. date: 1951
"The international quarterly of The Poetry Guild."
WU   UWM (RBR) V.1 no.1; v.2 no.1; v.3 no.1; v.4 no.2 (AUT1951-OCT/DEC1958); n. ser. v.1 no.1-4 (JAN/MAR1963-JUL/SEP1963).

Weapon. *New York.* 1518525
ISSN: 0511-4004 Beg. date: 1965
WU   UWM (RBR) No.1 (FAL/WIN1965).

Webb School of California, Claremont.   Sage. *See* Sage. 1509944
Claremont, Calif., Webb School of California.

Webster College, Webster Groves, Missouri. Webster 1286960
review. *See* Webster review. Webster Groves, Mo., Webster College.

Webster review. *Webster Groves, Mo., Webster College.* 1286958
WU   UWM (RBR) V.1-v.3 no.3 (SPR1974-1977).

Weed. *Toronto.* 1518538
ISSN: 0511-4101 Beg. date: 1966 End date: 1967
Ceased publication with no. 12, Nov./Dec. 1967.
WU   UWM (RBR) No.1-12 (1966-1967).

Weid. *Homestead, Fla., Olivant Press.* 1518540
ISSN: 0145-983X LCCN: 77-643260 Beg. date: 1972
"The sensibility revue."
Continues the Human voice with vol. 8 no. 1 (no. 33), March 1972.
WU   UWM (RBR) V.8-13 (no.33-48) (MAR1972-1977).

The Welsh review. *Cardiff, Wales.* 1518553
LCCN: 49-14156 Beg. date: 1939 End date: 1948
"A quarterly journal about Wales, its people, and their activities" (varies).
Suspended publication between Nov. 1939-March 1944.
Ceased publication with vol. 7 no. 4, Dec. 1948.
WU   UWM (RBR) V.5 no.2,4; v.6 no.1-3; v.7 (JUN1946-1948).

Wen. *Oxford.* 1518566
Beg. date: 1958
WU   UWM (RBR) No.[1]-6 ([1968]-1970).

Wesleyan College, Buckhannon, West Virginia. Laurel 1450067
review. *See* Laurel review. Buckhannon, W. Va., West Virginia Wesleyan College.

Wesleyan University, Middletown, Connecticut. Cardinal. 1431032
See Cardinal. Middletown, Conn., Wesleyan University.

Wessex. *Southampton, Eng., University College.* 1518579
Beg. date: 1928 End date: 1938
"An annual record of the movement for a University of Wessex."
Ceased publication with vol. 42 no. 2, 1938.
WU   UWM (RBR) No.1 (1928).

West coast poetry review. *Reno, Nev.* 1518594
ISSN: 0049-7215 LCCN: 78-618104 Beg. date: 1971
WU   UWM (RBR) V.1-v.5 no.1 (SUM1971-1976).

West coast review. *Burnaby, B.C., Simon Fraser University.* 1518603
ISSN: 0043-311X LCCN: 66-9940 Beg. date: 1966
"A tri-annual magazine of the arts."
WU   UWM (RBR) V.1-v.12 no.1 (1966-1977).

The West conscious review. *Millbrae, Calif., Scarecrow Books.* 1518629
Beg. date: 1975
WU   UWM (RBR) V.1 no.1-3 (1975-SUM1976).

West end. *New York.* 1518631
Beg. date: 1971
WU   UWM (RBR) V.1-2; v.3 no.1-2,4; v.4 no.1-2 (WIN1971-FAL1976).

West Essex Writers' Club. Manuscript. *See* Manuscript. 1495977
Dagenham, Essex, Eng., West Essex Writers' Club.

West Virginia. University. Appalachian review. *See* 1438153
Appalachian review. Morgantown, W. Va., West Virginia University.

West Virginia. University. West Virginia University 1518657
magazine. *See* West Virginia University magazine. Morgantown, W.Va., West Virginia University Foundation, Inc.

West Virginia Poetry Society. Echoes of West Virginia. *See* 1435500
Echoes of West Virginia. Huntington, W. Va.

The West Virginia University magazine. *Morgantown, W.Va.,* 1518644
West Virginia University Foundation, Inc.
ISSN: 0043-3349 Beg. date: 1969
WU   UWM (RBR) V.1 no.1-3; v.2; v.3 no.2,4 (SPR1969-SPR1972).

The Westbere review. *Haydenville, Mass., Morning Star* 1529841
Press.
Beg. date: 1977
WU   UWM (RBR) V.1 no.1 (SUM1977).

Westerly. *Nedlands, Australia, University of Western* 128559A
Australia Press.
ISSN: 0043-342X Beg. date: 1956
Issued by The Arts Union of the University of Western Australia, 1956- ; Department of English, University of Western Australia,
WU   UWM (RBR) 1959 no.1-1977 no.1

The Westerly review. *Westerly, R.I., Split-Leaf Press.* 151866A
Beg. date: 1976
WU   UWM (RBR) V.1 no.1-3 (1976).

The Western gate. *Buffalo, N.Y., Daniel Zimmerman.* 1518672
Beg. date: 1970
WU   UWM (RBR) No.1-2 (1970).

Western Reserve University, Cleveland. Polemic. *See* 1507826
Polemic. Cleveland.

Western world review. *Culver City, Calif., Western World* 1518685
Press.
ISSN: 0043-4299 Beg. date: 1965
"A non-partisan review and opinion journal."
WU   UWM (RBR) V.1 no.2-v.4 no.3; v.5 no.1-3; v.6 no.1 (1966-SPR1971).

The Westigan review of poetry. *Salt Lake City, etc.* 1518698
Beg. date: 1969
WU   UWM (RBR) V.1-v.3 no.3 (no.1-11) (1970-1977).

Westminster magazine. *Atlanta.* 0794541
LCCN: 58-39096
V. 34 no. 1 called also N. Ser. V. 1 no. 1.
Founded in 1911.
Absorbed Bozart in 1935, and called Bozart-Westminster, 1935-1938.
Ceased publication 1957.
WU   UWM (RBR) V.16 no.4; v.23 no.3; v.38 no.1-3; v.39 no.1; v.45 no.4; v.46 no.1-3 (DEC1931-AUT1956).

Westwind. *Los Angeles, ASUCLA Board of Communications.* 1518707
ISSN: 0508-6191 Beg. date: 1957
"UCLA's quarterly of the arts" (varies).
Supersedes Chimera.
WU   UWM (RBR) Winter 1975/1976-Summer 1977.

Westwind. *San Francisco, The Westwind Co.* 1518722
Beg. date: 1905 End date: 1912
Ceased publication with vol. 8 no. 5, May 1912.
WU   UWM (RBR) V.3 no.6; v.4 no.1-5; v.5 no.2,4; v.8 no.3 (DEC1909-MAR1912).

Weyfarers. *Bramley, Surrey, Eng., Guildford Poets Press.* 1518735
Beg. date: 1972
WU   UWM (RBR) No.1-19 (1972-1977).

What can this charlatan be trying to say? *See* Charlatan. 1428342
[Iowa City, Charlatan Publications.].

What's a nice hillbilly like you..? *Beckley, W.Va., Southern* 1518748
Appalachian Circuit of Antioch College.
WU   UWM (RBR) No.2-4 (n.d.-SPR1976).

What's happening. *New York.* 1514780
"A bi-monthly magazine published by a group of New York City teenagers" (varies).
WU   UWM (RBR) V.1 no.1-2,4 (SEP-DEC1965); Mar. 1966; v.2-v.4 no.4 (DEC1966-JUL1969); v.5 no.1 (WIN1970); Feb. 1970.

Wheels: a second cycle. *See* Wheels: an anthology of verse. 1230559
Oxford, etc., B.H. Blackwell, etc.

Wheels: a third cycle. *See* Wheels: an anthology of verse. 1230561
Oxford, etc., B.H. Blackwell, etc.

Wheels: an anthology of verse. *Oxford, etc., B.H. Blackwell,* 1230546
etc.
Beg. date: 1916 End date: 1921
Ceased publication with sixth cycle, 1921.
WU   UWM (RBR) No.1-3,5-6 (1916-1921).

Wheels, 1919, fourth cycle. *See* Wheels: an anthology of 1230574
verse. Oxford, etc., B.H. Blackwell, etc.

Wheels, 1920, fifth cycle. *See* Wheels: an anthology of verse. Oxford, etc., B.H. Blackwell, etc.   1230587

Wheels, 1921, sixth cycle. *See* Wheels: an anthology of verse. Oxford, etc., B.H. Blackwell, etc.   123059A

Whe're. *Toronto.*   1518776
ISSN: 0511-8700   Beg. date: 1966
"A magazine of location."
Ceased publication with no. 1, Summer 1966.
WU   UWM (RBR) No.1 (SUM1966).

Whetstone. *Philadelphia.*   0795232
ISSN: 0043-4833
"A literary quarterly" (varies).
Publication suspended 1961-1963.
WU   UWM (RBR) V.1-v.4 no.3 (1955-1964); n. ser. v.2 no.1; v.3 no.1-2; v.4 no.1-2; v.5 no.1-2 (FAL1968-FAL1971).

Whim. *Newark, New Jersey.*   0795258
LCCN: 10-17851
Merged into Papyrus.
WU   UWM (RBR) V.1-v.8 no.6 (1901-1905).

Whims. *New York, The Whims Co.*   1518789
Beg. date: 1896   End date: 1896
Ceased publication with vol. 2 no. 3, Sept. 1896.
WU   UWM (RBR) V.1 no.1-4; v.2 no.1-3 (JAN-SEP1896).

Whimsy. *See* Wwhimsy. St. Louis.   1515170

The Whirl. *Santa Fe, N.M., El Estudio Press.*   1518791
Beg. date: 1930
"Art-plus."
WU   UWM (RBR) No.1 (MAR151930).

White arms. *Fort Wayne, Ind.*   1518800
Beg. date: 1974
WU   UWM (RBR) No.1-2/3,6; one unnumbered issue (APR1974-NOV1976).

The White dove review. *Tulsa, Okla., The White Dove Press.*   1518813
ISSN: 0511-8743   Beg. date: 1959   End date: 1960
Ceased publication vol. 2 (no. 5), May/Aug. 1960.
WU   UWM (RBR) V.1 no.1-3; v.2 no.4-5 (1959-1960).

The White elephant. *[n.p.].*   1518826
Beg. date: 1971
WU   UWM (RBR) No.1-[3] (1971-1972).

White heap. *Cleveland, Falling Down Press.*   1518839
WU   UWM (RBR) No.2 (n.d.).

White lion poets. *[n.p.].*   1518841
Beg. date: 1975
WU   UWM (RBR) No.1 ([1975]).

White mule. *Tampa, Fla., White Mule.*   1518854
"A poetry journal."
WU   UWM One unnumbered, undated issue; v.2 no.2 (1976).

The White owl. *Philadelphia.*   1518867
Beg. date: 1901   End date: 1902
"A monthly magazine of short stories, witticism and poems" (varies).
Ceased publication with vol. 1 no. 7, June 1902.
WU   UWM (RBR) V.1 no.1-7 (NOV1901-JUN1902).

White pelican. *Edmonton, Alta.*   151887A
ISSN: 0049-7584   Beg. date: 1971
"A quarterly review of the arts."
WU   UWM (RBR) V.1-v.5 no.2 (WIN1971-1975).

White pine. *Buffalo, N.Y.*   1518882
Beg. date: 1974
WU   UWM (RBR) No.1-12 (1974-1977).

Whitehall Musical and Dramatic Society. Anthos. *See* Anthos. Dublin, Whitehall Musical and Dramatic Society.   1432758

Why. *New Orleans, Isolina Hafford.*   1518895
WU   UWM (RBR) V.2 no.3 (JUL/AUG1940).

Why? *See* Resistance. New York.   1504456

The Widening circle. *Columbus, Ohio.*   1518904
ISSN: 0363-3497   LCCN: 73-645750   Beg. date: 1973
WU   UWM (RBR) V.1 (WIN-FAL1973).

Wild dog. *San Francisco, etc.*   1518917
ISSN: 0511-9448   Beg. date: 1963
WU   UWM (RBR) V.1 no.1-9; v.2 no.10-19/20; v.3 no.21 (APR1963-MAR1966).

Wild hawk. *See* Plowshare. Woodstock, N.Y., Maverick Press.   1501177

Wild places. *Red Hook, N.J.*   1529854
Beg. date: 1976
Wu   UWM (RBR) V.1 no.1; v.2 no.1 (SPR1976,SPR1977).

Willamette University, Salem, Oregon. Jason. *See* Jason. [Salem, Ore.], Willamette University.   1438560

The William and Mary review. *Williamsburg, [Va.].*   0797532
ISSN: 0043-5600   LCCN: 67-4514
Formed by the union of Royalist and Seminar.
WU   UWM (RBR) V.2 no.1; v.6 no.1; v.8 no.2; v.9 no.1-2; v.10 no.1; v.11 no.1-2; v.12 no.1-2; v.13 no.1-3; v.14 no.1-2 (WIN1964-SPR1976).

Williams College. Department of English. Berkshire review. *See* Berkshire review. Williamstown, Mass., Department of English, Williams College.   1070651

The Willie. *San Francisco, Manic Press.*   151892A
ISSN: 0511-9847   Beg. date: 1967
WU   UWM (RBR) No.1-2 (SUM1967-SPR1968).

Willmore city. *Cardiff-by-the-sea, Calif., Alexander Associates.*   1518932
WU   UWM (RBR) No.2/3-4/5 (FAL1975-1976).

Win. *New York, Win Publishing Empire.*   0798208
ISSN: 0512-5375   Beg. date: 1965
Issued 1965-Oct. 2, 1967, by the Committee for Nonviolent Action and the New York Workshop in Nonviolence.
Issued Oct. 16, 1967-   by the War Resisters League in cooperation with the New York Workshop in Nonviolence.
1966-   called also Win peace and freedom thru nonviolent action.
WU   UWM (RBR) V.2 no.8-18,20-21; v.3 no.1-3,7-21; v.4 no.3-11,13-21; v.5 no.1-22; v.6 no.1-21; v.7 no.1-20; v.8 no.1-20 (APR1966-1972).

Win peace and freedom thru nonviolent action. *See* Win. New York,   1113752

Winchester College, Winchester, England. Caliban. *See* Caliban. Winchester, Hamps., Eng., Winchester College.   1441865

Winchester Poetry Circle. Winchester poets. *See* Winchester poets. Winchester, Hampshire, Eng., Winchester Poetry Circle.   1518958

Winchester poets. *Winchester, Hampshire, Eng., Winchester Poetry Circle.*   1518945
WU   UWM (RBR) 1968-Summer 1975.

Wind. *[Pikeville, Ky.].*   1518960
ISSN: 0361-2481   LCCN: 72-621269   Beg. date: 1971
WU   UWM (RBR) V.1-7 (no.1-25) (SPR1971-1977).

The Wind and the rain. *Nendeln, Kraus Reprint, 1969.*   0798236
LCCN: 49-51885
Originally published in London.
WU   UWM (RBR) V.1 no.2; v.2 no.2-4; v.3 no.1-2; v.4 no.4; v.5 no.1-2,4; v.6 no.3-4; v.7 no.1-2/3 (SUM1941-1951).

The Windless orchard. *Fort Wayne, Ind., Star Business Service.*   1518973
ISSN: 0043-5716   LCCN: 76-645976   Beg. date: 1970
WU   UWM (RBR) No.1-29 (FEB1970-1977).

The Windmill. *London.*   1518986
Beg. date: 1944   End date: 1948
Ceased publication with vol. 3 no. 2, 1948.
WU   UWM (RBR) V.1 no.1-2,4; v.2 no.6,8 (1944-1947).

The Window. *London, Hollywood, Villiers Publications.*   1518999
ISSN: 0508-8062   Beg. date: 1951   End date: 1955
Ceased publication with no. 9, 1955.
WU   UWM (RBR) No.1-3 (n.d.-n.d.); no.4-8 (FEB1952-FEB1955); no.9 (n.d.).

Window. *Takoma Park, Md., Window Press.*   1519006
Beg. date: 1976
WU   UWM (RBR) No.1-4 (SPR1976-1977).

Window, a quarterly magazine. *London, E. Partridge, Ltd.*   0798301
ISSN: 0043-5724
WU   UWM (RBR) V.1 no.1-4 (JAN-OCT1930).

Windsor, Ontario. University. French Department. Poetry, Windsor, poésie. *See* Poetry, Windsor, poésie. Windsor, Ontario, French Department, University of Windsor.   1507791

The Windsor quarterly. *Mena, Ark., etc., Commonwealth College, etc.* 1519019
Beg. date: 1933 End date: 1935
"Modern American literature."
Ceased publication with vol. 3 no. 1, Fall 1935.
Index: 1-3 in vol. 3 no. 1.
WU   UWM (RBR) V.1-v.3 no.1 (SPR1933-FAL1935).

Wine rings. *Sacramento, Wilton, Calif.* 1519047
ISSN: 0146-6356 Beg. date: 1975
WU   UWM (RBR) No.1-7 (SPR1975-1977).

The Winepress. *[n.p.], Social Education Centre.* 1519034
WU   UWM (RBR) One unnumbered, undated issue.

Winged purposes. *Lincoln Center, Mass.* 151905A
Beg. date: 1973
WU   UWM (RBR) V.1 no.1 (FAL/WIN1973).

The Winged word. *Brunswick, Me.* 1519062
LCCN: 45-50308 Beg. date: 1941
"A poetry quarterly."
WU   UWM (RBR) V.1-10 (AUT1941-WIN1952).

Wings. *New York.*
LCCN: 36-30384
"A quarterly of verse."
Ceased publication with vol. 14 no. 6, Summer 1960.
Each volume covers two years.
WU   UWM (RBR) V.1-v.14 no.6 (SPR1933-SUM1960).

Wisconsin. University. University Extension Division. *See* 0800657
Arts in Society. *Madison, University of Wisconsin Extension Division.*

Wisconsin. University--Green Bay. Extension Center. 1498394
Parnassus. *See* Parnassus. *Green Bay, Wisc., University of Wisconsin. Green Bay Extension Center.*

Wisconsin. University--Madison. Cheshire. *See* Cheshire. 1442004
Milwaukee, University of Wisconsin.

Wisconsin. University--Madison. Creative arts '67. *See* 1442177
Creative arts '67. *[Madison, Wisc.].*

Wisconsin. University--Madison. Literary preview. *See* 1493034
Literary preview. *Madison, Wis., Univ. of Wisconsin.*

Wisconsin. University--Madison. Madison review. *See* 1494249
Madison review. *[Madison, Wisc.], Department of English, University of Wisconsin.*

Wisconsin. University--Madison. New idea. *See* New idea. 1494762
Madison, Wisc., The University of Wisconsin.

Wisconsin. University--Madison. Arden Club. Rocking 150476A
horse. *See* Rocking horse. *Madison, Wisc., The Arden Club, University of Wisconsin, Madison.*

Wisconsin. University--Madison. Department of 1501922
Comparative Literature. Quixote. *See* Quixote. *Madison, Wisc., Dept. of Comparative Literature.*

Wisconsin. University--Madison. Department of English. 143847A
Bloodroot. *See* Bloodroot. *Madison, Wis., Dept. of English, Univ. of Wisconsin, and Memorial Union Directorate.*

Wisconsin. University--Madison. Department of English. 1496893
Modine gunch. *See* Modine gunch. *Madison, Wisc., Department of English, University of Wisconsin.*

Wisconsin. University--Milwaukee. Tempest. *See* Tempest. 1510832
Milwaukee, University of Wisconsin, Milwaukee.

Wisconsin Dramatic Society. Play-book. *See* Play-book. 1500250
Madison, Wisc., The Wisconsin Dramatic Society.

Wisconsin Fellowship of Poets. Hawk and whippoorwill 1439251
recalled. *See* Hawk and whippoorwill recalled. *Madison, Wis., Wisconsin Fellowship of Poets.*

Wisconsin Institute for Intermedia Studies. Madison area 1495622
magazine of the arts. *See* Madison area magazine of the arts. *Madison, Wisc., Madison Area Movement of the Arts (MAMA) and the Wisconsin Institute for Intermedia Studies.*

Wisconsin Poetry Alliance magazine. *Madison, Wis.* 1529867
Beg. date: 1973
Some issues have distinctive titles.
WU   UWM (RBR) No.1-3 (1973-1974?).

Wisconsin poetry magazine. *Wauwatosa, Wisc.* 1228519
ISSN: 0043-6607 Beg. date: 1954
WU   UWM (RBR) V.1 no.6; v.2 no.2-5; v.3 no.1-5; v.4 no.1-6; v.5 no.1-2,4-5; v.6 no.1 (n.d.-1960; n. ser. v.7 no.1; v.8 no.3; v.9 no.1; v.10 no.1 (1961-n.d.); suppl. Oct., Dec. 1957; June-July, Sept.. Nov. 1958.

Wisconsin Regional Writers Association. Creative 1431480
Wisconsin. *See* Creative Wisconsin. *Birnamwood, Wis. [etc.].*

Wisconsin Rural Writers Association. Creative Wisconsin. 1431493
See Creative Wisconsin. *Birnamwood, Wis. [etc.].*

Wisconsin's impact! *[n.p.].* 1519075
Beg. date: 1973
"A magazine/newsletter serving the needs of Wisconsin poets, especially members of Improving Poets Arriving at Critical Thought."
WU   UWM (RBR) V.1 no.1-3 (AUT1973-AUT1974).

Within the circle. *London.* 1514793
"The review of the London Writer Circle" (varies).
WU   UWM (RBR) No.95-121 (MAR1970-AUG1977).

The Wivenhoe Park review. *Colchester, Essex, Eng., Department of Literature, University of Essex.* 1519090
ISSN: 0043-7107 Beg. date: 1965 End date: 1968
Ceased publication with no. 3, 1968.
Superseded by Park.
WU   UWM (RBR) No.1-2 (WIN1965-[1967]).

Wloptoonakun. *New York, Bleb Press.* 1519112
"The good word."
WU   UWM (RBR) 1971.

Wolverhampton, England. Polytechnic Wolverhampton. 1437421
Forge. *See* Forge. *Wolverhampton, Eng., Polytechnic Wolverhampton.*

Wolverhampton College of Art. Department of Art History 1499029
and Contemporary Studies. Poetry workshop. *See* Poetry workshop. *Wolverhampton, Eng., Department of Art History and Contemporary Studies, Wolverhampton College of Art.*

Woman child. *See* Womanchild. *Ware, Mass.* 1519138

Womanchild. *Ware, Mass.* 1519125
Beg. date: 1976
WU   UWM (RBR) V.1 no.1 (SUM1976); Summer-Fall 1976.

Womansmith. *Massapequa, N.Y., Womansmith Inc.* 1519140
Beg. date: 1975
WU   UWM (RBR) V.1 no.1 (FAL1975).

Wombat. *Normanhurst, Australia.* 1519153
"A 'For We Are Young and Free' publication."
WU   UWM (RBR) No.2-4 (JUL1971-JUL1972); no.3A, a special poetry issue.

Women poems. *Lexington, Mass., Women/Poems Press.* 1519166
WU   UWM (RBR) No.3-4 (1974-1976).

Women's Poetry Collective. Gravida. *See* Gravida. 1436546
Hartsdale, N.Y.

The Wonewoc review. *Whitewater, Wisc.* 1519179
Beg. date: 1973
WU   UWM (RBR) V.1 no.1 (JAN1973).

Wood ibis. *Austin, Tex., etc., Place of Herons Press.* 1519181
Beg. date: 1975
"A journal of contemporary shamanism."
WU   UWM (RBR) No.1-2 (1975-1976).

The Woods-runner. *Sault Ste. Marie, Mich., Lake Superior State College, Publications Committee.* 1519194
Beg. date: 1970
"Combined with Ruffles & flourishes."
WU   UWM (RBR) V.3 no.11; v.4 no.14-27 (FEB1973-1977).

Worcester State College. Agora. *See* Agora. *[Worcester, Mass., Worcester State College].* 142961A

Word. *Albuquerque, N.M., University of New Mexico.* 1519216
ISSN: 0043-793X Beg. date: 1967
"A poetry broadsheet."
WU   UWM (RBR) V.1 no.1-5 (JAN-NOV1967).

Word. *Galexico, Calif., San Diego State College, Imperial Valley Campus.* 1519231
Beg. date: 1970
WU   UWM (RBR) V.1 no.1 (JAN1970).

The Word. *Hempstead, N.Y., Hofstra College.* 1519257
WU   UWM (RBR) May 1948; Nov. 1950; Apr., May, Fall 1952.

Word ensemble. *London.* 1519272
WU   UWM (RBR) One unnumbered, undated issue.

Word press. *Chula Vista, Calif.* 152987A
WU   UWM (RBR) Sept. 1968.

The Word-smith. *Philadelphia.*   1514843
   Beg. date: 1975
   WU   UWM (RBR) V.1 no.1/2 (SUM1975).

Wordjock. *Tipton, Ind.*   1519285
   ISSN: 0512-2090   Beg. date: 1967   End date: 1968
   "A magazine of poetry."
   Continued by Earthwords with no. 5, April 1970.
   WU   UWM (RBR) V.1 no.1-4 (SEP1967-NOV1968).

Words. *Boston.*   1514815
   Issued by the students of Emerson College in cooperation with the Department of English.
   WU   UWM (RBR) V.2 no.4-5 (MAR15-MAY151974).

Words. *Bramely, Surrey, Eng.*   1514830
   WU   UWM (RBR) No.5-20 (1974-1974).

Words etcetera. *Chula Vista, Calif., etc., Words Press.*   1529882
   Beg. date: 1971
   "A miscellany."
   WU   UWM (RBR) V.2 no.1 (1973).

Wordsmith. *See* Word-smith. Philadelphia.   1514856

Wordworks. *Altrincham, Cheshire, Eng., Michael Butterworth Publications.*   1514869
   ISSN: 0010-9142
   Supersedes Concentrate and Corridor, ISSN 0010-9142.
   WU   UWM (RBR) No.6-7 (1975-1976).

Work. *Detroit, Artists' Workshop Press.*   1514871
   ISSN: 0512-2120   Beg. date: 1965
   WU   UWM (RBR) No.1-5 (SUM1965-1968).

Works. *New York, A M S Press.*   0803494
   ISSN: 0043-812X
   WU   UWM (RBR) V.1-v.4 no.3 (AUT1967-SUM1974).

Workshop. *Brattleboro, Vt.*   1514884
   WU   UWM (RBR) No.23-25 (AUG1974-SUM/FAL1975).

Workshop. *London.*   1514897
   ISSN: 0043-8146   Beg. date: 1967
   Title varies: no. 1, July 1967, Writers' workshop.
   WU   UWM (RBR) No[1]-15,17-27 (1967-1975).

The World. *New York, The Poetry Project.*   1514919
   ISSN: 0043-8154
   "A New York City literary magazine."
   WU   UWM (RBR) No.2-3,5,7-23 (MAR1967-SUM1971).

World frontiers. *New York.*   1514921
   ISSN: 0509-240X   Beg. date: 1952   End date: 1953
   Ceased publication with vol. 2 no. 1, Summer 1953.
   WU   UWM (RBR) V.1-v.2 n o.2 (SPR1952-SUM1954).

World poets. *Charleston, Ill.*   1514934
   Wu   UWM (RBR) No.4-5,9-10,12-14,17 (1971-1975).

World review. *[London, E. Hulton, etc.].*   080539A
   LCCN: 37-37277   Beg. date: 1936
   Formed by the union of Review of reviews and World.
   Title varies: March-Aug. 1936, World review of reviews. Journal of the Federal Union Club, January-June 1940.
   Ceased publication with n. ser. no. 50, April/May 1953?
   WU   UWM (RBR) 1942-Apr./May 1953.

World review of reviews. *See* World review. *[London, E. Hulton, etc.].*   080544A

Wormwood review. *Storrs, Conn.*   0806052
   ISSN: 0043-9401   LCCN: 72-29491   Beg. date: 1960
   Wu   UWM (RBR) V.1-17 (no.1-66) (WIN1960-1977).

Writ. *Toronto, Writing Lab, Innis College, University of Toronto.*   1514947
   ISSN: 0316-3768   Beg. date: 1970
   Supersedes On the bias.
   WU   UWM (RBR) No.1-8 (SPR1970-1976).

Write on. *Pittsburgh, Northland Public Library Wirter's Workshop.*   1514962
   Beg. date: 1974
   WU   UWM (RBR) V.1 no.1-3; v.2 no.1-2 (SPR1974-DEC1975).

The Writer. *London, Bond Street Publishers, Ltd.*   1514975
   WU   UWM (RBR) Oct. 1969-Nov. 1972.

Writers cramp. *Rochester, N.Y.*   1514988
   WU   UWM (RBR) No.3 (JAN1976).

The Writer's exchange. *Frederic, Wisc.*   1514990
   ISSN: 0510-968X   Beg. date: 1961
   Continued —

Continued —
   WU   UWM (RBR) V.1-v.3 no.4 (1961-SUM/FAL1963); The Little companion to the writers exchange (unnumbered,undated).

Writer's forum. *New York.*   093167A
   Beg. date: 1965
   WU   UWM (RBR) V.1 no.1-2; v.2 no.3; v.3 no.4 (MAY1965-SPR1967).

Writers Forum, London. *And. See* And. London, Writers Forum.   1438021

Writers' Guild of Queensland. Expression. *See* Expression. Adelaide.   1441432

Writers in residence. *Bowling Green, Ohio.*   1515008
   WU   UWM (RBR) No.5 (FAL1975).

Writers International. Left review. *See* Left review. London, Writers International, British Section.   1505162

Writer's newsletter. *Bloomington, Ind., Indiana Writes.*   1529895
   Beg. date: 1977
   WU   UWM (RBR) July/Aug. 1977.

Writer's notes & quotes. *Fullerton, Calif. [etc.].*   1515010
   ISSN: 0043-955X   Beg. date: 1951
   "A friendly meeting-place for beginning & advanced writers."
   Title varies: vol. 1-vol. 6 no. 7, 1951-June 1957, Amateur notes & quotes.
   WU   UWM (RBR) V.7 no.1; v.8; v.9 no.1-2,4-6; v.10 no.1-3; v.12 no.1-2; v.13 no.2,4; v.14 no.1-3; v.15 no.2-4; v.16 no.2 (DEC1957-SEP1968).

Writers of the midlands. *Handsworth, Birmingham, Eng.*   1515036
   WU   UWM (RBR) V.1 no.1 (n.d.).

Writers of tomorrow. *[n.p.], Resurgam Books.*   1529917
   WU   UWM (RBR) No.2 (AUT1945). RBR holds second impression, Spring 1946.

Writer's review. *Birdlip, Gloucester, Eng., United Writer's Publications.*   151508A
   ISSN: 043-9568   Beg. date: 1963
   WU   UWM (RBR) V.2 no.4-v.3; v.4 no.1-2,4; v.5-v.6 no.2 (AUT1965-1969 (; no.23-34 (SPR1970-1973); July-Aug. 1974.

Writer's voice. *See* Guardino's gazette. New York.   1439957

The Writer's voice. *New York, Poets of America Publishing Co.*   1515092
   ISSN: 0509-3902   Beg. date: 1958
   Continued by Guardino's gazette.
   WU   UWM (RBR) V.1-2; v.3 no.2-9,11-12; v.4; v.5 no.1-7, 9,11-12; v.6 no.1-4,6-12; v.7 no.1-2 (JAN1958-FEB1964).

Writers' workshop. *See* Workshop. London.   1514906

Writers Workshop, Calcutta. Miscellany. *See* Miscellany. Calcutta, Writers Workshop.   0956422

Writers' Workshop, San Francisco. San Francisco Writers' Workshop magazine. *See* San Francisco Writers' Workshop magazine. San Francisco, Writers' Workshop, California Labor School.   1502290

Writers Workshop miscellany. *See* Miscellany. *Calcutta,*   1466031

Writing at Wyoming. *See* Sage. Laramie, University of Wyoming.   1224395

Writing from Sheffield. *[Sheffield, Eng?], Bookshop and Publishing Committee. Sheffield University Union of Students.*   1515127
   WU   UWM (RBR) May 1967; Jan. 1968.

Writing magazine. *Austin, Tex., St. Edward's University.*   1515101
   Beg. date: 196
   Also called Writing.
   WU   UWM (RBR) No.2-4,6 (SPR1963-APR1968).

Writing today. *London.*   151513A
   ISSN: 0509-3910   Beg. date: 1957
   WU   UWM (RBR) No.1-12 (JUL1957-MAR1962).

Writings. *New York, Media Publishing Center.*   1515142
   Beg. date: 1968
   Supersedes Mississippi Valley writing.
   Title includes date; i.e., Writings 1968.
   WU   UWM (RBR) No.1 (1968).

Wunderhorn musette. *New York.*   1515155
   Beg. date: 1955
   WU   UWM (RBR) No.1 (1955).

Wwhimsy. *St. Louis.*   1515168
   ISSN: 0509-4259   Beg. date: 1955   End date: 1956
   Cover title: W W.
   Ceased publication with vol. 2 no. 3, Dec. 1956.
Continued —

Continued —
WU UWM (RBR) V.1 no.4-5; v.2 no.1-3 (AUG1955-DEC1956).

Wyoming. University. Sage. *See* Sage. Laramie, University of Wyoming.   1224367

Wyoming. University. Department of English. Sage. *See* Sage. Laramie, University of Wyoming.   122437A

Wyoming. University. Department of English. Writing at Wyoming. *See* Sage. Laramie, University of Wyoming.   1224382

X

X; a journal of the arts. *Harrisburg, Pa.*   1515196
   Beg. date: 1977
   Accompanied by occasional chapbooks.
   WU   UWM (RBR) No.1 (SUM1977).

X; a quarterly review. *London, Barrie and Rockliff.*   0910990
   ISSN: 0512-6576   Beg. date: 1959   End date: 1962
   Ceased publication with vol. 2 no. 3, July 1962.
   WU   UWM (RBR) V.1-v.2 no.3 (NOV1959-JUL1962).

Xanadu. *Wantagh, N.Y., Long Island Poetry Collective.*   1515205
   ISSN: 0146-0463   LCCN: sc 77-732   Beg. date: 1975
   WU   UWM (RBR) V.1-v.2 no.4 (SUM1975-1977).

Xanthippe. *San Jose, Calif., Xanthippe Collective and the San Jose State University Women's Center.*   1515220
   Beg. date: 1971
   WU   UWM (RBR) No.1-3 (1971-MAR1976).

Xanthippe Collective.   Xanthippe. *See* Xanthippe. San   1515233
Jose, Calif., Xanthippe Collective and the San Jose State University Women's Center.

Xenia. *Bristol, Eng.*   1515261
   Beg. date: 197   End date: 1976
   Ceased publication with no. 9?, 1976.
   WU   UWM (RBR) No.2-9 (1973-1976).

Xenia. *Chicago.*   1515259
   Beg. date: 1965
   "A magazine of poetry and comment."
   WU   UWM (RBR) No.1 (FAL1965).

Y

Yale lit. *New Haven, Yale University.* 1155255
  Beg. date: 1971
  Continues Yale literary magazine with vol. 141 no. 1, Oct. 1971.
  WU   UWM (RBR) V.141-v.146 no.2 (OCT1971-JAN1977).

The Yale literary magazine (1836-1971). *New Haven, Yale University.* 0807659
  ISSN: 0044-0108 LCCN: 7-19863-4 Beg. date: 1836 End date: 1971
  Included in American Periodical Series.
  Continued by Yale lit with vol. 141 no. 1, Oct. 1971.
  WU   UWM (RBR) V.101 no.6; v.126 no.5; v.127 no.5; v.128 no.4/5; v.130 no.2-5/6; v.131; v.132 no.1,3-5; v.133 no.1-2,5-6; v.134-136; v.137 no.1; v.138,140 (FEB1936,1958-1971).

The Yale literary magazine (1977-). *New Haven, Yale University.* 1515274
  ISSN: 0148-4605 Beg. date: 1977
  Continues Yale lit with vol. 146 no. 3, Feb. 1977, resuming original title.
  WU   UWM (RBR) V.146 no.3-4 (FEB-APR1977).

Yale poetry review. *New Haven, Conn.* 0807687
  Beg. date: 1945 End date: 1948
  Ceased publication with no. 8, 1948.
  Superseded by Poetry New York with 1949.
  Index in v. 1 of Poetry, N.Y.
  WU   UWM (RBR) V.1 no.2-3,6 (AUT1945-1946).

Yale University. Yale lit. *See* Yale lit. New Haven, Yale University. 1155268

Yale University. *See* The Yale literary magazine (1836-1971). New Haven, Yale University. 0807871

Yanagi. *Sausalito, Calif., New College of California.* 1515287
  Beg. date: 1974
  WU   UWM (RBR) No.1-2 (MAY1974-APR1975).

Yankee poetry chapbook. *[Flushing, N.Y.], Leonard Twinem.* 151529A
  Beg. date: 1934 End date: 1935
  Ceased publication with Spring 1935.
  Absorbed by American poetry journal.
  WU   UWM (RBR) Summer, Autumn 1934.

Yardbird reader. *Berkeley, Calif., Yardbird Publishing Company, Inc.* 1515309
  ISSN: 0093-6103 LCCN: 73-75226 Beg. date: 1972
  WU   UWM (RBR) V.1-5 (1972-1976).

Yeah. *New York, Birth Press.* 1515311
  ISSN: 0513-2002 Beg. date: 1961
  "A chronicle of the last days."
  WU   UWM (RBR) No.1-10 (DEC1961-JUL1965).

Year magazine. *See* 1933: a year magazine. Philadelphia, J. Louis Stoll. 1515077

The Yellow book; an illustrated quarterly. *London; Boston [etc.]; E. Mathews and J. Lane; Copeland and Day, [etc.].* 0809407
  LCCN: 5-41105 Beg. date: 1894 End date: 1897
  Ceased publication with vol. 13, April 1897.
  Indexed by Reader's guide to periodical literature.
  WU   UWM (RBR) V.1-13 (APR1894-APR1897).

Yellow brick road. *Tempe, Ariz., Emerald City Press.* 1515324
  ISSN: 0361-8552 LCCN: 77-23 Beg. date: 1974
  "Dedicated to the proposition that in the absurd lurks reality."
  WU   UWM (RBR) No.1-9 (1974-1977).

Yellow butterfly poetry broadsides. *Las Cruces, N.M., The Yellow Butterfly Press.* 1515337
  Beg. date: 1973
  MnWU   UWM (RBR) No.1-8 (1973-1977).

Yellowjacket. *Oxford.* 151534A
  Beg. date: 1939 End date: 1939
  Ceased publication with vol. 1 no. 2, May 1939?
  WU   UWM (RBR) V.1 no.1 (MAR1939).

Yes. *Avoca, N.Y.* 1515352
  Beg. date: 1970 End date: 1975
  "A magazine of poetry."
  Ceased publication with vol. 5 no. 3, Summer 1975.
  WU   UWM (RBR) V.1-v.5 no.3 (AUT1970-SUM1975).

Yes. *Pierrefonds, Que. [etc.].* 1515365
  ISSN: 0044-0353 Beg. date: 1956
  Ceased publication with no. 19, April 1970.
  Superseded by Chien d'or.
  WU   UWM (RBR) V.1-v.2 no.3 (APR1956-FEB1958); no.8-17 (WIN1958/1959-OCT1969).

Yin times. *See* Yin times of Black Bart. Canyon, Calif., Black Bart Brigade. 1515380

The Yin times of Black Bart. *Canyon, Calif., Black Bart Brigade.* 1515378
  Beg. date: 1976
  "A networking."
  No. 1 called The Yin times.
  Supersedes Black Bart brigade.
  WU   UWM (RBR) No.1-2 (FEB1976-JAN1977).

York University, Toronto. Essays on Canadian writing. *See* Essays on Canadian writing. Downsview, Ont., York University. 1433947

York University, Toronto. Waves. *See* Waves. Downsview, Ont., York University. 151845A

York University, Toronto. Atkinson College. Exile. *See* Exile; a literary quarterly. Toronto, Atkinson College, York University. 1140796

Yorkshire Arts Association. Pennine platform. *See* Pennine platform. Wetherby, West Yorkshire, Eng. 1499687

Yorkshire Arts Association. Volt. *See* Volt. Luddenden Foot, York., Eng., Pennine Poets. 1517468

Yorkshire Arts Association. Yorkshire review. *See* Yorkshire review. Bradford, Eng., Yorkshire Arts Association. 1515402

Yorkshire Poets' Association. Intak'. *See* Intak'. Sheffield, Eng.? 1440951

Yorkshire review. *Bradford, Eng., Yorkshire Arts Association.* 1515393
  Beg. date: 1975
  "A magazine of literature and the arts."
  WU   UWM (RBR) No.1-4 (DEC1975-DEC1976).

You. *Santa Ana, Calif.* 1515415
  "A Teleta Alveretta publication."
  Title includes date; i.e., You 1967.
  WU   UWM (RBR) 1967-1968.

Young Men's Progressive Club. Bim. *See* Bim. [St. Michael, Barbados, Young Men's Progressive Club]. 1433135

Young Writers' Group. Cambridge writing. *See* Cambridge writing. Cambridge, Eng., Young Writers' Group. 1434309

Youth. *Chicago, Youth Publishing Co.* 1515428
  Beg. date: 1921
  "A magazine of the arts."
  WU   UWM (RBR) V.1 no.1,4 (1921).

Youths' Art and Culture Circle. Aesthetics. *See* Aesthetics. Bombay, Youths' Art and Culture Circle. 1429585

Yowl. *New York.* 1515430
  ISSN: 0513-3378 Beg. date: 196
  "A poetry publication."
  WU   UWM (RBR) No.5-6 (1964).

Yugen. *New York.* 152992A
  ISSN: 0513-6377 LCCN: 63-51226 Beg. date: 1958 End date: 1962
  Ceased publication with no. 8, 1962.
  WU   UWM (RBR) No.1-8 (1958-1962).

Yukoner. *Whitehorse, Yukon Territory.* 1515443
  Beg. date: 1962
  Absorbed Small world monthly with April 1965.
  WU   UWM (RBR) V.3 no.9-11; v.4 no.1-2 (SEP1965-MAR/APR1966); Sept.-Oct. 1966.

Z

Z. *New York, Z Press.*   1515456
Beg. date: 197
"Published via The Poetry Project at St. Marks Church-in-the-Bowery."
WU   UWM (RBR) No.1-[4] ([1973]-1975).

Zahir. *Newburyport, Mass., Diane Kruchkow.*   1515471
ISSN: 0049-8505   Beg. date: 1970
WU   UWM (RBR) V.1-v.2 no.3 (no.1-9) (WIN1970-1977).

Zanzibar magazine. *Madison, Wis.*   1515484
Beg. date: 1974
WU   UWM (RBR) No.1-3 (1974-SUM1975).

Zebra. *Bristol, Eng.*   1515497
ISSN: 0513-8833   Beg. date: 1954   End date: 1956
Ceased publication with vol. 2 no. 3, Winter 1955/1956.
WU   UWM (RBR) No.3-12 (MAR1954-JAN1955); v.2 no.1-3 (SUM1955-WIN1955/1956).

Zeitgeist. *East Lansing, Mich.*   1515506
ISSN: 0044-2119   Beg. date: 1965
"A quarterly journal of ideas."
WU   UWM (RBR) V.1-v.3 no.1 (SEP1965-1969).

Zephyrus image magazine. *San Francisco.*   1515519
Beg. date: 1972
WU   UWM (RBR) No.1 (1972?).

Zero. *New York, Zero Press.*   1223087
Beg. date: 1949
Suspended publication 1951-May 1954.
Continued by Zero anthology of literature and art with no. 8, 1956.
Index: nos. 1-6, 1949-1954, in no. 7.
WU   UWM (RBR) V.1-2 (no.1-7) (1949-SPR1956).

Zero anthology of literature and art. *See* Zero. New York, Zero Press.   122309A

Zero to nine. *See* 0 to 9. New York.   1515051

Zeugma. *Belmont, Mass., Merrill Kaitz.*   1515521
Beg. date: 1975
"A magazine of poetry and practical poetic theory."
WU   UWM (RBR) No.1-3 (1975-1976).

Ziggurat. *Milwaukee, Wis.*   1529932
Beg. date: 1968
WU   UWM (RBR) No.1-2 (1968-MAR1974).

Zimri. *[Glamorgan, Wales].*   1515534
Beg. date: 196
WU   UWM (RBR) No.2 (SUM1967).

ADDENDUM

Titles added between November 1, 1977 and June 30, 1979

A

Abundanza. San Francisco, Cal.
 Beg. date: 1978
 No. 1 (SUM1978).

After-Image. Towson, Md.
 Beg. date: 1978
 No. 1 (1978).

Aieee. Charlottesville, Va., Alphaville Academy of Archetypes.
 Beg. date: 1974
 No. 3,4,5/6 (JUN1975-1977).

Alembic: a magazine of poetry. Ithaca, New York.
 Beg. date: 1978
 No. 1-2 (1978).

Alive & Kicking. Jackson Heights, N.Y.
 ISSN: 0147-5762 Beg. date: 1976
 No. 1-2 (FAL1976-SPR1978).

Alley Cat Readings. Hermosa Beach, Cal., Bombshelter Press.
 Beg. date: 1975
 No. (1),2-5 (DEC1975-SEP1976).

Altadena Review. Altadena, Cal.
 ISSN: 0162-8208 Beg. date: 1978
 Vol.1, no. 1-2 (SUM1978-WIN1979).

Androgyne. San Francisco, Cal.
 Beg. date: 1971
 No. 2-4 (1976-1978).

Angelstone. Birmingham, Ala.
 Beg. date: 1978
 No. 1 (FAL/WIN1978/1979).

Annex 21. Omaha, Neb., University of Nebraska at Omaha, Community Writers' Workshop.
 Beg. date: 1978
 No. 1 (1978).

Another Chicago Magazine. Oak Park, Ill., Thunder's Mouth Press.
 Beg. date: 1977
 Vol. 1,3 (FAL1977-1978).

Aquila Rose. Saint Paul, Minn., Truck Press.
 Beg. date 1977
 No. 1-6 (1977-1978).

As Is. Bethesda, Md.
 Beg. date: 1971
 (SPR1978).

Ataraxia: a journal of wordcraft. Madison, Ga.
 Beg. date: 1973
 No. 7 (WIN1978).

Athaena: a collection of poetry. Ann Arbor, Mich.
 Beg. date: 1976
 No. (1),2-5 (1976-1977).

Austin Pulpwood. Austin, Tex.
 No. 5,6 (1976?-n.d.)

B

Back Bay View. Hingham, Mass., Back Bay View, Inc., Boston Center for Adult Education and Publishing Course.
 Beg. date: 1976
 Vol. 1, no. 1-3; v. 2, no. 1-2 (FAL 1976-SUM/FAL1978).

Bad Breath. Berkeley, Cal., As Is Press. Some issues published in conjunction with <u>As Is Times</u>.
 Beg. date: 1973
 No. 2, (3), n.n.4-5,6 (MAY1974-1976?).

Barataria. New Orleans, Barataria Press. Supersedes and continues the numbering of Barataria Review.
Beg. date: 1977
No. 3-4 (SPR/SUM1977-FAL1977).

Black Bart. Canyon, Cal.
Continues Yin Times of Black Bart and Black Bart Brigade.
Beg. date: 1979
No. 10 (JAN1979).

Black Beetle. Hove, East Sussex, England.
ISSN: 0140-9808 Beg. date: 1978?
No. 1-2 (1978?).

Black Review. Baltimore, Md., Blackberry Press.
Beg. date: 1978
No. 1 (1978).

Black Rooster. West Lafayette, Ind., Sparrow Press.
Beg. date: 1973
No. (1)-6 (JUN1973-May1978).

Blind Alley. Edinburg, Tex., Blind Alley Press.
Beg. date: 1978
V. 1, no. 1-3 (JAN-OCT1978).

Bloodroot. Grand Forks, N.Dak., Bloodroot, Inc.
ISSN: 0161-2506 Beg. Date: 1976
No. 1-6 (FAL1976-SPR1979).

Blue Buildings. Des Moines, Iowa, Duke University, Department of English.
Beg. date: 1978
No. 1-2 (1978-1979).

Blue Moon News. Tucson, Arizona, University of Arizona, Department of English.
Beg. date: 1976
V. 1, (1)-2; v. 2, No. 1 (SPR1976-1978).

Blue Ridge Review. Charlottesville, Va.
Beg. date: 1978
V. 1, no. 1/2-3 (1978-FAL1978).

Blue Unicorn: tri-quarterly of poetry. Kensington, Cal.
Beg. date: 1977
V.1,no. 1-3; v. 2, no. 1 (OCT1977-OCT1978).

Bogg. Filey, North Yorkshire, England, Fiasco Publications.
Beg. date: 1968.
No. 2-5; 37-41 (1969-1970; 1977-1979).

Bombay Gin. Boulder, Col.
Beg. date: 1976?
No. (3), 4, (5) (WIN/SPR1977-WIN/SPR 1978).

Brains. Valley View, Ill.
Beg. date: 1979
No. 1 (SPR1979).

Bridgend. N. Vancouver, B.C., Capilano College, Humanities Division.
Beg. date: 1977?
No. 1-3 (1977?-JUN1978).

Buffalo Gnats. Glen Rock, N.J., Buffalo Gnats Press
Beg. date: 1976
No. 1-5 (1976-1978.

Bug Tar. San Jose, Cal., Bug Tar Press.
Beg. date: 1977
No. 1-2 (SUM1977-FAL1979).

Bum News. Corby, Northants, England., Excello & bollard. Also entitled British Underground Magscene News.
ISSN: 0140-7236 Beg. date: 1977?
Nos. 4-10 (1978-1979).

Burnt River Primer. Cleveland, Ohio, Falling Down Press.
Beg. date: 1975?
No. (1)-(3) (1975?-1976?)

C

Calliope. Bristol, R.I., Roger Williams College, Division of Fine Arts.
Beg. date: 1977
V. 1, no. 1-2; v. 2, no. 1 (1977-1978).

Carousel. Glen Echo, Md., Writer's Center. Subtitle: Newsletter for Writer's Center Members.
Beg. date: 1976
7 issues (SEP?1978-MAY1979).

Carousel Quarterly of Poetry. Mount Laurel, N.J.
Beg. date: 1976
V. 4, no. 1 (SPR1979).

CCLM Newsletter. New York, Coordinating Council of Literary Magazines.
Beg. date: 1978
2 issues (MAY-DEC1978).

Chair. Billingham, Cleveland, England.
No. 4-7 (WIN1977-WIN1978).

Chicory. Ruffsdale, Pa., Rook Press.
Beg. date: 1978
V. 1, no. 1 (1978).

Chock. Canterbury, Kent, England., The University, Rutherford College.
ISSN: 0140-9794 Beg. date 1978?
No. 1-2 (1978?).

Chunga Review. Felch, Mich.
Beg. date: 1978
V. 1, no. 1-2 (1978-1979).

Cicada. Toronto, Ontario, Haiku Society of Canada.
ISSN: 0703-1831 CN: 78-39031
Beg. date: 1977
V. 1, no. 1-4; v. 2, no. 1-4; v. 3, no. 1 (APR1977-1979).

City Miner. Berkeley, Cal.
Beg. date: 1976
V. 1, no. 1-3; v. 2, no. 1-4; v. 3, no. 1-4 (no. 11) (SPR1976-1978).

Climate: a journal of Australasian writing. Wellington, New Zealand. Continues Mate.
Beg. date: 1978
No. 28 (AUT1978).

Clover Patch. Montrose, Pa.
Beg. date: 1973
No. 5-6 (WIN1977-SUM1977).

Clown War. Brooklyn, N.Y.
Beg. date: 1972
No. 20 (JAN1979).

Co-evolution Quarterly. Sausalito, Cal. Point Press.
Beg. date: 1974
No. 20-21 (WIN1978-SPR1979).

Connecticut Quarterly. Enfield, Conn., Asnuntuck Community College Press.
Beg. date: 1979
V. 1, no. 1 (1979).

Contrast. Westminster, Md., Western Maryland College.
Beg. date: 1960.
V. 22, no. 1-2 (1978-1979.

Coqui: an independent literary review. Carolina, Puerto Rico, Cibola Studio.
Beg. date: 1977
No. 1-4 (1977/1978-1979).

COSMEP Midwest Newsletter. West Branch, Iowa.
V. 2, no. 1-2 (OCT1978-JAN1979).

COSMEP South News: little presses in the South. Carrboro, N.C.
Beg. date: 1974
V. 4, no. 1-4; v. 5, no. 1-3 (MAR 1977-WIN/SPR1979).

Creel. New York.
Beg. date: 1979?
No. 1 (n.d.-1979?).

Croton Review. Croton-on-Hudson, N.Y.
Beg. date: 1978
V. 1, no. 1 (SUM1978).

Addendum   Little Magazine Collection - University of Wisconsin

Cultural Watchdog Newsletter. White
  Plains, N.Y.
  V. 2, no. 4/5 (1979).

Cumberlands. Pikeville, Ky., Pikeville
  College Press of the Appalachian
  Studies Center. Supersedes and con-
  tinues Twigs.
  Beg. date: 1977
  V. 14, no. (1); v. 15, no. 1-3
  (FAL1977-FAL/WIN1978)

D

Dancing Ledge Mercury. Stroud, Glou-
  cester, England, Dancing Ledge X
  Press, The Old Convent.
  Beg. date: 1977
  No. 1 (1977).

Davidson Miscellany. Davidson, N.C.
  Continues Miscellany.
  Beg. date: 1978
  V. 14, no. 1 (1978).

The Deep Earth Review. Chessington,
  Surrey, England.
  Beg. date: 1977?
  No. 1-2 (1977?-JAN1979).

Dico. Victoria, B.C., Canada.
  Beg. date: 1978/1979
  V. 1, no. 1 (1978/1979).

Dodgems. New York, Fido Publications.
  Beg. date: 1977
  No. 1-(2) (1977-n.d.).

Dodo. Sydney, New South Wales, Austra-
  lia, Sydney University.
  Beg. date: 1975
  V. 3, no. 1-2 (1977-1978?)

Dog. Maidstone, Kent, England.
  Beg. date: 1978
  1 issue, n.n. (1978).

Dreams. New York.
  No. 10 (1979).

Durak: the international magazine of
  poetry. Westlake, Cal.
  ISSN: 0163-6413 Beg. date: 1978
  No. 1-2 (1978-1979).

E

Energy Review: a creative arts magazine.
  Beg. date: 1977
  V.1, no. 1-3 (1977).

Et Cetera. Sinking Spring, Pa.
  V. 3, no. 1/2-3 (also numbered 9/10-
  11), (1978-1979).

Euterpe. New York, New York Literary
  Society.
  Beg. date: 1977
  V. 1, no. 1-3; v. 2, no. 2-3 (1977-
  1979).

Everyman His Own Football. Montreal.
  Beg. date: 1977
  1 issue, n.n. (1977).

F

Famous. Oakland, Cal.
  Beg. date: 1975
  2 issues (1975-1977).

Fiction Texas. Texas City, Tex.,
  College of the Mainland.
  Beg. date: 1978
  V. 1, no. 1 (1978).

Figment. Newton, Mass.
  Beg. date: 1970
  No. 1-7 (1970-1978).

Fireweed: a quarterly magazine of
  working-class and socialist arts.
  Lancaster, England.
  Beg. date: 1975
  No. 1-12 (SPR1975-APR1978).

Fish. Needham, Mass., Roxbury Poetry
  Enterprises.
  Beg. date: 1977
  Ceased publication with no. 1, 1977.
  No. 1 (1977).

Fit. Wilkes-Barre, Pa., Fit Press.
  Beg. date: 1979
  No. 1 (1979).

Flute. New York, The Subway Press.
  Beg. date: Fall 1975
  n.n. (FAL1975-WIN1977), 4 issues.

Follies. Pasadena, Cal.
  ISSN: 0162-721X Beg. date: 1975
  V. 4, no. 1-5 (OCT1978-1979).

Foothill Quarterly. Los Altos Hills,
  Cal., Foothill College.
  Beg. date: 1975
  V. 1, no. 1-4; v. 2, no. 1-4, v. 3,
  no. 1-2 (1975-1979).

Footprint Magazine. Somerville, N.J.
  Beg. date: Spring 1978
  no. (1)-2 (SPR1978-AUT1978).

Forms: a magazine of poetry and fine
  arts. Bethlehem, Pa.
  V. 1, no. 2 (1978).

Frogpond. New York, Haiku Society of
  America, Japan House.
  Beg. date: Feb. 1978
  V. 1, no. 1-4 (FEB-NOV1978).

Front. Kingston, Ontario, Canada.
  Beg. date: 1975
  No. 2 published jointly with It needs
  to be said.
  No. (1), 2-5 (1975-1978).

G

Gargoyle. Jamaica Plain, Mass.
  Subtitle: A Publication of the
  Cambridge Poets.
  Beg. date: Spring 1975.
  No. 1-9 (1975-1979).

Gargoyle. Rockville, Md., Paycock
  Press.
  ISSN: 0162-1149 Beg. date: Aug. 1976
  V. 1, no. 1-4; no. 5-10 (1976-1978).

Ghent Quarterly: a review of the arts.
  Norfolk, Va., St. Regis Press.
  Beg. date: Summer 1975
  No. 1 (1975).

Glitch. Groton, Conn.
  Beg. date: 1978?
  No. 1-2 (n.d.).

Graham House Review. Englewood, N.J.,
  Graham House Press.
  ISSN: 0145-7780 LCCN 77-649839
  Beg. date: Summer 1976
  V.1,no. 1, 3-4 (SUM1976-SPR1979).

Gramercy Review: a journal of contemporary poetry and fiction. Los Angeles.
  Beg. date: 1977
  V. 1, no. 3-4; v. 2, no. 1-4, v. 3,
  no. 1 (JUL1977-WIN1979).

Great River Review. Winona, Minn.
  ISSN: 0160-2144 Beg. date: 1977
  V. 1, no. 1-3 (1977-1978).

Green House. Dedham, Mass.
  ISSN: 0364-7641 LCCN: 76-647936
  Beg. date: Spring 1976
  V. 1, no. 1-3; v. 2, no. 1-2
  (SPR1976-SPR1979).

Gusto: a literary/poetry journal.
  Bronx, N.Y., Gusto Press.
  ISSN: 0190-2253 Beg. date: Summer
  1978
  V. 1, no. 1-4 (SUM1978-SPR1979).

H

Harvest. Farmington, Conn., Connecticut
  Writers League.
  Beg. date: 1974
  NO. (2),3-4 (1975-1977).

Harvest. Willowdale, Ontario, Canada.
  Beg. date: Summer 1977
  No. 1-5/6 (SUM1977-SEP1978).

Hawk-wind. Grafton, Wis.
  Beg. date: January 1979
  No. 1 (JAN1979).

High/coo: a quarterly of short poetry.
  West Lafayette, Ind.
  Beg date: 1976
  V. 2, no. 5-8; v. 3, no. 9-11 (AUG
  1977-FEB1979).

Hills. San Francisco, Cal.
  Beg. date: March 1973
  No. 1-5 (MAR1973-1978).

Addendum   Little Magazine Collection - University of Wisconsin

Hot Water Review. Philadelphia, Pa.
  Beg. date: 1976
  No. (1)-2 (1976-1977).

I

Image Magazine: a magazine of the arts.
  Fenton, Mo., Cornerstone Press.
  Beg. date: 1972
  SPR/SUM1975, FAL1976, APR/SUM1977,
  v. 6, no. 1, n.n.1978 (1975-1978).

Independent. Arlington, Mass.
  Beg. date: 1978
  V. 0, no. 1-2; v. 1, no. 1 (1978-
  JAN1979).

Ins & Outs: a magazine of awareness.
  Amsterdam, The Netherlands, Ins &
  Outs Publications.
  Beg. date: 1978
  V. 1, no. 1-3 (1978-WIN/SPR1979).

Intrinsic: poetry and poetics. Toronto,
  Ontario, Canada.
  ISSN: 0704-7290 Beg. date: Summer
  1977
  No. 1-4 (SUM1977-SPR1978.

J

Joe Soap's Canoe. Clare, Suffolk, En-
  gland, Syntaxophone Publications.
  Beg. Date: 1978
  No. 1-2 (OCT1978-FEB1979).

Journal. Chicago, Illinois, Journal
  Books, Fathom Press.
  Beg. date: 1976
  No. 1-2 (1976-1977).

K

Kaldron. Grover City, Cal., Rainbow
  Resin Press.
  Beg. date: 1976
  No. 2-8 (1977-1978/1979).

Kaleidoscope. London, England.
  Beg. date: 1973?
  No. 2,4-5 (1973?-1975).

Kencompotl. Ravenna, Ohio, Shelly's
  Press.
  Beg. date: May 1978
  No. 1-4 (1978).

Koff. New York, Consumptive Poets
  League.
  V. 2, no. 1; no. 3 (1978).

Kontakte. Toronto, Ontario, Canada,
  Phenomenon Press.
  Beg. date: 1976
  V. 1, no. 2-3; v. 2, no. 1-3 (DEC
  1976-1978).

Kudos. Leeds, England.
  Beg. date: 1979
  No. 1 (1979).

Kudzu. Cayce, South Carolina.
  Beg. date: 1977
  No. 1-8 (JUL1977-WIN1978/1979).

L

Lady-Unique-Inclination-Of-The-Night.
  New Brunswick, N.J., Sowing Circle
  Press.
  Beg. date: Autumn 1976
  Cycle 1-3 (1976-1978).

Lake Street Review. Minneapolis, Minn.
  Beg. date: 1976
  V. 1, no. 1; no. 2-6 (SPR/SUM1976-
  WIN1979).

Language. New York
  Beg. date: 1978
  V. 1, no. 1-5 (1978).

LCAN Newsletter. San Francisco, Cal.
  The Commentator's Press.
  ISSN: 0162-9522 Beg. date: 1977
  V. 2, no. 6 (1978).

Letters Magazine. Stonington, Maine.
  n.n., 11 issues (APR1975-SEP/JAN1977/
  1978).

Limberlost Review: a magazine of poetry.
Pocatello, Idaho, Idaho State University, Department of English.
Beg. date: 1976
V. 1, no. 1-6 (FAL1976-1979).

Longhouse. Brattleboro, Vt.
Beg. date: Spring 1976
n.n., 6 issues (SPR1976-SPR1978).

Lore-X. Brownwood, Tex.
Beg. date: 1977
V. 1, no. 1-4; v. 2. no. 1-4 (1977-1978).

Lost Glove. New York.
Beg. date: 1977
V. 1, no. 1 (1977).

Louisville Review. Louisville, Ky., University of Louisville.
ISSN: 0148-3250 LCCN: 77-641327
Beg. date: Fall 1976
No. 1-5 (FAL1976-1978.

M

Maelstrom Review. Longbeach, Cal., Nausea Publications/Russ Haas Press.
V. 4, no. 2/3 (SPR/SUM1978).

Mag City. New York
Beg. date: 1977
No. 1-6 (1977-1979).

Mamashee: a literary quarterly. Inwood, Ontario, Canada.
ISSN: 0702-7575 CN: 78-30560
Beg. date: 1977
V. 1, no. 2-4; v. 2, no. 1-4 (1977-1978)

Manassas Review. Manassas, Va. Northern Virginia Community College - Manassas Campus.
Beg. date: 1977
V. 1, no. 1-2 (1977-1978)

Mars. London, England.
Beg. date: 1977
No. 1-2 (1977-?)

Maxy's Journal. Nashville, Tenn., Truedog Press.
Beg. date: 1978
No. 1-2 (1978-1979).

Meantime. Cambridge, England.
Beg. date: 1977
No. 1 (1977).

Mini Review. Long Beach, Cal.
Beg. date: 1977
V. 1, no. 1-2 (1977).

Missouri Review. Columbia, Mo., University of Missouri-Columbia, Department of English.
ISSN: 0191-1961 LCCN: 79-642599
Beg. date: 1978
V. 1, no. 1; v. 2, no. 1 (1978).

Mixed Voices. New York, Olive Press.
Beg. date: Fall 1977
V. 1, no. 1-3 (1977-1978).

Mondo: a river city journal. Austin, Tex., Orpheus Press.
Beg. date: January 1978
V. 1, no. 1-3 (1978).

Montreal Poems. Dewittville, Quebec, Canada, Sunken Press Forum.
Title varies: Poésie de Montréal.
Beg. date: 1974
ISSN: 0702-7184 CN: 77-32243
No. 3-4 (WIN1976-WIN1978).

Moody Street Irregulars: a Kerouac newsletter. Clarence Center, N.Y.
Beg. date: Winter 1978
V. 1, no. 1-3 (1978-1979)

Moonshine Review. Flowery Branch, Ga.
Beg. date: 1978
No. 1 (1978).

Moosehead Review. Waterville, Quebec, Canada.
Beg. date: 1977
V. 1, no. 1-2 (1977-1978).

Mota: museum of temporary art. Washington, D.C.
ISSN: 0149-4902
No. 16 (1978).

Motheroot Journal: a women's review of small presses. Pittsburgh, Pa.
Beg. date: Fall 1978
n.n. (FAL1978).

Mountain Review. Whitesburg, Ky.
ISSN: 0145-546X LCCN: 76-649176
Beg. date: 1974
V. 4, no. 1-3 (178-1979).

MRB Network: Madison Review of Books. Madison, Wis.
Beg. date: 1979
V. 1, no. 1 (1979).

Mugshots. Hayes, Middlesex, England, Poet & Peasant Books.
Beg. date: 1976
No. 1-12 (1976-1977).

N

El Nahuatzen. Iowa City, Iowa, University of Iowa.
ISSN: 0162-9085 Beg. date: 1978
V. 1, no. 1 (1978).

New Deep City Press: San Francisco's Taxi Horizon. San Francisco, Cal.
No. 11 (1978).

New Earth Review. New York.
Supersedes and continues the numbering of New York Poetry.
V. 1, no. 2-4 (1975-1977).

New England Review. Hanover, N.H.
ISSN: 0164-3177 LCCN: 79-644868
Beg. date: Autumn 1978
V. 1, no. 1-3 (1978-1979).

New Hope. Merseyside, England, Headland Publications.
Beg. date: 1978
Supersedes and incorporates Hallamshire & Osgoldcross Poetry Express and Promontory.
No. 1 (1978).

New Jersey Poetry Monthly. Saddle Brook, N.J., New Jersey Poetry Press.
Beg. date: April 1977
ISSN 0146-1087
V. 1, no. 1-9; v. 2, no. 1-11; v. 3, no. 1 (1977-1979.

New Journal. Austin, Tex.
Beg. date: 1978
Annual publication.
1 issue (1978)

New Quarterly Cave. Hamilton, New Zealand.
LCCN 76-647578 Beg. date: 1976
"An International Review of Arts and Ideas." Supersedes Cave. Ceased publication with vol. 2, no. 4 (Oct. 1977). Continued by Pacific Quarterly.
V. 1, no. 1-4,; v. 2, no. 1-4 (JAN1976-OCT1977).

New World Journal. Berkeley, Cal., Turtle Island Foundation.
Beg. date: 1975
Published by the Netzahaucoyotl Historical Society.
V. 1, no. 1-2/3 (1975-1977).

New Yorkshire Writing. West Yorkshire, England.
Beg. date: Summer 1977
No. 2-7 (1977-1979).

Nit & Wit: a monthly literary arts magazine. Chicago, Ill.
Beg. date: 1977
V. 1, no. 1-3 (1977-1978).

Noon At Night Magazine. Iola, Wis.
Beg. date: 1978
No. 1 (1978).

North Carolina Review. Raleigh, N.C., The N. C. Review Press.
Beg. date: Winter 1976
1 issue (WIN1976).

Northeast Journal. Providence, R.I.
Beg. date: 1978
Supersedes Harbinger.
V. 1, no. 1 (1978).

Northern Woman Journal. Thunder Bay Ontario, Canada.
V. 4, no. 2-6; v. 5, 1-2 (FEB1978-APR/MAY1979).

Little Magazine Collection - University of Wisconsin   Addendum

O

On the Cusp. Battleground, Ind., Prophet's Rock Press.
Beg. date: 1977
1 issue (SPR1977).

The Open Reader. Sausalito, Cal., In Between Books.
Beg. date: 1977
No. 1-3 (1977).

Origin. Series 4. Kyoto, Japan.
Beg. date: 1977
See: Origin, Series 2 and 3.
No. 1-7 (1977-1979).

Outcrowd. Maidstone, Kent, England
Beg. date: 1975
Unnumbered issues each with individual title: Slugs, Uncle Nasty's Original Pork Pies (2 issues), Gazund.
4 issues (1975-1978).

Ozark Review. Piedmont, Mo.
Beg. date: 1978
V. 1, no. 1-2 (1978).

P

Pacific Quarterly. Hamilton, New Zealand.
ISSN: 0110-3970 Beg. date: Jan. 1978
Supersedes and continues the numbering of New Quarterly Cave.
V. 3, no. 1-4 (1978).

Panda. Banbury, Oxon, England, Panda Press.
Folios no. 14-36 (1978).

Paragraph. San Francisco, Cal., Antares Foundation.
Beg. date: 1978
"A quarterly of gay fiction."
No. 1 (1978).

Parchment. Waupaca, Wis.
Beg. date: 1979
V. 1, no. 1-3 (1979).

Perfect Bound. Cambridge, England.
Beg. date: 1976
No. (1-2), 3-7 (1976-1979).

Periodics: a magazine devoted to prose. Vancouver, B.C., Canada.
Beg. date: 1977
No. 1-4 (1977-1978).

Permafrost. Fairbanks, Alaska.
Beg. date: 1977
V. 1, no. 1-3; v. 2, no. 1 (1977-1978).

Pikestaff Forum. Normal, Ill., Pikestaff Publications.
ISSN: 0192-8716 Beg. date: 1978
No. 1 (1978).

Plucked Chicken. Morgantown, W.VA.
Beg.date: 1977
No. 1-3 (1977-1978).

Plum. New York.
Beg. date: 1978
No. 1 (1978).

Plumbers Ink. Honolulu, Hi., Plumbers Ink Press
Beg. date: 1977
V. 1, no. 1 (1977).

Poetalk/Poemphlet. Berkeley, Cal., Bay Area Poets Coalition.
V. 4, no. 8-9 (1979).

Poetry &. Chicago, Ill.
Beg. date: 1976
V. 1, no 1-11; v. 2, no. 1-12 (1976-1978).

Poetry Project Newsletter. New York, St. Mark's Church.
No. 58-62 (1978-1979).

Poetry Toronto Newsletter. Toronto, Ontario, Canada.
ISSN: 0703-7023 CN: 77-33486
Beg. date: April 1975
no. 9-11; 37-40 (1976-1979).

Addendum   Little Magazine Collection - University of Wisconsin

Poets. New York.
   Beg. date: 1978
   V. 1, no. 1-5 (1978).

Poets in the South: Conversation within the word. Tampa, Fla., New Collage Press.
   Beg. date: 1977
   University of South Florida, Center for Writers.
   V. 1, no. 1-2 (1977-1978).

Press Pigeons. Crumpsall, Manchester, England.
   No. 2-3 (1977).

Puck's Corner. Gloucester, Mass.
   Beg. date: 1978.
   V. 1, no. 1-8; v. 2, no. 1 (1978-1979).

Purple Patch. West Bromwich, West Midlands, England.
   No. 4-11 (n.d.- 1979?).

Q

Quarterly West. Salt Lake City, Utah.
   Beg. date: Fall 1976
   No. 1-8 (1976-1979).

Quindaro. Kansas City, Kans.
   Beg. date: 1978
   no. 1-3 (1978-1979).

Qwertyuiop. Columbus, Ohio, Reductio Ad Asparagus Press.
   Beg. date: 1978
   No. 1 (1978).

R

Rawz. London, England.
   Beg. date: 1977
   No. 1 (1977).

Readout Poetry. Hyattsville, Md.
   Beg. date: (Feb. 1976)
   Ceased publication with v. 2, no. 2, Fall 1977.
   V. 1, no. 1-5; v. 2, no. 1-2 (n.d.- FEB1976?-FAL1977).

Red Balloon Poetry Conspiracy. Brooklyn, N.Y.
   Beg. date: 1975
   No. 1-5, 1975- 1978/1979).

Red M(irage): a quarterly magazine of the experimental. Brooklyn, N.Y., Red Herring Press.
   Beg. date: 1977
   No. 1 (1977).

Renegade. New York.
   No. 1 (1978?).

Review Ottawa. Ottawa, Canada, Commoners Publishing Society
   ISSN: 0703-4563 CN: 79-30071
   Beg. date: Autmun 1977
   V. 1, no. 1 (AUT1977).

Rhino. Bannockburn, Ill.
   Beg. date: 1976
   Ceased publication with v.2, no. 1, 1978.
   V. 1, no. 2-3; v. 2, no. 1 (1977-1978).

Riverrun. Cook's Hill, New South Wales, Australia, Riverrun Press.
   Beg. date: 1976
   V. 1, no. 1-4 (1976-1977/1978).

RiverSedge. Edinburg, Tex.
   Beg. date: 1977
   "A journal of art, poetry, and prose from the Lower Rio Grande Valley of Texas.
   V. 1, no. 1-4; v. 2, no. 1-2 (1977-1978).

River Styx. St. Louis, Mo., Big River Association.
   ISSN: 0149-8851 Beg. date: 1975
   No. 1-5 (1975-1979).

Roof. New York, Segue Press.
   ISSN: 0163-0687 Beg. date: Summer 1976
   V. 1, no. 2-6; v. 2, no. 3-4 (also 7-8) (1976-1978).

Room: a women's literary journal. San Francisco, Cal.
Beg. date: 1976
V. 1, no. 1-2/3 (1976-1976/1977).

S

Salome: a literary dance magazine. Chicago, Ill.
Beg. date: 1976
No. 1/2, 7, 8/9, 10 (1976-n.d.1978?).

Salt Cedar. Fort Collins, Col., Tamarix House.
Beg. date: 1977
No. 1-2 (1977-1978).

San Fernando Poetry Journal. Northridge, Cal., Kent Publications.
Beg. date: 1979
V. 1, no. 1 (1979).

San Jose Studies. San Jose, Cal.
Beg. date: Feb. 1975
V. 1, no. 1-3; v. 2, no. 1-3; v. 3, no. 1-3; v. 4, no. 1-3; v. 5, no. 1 (1975-1979), and a 1976 special issue, a 1977 special issue.

San Marcos Review. Albuquerque, N.M., San Marcos Press.
No. 1-2 (n.d.1976?-1978).

Sands: a literary review. Dallas, Tex.
Beg. date: 1978
Continues Sand.
1 issue (1978).

Scratch. Cleveland, Ohio, Mostly Broken Scabs Press/Falling Down Press.
2 issues (n.d.).

Seattle Review. Seattle Wash.
ISSN: 0147-6629 Beg. date: Fall 1978
University of Washington
V. 1, no. 1-2 (1978).

Second Growth. Johnson City, Tenn.
Beg. date: 1975
"Appalachian Nature and Culture."
2 different issues identified as V. 1, no. 1 (1975).

A Selected Few/The People's Gallery Bellerose, N.Y.
Beg. date: 1970
V. 4, no. 1-2; v. 5, no. 1-2; v. 6, no. 1-2; v. 7, no. 1; v.8, no. 1 (1973-1977).

Sez. Minneapolis, Minn., Shadow Press.
ISSN: 0190-3640 Beg. date: Winter 1978
"A multi-racial journal of poetry & people's culture."
No. 1 (WIN1978).

Shankpainter. Provincetown, Mass., Fine Arts Work Center in Provincetown, Work Center Press.
Beg. date: 1969
No. 3-5, 8-11, 15-18 (1970-1979).

Sheaf: a magazine of contemporary writing. San Francisco, Cal.
Beg. date: 1977
V. 1, no. 1-2 (1977-1978).

Shelly's. Ravenna, Ohio, Shelly's Press.
Beg. date: 1974
No. (1) 2-4, 6-8 (1974-1978).

Silver Vain: a literary magazine. Park City, Utah, Pi Right Press.
ISSN: 0147-6122 LCCN: 77-641755
Beg. date: Spring 1977
No. 1-3 (1977-1978).

Silverfish Review. Eugene, Ore.
ISSN: 0164-1085 Beg. date: January 1979
No. 1 (JAN1979).

Sing Heavenly Muse. Minneapolis, Minn.
Beg. date: 1978
"Women's poetry and prose."
No. 1-2 (1978).

Skullpolish. Santa Ana, Cal., Broken Arrow Press.
Beg. date: 1977
V. 1, no. 1-3 (1977-1978).

Addendum	Little Magazine Collection - University of Wisconsin

Slackwater Review. Lewiston, Idaho, Confluence Press.
ISSN: 0160-7677   LCCN: 78-642353
Beg. date: 1976
"A Northwest magazine of the arts."
V. 1, no. 1-2; v. 2, no. 1-2; special issue (1977-1978).

Slick Press Poetry/Fiction Magazine. Chicago, Ill.
No. 6-9 (1978).

Slow Dancer. Crouch End, London, England.
Beg. date: 1977
No. 1-3 (1977-1978).

Slow Loris Reader. Pittsburgh, Pa.
ISSN: 0191-5703   Beg. date: 1979
V. 1, no. 1/2 (1979).

Small Moon. Boston, Mass., Poetry Cooperative of Boston.
Beg. date: 1975
"A journal of the Poetry Cooperative of Boston."
No. 1-6 (1975-1978?)

Small Press Novels & Novellas. New Berlin, N.Y., Molly Yes Press.
Beg. date: 1978
V. 1, no. 1-5; v. 2, no. 1 (also no. 6) (1978-1979).

Smudge. Detroit, Mich.
Beg. date: 1978
No. 1-4 (1978-1978/1979).

Sniffin Flowers. Romford, Essex, England.
No. 3 (1978?).

Soft Times. Milwaukee, Wis., O Press/Heavy Evidence.
No. 3 (1976).

Solana: a women's forum. St. Louis, Mo.
Beg. date: 1976
V. 1, no. 1-2; v. 2, no. 1 (1976-1978).

Soundings. Salem, Mass., Salem State College.
Beg. date: 1978
V. 1, no. 1-2 (1978).

Source. Jamaica, N.Y., Queens Council on the Arts, Literary Arts Division.
Beg. date: 1976
V. 1, no. 1-2; v. 2, no. 1-2 (1976-n.d.1979?).

South Shore. AuTrain, Mich.
ISSN: 0149-6824   Beg. date: 1977
V. 1, no. 1-2 (1977-1978).

Speakeasy. Iowa City, Iowa.
Beg. date: 1976
No. 1-3 (1976-1978).

Spondee. Hammond, Ind.
Beg. date: 1977
V. 1, n.n.-2 (1977).

Spring. Syracuse, N.Y.
Beg. date: 1979
No. 1 (1979).

Stable Diet. Suffolk, England.
Beg. date: July 1977.
Published in conjunction with Stable; no. 2 incorporated in Stable, no. 5.
No. 1 (JUL1977).

Start. Burslen, Stoke-on-Trent, England.
Beg. date: 1978
No. 1-4 (1978-1979).

Stony Hills. Newburyport, Mass.
ISSN: 0146-2067   Beg. date: 1977
V. 1, no. 1-3 (1977-1978).

Stony Thursday Book. Rath Bhane, Limerick, Ireland.
Beg. date: 1975
No. 2-5 (1976-1977/1978).

Sunrise Magazine. Red Deer, Alberta, Canada.
Beg. date: July 1978
No. 1 (JUL1978).

Survivor. Rochester, N.Y., Morning Glory Media, Inc.
Beg. date: 1977
2 issues, n.n., V. 2, no. 1 (1978).

Syncline. Chicago, Ill., Brachio Press.
  ISSN: 0163-6375 Beg. date: 1977
  2 issues, n.n. (1977).

T

Tailings. Houghton, Mich.
  Beg. date: 1977
  Michigan Technological University,
  Humanities Department.
  V. 1, no. 1 (1977).

Tamarack. Potsdam, N.Y., Banjo Press.
  Beg. date: 1978
  No. 1 (1978).

Tamarisk. Ramsey, N.J., Tamarisk Press.
  Supersedes Apocalypse.
  V. 2, no. 1-2 (1978).

Tawte. Berkeley, Cal., Thorp Springs
  Press.
  Beg. date: 1974
  "A journal of Texas culture; Texas
  artists, writers, and thinkers in
  exile."
  2 issues, n.n. (1974-1975).

Tendril. Green Harbor, Mass.
  Beg. date: Winter 1977/1978
  No. 1-4 (1977/1978-1979).

Tequila Press Poetry Review. Long Beach,
  Cal.
  Beg. date: 1977
  No. 1-3 (1977-1978).

Text. New York.
  Beg. date: 1976/1977
  No. 1-10 (1976/1977-1978/1979).

Third Eye. Williamsville, N.Y., Third
  Eye Publications.
  Beg. date: June 1976
  No. 1-9 (JUN1976-WIN1978/1979).

Thorn Apple. Las Vegas, Nev.
  Beg. date: 1977
  V. 1, no. 1, n.n. (1977-SUM1978).

Three Sisters. Washington, D.C.
  Beg. date: Fall 1971
  Georgetown University
  V. 6, no. 1-3, n.n.; v. 7, 1-2 (1977-
  1978).

Tinderbox. Mt. Pleasant, S.C.
  Beg. date: 1978
  V. 1, no. 3-4; v. 2, no. 1 (1978-
  1979).

Tiotis Poetry News. Fort Myers, Fla.,
  M.O.P. Press.
  Beg. date: 1979
  V. 1, no. 1-2 (1979).

Tooth of Time Review. Guadalupita, N.M.,
  Tooth of Time Publications.
  Beg. date: 1974
  No. 4-7 (1976-1978).

Touchstone. Houston, Tex.
  Beg. date: 1976
  V. 3, no. 2 (n.d.)

Truly Fine Press. Bemidji, Minn.
  Beg. date: 1976
  No. 2-3 (1977-1978).

23 Club Series: all new fits printed.
  Buffalo, N.Y., Intrepid Press.
  Beg. date: 1971
  No. 1 (1971).

Twisted Wrist. Hebden Bridge, West
  Yorkshire, England
  Beg. date: 1977
  No. 1-3 (1977-1978).

Two Hands News. Chicago, Ill.
  Beg. date: 1976
  No. 5, 17 (1976-1978).

Two Steps In: a journal of the arts.
  Palo Alto, Cal.
  V. 2, no. 2 (1978).

U

US1 Worksheets. Roosevelt, N.J., Bird
  in the Bush Press
  Beg. date: 1973
  No. 1-11 (1973-1978).

Ululatus. Fort Smith, Ark., Ululatus,
  Inc.
  Beg. date: 1978
  V. 1, no. 1-3 (1978-1979).

Addendum   Little Magazine Collection - University of Wisconsin

United Artists. Lenox, Mass.
  Beg. date: November 1977
  No. 1-6 (1977-1979).

Urbane Gorilla. Sheffield, England, Raven Publications.
  Beg. date: 1970
  No. 2-3,4/5,6-8 (1974-1978).

Urthkin. Los Angeles, Cal.
  ISSN: 0163-3295 Beg. date: 1978
  Subtitle: Prose/Verse
  No. 1-2 (1978-1979).

Uwharrie Review. Albermarle, N.C., Stanley Arts Council.
  Beg. date: 1974
  V.1, no. 1; v.2, no. 1; v.3, no. 1-2 1974-1978).

V

Valhalla. Birmingham, Ala., Ragnarok Press.
  Beg. date: 1972
  No. 1-2,4 (1972-1977).

Vanishing Cab. San Francisco, Cal.
  No. 2 (1977).

Village Idiot. Santa Barbara, Cal., Mudborn Press.
  Beg. date: 1975
  No. 2-3,n.n.(5-6) (1976-1978).

Vital Statistics. Eugene, Ore., Wolf Run Books.
  ISSN: 0164-0151 Beg. date: 1978
  No. 1-2 (1978-1979).

Voices. Droylsden, Manchester, England, Manchester Unity of Arts Society.
  Beg. date: 1973?
  Subtitle varies: Verse and Prose; Working Class Poetry and Prose with a Socialist Appeal.
  No. 1-6; n.s. 1-5 (also numbered 7-11), no. 8 (14) (1973-1977).

W

Wee Giant. Hamilton, Ontario, Canada., Wee Giant Press.
  ISSN: 0702-4894 CN: 78-30117
  Beg. date: Autumn 1977
  "A wee magazine devoted to the arts."
  V. 1, no. 1-3; v. 2, no. 1-3 (1977-1979).

West Branch. Lewisburg, Pa.
  ISSN: 0149-6441 Beg. date: Fall 1977
  Bucknell University, Department of English.
  No. 1-4 (FAL1977-1979).

Western Poetry Quarterly. Laguna Hills, Cal., Western Poetry Press.
  Beg. date: 1973
  V. 4, no. 4; v. 5, no. 1-4; v. 6, no. 1-2 (1977-1979).

Whetstone: a Southwest poetry magazine. St. David, Arizona, San Pedro Press.
  Beg. date: 1978
  No. 1-3 (1978).

White Heap. Cleveland, Ohio, Falling Down Press.
  No. 1-3 (n.d.-1977).

Whitewalls. Chicago, Ill., Whitewalls, Inc.
  Beg. date: 1978
  No. 1-2 (1978-1979).

Wolfsong. Iola, Wis.
  Beg. date: 1978
  Spersedes River Bottom.
  No. 1-4 (1978).

Wolly of Swot. Hove, Sussex, England.
  Beg. date: September 1977
  No. 1-2 (1977-1978?).

Women Talking, Women Listening. Dublin, Cal.
  Beg. date: 1975
  Published with supplements.
  V. 1-4 (1975-1978).

Little Magazine Collection - University of Wisconsin   Addendum

Woodstock Poetry Review. Woodstock,
  N.Y., Aesopus Press.
  Beg. date: 1977
  No. 4 (1978).

Words Worth. London, England.
  Beg. date: 1978
  V. 1, no. 1-2 (1978-1979?).

Writers News Manitoba. Winnipeg,
  Manitoba, Canada.
  ISSN: 0707-3852 CN: 79-30424
  No. 1-5 (1978-1979).

Writing. La Mesa,Cal., Associated
  Creative Writers.
  ISSN: 0163-5530 Beg. date: 1979
  V. 1, no. 1-2 (1979).

Writings From The Great Plains.
  Scottsbluff, Neb., Panhandle Press.
  Beg. date: 1977
  V. 1, no. 1-2 (1977-1978).

Y

Yakima. Yakima, Wash.
  Beg. date: 1978
  No. 1-2 (1978).

Y'Bird. Berkeley, Cal.
  Beg. date: 1977
  V. 1, no. 1-2 (1977-1978).

Your Friendly Fascist. Darlington,
  New South Wales, Australia.
  No. 12-13,15-17 (n.d.)

Z

Zone. Brooklyn, N.Y., Zonepress.
  ISSN: 0162-1904 Beg. Date: 1977
  No. 1-3 (1977-1978).

Ref
Z
6944
L5
W57
1979

APR 2 1981